# Population Growth and Economic Development: Issues and Evidence

# Social Demography

Series Editors  Doris P. Slesinger
James A. Sweet
Karl E. Taeuber

Center for Demography and Ecology
University of Wisconsin-Madison

*Procedural History of the 1940 Census of Housing and Population*
Robert M. Jenkins

*Population Growth and Economic Development: Issues and Evidence*
Edited by D. Gale Johnson and Ronald D. Lee

*Thailand's Reproductive Revolution: Rapid Fertility Decline in a Third-World Setting*
John Knodel, Aphichat Chamratrithirong, and Nibhon Debavalya

*Prolonged Connections: The Rise of the Extended Family in Nineteenth-Century England and America*
Steven Ruggles

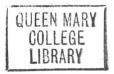

# Population Growth and Economic Development: Issues and Evidence

Edited by D. Gale Johnson and Ronald D. Lee

Working Group on Population Growth
and Economic Development

Committee on Population

Commission on Behavioral and Social Sciences
and Education

National Research Council

The University of Wisconsin Press

Published 1987

The University of Wisconsin Press
114 North Murray Street
Madison, Wisconsin 53715

The University of Wisconsin Press, Ltd.
1 Gower Street
London WC1E 6Ha, England

Library of Congress Cataloging-in-Publication Data
Population growth and economic development.
    (Social demography)
    "Working Group on Population Growth and Economic Development;
Committee on Population, Commission on Behavioral and Social
Sciences and Education, National Research Council."
    Includes bibliographical references.
    1. Developing countries--Population. 2. Food supply--
Developing countries. 3. Labor supply--Developing countries.
4. Natural resources--Developing countries. 5. Developing
countries--Economic policy.
I. Johnson, D. Gale (David Gale), 1916-      .
II. Lee, Ronald Demos, 1941      . III. National
Research Council (U.S.). Working Group on Population
Growth and Economic Development. IV. National Research
Council (U.S.). Committee on Population. V. Series.
HB884.P66547 1987     338.9'009172'4    86-40447
ISBN 0-299-11130-X

# Contents

CONTRIBUTORS                                                          vii

WORKING GROUP ON POPULATION GROWTH AND ECONOMIC
   DEVELOPMENT                                                         ix

COMMITTEE ON POPULATION                                                x

PREFACE                                                               xi


I  FOOD, AGRARIAN SYSTEMS, AND RURAL DEVELOPMENT

   1  Population and Food                                              3
         T.N. Srinivasan

   2  Population Density and Agricultural
      Intensification:  A Study of the Evolution of
      Technologies in Tropical Agriculture                            27
         Prabhu L. Pingali and Hans P. Binswanger

   3  Population Growth and Agricultural Productivity                  57
         Yujiro Hayami and Vernon W. Ruttan


II  LABOR, URBANIZATION, AND THE NONAGRICULTURAL SECTOR

   4  Population Growth, Labor Supply, and Employment
      in Developing Countries                                         105
         David E. Bloom and Richard B. Freeman

   5  The Impacts of Urban Population Growth on Urban
      Labor Markets and the Costs of Urban Service
      Delivery:  A Review                                             149
         Mark R. Montgomery

   6  Industrialization and Urbanization:  International
      Experience                                                      189
         J. Vernon Henderson

7   Population and Technical Change in the
    Manufacturing Sector of Developing Countries        225
        Jeffrey James


III   NATURAL RESOURCES

    8   Natural Resource Scarcity:  A Global Survey        259
            F. Landis MacKellar and Daniel R. Vining, Jr.

    9   Natural Resources, Population Growth, and
        Economic Well-Being                                331
            Margaret E. Slade

IV   HUMAN RESOURCES

    10  The Effect of Family Size on Family Welfare:
        What Do We Know?                                   373
            Elizabeth M. King

    11  School Expenditures and Enrollments, 1960-80:
        The Effects of Income, Prices, and Population
        Growth                                             413
            T. Paul Schultz


V   MACROECONOMIC ISSUES AND MODELS

    12  The Impact of Population Growth on Economic
        Growth in Developing Nations:  The Evidence
        from Macroeconomic-Demographic Models              479
            Dennis A. Ahlburg

    13  National Saving Rates and Population Growth:
        A New Model and New Evidence                       523
            Andrew Mason

    14  Trade and Capital Mobility in a World of
        Diverging Populations                              561
            Alan V. Deardorff

    15  Distribution Issues in the Relationship Between
        Population Growth and Economic Development         589
            David Lam


VI   WELFARE AND ETHICS

    16  The Ethical Foundations of Population Policy       631
            Partha Dasgupta

    17  Externalities and Population                        661
            Robert J. Willis

# Contributors

DENNIS A. AHLBURG, Department of Industrial Relations, University of Minnesota
HANS P. BINSWANGER, Employment and Rural Development Division, The World Bank, Washington, D.C.
DAVID E. BLOOM, Department of Economics, Harvard University
PARTHA DASGUPTA, Facutly of Economics and Politics, University of Cambridge
RICHARD B. FREEMAN, Department of Economics, Harvard University
ALAN V. DEARDORFF, Department of Economics, University of Michigan
YUJIRO HAYAMI, Faculty of Economics, Tokyo Metropolitan University
J. VERNON HENDERSON, Department of Economics, Brown University
JEFFREY JAMES, World Development Institute, Boston University
ELIZABETH M. KING, The Rand Corporation, Santa Monica, California
DAVID LAM, Department of Economics, University of Michigan
F. LANDIS MACKELLAR, Department of Economics, Queens College
ANDREW MASON, East-West Population Institute, Honolulu
MARK R. MONTGOMERY, Office of Population Research, Princeton University
PRABHU L. PINGALI, International Bank for Reconstruction and Development, The World Bank, Washington, D.C.
VERNON W. RUTTAN, Department of Agricultural and Applied Economics, University of Minnesota
T. PAUL SCHULTZ, Department of Economics, Yale University
MARGARET E. SLADE, Department of Economics, University of British Columbia
T.N. SRINIVASAN, Department of Economics, Yale University
DANIEL R. VINING, JR., Department of Regional Sciences, University of Pennsylvania
ROBERT J. WILLIS, Department of Economics, State University of New York, Stonybrook

# Working Group on Population Growth and Economic Development

D. GALE JOHNSON (Cochair), Department of Economics, University of
    Chicago
RONALD D. LEE (Cochair), Graduate Group in Demography, University
    of California, Berkeley
NANCY BIRDSALL, Population, Health, and Nutrition Department, The
    World Bank, Washington, D.C.
RODOLFO A. BULATAO, Population, Health, and Nutrition Department,
    The World Bank, Washington, D.C.
EVA MUELLER, Population Studies Center, University of Michigan
SAMUEL H. PRESTON, Population Studies Center, University of
    Pennsylvania
T. PAUL SCHULTZ, Department of Economics, Yale University
T.N. SRINIVASAN, Department of Economics, Yale University
ANNE D. WILLIAMS, Department of Economics, Bates College


KENNETH M. CHOMITZ, National Research Council Fellow
GEOFFREY GREENE, Research Associate

# Committee on Population

x

# Preface

The 17 chapters in this volume review the available empirical evidence on the complex set of interrelationships between population growth and economic development in developing countries from a variety of perspectives. The issues examined include the relationship between population growth and natural resources; agriculture; savings, investment and trade; health, education, and welfare; and labor and urbanization. In addition, several chapters attempt to unravel the conceptual issues involved in understanding how population change affects economic development.

These chapters were prepared for the Working Group on Population Growth and Economic Development which was formed by the Committee on Population to prepare a scientific assessment of the impact of population growth on economic development. The working group's assessment was published by the National Academy Press in a report entitled Population Growth and Economic Development: Policy Questions. The working group concluded that slower population growth would, on balance, benefit most developing countries and that the positive effects of slower population growth on economic development would be clearest in the poorest and most densely populated countries. But the working group also reported that drawing firm conclusions about the overall impact of slower population growth is difficult because the research base is inadequate. Studies completed to date are frequently based on limited samples and data of poor quality, as well as on only partial and occasionally inappropriate conceptual models and statistical techniques. Simply put, the scientific literature contains few adequate studies of the effects of slower population growth in developing countries.

The summary report and this collection of chapters are part of a larger research program undertaken by the Committee on Population. A second working group has examined the effectiveness of family planning in developing countries. The publications of that group provide important additional information about the costs of lowering fertility.

The National Research Council (NRC) has had a long-standing interest in the consequences of population growth, in particular, its impact on the economic prospects of poor countries. In 1963 an NRC panel published a report entitled The Growth of World Population. Then, as now, the population of developing countries was increasing at about 2 percent a year. The panel found that rapid population growth was generally harmful to the economies of developing countries. In 1971 another panel, commissioned by the Foreign Secretary of the National Academy of Sciences and supported by the Agency for International Development (AID), again examined the relationship between population growth and economic development and reached similar conclusions. Continuing questions about the consequences of different levels and patterns of population growth for the economic prospects of poor countries led AID in 1983 to ask the NRC to undertake a new assessment of the relationship between population growth and economic development. The William and Flora Hewlett Foundation and the Rockefeller Foundation also supported the project, as did the National Academy of Sciences and the National Academy of Engineering through the NRC Fund.*

Each author of a chapter in this volume was asked to provide a critical summary of the state of knowledge on some aspect of the consequences of population change for developing countries. Taken together, the chapters provide a review of much, although not all, of the literature on the subject. In addition to a review of the literature, many of the chapters contain original theoretical or empirical research. It is our hope that these chapters will encourage others to study the detailed consequences of demographic change for social and economic development.

The volume is divided into six sections. The first four cover the relationship between population growth and a series of specific development issues. More general macroeconomic models and related issues are reviewed in the fifth section, and the collection concludes with two chapters on important conceptual issues related to the impact of population growth.

---

*The National Research Council (NRC) Fund is a pool of private, discretionary, nonfederal funds that is used to support a program of Academy-initiated studies of national issues in which science and technology figure significantly. The NRC Fund consists of contributions from a consortium of private foundations including the Carnegie Corporation of New York, the Charles E. Culpepper Foundation, the William and Flora Hewlett Foundation, the John D. and Catherine T. MacArthur Foundation, the Andrew W. Mellon Foundation, the Rockefeller Foundation, and the Alfred P. Sloan Foundation; the Academy Industry Program, which seeks annual contributions from companies that are concerned with the health of U.S. science and technology and with public policy issues with technology content; and the National Academy of Sciences and the National Academy of Engineering endowments.

The Working Group on Population Growth and Economic Development and the Committee on Population are grateful to the authors of these chapters for their diligence. Each of these chapters has been reviewed, sometimes several times, by members of the working group and the committee as well as by other experts. This effort to ensure the highest quality publication is appreciated.

We also wish to express our thanks to other members of the committee staff who helped organize the working group and provided support throughout the course of the project: Robert J. Lapham and Peter J. Donaldson, study directors at the beginning and the end of the project; Diane Lindley, research assistant; Cheryl Hailey, administrative secretary; Elaine McGarraugh and Rona Briere, editors, and Brent Wolff, Institute for Resource Development Inc., for his contribution with the graphics. Particular thanks are due to Geoffrey Greene and Kenneth M. Chomitz, members of the committee staff, who provided valuable assistance throughout the project.

G. Gale Johnson and
Ronald D. Lee, Cochairs
Working Group on Population
 Growth and Economic Development

# I. Food, Agrarian Systems, and Rural Development

# 1

# Population and Food

## T. N. Srinivasan

INTRODUCTION

The impact of population size on the demand for and supply of food in developing countries has long attracted the attention of economists and demographers.

One could distinguish several channels of influence in each direction in the relationship between population and food. First, population growth, and hence the size of the future population, obviously affects the demand for food. With growth of income kept unchanged, an exogenous increase in the rate of growth of a population will imply a slower growth of income per head and a slower growth of its per capita food demand. However, as long as the elasticity of per capita food demand with respect to income is less than unity, the rate of growth of total demand for food will increase with an increase in the rate of growth of population. Second, to the extent that demand elasticities differ across socioeconomic groups, changes in income distribution will have an impact on food demand even if aggregate income growth is kept constant and the process of population growth itself could alter income distribution. Finally, population growth could affect food supplies in several ways: by changing potential labor force size and quality; by changing the availabilities (per worker) of other inputs, such as land, through changes in the size distribution of farms and the extent of land fragmentation; by influencing the technology of cultivation (Boserup, 1965, 1981; Simon, 1981); and by influencing the environment through changes in the process of soil erosion and degradation, thereby affecting yields.

This chapter is a summary of a paper prepared for a conference on population, food, and rural development, New Delhi, India, December, 1984, sponsored by the International Union for the Scientific Study of Population. I wish to thank Paul Demeny, Richard Easterlin, Geoff Greene, Gale Johnson, Allen Kelley, Ronald Lee, Hans Linneman, Eva Mueller, and Julian Simon for their comments on earlier drafts.

        In the opposite direction, there is of course the potential
Malthusian relationship between the availability of food,
fertility, and mortality.  It has been pointed out (World Bank,
1982) that a majority of the world's poor are either landless
agricultural laborers or cultivators with small land holdings.
Moreover, the poor have higher fertility rates, while fertility
is influenced by household income-earning opportunities, particularly for women.  To the extent that the process of growth of
agricultural output affects land tenure, farm-size distribution,
and income-earning opportunities, fertility rates and population
growth rates may be affected as well.
        A great many attempts have been made to model quantitatively
the food-population nexus.  The resulting models vary greatly in
sophistication, ranging from simple trend analyses and mechanical
models devoid of economic content (e.g., Forrester, 1971; Meadows
et al., 1972) to dynamic general equilibrium models, such as the
International Institute for Applied Systems Analysis (IIASA)
system (Parikh and Rabar, 1981; Shah et al., 1984).  All fall
short of an ideal model fully describing the interdependecies
among population growth; technological and environmental change;
and the evolution of prices, output, income distribution, and
trade.  However, despite their inevitable shortcomings, some of
the more sophisticated models provide the best available basis
for projecting the future of the world food economy.  This
chapter briefly describes the methods and conclusions of four
important world food models:  studies based on population
carrying capacity (the maximum population that can be sustained
indefinitely into the future) and projections of population
size; Food and Agriculture Organization (FAO) projections; the
grain-oilseed-livestock model underlying the food supply-demand
projections of the Global 2000 Report; and the linked system of
country models under the auspices of IIASA.  (For a more extended
discussion, see Srinivasan, 1986.)  The discussion then turns to
feedback effects in the food-population nexus that these models
either address inadequately or neglect altogether, and sets
forth the implications of these effects for understanding the
relation of population to food production and consumption.  In a
final section, conclusions are presented.


WORLD FOOD MODELS

Population Carrying Capacity and Projections of Population Size

It is tempting to compare the projected population, say, by the
year 2050 (see Table 1) with the potential for feeding this
population.  Some of the early attempts (reviewed by Shah et al.,
1984) estimated potential arable land and yield per hectare in
different regions of the world to arrive at an estimate of
potential output in grain-equivalent units, which was then
divided by an assumed consumption level per head to obtain an
estimate of the maximum population that could be sustained.
These estimates depended on variations in the three inputs:

TABLE 1  Population Projections (in millions)

| Country Grouping | Standard Projection | | | Rapid Fertility Decline | | Rapid Fertility and Mortality Decline | |
|---|---|---|---|---|---|---|---|
| | Mid-1982 | 2000 | 2050 | 2000 | 2050 | 2000 | 2050 |
| Low-Income Countries | 2276 | 3107 | 5092 | 2917 | 4021 | 2931 | 4225 |
| China | 1008 | 1196 | 1450 | 1196 | 1450 | 1185 | 1462 |
| India | 717 | 994 | 1513 | 927 | 1313 | 938 | 1406 |
| Bangladesh | 93 | 157 | 357 | 136 | 212 | 139 | 230 |
| Pakistan | 87 | 140 | 302 | 120 | 181 | 122 | 197 |
| Middle-Income Countries | 1120 | 1695 | 3144 | 1542 | 2321 | 1556 | 2437 |
| Indonesia | 153 | 212 | 330 | 197 | 285 | 109 | 289 |
| Nigeria | 91 | 169 | 471 | 143 | 243 | 147 | 265 |
| Brazil | 127 | 181 | 279 | 168 | 239 | 169 | 247 |
| Mexico | 73 | 109 | 182 | 101 | 155 | 101 | 160 |
| High-Income Oil-Exporting Countries | 17 | 33 | 77 | 30 | 46 | 30 | 49 |
| Industrial Market Economies | 723 | 780 | | | | | |
| U.S. | 232 | 259 | | | | | |
| Japan | 118 | 128 | | | | | |
| Eastern European Nonmarket Economies | 384 | 431 | | | | | |
| U.S.S.R | 270 | 306 | | | | | |
| Total[a] | 4520 | 6046 | | | | | |

[a]Excludes countries with population less than 1 million.

Source:  World Bank (1984).

estimates of arable land, yield per hectare, and per capita consumption needs. The range was enormous, from a low estimate of 902 million by Pearson and Harper in 1945 to 147 billion by Clark in 1967 (Shah et al., 1984:5).

A study on population carrying capacities undertaken jointly by FAO, the United Nations Fund for Population Activities (UNFPA), and IIASA (Higgins et al., 1983; Shah et al., 1984) uses a more disaggregated data base and superior methodology, though it excludes some major countries, including China. It combines a climate map providing spatial information on temperature and moisture conditions with a soil map providing spatial data on soil texture, slope, and phase, then divides the study area into grids of 100 square kilometers each. In all, 14 major climates during growing period are distinguished, and 15 most widely grown food crops are considered. Three alternative levels of farm technology are postulated, varying from no change in existing cropping patterns, no use of fertilizers and pesticides, and no mechanization to optimum use of plant genetic potential, along with needed fertilizers and pesticides and full mechanization.

The production potential in each soil-climate grid is determined by the soil characteristics, climate, growing season
length, technology, and cropping pattern, together with the
requirement that production be sustainable (i.e., through appropriate fallowing techniques and soil conservation measures).
These factors are aggregated to yield production potential for
each country. The deduction of seed, feed, and wastage provides
an estimate of the potential output available for human consumption for each crop. Livestock production potential is also
assessed under the assumptions that only grassland will be used
to support herds and that crop residues and by-products will be
used in addition (Shah et al., 1984:32). The maximum population
that can be supported is estimated given average calorie and
protein requirements based on the 1973 recommendations of a
committee of FAO and World Health Organization (WHO) experts, the
projected age and sex distribution of the population of a country, and the food production available for human consumption in
terms of energy and protein. The results are shown in Table 2.

What inference can one draw from this study? It would appear
that the technological capability and land resources needed to
sustain a population of as high as 33 billion (or nearly 9 times
the projected population of 3.6 billion in the year 2000) exist
in the five regions of the developing world, excluding China.
However, this conclusion by itself is no cause for complacency
since there is virtually no economic analysis underlying these
projections. Farming is done by millions of individual peasants
concerned with their private economic interest. Given the prices
for inputs and outputs they face and the constraints to which
they are subject, they will not produce a particular set and
level of crop outputs merely because it is agroclimatically and
technologically feasible to do so. In particular, the investments in land, capital equipment, livestock, technical skills,
and knowledge needed to attain the potential output will not be
forthcoming unless the returns are adequate.

As noted in Table 2, the study identifies "critical" countries that are not projected to be self-sufficient in meeting
basic food needs. However, asking whether each country or region
within a country has the potential to sustain its projected year
2000 or stationary population ignores the economic cost of such
autarkic development even if it were feasible. Furthermore,
fundamental ideas of comparative advantage and gain from trade
between regions within a country and between countries are absent
in the analysis. At best, the study is useful in pinpointing
countries where, with a technology that raises the output per
unit of land to the fullest extent, even the current level of
population cannot be sustained by a sole reliance on home
production. Such observations may be taken as indicating a need
for the out-migration of part of a country's population, or for
investment in the production of exports to pay for food imports,
or some combination of both.

The FAO'S Agriculture Toward the Year 2000

The FAO published its projections for the year 2000 in Agriculture: Toward 2000 (FAO, 1981). This study individually covers 90 developing countries, accounting for 98 percent of the developing country population outside of China, and summarily covers 34 developed countries. It analyzes the implications for agriculture of three major scenarios: a trend scenario representing a continuation of trends since the early 1960s; a modest improvement over these trends (scenario B) and a more ambitious but still feasible rate of growth (scenario A). While the agronomic and technical bases for the projections are perhaps stronger than their economic basis, the latter shows an improvement over studies of population carrying capacity. On the other hand, although the study emphasizes that access to productive assets, particularly land and credit, must be widely shared for successful agricultural development to take place, it does not address the existing distortions, implicitly assuming that they will continue. The medium variant of the U.N. population projections is common to all of the scenarios. The demand for agricultural products is driven mostly by exogenously specified income and population trends, except that caloric intake per capita is not allowed to fall in countries with declining trends and not allowed to exceed certain upper bounds in countries with rising trends. Production estimates are based on projections of land and water resources, investment, and increases in yield per hectare of land.

The results are given in Table 3. The study concludes that a doubling of agricultural production in 20 years in the ambitious scenario A (and an 80 percent increase in the less ambitious scenario B) depends on a tremendous transformation of agriculture in all developing countries. This transformation is no less than "almost an agricultural revolution, involving widespread modernization in technology and techniques, and based primarily on a massive increase in inputs into agriculture (well over doubling annual investment and no less than tripling current inputs alone in Scenario A) . . . and pursued with an increased awareness of the need to conserve the environment and avoid undesirable social consequences" (FAO, 1981:57). Yet even if this ambitious task is accomplished, the study concludes that 260 million people (390 million in scenario B) in 86 of the 90 study countries, constituting 7 percent of these countries' population, will be seriously undernourished in the year 2000; in 3 of the countries, more than 15 percent of the population will be seriously undernourished.

The FAO study briefly addresses the question of whether different rates of population growth than those assumed would materially modify the results (FAO, 1981:42). Depending on where the variations occurred, the results would be changed substantially: a speeding up of population growth in already poor countries with weak agricultural and economic growth prospects could be disastrous; on the other hand, a slowing down of population growth could reduce the cereal import requirements

TABLE 2   Population Carrying Capacities (in millions)

| Region | Level of Farming Technology | | |
|---|---|---|---|
| | Low | Intermediate | High |
| **Africa** | | | |
| Number of Critical Countries | 29 | 12 | 4 |
| Limited countries | 4 | 7 | 4 |
| Surplus countries | 18 | 32 | 43 |
| Population Carrying Capacity | | | |
| Critical countries | 209 (466) | 62 (110) | 9 (11) |
| Limited countries | 68 (62) | 340 (258) | 70 (52) |
| Surplus countries | 977 (252) | 4087 (412) | 12789 (717) |
| All Countries | 1254 (780) | 4489 (780) | 12868 (780) |
| **Southwest Asia** | | | |
| Number of Critical Countries | 14 | 14 | 11 |
| Limited countries | 1 | -- | 3 |
| Surplus countries | -- | 1 | 1 |
| Population Carrying Capacity | | | |
| Critical countries | 87 (195) | 116 (195) | 47 (89) |
| Limited countries | 93 (69) | -- | 118 (106) |
| Surplus countries | -- | 121 (69) | 159 (69) |
| All Countries | 180 (264) | 237 (264) | 324 (264) |
| **Southeast Asia** | | | |
| Number of Critical Countries | 6 | 2 | 1 |
| Limited countries | 4 | -- | 1 |
| Surplus countries | 6 | 14 | 14 |
| Population Carrying Capacity | | | |
| Critical countries | 270 (341) | 148 (156) | (3) |
| Limited countries | 1492 (1190) | -- | 185 (153) |
| Surplus countries | 702 (407) | 4210 (1782) | 6149 (1782) |
| All Countries | 2464 (1938) | 4358 (1938) | 6334 (1938) |
| **Central America** | | | |
| Number of Critical Countries | 14 | 7 | 2 |
| Limited countries | 2 | -- | 1 |
| Surplus countries | 5 | 14 | 18 |
| Population Carrying Capacity | | | |
| Critical countries | 34 (52) | 17 (24) | 1 (2) |
| Limited countries | 194 (139) | -- | 11 (10) |
| Surplus countries | 64 (24) | 540 (191) | 1281 (203) |
| All Countries | 292 (215) | 557 (215) | 1293 (215) |
| **South America** | | | |
| Number of Surplus Countries | 13 | 13 | 13 |
| Population Carrying Capacity | | | |
| Surplus countries | 1418 (393) | 5288 (393) | 12375 (393) |

TABLE 2 (continued)

| Region | Level of Farming Technology | | |
|---|---|---|---|
| | Low | Intermediate | High |
| **All Regions** | | | |
| Number of Critical Countries | 63 | 35 | 18 |
| Limited countries | 11 | 7 | 9 |
| Surplus countries | 42 | 74 | 89 |
| **Population Carrying Capacity** | | | |
| Critical countries | 600 (1054) | 343 (485) | 58 (105) |
| Limited countries | 1847 (1460) | 340 (258) | 384 (321) |
| Surplus countries | 3161 (1076) | 14246 (2847) | 32753 (3164) |
| All Countries | 5603 (3590) | 14928 (3590) | 33194 (3590) |

Notes:  Figures in parentheses denote the projected population by year 2000.
In this table, "critical" countries are those that could not meet the basic food need of their populations, even if all their arable land were devoted to growing food crops.  "Limited" countries are those that cannot meet these needs if part of their arable land has to be diverted to produce other food and nonfood cash crops; that is, if a third of the arable land in these countries is assumed to be devoted to nonfood or food crops other than the basic 15, then their projected populations by the year 2000 would exceed their estimated carrying capacity.  Finally, "surplus" countries are those that meet their food as well as other nonfood crop requirements.

Source:  Shah et al. (1984:Tables 14-18).

of cereal-importing countries and the number of those seriously undernourished in the population.

The study also attempts a longer-term projection up to the year 2055.  With population in the developing world (including China) increasing by more than 60 percent over its level in the year 2000, agricultural production would have to be nearly three times its 2000 level, and nearly five times its 1980 level. Since only a few countries have reserves of arable land and water, production increase would become geographically more concentrated, and international trade would be more significant. Food importers would have to rely on rapid growth in production and exports of nonagricultural products to finance their food imports.  The study recognizes (without attempting to quantify) the environmental implications of the strategy of rapidly expanding agricultural output based on a technology intensive in the use of irrigation, chemical fertilizers, and energy, particularly as regards soil quality and erosion, and water pollution. It is suggested that there is an intertemporal trade-off between reducing the poverty of the present generation and protecting the quality of the environment bequeathed to future generations in developing countries, and that in this trade-off, given the extreme poverty in some countries, the present generation should perhaps be favored.

Srinivasan

TABLE 3  Agriculture Toward 2000:  Projection

| Variable | 1980 | 1990 | 2000 |
|---|---|---|---|
| Population (in millions) | | | |
|   90 Developing Countries | 2259 | 2906 | 3630 |
|   (included in the study) | | | |
|   Other Developing Countries | 993 | 1121 | 1244 |
|   (including China) | | | |
|   Developed Countries | 1163 | 1248 | 1325 |
|   World | 4415 | 5275 | 6199 |
| Population Growth Rates[a] | | | |
|   (percent per year) | | | |
|   90 Developing Countries | 2.5 | 2.3 | |
|   Other Developing Countries | 1.2 | 1.0 | |
|   Developed Countries | 0.7 | 0.6 | |
|   World | 1.6 | 1.7 | |
| GDP Growth Rate[b] | | | |
|   (percent per year) | | | |
|   90 Developing Countries | | | |
|     Scenario A | 6.8 | 7.2 | |
|     Scenario B | 5.6 | 5.8 | |
|   Developed Countries | | | |
|     Scenario A | 3.7 | 3.1 | |
|     Scenario B | 3.8 | 3.2 | |
| Caloric Intake Per Capita | | | |
|   (kilo cals per days) | | | |
|   90 Developing Countries | 2180 | | |
|     Continuation of trends | | 2330 | 2370 |
|     Scenario A | | 2445 | 2635 |
|     Scenario B | | 2380 | 2500 |
|   Developed Countries | 3315 | 3415 | 3475 |
| Production of Cereals | | | |
|   (million tons) | | | |
|   90 Developing Countries | 382[a] | | |
|     Continuation of trends | | 518 | 636 |
|     Scenario A | | 569 | 786 |
|     Scenario B | | 538 | 696 |
|   Developed Countries | 818[a] | | |
|     Continuation of trends | | | 1102 |
|     Scenario A | | | 1017 |
|     Scenario B | | | 1069 |
| Net Trade in Cereals | | | |
|   (million tons) | | | |
|   90 Developing Countries | -36[a] | | |
|     Continuation of trends | | -72 | -132 |
|     Scenario A | | -57 | -64 |
|     Scenario B | | -67 | -105 |

TABLE 3 (continued)

| Variable | 1980 | 1990 | 2000 |
|---|---|---|---|
| Other Developing Countries (including China) | -16 | | |
|   Scenario A | | -15 | -17 |
|   Scenario B | | -19 | -27 |
| All Developed Countries | -52 | | |
|   Scenario A | | -72 | -81 |
|   Scenario B | | -86 | -132 |
| Available Land (hectares per capita) | | | |
|   90 Developing Countries | | 0.29 | 0.25 |

[a]Average for 1976-79.
[b]The first and second columns refer respectively to average
annual growth rates during 1980-90 and 1990-2000.

Source: FAO (1981:Table 3.10 and Statistical Annex Tables
3 and 5).


The Global 2000 Report

The grain-oilseed-livestock (GOL) submodel of the Global 2000
Report (Council on Environmental Quality, 1981) (hereafter The
Report), is an econometric model describing demand, supply, and
trade as related to grains, oilseed, and livestock. The
exogenous variables include (regional) population and income
growth rates, and variables describing agricultural and trade
policy, as well as weather. Endogenous variables include prices
at which trade takes place, supply, demand, and the like. The
supply equations reflect technology (i.e., input-output
relationships) and producer behavior. The full model consists
of three submodels for projecting arable area, total food
production and consumption, and fertilizer use. The purpose of
the model is to project world population, consumption, trade,
and prices of grain, oilseed, and livestock products for 1995
and 2000.
   However, it is important to keep in mind that the mutual
feedback effects among population, resources, and the environment
are not fully allowed for in the resulting projections which are
"based largely on extrapolations of past trends" (Council on
Environmental Quality, 1981:4). This drawback should be kept in
mind in interpreting the results. On the other hand, while the
model's coverage is more extensive with respect to grains and
less with respect to livestock, it is still impressive in its
commodity, regional, and price detail. It should also be noted
that this model belongs to the static equilibrium genre, and
therefore its projections, say for 1995, are independent of its
projections for any other year, say 2000.

The crucial assumptions underlying the projections are as
follows:

- No major man-made or natural shocks will occur; in particular, no climatic change is projected, though the
  scenarios include "optimistic" and "pessimistic" weather
  assumptions.

- Yields per hectare of land will evolve at rates comparable
  to their historic evolution since 1950.

- Protectionist agricultural policies in Western Europe and
  the political determination of U.S. trade with China,
  Eastern Europe, and the U.S.S.R. will continue.

Three alternative scenarios are simulated:

- Alternative I is the reference or baseline scenario in
  which growth rates of world population and per capita
  income assume their median values of 1.8 percent and 1.5
  percent, respectively, between 1975 and 2000. No change
  in weather is assumed as compared to 1950-75. Energy
  prices are assumed either to remain unchanged at their
  1974-76 real levels or, alternatively, to double by 2000.

- Alternative II is the optimistic scenario, with lower
  population growth (1.5 percent) and higher per capita
  income growth (2.4 percent). Weather is assumed to be
  more favorable than during 1950-75, thereby increasing
  yields. Energy prices are kept unchanged relative to
  their 1974-76 real level.

- Alternative III is the pessimistic scenario, with population growth high (2.1 percent), per capita income growth
  low (0.7 percent), and unfavorable weather resulting in
  lower yields. Real energy prices more than double in this
  scenario by the year 2000 relative to their 1974-76
  values.

The resulting projections (Tables 4 and 5) show that even in
the pessimistic third alternative, the consumption of food is
higher by about 4 percent in the year 2000 than its 1969-71
level, though grain consumption is lower by about 3 percent than
its 1969-71 level of 311 kilograms per capita. Under the
baseline Alternative I, per capita food consumption in 2000 is
higher compared to 1969-71 by 14.5 percent and 17.0 percent,
respectively, depending on whether real energy prices more than
double between 1974-76 and 2000 or stay constant. Grain consumption is higher by 10.3 percent and 13.2 percent, respectively, under the same circumstances. Per capita caloric
consumption in 2000 in less developed countries as a whole
remains unchanged at its 1969-71 level under the pessimistic
third alternative and increases by 7.6 percent to 9.5 percent

TABLE 4   Food Production, Consumption, Trade, and Price in the Year 2000

| Development Status and Variable | Alternative I | Alternative II | Alternative III |
|---|---|---|---|
| **Industrialized Countries** | | | |
| Population growth rate (% per year) | 0.52 | 0.34 | 0.71 |
| Per capita income growth rate (% per year) | 2.57 | 3.35 | 1.77 |
| Grain production (million metric tons) | 739.7-679.1 | 730.0 | 683.3 |
| Grain consumption (million metric tons) | 648.1-610.8 | 689.6 | 590.2 |
| Grain trade (million metric tons) | +91.3-+68.3 | +42.4 | +93.1 |
| Food production index (1969-71 = 100) | 157.0-143.7 | 157.1 | 143.5 |
| Food consumption index (1969-71 = 100) | 155.8-147.7 | 165.7 | 143.6 |
| **Centrally Planned Economies** | | | |
| Population growth rate (% per year) | 1.21 | 0.94 | 1.43 |
| Per capita income growth rate (% per year) | 2.01 | 3.00 | 1.03 |
| Grain production (million metric tons) | 722.0 | 746.0 | 691.0 |
| Grain consumption (million metric tons) | 758.5 | 755.4 | 730.0 |
| Grain trade (million metric tons) | -36.5 | -9.4 | -39.4 |
| Food production index (1969-71 = 100) | 174.0 | 179.5 | 166.1 |
| Food consumption index (1969-71 = 100) | 179.9 | 179.2 | 173.2 |
| **Less Developed Countries** | | | |
| Population growth rate (% per year) | 2.37 | 2.04 | 2.71 |
| Per capita income growth rate (% per year) | 2.01 | 3.00 | 1.03 |
| Grain production (million metric tons) | 735.0-740.6 | 757.0 | 745.3 |
| Grain consumption (million metric tons) | 789.8-772.4 | 790.4 | 799.4 |
| Grain trade (million metric tons) | -54.8-31.8 | -33.4 | -54.1 |
| Food production index (1969-71 = 100) | 244.5-247.7 | 268.2 | 246.4 |
| Food consumption index (1969-71 = 100) | 247.8-242.8 | 261.2 | 249.0 |
| **World Market Weighted Real Food Prices** (Index 1969-71 = 100) | 145-195 | 130 | 215 |
| **World Exports of Grain** (million metric tons) | 221-219 | 178 | 239 |

Source:  Council on Environmental Quality (1981:Vol. 2:78, 91-92, and 96, Tables 6-1, 6-2, 6-7, and 6-11).

TABLE 5  Per Capita Grain and Food Consumption and Daily Caloric Intake in the Year 2000

| Region | Alternative I Grain (kgs.) | Alternative I Food Index (1969-71=100) | Alternative II Grain (kgs.) | Alternative II Food Index (1969-71=100) | Alternative III Grain (kgs.) | Alternative III Food Index (1969-71=100) |
|---|---|---|---|---|---|---|
| Industrialized Countries | 735.0-692.4 | 127.7-121.2 | 798.3 | 139.1 | 619.2 | 110.0 |
| United States | 1183.3-1111.5 | 135.9-128.3 | 1363.3 | 147.7 | 1154.8 | 107.9 |
| Western Europe | 581.7-548.8 | 121.4-115.5 | 599.0 | 124.5 | 518.2 | 110.1 |
| Japan | 484.4-452.3 | 164.2-154.2 | 481.2 | 163.2 | 401.1 | 138.3 |
| Centrally Planned Countries | 473.9 | 135.8 | 495.1 | 138.4 | 396.5 | 119.0 |
| USSR | 949.9 | 141.4 | 976.4 | 145.2 | 828.4 | 123.7 |
| Eastern Europe | 997.6 | 152.1 | 1012.1 | 154.2 | 920.8 | 141.2 |
| China | 267.8 | 119.1 | 281.8 | 124.7 | 220.0 | 99.9 |
| Less Developed Countries | 210.2-205.5 | 111.0-108.6 | 219.4 | 116.7 | 189.5 | 99.9 |
| Latin America | 282.8-278.1 | 127.1-125.1 | 306.6 | 136.7 | 243.8 | 110.8 |
| N. Africa/Middle East | 301.8-292.8 | 105.9-102.2 | 318.6 | 112.9 | 283.7 | 98.4 |
| Other African LDCs | 112.5-112.0 | 81.3-80.9 | 119.1 | 86.3 | 108.8 | 78.5 |
| South Asia | 186.7-181.0 | 109.2-105.8 | 192.4 | 112.5 | 164.9 | 96.4 |
| Southeast Asia | 233.2-228.5 | 117.1-114.6 | 237.1 | 119.2 | 217.9 | 110.0 |
| East Asia | 219.5-217.3 | 128.7-127.3 | 221.3 | 129.7 | 195.5 | 114.2 |
| World | 352.0-343.2 | 117.0-114.5 | 373.0 | 126.0 | 302.0 | 104.0 |

| Daily Caloric Consumption in Less Developed Countries | 1969-71 | Alternative I | Alternative II | Alternative III |
|---|---|---|---|---|
| Developed Countries | 2165 | 2370-2330 | 2390 | 2165 |
| Latin America | 2525 | 2975-2905 | 3080 | 2710 |
| N. Africa/Middle East | 2421 | 2530-2460 | 2655 | 2390 |
| Other African LDCs | 2139 | 1840-1830 | 1920 | 1800 |
| South Asia | 2036 | 2180-2130 | 2230 | 1985 |
| Southeast Asia | 2174 | 2400-2365 | 2425 | 2310 |
| East Asia | 2140 | 2505-2480 | 2520 | 2320 |

Source:  Council on Environmental Quality (1981:Vol. 2:93-95, Tables 6-8 and 6-9).

14

under the baseline alternative, depending on the trend in
petroleum prices, although there are enormous regional
variations. The sub-Saharan African countries appear to fare
the worst: even in the optimistic second alternative, their per
capita food consumption in the year 2000 is lower by 13.7 percent
compared to its 1969-71 level and by a larger 18.7 percent to
19.1 percent under the baseline alternative. In South Asia and
North Africa, only the pessimistic scenario leads to a decline
in food consumption per capita of 3.6 percent and 1.6 percent,
respectively, in 2000 as compared to 1969-71. Thus it would
appear that, except for sub-Saharan Africa, the world has the
physical and economic capacity to produce enough food to meet
modest increases in demand through 2000.

The Report points out that the ability to sustain these
modest increases arises from substantial increases in the
resources committed to food production, as well as impressive
increases in gains in resource productivity through wider
adoption of improved technology and the use of land-augmenting
inputs such as fertilizers and pesticides. In fact, even though
arable land per capita declines 36 percent between 1975 and
2000, food production roughly doubles over the same period
because of a tripling of fertilizer use. However, achieving
such an intensification in input usage is expensive, besides
being a formidable task. This is because increasing fertilizer
use depends to a significant extent on irrigation, and the
creation of irrigation capacity is likely to be capital-
intensive. Operating the capacity created and producing the
fertilizers needed are both energy-intensive. Managing irrigation systems efficiently is also skill-intensive. Moreover, The
Report recognizes that the effort to increase food output through
the expansion of arable area, the extension of irrigation, and
the use of chemical fertilizers and pesticides would have an
impact on the environment, particularly in terms of deforestation, desertification, soil degradation (increasing salinity and
erosion), chemical pollution of surface and ground waters, and
the like. However, The Report concludes that these problems,
though serious, are manageable, although it does not relate
trends in such areas as population, income, and industrialization
to the probability of long-term cooling or warming.

Since supplies and demands do not balance at the regional
and country levels, there is a substantial increase in international trade. The extent of this increase by the year 2000
varies among the alternatives from 63 to 110 percent over the
1973-75 level. The implication is that food-importing countries
would have to export other commodities to finance such massive
increases in their food imports. Since developing-country food
importers account for 36 to 43 percent of world imports in the
year 2000, this financing problem is indeed a serious one. Apart
from the problem of generating exportable surpluses, the task of
converting these into export earnings is likely to prove daunting
if protectionist trends in the developed world intensify. The
political determination of U.S. policies regarding grain trade
and agricultural protectionism in Europe may continue, and it

would be naive to pretend that this would have no serious consequences.


The Systems Models of IIASA

Unlike the static partial equilibrium GOL model of The Report, the IIASA system of models is of the dynamic general equilibrium genre. It consists of a set of country models, some put together by research groups within each country with a substantial degree of disaggregation and others built by the research team of the Ford and Agriculture Project (FAP) of IIASA. The 22 country and regional models were designed in such a way that they could be aggregated to a global ten-sector model, distinguishing nine agriculture and livestock product sectors, and a single sector covering all nonagricultural activities (see Parikh and Rabar, 1981, for details).

Each aggregated country model consists of a supply module and a demand module. In some country models, several groups of agents (rural, urban, income classes, etc.) are distinguished, each endowed with its own preferences and claims to output. Several government policies are modeled, such as tariffs that establish a wedge between domestic and international prices, export and import quotas, buffer stock operations, domestic rationing and public food procurement and distribution systems, and income transfers between agents. The models are solved year by year for prices, output, investment, and trade, given the previous year's values for these variables. Population growth is exogenously specified in all of the models; however, in some, labor force participation rates and rural-urban migration are endogenized through simple income-related behavioral equations.

The data base for the models included the FAO's supply utilization accounts for about 1,000 commodities for the period 1961-76, which were aggregated to suit the models' sectoral classification. The models were calibrated (i.e., free parameters were chosen) so as to reproduce the observed prices, outputs, and trade flows of the period 1970-76 as closely as possible. Then the models were run in a simulation mode for the period 1977-2000.

The results are shown in Table 6. Even though the methodology of the IIASA models is different from and many ways superior to that of the model used for The Report, the results are broadly similar. While The Report projects a global population for the year 2000 varying from 5.9 billion in Alternative II to 6.7 billion in Alternative III, with a figure of 6.4 billion for the reference Alternative I, IIASA projects a figure of 6.1 billion for its reference run. The gross national product (GNP) growth rates are endogenous in the IIASA model, while they are exogenous in The Report, with the IIASA growth rates being somewhat higher. The output of all grains in the year 2000 for the IIASA models is 1.96 billion tons, as compared to the range of 2.12 to 2.23 billion tons in The Report. Total exports of grain in the year 2000 are on the order of 152 million tons in

the IIASA models (Table 6), and from 178 to 239 million tons in
The Report (Table 4). It is understandable that the volume of
trade is higher in The Report than in the IIASA projections
since the former model, being of the static partial equilibrium
kind, limits the extent of adjustment to changing prices. Given
that the country groupings in the two models are different, a
direct comparison of their results may not be appropriate.
Still, it would appear that if we use caloric intake as an
indicator of welfare, prospects for the developing countries as
a whole are somewhat better in the IIASA projections than in
those of The Report.

The India model of the IIASA system is more elaborate than
the others in that it distinguishes five income (more precisely,
per capita real consumption expenditure) groups among rural and
urban households. All households within each group have the
same function, represented by a Stone-Geary linear expenditure
system. The distribution of households according to per capita
household consumer expenditures is assumed to be log-normal. In
this model, population growth is exogenously specified and
influences only the demand module. Three alternative growth
paths are specified: Alternative I corresponds to IIASA's
reference projection, Alternative II corresponds to the standard
projections for year the 2000, and Alternative III corresponds
to the rapid fertility decline and standard mortality decline
projection of The World Bank (1984). There is a difference of
121 million persons between the projections of Alternatives I
and III by the year 2000. The model is run in a stand-alone
mode, with the time path of international prices faced by India
exogenously specified to be the same as that emerging as the
equilibrium path in the world model reference run. Since
population influences only per capita income and demand and not
the production process, the differences between the alternatives
are not large (see Table 7). As is to be expected, Alternative
III, with the slowest population growth, leads to a minuscule
speeding up of the rate of growth of real gross domestic product
(GDP). However, the impact on caloric intake and on the distribution of population among expenditure groups is more percep-
tible. In general, for all groups, caloric intake increases as
population growth decreases and the distribution of income
improves, with a higher proportion of the population moving to
richer expenditure classes, particularly in the urban areas.


THE NEGLECTED FEEDBACK EFFECTS

In all the projections reviewed above, population growth is
exogenous. Also ignored are the effects, if any, of exogenous
population growth on the environment through desertification and
soil erosion; the effects on climate in general, and frequency
of severe droughts and floods in particular; and the effects on
farm size and the fragmentation of holdings due to subdivisions
of land within families. Writers such as Lester Brown of The
World Watch Institute argue that "as world population expands,

TABLE 6  Projections from IIASA Basic Linked System

| Variable | Year | OECD | CMEA | Developing Countries | | | | World (including others) |
|---|---|---|---|---|---|---|---|---|
| | | | | Mid-Income | Low Mid-Income | Low Income | All | |
| Population (3-year average up to indicated year) | 1980 | 648 | 375 | 389 | 695 | 2076 | 3160 | 4338 |
| | 1990 | 701 | 406 | 502 | 891 | 2513 | 3906 | 5186 |
| | 2000 | 754 | 437 | 637 | 1119 | 3023 | 4776 | 6106 |
| Rate of Growth of Population (% per year) | 1971-80 | 0.79 | 0.90 | 2.63 | 2.58 | 2.12 | 2.28 | 1.84 |
| | 1980-90 | 0.79 | 0.80 | 2.59 | 2.51 | 1.91 | 2.13 | 1.80 |
| | 1990-2000 | 0.73 | 0.71 | 2.38 | 2.28 | 1.86 | 2.03 | 1.63 |
| Rate of Growth of Real GDP (% per year) | 1971-80 | 3.94 | 5.99 | 6.24 | 6.09 | 5.24 | 5.77 | 4.63 |
| | 1980-90 | 3.57 | 5.33 | 5.89 | 5.70 | 5.09 | 5.51 | 4.31 |
| | 1990-2000 | 3.15 | 4.87 | 5.84 | 5.67 | 4.80 | 5.39 | 4.04 |
| Daily Caloric Intake (kilocalories)[a] | 1980 | 3335 | 3619 | 2712 | 2369 | 2310 | 2373 | 2595 |
| | 1990 | 3454 | 3628 | 2913 | 2509 | 2448 | 2522 | 2706 |
| | 2000 | 3550 | 3580 | 3059 | 2626 | 2552 | 2637 | 2787 |
| Production of Wheat[a] | 1980 | 136 | 127 | 26 | 21 | 84 | 131 | 414 |
| | 1990 | 181 | 141 | 31 | 27 | 112 | 170 | 519 |
| | 2000 | 212 | 156 | 36 | 32 | 139 | 207 | 564 |
| Production of Rice[a] | 1980 | 15 | 1 | 10 | 52 | 158 | 220 | 241 |
| | 1990 | 16 | 2 | 13 | 67 | 195 | 275 | 298 |
| | 2000 | 18 | 2 | 16 | 89 | 224 | 329 | 355 |

| | | | | | | | | |
|---|---|---|---|---|---|---|---|---|
| Production of Coarse Grains[a] | 1980 | 315 | 172 | 60 | 48 | 120 | 228 | 757 |
| | 1990 | 366 | 193 | 75 | 63 | 142 | 280 | 894 |
| | 2000 | 429 | 199 | 91 | 182 | 172 | 345 | 1040 |
| Production of all Grains[a] (indicated year) | 1980 | 466 | 300 | 96 | 121 | 362 | 579 | 1412 |
| | 1990 | 563 | 336 | 119 | 157 | 449 | 725 | 1711 |
| | 2000 | 669 | 357 | 143 | 203 | 535 | 881 | 1959 |
| Net Exports: Wheat[a] (indicated year) | 1980 | 55 | -20 | -10 | -14 | -12 | -36 | |
| | 1990 | 84 | -22 | -17 | -23 | -25 | -65 | |
| | 2000 | 102 | -16 | -25 | -36 | -40 | -101 | |
| Net Exports: Rice[a] (indicated year) | 1980 | 2 | -1 | -1 | -2 | 3 | -- | |
| | 1990 | 2 | -1 | -3 | -7 | 8 | -2 | |
| | 2000 | 2 | -- | -5 | -5 | 5 | -5 | |
| Net Exports: Coarse Grains[a] (indicated year) million metric tons) | 1980 | 40 | -13 | 9 | -5 | -10 | -6 | |
| | 1990 | 35 | -14 | 3 | -10 | -23 | -30 | |
| | 2000 | 48 | -12 | -8 | -19 | -39 | -67 | |
| Net Exports: All Grains | 2000 | 152 | -28 | -38 | -60 | -74 | -173 | |

[a]Three-year average up to indicated year.

Source: Food and Agriculture Project (FAP), IIASA, private communication, June, 1984. Results are preliminary and likely to change; not to be quoted without permission of Project Leader, FAP, IIASA.

TABLE 7   Projections from India Model of IIASA

| Variable | Year | Alternative I | Alternative II | Alternative III |
|---|---|---|---|---|
| Population | 1980 | 674 | 672 | 670 |
| (in millions) | 1990 | 843 | 813 | 788 |
| | 2000 | 1048 | 995 | 927 |
| Rate of Growth of | 1971-2000 | 2.249 | 2.057 | 1.808 |
| Population (% per | 1980-2000 | 2.232 | 1.980 | 1.637 |
| year) | 1990-2000 | 2.206 | 1.980 | 1.637 |
| Rate of Growth of | 1971-2000 | 4.746 | 4.752 | 4.756 |
| Real GDP (% per | 1980-2000 | 5.349 | 5.356 | 5.363 |
| year) | 1990-2000 | 6.077 | 6.090 | 6.100 |
| Production of Wheat | 1980 | 33 | 33 | 33 |
| (million metric | 1990 | 57 | 57 | 57 |
| tons) | 2000 | 85 | 84 | 83 |
| Production of Rice | 1980 | 47 | 47 | 47 |
| (million metric | 1990 | 68 | 68 | 68 |
| tons) | 2000 | 92 | 92 | 92 |
| Production of | 1980 | 26 | 26 | 26 |
| Coarse Grains | 1990 | 32 | 32 | 32 |
| (million metric | 2000 | 35 | 34 | 34 |
| tons) | | | | |
| Production of all | 1980 | 106 | 106 | 106 |
| Grains (million | 1990 | 157 | 157 | 157 |
| metric tons) | 2000 | 212 | 210 | 209 |
| Daily Caloric Intake | | | | |
| Rural Group 1 | 1990 | 1018(28) | 1024(27) | 1030(26) |
| | 2000 | 1111(20) | 1152(18) | 1183(16) |
| Rural Group 2 | 1990 | 1958(17) | 1959(17) | 1961(17) |
| | 2000 | 2125(16) | 2159(16) | 2184(15) |
| Rural Group 3 | 1990 | 2584(19) | 2588(19) | 2591(19) |
| | 2000 | 2840(20) | 2872(20) | 2897(20) |
| Rural Group 4 | 1990 | 2659(20) | 2674(20) | 2693(20) |
| | 2000 | 2927(23) | 2937(23) | 2988(23) |
| Rural Group 5 | 1990 | 3789(17) | 3837(17) | 3898(18) |
| | 2000 | 3911(22) | 4013(23) | 4174(25) |
| Urban Group 1 | 1990 | 1170(2.1) | 1172(1.0) | 1178(0.9) |
| | 2000 | 1173(0.5) | 1217(0.4) | 1261(0.3) |
| Urban Group 2 | 1990 | 1654(5.7) | 1657(5.3) | 1664(4.9) |
| | 2000 | 1689(3.4) | 1726(2.9) | 1766(2.3) |
| Urban Group 3 | 1990 | 2029(17) | 2039(16) | 2052(15) |
| | 2000 | 2040(13) | 2073(12) | 2115(11) |
| Urban Group 4 | 1990 | 2379(35) | 2396(35) | 2419(34) |
| | 2000 | 2352(34) | 2397(33) | 2456(32) |
| Urban Group 5 | 1990 | 3102(41) | 3145(43) | 3200(44) |
| | 2000 | 3010(49) | 3091(51) | 3209(55) |

Note:  Figures in parentheses represent the population of each class in
rural and urban areas as a percent of the total rural and urban
population, respectively, in 1990 and 2000.

Source:  Food and Agriculture Project (FAP), IIASA, private communication,
June, 1984.  Results are preliminary and likely to change; are not to be
quoted without permission of Project Leader, FAP, IIASA.

the shrinking cropland area per person and the reduction in average soil depth by erosion combine to steadily reduce the per capita availability of topsoil for food production" (Brown et al., 1984:189). After pointing out that expanding food supplies may be progressively costly relative to real incomes (particularly of the poor), the authors conclude (p. 193) that "nothing less than a wholesale reexamination and reordering of social and economic priorities--giving agriculture and family planning the emphasis they deserve--will get the world back on an economic and demographic path that will reduce hunger (rather) than increase it."

Apart from doubtful empirical support for estimates of global soil erosion and degradation, the above formulation of the impact of population growth ignores the response of private agents to market signals, as well as social action that can prevent such a grim situation from arising. As Kelley (1984) points out, there are essentially only two prima facie plausible arguments that can be advanced to support the hypothesis that rapid population growth will necessarily lead to disaster. The first of these arguments holds that rapid population growth, by extending cultivation to marginal lands and increasing intensive cultivation in intramarginal lands, will lead to a progressively increasing relative price of food because of diminishing returns to factors other than land. However, this argument assumes the following: reserves of arable land are nearly exhausted; technical change that can mitigate diminishing returns will not occur; and the benign effect of rising incomes on the rate of decrease in population growth, if any, will be too slow-acting relative to the malign effect of the rising cost of food on the health and nutritional status of the poorer groups in the population. The second argument rests on the belief that natural resources (including the environment) are exhaustible in the sense that real marginal costs of use will eventually rise steeply, and the possibilities for exploiting substitutes for relatively abundant natural resources and/or primary factors such as capital and labor are limited.

Simon (1981) has persuasively argued that empirical support for these arguments is almost nonexistent. In his view, available data suggest that the real cost of food (as well as that of many other natural resources) has been falling rather than rising. There are still reserves of unutilized arable land in some areas of the world (particularly in South America), and the potential for increasing yields by increasing cropping intensity (i.e., through multiple cropping) is far from exhausted. Further, the potential for raising output in many parts of the developing world through the adoption of known superior technology has yet to be fully realized. In addition, evidence for induced innovation (Ruttan and Hayami, 1984; Hayami and Kikuchi; 1981) suggests that the processes of technical and institutional change themselves will be responsive to emerging scarcities. In any case, the fact that the relative prices of food and many natural resources have not risen, and in many cases have fallen, suggests that diminishing returns and resource depletion have so far been kept at bay.

Even among those who do not foresee rapid population growth
as a problem in the long run, some would still recognize that
there may be an "adjustment" problem in the short and medium
runs.  Ruling out "adjustment" through Malthusian "natural
checks" or coercive controls over the childbearing decisions of
couples, it is possible that (in the absence of noncoercive
policy instruments that influence population growth) there may
be no feasible path that would take the society from its initial
position to the steady state.  This is so, even though the long-
run sustainable (i.e., steady state) level of population may be
substantially larger than the current level, and the standard of
living associated with the long-run steady state may be much
better.  One reason advanced for this is the belief that rapid
population growth reduces savings and investment, possibly
delaying or precluding the attainment of the steady state.
After many studies, however, empirical evidence on the negative
impact of population growth on savings and investment is, at
best, inconclusive.  A more serious problem in many developing
countries is that inappropriate public policy interventions have
blunted and distorted the incentives of farmers to enlarge food
supplies.  Even in countries whose public policy has included
substantial investment in irrigation works, the development of
location-specific agricultural technology (including superior
crop varieties), the diffusion of such technology through
extension and subsidized credit, and the like, the design of
these policies and the management of the facilities created have
been so poor that any benefits and their distribution among
socioeconomic groups in the rural population have been reduced.
As contrasted with the empirical support for many of the arguments about the deleterious consequences of rapid population
growth, the empirical evidence on the cost of ill-conceived
public policy interventions in agriculture in developing
countries in Africa, Asia, and Latin America is strong and well
documented.


CONCLUSIONS

It would appear from the projections of the various models
reviewed above that the demand for food that is likely to arise
from anticipated income and population growth can be met without
a substantial increase in the relative price of food.  However,
this conclusion must be qualified for several reasons.  Even
though alternative income and population growth scenarios are
analyzed in almost all the models, in none of the models is population growth endogenous, and only in the IIASA model is income
growth endogenous.  Endogenizing population growth is very likely
to increase the chances for long-run viability of the system.
Adjustment to incipient excess demands or supplies of goods and
factors through relative price changes is exploited to the
greatest extent in the IIASA system of models, but to lesser and
varying degrees in other models.  The process of technical change
is very crudely modeled, if at all, and is independent of popula-

tion growth. Except for the IIASA system, all the models are
static; even in the former, however, the modeling of the process
of investment in capacity creation appears to be rudimentary, and
future returns from investing in alternative activities do not
appear to influence the pattern of investment.

Further, there are several possible channels for the influence of population growth on the production capacity of the
economy in general, and food and agriculture in particular, not
all of which have been taken into account in the projections
reviewed. One of the more important among these is the process
of the shift of labor away from agriculture. In most of the
presently developed countries, the agricultural share of employment is less than 10 percent, and in some of the developing
countries it has fallen substantially in the post-World War II
era. Yet in India, it has hardly changed in over 100 years from
about 70 percent, even though the share of agriculture in GDP has
steeply declined. The situation in Bangladesh is no better,
while the proportion of the labor force employed in agriculture
in China is only marginally less than that in India according to
the World Bank (1984:258, Table 21). If the proportion of a
rapidly growing (because of population growth) labor force
employed in agriculture remains virtually unchanged while the
share of domestic products originating in agriculture falls,
income disparities between agricultural and nonagricultural
workers will widen in the absence of massive transfers. However,
failure to reduce the pressure on agriculture would seem to
emerge, not from rapid population growth per se, but from the
strategy of industrialization that increased the capital intensity of production outside agriculture, thereby limiting the
scope of expanding nonagricultural employment.

It was mentioned earlier that the pattern of land-holdings
(in terms of the size distribution of farms), land tenure, and
other institutional arrangements in agriculture may be influenced
by population growth and technical change. Such institutional
changes may, in turn, affect the distribution of real incomes
(or "income entitlements" as Sen (1981) put it) and access to
food. Incorporating these factors into the formal methodology
of projections is not simple, if not for any other reason than
because the theory of endogenous institutional change is in its
infancy. Yet these factors could be far more significant than
those included in the projection models.

It is obviously impossible to give a satisfactory quantitative answer to the question of whether prospects for accommodating increasing population at a reasonable level of living
would improve or worsen if one were to generalize the projection
models by suitably including several of the above factors
without doing such an exercise. However, a qualitative and
somewhat speculative answer can be given. The viability of the
system can only be enhanced by recognition and utilization of
the proven strength of the price system in two areas: first, in
considerably reducing, if not eliminating altogether, any
incipient imbalances between supplies and demands in the short
run; second, and more important, in providing appropriate

signals for directing investments so as to ensure long-run
balance-formulation models and policies.  The influence of
technical change, particularly of the endogenous or induced
variety, is also likely to be in the same direction.  Many
structural rigidities and development policies that reduce the
static and dynamic efficiency of resource use are rarely
reflected in the models; therefore, both static, one-and-for-all
and continuing, dynamic gains from the removal of these policies
are neglected.  This again works toward underestimation of the
potential strength and long-run viability of the system.  On the
other hand, in the absence of a satisfactory theory of institutional change, it is difficult to assess even qualitatively
whether such change will be orderly and whether the burdens of
adjustment will be distributed in proportion to the capacity to
bear them.  For instance, demographic pressures can lead to an
increase in landlessness and unviable, fragmented land holdings.
Unless institutions and policy makers respond by encouraging the
consolidation of fragmented holdings, ensuring access to land
through tenancy arrangements, and augmenting income-earning
opportunities outside agriculture, the extent of poverty and
food insecurity among the poor may increase and eventually
threaten political stability.  In such a situation, it is difficult to say whether an easing of demographic pressures will
merely postpone the day of political reckoning or will provide
an extended period during which institutions can respond
positively.

Normal fluctuations in food supply, whether they relate to
output or to terms of trade, must be addressed by other means,
and population growth has little to do with them.  How the
available food is distributed among the population will depend
on the institutional arrangements relating to production and
exchange.  For instance, in a market economy, an individual must
have enough purchasing power through his "income entitlements"
to be able to afford a diet above starvation level.  The nature
of transportation, storage, and distribution networks is also
important.  As shown by recent tragic events in Ethiopia, in the
absence of such networks, food shipped by the rest of the world
will not reach the starving.  These elementary relationships
between institutional arrangements and access to food, along
with their implications for understanding episodes of famine,
are elegantly elaborated in Sen (1981).  It would appear from
his analysis that the main cause of such episodes has not been
shortage of food or rapid population growth, but colossal policy
failures in areas unrelated to population growth.

Once again, with the famine raging in Ethiopia, some
observers continue to assert that, while successive droughts
have contributed, rapid population growth and its alleged
consequences (e.g., desertification and the abandonment of
traditional methods of cultivation in favor of others that are
ecologically damaging) are behind the tragedy, and further that
desertification may even be responsible for the droughts.
However, as in earlier episodes, policy failures, particularly
in distorting incentives, may have more to do with the tragedy

than slower-acting, long-term ecological processes. A comparison
between the recent experiences of Tanzania and Zimbabwe in coping
with drought indeed suggests that the former's policies contributed significantly to their relative lack of success. The cause
of eliminating starvation and hunger in the world in a not-too-
distant future will be ill served if, instead of analyzing
avoidable policy failures, policy makers turn their attention to
attempts at changing an admittedly slow-acting process of interaction between population growth and the food economy. This is
not to deny the modest improvements in income distribution and
in the extent of undernourishment resulting from an exogenous
reduction in the rate of population growth, as shown by some of
the models reviewed here; rather, it is to point out that the
pay-off to the correction of policy failures is likely to be
more rapid and perhaps greater.


REFERENCES


Boserup, E. (1965)  The Conditions of Agricultural Progress.
    Winchester, Mass.:  Allen and Unwin Press.
Boserup, E. (1981)  Population and Technological Change:  A Study
    of Long Term Trends.  Chicago:  University of Chicago Press.
Brown, L., L. Starke, and E. Wolfe (1984)  State of the World
    1984.  A Worldwatch Institute Report on Progress Toward a
    Sustainable Society.  New York:  W.W. Norton & Co.
Council on Environmental Quality (1981)  Entering the Twenty-
    First Century:  The Global Report 2000 to the President,
    Vol. 1 and 2.  Washington, D.C.:  U.S. Government Printing
    Office.
Food and Agriculture Organization (1981)  Agriculture Toward
    2000.  Rome:  Food and Agriculture Organization.
Forrester, J.W. (1971)  World Dynamics.  Cambridge, Mass.:
    Wright-Allen Press.
Hayami Y., and M. Kikuchi (1981)  Asian Village Economy at the
    Cross Roads:  An Economic Approach to Institutional Change.
    Baltimore, Md.:  The Johns Hopkins University Press.
Higgins, G.M., A.H. Kassam, L. Naiken, G. Fischer, and M.M. Shah
    (1983)  Potential Population Supporting Capacities of Lands
    in the Developing World.  Technical Report FPA/INT/513 of
    Project Land Resources for Population of the Future, FAO,
    Rome.
International Food Policy Research Institute (1977)  Food Needs
    of Developing Countries:  Projections of Production and
    Consumption in 1990.  Report 3, International Food Policy
    Research Institute, Washington, D.C.
Kelley, A. (1984)  The Population Debate:  A Status Report and
    Revisionist Reinterpretation.  Mimeo, Centre for Demographic
    Studies, Duke University.
Meadows, D.H., D.L. Meadows, J. Randers, and W.W. Behrens III
    (1972)  The Limits to Growth.  New York:  Universe Books.

Parikh, K.S., and F. Rabar, eds. (1981)  Food for All in a
    Sustainable  World:  The IIASA Food and Agriculture
    Problem.  Laxenburg, Austria:  International Institute for
    Applied Systems Analysis.
Ruttan, V.W., and Y. Hayami (1984)  Towards a theory of induced
    innovation.  Journal of Development Studies 20(4):203-223.
Sen, A.K. (1981) Poverty and Famines.  London:  Oxford University
    Press.
Shah, M.M., G. Fischer, G.M. Higgins, A.H. Kassam, and L. Naiken
    (1984)  People, Land and Food Production:  Potentials in the
    Developing World.  Laxenburg, Austria:  International
    Institute for Applied Systems Analysis.
Simon, J. (1981)  The Ultimate Resource.  Princeton, N.J.:
    Princeton University Press.
Srinivasin, T.N. (1986)  Population and food.  In B. Arthur and
    R. Lee, eds., Population, Food and Rural Development.  New
    York:  Oxford University Press.
World Bank (1982)  World Development Report.  New York:  Oxford
    University Press.
World Bank (1984)  World Development Report.  New York:  Oxford
    University Press.

# 2
# Population Density and Agricultural Intensification: A Study of the Evolution of Technologies in Tropical Agriculture

Prabhu L. Pingali
Hans P. Binswanger

INTRODUCTION

This chapter describes the process by which agricultural societies have traditionally coped with increasing population densities. It explores the impact of population density on the overall nature of the farming system, on land use patterns and yields, on the location and nature of land investments, on the use of mechanical technology, and on the production of organic fertilizers. In the process, it also briefly addresses causes of agricultural intensification other than population growth and the problem of environmental degradation that can result from population growth.

The focus of the chapter is on how societies have been able to achieve agricultural growth resulting from farmer-based innovations rather than science-based inputs. Adaptation of the farming systems, the invention of new technologies, and related investments were--and continue to be--generated by farmers themselves. Identical or strikingly similar solutions to the need for increasing food production from a given area of land have been found independently in many places all over the world. Moreover, these solutions have often been sufficient to cope with the relatively low historic rates of growth in demand from increasing populations; in many cases they have also allowed for rising levels of food consumption. We should note, however, that other research (Binswanger and Ruttan, 1978; Hayami and Ruttan, 1985) clearly shows that farmers' own methods of technology discovery and land investment have not been sufficient to accommodate modern rates of growth in demand in developed countries where land frontiers are exhausted. These countries have been able to achieve high rates of agricultural growth only by adding science-based technologies--fertilizers, pesticides, high-yielding varieties, etc.--to farmer-generated technologies. These issues, and in particular the process and institutions required for generating the science-based technologies, are described in greater detail in Chapter 3 in this volume.

A casual look at farming systems across the world--from the annual and multicropping systems in South and Southeast Asia to the forest fallow systems in parts of West Africa--leads to an understanding of the positive relationship between population density and the intensity of farming. Boserup (1965) insisted that population pressure is the main determinant of agricultural intensification. General support for this proposition has been provided by specific case studies by Clarke (1966), Gleave and White (1969), Basehart (1973), and Brown and Podolejsky (1976). Turner et al. (1977) provide empirical support for the relationship between population density and farming intensity using cross-sectional data from 29 locations across the world. However, the relationship among farming intensity, agricultural technology, and labor use is not so obvious. Boserup (1965) shows a historic link between intensity of cultivation on the one hand and the level of mechanical technology, land investments, and organic fertilizer inputs on the other hand. This chapter explores the evolution of farming systems from the extensive to the intensive margin and associated increases in the number and intensity of the tasks performed.

The discussion below empirically verifies that intensification of the farming system leads to longer working hours and increased labor input per hectare of crop production. The transition from handhoes to animal-drawn plows and tractors is also shown to be directly associated with intensification of the farming system and increased labor requirements. This chapter shows that labor-saving benefits, rather than yield increases, are the overriding determinant in the transition to animal and mechanical power.

The discussion below first addresses the relationship between population density and the intensity of land use, then the pattern of labor use with intensity of farming, and next labor use and the evolution of tool systems. These sections are followed by an empirical analysis. In a final section, conclusions are presented.


POPULATION DENSITY AND THE INTENSITY OF LAND USE

The existence of a positive correlation between population density and the intensity of land use has been shown by Boserup (1965, 1980). She argues from the premise that during the neolithic period, forests covered a much larger part of the land surface than is the case today. The replacement of forests by bush and grassland was caused by (among other things) a reduction in fallow periods due to increasing population densities: "The invasion of forest and bush by grass is more likely to happen when an increasing population of long fallow cultivators cultivate the land with more and more frequent intervals" (Boserup, 1965:20).

Table 1 presents the relationship between population density and the intensity of the agricultural system. At very sparse population densities, up to 4 persons/square kilometer, the prevailing form of farming is the forest fallow system. A plot of forest land is cleared and cultivated for 1 or 2 years and then

TABLE 1  Food Supply Systems in the Tropics

| Food Supply Systema | Farming Intensity (R-value)b | Population Density Group Persons/kmc | Climatic Zoned | Tools Used |
|---|---|---|---|---|
| Gathering | 0 | 0-4 | | |
| Forest Fallow | 0-10 | 0-4 | Humid | Axe, matchet, and digging stick |
| Bush Fallow | 10-40 | 4-64 | Humid and semihumid | Axe, matchet, digging stick, and hoe |
| Short Fallow | 40-80 | 16-64 | Semihumid, semiarid, and high-altitude | Hoes and animal traction |
| Annual Cropping | 80-120 | 64-256 | Semihumid, semiarid, and high-altitude | Animal traction and tractors |

Notes: The food supply systems are not mutually exclusive. It is quite possible for two or more of the systems to exist concurrently (e.g., cultivation in concentric rings of various lengths of fallow, as in Senegal).
   The population density figures are only approximations; the exact numbers depend on location-specific soil fertility and agroclimatic conditions.

aDescription of food supply systems:
Gathering--wild plants, roots, fruits, nuts.
Forest fallow--1 or 2 crops followed by 15-25 years of fallow.
Bush fallow--2 or more crops followed by 8-10 years of fallow.
Short fallow--1 or 2 crops followed by 1 or 2 years of fallow; also known as grass fallow.
Annual cropping--1 crop each year.
Multicropping--2 or more crops in the same field each year.
bR equals number of years of cultivation times 100 divided by number of years of cultivation plus number of years of fallow (Ruthenberg, 1980:16; Boserup, 1980:23).
cBoserup (1980:19).
dRuthenberg (1980).

allowed to lie fallow for 20-25 years; this period of fallow is sufficient to allow forest regrowth. An increase in population density will result in a reduction in the period of fallow, and eventually the forest land will degenerate to bush savannah. Bush fallow is characterized by cultivation of a plot of land for 2-6 years, followed by 6-10 years of fallow; this period of fallow is too short to allow forest regrowth. Increasing population densities are associated with longer periods of continuous cultivation and shorter fallow periods. Eventually, the fallow period becomes too short for anything but grass growth. The transition to grass fallow occurs at population densities of around 16-64 persons per square kilometer. Further increases in population result in the movement to annual cultivation and multicropping, the most intensive systems of cultivation.

The above discussion leads to the broad generalization that for given agroclimatic conditions, increases in population density will gradually move the agricultural system from forest fallow to annual cultivation and even multicropping. The reasons for population concentration and/or growth and the consequent decline in arable land per capita are discussed below.

## Population Growth, Markets, and Other Determinants of Intensification

Since the turn of this century, we have observed a substantial increase in the natural rate of population growth across the world, mainly due to a sharp decline in the death rates caused by rapid advances in public health services. At the worldwide level, and at the level of a specific country, the decline in arable land per capita must be attributed primarily to this general increase in population. Within a country and within regions, however, population concentrations vary by soil fertility, altitude, and market accessibility. These intracountry variations are briefly discussed below, with examples primarily from sub-Saharan Africa. Table 2 shows the major causes and consequences of population concentration.

Since marginal productivity of labor is relatively higher on more fertile soils, one would expect immigration from less-endowed areas leading to reductions in cultivable areas per capita. Ada district in Ethiopia, Nyanza Province in Kenya, and the southern province of Zambia are a few examples of fertile areas that are relatively densely populated and intensively cultivated. High-altitude areas are similarly densely populated because of immigration from the lowlands due to lower disease incidence (notably malaria and sleeping sickness). Population concentrations on the Ethiopian and Kenyan highlands are popular examples of this phenomenon.

Given suitable soil conditions, areas with better access to markets, either through transport networks or proximity to urban centers, will be more intensively cultivated. Intensification occurs for two reasons:

- Higher prices and elastic demand for exportables imply that the marginal utility of effort increases; hence farmers in the region will begin cultivating larger areas.

- Higher returns to labor encourage immigration into the area from neighboring regions with higher transport costs.

TABLE 2 Causes and Consequences of Population Concentration

| Variable | Causes | Direct Consequence | Implications |
|---|---|---|---|
| Natural Population Growth | Improved public health and lack of emigration | | Reduction in fallow periods; Movement from shifting to permanent cultivation |
| Soil Fertility | Immigration to capture the benefits of higher returns to labor input | | Mechanization; Plowing: where agroclimatic and soil conditions make it profitable |
| Transport Facilities[a] | Immigration to capture the benefits of reduced transport costs | Reduction in available area per capita | Transport: where markets exist for food and other crops |
| Urban Demand[a] | Immigration to capture the benefits of market proximity | | Milling: in response to higher opportunity cost of time for female household members |
| Health | Avoidance of malaria and tsetse fly; immigration to cooler highlands | | Land investments; For soil fertility, drainage, terracing, etc.; increase in the marginal lands brought under cultivation |
| Historic | Tribal war/slave trade; immigration to inaccessible highlands | | Land rights; From general use rights to specific land rights |
| Land Laws, Rights | Restrictions on the right to open new land | | |

[a] In the case of improved transport facilities and urban demand, one may observe an expansion in the area under cultivation in the absence of immigration.

31

Intensive groundnut production in Senegal, maize production
in Kenya and Zambia, and cotton production in Uganda have all
followed the installation of the railway and have been mainly
concentrated in areas close to the railway line. Similarly,
agricultural production around Kano, Lagos, Nairobi, Kampala, and
other urban centers is extremely intensive as compared to other
areas. It should be noted that agricultural intensification in
response to improved market access could occur even under low
population densities as a result of individual farmers' expanding
their area under marketed crops. The consequences of intensification in these circumstances do not differ from those in areas
with high population densities.

Finally, it should be noted that inter- and intra-country
variations in population densities, especially in sub-Saharan
Africa, have historically been caused by tribal warfare and slave
trade, resulting in population concentrations in relatively inaccessible highlands. Population concentration on the high plateau of Rwanda and Burundi was in response to the incursions of
slave traders and health concerns. Similar migrations from the
lowlands to the Mandara Mountains in Cameroon, the Jos Plateau
in Nigeria, and the Rift Valley in Kenya and Tanzania have been
based on the desire for personal security. Subsequent natural
population growth has made many of these areas the most densely
populated parts of Africa.

Agricultural Intensification and Soil Preferences

The intensification of agricultural systems is constrained by
climatic and soil factors. Table 1 illustrates the impact of
climatic factors on the intensification of the agricultural
system. For given agroclimatic conditions, the extent of intensification is conditional on the relative responsiveness of the
soils to inputs associated with intensive production, such as
land improvements, manure, and fertilizers. The responsiveness
to intensification is generally higher on soils with higher
water- and nutrient-holding capacity, primarily because higher
water-holding capacity reduces drought risk. Water-holding
capacity is higher the deeper the soils and the higher their
clay content; it is low on shallow sandy soils.

Figure 1 presents the differences in soil types across a
toposequence for given agroclimatic conditions. Soils on the
upper slopes are relatively light and easy to work by hand;
tillage requirements are minimal on these soils. The clay
content and hence the heaviness of the soils increase as one goes
down the toposequence, and therefore power requirements for land
preparation increase. Movement down the slope also reduces yield
risks because of the increased water retention capacity of the
soils. The soils are heaviest in the depressions and marshes at
the bottom of the toposequence. These bottom lands, or bas
fonds, are often extremely difficult to prepare by hand and are
often impossible to cultivate in the absence of investments in
water control and drainage. The extremely high labor require-

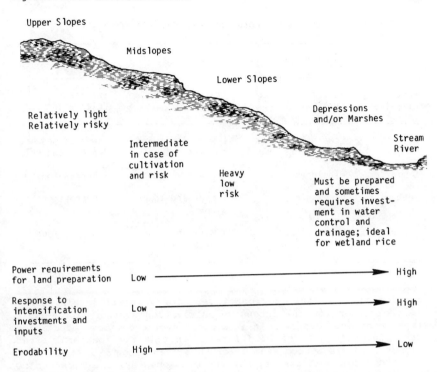

FIGURE 1   Toposequence and Soil Type

ments for capital investments and land preparation make the
bottom lands the least preferred for cultivation under low population densities, and they are often found to be under fallow.
As population densities increase, however, the bottom lands become intensively cultivated because of the relatively higher
returns offered to labor and land investments, especially in rice
cultivation. Also, as population densities increase, labor
supply increases make it possible to undertake the necessary
labor-intensive investments in irrigation, drainage, and the
like.

Soil type differences across a toposequence that are
characterized here could be microvariations limited to a few
hundred meters or a few kilometers, or they could be macro-
variations in which entire regions are part of one level of the
toposequence. For example, the northeastern part of Thailand
can be characterized as the upper slopes and the central plains
of Thailand as the lower slopes and valley bottoms. Preferences
for cultivating different points of the toposequence are dependent on the agroclimatic conditions. Table 3 presents soil preferences by farming intensity and agroclimatic zones. Under arid
conditions, lower slopes and depressions are the only lands that
can be cultivated because only here is water retention capacity

TABLE 3  Farming Intensity, Agroclimates, and Soil Preferences

|  | Farming Intensity | | |
| --- | --- | --- | --- |
| Agro-climates | Forest and Bush Fallow | Grass Fallow | Permanent Cultivation |
| Arid | Lower slopes and depressions only | Lower slopes and depressions only | Lower slopes and depressions only |
| Semiarid | Midslopes | + Lower slopes | + Depressions |
| Subhumid | Upper slopes | + Mid- and lower slopes | + Depressions |
| Humid | Upper slopes | + Mid- and lower slopes | + Depressions |

sufficient to sustain a crop at very low rainfall levels. This is the reason for the intensive cultivation systems of an oasis type that one observes in arid areas even under low population densities. Pockets of arid farming in primarily pastoral areas of Botswana are a good example of this phenomenon.

Under semiarid conditions, the midslopes are the first to be cultivated. As population densities increase, cultivation replaces grazing on the lower slopes and eventually in the depressions. Power sources for tillage are first used in the bottom lands, generally around the time when population pressure makes these lands valuable for cultivation. The reversal of land preferences is quite dramatic: in the semiarid zones of Africa, where population density is low, the lower slopes and depressions are left for grazing and contribute only minimally to food supply; in the semiarid zones of India, on the other hand, the depressions are intensively cultivated, usually with rice, using elaborate irrigation systems and animal traction.

Yield risks due to low water availability are not a major problem in the subhumid and humid tropics; hence, one finds cultivation starting at the upper slopes and gradually moving downward as population pressure increases. At high population densities, the swamps and depressions become the most important land sources for food production, often associated with extremely intensive rice production. One observes such labor-intensive rice production in South and Southeast Asia and could expect the same for Africa as population densities increase.

Population pressure leads to a sharp reversal in the preference (price) for different types of land in all but the arid zones. As population densities increase, one observes the cultivation of land that requires substantially higher labor input, but at the same time is more responsive to the extra inputs.

The Soil Degradation Problem

Soil degradation is defined here as soil erosion and loss in soil fertility associated with intensive cultivation, overgrazing, and deforestation. Soil degradation is not a universal problem. First, the threat of soil degradation varies enormously by soil type and with differences in temperature, rainfall regimes, and slope. Second, appropriate land use and land investments can prevent the problem, even on high-risk soils. Therefore, degradation problems are mainly restricted to areas where the rate of return to preventive land investments (such as terracing) is low. Incentives for corrective land investments depend on the relative land endowments of the region and on whether potentially degradable land is under private or communal control.

The previous section addressed the process of agricultural intensification along the toposequence, and the conclusion was that the response to intensification is highest on the heavier soils on the lower slopes and valley bottoms. However, the very forces of intensification that lead to land investments lower down in the toposequence may simultaneously cause higher levels of degradation on the upper parts of the toposequence. The mechanics of this process and the conditions under which the problem can be corrected are briefly described below; Table 4 presents the consequences of intensification.

Under low population densities, the farmer chooses between yields and labor requirements. As population densities increase, forest cover is reduced, the cultivated area expands toward lower slopes, and the supply of pasture land and forest products decreases. Farmers will attempt to increase their private rights in plots, especially in the lower areas, where drainage investments are required and where erosion problems are absent or minimal. On the midslopes, the return to land investments is often sufficient to induce--where necessary--private investment in controlled drainage, bunding, or even terracing. Since some of these investments must be carried out on the basis of small watersheds, problems can arise when fragmentation of land is excessive and the required group action for these investments is not forthcoming. When population densities rise, better investment in irrigation may also occur on the midslopes.

It is on shallow soils of the upper slopes that erosion problems are most likely to arise. Several mechanisms are involved. In regions with small endowments of low-lying areas, the cultivated area will expand into the shallow upper slopes which were previously used for pasture and/or as communal forests. However, yields are low, and the payoffs to erosion control or intensive inputs are low as well. Unlike the case of the midslopes, and despite privatization, individual initiative cannot arrest the process of degradation because of the low return to control measures. A low-yield/low-input equilibrium will emerge; these low yields and low input levels may coexist in the same village with high levels of inputs and yields in small pockets of low-lying areas.

TABLE 4   Impact of Population Growth and Growing Markets

| Lower Slopes and Depressions | Midslopes | Upper Slopes |
|---|---|---|
| Rapid Privatization | Attempts to privatize | If privatization possible |
| Investment in Drainage, Irrigation, etc. | More permanent cultivation | Where crop options in lower slopes are limited:<br>- land uses for crops at mini- |
| High Use of Inputs | Investment in erosion control, perhaps irrigation | mal levels of investment and purchased inputs (low payoff)<br>- very low yield equilibrium |
| High Payoffs to Inputs Investments | High levels of input use<br><br>Potential difficulties with erosion control because of fragmentation | Where crop options exist elsewhere in village or region, people will use the land for grazing or forestry; no problem of degradation<br><br>If left as common for pasture and forestry<br><br>Overgrazing and overcutting problem (must be solved by controlling access)<br>Absence of investment and reinvestment (must be solved by community action or government intervention)<br>If no corrective actions, serious degradation |

Where cropping opportunities exist in abundant low-lying areas or midslopes, the upper slopes will continue to be used as pastures and/or forests. Where privatization is not possible, common property resource problems arise, which are aggravated as the supply of forest products and pastures declines rapidly in the better land areas. Without controlled access to the areas or privatization of the lands, overgrazing and overcutting of wood will expose the land to degradation. Private ownership provides incentives both for controlled access and for investment in erosion control and/or tree planting; however, it may deprive large segments of the population of their former use rights. Where privatization is infeasible or undesirable, community action or government intervention is required both for control of access and for investments in erosion control and forest replanting. Difficult dilemmas frequently arise as traditional users are threatened with a loss of their use rights. Societies are often incapable of solving these ownership or access control problems before serious damage has occurred.

The extent and magnitude of the degradation problem varies by the agroclimatic zone. The general principle here is that the rate of return to land investments varies by agroclimatic zone,

TABLE 5  Payoffs to Land Investments and Potential Soil Degradation by
Agroclimates

| Agroclimate Zone | Upper Slopes | Midslopes | Lower Slopes and Depressions |
|---|---|---|---|
| Arid | Payoffs: low | Payoffs: low | Payoffs: high |
| | Degradation: high when land endowments low and/or when communal access problem not solved | Degradation: high when land endowments low and/or when communal access problem not solved | Degradation: low |
| Semiarid | Payoffs: low | Payoffs: moderate | Payoffs: high |
| | Degradation: high when land endowments low and/or when communal access problem not solved | Degradation: low when privatized and externality problem solved | Degradation: low |
| Subhumid and Humid | Payoffs: moderate | Payoffs: high | Payoffs: high |
| | Degradation: low when privatized and used predominantly for tree crops | Degradation: low when privatized and used for a combination of tree and field crops | Degradation: low |

and the problem of degradation is highest in those zones where
the returns to such investments are the lowest.  Table 5 shows
the payoffs to land investment and potential degradation by toposequence and agroclimatic zone.  In the context of agroclimates,
there are two problem areas that should be emphasized here:  on
the one hand, regeneration of vegetation is extremely slow in the
arid zones, while on the other hand, continuous cultivation in
the humid tropics could cause severe leaching and soil acidification problems.  Accordingly, the medium rainfall zones between
1,000-1,500 mm are the most suitable for continuous field crop
production.

The mid- and upper slopes in the arid zones have very low
returns to investment and if used for cropping are highly susceptible to degradation.  Where these lands are used for communal
grazing, they could be subject to overgrazing, particularly in
drought years by transhumant cattle.

In the semiarid tropics, because of privatization and moderate returns to land investments in the midslopes, soil degradation is reasonably well controlled.  The problem areas in the
semiarid zones are the upper slopes, which, depending on the
region's land endowments, could be used either for grazing and
forestry or for low-yield crop production.  As discussed earlier,
these upper slopes could suffer from degradation either through
an inability to control access, or through permanent cultivation
on extremely marginal land.

In the subhumid and humid tropics, the rate of return to land investment is high even on the upper slopes. The problem of degradation can be controlled more easily by individual initiative in these zones. By choosing appropriate combinations of tree and field crops across a toposequence, an individual farmer could possibly control for erosion and leaching, and maintain long-term soil quality. The major problem of the humid and subhumid tropics is one of deforestation since as population densities increase, the demand for arable land leads to a recession in forest areas.

The discussion up to now has highlighted mainly long-term consequences, assuming that short-term adjustments in land use and the evolution of an institutional framework for rights of usage occur smoothly. Where institutional changes such as privatization and land tenancy do not occur rapidly, one could observe severe short-run soil degradation irrespective of agroclimates, land endowments, or the toposequence, except possibly on the bottomlands.


PATTERN OF LABOR USE WITH INTENSITY OF FARMING

The total labor input per hectare on a given crop is positively correlated with the intensity of farming, holding technology constant. Table 6 presents examples of labor use with farming intensity in rice cultivation. The movement from forest fallow to annual cultivation in West Africa using the hoe results in an increase in total labor input per hectare from 770 hours in Liberia to 3,300 hours in Cameroon. This increase in labor input occurs because of an increase in the intensity with which certain tasks have to be performed (for example, land preparation and weeding) and because of an increase in the number of operations performed (e.g., manuring, irrigation). A discussion of labor use across intensities of farming is provided below. Table 7 presents the increase in operations performed with the intensification of the farming system.

In the forest and bush fallow systems of cultivation, land clearing, planting, and harvesting are the major tasks performed. Fire is the most prevalent technique used for land clearance; this form of land clearance, in addition to regenerating the soil, also removes all weed growth. Land clearance by fire requires very low levels of labor input: 300 to 400 hours per hectare for forest fallow systems in Liberia and Ivory Coast. Being under tree cover, the ground is soft, and hence no further land preparation is required prior to sowing with the help of a digging stick or a handhoe. Such systems of cultivation require almost no weeding or interculture, and the period between planting and harvesting is virtually task-free.

As the fallow period becomes shorter and the land under fallow becomes grassy, fire can no longer be used for land clearance. Since fire cannot get rid of grass roots, grasses persist through the growing season. The intensive use of a hoe for land preparation becomes essential in order to clear the

| Country<br>Region<br>Intensity of Farming<br>Technique | Liberia<br>Gbanga<br>11<br>Hoe | Ivory Coast<br>Man<br>24<br>Hoe | Ghana<br>Begora<br>40<br>Hoe | Cameroon<br>Bamunka<br>100<br>Hoe | India<br>Ferozepore<br>121<br>Animal Plow | Java<br>Subang<br>200<br>Animal Plow | Philippines<br>Laguna<br>180<br>Tractor |
|---|---|---|---|---|---|---|---|
| **Time/Operation (hours/hectare)** | | | | | | | |
| Land Clearing | 418.4 | 300.8 | 665 | -- | -- | -- | -- |
| Land Preparation | -- | -- | -- | 714 | 86.4 | 494.4 | 73.6 |
| Sowing/Planting | 107.2 | 142.4 | 207 | 536.8 | 129.6 | 146 | 80.0 |
| Fertilizing and Manuring | -- | -- | -- | -- | 12.8 | -- | -- |
| Weeding | 36.8 | 292 | 276.8 | 113 | 57.6 | 218 | 213 |
| Plant Protection | 44 | 222 | -- | 1,393 | | -- | 96 |
| Harvesting | 164 | 218.4 | 280 | 264 | 128.8 | 324.4 | 222.4 |
| Threshing | -- | 84 | -- | 280 | 76.8 | 70 | -- |
| Other | -- | -- | -- | -- | 136[a] | -- | -- |
| Total | 770 | 1,259.2 | 1,432 | 3,300 | 627.2 | 1,252 | 685 |

[a] Irrigation.

TABLE 7 Comparison of Operations and Technology Across Farming Systems

| Operation | Forest Fallow | Bush Fallow | Short Fallow | Annual Cropping | Multicropping |
|---|---|---|---|---|---|
| Land Clearance | Fire | Fire | None | None | None |
| Land Preparation | No land preparation; digging sticks used to plant roots and sow seeds | Land loosened using hoes and digging sticks | Use of plow for preparing land | Animal-drawn plows and tractors | Animal-drawn plows and tractors |
| Manure Use | - Ash<br>- Household refuse for garden plots | Ash, burnt or unburnt leaves, other vegetable matter, and turf brought from surrounding land | - Animal and human waste<br>- Green manuring<br>- Composts<br>- Silt from canals | - Animal and human waste<br>- Composting<br>- Cultivation of green manure crops<br>- Chemical fertilizer | - Animal and human waste<br>- Composting<br>- Cultivation of green manure<br>- Chemical fertilizer |
| Weeding | Minimal | Required as length of fallow decreases | Weeding required during growing season | Intensive weeding required during growing season | Intensive weeding required during growing season |
| Use of Animals in Farming | None | As length of fallow decreases, animal drawn plows begin to appear | - Plowing<br>- Transport<br>- Interculture | - Plowing<br>- Transport<br>- Interculture<br>- Postharvest tasks<br>- Irrigation | Plowing, transport, interculture, postharvest tasks, irrigation |
| Seasonality of Labor Demand | None | None | Land preparation, weeding, and harvesting | Acute seasonal labor demand concentrated around the rainy season and harvest period | Acute seasonal labor demand concentrated around land preparation, weeding, harvest, and postharvest tasks |
| Fodder Supply | None | Emergence of grazing land | Abundant free grazing land | Free grazing during fallow period, crop residues | Intensive fodder management and fodder crop production |

grass roots.  Land preparation and sowing take up almost 40 percent of the total labor input for the annual cultivation of rice in Cameroon.  Under short fallow systems of cultivation, early-season weeding and plant protection become pronounced; also, manure use is required to complement fallow periods for maintaining soil fertility.

Permanent cultivation of land requires labor investments for irrigation, drainage, leveling, or terracing, and for the development of more evolved manuring techniques.  Permanent cultivation also requires extremely intensive land preparation and interculture.

In the intensification of the pattern of land use, one observes an increase in agricultural employment and in yields per hectare.  However, intensification of farming in the absence of a change in tools used would probably lead to a decline in yield per man-hour.  This can be deduced from the observation that the greater proportion of the additional labor input is used for maintaining soil fertility, weeding, and protecting plants.  In other words, it is possible to hypothesize that labor input per hectare increases at a faster rate than yield per hectare in the movement to more intensive systems of farming.

## LABOR USE AND THE EVOLUTION OF TOOL SYSTEMS

The transition from digging sticks and handhoes to the plow is closely correlated with the intensity of farming.  The emergence of mechanical tillage is generally observed at late bush fallow and early grass fallow stages, and not before.  The switch from one set of tools to the next occurs when the resulting labor-saving benefits exceed the costs of switching to new tools.

The simplest form of agricultural tool, the digging stick, is most useful in the very extensive forest and bush fallow systems where no land preparation is required.  As the bush cover begins to recede, the ground needs to be loosened before sowing, and at this stage handhoes replace digging sticks.  Handhoes are used for land preparation and weeding in the latter stages of bush fallow, in grass fallow, and even in some instances of annual cultivation.  Land preparation using the hoe becomes extremely labor-intensive and tedious by the grass fallow stage, especially because of the persistence of grass weeds. "The use of a plow for land preparation becomes indispensible at this stage" (Boserup 1965:240).  A switch to the plow during grass fallow results in a substantial reduction in the amount of labor input required for land preparation.  The net benefits of switching from the hoe to the plow are conditional on soil types and topography; the benefits are lower for sandy soils and for hilly terrain.

The above discussion on the evolution from handhoes to animal-drawn plows is formalized in Figure 2.  This figure compares labor costs under hand- and animal-powered cultivation systems and shows the point where animal traction is the dominant technology.

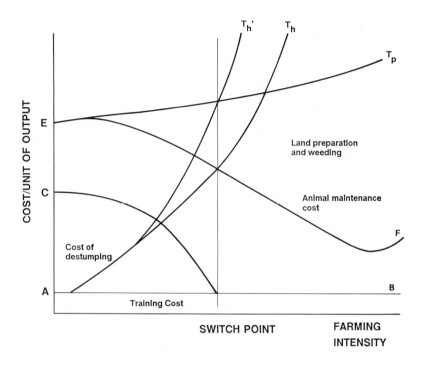

FIGURE 2   A Comparison of Labor Costs Under Hand- and Animal-
Powered Cultivation

Notes:
$T_p$:  total labor costs for land prepared, early-season
       weeding, and manuring using animal traction.
$T_h$:  labor costs for land preparation and early-season
       weeding using handhoes.
$T_h'$  $T_h$ plus labor costs for maintaining soil fertility
       without manure from draft animals.
Switch Point:  farming intensity at which animal traction
       become the dominant technology.

    The overhead labor costs in the transition from hand to
animal power include the cost of training the animals, the cost
of destumping and leveling the fields, and the cost of feeding
and maintaining the animals on a year--round basis.  The cost of
training  the animals is independent of the intensity of farming.
The cost of destumping is extremely high under forest and early
bush fallow systems because of the high density of stumps per
unit area and a highly developed root network that is difficult
to remove.  As the length of fallow decreases, the costs of de-

stumping decline because of reduced tree and root density; destumping requirements are minimal by the grass fallow stage. The
cost of the feeding and caretaking of the draft animals is also
very high during forest and early bush fallow, primarily because
of the lack of grazing land, as well as the prevalence of di-
seases such as trypanasomiasis. As the fallow becomes grassy,
grazing land becomes prevalent and so does animal ownership;
hence the costs of maintaining draft animals decline. By the
annual cultivation stage, however, grazing land becomes a limiting factor necessitating the production of fodder crops, which
in turn leads to an increase in the cost of feeding and maintaining draft animals. The total cost of using draft animals for
land preparation, early season weeding, and manuring is given by
the curve $T_p$.

As discussed earlier, the labor costs for cultivation using
hand tools rise rapidly as farming intensity increases. This is
mainly because of the increased effort required for preparing the
land, weeding, and maintaining soil fertility. $T_h$ shows total
labor costs using handhoes for land preparation and weeding,
while $T_h'$ adds in the cost of maintaining soil fertility. The
shape of the $T_h'$ curve depends on (1) the ease of producing
compost, (2) the rate of decay of organic matter, and (3) the
cost of chemical fertilizer. In humid and subhumid areas, it is
easier to produce compost and manure relative to semi-arid and
arid areas because of an abundance of natural vegetation; hence,
the labor costs involved in the production of manure are lower,
and the $T_h'$ curve is flatter. In hot tropical areas, the very
high temperatures cause the organic matter to decay at a faster
rate relative to the more temperate highlands; thus, these areas
require additional compost and manure inputs, making the $T_h'$
curve steeper. The cheaper chemical fertilizers are the flatter
the $T_h'$ curve becomes because of the substitution of fertilizers for labor-intensive manure production.

Animal-drawn plows are the dominant technology at the point
where the costs of hand cultivation exceed those of the transition to animal power. This switch point is shown in Figure 2.
This discussion illustrates the following conclusions:

- The transition to animal-drawn plows would not be cost-
  effective in forest and bush fallow systems because of
  the very high overhead labor costs required for
  destumping and animal maintenance.

- There is a distinct point in the evolution of agricultural systems at which animal draft power becomes
  economically feasible.

- This dominance point is conditional on soil types and
  soil fertility: the transition would occur sooner for
  hard-to-work soils (clays) and for soils that require
  high labor input for maintaining soil fertility.

The complementarity between animal traction and manure use implied in the third conclusion above is explained by the inverse relationship between farming intensity and soil fertility, and by the increased availability of manure when draft animals are introduced into the farming system. Fertilizers tend to substitute for manure around the annual cultivation and multicropping stages.

The transition from animal plows to tractors is explained better in terms of the choice of techniques rather than the evolution of farming systems. Factors that determine this transition are capital availability, economic efficiency of tractor use, labor cost, and peak season labor scarcity. Tractors generally emerge as feasible alternatives to animal-drawn plows at the stage of permanent cultivation of land; land preparation and transport are usually the first operations for which tractors are used. For a detailed analysis of the evolution of tool systems in sub-Saharan Africa, see Pingali et al. (1985).


EMPIRICAL ANALYSIS

Examples cited in the prior sections of this chapter are primarily from sub-Saharan Africa. These examples are part of a compilation of cases for a research project on agricultural mechanization and the evolution of farming systems in sub-Saharan Africa (see Pingali et al., 1985). For the empirical work presented below, a worldwide data set assembled from several research studies and surveys was used. This data set, presented in the Appendix Table, contains information on farming intensity, labor use, mechanization, fertilizer use, land investments, and yields for 52 specific locations in Africa, Asia, and Latin America.

This section provides a sequence of empirical results that relate to the effects of an increase in farming intensity, a change in tools used, and increased land investments on labor use per hectare, yields, labor productivity, and fertilizer use. Empirical tests are provided for the following hypotheses:

- For a given set of tools, higher intensities of farming are associated with higher levels of labor input.

- A change in the set of tools leads to a reduction in labor input.

- A change in the set of tools is induced by the labor-saving rather than yield benefits.

- The use of organic and chemical fertilizers is directly related to the intensity of farming.

Intensity of farming or land use was measured by the R-value, as defined as follows:

$$R\text{-value} = \frac{\text{crop cycles/year} * \text{years of cultivation} * 100}{\text{years of cultivation} + \text{years of fallow}}$$

In other words, intensity of farming can be defined as the percentage of time in the rotation cycle that a plot of land is devoted to cropping. The R-value can range from less than 10 percent for forest fallow cultivation to over 200 percent for multicropping. (Table 9 presents the approximate R-values for different intensities of farming.)

Mechanization is defined as the substitution of animal and tractor power for hand cultivation. Dummy variables are used for animal traction, tractor use, land investments, and fertilizer use. Land investments include destumping, leveling, drainage, irrigation, and the like, while the fertilizer use variable includes both organic and chemical fertilizers. Labor input is measured in hours per hectare, and yield is measured per hectare and per labor hour.

Farming Intensity and Technologies Used

Table 8 is a frequency table of technologies used with farming intensity. As hypothesized plow use becomes significant at the grass fallow stage, 63 percent of the grass fallow cases use plows, while all the forest and bush fallow cases use handhoes. By the annual cultivation stage, 87 percent of all cases use the plow. The use of animal power increases through the multicropping stage, in which 63 percent of the cases use animal-drawn plows. The use of fertilizers and investments in land also increase with farming intensity. While none of the forest and/or

TABLE 8  A Frequency Table of Farming Intensity and Technologies Used

| Technology | Forest and Bush Fallow | Grass Fallow | Annual | Multi-cropping |
|---|---|---|---|---|
| Animal Traction | 0 | .50 | .55 | .63 |
| Tractor | 0 | .13 | .32 | .21 |
| Total Plow Use | 0 | .63 | .87 | .84 |
| Land Investments | 0 | 0 | .64 | .74 |
| Fertilizers | 0 | .75 | .91 | .95 |
| Number of Observations | 8 | 8 | 22 | 19 |

TABLE 9  Labor Use in Cultivation[a] with Farming Intensity, Mechanization, and Land Investments

| Dependent Variable | Log Labor Use per Hectare |
| --- | --- |
| Log Farming Intensity | 0.456[b] (0.132) |
| Animal Traction | -0.96[b] (0.23) |
| Tractor | -1.14[b] (0.27) |
| Land Investments | 0.057 (0.20) |
| Intercept | 5.46 |
| $R^2$ | 0.33 |
| Number of Observations | 56 |

[a]Does not include labor use in overhead activities such as land investments and animal or machine maintenance.
[b]Significant at 1 percent.

bush fallow cases use any of the technologies, the use of animal traction and fertilizers, along with capital investments in land, becomes very pronounced in the multicropping stage. The use of tractors, though not observed in the forest and bush fallow stages, does not show an increasing trend with farming intensity; this is in accordance with the proposition that the choice between animal traction and tractor use cannot be explained in terms of the evolution of farming systems.

Labor Use and Farming Intensity

A log-linear regression was used to test the hypothesis of a positive correlation between labor use and farming intensity. The results of this regression are presented in Table 9. Intercept dummies were used for animal traction, tractor use, and land investments. This is not a perfect inquiry, however, since causality could not be established.

The hypothesis that the transition to more intensive farming systems is associated with longer working hours is validated. A 10 percent increase in farming intensity is associated with a 4.6 percent increase in labor use per hectare. When the data set was separated by each type of tool and the coefficient on farming intensity estimated, it was found that the relationship between farming intensity and labor use holds true irrespective of the types of tools used, although the null hypothesis of equality of coefficients could not be rejected. Animal traction and tractor use act as intercept shifters. For given intensity of farming, the switch to animal traction or tractors significantly reduces the total labor use per hectare. Land investments were not found to significantly affect labor use in cultivation. However, the labor use data generally did not include the time spent for investments such as destumping, leveling, and irrigation, or for the maintenance of animals and machines; this overhead labor obviously does increase with land investments.

Figure 3 shows the relationship between intensity of farming and labor use, and the effect of the mechanization shifters. Cultivation using a handhoe is prevalent up to an R-value of 50. Hand cultivation persists beyond this level of intensity in areas where animal traction is not feasible, such as mountainous areas (Lumle, Nepal) or tsetse fly areas (Agnale, Ethiopia and Bamunka, Cameroon). There is a definite switch to animal traction at an R-value of 50. As hypothesized, this is the grass fallow stage, and fields are free of stumps. There does not seem to be an upper bound for animal traction, which is observed even at an R-value of 200. Farming intensities at which tractor cultivation becomes feasible are the same as those for animal traction (R-value greater than 50). This data set supports the proposition that the switch from animal traction to tractor use is not explained by the evolution in farming systems.

Yields, Labor Productivity, and Farming Intensity

Results presented in Table 10 validate the hypothesis that yield per hectare and fertilizer use rise with farming intensity, holding the level of mechanization constant. For a 10 percent increase in farming intensity, yield per hectare increases by 3.9 percent. The level of mechanization was found to have no significant effect on yield per hectare. Capital investments in land, on the other hand, were found to have a significant positive effect on yields: these investments, primarily irrigation, raise yields by 30 percent for a given intensity of farming.

Increases in farming intensity were found to have no significant effect on yield per man-hour, although the negative sign on the coefficient was as hypothesized. The tools used have a significant positive effect on yield per man-hour or labor productivity. A switch from hand cultivation to animal traction increases yield per man-hour by 78 percent, while a further switch to tractor use increases yield by an additional 42 percent for given intensity of farming.

Increase in farming intensity was found to have no significant effect on yield per man-hour, although the negative sign on the coefficient is as hypothesized. The decline in yield per

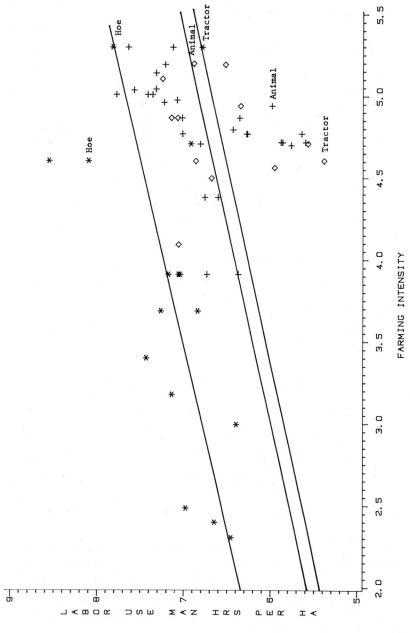

FARMING INTENSITY

48

TABLE 10  Farming Intensity Related to Yield per Hectare, Yield per
Hour of Cultivation Labor, and Fertilizer Use

| Dependent Variable | Log Yield/ha | Log Yield/ Hour of Culti- vation Labor | Fertilizer Use |
|---|---|---|---|
| Log Farming Intensity | 0.389[a] (0.097) | -0.068 (0.15) | 0.24[a] (0.06) |
| Animal Traction | -0.179 (0.17) | 0.78[a] (0.26) | 0.369[a] (0.105) |
| Tractor | 0.068 (0.20) | 1.20[a] (0.31) | 0.407[a] (0.12) |
| Land Investments | 0.299[b] (0.148) | 0.24 (0.23) | 0.037 (0.09) |
| Intercept | 5.69 | 0.24 | -0.57 |
| $R^2$ | 0.45 | 0.38 | 0.62 |
| Number of Observations | 56 | 56 | 56 |

[a]Significant at 1 percent.
[b]Significant at 5 percent.

man-hour of cultivation labor is presumably prevented by additional capital investments in land, and the movement to heavier
soils that are more responsive to intensification inputs.  The
additional labor required for investments in land is not reflected in this data set.  It is likely that yield per man-hour
of total labor (cultivation and overhead) would show the
hypothesized declining trend.

As discussed earlier, higher population densities lead to a
movement to heavier bottom land soils.  These soils require high
levels of labor input for investments in drainage and water
control; however, once those investments have been made, these
soils provide substantially higher yields, especially for rice,
than do the lighter and easier-to-work soils.  It is possible
that the negative effect on labor productivity imposed by the
higher overhead labor requirements is offset to a large extent
by the higher yields, especially on the heavier, bottom land
soils.[1]

Increases in farming intensity were found to have a positive
effect on the use of organic and chemical fertilizers.  For a 10
percent increase in farming intensity, fertilizer use increases
by 2.4 percent.  The level of mechanization has a significant
positive effect on fertilizer use: a switch from handhoes to

animal traction is accompanied by a 37 percent increase in fertilizer use per hectare; a further switch to tractors increases
fertilizer use by an additional 5 percent. Land investments were
found to have no significant effect on fertilizer use, although
the positive sign is as expected.


CONCLUSIONS

The overriding question behind this chapter is whether or not we
can expect rapid population growth to be associated with declining levels of welfare of the agricultural population in the
developing world. This obviously depends on many other issues
than the purely agricultural factors discussed here. However,
the following points can be made:

    Far from being immobile and technologically stagnant,
        "traditional" societies have responded to changes in
        population densities and external markets with changes
        in farming systems and land-use patterns, as well as
        technological change, in systematic and predictable
        patterns.

   •    These changes are generally associated with increased
        labor requirements per hectare of cultivated area.
        Animal-drawn mechanization has been used systematically
        to reduce these labor requirements when farming systems
        have reached the stages of annual cultivation. Increased
        labor requirements, however, arise not only from the
        actual labor used in cultivation, but also from overhead
        labor required for building and maintaining soil improve-
        ments and irrigation facilities. Maintenance of draft
        animals and tools also leads to increased labor require-
        ments, as do the gathering and preparation of organic
        manure.

   •    With the data set from developing countries used here, a
        mild decrease was found in labor productivity per hour of
        cultivation labor, although this decrease was not statis-
        tically significant. However, cultivation labor does not
        include overhead labor, and if there were data on over-
        head labor, the results would point more conclusively to
        declining labor productivity.

   •    Declines in labor productivity should not, however, be
        expected uniformly across regions. They would not be
        dramatic in regions that are well endowed with land and
        where yields respond well to land investments and
        intensification inputs. In regions with mostly marginal
        lands, however, the decline would be substantial. Such
        regions often emerge as sources of large migrant streams
        to better-endowed regions or countries.

• Regions with large endowments of marginal lands are also
  those in which soil degradation problems are likely to
  be most severe. Such problems can be reduced or overcome
  by the development of institutions or organizations that
  limit cropping and control access to grazing or forestry
  resources, as well as undertake investments in erosion
  control and forestry. The establishment of private
  property rights also reduces, though may not eliminate,
  the problem. However, societies frequently find it very
  difficult to undertake the required institutional
  changes, since the established rights of very poor people
  must often be rearranged and limited. Historically,
  the solution has frequently been a simple abolishment of
  the rights of tribal groups in favor of more enterprising
  permanent cultivators.

• As we know from research on developed countries, declines
  in labor productivity can be offset and more than offset
  by mechanical inputs and modern biological technologies.
  All countries of the developed world have achieved rates
  of labor and land productivity sufficient to outstrip
  their rates of population growth. This cannot, however,
  be cause for assuming that rapid population growth
  presents no problem. First of all, developing country
  population growth rates exceed historical rates in
  developed countries susbtantially. Moreover, the biological technologies required often have to be invented;
  they cannot simply be pulled from a shelf. In a number
  of countries, the institutional capacity to invent these
  technologies is rudimentary at best. Even the mechanical
  technologies require adaptive learning. They also
  require capital accumulation of a magnitude that is very
  hard to achieve given the current capital endowments of
  the societies involved.

• The potential problems of declining labor productivity
  and environmental degradation are not problems of <u>levels
  of population densities</u>. Given sufficient time, it is
  likely that a combination of farmer inventions, savings,
  and the development of research institutions and
  institutions for dealing with soil degradation issues
  will be able to accommodate much more than the current
  population in most countries, especially in many of the
  low-density ones. However, if all these changes are
  required quickly and simultaneously because of rapid
  population growth rates, they may emerge at too slow a
  pace to prevent a decline in human welfare.

NOTE

1   Kenneth Chomitz of the National Research Council reran our
    regressions on the rice-only subsample of 40 observations.
    The coefficients on the use of animal and mechanical traction
    are similar to those on the combined-crop sample and retain
    their high level of significance. However, the elasticity
    of labor productivity with respect to intensification changes
    from -0.07 (t = 0.45) to -0.21 (t = 1.11). At the same time,
    the coefficient on land investments is boosted from 0.24
    (t = 1.04) to 0.45 (t = 1.47). These results are consistent
    with the point made here that heavier soils (typically rice
    lands) have higher overhead labor requirements for invest-
    ments in water control and drainage, but are also very
    responsive to intensification inputs.

REFERENCES

Basehart, W. (1973) Cultivation intensity, settlement patterns,
    and homestead forms among the Matengo of Tanzania. Ethnology
    12:71.
Binswanger, H.P., and V.W. Ruttan (1978) Induced Innovation:
    Technology Institutions and Development. Baltimore, Md.:
    The Johns Hopkins University Press.
Boserup, E. (1965) The Conditions of Agricultural Growth.
    Chicago: Aldine Publishing Company.
Boserup, E. (1980) Population and Technological Change: A Study
    of Long-Term Trends. Chicago: University of Chicago Press.
Brown, P., and A. Podolejsky (1976) Population density, agricul-
    tural intensity, land tenure and group size in the New Guinea
    highlands. Ethnology 15:211-238.
Buck, J.L. (1937) Land Utilization in China. Nanking: Univer-
    sity of Nanking.
Cain, M.T. (1980) The economic activities of children in a
    village in Bangladesh in rural household studies in Asia.
    In H.P. Binswanger et al., eds., Rural Household Studies in
    Asia. Singapore: Singapore University Press.
Clarke, W.C. (1966) From extensive to intensive shifting culti-
    vation: a succession from New Guinea. Ethnology 5:347-359.
Gleave, M.B., and H.P. White (1969) Population density and agri-
    cultural systems in West Africa. In M.F. Thomas and G.W.
    Whittington, eds., Environment and Land Use in West Africa.
    London: Methuen & Co.
Green, D.A.G. (1971) Agricultural Mechanization in Ethiopia: An
    Economic Analysis of Four Case Studies. Unpublished Ph.D.
    thesis, Michigan State University.
Hayami, Y., and V.W. Ruttan (1985) Agricultural Development: An
    International Perspective, revised ed. Baltimore, Md.: The
    Johns Hopkins University Press.
India, Government of (1960) Studies in the Economics of Farm
    Management in West Bengal. New Delhi, India: Ministry of
    Agriculure.

India, Government of (1974a) Studies in the Economics of Farm Management in Cuttack District (Orrisa). New Delhi, India: Ministry of Agriculure.

India, Government of (1974b) Studies in the Economics of Farm Management in Ferozepur District (Punjab). New Delhi, India: Ministry of Agriculure.

India, Government of (1974c) Studies in the Economics of Farm Management in Muzaffarnagar District, Uttar Pradesh. New Delhi, India: Ministry of Agriculure.

India, Government of (1974d) Studies in the Economics of Farm Management in Thanjavur (Tamilnadu). New Delhi, India: Ministry of Agriculure.

India, Government of (1976a) Studies in the Economics of Farm Management in Coimbatore District (Tamilnadu). New Delhi, India: Ministry of Agriculure.

India, Government of (1976b) Studies in the Economics of Farm Management in Surat-Bulsar (Gujarat). New Delhi, India: Ministry of Agriculure.

India, Government of (1977) Studies in the Economics of Farm Management in Nowgong District (Assam). New Delhi, India: Ministry of Agriculure.

Jodha, N.S. (1982) Some Aspects of Traditional Farming Systems in Kilosa Area of Tanzania. Hyderabad, India: ICRISAT.

Johnson, S.L. (1979) Changing patterns of maize utilization in western Kenya. In E.F. Moran, ed., Changing Agricultural Systems in Africa. Williamsburg, Va.: College of William and Mary.

Kikuchi, M.A. Hafid, C. Saleh, S. Hartoyo, and Y. Hayami (1980) Changes in Community Institutions and Income Distribution in a West Java Village. IRRI Research Paper Series No 50, International Rice Research Institute, Los Banos, Philippines.

Lassiter, G.C. (1981) Cropping Enterprises in Eastern Upper Volta. African Rural Economy Working Paper No. 35, Michigan State University, East Lansing, Michigan.

Naseem, S.M. (1980) Regional Variation and Structural Changes: Their Effect on Labor Absorption in Pakistan's Agriculture in Employment Expansion in Asian Agriculture, Asian Employment Program. Bangkok: International Labour Organisation.

Pingali, P.L., Y. Bigot, and H. Binswanger (1985) Agricultural Mechanization and the Evolution of Farming Systems in Sub-Saharan Africa. Agricultural Research Unit, Paper No. ARU40. Washington, D.C.: The World Bank.

Pudasaini, S.P. (1979) Farm Mechanization, Employment, and Income in Nepal: Traditional and Mechanized Farming in Bara District. IRRI Research Paper Series No 38, International Rice Research Institute, Los Banos, Philippines.

Purcal, J.T. (1971) Rice Economy: A Case Study of Four Villages in West Malaysia. Kuala Lumpur: University of Malaya.

Ruthenberg, H. (1980) Farming Systems in the Tropics, 3rd ed. Oxford: Clarendon Press.

Singh, I.J. (1976) A Note on the Economics of Agricultural Mechanization: Studies in Employment and Rural Development. World Bank Working Paper No. 33, The World Bank, Washington, D.C.

Smith, J., and F.E. Gascon (1979)   The Effect of New Rice Techno-
    logy on Family Labor Utilization in Laguna.   IRRI Research
    Paper Series No. 42, International Rice Research Institute,
    Los Banos, Philippines.
Spencer, D.S.C., and D. Byerlee (1977)   Small Farms in West
    Africa:   A Descriptive Analysis of Employment, Incomes, and
    Productivity in Sierra Leone.   African Rural Economy Working
    Paper No. 19, Michigan State University, East Lansing,
    Michigan.
Turner, B.L., R.Q. Hanham, and A.V. Portararo (1977)   Population
    pressure and agricultural intensity.   Annals of the Associa-
    tion of American Geographers 67(3):384-396.
Wickramasekara, P. (1980)   Labor Absorption in Paddy Cultivation
    in Sri Lanka in Employment Expansion in Asian Agriculture.
    Asian Employment Programme.   Bangkok:   International Labour
    Organisation.

APPENDIX TABLE  Data on Farming Intensity, Mechanization, Labor Use, and Yield

| Country, Area | Crop | Farming Intensity | Mechanization | Labor Use | Yield Per Man Hour | Yield Per Hectare | Land Investments | Fertilizer Use | Source of Data |
|---|---|---|---|---|---|---|---|---|---|
| Sri Lanka, South | Rice | 130 | Animal | 1126 | 2.19 | 2466 | Yes | Yes | Wickramasekara (1980) |
| India, Ferozepur | Rice | 121 | Animal | 627 | 3.38 | 2401 | Yes | Yes | India (1974b) |
| India, Coimbatore | Rice | 143 | Animal | 1386 | 2.16 | 2994 | Yes | Yes | India (1976a) |
| India, Surat | Rice | 118 | Animal | 1119 | 1.26 | 1410 | Yes | Yes | India (1976b) |
| Bangladesh, Chargopalpur | Rice | 150 | Animal | 2400 | 1.09 | 2616 | No | Yes | Cain (1980) |
| Pakistan, Punjab | Rice | 112 | Animal | 360 | 4.97 | 1789 | Yes | Yes | Naseem (1980) |
| Pakistan, Sind | Rice | 118 | Animal | 536 | 3.32 | 1780 | Yes | Yes | Naseem (1980) |
| Upper Volta, Eastern | Rice | 50 | Animal | 845 | 0.92 | 777 | No | Yes | Lassiter (1981) |
| India, Assam | Rice | 130 | Animal | 581 | 2.70 | 1569 | No | Yes | Ruthenberg (1980) |
| Bangladesh, Comilla | Rice | 150 | Animal | 1583 | 2.34 | 3704 | No | Yes | Ruthenberg (1980) |
| Philippines, Laguna | Rice | 180 | Animal | 1368 | 1.80 | 2462 | Yes | Yes | Smith and Gascon (1979) |
| Java, Subang | Rice | 200 | Animal | 1252 | 2.30 | 2880 | Yes | Yes | Kikuchi et al. (1980) |
| Nepal, Bara | Rice | 134 | Animal | 1192 | 1.40 | 1669 | Yes | Yes | Pudasaini (1979) |
| Nepal, Bara | Rice | 155 | Animal | 1523 | 1.40 | 2132 | Yes | Yes | Pudasaini (1979) |
| India, Bengal | Rice | 200 | Animal | 2098 | 0.80 | 1678 | Yes | Yes | India (1960) |
| India, Thanjavar | Rice | 150 | Animal | 1671 | 1.40 | 2339 | Yes | Yes | India (1974d) |
| China, Yangtze | Rice | 171 | Animal | 1518 | 2.25 | 3416 | Yes | Yes | Buck (1937) |
| China, Szechuan | Rice | 154 | Animal | 1960 | 1.95 | 3822 | Yes | Yes | Buck (1937) |
| Kenya, Migori | Maize | 80 | Animal | 864 | 2.60 | 2246 | No | Yes | Johnson (1979) |
| Tanzania, Sukumaland | Maize | 111 | Animal | 912 | 1.80 | 1642 | No | Yes | Singh (1976) |
| India, Muzaffarnagar | Maize | 140 | Animal | 399 | 4.70 | 1875 | Yes | Yes | India (1974c) |
| Pakistan | Maize | 110 | Animal | 320 | 3.50 | 1120 | No | Yes | Naseem (1980) |
| Upper Volta, Eastern | Maize | 50 | Animal | 589 | 1.35 | 795 | No | Yes | Lassiter (1981) |
| Kenya, Migori | Maize | 80 | Animal | 744 | 1.80 | 1339 | No | No | Johnson (1979) |
| Pakistan, Sind | Rice | 118 | Animal | 530 | 3.35 | 1767 | Yes | Yes | Naseem (1980) |
| Pakistan, Punjab | Rice | 112 | Animal | 276 | 7.03 | 1943 | Yes | Yes | Naseem (1980) |
| Pakistan, Sind | Rice | 118 | Animal | 284 | 7.14 | 2026 | Yes | Yes | Naseem (1980) |
| Pakistan, Punjab | Rice | 112 | Animal | 354 | 8.10 | 2688 | Yes | Yes | Naseem (1980) |
| Sierra Leone, Bum | Rice | 12 | Hoe | 1072 | 1.15 | 1233 | Yes | No | Ruthenberg (1980) |
| Liberia, Gbanga | Rice | 11 | Hoe | 770 | 1.26 | 970 | No | No | Ruthenberg (1980) |
| Ivory Coast, Man | Rice | 24 | Hoe | 1259 | 1.38 | 1737 | No | No | Ruthenberg (1980) |
| Cameroon, Begang | Rice | 30 | Hoe | 1691 | 0.45 | 761 | No | No | Ruthenberg (1980) |
| Nepal, Lumle | Rice | 100 | Hoe | 5208 | 0.42 | 2187 | Yes | Yes | Ruthenberg (1980) |
| Cameroon, Bamunka | Rice | 100 | Hoe | 3301 | 0.48 | 1584 | No | No | Ruthenberg (1980) |
| Philippines, Iloilo | Rice | 200 | Hoe | 2504 | 1.35 | 3380 | No | Yes | Ruthenberg (1980) |
| Philippines, Iloilo | Rice | 300 | Hoe | 4579 | 0.86 | 3938 | No | Yes | Ruthenberg (1980) |

APPENDIX TABLE (continued)

| Country, Area | Crop | Farming Intensity | Mechanization | Labor Use | Yield Per Man Hour | Yield Per Hectare | Land Investments | Fertilizer Use | Source of Data |
|---|---|---|---|---|---|---|---|---|---|
| Tanzania, Sukumaland | Maize | 111 | Hoe | 1256 | 1.20 | 1219 | No | Yes | Singh (1976) |
| Ethiopia, Agnale | Maize | 200 | Hoe | 895 | 3.91 | 3499 | No | No | Green (1971) |
| Brazil, Castanaha | Maize | 10 | Hoe | 636 | 0.94 | 598 | No | No | Ruthenberg (1980) |
| Ghana | Maize | 20 | Hoe | 600 | 3.17 | 1902 | No | No | Ruthenberg (1980) |
| Ghana, Begora | Maize | 40 | Hoe | 1432 | 1.03 | 1475 | No | No | Ruthenberg (1980) |
| Tanzania, Kilosa | Maize | 40 | Hoe | 936 | 1.20 | 1123 | No | No | Jodha (1982) |
| Upper Volta, Eastern | Maize | 50 | Hoe | 1147 | 0.51 | 585 | No | Yes | Lassiter (1981) |
| Kenya, Kilifi | Maize | 50 | Hoe | 1169 | 0.55 | 643 | No | No | Ruthenberg (1980) |
| Upper Volta, Eastern | Rice | 50 | Hoe | 1314 | 0.75 | 986 | No | Yes | Lassiter (1981) |
| Taiwan, Central | Rice | 181 | Tractor | 984 | 3.39 | 3336 | Yes | Yes | Ruthenberg (1980) |
| Peru, Tinachones | Rice | 100 | Tractor | 960 | 7.29 | 6998 | Yes | Yes | Ruthenberg (1980) |
| Brazil, Rio Grande | Rice | 100 | Tractor | 219 | 19.18 | 4200 | Yes | Yes | Ruthenberg (1980) |
| Phillippines, Laguna | Rice | 180 | Tractor | 685 | 5.99 | 4103 | Yes | Yes | Smith and Gascon (1979) |
| Nepal, Bara | Rice | 165 | Tractor | 1411 | 1.56 | 2201 | Yes | Yes | Pudasaini (1979) |
| Tanzania, Sukumaland | Maize | 111 | Tractor | 264 | 2.20 | 581 | No | Yes | Singh (1976) |
| Thailand, Ampur | Maize | 96 | Tractor | 387 | 8.19 | 3170 | No | Yes | Ruthenberg (1980) |
| Sri Lanka, Minipe | Rice | 130 | Tractor | 1183 | 2.50 | 2956 | Yes | Yes | Wickramasekara (1980) |
| Sri Lanka, Yala | Rice | 130 | Tractor | 1272 | 2.04 | 2595 | Yes | Yes | Wickramasekara (1980) |
| Sierra Leone, Bolilands | Rice | 60 | Tractor | 1169 | 1.37 | 1602 | No | Yes | Spencer and Byerlee (1977) |
| Malaysia | Rice | 90 | Tractor | 801 | 3.94 | 3156 | | | Purcal (1971) |
| India, Orrisa | Rice | 140 | Tractor | 574 | 2.60 | 1492 | Yes | Yes | India (1974a) |

# 3
# Population Growth and Agricultural Productivity

Yujiro Hayami
Vernon W. Ruttan

INTRODUCTION

Between 1960 and 1980, world population increased from approximately 3.0 to 4.4 billion persons. The annual rate of population growth during this period--1.9 percent per year--was higher than at any previous period in human history. During this same period, concern about the relationship between population growth and development reemerged as a major theme in development thought and policy.

In the classical model of economic development, population growth was believed to be dependent on the quality of agricultural resources. Diminishing returns to increments of labor and capital applied to a constant quality of land were both a source of poverty and a constraint on growth. In contemporary discussion, this perspective has provided the primary theoretical foundations for the "limits to growth" literature. A major thrust of much of the theorizing in the "dual economy" tradition was to identify the conditions that would permit a poor society to escape from a Malthusian trap in which the marginal productivity of labor in rural areas was at or below the subsistence wage rate. At a more popular level, the "population bomb" has been blamed for many or even most of the ills of the world--including hunger, poverty, war, and population and psychological stress.

The perspective on the relationship between population growth and agricultural productivity that emerges from more recent development thought is much more complex. In the theory of induced innovation, for example, changes in relative resource endowments, such as shifts in the ratio of agricultural labor to land, are viewed as directing technical change along a path that permits

This chapter draws on material from our book, Agricultural Development: An International Perspective, rev. ed. (Baltimore: Johns Hopkins University Press, 1985). An earlier draft of this paper was presented at the symposium, "Technological Prospects and Population Trends," American Association for the Advancement of Science, New York, May 25, 1984.

the substitution of relatively abundant factors for the relatively scarce factors of production. This perspective thus
directs attention to the conditions under which the growth of
population induces agricultural productivity growth and to the
conditions under which resource endowments, which act as a constraint on the growth of productivity in rural areas, are released by advances in technology.

INDUCED TECHNICAL CHANGE

The process by which technical change is generated has traditionally been treated as exogenous to the economic system--as a product of autonomous advances in scientific and technical knowledge. Over the last several decades, advances in economic
theory and the accumulation of empirical evidence have tended to
confirm that the rate and direction of technical change can be
interpreted as largely endogenous to the economic system--as
induced by differences or changes in the conditions of factor
supply and product demand. In agriculture, the constraints
imposed on development by an inelastic supply of land may be
offset by advances in biological technology; the constraints
imposed by an inelastic supply of labor may be offset by
advances in mechanical technology.

Theories of induced innovation have been developed mainly
within the framework of the theory of the firm. There have been
two traditions in the attempt to incorporate into economic theory
the innovative behavior of profit-maximizing firms. One is the
Hicks tradition, which focused on the factor-saving bias induced
by changes in relative factor prices resulting from changes in
relative resource scarcities (Hicks, 1932).[1] The other is the
Schmookler-Griliches tradition, which focused on the influence
of the growth of product demand on the rate of technical change
(Griliches, 1957; Schmookler, 1962, 1966).[2]

In the dynamic process of economic development, changes in
product demand and relative factor prices are inseparably related. For example, when food demand rises because of growth in
population or per capita income, or both, the demand for factor
inputs in food production increases more or less proportionally.
When increases in factor demands are confronted with different
elasticities in the supply of production factors, the result is
changes in relative factor prices. The different rates of change
in factor prices result, in turn, in changes in the level of income and income distribution among factor owners, thereby affecting the aggregate product demand. A fully developed general-
equilibrium induced innovation model capable of explaining the
dynamic process of agricultural development should incorporate
the mechanisms by which changes in both product demand and factor
endowments interact to influence the rate and direction of technological change.[3]

We do not, of course, regard technical change as wholly induced by economic forces. In addition to the effects of changes
(or differences) in resource endowments and growth in demand,

technical change may occur in response to autonomous advances in
scientific knowledge.  Progress in general science that lowers
the "cost" of technical and institutional innovations may have
influences on technical change that are unrelated to changes in
factor proportions and product demand.  Even so, the rate of
adoption and impact on productivity of such autonomous or exogenous changes in technology will be strongly influenced by
conditions of resource supply and product demand.

A model of induced technical innovation in agriculture is
illustrated in Figure 1.  This model incorporates the characteristics of both factor substitution and complementarity associated
with advances in biological and mechanical technologies.

The process of advance in mechanical technology is shown in
the left-hand panel of Figure 1.  $I_0^*$ represents the innovation possibility curve (IPC) at time zero; it is the envelope of
less elastic unit isoquants that correspond, for example, to different types of harvesting machinery.  A certain technology--a
reaper, for example--represented by $I_0$ is invented when the
price ratio XX prevails for some time.  Correspondingly, the
minimum-cost equilibrium point is determined at P with a certain
optimal combination of land, labor, and nonhuman power to operate
the reaper.  In general, the technology that permits cultivation
of a larger area per worker requires a higher animal or mechanical power per worker.  This implies a complementary relationship
between land and power, which may be drawn as a line representing
a certain combination of land and power (A, M).  In this
simplified presentation, land-cum-power is assumed to be substi-

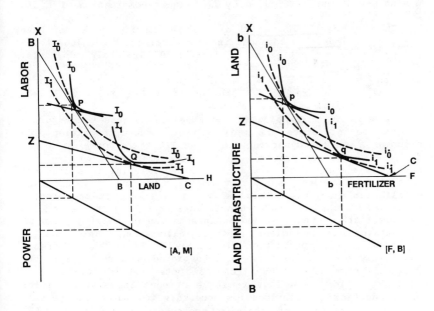

FIGURE 1   A Model of Induced Technical Change in Agriculture

tuted for labor in response to a change in wage relative to an index of land and power prices, though, of course, in actual practice land and power are substitutable to some extent.

$I_1^i$ represents the IPC of period 1. Let us assume that from period 0 to 1, labor becomes more scarce relative to land, for example, because of labor outmigration to industry in the course of economic development, resulting in a decline in land rent relative to wage rates. Also assume that the price of power declines relative to the wage rate for labor because of the supply of a cheaper power source from industry. The change in the price ratio from XX to ZZ induces the invention of another technology--such as the combine--represented by $I_1$, which enables a farm worker to cultivate a greater land area using a greater amount of power.

The process of advance in biological technology is illustrated in the right-hand panel of Figure 1. Here, $i_0^*$ represents an IPC embracing less elastic land-fertilizer isoquants, such as $i_0$, corresponding to different crop varieties and cultural practices. When the fertilizer-land price ratio declines from xx to zz from time period 0 to 1, a new technology--a more fertilizer-responsive variety, for example--represented by $i_1$ is developed along $i_1^*$, the IPC of time 1. In general, the technology that facilitates the substitution of fertilizer for land, such as fertilizer-responsive, high-yielding crop varieties, requires better control of water and better land management. This suggests a complementary relationship between fertilizer and land infrastructure in the form of irrigation and drainage systems, as implied by the linear combination of F and B.

In the model of induced innovation in Figure 1, we have treated the impact of advances in mechanical and biological technology on factor ratios as if they were completely separable. This is clearly an oversimplification. It is not essential to the induced technical change model that change in the land-labor ratio be a direct response to the price of land relative to the wage rate (Thirtle, 1985a, 1985b).

It would be misleading if the model illustrated in Figure 1 were to be interpreted as implying that induced innovation proceeds as a smooth adjustment along the IPC in response to change in relative factor prices. In the dynamic process of development, the emergence of imbalance or disequilibrium is a critical element in inducing technical change and economic growth. Disequilibrium among the several elements or stages in the process of technical change creates constraints that focus the attention of scientists, inventors, and administrators on solving problems to attain more efficient resource allocation. The dramatic advances in rice production technology in South and Southeast Asia since the mid-1960s can be interpreted as a response to the disequilibrium between the technical potential for advances in rice production technology, and the changes in relative factor and product price relationships necessary to induce the generation and diffusion of the new technology. Rice yields had remained low before the mid-1960s in spite of substantial de-

clines in the fertilizer-land and fertilizer-rice price ratios.
The movement to a new position on a "meta-production function"
was delayed until, following the dislocations of World War II and
of decolonization, the needed investments were made in experiment
station capacity so that the prototype technology available in
Japan and other temperate rice-growing areas could be adapted to
the agroclimatic and socioeconomic environments of South and
Southeast Asia (Hayami and Ruttan, 1985). One implication of the
model illustrated in Figure 1 is that alternative paths of technical change can be expected to emerge in response to differences
or changes in relative resource endowments. Figure 2 shows the
changes in partial productivity ratios, output per worker, and
output per hectare for a large number of both developed and developing countries for 1960-80. Three distinct, long-term growth
paths are apparent in Figure 2: (1) a new continent growth path;
(2) a European growth path; and (3) an Asian path. The new continent path includes countries with relatively high land-labor
ratios, while the Asian path includes countries with relatively
low land-labor ratios. The long-term historical growth paths for
selected countries are plotted in Figure 3: the historical path
for the United States passes through the scatter of points for
the new continent countries; the path for Japan passes through
the scatter points for the African and Asian countries; and the
historical paths for Denmark, France, and the United Kingdom pass
through the scatter of points for the European countries.
    We hypothesize that movement along the vertical axis is
dominated by advances in biological technology that facilitate
the use of land substitutes for land. Movement along the horizontal axis is dominated by advances in mechanical technology
that permit the substitution of power for labor. The next
section summarizes the results of attempts to provide more
rigorous tests of the induced innovation hypothesis.


RESOURCE CONSTRAINTS AND TECHNICAL CHANGE: JAPAN AND THE UNITED
STATES

Our initial tests of the induced innovation hypothesis were
against the experience of the United States and Japan for the
period 1880-1960. Additional tests have been conducted against
the experience of other developed and developing countries. In
a recent publication, we extended the Japan-United States tests
from 1880-1960 to 1880-1980.[4]
    Japan and the United States are characterized by extreme
differences in relative endowments of land and labor (Table 1).
In 1880, total agricultural land area per male worker was more
than 60 times as large in the United States as in Japan, and
arable land area per worker was about 20 times as large. These
differences have widened over time. By 1980, total agricultural
land area per male worker was more than 100 times as large and
arable land area per male worker about 50 times as large in the
United States as in Japan.

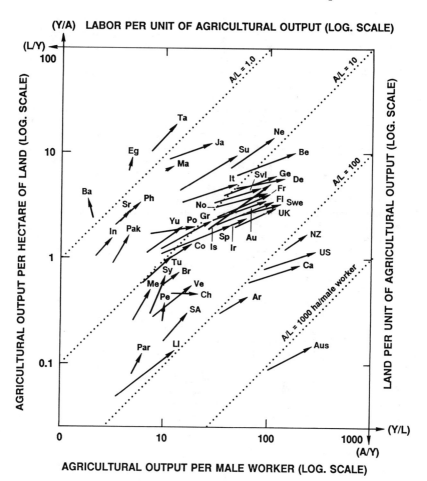

**(Y/A)  LABOR PER UNIT OF AGRICULTURAL OUTPUT (LOG. SCALE)**

**AGRICULTURAL OUTPUT PER MALE WORKER (LOG. SCALE)**

FIGURE 2    International Comparison of Labor and Land
Productivities in Agriculture

Source:  Hayami and Ruttan (1985:Chapter 5).

---

Symbol Key for Figures 2 and 3

| | | | |
|---|---|---|---|
| Ar: | Argentina | Ch: | Chile |
| Aus: | Australia | Co: | Colombia |
| Au: | Austria | De: | Denmark |
| Ba: | Bangladesh | Eg: | Egypt |
| Be: | Belgium (and Luxemburg) | Fi: | Finland |
| Br: | Brazil | Fr: | France |
| Ca: | Canada | Ge: | Germany, F.R. |

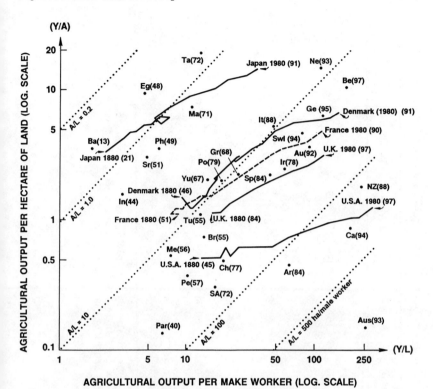

FIGURE 3  Historical Growth Paths of Agricultural Productivity
of Denmark, France, Japan, the United Kingdom, and the United
States for 1880-1980 Compared with Intercountry Cross-Section
Observations of Selected Countries in 1980

Source:  Hayami and Ruttan (1985:Chapter 5).

| Gr : | Greece | Ph : | Philippines |
|------|--------|------|-------------|
| In: | India | Po : | Portugal |
| Ir : | Ireland | SA: | South Africa |
| Is: | Israel | Sp: | Spain |
| It: | Italy | Sr: | Sri Lanka |
| Ja: | Japan | Su: | Surinum |
| Li: | Libya | Swe : | Sweden |
| Ma: | Mauritius | Swi: | Switzerland |
| Me: | Mexico | Sy: | Syria |
| Ne: | Netherlands | Ta : | Taiwan |
| NZ: | New Zealand | Tu: | Turkey |
| No: | Norway | UK: | U.K. |
| Pak: | Pakistan | USA: | U.S.A. |
| Par: | Paraguay | Ve : | Venezuela |
| Pe : | Peru | Yu: | Yugoslavia |

Hayami and Ruttan

TABLE 1 Land-Labor Endowments and Relative Prices in Agriculture: United States and Japan, Selected Years

| Variable | 1880 | 1900 | 1920 | 1940 | 1960 | 1980 |
|---|---|---|---|---|---|---|
| **United States** | | | | | | |
| (1) Agricultural land area (million ha.) | 327 | 465 | 458 | 452 | 440 | 427 |
| (2) Arable land area (million ha.) | 93 | 157 | 194 | 189 | 185 | 191 |
| (3) Number of male farm workers (thousand) | 7,959 | 9,880 | 10,221 | 8,487 | 3,973 | 1,792 |
| (4) (1)/(3) (ha./worker) | 41 | 47 | 45 | 50 | 111 | 238 |
| (5) (2)/(3) (ha./worker) | 12 | 16 | 19 | 22 | 47 | 107 |
| (6) Value of arable land ($/ha.) | 109 | 106 | 341 | 178 | 696 | 3,393 |
| (7) Farm wage rate ($/day) | 0.90 | 1.00 | 3.30 | 1.60 | 6.60 | 25.31 |
| (8) (6)/(7) (days/ha.) | 188 | 106 | 103 | 111 | 105 | 134 |
| **Japan** | | | | | | |
| (9) Agricultural land area (thousand ha.)[a] | 5,509 | 6,032 | 6,958 | 7,102 | 7,042 | 5,729 |
| (10) Arable land area (thousand ha.) | 4,749 | 5,200 | 5,998 | 6,122 | 6,071 | 5,461 |
| (11) Number of male farm workers (thousand) | 8,336 | 8,483 | 7,577 | 6,362 | 6,230 | 2,674 |
| (12) (9)/(11) (ha./worker) | 0.66 | 0.71 | 0.92 | 1.12 | 1.13 | 2.14 |
| (13) (10)/(11) (ha./worker) | 0.57 | 0.61 | 0.79 | 0.96 | 0.97 | 2.04 |
| (14) Value of arable land (yen/ha.) | 343 | 917 | 3,882 | 4,709 | 1,415,000 | 7,642,000 |
| (15) Farm wage rate (yen/day) | 0.22 | 0.31 | 1.39 | 1.90 | 440 | 5,054 |
| (16) (14)/(15) (days/ha.) | 1,559 | 2,958 | 2,793 | 2,478 | 3,216 | 1,512 |

[a]Agricultural land areas in Japan for 1880-1960 are estimated by multiplying arable land areas by 1.16, the ratio of agricultural land area to arable land area in the 1960 Census of Agriculture; this conversion factor changed to 1.05 for 1980 based on the 1980 Census of Agriculture.

Source: Hayami and Ruttan (1985:Chap. 7).

The relative prices of land and labor also differed sharply in the two countries. In 1880, to buy a hectare of arable land (compare rows 8 and 16 in Table 1), a Japanese hired farm worker would have had to work 8 times as many days as a U.S. farm worker. In the United States, the price of labor rose relative to the price of land, particularly between 1880 and 1920; in Japan, the price of land rose sharply relative to the price of labor, particularly between 1880 and 1900. By 1960, a Japanese farm worker would have had to work 30 times as many days as a U.S. farm worker to buy one hectare of arable land. This gap was reduced after 1960, partly because of extremely rapid increases in wage rates in Japan during the two decades of "miraculous" economic growth. In the United States, land prices rose sharply in the postwar period, primarily because of the rising demand for land for nonagricultural uses and the expectation of continued inflation. Yet in 1980, a Japanese farm worker still would have had to work 11 times as many days as a U.S. worker to buy one hectare of land.

In spite of these substantial differences in land area per worker and in the relative prices of land and labor, both the United States and Japan experienced relatively rapid rates of growth in production and productivity in agriculture (Table 2). Overall agricultural growth for the entire 100-year period was very similar in the two countries. In both countries, total agricultural output increased at an annual compound rate of 1.6 percent, total inputs (aggregate of conventional inputs) increased at 0.7 percent, and total factor productivity (total output divided by total input) increased at an annual rate of 0.9 percent. Meanwhile, labor productivity measured by agricultural output per male worker increased at rates of 3.1 percent per year in the United States and 2.7 percent in Japan. It is remarkable that the overall growth rates in output and productivity were so similar despite the extremely different factor proportions that characterize the two countries.

In the last section, we hypothesized that agricultural growth in the United States and Japan during the period 1880-1980 can best be understood when viewed as a dynamic factor substitution process. Factors have been substituted for each other along a metaproduction function in response to long-run trends in relative factor prices. Each point on the metaproduction surface is characterized by a technology that can be described in terms of specific sources of power and types of machinery.

The movements along the metaproduction function may be inferred from Figures 4 and 5, in which U.S. and Japanese data on the relationship between farm draft power (from both tractors and draft animals) per male worker and the machinery-labor price ratio, and between fertilizer input per hectare of arable land and the fertilizer-land price ratio, are plotted. Despite the enormous differences in climate and other environmental conditions, the relation between these variables is almost identical in both countries. This suggests that U.S. and Japanese agricultural growth has involved a movement along a common metaproduction function.

ttan

TABLE 2  Annual Compound Rates of Growth in Output, Input, Productivity, and Factor Proportions in U.S. and Japanese Agriculture:  1880-1980, Selected Periods (in percent)

| Variable | Period 1880 to 1900 | 1900 to 1920 | 1920 to 1940 | 1940 to 1960 | 1960 to 1980 | Whole Period 1880 to 1980 |
|---|---|---|---|---|---|---|
| **United States** | | | | | | |
| Output (net of seeds and feed) | 2.2 | 0.8 | 1.3 | 1.9 | 1.9 | 1.6 |
| Total input | 1.6 | 1.4 | 0.2 | 0.1 | 0.3 | 0.7 |
| Total productivity (output/total input) | 0.6 | -0.7 | 1.1 | 1.9 | 1.6 | 0.9 |
| Number of male workers | 1.1 | 0.2 | -0.9 | -3.7 | -3.8 | -1.5 |
| Output per male worker | 1.1 | 0.6 | 2.2 | 5.9 | 6.1 | 3.1 |
| Agricultural land area | 1.8 | -0.1 | -0.4 | 0.2 | -0.2 | 0.3 |
| Arable land area | 2.7 | 1.1 | -0.1 | -0.1 | 0.1 | 0.7 |
| Output per ha. of agricultural land | 0.4 | 0.8 | 1.7 | 1.7 | 2.1 | 1.3 |
| Output per ha. of arable land | -0.4 | -0.3 | 1.4 | 2.0 | 1.8 | 0.9 |
| Agricultural land area per male worker | 0.7 | -0.3 | 0.5 | 4.1 | 3.9 | 1.8 |
| Arable land per male worker | 1.5 | 0.9 | 0.8 | 3.8 | 4.2 | 2.2 |
| **Japan** | | | | | | |
| Output (net of seeds and feed) | 1.6 | 2.0 | 0.7 | 1.8 | 1.9 | 1.6 |
| Total input | 0.4 | 0.5 | 0.3 | 1.6 | 1.0 | 0.7 |
| Total productivity | 1.2 | 1.5 | 0.4 | 0.2 | 0.9 | 0.9 |
| Number of male workers | 0.1 | -0.6 | -0.9 | -0.1 | -4.2 | -1.1 |
| Output per male worker | 1.5 | 2.6 | 1.6 | 1.9 | 6.3 | 2.7 |
| Arable land area (=agric. land area) | 0.4 | 0.7 | 0.1 | -0.04 | -0.5 | 0.1 |
| Output per ha. of arable land | 1.2 | 1.3 | 0.6 | 1.8 | 2.4 | 1.5 |
| Arable land area per male worker | 0.4 | 1.3 | 1.0 | 0.1 | 3.8 | 1.2 |

Source:  Hayami and Ruttan (1985:Chap. 7).

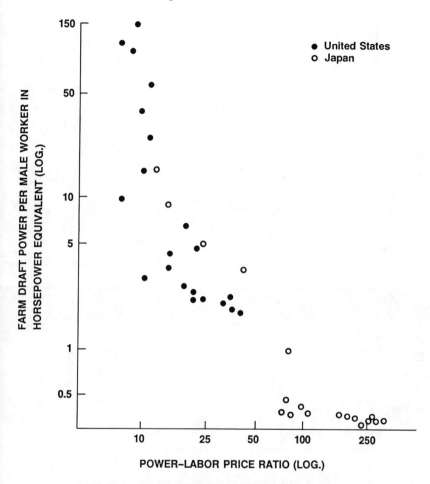

FIGURE 4   Relation Between Farm Draft Power Per Male Worker and
Power-Labor Price Ratio, the United States and Japan, Quinquennial Observations for 1880-1980

Note:  Equals hectares of work days that can be purchased by one
horsepower of tractor or draft animal.

Source:  Hayami and Ruttan (1985:Chapter 7).


As a test of this hypothesis, we have tried to determine the
extent to which the variations in factor proportions, as measured
by the land-labor, power-labor, and fertilizer-land ratios, can
be explained by changes in factor price ratios.  In a situation
characterized by a fixed technology, it seems reasonable to
presume that the elasticities of substitution among factors are

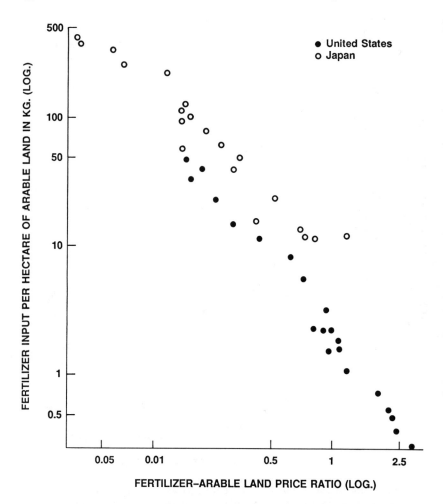

FIGURE 5   Relation Between Fertilizer Input per Hectare of
Arable Land and Fertilizer-Arable Land Price Ratio, the United
States and Japan, Quinquennial Observations for 1880-1980

Note:   Equals hectares of arable land that can be purchased by
one ton of $N + P_{20t} + K_20$ contained in commercial
fertilizers.

Source:   Hayami and Ruttan (1985:Chapter 7).

small. This permits us to infer that innovations were induced if the variations in these factor proportions are explained consistently by the changes in price ratios. The historically observed changes in those factor proportions in the United States and Japan are so large that it is hardly conceivable that these changes represent substitution along a given production surface describing a constant technology.

To specify the regression form adequately, we have to be able to infer the shape of the underlying metaproduction function, as well as the functional form of the relationship between changes in the production function and in factor price ratios. Because of a lack of adequate a priori information, we have simply specified the regression in log-linear form without much claim for theoretical justification. If we can assume that the production function is linear and homogeneous, the factor proportions can be expressed as factor price ratios alone and are independent of product prices.

Considering the crudeness of the data and the purpose of this analysis, we used quinquennial observations (stock variables measured at 5-year intervals and flow variables averaged for 5 years) instead of annual observations for the regression analysis. A crude form of adjustment is built into our model, since our data are quinquennial observations, and prices are generally measured as the averages of the past 5 years preceding the year when the quantities are measured (for example, the number of workers in 1910 is associated with the 1906-10 average wage).

The results of regression analyses are summarized in Tables 3, 4, 5, and 6. Tables 3 and 4 present the regressions for land-labor and power-land proportions. In those regressions, we originally included other variables, such as the fertilizer-labor price ratio and the exponential time trend. However, probably because of high intercorrelations, the coefficients for those variables either were nonsignificant or resulted in implausible results for the other coefficients. Those variables were therefore dropped in the subsequent analysis.

Table 3 shows the results for the United States. A major anomaly in our initial U.S. regressions on land-labor and power-land ratios (not shown) was that very poor results were obtained for signs and significance levels of estimated coefficients, coefficients of determination, and the Durbin-Watson statistics when the regressions were estimated for 1880-1980, yet good results were obtained for 1880-1960 (Hayami and Ruttan, 1971). This anomaly seems to be explained by the deficiency of data on land prices. We measured land price by the average unit of land in farms. This is a measure of the price of land as a stock, but not the price of the service of land for agricultural production. As is well known, agricultural land prices in the United States diverged rapidly from agricultural land rents during 1960-80 because of the rising demand for nonagricultural uses and the expectation of continued inflation.[5] As a result, the stock price of land rose relative to the farm wage rate after 1960. However, land rents seem to have declined relative to the farm

TABLE 3 Regressions of Land-Labor Ratios and Power-Labor Ratios on Relative Factor Prices: United States, 1880-1980, Quinquennial Observations

| Regression Number | Dependent Variable | Coefficients of Price | | | Coeff. of Det. ($\bar{R}^2$) | S.E. | Durbin-Watson Statistics |
| --- | --- | --- | --- | --- | --- | --- | --- |
| | | Land Relative to Farm Wage | Machinery Relative to Farm Wage | Time Dummy | | | |
| | Land-Labor Ratios | | | | | | |
| (W 1) | Agricultural land per male worker | -.248 (.191) | -.313 (.107) | .984 (.118) | .922 | .155 | 1.82 |
| (W 2) | Arable land per male worker | -.042 (.182) | -.592 (.102) | .902 (.112) | .945 | .148 | 1.92 |
| (W 3) | Agricultural land per work-hour | -.182 (.206) | -.267 (.115) | .971 (.127) | .898 | .167 | 1.55 |
| (W 4) | Arable land per work-hour | .024 (.195) | -.545 (.109) | .889 (.120) | .929 | .158 | 1.67 |
| | Power-Labor Ratios | | | | | | |
| (W 5) | Horsepower per male worker | -1.040 (.466) | -1.060 (.261) | 1.839 (.287) | .928 | .378 | 1.73 |
| (W 6) | Horsepower per work-hour | -.974 (.480) | -1.013 (.269) | 1.826 (.295) | .919 | .389 | 1.65 |

Note: Equations are linear in logarithm. Standard errors of the estimated coefficients are in parentheses. The time dummy variable is zero for 1880-1960 and one for 1965-1980.

Source: Hayami and Ruttan (1985:Chap. 7).

TABLE 4 Regressions of Land-Labor Ratios and Power-Labor Ratios on Relative Factor Prices: Japan, 1880-1980, Quinquennial Observations

| Regression Number | Dependent Variable | Coefficients of Price | | Coeff. of Det. ($\bar{R}^2$) | S.E. | Durbin-Watson Statistics |
| | | Land Relative to Farm Wage | Machinery Relative to Farm Wage | | | |
|---|---|---|---|---|---|---|
| | **Land-Labor Ratios** | | | | | |
| (W 7) | Agricultural land per male worker | -.147 (-.068) | -.408 (.034) | .893 | .123 | 1.00 |
| (W 8) | Arable land per male worker | .069 (.067) | -.354 (.060) | .680 | .215 | .48 |
| | **Power-Labor Ratios** | | | | | |
| (W 9) | Horsepower per male worker | .221 (.375) | -1.146 (.188) | .695 | .675 | .37 |
| (W 10) | Horsepower per work-hour | .143 (.430) | -1.091 (.216) | .615 | .773 | 1.74 |

Note: Equations are linear in logarithm. Standard errors of the estimated coefficients are in parentheses.

Source: Hayami and Ruttan (1985:Chap. 7).

71

wage rate, although the national aggregate time-series data on agricultural land rents are not yet available.

To adjust for the divergence between the stock and the service prices of agricultural land, the regressions in Table 3 include a time dummy variable, which is specified as zero for 1880-1960 and one after 1960. About 90 percent of the variation in the land-labor ratio and in the power-labor ratio is explained by the changes in their price ratios together with the dummy variables. The coefficients are all negative, except the land-price coefficient in regression (W4). Such results indicate that the marked increases in land and power per worker in U.S. agriculture over the past 100 years have been closely associated with declines in the prices of land and of power and machinery relative to the farm wage rate. The hypothesis that land and power should be treated as complementary factors is confirmed by the negative coefficients. This seems to indicate that, in addition to the complementarity along a fixed production surface, mechanical innovations that raise the marginal rate of substitution of power for labor tend also to raise the marginal rate of substitution of land for labor.

The results from using the same regressions for Japan (Table 4) are greatly inferior in terms of statistical criteria, probably because the ranges of observed variation in the land-labor and power-labor ratios are too small in Japan to permit the detection of meaningful relationships between the factor proportions and price ratios. These inferior results may also reflect the fact that the mechanical innovations in Japan were developed and adopted primarily to increase yield, rather than as a substitute for labor, for the period before World War II.

Table 5 presents results for the United States of the regression analyses of the determinants of fertilizer input per hectare of arable land. These results indicate that variations in the fertilizer-land price ratio alone explain more than 90 percent of the variation in fertilizer use. They also show that the wage-land price ratio is a significant variable, indicating a substitution relationship between fertilizer and labor. Over a certain range, fertilizer input can be substituted for human care for plants (for example, weeding). A more important factor in Japanese history would be the effects of the substitution of commercial fertilizer for the labor allocated to the production of self-supplied fertilizers, such as animal and green manure.[6]

A comparison of Table 5 with Table 6 indicates a striking similarity in the structure of demand for fertilizer in the United States and Japan. The results in these two tables seem to suggest that, despite enormous differences in climate, initial factor endowments, and social and economic institutions and organizations in the two countries, the agricultural production function, the inducement mechanism of innovations, and the response of farmers to economic opportunities have been essentially the same.

The results of the statistical analysis are clearly consistent with the hypothesis stated at the beginning of this section. In both Japan and the United States, factors have been

TABLE 5 Regressions of Fertilizer Input per Hectare of Arable Land on Relative Factor Prices: United States, 1880-1980, Quinquennial Observations

|  | Coefficients of Price | | | | | |
| --- | --- | --- | --- | --- | --- | --- |
| Regression Number | Fertilizer Relative to Land | Labor Relative to Land | Machinery Relative to Land | Coeff. of Det. ($\bar{R}^2$) | S.E. | Durbin-Watson Statistics |
| (W 11) | -1.512 (.119) | .850 (.212) | -.025 (.233) | .983 | .177 | 2.02 |
| (W 12) | -1.521 (.053) | .843 (.216) | -- | .984 | .189 | 2.02 |
| (W 13) | -1.641 (.063) | -- | -- | .972 | .250 | .88 |
| (W 14) | -1.295 (.092) | 1.118 (.129) | -.066 (.176) | .991 | .129 | 2.01 |
| (W 15) | -1.328 (.038) | 1.076 (.114) | -- | .992 | .134 | 2.04 |
| (W 16) | -1.524 (.075) | -- | -- | .954 | .318 | 1.04 |

Note: Equations are linear in logarithm. Standard errors of the estimated coefficients are in parentheses.

Source: Hayami and Ruttan (1985:Chap. 7).

TABLE 6  Regressions of Fertilizer Input per Hectare of Arable Land on Relative Factor Prices: Japan, 1880-1980, Quinquennial Observations

| Regression Number | Coefficients of Price | | | Coeff. of Det. ($\bar{R}^2$) | S.E. | Durbin-Watson Statistics |
|---|---|---|---|---|---|---|
| | Fertilizer Relative to Land | Labor Relative to Land | Machinery Relative to Land | | | |
| (W 17) | -1.033 (.347) | .432 (.209) | .019 (.487) | .884 | .388 | 1.67 |
| (W 18) | -1.020 (.082) | .427 (.173) | -- | .891 | .388 | 1.67 |
| (W 19) | -1.037 (.093) | -- | -- | .862 | .449 | 1.29 |
| (W 20) | -1.626 (.311) | .496 (.180) | .906 (.437) | .909 | .345 | .63 |
| (W 21) | -1.001 (.082) | .587 (.190) | -- | .892 | .386 | 1.06 |
| (W 22) | -1.028 (.098) | -- | -- | .844 | .477 | 1.07 |

Note:  Equations are linear in logarithm.  Standard errors of the estimated coefficients are in parentheses.

Source:  Hayami and Ruttan (1985:Chap. 7).

substituted for each other along a metaproduction function, primarily in response to long-run trends in factor prices.

The test of the induced technical change hypothesis presented in Tables 3, 4, 5, and 6 has established rather clearly its plausibility. To test the hypothesis more rigorously, it is necessary to decompose changes in factor proportions into (1) the effect of factor substitution along a fixed-technology iso-quant in response to changes in relative factor prices, and (2) the effect of biased technical change. In addition, it is necessary to see whether the biased technical change effect is in the same direction as the price-induced factor substitution effect.

A method for measuring biases of technical change with many factors of production was originally developed by Hans Binswanger (1974b, 1978b) using the transcendental logarithmic (translog) function. This method has found a number of applications in the analysis of agricultural production.[7] In the present study, we employ a two-level constant elasticity of substitution (CES) production function, which is more robust in estimation and more clear-cut in interpretation than the translog function.[8] The results are shown in Figure 6.

The cumulative changes in factor shares resulting from biased technical change are compared in Figure 6 for both the United States and Japan. As measured by these changes, the absolute effects of biased technical change on the agricultural production cost structure are quite different for the United States and Japan. In the United States, biased technical change resulted in a major increase in the share of power in total production cost and an associated decrease in the share of labor. Although the rate of increase in fertilizer-using bias was high, its absolute effect on the factor-share structure was relatively small because the initial factor share for fertilizer was very small. It seems clear that the dominant effects of biased technical change in U.S. agriculture on the production structure were labor-saving and power (cum machinery)-using throughout the entire period of analysis.

In contrast, in Japan, the absolute effect of factor-using bias on factor shares was largest for fertilizer and second largest for power, and the factor-saving effect was the largest for labor for the entire period. Until about 1915, the dominant effects of biased technical change were land-saving and labor-using. It seems clear that, during the early period in which labor was relatively abundant and land represented the major constraint on agricultural production, the primary efforts of technological development in Japan were directed to facilitating the substitution of labor for land. Later, as wage rates rose, mainly because of increased labor demand from the nonagricultural sectors, productivity growth seems to have been redirected in a labor-saving direction by technical changes that facilitated the substitution of power and fertilizer for labor.

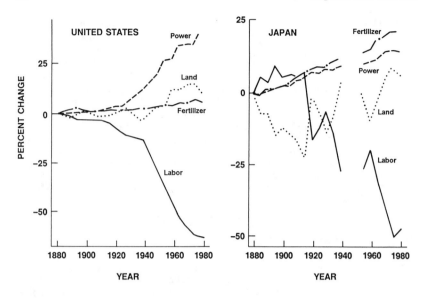

FIGURE 6   Cumulative Changes in Factor Shares Owing to Biased
Technical Change in Agriculture ($B_{it}$), United States and
Japan, 1880-1980

Source:   Hayami and Ruttan (1985:Chapter 7).


POPULATION PRESSURE AND LAND INFRASTRUCTURE DEVELOPMENT

In the previous section, we tested the induced innovation hypothesis against the agricultural history of the United States and
Japan.   In Japan, investments in biological technology and complementary investments in land infrastructure development resulted
in a relaxation of the land resource constraint on agricultural
development, particularly during the first several decades of the
period studied.   The Japanese experience is particularly relevant
for contemporary experience in countries characterized by a high
and rising pressure of population against land resources.[9]   In
this section, we draw on recent Philippine experience to illustrate the interrelationships among resource endowments, land infrastructure investment, and technical change in a contemporary
setting.[10]
     Until the end of the 1950s, Philippine agriculture followed
the traditional vent-for-surplus pattern of agricultural development characteristic of much of Southeast Asia.   Growth was
brought about primarily by expansion of the cultivated area in
response to an increased world demand for export crops.   The area
planted to food staples, such as rice and corn, was then increased in response to the growth in domestic demand resulting
from the export-stimulated growth in income and population.   Rice

and corn yields were low, and there was little growth in yield
per hectare.  Some efforts had been made to increase the yield
of plantation crops (notably by introducing improved sugarcane
varieties from Java and Hawaii), but the possibility of increasing the yields of food staples was largely ignored.  Expansion of the area under cultivation at a rate rapid enough to
absorb the growing labor force was possible as long as large
unused land areas existed.

With the rapid growth of population after World War II, the
supply of unexploited land became progressively exhausted.
Toward the end of the 1950s, the rate of expansion of cultivated
land began to decline in the Philippines, but the number of
workers in agriculture continued to grow at about the same rate,
as shown in Figure 7.  As a result, cultivated area per worker
began to decline.  The development of irrigation facilities was
accelerated during this period; the expansion of the irrigation
system since the 1950s has made an important contribution to the
rapid diffusion of modern semidwarf varieties of rice since the
mid-1960s.

This transition was accompanied by a major change in the
pattern of growth in agricultural output and factor use (Table
7).  During the 1950s, the rapid growth of output, 4.1 percent
per year, was accompanied by a 3.4 percent annual increase in
land area under cultivation.  Expansion of area cultivated
accounted for more than 80 percent of output growth; increases
in yield per hectare of cultivated land area accounted for less
than 20 percent.  The agricultural labor force (number of farm
workers) increased at an annual rate of 2.7 percent.  Approximately one-half of the gain in labor productivity (1.5 percent
per year) was explained by the increase in area per worker.

The pattern of agricultural growth in the 1960s is in sharp
contrast to that of the previous decade.  The rate of expansion
of cultivated area dropped by almost one-half, but population
growth did not drop appreciably.  Increases in labor productivity became totally dependent on increases in land productivity.
The data in Table 7 clearly suggest that Philippine agriculture
experienced a transition from a traditional growth pattern, based
on the expansion of cultivated area, to a new pattern based on
increase in land productivity.

Another remarkable aspect of the change in growth pattern is
that the application of modern inputs and technology, which had
previously been limited to export crops, became increasingly
focused on food crops.  During the 1950s, the increases in yields
per hectare were confined to export crops such as sugar; during
the 1960s, the yields per hectare of food crops for domestic consumption began to increase (Table 8).

Such contrasts seem to reflect a basic change in the direction of the growth of Philippine agriculture.  The demand-induced
technical changes that previously had been generated by world
demand for export crops were complemented during the 1960s by
rapid growth in domestic demand for food crops, generated by the
population explosion.  This trend was reinforced by a factor-
price-induced demand for yield-increasing infrastructure

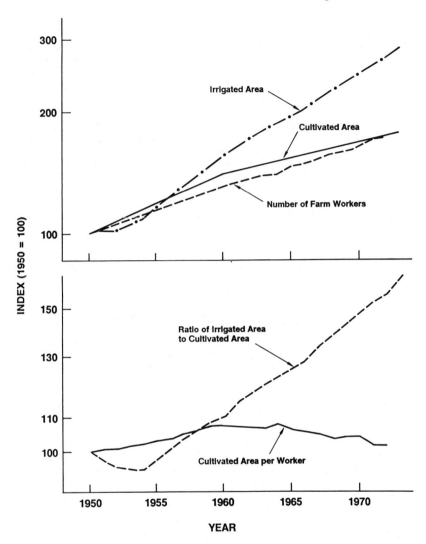

FIGURE 7  Comparisons in the Trends of Cultivated and Irrigated
Land Areas and of Number of Farm Workers in the Philippines,
Three-Year Moving Averages, Semilog Scale

Source:  Hayami and Kikuchi (1978:71).

TABLE 7  Contribution of Area and Land Productivity to the Growth in Output and Labor Productivity in Philippine Agriculture (in percent)

| Variable | 1948-52 to 1958-62 | | 1958-62 to 1968-72 | | 1968-72 to 1978-82 | |
|---|---|---|---|---|---|---|
| | Annual Growth Rate | Relative Contribution | Annual Growth Rate | Relative Contribution | Annual Growth Rate | Relative Contribution |
| Total Agricultural Output | 5.1 | 100 | 3.2 | 100 | 6.2 | 100 |
| Cultivated land area | 3.3 | 65 | 1.4 | 44 | -0.6 | -10 |
| Output per ha. of cultivated land area | 1.8 | 35 | 1.8 | 56 | 6.8 | 110 |
| Agricultural Output Per Farm Worker | 2.7 | 100 | 0.8 | 100 | 3.8 | 100 |
| Cultivated land area per farm worker | 0.9 | 33 | -1.0 | -125 | -3.0 | 79 |
| Output per ha. of cultivated land area | 1.8 | 67 | 1.8 | 225 | 6.8 | 179 |

Source:  David et al. (1984).

TABLE 8   Contribution of Area and Yield to Growth in Total Output
of Rice and Sugar in the Philippines (in percent)

|  | Annual Growth Rate | | | Relative Contribution | | |
|---|---|---|---|---|---|---|
|  | Output | Area | Yield | Output | Area | Yield |
| 1948-52 to 1958-62 |  |  |  |  |  |  |
| Rice | 3.5 | 3.5 | -0.05 | 100 | 101 | -1 |
| Sugar | 6.2 | 4.6 | 1.5 | 100 | 75 | 25 |
| 1958-62 to 1968-72 |  |  |  |  |  |  |
| Rice | 3.2 | 0.1 | 3.1 | 100 | 3 | 97 |
| Sugar | 3.7 | 4.8 | -1.1 | 100 | 130 | -30 |
| 1968-72 to 1978-82 |  |  |  |  |  |  |
| Rice | 4.3 | 0.7 | 3.6 | 100 | 17 | 83 |
| Sugar | 2.3 | 1.3 | 1.0 | 100 | 57 | 43 |

Source:   David et al. (1984).

investment and technical innovation.  The nature of this "epochal
change" in the growth pattern of Philippine agriculture is comparable to the experience of Taiwan agriculture during the period
between the two world wars. Agricultural growth in Taiwan before
the mid-1920s was based primarily on expansion of area cultivated.   Increases in output per worker were associated with increases in cultivated area per worker. As population growth in
Taiwan rose from 1 percent per year during the 1910s to 2.5 percent per year in the 1930s, the area for possible expansion was
exhausted, and the land-labor ratio began to decline.   At the
same time, there was a spurt in land productivity.  The growth
in yield per hectare of cultivated land was brought about by
increased cropping intensity and the development and diffusion
of Ponlai varieties.  The increase in the intensity of land use
was based on investment in irrigation, which was accelerated
during the 1910s.   As a result, agricultural output and productivity in Taiwan continued to rise in spite of the decline in
the land-labor ratio.
    The similarity of the Philippine and Taiwan experiences is
demonstrated in Figure 8.  Both Taiwan and the Philippines moved
to higher levels of labor productivity (iso-labor-productivity
curves are represented by plotted contours) through changes in
land productivity (Y/A) and land area per worker (A/L).  It is
clear that the turning point in agricultural growth from a pattern based on area expansion to one based on yield increases
occurred in Taiwan in the mid-1920s and in the Philippines in
the late 1950s.  The change in the agricultural growth pattern
in both countries seems to have occurred in response to population pressure on land.

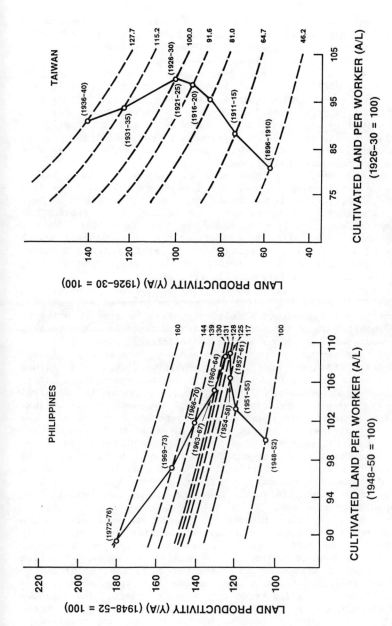

FIGURE 8 Historical Growth Paths of Labor Productivity in Relation to Land Productivity and Land–Labor Ratio in the Philippines and Taiwan

Source: David et al. (1984).

81

The epochal change in the agricultural growth momentum in
the Philippines between the 1950s and 1960s is clearly reflected
in the spurt in rice yield per hectare in the latter period.
Figure 9 compares the trend in rice yield per hectare in the
Philippines for 1950-79 with the trends of Japan, Taiwan, and
Korea before World War II. It is apparent that the spurt in rice
yield in the Philippines since the 1960s was similar to that
experienced in Taiwan and Korea during the interwar period.[11]

The Philippine experience, combined with similar experiences
in Japan, Korea, and Taiwan, suggests a common underlying process
of increases in land productivity in response to growing
population pressure against land resources.

Increase in land productivity from improving land infrastructure and developing seed-fertilizer technology has the same
effect on agricultural output as expansion in cultivated land
area. The former may be called "internal land augmentation," as
opposed to "external land augmentation" for the latter. We can
conceptualize the shifts in the momentum of agricultural output
growth from external to internal land augmentation, as observed
in the histories of Japan, Taiwan, Korea, and the Philippines,
along the lines illustrated in Figure 10.

As population pressure pushes the cultivation frontier into
marginal cost areas, we expect the marginal cost of agricultural
production via expansion of cultivated area to rise relative to
the marginal cost of production via intensification. Eventually,
the economy will reach a stage at which internal land
augmentation becomes a less costly means of increasing agricultural output than external land augmentation. Curve A in Figure
10 represents the marginal cost of increasing agricultural output
or income by opening new land; Curve I represents the marginal
cost of raising agricultural production by constructing irrigation facilities. With abundant land resources, Curve A will remain horizontal and below Curve I, indicating a relative advantage of external expansion over internal augmentation. As unused
land resources are exhausted and the cultivation frontier moves
from superior land to inferior land, Curve A will rise and cross
Curve I. When the economy reaches the crossover point, irrigation becomes a more profitable base for agricultural growth than
the opening of new land.

As the area under irrigation expands, however, irrigation
development moves from the relatively easier and less costly
projects to the more difficult and more costly. As a result,
the marginal cost of adding irrigated area increases. The rise
in the cost of irrigation will eventually reduce the incentive
to invest in land infrastructure. At the same time, other forces
act to offset the rising trend in irrigation costs. The improvement of irrigation permits the introduction of new seed-
fertilizer technology. Because of their high complementarity,
the use of fertilizers and improved seeds reduces the cost of
irrigation required to produce a unit of additional output, as
is illustrated in Figure 10 by the shift of the irrigation cost
curve downward from I to I'. Curve A may also be affected to
some extent by biological and chemical innovations, but their

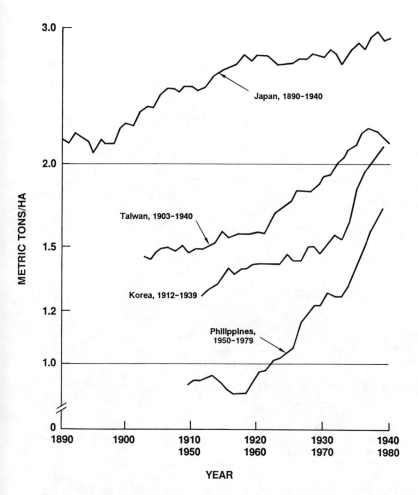

FIGURE 9  Brown Rice Yield per Hectare Planted in Japan,
Taiwan, Korea, and the Philippines, Five-Year Moving Averages

Sources:  Kikuchi and Hayami (1978:847); Palacpac (1982).


impacts on Curve I will be much larger because of the strong
complementarity between irrigation and the seed-fertilizer response functions.  The increased advantage of irrigation over
expansion of external area increases the incentive to invest in
land infrastructure.12
    In accordance with our hypothesis, the modern agricultural
histories of Japan, Taiwan, Korea, and the Philippines may be
reinterpreted as follows.  Before modern economic growth began
in the Meiji period, Japan was already located to the right of

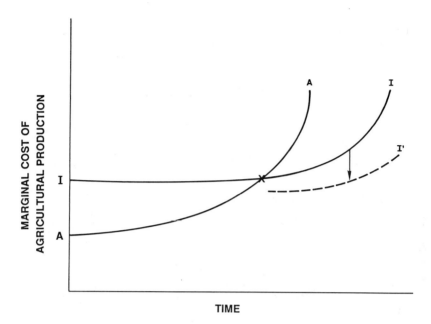

FIGURE 10   Hypothetical Relations Between the Marginal Cost
Curves of Agricultural Production by Opening New Land (A) and by
Building Irrigation Systems (I, I')

Source: Kikuchi and Hayami (1978:853).


the crossover point in Figure 10 as a result of gradual population growth in the feudal Tokugawa period.  However, because the
shift was very gradual, there was sufficient time so that village
communities could develop an organizational capacity to mobilize
communal labor for building and maintaining local irrigation
facilities.  Feudal lords had also taken the responsibility for
controlling rivers and major irrigation systems.  A decentralized
power structure that permitted economic and political competition
among the holders of feudal fiefs contributed to the response of
the rulers regarding the possibilities of local economic development.  As a result, Meiji Japan inherited a well-developed irrigation infrastructure.  The stage had been set for a move from
Curve I to Curve I' through development of the high-yielding
seed-fertilizer technology.
     It appears that Korea was also located to the right of the
crossover point before its modern agricultural growth began.
Partly because of the incapacity of the Yi dynasty in its late
stage, and partly because of the highly centralized despotic
structure of the government, the irrigation infrastructure had
not been properly developed.  Therefore, initial large-scale
investment in irrigation was required before the shift from
Curve I to Curve I' could begin.

Taiwan's economy, in contrast, seems to have reached the crossover point in the late 1910s. The increase in government investment in irrigation during this period, supported by the budget surplus of the colonial government, played a large role. However, an even more basic factor appears to have been the increase in the relative advantage of irrigation over land opening. The government irrigation investment provided the conditions for shifting from I to I' in the 1920s and 1930s.

The Philippines seems to have reached the crossover point only in the late 1950s. The nationalistic desire to achieve self-sufficiency in food, together with foreign exchange considerations, helped focus public attention on the need to invest in irrigation, which had become a relatively less costly means of increasing rice output. The conditions necessary to induce a shift from I to I' in the mid-1960s had thus been established.


POPULATION PRESSURE, LAND RESOURCE CONSTRAINTS, AND TECHNICAL CHANGE AND DEVELOPMENT: TWO VILLAGES IN INDONESIA

The implications of the process of agricultural development for factor productivity and income distribution at the village level as outlined in this chapter have been the subject of much debate. Since biological technology saves land by permitting more intensive use of labor and of biological and chemical inputs, it might be expected to contribute to a more favorable income distribution in rural communities. Nonetheless, the new seed-fertilizer technology has often been criticized for benefiting landlords at the expense of tenants and laborers, on the grounds that land rents have increased where modern crop varieties have been introduced. These arguments have often ignored the effects of rapid population growth, which has induced the intensification of crop production on factor returns.

Empirical evidence shows that the adoption of modern varieties (MVs) (combined with irrigation and fertilizer) has generally resulted in increases in labor demand, even in areas where it has been accompanied by concurrent progress in mechanization. We do, however, see a real danger of growing inequality in rural areas, not because of new technology, but because of insufficient progress in its development and diffusion. If technological progress is not sufficiently rapid, the increase in labor demand will fail to keep up with the increase in labor supply arising from rapid population growth.

This point is demonstrated with remarkable clarity in a comparative analysis by Yujiro Hayami and Masao Kikuchi of two villages located in the same geographic district in Java--one characterized by technological stagnation and the other by significant technological progress (Hayami and Kikuchi, 1981). A comparison of the two cases shows the separate effects of technological change and population growth.

The two villages chosen for the comparative analysis are located in the Regency (kabupaten) of Subang in West Java,

adjacent to the north of the Bandung Regency and about 120 km
east of Jakarta. One village is located at the foot of the
mountains in the southern part of the Subang Regency and is
identified as the South Village; much of the land belonging to
this village consists of terraced rice fields. The other
village, identified as the North Village, is located about 20 km
south of the South Village and is on a completely flat coastal
plain along the Java Sea. These two were among villages covered
by the Rice Intensification Survey (Intensifikasi Padi Sawah),
which was conducted by the Agro-Economic Survey of Indonesia
during 1968-72. The data collected from this survey provide the
initial benchmark information. New surveys were conducted during
January 1979 in the South Village and during November-December
1979 in the North Village.


Population Pressure and Technological Change

Java is known for its extremely high population density. The two
villages under study are also characterized by very unfavorable
man-land ratios. In the South Village, as many as 419 persons
obtained their primary subsistence from only about 25 hectares of
wet rice (Sawah). The situation was somewhat better in the North
Village, whose population of 774 persons had 64 hectares of rice
land. In addition to the wet rice fields, the South Village had
three hectares devoted to home gardens and fish ponds and the
North Village had eight.
    Although the population density was higher in the South
Village, the rate of population growth seems to have been much
faster in the North Village. Data on the number of children per
mother (Table 9) suggest that over the past 40 years, the natural
rate of population growth in the South Village declined from
about 3 percent per year to 1 percent. There was no indication
of a significant inflow of migrants. Although data for the
higher age brackets are not available, a comparison of the
average numbers of children per mother suggests that the natural
rate of population growth was much faster in the North Village
than in the South Village; moreover, there were a large number
of migrants into the North Village. Older villagers recalled
that in 1940 there were about 40 households. At the time of our
survey, that number had increased to 191. Assuming no change in
average family size, the rate of population growth for the past
four decades was in the neighborhood of 4 percent per year.
    These demographic differences can be explained by the dif-
ferent histories of settlement and technological change in the
two villages. The South Village is old; no one could recall
when it was first settled. The North Village was settled after
1920. The settlement was late because it was more difficult to
build a gravity irrigation system with only local resources in
the flat coastal plain than in the small mountain valley where
the South Village was located.

TABLE 9  Average Numbers of Surviving Children per Mother by Mother's Age and the Estimates of the Natural Rates of Population Growth in the South and North Villages in the Regency of Subang, West Java, Indonesia

| | South Village | | North Village | |
|---|---|---|---|---|
| Mother's Age | Children per Mother (n) No. | Population Growth Rate[a] (r) %/year | Children per Mother (n) No. | Population Growth Rate[a] (r) %/year |
| 80 Years and Above | 4.80 | 3.0 | n.a. | -- |
| 60-79 | 3.93 | 2.3 | n.a. | -- |
| 50-69 | 3.49 | 1.9 | n.a. | -- |
| 40-49 | 2.71 | 1.0 | 3.25 | 1.6 |
| (36-45) | (2.48) | (0.7) | (3.16) | (1.5) |
| 30-39 | 1.95 | -- | 2.57 | -- |
| 20-29 | 0.84 | -- | 1.80 | -- |

[a]Calculated by the formula: $n = 2(1 + r)^{30}$, assuming 30 years for the period of mothers' reproductive capacity.

Source: Hayami and Kikuchi (1981).

The economy of the South Village experienced little change in recent times. The local irrigation systems had been well developed as long as people could remember and permitted rice production on about 90 percent of the paddy field area, even in dry seasons. There had been no significant improvements in the system and no expansion in the cultivated area since World War II. Growing population pressure resulted in increased fragmentation of landholdings through inheritance; the number of landless and near-landless families increased.

MVs were introduced in the late 1960s under the Bimas Program, a nationwide effort to intensify rice production based on a package of modern inputs, credit, and extension. However, because the first MVs introduced were highly susceptible to the brown planthopper and tungro, a virus disease, many farmers who tried them shifted back to traditional varieties. From 1968-71 to 1978, the MV adoption rate increased slowly from 11 to 14 percent, although as many as 83 percent of the farmers had tried MVs at least once. As a result, the average rice yield per hectare increased only slightly, from 2.6 to 2.9 tons per hectare.13

The population pressure on limited land resources under a stable technology apparently reached a saturation point by the 1950s. The data in Table 9 indicate that the villagers responded by reducing their birth rate even before 1975, when a government birth control program was introduced. Villagers indicated that many wives had practiced abortion by indigenous

methods that were often harmful to their health. The South
Village appears to be an example of the impact of the Malthusian
check on population growth.

In contrast to the stagnation in the South Village, the
economy of the North Village was highly dynamic. The initial
settlers opened the land and practiced an extensive system of
rainfed rice production. Because rice yields under the rainfed
system were very low, a relatively large farm was required to
meet the subsistence needs of a family. The population density
was low by Java standards until the Jatiluhur Irrigation System,
the largest irrigation system in Indonesia, was extended to the
village.

The Jatiluhur System had a dramatic impact on the economy of
the North Village. Major laterals were built by 1968, but it was
not until 1972 that secondary and tertiary laterals were completed and the entire area of the village became suitable for
rice double-cropping. In 1968-71, double-cropping was practiced
on about half of the rice land; by 1979, the whole area was
double-cropped.

The introduction of double-cropping rice production was
facilitated by the diffusion of early-maturing and nonphoto-
sensitive MVs. According to the Rice Intensification Survey, 7
percent of farmers planted MVs in 1968-71; that ratio rose to 100
percent in 1978-79. There was no difference in the MV adoption
rate among farm-size and tenure classes. The MVs commonly used
in 1979 were IRRI varieties (IR26, IR36, IR38) and the Asahan
variety developed by the Central Agricultural Experiment Station
at Sukamandi, located near the North Village.

With the diffusion of MVs and the increased application of
fertilizer, the average yield per hectare of rice crop increased
from 2.4 tons in 1968-71 to 3.5 tons in 1978-79, while the cropping index rose from 1.5 to 2.0. Thus the average rice output
per hectare of rice land per year rose by more than 80 percent
between 1968 and 1978.


Employment, Wages, and Factor Shares

The different patterns of technological progress (defined here
broadly as a shift in the production function resulting from
both irrigation improvement and MV diffusion) between the two
villages were reflected in sharp differences in the use of rice
production inputs and in input prices (Tables 10 and 11).

In the South Village, where technology was stagnant, the
input of fertilizer per hectare of crop area increased at a rate
lower than the rate of decline in the real price of fertilizer.
In the North Village, where the fertilizer-responsive MVs were
widely adopted, the per-hectare input of fertilizer increased at
a rate six times as fast as the rate of decline in the price of
fertilizer.

Changes in the use of labor and animal power in relation to
their price changes also produced dramatic contrasts. In the
South Village, an increase in labor input was associated with a

TABLE 10 Changes in Inputs per Hectare of Rice Crop Area and Input
Prices for Rice Production in the South Village, 1968-71 to 1978

| Input | 1968-71[a] | 1978[b] | Percent Change from 1968-71 to 1978 |
|---|---|---|---|
| Inputs | | | |
| Fertilizer (kg/ha) | 191 | 229 | 20 |
| Labor (hours/ha) | | | |
| Land preparation | 420 | 494 | 18 |
| Total (preharvest) | 736 | 928 | 26 |
| Carabao and cattle for land preparation (days/ha) | 16.4 | 9.2 | -44 |
| Real Input Prices (in paddy)[c] | | | |
| Fertilizer (kg/kg) | 1.5 | 1.1 | -27 |
| Labor wage (kg/day)[d] | 9.5 | 8.5 | -11 |
| Carabao rental (kg/day) | 6.2 | 9.5 | 53 |

[a]Averages for wet and dry season.
[b]Dry season.
[c]Nominal price divided by paddy price.
[d]Wage for land preparation, assuming eight hours per day: includes
meals.

Source: Hayami and Kikuchi (1981).

decline in the real wage rate. Meanwhile, a rise in the real
rental rate of draft animals (carabao and cattle) resulted in a
sharp decline in the use of animal power. As a result, because
of the decline in the labor wage rate relative to animal rental
costs, hand hoeing was substituted for animal plowing and
harrowing. It is clear that the population pressure on land
under a stagnant technology resulted in a decline in the value
of human labor relative to the values of both capital and food.
   In contrast, in the North Village higher labor inputs were
associated with a significant increase in the real wage rate.
The average labor input per hectare of rice area per year increased more than 40 percent over the decade as a result of the
increase in the multiple-cropping index (figures in parentheses
in the last column of Table 11). At the same time, the use of
animal power increased even more rapidly than the use of human
labor, despite a rapid rise in the real cost of animal rental.
It is clear that the increase in demand for labor owing to technological progress outpaced the increase in labor supply owing
to population growth. As a result, the real wage rate rose in
spite of the effort to substitute capital (animal power) for
human labor.
   How were the major differences in technological change reflected in different patterns of income distribution between the

TABLE 11  Changes in Inputs per Hectare of Rice Crop Area and Input
Prices for Rice Production in the North Village, 1968-71 to 1978

| Input | 1968-71[a] | 1978-79[b] | Percent Change from 1968-71 to 1978-79 |
|---|---|---|---|
| **Inputs** | | | |
| Fertilizer (kg/ha)[c] | 75 | 209 | 179 |
| Labor (hours/ha) | | | |
|   Land preparation | 219 | 223 | 6 (42)[g] |
|   Total (preharvest) | 638 | 701 | 10 (46)[g] |
| Carabao and cattle for land | | | |
|   preparation (days/ha)[d] | 9.6 | 13.2 | 38 (83)[g] |
| **Real Input Prices (in paddy)[e]** | | | |
| Fertilizer (kg/kg) | 1.5 | 1.0 | -33 |
| Labor wage (kg/day)[f] | 7.9 | 11.5 | 46 |
| Carabao rental (kg/day)[d] | 8.8 | 14.1 | 60 |

[a]Averages for wet and dry season.
[b]Averages for 1978-79 wet season and 1979 dry season.
[c]Urea and TPS.
[d]Data for wet season only.
[e]Nominal price divided by paddy price.
[f]Wage for land preparation, assuming eight hours per day: includes meals.
[g]Outside of parentheses are the rates of increase in labor input per ha of cropped area. Inside of parentheses are the rates of increase per ha of paddy field area per year.

Source:  Hayami and Kikuchi (1981).

South and North villages? Estimates of changes in the average
factor shares of rice output per hectare of crop area in the two
villages are shown in Tables 12 and 13. The factor payments are
expressed in terms of paddy (rough rice) by multiplying factor
inputs by factor-product price ratios.

In the South Village, the average rice yield per hectare
increased by about 10 percent from 1968-71 to 1978. Both the
payment to hired labor and the imputed cost of family labor increased by less than 5 percent. For owner farmers, operators'
surplus (residual) rose sharply. For tenant farmers, operators'
surplus was almost zero, and land rent paid to landlords was
equivalent to the owner farmers' surplus. These results indicate
that for the owner farmers, the operators' surplus consisted
mainly of the return to their land; this implies an increase in
the economic rent to land. The decline in the relative share to
labor and the rise in the relative share to land imply that the
income position of landlords and large owner farmers rose relative to that of marginal farmers, tenants, and agricultural
laborers.

TABLE 12  Changes in Factor Payments and Factor Shares in Rice Production per Hectare of Crop Area in the South Village, 1968-71 to 1978

| | Factor Payment (kg/ha) | | | Factor Share (percent) | | |
|---|---|---|---|---|---|---|
| | | 1978[b] | | | 1978 | |
| Factor | 1968-71[a] Owner | Owner[c] | Tenant[d] | 1968-71 Owner | Owner | Tenant |
| Rice Output | 2,600 | 2,942 | 3,080 | 100.0 | 100.0 | 100.0 |
| Factor Payment[e] | | | | | | |
| Current input[f] | 345 | 293 | 321 | 13.3 | 10.0 | 10.4 |
| Capital[g] | 136 | 125 | 76 | 5.2 | 4.2 | 2.5 |
| Labor | 1,257 | 1,301 | 1,341 | 48.3 | 44.2 | 43.5 |
| (family) | (427)[h] | (438) | (476) | (16.4) | (14.9) | (15.4) |
| (hired) | (830)[h] | (863) | (865) | (31.9) | (29.3) | (28.1) |
| Land | 0 | 0 | 1,262 | 0 | 0 | 41.0 |
| Operators' surplus | 2.6 | 862 | 1,223 | 80 | 33.2 | 41.6 |

[a]Averages for wet and dry season.
[b]1978 dry season.
[c]Averages of 74 owner farmers cultivating 20.4 ha.
[d]Averages of 9 tenant operators cultivating 1.8 ha.
[e]Factor payments converted to paddy equivalents by the factor-output price ratios.
[f]Seeds, fertilizers, and chemicals.
[g]Animal rental and irrigation fee.
[h]Assume the same composition of family and hired labor as for 1978.

Source:  Hayami and Kikuchi (1981).

It seems likely that the size distribution of income became even more skewed than the data in Table 12 indicate.  From 1968-71 to 1978, the number of landless and near-landless households in the South Village increased faster than the number of farmers. Therefore, the share of income per landless household probably declined by a greater extent than the share of labor income per hectare.  It is highly likely that per household or per capita income from rice production for landless and near-landless households declined in absolute terms even though the rice income per hectare increased slightly.

The situation was very different in the North Village.  There the average yield per hectare per year, over both the wet and dry seasons, increased by more than 80 percent.  In spite of the rapid increase in output, the relative share of labor stayed almost constant.  Meanwhile, current inputs and capital shares increased.  The operators' surplus of owner farmers declined.

The operators' surplus for tenant farmers was almost zero, and the land rent paid to landlords was equivalent to the owner farmers' surplus.  This implies that the operators' surplus for

TABLE 13  Changes in Factor Payments and Factor Shares in Rice Production per Hectare of Crop Area in the North Village, 1968-71 to 1978-79

| Factor | Factor Payment (kg/ha) | | | Factor Share (percent) | | |
| | 1968-71[a] Owner | 1978-79[b] | | 1968-71[a] Owner | 1978-79[b] | |
| | | Owner | Tenant[c] | | Owner | Tenant[c] |
| --- | --- | --- | --- | --- | --- | --- |
| Rice Output | 2,342 | 3,203 | 3,272 | 100.0 | 100.0 | 100.0 |
| Factor Payment[d] | | | | | | |
| Current input[e] | 152 | 300 | 280 | 6.5 | 9.4 | 8.5 |
| Capital[f] | 47 | 154 | 154 | 2.0 | 4.8 | 4.7 |
| Labor | 947 | 1,322 | 1,295 | 40.4 | 41.0 | 39.6 |
| (family) | (117) | (252) | (357) | ( 5.0) | ( 7.9) | (10.9) |
| (hired) | (830) | (1,070) | (938) | (35.4) | (33.4) | (28.7) |
| Land | 0 | 0 | 1,495 | 0 | 0 | 45.7 |
| Operators' surplus | 1,196 | 1,427 | 48 | 51.1 | 44.5 | 1.5 |

[a]Averages for wet and dry season.
[b]Averages of 1978-79 wet season and 1979 dry season.
[c]Data for share tenants.
[d]Factor payments converted to paddy equivalents by the factor-output price ratios.
[e]Seeds, fertilizers, and chemicals.
[f]Animal and machine rental and irrigation fee.

Source:  Hayami and Kikuchi (1981).

owner farmers consisted mainly of the return to their land. Thus the results in Table 13 are consistent with the hypothesis that technological progress in this village was biased in a land-saving and capital-using direction and was more or less neutral with respect to the use of labor.  These results for the North Village are in sharp contrast to those for the South Village, where the share of land increased sharply at the expense of the labor share.

The comparison of these two villages shows clearly as follows: that growing poverty and inequality are almost certain to result if efforts to generate technological progress are insufficient to overcome the decreasing return to labor resulting from growing population pressure on land.

PERSPECTIVE

In the agriculture of developing countries, with land becoming increasingly scarce and expensive relative to labor as population pressure against land resources increases, the development of biological and chemical technologies is the most efficient

way to promote agricultural growth. Technological progress of
this type tends to make small-scale operations relatively more
efficient. It thereby induces an agrarian structure characterized by a unimodal distribution of small family farms, rather
than a bimodal distribution consisting of large commercial
farmers and large numbers of landless or near-landless laborers.
Moreover, because biological and chemical technologies tend to
be generally biased, or at least neutral, toward labor use, they
help counteract the effect of population pressure on land rent
and wages. In a broad perspective, the emergence of the green
revolution technology can be considered a worldwide response to
the demand for more intensive land use associated with the growth
of population relative to land resources.

The question is frequently raised as to whether advances in
indigenous technology induced by population density, along the
lines outlined by Boserup (1965), would be sufficient to sustain
rising levels of per capita income and consumption. Such advances, however, have rarely been rapid enough to do more than
slow the rate of decline in labor productivity. However, a
decline in labor productivity, measured in terms of output per
hour or per day, if accompanied by an increase in the number of
hours or days worked per year, is not incompatible with a rise
in annual output or income per worker (see footnote 9). This
was the classic pattern followed in the wet rice cultivation
areas of East Asia during the shift from upland to rainfed rice
production, and then from rainfed to irrigated rice production.
In the long run, however, even with relatively slow growth in
population and labor force, output or income per worker or per
year tends to stagnate or decline as the rate of indigenous
technical change in response to population growth declines.

The association between more intensive cultivation and declining levels of labor productivity under conditions of rapid
population growth has, at times, been reversed by a combination
of technology transfer and institutionalization of the domestic
capacity to adapt and invent biological and chemical technologies. This view is consistent with the green revolution
experience in East, Southeast, and South Asia. If rapid population growth continues indefinitely, however, these gains will
be difficult to maintain. For example, we have no experience
with countries that have been able to maintain a rate of growth
in agricultural output in the range of 4 percent per year or
above over a sustained period. It has, however, been possible
to achieve rates of growth in labor productivity in the 4 percent
range or above in situations characterized by both growth in output per unit area and declining farm employment. In the United
States, labor productivity growth in the range of 6 percent per
year has been achieved as the result of increases in output per
unit of land area of approximately 2 percent yer year and increases in area cultivated per worker of approximately 4 percent
per year.

The development of more productive biological and chemical
technologies capable of offsetting the effect of growing population pressure appears to be a necessary condition for the simul-

taneous achievement of both growth and equity in developing
countries today.  If developing countries fail to achieve sufficiently rapid technological progress, greater poverty and inequity
in rural areas will be the inevitable result.  As the growth of
population presses against limited land resources under existing
technology, the cultivation frontier is forced onto more marginal
land.  Greater amounts of labor must be applied per unit of cultivated land, with the result that the cost of food production
increases and food prices rise.  The long-run effect will be, as
in the South Village in the Indonesian study, the reduction of
wages to a subsistence level, with the available surpluses
captured by landlords in the form of land rent.

MV technology, enthusiastically heralded as the green
revolution, has often been regarded as a source of inequity in
rural incomes.  This view is generally inconsistent with the
green revolution experience.  The MV technology diffused rapidly
among farmers irrespective of farm size and land tenure in the
areas where it was superior to traditional technology.  There are
numerous cases, however, where small or poor farmers lagged significantly behind the large or wealthy farmers in the adoption
of MVs and related inputs.  Such cases are largely a reflection
of institutional rather than technical bias.  Institutional re-
forms are necessary to partition equitably the new income streams
generated by an appropriate technology.

A relevant question, given the extreme inequality in wealth
and power in many developing countries, is whether the development of the green revolution technology should have been withheld
because of its possible adverse effect on income distribution.
Even the most severe critics of the green revolution technology
have seldom been willing to advocate such a policy.  MV technology has been diffusing in Asia with sufficient speed to shift
the product demand and the labor supply schedules significantly.
There have been substantial gains to both producers and consumers.  In the absence of the new technology, many developing
countries would have moved several steps closer to the Ricardian
trap of economic stagnation and even greater stress over the
distribution of income.  The conclusion that should be drawn
from this experience is not that growth has been "immizerizing,"
but that stagnation has.

A further reason for encouraging the development and
diffusion of new biological and chemical technologies, even in
societies characterized by inequitable distribution of economic
and political resources, is that the new income streams generated
by technical change represent a powerful source of demand for
institutional change.  It seems clear that in many countries,
the potential gains from the new technology have generated
effective demand for institutional reform.  The gains from the
new technology can be fully realized only if land tenure, water
management, and credit institutions perform effectively.  Markets
for the inputs that embody the new technology--seeds, fertilizer,
and pesticides--must perform efficiently.  Product markets in
which prices are distorted against either producers or consumers
fail to generate the potential gains from new technology.  In a

society in which technology is static and marketable surpluses are not increasing, there are few gains, either to producers or consumers, from the reform of market institutions. However, when rapid growth of production and of productivity becomes possible, the gains become larger, and the incentives that act to induce institutional reforms become more powerful. Similarly, unless the potential gains from land tenure and other institutional re-forms are enhanced by technical change, it will be difficult to generate the effort needed to bring about the reforms.

We do not argue, of course, that the dialectical interaction between technical and institutional innovation always functions to enhance both growth and equity. Simon Kuznets (1955) and others have documented the tendency for income distribution to worsen during the initial stages of development (see also Bacha, 1979).14 The potential gains from technical change set in motion both private and bureaucratic efforts to capture those gains in the form of institutional rents, rather than allowing the market to partition the gains among factor owners and con-sumers. The possibilities for bias in institutional innovation are greatest in societies with highly unequal distribution of economic and political resources.

We should emphasize that even the most appropriate technical changes have a limited impact on the growth and distribution of income in rural areas when unaccompanied by effective development efforts in other sectors. Growth in rural incomes and in returns to labor is critically dependent on rapid growth in nonagricul-tural employment opportunities and on effective intersector labor markets. We do not argue, therefore, that rapid and appropriate growth in agricultural productivity is a solution to either the income level or income distribution problem in rural areas. We do insist that it is a necessary condition.

NOTES

1  Interest by economists in the issue opened up by Hicks lagged until the 1960s. Two papers by William Fellner (1961, 1962) were particularly important in directing attention to the issue of induced technical change. This was followed by an extended dialogue over the theoretical foundations and macroeconomic implications of induced tech-nical change, beginning with the article by Kennedy (1964, 1966, 1967) and continuing with Samuelson (1965, 1966), Ahmad (1966, 1967a, 1967b), and Fellner (1967). For other contributions see Drandakis and Phelps (1966), Conlisk (1969), and van de Klundent and de Groot (1971). For reviews of this and related literature see Wan (1971), Nordhaus (1973), and Binswanger (1978a).

2  Mowery and Rosenberg (1979:104) have argued that in a number of recent studies, "the notion that market demand forces 'govern' the innovation process is simply not demonstrated by the empirical analyses which have claimed to support that conclusion." In a recent study, however, Scherer (1982:

230), using a more complete data base, concludes that "the relationship between demand-pull indices and associated patent flows is positive and statistically significant."

3    Hans P. Binswanger (1974a, 1978c) has developed an induced innovation model incorporating a research production function. By assuming decreasing marginal productivity of research resources in applied research and development, he was able to construct a model of induced factor-saving bias in technical change based on the profit-maximizing behavior of the firm, without resorting to the restrictive assumption of the fixed research budget of the Kennedy model. Binswanger also incorporates into the model the effect of product demand on research resource allocation. In his model, the growth in product demand increases the marginal value product of resources devoted to research, thereby increasing the optimal level of research expenditure for the profit-maximizing firm. The larger research budget implies a shift of the innovation possibility curve (IPC), defined as an envelope of unit isoquants corresponding to the alternative technologies that can potentially be developed for a given research budget at a given state of the art, toward the origin. In the Binswanger model, technical change is ʹguided along the IPC by changes in relative factor prices, while the IPC itself is induced to shift inward toward the origin by the growth in product demand. Thus he was able to incorporate both the Hicks approach, which focused on the effect of relative factor prices on factor-saving bias, and the Schmookler-Griliches approach, which focused on the effect of product demand on the rate of technological change, into a single model of induced technical change.

4    This section draws heavily on Hayami and Ruttan (1971) and on Kawagoe et al. (1983). Our earlier results for 1880-1960 have been compared with the experience of Denmark, France, Germany, and the United Kingdom by Weber (1977), Wade (1981), and Ruttan et al. (1978).

5    For the divergence between agricultural land prices and land rents in the United States since 1960, see Doll and Widdows (1982).

6    Biological innovations represented by improvements in crop varieties, characterized by greater response to fertilizer, tend to be land-saving and labor-using. The yield potential of the improved varieties is typically achieved only when high levels of fertilization are combined with high levels of crop husbandry and water management. Thus the introduction of high-yielding varieties enhances the substitution of fertilizer and labor for land. On the other hand, in an environment of rising wage rates, the substitution of commercial fertilizers for plant and animal manures may have significant labor-saving effects. In Japan, the production of such self-supplied fertilizers as manure, green manure, compost, and night soil has traditionally occupied a significant portion of a farmer's work hours. With the in-

creased supply of commercial fertilizers, farmers have
diverted their labor to improvements in cultural practices,
such as better seedbed preparation and weed control.

7   The Binswanger method was applied to Japanese agriculture
by Kako (1978) and Nghiep (1979).

8   The two-level CES production function was originally
developed by Sato (1967). This production function was
first applied to the analysis of Japanese agriculture by
Shintani and Hayami (1975). More recently, the two-level
CES production function was advocated for its relevance to
the analysis of agricultural production in general by Kaneda
(1982). According to Kaneda, the two-level CES function has
advantages over the translog function in parsimony in parameters, ease of interpretation and computation, and inter-
polative and extrapolative robustness. For an earlier
attempt to adapt the CES production function to estimating
elasticities of substitution among more than two factors,
see Roe and Yeung (1978).

9   The argument that population growth is a necessary condition
for the development of intensive systems of agricultural
production has been argued most forcefully by Boserup (1965,
1981). The Boserup argument that a labor-intensive system
of agricultural production was essential for the production
of the agricultural surpluses necessary for the emergence of
urban civilization in Mesopotamia, Mesoamerica, and East
Asia appears to be firmly grounded in economic history. The
impact of population growth on inducing indigenous improvements in agricultural technology in contemporary peasant
societies has also been documented by Boserup. Her insis-
tence on the importance of population growth in inducing
the development of intensive systems of agricultural production is an important correction to the view that agricultural technology in primitive or traditional societies
was essentially static.

The experience of preindustrial Western Europe suggests,
however, a somewhat less optimistic view of the relationship
between population and economic growth. According to Lee
(1980:547), the economy of preindustrial England "could
absorb population growth at about 0.4 percent per year with
little effect; deviations above or below this trend, however, had dramatic consequences . . . a 10 percent increase
in population depressed wages by 22 percent; raised rents
by 19 percent; lowered industrial prices relative to agricultural prices by 17 percent; raised the rates of industrial agricultural production by 13 percent; and lowered
labor's share of national income by 14 percent."

10  This section draws heavily on Hayami et al. (1976). This
and the next section draw heavily on Kikuchi and Hayami
(1978). For more detail on the history of land infrastructure development in Japan, see Hayami et al. (1975).

11  The critical importance of irrigation for the introduction
of seed-fertilizer technology in monsoon Asia has been emphasized by Ishikawa (1967) and by Hsieh and Ruttan (1967).

12  Other stylized models would be appropriate under other eco-
    logical conditions or different land-labor resource endow-
    ments.  In the more humid upland farming areas of North
    America, for example, the closing of the frontier was
    followed initially by the development of yield-increasing
    crop varieties, and only later by supplemental irrigation
    and more intensive tillage practices.  In arid-region agri-
    culture, irrigation and other forms of water management
    might be expected to precede the development of high-
    yielding varieties by a much longer time than in the more
    humid areas of East and Southeast Asia.  See, for example,
    Richards (1982).
13  On revisiting the South Village in 1984, the staff of the
    Agro-Economic Research Center found indications that modern
    rice varieties have been widely adopted.  The initial ex-
    perience with the brown planthopper and tungro-susceptible
    varieties apparently contributed to cautious acceptance of
    the new brown planthopper and tungro-resistant varieties.
14  Kuznets (1980) has also emphasized that a successful devel-
    oped country has had to acquire the capacity both to encour-
    age technological innovation and to design institutions that
    can accommodate the uneven distributional impact of technol-
    ogy on different social groups.

REFERENCES

Ahmad, S. (1966)  On the theory of induced invention.  Economic
    Journal 76:343-357.
Ahmad, S. (1967a)  A rejoinder to Professor Fellner.  Economic
    Journal 77:960-963.
Ahmad, S. (1967b)  Reply to Professor Fellner.  Economic Journal
    77:664-665.
Bacha, E.L. (1979)  The Kuznets curve and beyond:  growth and
    changes in inequalities.  Pp. 52-71 in E. Malinvaud, ed.,
    Economic Growth and Resources, Vol. 1, The Major Issues.
    Proceedings of the Fifth World Congress of the Inter-
    national Economic Association, Tokyo, Japan, 1977.  New
    York:  St. Martin's Press.
Binswanger, H.P. (1974a)  A microeconomic approach to induced
    innovation.  Economic Journal 84:940-958.
Binswanger, H.P. (1974b)  The measurement of technical change
    biases with many factors of production.  American Economic
    Review 64:964-976.
Binswanger, H.P. (1978a)  Induced technical change:  evolution of
    thought.  Pp. 13-43 in H.P. Binswanger and V.W. Ruttan et
    al., eds., Induced Innovation:  Technology, Institutions and
    Development.  Baltimore, Md.:  The Johns Hopkins University
    Press.
Binswanger, H.P. (1978b)  Measured biases of technical change:
    the United States.  Pp. 215-242 in H.P. Binswanger and V.W.
    Ruttan et al., eds., Induced Innovation:  Technology, Insti-
    tutions and Development.  Baltimore, Md.:  The Johns Hopkins
    University Press.

Binswanger, H.P. (1978c)  The microeconomics of induced technical
  change.  Pp. 91-127 in H.P. Binswanger and V.W. Ruttan et
  al., eds., Induced Innovation:  Technology, Institutions and
  Development.  Baltimore, Md.:  The Johns Hopkins University
  Press.
Boserup, E. (1965)  The Conditions of Agricultural Growth:  The
  Economics of Agrarian Change and Population Press.  Chicago:
  Aldine.
Boserup, E. (1981)  Population and Technical Change:  A Study of
  Long-Term Trends.  Chicago:  University of Chicago Press.
Conlisk, J. (1969)  A neoclassical growth model with endogenously
  positioned technical change frontier.  Economic Journal 79:
  348-362.
David, C.C., R. Barker, and A. Palacpac (1984)  The Nature of
  Productivity Growth in Philippine Agriculture, 1948-1982.
  Paper presented at the Symposium on Agricultural
  Productivity Measurement and Analysis, Asian Productivity
  Organization, Tokyo, Japan.
Doll, J.P., and Widdows, R. (1982)  A Comparison of Cash Rent and
  Land Values for Selected U.S. Farming Regions.  Washington,
  D.C.:  U.S. Department of Agriculture.
Drandakis, E.M., and E.S. Phelps (1966)  A model of induced in-
  vention, growth and distribution.  Economic Journal 76:823-
  840.
Fellner, W. (1961)  Two propositions in the theory of induced
  innovations.  Economic Journal (6):305-308.
Fellner, W. (1962)  Does the market direct the relative factor-
  saving effects of technological progress?  Pp. 171-193 in
  R.R. Nelson, ed., The Rate and Direction of Inventive
  Activity.  Princeton, N.J.:  Princeton University Press.
Fellner, W. (1967)  Comment on the induced bias.  Economic
  Journal 77:662-664.
Griliches, Z. (1957)  Hybrid corn:  an exploration in the
  economics of technical change.  Econometrica 25:501-522.
Hayami, Y., and M. Kikuchi (1978)  Investment inducements to
  public infrastructure:  irrigation in the Philippines.
  Review of Economics and Statistics 60:70-84.
Hayami, Y., and M. Kikuchi (1981)  Asian Village Economy at the
  Crossroads:  An Economic Approach to Institutional Change.
  Baltimore, Md.:  The Johns Hopkins University Press and
  Tokyo:  University of Tokyo Press.
Hayami, Y., and V.W. Ruttan (1971)  Factor prices and technical
  change in agricultural development:  the United States and
  Japan, 1880-1960.  Journal of Political Economy 78:1115-1141.
Hayami, Y., and V.W. Ruttan (1985)  Agricultural Development:  An
  International Perspective.  Baltimore, Md.:  The Johns
  Hopkins University Press.
Hayami, Y., with M. Akino, M. Shintani, and S. Yamada (1975)  A
  Century of Agricultural Growth in Japan.  Minneapolis,
  Minn.:  University of Minnesota Press and Tokyo:  University
  of Tokyo Press.
Hayami, Y., C.C. David, P. Flores, and Masaokikuchi (1976)
  Agricultural growth against a land resource constraint:  the
  Philippine experience.  Australian Journal of Agricul- tural
  Economics 20:144-159.

Hicks, J.R. (1932)  The Theory of Wages.  London:  MacMillan &
    Co.
Hsieh, S.-C., and V.W. Ruttan (1967)  Environmental technological
    and institutional factors in the growth of rice production:
    Philippines, Thailand, and Taiwan.  Food Research Institute
    Studies 7:307-341.
Ishikawa, S. (1967)  Economic Development in Asian Perspective.
    Tokyo:  Kinokuniya Bookstore, Co.
Kako, T. (1978)  Decomposition analysis of derived demand for
    factor inputs:  the case of rice production in Japan.
    American Journal of Agricultural Economics 60:628-635.
Kaneda, H. (1982)  Specification of production functions for
    analyzing technical change and factor inputs in agricul-
    tural development.  Journal of Development Economics 11:
    97-108.
Kawagoe, T., K. Otsuka, and Y. Hayami (1983)  Induced Biases of
    Technical Change in Agriculture:  The United States and
    Japan, 1880-1980.  Unpublished manuscript, Tokyo Metro-
    politan University.
Kennedy, C. (1964)  Induced bias in innovation and the theory of
    distribution.  Economic Journal 74:541-547.
Kennedy, C. (1966)  Samuelson on induced innovation.  Review of
    Economics and Statistics 48:442-444.
Kennedy, C. (1967)  On the theory of induced invention--a reply.
    Economic Journal 77:958-960.
Kikuchi, M., and Hayami, Y. (1978)  Agricultural growth against
    a land resource constraint:  a comparative history of Japan,
    Taiwan, Korea, and the Philippines.  Journal of Economic
    History 38:839-864.
Kuznets, S. (1955)  Economic growth and income inequality.
    American Economic Review 45:1-28.
Kuznets, S. (1980)  Driving forces of economic growth:  what can
    we learn from history?  Weltwirtschaftliches Archiv 16:409-
    431.
Lee, R.D. (1980)  A historical perspective on economic aspects
    of population explosion:  the case of pre-industrial
    England.  In R.H. Easterlin, ed., Population and Economic
    Change in Developing Countries.  Chicago:  University of
    Chicago Press.
Lee, T.-h. (1971)  Intersectoral Capital Flows in the Economic
    Development of Taiwan, 1895-1960.  Ithaca, N.Y.:  Cornell
    University Press.
Mowery, D., and N. Rosenberg (1979)  The influence of market
    demand upon innovation:  a critical review of some recent
    empirical studies.  Research Policy 8:102-153.
Nghiep, L.T. (1979)  The structure and changes of technology in
    prewar Japanese agriculture.  American Journal of Agricul-
    tural Economics 61:687-693
Nordhaus, W.D. (1973)  Some skeptical thoughts on the theory of
    induced innovation.  Quarterly Journal of Economics 87:208-
    219.
Palacpac, A.C. (1982)  World Rice Statistics.  Los Banos,
    Philippines:  International Rice Research Institute.

Richards, A. (1982) Egypt's Agricultural Development, 1800-1980: Technical and Social Change. Boulder, Colo.: Westview Press.

Roe, T., and P. Yeung (1978) A CES test of induced technical change: Japan. Pp. 243-260 in H.P. Binswanger and V.W. Ruttan et al., eds., Induced Innovation: Technology, Institutions and Development. Baltimore, Md.: The Johns Hopkins University Press.

Ruttan, V.W., H.D. Binswanger, Y. Hayami, W.W. Wade, and A. Weber (1978) Factor productivity and growth. Pp. 44-87 in H.P. Binswanger and V.W. Ruttan et al., eds., Induced Innovation: Technology, Institutions and Development. Baltimore, Md.: The Johns Hopkins University Press.

Samuelson, P.A. (1965) A theory of induced innovation along Kennedy-Weisacher lines. Review of Economics and Statistics 47:343-356.

Samuelson, P.A. (1966) Rejoinder: agreements, disagreements, doubts and the case of induced Harrod-neutral technical change. Review of Economics and Statistics 48:444-448.

Sato, K. (1967) A two-level constant-elasticity-of-substitution production function. Review of Economic Studies 34:201-218.

Scherer, F.M. (1982) Demand pull and technological invention: Schmookler revisited. Journal of Industrial Economics 30: 225-238.

Schmookler, J. (1962) Changes in industry and in the state of knowledge as determinants of industrial invention. Pp. 195-231 in Nelson, ed., Rate and Direction of Inventive Activity. Princeton, N.J.: Princeton University Press.

Schmookler, J. (1966) Invention and Economic Growth. Cambridge, Mass.: Harvard University Press.

Shintani, M., and Y. Hayami (1975) Factor combination and biased technical change in agriculture. Pp. 228-248 in Economic Development of Modern Japan. Tokyo: Toyokeizaishimposha.

Thirtle, C.G. (1985a) Induced innovation in United States field crops, 1939-78. Journal of Agricultural Economics 36:(1): 1-14.

Thirtle, C.G. (1985b) The microeconomic approach to induced innovation: a reformulation of the Hayami and Ruttan model. Manchester School of Economic and Social Studies.

Van de Klundent, Th., and R.J. de Groot (1977) Economic growth and induced technical progress. De Economist (The Netherlands) 125:505-524.

Wade, W.W. (1981) Institutional Determinants of Technical Change and Agricultural Productivity Growth: Denmark, France and Great Britain, 1870-1965. New York: Arno Press.

Wan, H.Y., Jr. (1971) Economic Growth. New York: Harcourt, Brace, Javonovich.

Weber, A. (1977) Productivity in German agriculture, 1950 to 1970, with comparisons to the development of Japan and the United States. In P. Andreou, ed., Rural Development Economics. Nairobi: East African Literature Bureau.

# II. Labor, Urbanization, and the Nonagricultural Sector

# 4

## Population Growth, Labor Supply, and Employment in Developing Countries

David E. Bloom
Richard B. Freeman

ABSTRACT

The economies of the less developed countries are about to face
perhaps the greatest challenge in their histories:  generating a
sufficient number of jobs at reasonable wages to absorb their
rapidly growing populations into productive employment.  In terms
of absolute magnitude, this challenge has no precedent in human
history.  In some respects, this challenge is also unprecedented
in terms of its nature, given, on the one hand, the limited
availability of natural resources in many countries, and, on the
other hand, the widespread availability of advanced technology.
    This chapter examines the nature and magnitude of the prin-
cipal effects of population growth on labor supply and employment
in the developing economies of the world.  On the supply side of
labor markets, it addresses key features of the interrelations
between population growth and the labor force.  These include the
lags between population growth and labor force participation; the
independent effects on labor supply of accelerated population
growth due to changes in fertility, mortality, and migration;
patterns and trends in labor force participation rates; and
gender differences in labor supply behavior.  On the demand
side, it describes and analyzes the nature of labor markets in
developing economies and attempts to identify the key factors
that condition their labor absorption capacity.  Descriptive
statistics on the characteristics of developing country labor
markets and on the relationships between population growth, labor
supply, employment shifts, and growth of output per worker are
presented and discussed.  The key result of the analysis is that,
despite the unprecedented magnitude of population growth and the
existence of imperfections in labor markets, developing economies
tended to shift between 1960 and 1980 from low-productivity

We thank reviewers from the Committee on Population at the
National Academy of Sciences for useful comments.  We also thank
Vijaya Ramachandran for excellent research assistance and for
especially helpful discussions and suggestions.

agriculture to the higher-productivity service and industrial
sectors, and, albeit with some exceptions, to raise real income
per capita.

With respect to developing countries' prospects for the
remainder of this century, the chapter also concludes that
Malthusian disasters will not necessarily be the result of forecasted population growth, provided the developing economies can
generate human and physical capital investments of relative
magnitudes comparable to those of the past two decades. However,
on the basis of past history, the middle-income developing
countries are likely to perform better in this respect than the
low-income countries, some of which may need considerable help
if they are to absorb increased population while shifting labor
to more productive sectors and raising output per worker.


INTRODUCTION

The population of today's less developed countries increased by
roughly 1.2 billion people between 1960 and 1980. This increase
is larger than the 1984 population of all of the more developed
countries of the world combined.[1] It is also more than twice
the 1984 population of Africa, and three times the 1984 population of Latin America. By the end of this century, all of the
surviving children of this global baby boom will have reached
working ages. In the first 20 years of the next century, this
pattern will repeat itself, but with even larger numbers.
Between 1980 and the year 2000, 1.7 billion people are expected
to be added to the populations of today's developing countries.
This increase is roughly equal to the total population of the
less developed world as recently as 1950.[2]

As these projections and comparisons make clear, the
economies of the less developed countries are about to face
perhaps the greatest challenge in their histories: generating a
sufficient number of jobs at reasonable wages to absorb their
rapidly growing populations into productive employment. In
absolute magnitude, this challenge has no precedent in human
history. In some respects, this challenge is also unprecedented
in nature, given, on the one hand, the limited availability of
natural resources (and especially land) in many countries and,
on the other hand, the widespread availability of advanced
technology.

The purpose of this chapter is to examine the nature and
magnitude of the principal effects of population growth on labor
supply and employment in the developing economies of the world.
This is done mainly through analysis of the effect of population
growth on the operation and evolution of developing country labor
markets. On the supply side of the market, the chapter discusses
key features of the interrelations between population growth and
the labor force. These include the lags between population
growth and labor force participation; the independent effects on
labor supply of accelerated population growth due to changes in
fertility, mortality, and migration; patterns and trends in labor

force participation rates; and gender differences in labor supply
behavior.  On the demand side of the market, the nature of labor
markets in developing economies is described and analyzed, and an
attempt is made to identify the key factors that condition their
labor absorption capacity.

Although it is tempting to try, the chapter does not provide
a comprehensive empirical description of the structural labor
supply and labor demand changes that result from rapid population
growth.  Cross-country experiences vary too widely, and data on
many key variables are too sketchy and unreliable.  Moreover, a
review of existing literature indicates that there is no standard
pattern of labor market responses to population growth to which
a large number of countries closely conform.  However, the descriptive analysis is buttressed by a discussion of a range of
country-specific experiences.

In proceeding this way, we may clarify some of the labor
market issues that are central to the ongoing debate between two
groups of leading students of the relationship between population
and development:  the population pessimists and the population
optimists.[3]  On the one hand, the pessimists advance the view
that rapid population growth hinders the growth of income per
capita, thereby reducing rates of saving and investment, and
resulting in mass underemployment, unemployment, and poverty.
The optimists, on the other hand, stress the point that population growth can stimulate both technological change and the
adoption of techniques that realize economies of scale, and
therefore promote economic growth.  Indeed, cross-country
correlations between growth in income per head and the rate of
population growth are typically quite weak,[4] and there are a
number of countries that have simultaneously experienced rapid
growth of both their economies and populations.  Until the 1930s,
moreover, population tended to grow more rapidly in countries
with more rapid productivity growth, most notably of course in
the areas settled by European immigrants.

As the chapter tries to make clear, these alternative views
are overly simplistic.  Population and labor force growth are not
necessarily related strongly to labor absorption.  Other factors,
including labor market imperfections and technical considerations
relating to the marginal productivity of labor in agriculture,
are also key conditioning variables.

The next section addresses the relationship between population growth and labor supply and analyzes selected descriptive
statistics.  In the following section, the nature of labor
demand in models of developing country labor markets is discussed.  The chapter then analyzes descriptive statistics on
structural changes in employment in less developed economies and
on the growth of employment relative to the growth of output per
capita.  This section presents our chief optimistic finding that,
despite the unprecedented population growth in developing
countries in the 1960-80 period, the countries were generally
able to "absorb" the new labor supply at increased productivity
and with a shift toward more productive employment.  In the next
section, a discussion of recent labor market experiences in a

number of individual developing countries is presented. The
final section outlines conclusions and offers some speculations
on the ability of developing economies to absorb the massive
numbers of workers who will enter their labor markets in the
next few decades.


POPULATION GROWTH AND LABOR SUPPLY

Conceptual Interrelations

The purpose of this section is to identify and discuss the
principal linkages between population growth and labor supply.
In so doing, it considers labor supply simply in terms of published labor force participation rates (i.e., the ratio of
individuals who are either employed or unemployed, but seeking
work, to employed, unemployed, and economically inactive
individuals). The discussion overlooks issues relating to the
number of hours people work; measurement problems related to the
determination of whether individuals are, or would like to be,
"economically active"; and qualitative characteristics of members
of the labor force, such as their ability and motivation.
Although these characteristics of a working population are
obviously important determinants of an economy's productive
capacity, the measurement issues they raise are simply beyond
the scope of this chapter.[5]
    Generally speaking, the labor supply forthcoming from any
population depends on the size of the population, broken down
into different sex and age groups, and the participation rates
for each of those groups. Whereas population size by age and
sex is directly determined by population growth (and, more
specifically, by the history of fertility, mortality, and
migration patterns), participation rates tend to be more
economically and culturally determined. For example, labor
force participation is nearly universal for prime-aged males in
less developed economies, whereas its incidence is considerably
lower for younger and older men. Participation rates for these
latter groups also exhibit considerable variability over time
and across countries. In addition, although it is well known
that published labor force participation rates for women are
poor indicators of their economic activity levels (especially in
countries in which women work predominantly in agriculture),
these rates tend to vary widely across countries and over time,
and to be lower at each age than corresponding rates for men.
Nevertheless, it is undoubtedly the case that labor force participation rates are themselves influenced by the same fertility,
mortality, and migration patterns that determine population
size. Thus, in discussing the effects of population growth on
labor supply, it is important to distinguish between pure
"accounting" effects and other effects that are fundamentally
"behavioral" in nature.
    There are three main points to be made about the inter-
relationship between population growth (and changes in

population growth) and labor supply. (1) Population growth will affect labor supply with a lag whose length depends on the reasons underlying the growth; in particular, an acceleration of population growth because of an increase in net in-migration or a decline in mortality will have a different impact on the labor force than an acceleration of population growth that results from an increase in fertility. (2) Fertility and mortality levels are important determinants of labor supply, independently of their relation to each other. (3) Fertility increase and mortality decline are likely to have an immediate effect on labor supply through their "behavioral" effects on labor force participation rates. We will consider each of these points in turn.

(1) It is well known that population growth will tend to have a lagged effect on labor supply. For example, if population growth is the result of relatively high fertility or of an age distribution that is heavily concentrated in the childbearing years, the growth in any year will have its impact focused at age 0 of the age distribution. Thus, it will take at least 10 to 15 years before the effects of a particular year's population growth even begin to be felt in the labor force. It will probably be more like 20 to 25 years before the net additions to the population begin to have a substantial impact on its labor force.[6]

On the other hand, if population growth is mainly the result of substantial in-migration, its principal effect on labor supply will not be lagged since migration propensities tend to be relatively low before the teenage years. Although in-migration is a relatively small contributor to population growth in most developing countries, this point also applies to regions within a country. In other words, population growth resulting from an excess of births over deaths in rural portions of an economy may create pressures for migration to urban areas. To the extent that the migrants tend to be of working age, population growth in the urban areas will have an immediate--as opposed to a lagged-- effect on labor force growth.[7]

(2) Although changes in levels of fertility and mortality will both affect population growth rates, they will do so in ways that tend to have different labor force implications. For example, an acceleration of population growth because of an increase in fertility will result in a more steeply sloped age distribution and a higher dependency burden, both immediately and when the population achieves a stable form. In contrast, an acceleration of population growth due to a mortality decline may steepen the age distribution somewhat and increase the dependency burden of the population, but not by as much as a fertility increase. This difference arises because the effects of mortality decline are not concentrated at one point on the age distribution, but rather spread out across the age distribution. In fact, mortality declines will affect the age distribution differently at different initial levels of mortality. For example, it is well known that mortality reductions in high-mortality populations are enjoyed mainly by infants and young children, whereas mortality reductions in middle-mortality populations are more evenly spread throughout the age

110                                        Bloom and Freeman

distribution.  (In low-mortality populations, mortality declines
are largely concentrated at the oldest ages, where labor force
participation rates are quite low.)  Thus, mortality declines in
high-mortality populations will be analogous to fertility
increases, and will therefore have labor supply effects that
have long lags.  In contrast, mortality declines in middle-
mortality populations will be more immediately felt throughout
the age distribution.

Because changes in mortality and fertility tend to affect an
age distribution differentially, even holding constant the rate
of natural increase in a stable population, fertility and mortality levels are potentially important determinants of the
proportion of a population in the working ages.  To illustrate
this point, consider the example of the two West model stable
populations presented in McNicoll (1984a:187).  The first
population has a birth rate of 4.5 percent and a death rate of
2.0 percent, while the second has a birth rate of 3.0 percent
and a death rate of 0.5 percent.  Thus, both populations have
identical rates of increase.  However, they do not have identical
age distributions:  in the first population, 54 percent of the
population falls between ages 15 and 64; in the second, 57
percent of the population is of working age.  Although this
difference in the age distributions is not particularly large,
it does illustrate the point that fertility and mortality levels
have an effect on the age distribution--and therefore on the
labor force--that is independent of their crude difference.

(3) The final point about the effect of population growth on
labor supply relates to the behavioral relationships between
fertility and mortality levels and changes, and labor force
participation rates.  To begin with, it must be recognized that
childrearing and labor force participation are both time-
intensive activities in developed and developing countries alike.
It is, however, difficult to generalize about the extent to which
women can engage in them both simultaneously.  For example, in
some high-fertility populations, women are constrained either
from working at all or from working away from the home; in other
high-fertility populations, women are able to spend a great deal
of time working outside the home by having the older children
take care of the young ones.  Despite the difficulty of
generalizing, the possibility of combining children and work is
greater in rural areas of developing countries than in urban
areas since the workplace and the home are not separated by as
much time and distance in the former.  In addition, women have
relatively more freedom to work, at least for a greater portion
of their lives, in low-fertility populations.  Thus, a decline
in fertility may have an immediate impact on the size of the
labor force because of its effect on the participation rates of
women.  Empirical evidence on this point is mixed, however, with
participation rates of women aged 30-45 increasing after fertility declines in some countries, and decreasing in others.  As
noted above, this suggests that labor force participation rates
of women, which can be an important component of overall participation rates, are determined not just economically, but also

culturally, in many developing economies. Of course, this conclusion is weakened to the extent that the types of jobs women do
are also culturally and economically determined, since some
economic activities are better measured than others (i.e.,
"disguised employment" may be an important issue).[8]
     Mortality changes may also have an effect on the labor force.
In this case, however, the effect does not operate entirely
through the effect of mortality decline on age-specific participation rates, but also operates through the positive effect of
declining morbidity on the quality and productivity of the labor
force. Of course, to the extent that a decline in mortality is
perceived by individuals as extending their worklife horizons, it
may also provide greater incentives for undertaking human capital
investments. Whereas such investments will tend to contribute to
the overall quality of the labor force, they will also tend to
delay the entry of individuals into the labor force and therefore
reduce aggregate participation rates. Indeed, one of the few
patterns in labor force participation rates that has been
observed with some degree of regularity in different developing
economies is the declining rate of labor force participation for
both men and women at the younger ages, a trend that is highly
correlated with the expansion of developing countries'
educational systems.


Empirical Patterns

This section presents and discusses evidence on the linkages
between population growth and the size and the structure of the
labor force in developing countries. Most of the statistics
analyzed are drawn from various publications of the World Bank,
although some were originally produced by the United Nations or
the International Labour Organisation (ILO). Countries are
grouped in two conventional ways for purposes of this analysis:
by income group and geographic location.
     The income classification is based on levels of gross
national product (GNP) per capita for most countries, with other
characteristics thought to be correlated with income group used
to classify countries for which per capita GNP data are either
unreliable or unavailable. The figures for low-income developing
economies are based on data for 34 countries whose 1982 per
capita GNP was less than $410 (U.S.) (average income per capita
for these countries is $250 [U.S.]). The figures for lower
middle-income economies are based on data for 38 countries whose
1982 per capita GNP exceeded $410 (U.S.) but was less than $1,650
(U.S.) (average per capita income for these countries is $840
[(U.S.]). The figures for the upper middle-income developing
economies are based on data for 22 developing economies with GNP
per capita in excess of $1,650 (U.S.) (average per capita income
is $2,490). Finally, the figures for the industrial market
economies are based on data for 19 countries that had an average
GNP per capita of $11,070.

TABLE 1  Growth Rates of Population and Labor Force, by Income Group

| Type of Economy | 1982 Population (in millions) | Average Annual Population Growth Rates (in percent) | | Difference in Average Annual Labor Force Growth Rates (in percent) | | Growth Rates (labor force population) | |
|---|---|---|---|---|---|---|---|
| | | 1960-70 | 1970-82 | 1960-70 | 1970-82 | 1960-70 | 1970-82 |
| Low-Income Developing | 2,266.5 | 2.3 | 1.9 | 1.7 | 2.0 | -0.6 | 0.1 |
| China | 1,008.2 | 2.3 | 1.4 | 1.7 | 1.8 | -0.6 | 0.4 |
| India | 717.0 | 2.3 | 2.3 | 1.7 | 2.1 | -0.6 | -0.2 |
| Other low-income | 541.3 | 2.5 | 2.6 | 1.8 | 2.3 | -0.7 | -0.3 |
| Lower Middle-Income Developing | 669.6 | 2.5 | 2.5 | 1.9 | 2.4 | -0.6 | -0.1 |
| Upper Middle-Income Developing | 488.7 | 2.6 | 2.3 | 2.3 | 2.3 | -0.3 | 0.0 |
| Industrial Market | 722.9 | 1.1 | 0.7 | 1.2 | 1.2 | 0.1 | 0.5 |

Source:  World Bank (1984).

The geographic grouping of developing economies also follows the standard World Bank classification. Thus, countries are grouped into the following regions: (1) sub-Saharan Africa, 34 countries; (2) Middle East and North Africa, 11 countries; (3) East Asia and Pacific, 14 countries; (4) South Asia, 8 countries; (6) Latin America and Caribbean, 22 countries; and (6) South Europe, 5 countries. All of the countries represented in our tables are listed individually by income group and geographic region in Appendix Tables A.1 and A.2. All of the population, labor force, and output statistics reported represent weighted averages of the individual country statistics, with 1960, 1970, or 1980 population sizes used to construct the weights. For the low-income developing countries, statistics are reported both separately and together for China, India, and other low-income countries.

Table 1 presents growth rates of population and labor force by countries grouped according to income. The statistics in this table reveal several interesting patterns.

First, with the exception of China after 1970, population growth rates for the low-income and lower middle-income developing countries have been extremely high since 1960 (i.e., implied doubling times are less than 30 years). Population growth rates in the upper middle-income developing countries have also been quite high, although they are showing some evidence of moderating. In contrast, the decline in the growth rate for China is substantial. Indeed, this decline is larger in proportionate terms (e.g., from an implied doubling time of 30 years in 1960-70 to 50 years in 1970-82) than for the industrial market economies (which had an implied doubling time of 100 years during the 1970-82 period).

Second, declining population growth rates in the 1970s have not yet shown up in the form of declining labor force growth rates for China, the upper middle-income developing economies, or the industrial market economies. This pattern illustrates the point made in the preceding subsection about the existence of a time lag between population growth and labor force growth.

The third noteworthy pattern in Table 1 is that during the 1960-82 period, none of the groups of developing countries (with the single exception of China in the 1970s) experienced labor force growth in excess of population growth. If there had been either no technological progress in this period or no increases in capital per worker, these economies' productive capacities per capita would have declined between 1960 and 1982. Nonetheless, the difference between population and labor force growth rates decreased for the developing economies between the 1960s and the 1970s. This decrease reflects the age distribution effects of population growth prior to 1960 and suggests that the secular deterioration of developing economies' ratios of labor force to total population is slowing. In China, this decline was actually reversed as labor force growth exceeded population growth during the 1970s.

Finally, one pattern not revealed in Table 1, but worthy of note, relates to the considerable variability of population and

TABLE 2   Labor Force Participation Rates for Males and
Females, by Income Group

| Type of Economy | Male 1960 | Male 1980[a] | Female 1960 | Female 1980[a] |
|---|---|---|---|---|
| Low-Income Developing | 56.6 | 54.4 | 31.5 | 29.5 |
| Middle-Income Developing | 53.4 | 49.4 | 19.5 | 19.7 |
| Industrial Market | 59.2 | 59.0 | 27.0 | 32.5 |

[a]Circa 1980.

Source:  World Bank (1983).

labor force growth rates among countries within the same income
group.   For example, among the low-income economies, Kenya and
Mozambique had population growth rates of 4.0 and 4.3 percent
between 1970 and 1982, while Sri Lanka and Haiti had growth rates
of 1.7 percent.   As another example, among the upper middle-
income economies, Syria, Venezuela, and Iraq had population
growth rates of about 3.6 percent from 1970 to 1982, roughly nine
times the rate of 0.4 percent in Uruguay and more than twice the
rates in Argentina, Chile, and North Korea.
     Table 2 presents male and female labor force participation
rates for a somewhat abridged income grouping of economies.   One
striking feature of these statistics is that the labor force
participation rates of men in industrial market economies
exceeded those of men in the two groups of developing economies
in both 1960 and 1980.   This differential results from the
relatively older age distributions of the industrial market
economies, a consequence of their lower rates of population
growth.   This pattern is especially interesting given that labor
force participation rates for men tend to fall at the young and
old ages as development proceeds (see Durand, 1975).   In this
case, the demography of the age structure dominates the
behavioral factors in determining aggregate labor force
participation.
     A second apparent regularity in Table 2 is that the labor
force participation rates for males in the middle-income
developing countries are lower than those in the low-income
countries.   In addition, participation rates in both groups of
countries have declined over time.   These findings seem to
reflect two facts:   (1) population growth was substantial in
both groups of developing economies in the 1950s and 1960s (as
they began their demographic transitions), thereby tending to
raise the youth share of their populations; and (2) population
growth was relatively greater in the middle-income countries

than in the low-income countries in the 1950s and 1960s, resulting in a greater increase in the youth proportions of the populations of the former countries (and consequently a greater decline in their male labor force participation rates).

Turning now to the labor force participation rates for females, we observe a slight decline from 1960 to 1980 for the low-income developing countries, most likely due to the effect of population growth on the age distribution. On the other hand, we observe a stable pattern in the middle-income developing countries, although the participation rates are substantially below those of the low-income developing countries. Whether this difference is a consequence of the notoriously poor data on female labor force participation in developing countries and problems of labor force definition in countries with large agricultural sectors, or whether it indicates a tendency for women to withdraw from the labor force as development proceeds, is unclear. It is also unclear whether this pattern is due to some omitted factors that affect the labor force participation of women and that are correlated with income group.

To get some idea of the extent to which the striking differences in the labor force participation rates of women in low- and middle-income developing countries are due to an omitted variable problem, Table 3 reports participation rates in 1960 and 1980, broken down by geographic region. As this table makes clear, there is considerable variation in female participation rates across regions, although those rates are quite stable within regions but over time. In 1980, for example, participation rates for women ranged from 5.6 percent in the Middle Eastern and North African countries to 33.5 percent for East Asian and Pacific countries (which is even slightly greater than the average rate for the industrial market economies). This pattern suggests that the dramatically different female labor force participation rates across income groups reported in Table 2 may be due to geographic participation differences that are correlated with income group or culture, as discussed earlier. Indeed, examination of the country breakdown (by income group and geographic region) in Appendix Table A.1 seems to confirm this supposition since none of the Middle Eastern and North African countries and only one of the Latin American and Caribbean countries--the two geographic groups with the lower participation rates--fall into the low-income developing category. Nonetheless, this conclusion is offered tentatively since the data on female labor force participation rates in these countries are thought to be especially poor.

Table 3 is also interesting with regard to the participation patterns for men. In particular, the participation rates are declining over time for all regions except East Asia and the Pacific. In addition, and in contrast to the pattern for women, male labor force participation rates exhibit relatively small differences across the developing countries.

As a basis for comparison, Table 3 also presents labor force participation rates for males and females in 1960 and 1980 in selected developed economies. Since these participation rates

TABLE 3  Labor Force Participation Rates for Males and Females,
by Geographic Region and for Selected Countries

|                                   | Male | | Female | |
|-----------------------------------|------|------|------|------|
| Geographic Region                 | 1960 | 1980 | 1960 | 1980 |
| **Developing Economies** (all ages) | | | | |
| Region | | | | |
| Africa south of Sahara            | 55.3 | 50.2 | 31.8 | 28.1 |
| Middle East and North Africa      | 51.6 | 45.4 | 4.5  | 5.6  |
| East Asia and Pacific             | 55.3 | 55.5 | 34.5 | 33.5 |
| South Asia                        | 57.1 | 52.0 | 24.4 | 22.8 |
| Latin America and Caribbean       | 52.9 | 49.8 | 12.5 | 14.8 |
| South Europe                      | 60.3 | 55.2 | 31.9 | 29.1 |
| **Developed Economies** (ages 15+) | | | | |
| Country | | | | |
| United States                     | 83.3  | 77.4 | 37.7  | 51.5 |
| Canada                            | 82.8  | 78.3 | 30.1  | 50.3 |
| Australia                         | 85.3[a] | 79.2 | 33.8[a] | 45.5 |
| Japan                             | 84.2  | 79.6 | 49.3  | 46.6 |
| France                            | 81.4  | 70.6 | 40.1  | 42.7 |
| Germany                           | 82.7  | 70.4 | 40.3  | 38.2 |
| Great Britain                     | 88.1  | 79.2 | 28.6  | 29.9 |
| Italy                             | 82.0  | 67.8 | 28.6  | 29.9 |
| Sweden                            | 87.1[b] | 74.9 | 46.8[b] | 59.9 |

[a]Datum for 1964.
[b]Datum for 1961.

Sources:  Developing economy data:  World Bank (1983).
Developed countries:  U.S. Department of Labor (1983).

are computed relative to the population aged 15 (or 16) and over,
they are not comparable in their levels to the rates for the
developing countries.  However, the rates for men do show about
the same degree of variation across countries and a similar
tendency to decline over time.  In the case of the developed
countries, the declines are largely due to increased educational
attainment, resulting in delayed entry into the labor force, and
to a decline in the age of retirement.  (For some countries, the
declines are also partly the result of post-World War II baby-
booms and their tendency to lower the age of the labor force.)
To the extent that these patterns in the developed countries may
be taken to foreshadow trends in the developing countries, we
see that development carries with it forces that ease the burden
on labor markets to adjust to rapid population growth.

In contrast to the rates for men, the participation rates for women in the developed economies show mixed trends over time. For example, participation rates climbed substantially between 1960 and 1980 in the United States, Canada, Australia, the United Kingdom, and Sweden. During these same years, however, the rates increased little or declined in Japan, France, Germany, and Italy. This pattern for the industrial economies tends to confirm the point made in the preceding subsection about participation rates for females tending to be much more culture-specific than those for men. It also adds a good deal of uncertainty to any attempts to project female labor force participation rates for the developing economies.

Finally, turning back to demographic issues, consider the figures in Table 4, which presents the percent of the population aged 15-64 (an approximate measure of the working ages) by income group. The statistics in this table show a large increase for China, reflecting its declining population growth rate. They also show that developing countries have smaller proportions of their populations at the working ages than the industrial market economies; this is a reflection of their relatively high population growth rates, which tend to increase the share of youth in their populations. The fact that the dependency burden (i.e., the inverse of the proportions shown in Table 4) in the developing countries is so high is, of course, a hindrance to development in two main ways. First, the high dependency burden indicates that these economies must sustain themselves on the income that can be generated by a relatively small proportion of their populations. Second, because most of the dependency burden in these rapidly growing populations is associated with the young, there is a relatively great need to invest social savings in welfare capital, such as schools and hospitals, for persons out of the workforce, as opposed to physical capital for persons in the workforce.

TABLE 4   Percent of Population Aged 15-64, by Income Group

| Type of Economy | 1960 | 1982 |
|---|---|---|
| Low-Income Developing | 55 | 59 |
|    China | 56 | 63 |
|    India | 54 | 57 |
|    Other low-income | 54 | 53 |
| Lower Middle-Income Developing | 54 | 55 |
| Upper Middle-income Developing | 55 | 57 |
| Industrial Market | 63 | 66 |

Source:  World Bank (1984).

LABOR SUPPLY AND EMPLOYMENT

Modeling the relationship between population growth and employment is a problem that is not uniquely of interest in the
developing country context. Following World War II, a number of
industrialized countries, including the United States, Canada,
and Australia, experienced baby booms in which population growth
was substantial. As the baby boom generations in those countries
began to reach labor force age, a theoretical and empirical
literature on the labor market effects of large cohort size was
spawned. The basic premise of that literature is quite simple:
large cohort size suggests an outward shift of labor supply that
has adverse implications for the labor market experience of the
large cohorts relative to that of smaller cohorts. Moreover,
there are two key dimensions along which these adverse implications may be observed: wages and employment (or unemployment).
    One of the most interesting empirical findings of the baby
boom literature relates to the considerable diversity that
appears to exist across countries in the nature of their adjustment to large-sized cohorts. For example, some countries
(including the United States) appear to have adjusted to the
baby boom mainly through a lowering of relative wages, whereas
the adjustment in other countries (including Canada) has
primarily taken the form of diminished employment opportunities
for members of the baby boom cohorts. Perhaps the main lesson
to learn from this diversity of experience is that labor market
responses to population growth are not necessarily dictated by a
simple supply-demand model that is common across countries.
Rather, different countries may have differently sloped labor
supply and labor demand curves, different industrial mixes, and
different labor market institutions and policies (e.g., minimum
wages, government incentives to join the military or to stay in
school) that result in different responses. Empirical work,
however, does seem to bear out the theoretical notion that either
wages or employment opportunities (or both) suffer as a result of
an outward shift of labor supply that results from past population growth.[9]
    These lessons about the labor market responses of industrial
economies to population growth are also applicable to the experience of developing economies. Indeed, institutional factors and
the slope of labor demand curves are crucial determinants of the
capacity of developing economies to absorb growing populations
into productive employment. In addition, as in the case of the
developed economies, there seems to be considerable variation in
the less developed economies with regard to the nature and
operation of their labor markets, making it difficult to reach
any general conclusions about the effects of rapid population
growth on employment in developing countries.[10] However,
several economic models of this relationship do shed light on
the key variables that determine whether labor markets have more
or less "absorptive" capacity.
    To begin with, a standard one-sector neoclassical model of
the labor market suggests that the degree to which population

growth will be absorbed into employment will depend on the slope of the aggregate labor demand curve. (For example, if labor demand is perfectly inelastic, an increase in labor supply will not be absorbed as increased employment; in addition, employed individuals will take wage cuts, unless there is a minimum wage, in which case there may be substantial involuntary unemployment.) However, the theoretical literature on developing country labor markets does not focus on the slope of labor demand curves. Instead, it is largely oriented toward analyzing a feature of developing country labor markets that is thought to be critical to their operation--their dual nature. The dual sectors of a developing country labor market have been referred to by a variety of names: one sector is usually referred to as agricultural, rural, noncommercial, peasant, traditional, or backward; the other is usually referred to as capitalistic, nonagricultural, commercial, formal, modern, or urban. More recently, distinctions have been made between a formal and informal sector within the urban economy, creating a trichotomy: agricultural, informal urban, and formal urban (of which more will be said later). While there is considerable debate over the extent of mobility among the sectors and over the causes and meaning of potentially large income differences between sectors, their economic differences are important in any assessment of how the labor market will "absorb" population increases. Without losing ourselves in the semantics of the issue, we may merely note that the key distinguishing feature of the sectors is the nature of their dominant production units: in the traditional agricultural and urban informal sectors, the production unit (e.g., a household) is characterized by self-employment and small-scale enterprise employment (exclusive of plantations); the chief characteristic of the production unit in the modern sector is that it is based on labor hired on a contractual basis. (See Ranis and Fei [1984] for further discussion of this point.)

The earliest of the popular two-sector models is due to Arthur Lewis (1954, 1958). According to the Lewis model, the main characteristic of the traditional-sector labor market is the presence of surplus (or excess, or redundant) labor. In one extreme version of this model, the marginal product of labor (i.e., the derivative of output with respect to the number of workers) in the traditional sector is zero. In other words, all members of a household who are able to work do so, and they share the output with the entire household. Moreover, it is assumed that each production unit attains the maximal level of output possible from its nonlabor resources, given its production technology. If the number of working members of a household increases, each member either works fewer hours (Sen, 1968) or expends less effort for the same number of hours (Leibenstein, 1978). This is the sense in which the marginal product of additional laborers is zero. In a less extreme version of this model, the marginal product of labor is viewed as being less than the average product (which is the wage received by the household's workers). It makes little difference to the qualitative implications of Lewis' model which assumption is correct.

The capitalist sector in the Lewis model closely resembles a
neoclassical labor market.  Employers have garden-variety down-
ward-sloping labor demand curves, and they hire labor to the
point at which the marginal product of labor equals the market
wage.  This wage will be determined by the nature of alternative job opportunities available to modern-sector workers.  Thus,
in a closed and frictionless economy, the market wage in the
modern sector will equal the average product in the agricultural
sector.  However, because of the transaction costs associated
with migration to the modern sector, most models of developing
economy labor markets view modern-sector wages as being greater
than the average product of labor.  This feature of the theoretical models is consistent with empirical evidence that demonstrates the existence of a positive wage differential between
the industrial and agricultural sector in most, though not all,
developing countries (see Table 5), as well as uniformly higher
output per worker in industry and services relative to
agriculture (see Table 11).

Within the context of this two-sector model, one can easily
identify the linkages between population growth and labor
absorption.  In particular, at early stages of development, the
supply of labor to the modern sector is horizontal at a
relatively low wage because of the existence of surplus labor in
the agricultural sector.  Enterprises will thus earn relatively
high profits, a substantial fraction of which they are assumed
to reinvest.  Consequently, capital formation will be relatively
great in the labor surplus economy and will lead to further
outward expansion of labor demand, thereby resulting in the
dynamic expansion of employment.  Thus, a large population in
the agricultural sector promotes the growth of industry by
making available a large supply of low-wage labor.[11]

In terms of its dynamic properties, the economy described by
this simple model does not continually experience rapid economic
growth.  Eventually, the modern sector draws enough labor out of
the traditional sector so that the marginal product of labor in
the agricultural sector equals its average product.  Beyond this
point, as capital formation leads to further economic expansion,
alternative opportunities will improve for both potential and
actual modern-sector workers, and urban wages will rise.  This
will, of course, tend to moderate the further growth of employ-
ment--although it will not curtail it completely.  Moreover,
during this second phase of development (i.e., beyond the point
at which the aggregate labor supply curve begins to slope
upward), the importance of distinguishing between the two sectors
of the economy is lost because both behave neoclassically.
Naturally, reaching this turning point does not signify that an
economy is no longer developing.  More interesting to analyze,
because it seems to characterize the experience of a greater
number of developing countries, is the effect of rapid population
growth on the labor market before an economy reaches its "turning
point."  Here, the basic idea is that population growth leads to
a fall in average product in the agricultural sector, which may
lead to a fall in the industrial sector wage, although the more

TABLE 5   Ratio of Average Agricultural to Average
Manufacturing Wages

| Country | 1968 | 1974 | 1979 |
|---|---|---|---|
| Argentina | 0.64[a,b] | 0.64[a,b,c] | 0.69[d] |
| Barbados[a] | 0.66 | 0.71 | -- |
| Burma | 1.31[a] | 1.21[a] | 1.22 |
| Colombia | 0.38[a] | 0.45[f] | 0.46 |
| Costa Rica[b] | -- | 0.50 | 0.50 |
| Chile[a,b] | 0.26 | 0.21[c] | 0.34 |
| Cyprus[a] | 1.24 | 1.10 | 0.71 |
| El Salvador[a] | -- | 0.30 | 0.30 |
| Guyana | 0.97[a] | 0.84[a] | 0.72 |
| Malawi | 0.33 | 0.29 | 0.28 |
| Mauritius | 0.97 | 1.31 | 1.52 |
| Mexico[b] | 0.31[a] | 0.33[f] | 0.37 |
| Morocco[a,b] | 0.51 | 0.30 | -- |
| Sri Lanka[a] | 0.44 | 0.41 | 0.53 |
| Syria[b] | 0.75[g] | 0.40 | 0.39[d] |
| Zambia[h] | 0.55 | 0.41 | 0.42[d] |

[a]Males only.
[b]Minimum rates.
[c]1973.
[d]1977.
[e]1976.
[f]1975.
[g]1969.
[h]Zambian nationals only.

Source:  International Labour Office (1975, 1981).

important effect of population growth is that it extends the
horizontal portion of the labor supply curve faced by the
industrial-sector employers.  Thus, by expanding the reservoir
from which modern-sector firms are able to hire labor, and
perhaps making that labor even cheaper, population growth postpones the point at which wages increase, and leads to a decline
in living standards in both the agricultural and industrial
sectors along the way.  In addition, as the discussion makes
clear, to focus only on the absorption problem associated with
population growth may be a bit misguided, since, in both dual
and neoclassical economies, an increase in population may be
substantially or even completely absorbed into the employed
labor force at the cost of reduced wages and living standards.

Although the main implication of this basic model is that
population growth slows the rate at which surplus labor decreases
and postpones the elimination of dualism and a rise in living
standards, this model can be (and has been) complicated in a
variety of ways that have significant implications for the
relationship between population growth and employment.  The
remainder of this section will not attempt a comprehensive

review of the many twists on the Lewis model, but will address
the main variations.[12]

First, one of the most widely observed facts about the
operation of developing country labor markets is that the
difference between modern-sector and agricultural-sector wages
exceeds the amount that would cover transaction costs associated
with movement from one sector to the other. In some cases, the
excess is substantial (see Table 5). A common explanation of
these wide differentials is the existence of labor market
imperfections in the modern sector. For example, it is often
argued that modern-sector wages are set institutionally by the
government at artificially high levels, perhaps because of trade
union pressure or politics associated with other interest groups.
To the extent that wages are maintained at artificially high
levels, employment will be lower than it would otherwise have
been, and capital formation will proceed at a slower rate.[13]

Table 6 presents some readily available information on one
such imperfection--the minimum wage. At the present time,
minimum wages, which were introduced into most developed
countries relatively late in their economic histories, are found
in virtually all developing countries, although the level and
enforcement of the minimum varies substantially across those
countries. The figures in the table show that minimum wages in
developing countries are typically set at 30-50 percent of manufacturing wages, comparable to the levels of minimum wages in
developed countries relative to their manufacturing wages. Note
also that minimum wages are probably enforced solely in the
larger modern-sector enterprises, and thus affect not so much
levels of total employment as employment in those enterprises.

Of equal or greater importance than minimum wages in creating
dualistic labor market structures are the government pay policies
in many developing countries. As Table 7 shows, public-sector
employment constitutes a relatively large proportion of nonagricultural employment in many developing countries and, ipso
facto, an even larger proportion of formal modern-sector
employment. The proportions far exceed those in currently
developed countries at a similar stage in their economic
histories, giving government pay policy a potentially important
role in creating and maintaining dualistic markets. Finally, as
Table 8 shows, government pay in developing countries has tended
to be much larger than per capita income, with the differences
greatest in the poorest countries. Until the 1980s, the "overpaid civil servant" was often cited as a problem in African
countries.

One might expect that the effectiveness of policies in
altering modern-sector wages relative to those elsewhere would
be extensively studied, with firm research conclusions; in fact,
however, there are only scattered studies for developing
countries, and no clear consensus on either the direction or
effectiveness of the policies. According to one leading scholar,
"The experiences of the various countries have called attention
to the importance of the role of government in creating wage

distortions" (Gregory, 1975:121). In a similar vein, another
analyst contends that "the root of the wage problem lies in one
fact: the export giants and local monopolies are willing . . .
to pay high wages" (Berg, 1970:296). By contrast, another
scholar argues that "the high wage policy that allegedly
characterizes LDCs . . . is a misrepresentation" (Webb, 1977:
246). With respect to unionism, while many attribute high wages
in Africa to union influence, some studies have found lower wages
in unionized sectors, suggesting that organized sectors are more
amenable to income policies (House and Rempel, 1976). In his
summary of the debate, Webb (1977:237-238) cited studies showing
both "the role of active or permissive government wage and
unionization policies" in raising wages and the converse, with
lack of enforcement of policies (such as those regulating minimum
wages) making nominal policy-initiated wage increases ineffec-
tive. In her analysis, Krueger (1983:146-147) notes "how little
is known" about labor market distortions due to policies.

A second widely observed fact about the operation of
developing country labor markets is that rates of rural-to-urban
migration have tended to exceed the absorptive capacity of the
modern sector, leading to growth of the "informal sector." This
fact is consistent with the point made earlier about the differential between industrial- and agricultural-sector wages, given
that migration is generated by a Harris-Todaro type of migration
model (or some variant thereof). According to that genre of
models, migration flows do not equalize observed wages across
sectors; rather, they equalize expected wages. Thus, given the
existence of rural-urban wage differences in excess of the amount
due to transaction costs, the migration flow to the modern sector
will surpass the latter's ability to absorb additional labor
(i.e., because equilibrium is reached when the probability of
securing employment in the modern sector times the modern-sector
wage is equal to the actual wage in the rural sector plus
mobility costs).

If rural-urban migration is generated according to a Harris-
Todaro type of model, migration flows will tend to be greater the
higher are institutionally determined wages in the modern sector.
However, since industry is unable to absorb labor as fast as it
arrives, one would expect to observe substantial urban unemployment, which turns out not to be the case. Instead, we have
observed the rise of a tertiary sector in urban areas--an
informal sector in which individuals queued up for high-wage
industrial employment work as handicraftsmen, artisans, and
suppliers of a variety of personal services. To the extent that
this group of workers is underutilized, they may be viewed as a
group of "disguised unemployed" workers in the urban sector.

Several additional comments about the urban informal sector
also seem in order. First, it is widely hypothesized that the
informal sector arises because of the way in which labor markets
operate in developing countries, with institutionally fixed
wages in excess of market wages. This feature of urban labor
markets suggests that both measured unemployment and the growth
rate of the urban labor force are poor measures of the absorption

TABLE 6    Cross-Section Variation in Minimum Wages

| Country | Year | Minimum | World Bank Data Avg. Manuf. Wages | Ratio | ILO Data Avg. Manuf. Wages | Ratio |
|---------|------|---------|--------------|-------|--------------|-------|
| Algeria (dinars/hr.) | 1975 | 2.08 | -- | -- | 3.13 | 0.66 |
| Argentina (peso/mo.) | 1976 | 7608 | -- | -- | 12,896.00 | 0.59 |
| Brazil (cruzeiro/mo.) | 1974 | 355 | 1,151.34 | 0.31 | -- | -- |
| Cameroon (CFA/hr.) | 1976 | 64 | 188.24 | 0.34 | -- | -- |
| Central African Republic (CAF/hr.) | 1976 | 35.60 | 135.56 | 0.26 | -- | -- |
| Colombia (peso/mo.) | 1977 | 1573 | 7,090.98 | 0.22 | 4,005.30 | 0.39 |
| Costa Rica (colones/mo.) | 1975 | 585 | 1,001.52 | 0.58 | 1,123.00 | 0.52 |
| Ecuador (sucres/mo.) | 1977 | 1500 | 4,494.01 | 0.33 | 4,022.20 | 0.37 |
| El Salvador (culones/mo.) | 1977 | 186 | 386.36 | 0.48 | 297.44[a] | 0.62 |
| Egypt (piastre/day) | 1976 | 40 | 153.85 | 0.26 | 108.11 | 0.37 |
| Ghana (pesewa/day) | 1977 | 400 | 781.26 | 0.51 | -- | -- |
| Guatemala (quetzal/mo.) | 1975 | 57 | 177.31 | 0.49 | 93.69 | 0.61 |
| Ivory Coast (CFA/hr.) | 1977 | 115 | 289.40 | 0.40 | -- | -- |
| Kenya (shillings/mo.) | 1977 | 350 | 977.82 | 0.36 | 978.30 | 0.36 |
| Libya (dinars/day) | 1976 | 2.00 | 4.24 | 0.47 | -- | -- |
| Mexico (peso/mo.) | 1977 | 2766 | 6,832.36 | 0.40 | 4,984.20 | 0.55 |
| Panama (balboa/mo.) | 1977 | 114 | 295.59 | 0.39 | 237.21 | 0.48 |
| Papua New Guinea (kina/wk.) | 1977 | 28.46 | 58.30 | 0.49 | -- | -- |
| Peru (sol/mo.) | 1975 | 3270 | 10,784.99 | 0.30 | 5,525.00 | 0.59 |

Labor Supply and Employment

TABLE 6 (continued)

| Country | Year | Minimum | World Bank Avg. Manuf. Wages | Ratio | ILO Avg. Manuf. Wages | Ratio |
|---------|------|---------|------------------|-------|------------------|-------|
| Philippines (peso/day) | 1977 | 15.18 | 27.99 | 0.54 | -- | -- |
| Sri Lanka (rupee/day) | 1977 | 8.96 | -- | -- | 19.05 | 0.47 |
| Tanzania (shillings/mo.) | 1974 | 340 | 563.90 | 0.60 | -- | -- |
| Tunisia (dinar/hr.) | 1977 | 0.193 | 0.46 | 0.43 | -- | -- |
| Turkey (lira/day) | 1977 | 60 | 238.58 | 0.25 | 127.52 | 0.47 |
| Uruguay (new peso/mo.) | 1977 | 312.2 | 504.12 | 0.62 | -- | -- |
| Zambia (angwee/hr.) | 1975 | 16 | 62.92 | 0.25 | 47.06 | 0.34 |

[a]Males only.

Sources: Minimum wages: Starr (1981); for Chile, Instituto Nacional de Estadisticas (1977). Manufacturing wages: United Nations (1968-1980); Industrial surveys and censuses of various countries; International Labour Office (1981, 1975).

power of an economy. In other words, informal-sector employees work in a labor market that is perhaps more closely akin to the traditional sector than to the modern sector. However, two features of the informal sector do suggest that it is a positive force in the development process. First, to the extent that one factor limiting the absorption of workers into industry is their lack of understanding of the culture of the urban sector (e.g., requisite work habits and other skills), the presence of a traditional-like sector in an urban area can serve as a massive training and acculturation program that partially eases hiring constraints faced by employers. Second, largely because of the high cost of housing in urban areas, the distance between home and work, and the fragmentation of family units that often accompanies rural-urban migration, urban dwellers tend to have lower fertility than rural dwellers (although there seems to be no definitive evidence on this often-asserted point). Thus, growth of the informal sector may help to curb population growth. The upshot of all this, then, is that population growth seems to be transforming the structure of developing country labor markets from dual-sector to tri-sector in nature. This in turn has two

TABLE 7   Public-Sector Employment as Share of
Nonagricultural Employment

| Type of Economy | 1979-80 |
| --- | --- |
| Low-Income Developing Countries | |
| Computed average of all countries except India and China | 54.4 |
| India | 72.0 |
| Lower Middle-Income Developing | 43.5 |
| Upper Middle-Income Developing | 22.8 |

Source:   Tabulated from Heller and Tait (1983).

main implications:   (1) that new measures of labor absorption
are needed, and (2) that a tri-sector labor market may be an
efficient mechanism for helping to curtail population growth and
channeling surplus agricultural labor into industry, thereby
promoting development.

The final major wrinkle on the basic Lewis model relates to
the dynamics of technological and institutional change in
developing economies.   In the original version of the model,
production functions were assumed to be stable over time.
However, it has been argued that population growth stimulates
technological progress and makes possible the realization of
economies of scale that provide incentives for the adoption of
more efficient techniques and institutional arrangements (see
Binswanger, 1979; Boserup, 1981; and Hayami and Ruttan, 1985).
It has also been argued, although without supporting evidence,
that population growth leads to the birth of more "geniuses,"
some of whom may contribute to technological progress and others
of whom may determine how to reorganize production in a way that
effectively taps the productive capacity of excess rural labor
(see Kuznets, 1965; Simon, 1981).   Taken together, these notions
suggest that population growth promotes development by moving an
economy's production possibility frontier outward.   Although it
is of critical importance to know whether this outward shift is
greater than or less than some appropriate measure of the
increase in population, these ideas cannot be refuted at a
theoretical level; however, in an excellent review of existing
studies of these issues, McNicoll (1984a) concludes that the
evidence so far is mixed.[14]

A second technology-related issue involves recent attempts
to identify a key difference between the past experience of
today's developed economies and the prospective experience of
today's developing economies.   Briefly, the argument is that
countries trying to develop today are doing so in the context of
surplus labor and readily transferable capital-intensive tech-

TABLE 8   Public-Sector and Government Average Wage
Relative to Per Capita Income

| Type of Economy | 1979-80 |
| --- | --- |
| Low-Income Developing Countries | |
| Computed average of all countries except India and China | 6.61 |
| India | 4.80 |
| Lower Middle-Income Developing | 4.84 |
| Upper Middle-Income Developing | 2.94 |

Source:   Tabulated from Heller and Tait (1983).

nologies.   In contrast, the development experience of today's
industrial market economies was generally characterized by labor
shortages and less advanced technologies.   In other words, while
industrial market economies adjusted to their situation by
developing labor-saving technology, today's developing economies
would probably be best off developing labor-intensive methods of
production.   However, the presence of already-developed
transferable technologies from the industrial economies, with
scarce capital to back it up, substantially eliminates those
incentives.   Thus, it has been argued that patterns of
technological development and utilization today are tending to
reduce the absorptive capacity of developing economies since
industrialization is taking place without labor absorption.[15]
     To sum up the main point of this section, at a theoretical
level, population and labor force growth are not necessarily
strongly related to labor absorption.   A variety of factors
condition the absorptive ability of an economy, allowing some
analysts to argue that economies can readily absorb a large
increase in the labor force (under specified conditions) and
others to argue the converse (also under specified conditions).
The issue is an empirical one; observed historical experience
can contribute significantly to an assessment of the optimistic
and pessimistic views of the effects of rapid population growth.


POPULATION AND EMPLOYMENT, 1960-1980

As the preceding section makes clear, a central indicator of the
pace at which a developing economy is absorbing labor is the
rate at which its sectoral balance is shifted from agricultural
to nonagricultural employment.   This section presents and
discusses a series of statistics on these shifts, using World
Bank data to examine differentials across both income groups and
geographic regions.   The three sectors on which the discussion

will focus are the agricultural, industrial, and service sectors. The agricultural sector encompasses forestry, hunting, and fishing, in addition to agriculture.[16] The industrial sector comprises manufacturing, mining, construction, and utilities. Services are defined as a residual category of economic activity (i.e., not agriculture or industry, as defined above). Although the focus is mainly on the expansion of the industrial and service sectors, this is not meant to suggest that agricultural development is of little consequence. Indeed, increases in productivity in the agricultural sector, which are also discussed, usually precede and are the primary cause of sectoral shifts in employment.[17]

The key result of the analysis is as follows: in the 1960-80 period, despite the unprecedented magnitude of population growth and the existence of imperfections in labor markets, developing countries tended to shift from low-productivity agriculture to the higher-productivity service sector and to a slightly lesser extent to the high-productivity industrial sector, and to raise income per head, although with some exceptions (e.g., some African countries). The discussion here does not address the question of whether these changes could have been more extensive in some counterfactual world with slower growth of population and labor force.

Table 9 reports the distribution of the labor force across economic sectors in 1960 and 1980, by country income categories. A number of patterns are revealed by this table. First is the well-known fact that the fraction of the labor force engaged in agricultural production is inversely related to the stage of development. In addition, there was a decrease in the share of the labor force in agriculture between 1960 and 1980 for all income groups in Table 9. However, with the exception of the upper middle-income developing economies, agriculture has been and remains the largest utilizer of labor in the developing economies. Even in the upper middle-income countries, the proportion of the labor force in agriculture was five times that in the industrial market economies in 1980.[18]

Second, Table 9 reveals that the relative decline of agriculture coincided mainly with growth in the share of the labor force in the service sector, which tended to be larger in size than the industrial sector in both 1960 and 1980. It is interesting to note, however, an important exception to the pattern of services comprising a larger share of the labor force than industry--China (in 1980), in which this pattern is reversed, and substantially so. With regard to country-specific differences, the statistics for India are also interesting insofar as they show a relatively small decline between 1960 and 1980 in the proportion of the labor force in agriculture.

Table 10 is similar to Table 9, except that the sectoral labor force shares are reported for developing countries grouped by geographic region rather than income. This table indicates the existence of large differences across regions in the sectoral share distributions. For example, the agricultural sector is

TABLE 9   Distribution of Labor Force Across Economic Sectors, by Income
Group

| Type of Economy | Percent of Labor Force | | | | | |
|---|---|---|---|---|---|---|
| | Agriculture | | Industry | | Services | |
| | 1960 | 1980 | 1960 | 1980 | 1960 | 1980 |
| Low-Income Developing[a] | 77 | 72 | 9 | 13 | 14 | 15 |
| China | n.a. | 69 | n.a. | 19 | n.a. | 12 |
| India | 74 | 71 | 11 | 13 | 15 | 16 |
| Other low-income | 82 | 73 | 7 | 11 | 11 | 16 |
| Lower Middle-Income Developing | 71 | 56 | 11 | 16 | 18 | 28 |
| Upper Middle-Income Developing | 49 | 30 | 20 | 28 | 31 | 42 |
| Industrial Market | 18 | 6 | 38 | 38 | 44 | 56 |

Note:   n.a. indicates not available.

[a]Figures for 1960 do not include data for China.

Source:   World Bank (1983).

substantially more dominant in South Asia and sub-Saharan Africa
in both 1960 and 1980 than it is in the Middle East and North
Africa and in Latin America and the Caribbean.  Table 10 also
indicates that the decline of the labor force share in agriculture between 1960 and 1980 was associated with an increase in
the labor force share in both industry and services--in all
regions.  However, there were some differentials in the extent
of decline in agriculture and the relative expansion of industry
and services.  For example, the biggest decline in agriculture
was in the South European countries, while the smallest decline
was in the South Asian countries.  Of the regions experiencing
the largest declines in agriculture, services tended to grow the
most, although not necessarily in proportionate terms.  In this
regard, the Middle East and North Africa stand out, insofar as
their moderate decline in agriculture was associated with a
growth rate in industry that exceeded that in services.

Taken together, Tables 9 and 10 indicate the existence of
differences in both income groups and regions in the sectoral
distribution of the labor force.  These tables also provide
evidence of changes over time, only some of which have been
uniform across income groups and geographic regions.

It is important to note that the shifts in the labor force
distribution shown in Tables 9 and 10 have contributed to
increased income per capita in developing countries.  This is

TABLE 10  Distribution of Labor Force Across Economic Sectors, by
Geographic Region

| | Percent of Labor Force | | | | | |
| | Agriculture | | Industry | | Services | |
| Geographic Region | 1960 | 1980 | 1960 | 1980 | 1960 | 1980 |
|---|---|---|---|---|---|---|
| Africa South of Sahara | 77.6 | 67.4 | 8.8 | 13.4 | 13.6 | 19.2 |
| Middle East and North Africa | 58.6 | 42.4 | 16.1 | 27.8 | 25.3 | 29.8 |
| East Asia and Pacific[a] | 71.1 | 53.2 | 9.5 | 16.9 | 19.4 | 29.9 |
| South Asia | 74.4 | 68.9 | 10.6 | 13.2 | 15.0 | 17.9 |
| Latin America and Caribbean | 48.8 | 31.9 | 19.2 | 23.7 | 32.0 | 44.4 |
| South Europe | 64.0 | 40.7 | 17.3 | 23.4 | 18.7 | 35.9 |

[a]Excludes China.

Source:  World Bank (1983).


illustrated by a two-part calculation:   first, relative labor
productivity in each sector has been estimated; second, the
impact of changes in labor force allocation across sectors on
the growth of economy-wide productivity has been evaluated.
Table 11 reports the results of the first calculation.  It shows
the ratio of gross domestic product (GDP) per worker in agriculture, industry, and services to the economy-wide GDP per
worker.   Figures greater than 1.0 indicate that a sector has
above-average productivity, while figures below 1.0 indicate the
reverse.   In all income groups of economies, agriculture has
below-average productivity; in all but the industrial market
economies, industry has markedly higher average productivity, as
do services.   There is, moreover, a general tendency for the
industry-to-all-economy differential to fall as agriculture's
share of the labor force drops.
     Table 12 provides estimates of the contribution of the labor
force shifts shown in Table 9 to the growth of GDP per worker
from 1960 to 1980.  It uses 1960 relative GDP per worker and 1980
relative GDP per worker as "productivity weights" to evaluate the
shift.   The results show that in the developing countries (with
the exception of India), changes in the sectoral distribution of
the labor force have contributed significantly to the growth of
overall labor productivity:  a 21-25 percent increase in middle-
income developing countries, and a 14-16 percent increase in low-
income countries exclusive of China and India.  With productivity

TABLE 11  Gross Domestic Product per Worker for Each Sector Relative to
the Economy, 1960-80

| Type of Economy | Agriculture 1960 | Agriculture 1980 | Industry 1960 | Industry 1980 | Services 1960 | Services 1980 |
|---|---|---|---|---|---|---|
| Low-Income Economies[a] | 0.64 | 0.50 | 2.89 | 2.69 | 1.79 | 1.93 |
| China | n.a. | 0.49 | n.a. | 2.47 | n.a. | 1.83 |
| India | 0.68 | 0.52 | 1.82 | 2.00 | 2.00 | 2.31 |
| Other low-income | 0.60 | 0.62 | 1.33 | 1.55 | 3.54 | 2.38 |
| Lower Middle-Income Developing[b] | 0.52 | 0.41 | 2.00 | 2.19 | 2.28 | 1.50 |
| Upper Middle-Income Developing[b] | 0.37 | 0.37 | 1.65 | 1.46 | 1.59 | 1.14 |
| Industrial Market | 0.33 | 0.67 | 1.05 | 0.97 | 1.23 | 1.11 |

Note:  n.a. indicates not applicable.

[a]Figures for 1960 do not include China.
[b]1982 GDP share by 1980 labor share for 1980.

Sources:  World Bank (1982); Table 9.

growth over the period of nearly 150 percent in middle-income
developing countries and about 100 percent in low-income
countries, the observed ability of the labor markets to shift
labor to the relatively more productive sectors despite rapid
population growth contributed from one-tenth to one-fifth of
observed overall productivity growth.

The next issue that needs to be addressed goes beyond estab-
lishing the existence of patterns or changes in the sectoral
distribution of the labor force.  Rather, it involves assessing
whether or not developing countries have been expanding their
productive capacities within sectors.  In other words, have the
sectoral shifts affected output per worker, within or between
sectors, as in the simple Lewis model?

Table 13 provides us with a preliminary answer to this
question.  This table presents statistics by country income
groups on the growth of GDP and the labor force between 1960 and
1980, broken down by economic sector.  Presumably, if economic
development were not taking place, one would expect this table
to reveal GDP growth falling short of labor force growth.  One
would also expect to see little evidence of growth in the agricultural sector's share of GDP due to the presence of surplus
labor.  Alternatively, agricultural productivity (i.e., the
difference between the growth of GDP from agriculture and the
growth of the agricultural labor force) would tend to be stable

TABLE 12  Estimates of the Contribution of Shifts in Sectoral
Distribution of Labor to Growth of GDP per Worker, 1960-80

| Type of Economy | Percentage Change in GDP per Worker Using | |
| --- | --- | --- |
| | 1960 Relative GDP by Sector | 1980 Relative GDP by Sector |
| Low-Income Economies | 10.5 | 11.5 |
| China | -- | -- |
| India | 3.9 | 5.2 |
| Other low-income | 15.1 | 13.8 |
| Lower Middle-Income Developing | 25.0 | 23.2 |
| Upper Middle-Income Developing | 24.1 | 21.0 |
| Industrial Market | 10.8 | 2.3 |

Sources:  Tables 9 and 11, calculated by applying 1980
distribution of labor force to 1960 relative GDPs per worker and
1960 distribution of labor force to 1980 relative GDPs per worker.

or decline over time.  Finally, one would expect to observe
little growth in the share of GDP coming from industry because
of the slow growth of capital, and little growth in the share of
GDP coming from services because of the slow emergence of an
informal sector.

Table 13 is highly illuminating on all of these points.  Over
the 1960-80 period, GDP growth actually exceeded labor force
growth in all three economic sectors and for all income groups
of economies.  Thus, GDP per member of the labor force, a crude
measure of productivity, increased over time.  However, the
magnitude of the increase was relatively small in the agricultural sector.  For example, in low-income developing countries,
GDP associated with agricultural output grew 56 percent between
1960 and 1980, while the agricultural labor force grew by about
35 percent.  In other words, output per labor force member grew
by roughly one-fifth over this 20-year period.  In comparison to
this figure, output per labor force member grew four times as
much in the industrial and service sectors of low-income developing economies.  For middle-income developing economies, agricultural output per agricultural labor force member grew by
about 75 percent between 1960 and 1980.  In comparison, this
measure of productivity grew by approximately 140 percent in
industry and 60 percent in services.  This last figure is
particularly interesting since it indicates that productivity
growth in the service sector was less than that in agriculture
in the middle-income developing economies.  However, this pattern

TABLE 13 Growth of Product and Labor Force by Sector, 1960–80 (in percent)

| Type of Economy | Growth of Real GDP, 1960–80 | | | | Growth of Labor Force, 1960–80 | | | |
|---|---|---|---|---|---|---|---|---|
| | Overall | Agriculture | Industry | Services | Overall | Agriculture | Industry | Services |
| Low-Income Developing | 141.2 | 56.1 | 189.9 | 134.3 | 44.3 | 34.9 | 108.4 | 54.6 |
| Middle-Income Developing | 203.0 | 89.6 | 258.8 | 191.8 | 56.0 | 15.7 | 118.4 | 130.6 |
| Industrial Market | 116.7 | 37.4 | 123.3 | 127.9 | 26.9 | -42.2 | 26.9 | 61.5 |

Source: Authors' calculations using data from World Bank (1983, 1984).

133

is more an indication that agricultural productivity growth was large than an indication that service productivity growth was small. For example, the productivity growth figures for agriculture and services in the middle-income developing countries are extremely close to those for the industrial market economies. Perhaps the pattern of agricultural productivity growth in middle-income developing countries signifies that population growth either has stimulated technological change, or has reached the point at which these countries have sufficient incentives to adopt more efficient production techniques or economic institutions. It also seems worth noting that overall GDP growth per labor force member grew more in the middle-income developing countries between 1960 and 1980 than in the low-income developing economies or the industrial market economies, where roughly equal growth rates were attained.

Overall, then, although the tables presented in this section do not permit us to distinguish between alternative theoretical views of the relationship between population growth and employment, they do not paint a particularly dire picture of developing countries' labor absorption prospects. The evidence for the rapid growth of the size of the nonagricultural sectors, and for the growing productivity of workers in those sectors, suggests that developing countries have, in fact, been able to absorb considerable additions to their populations into productive employment. Although the road ahead does look rockier for the low-income than for the middle-income developing countries, labor market structures in both groups of economies seem to be geared up for at least some further expansion.


COUNTRY-SPECIFIC EXPERIENCES[19]


The preceding three sections have presented a broad overview of the central relationships between population growth, labor supply, and employment in developing countries. They also reviewed aggregate indicators of many of those relationships, using data for different income and geographic groups of countries. An important caveat to these sections is that they reflect general tendencies and not necessarily the experience of any particular country. In other words, a particular country's culture, labor market institutions, international trade policies, stock of natural resources, etc. may have considerable influence on the extent to which (1) population growth leads to increased labor supply, and (2) increased labor supply is absorbed into productive employment. The purpose of this section is to document this claim with examples of the recent labor market experiences of a selected number of developing countries. While identifying all of the country-specific factors that can influence labor absorption is beyond the scope of this chapter, an attempt is made to list some of the main ones and to provide illustrative examples. In this connection, the discussion focuses on the role played by (1) external sources of demand for a particular economy's labor, (2) the availability of land and other natural resources, and (3) governmental policies that directly or indirectly impinge on the labor market.

In the simple theoretical models of developing country labor markets outlined in earlier sections, it was assumed that the economies were closed, i.e., that all labor absorption would take place domestically. However, the recent experience of several developing countries demonstrates that, to a substantial extent, this need not be the case in practice. For example, the economies of India, the Philippines, and Egypt have all been affected by the substantial emigration of their resident labor forces to the oil-rich Arab economies. To illustrate, it is estimated that there were 1-2 million Egyptians working abroad at the beginning of this decade, a magnitude equal to between 10 and 20 percent of Egypt's resident labor force. This massive emigration has both positive and negative implications for the Egyptian economy. On the positive side, the substantial absorption of labor into relatively high-wage employment externally has resulted in a sharp decline in agricultural employment, accompanied by an increase in agricultural wages and the onset of a trend toward capital intensity and higher productivity in agricultural production. In addition, these high-wage emigrants (the majority of them being skilled construction workers) have tended to remit substantial portions of their earnings to their relatives in Egypt (with remittances amounting to 10 percent of Egypt's GDP in 1980), thereby providing a major source of foreign exchange and a major stimulus to domestic demand.[20] On the other hand, the massive emigration of Egyptian labor has increased the dependence of the Egyptian economy on the world price of oil and on the construction boom in the Arab countries. Moreover, it appears that the structural transformation of Egyptian agricultural production has reduced its labor absorption capacity, which could be important under conditions of massive return migration.

A second key factor affecting the labor absorption capacity of a developing economy is the size and characteristics of its stock of idle land and other natural resources. In particular, labor absorption in developing economies is generally associated with a transition from predominantly agricultural to nonagricultural production and employment. However, the agricultural sectors of several developing economies have exhibited great labor absorption capacity. A good example is Mexico, which experienced a five-fold increase in the area of its land under cultivation from 1940 to 1970; Mexico also experienced rapid population growth during those years and growth of GNP per capita that was above the average for countries in its income group. However, starting in the late 1960s, Mexico's safety valve for labor absorption began to close up as its supply of unfarmed arable land began to disappear. As a consequence, growth of GNP per capita was below average for Mexico in the 1970s. Moreover, population and labor force growth in Mexico have continued to be substantial and have resulted in fairly massive increases in rural-urban migration. Indeed, this migration far exceeds the absorptive capacity of the industrial sector of the Mexican economy, and has resulted in the swelling of the informal urban sector and the steady flow of both legal and illegal emigration to the United States. Thus, Mexico no longer seems to provide an excellent counterexample to the pessimistic view that population growth hinders development (see Coale, 1978).

Another country that seems to be enjoying some degree of development despite rapid population growth is Kenya, a low-income developing country that had a population growth rate of 4.0 percent from 1970-82. Labor absorption in Kenya has been high, despite industrial wage levels that are considerably higher than agricultural-sector wages, as well as the presence of substantial urban unemployment. To a large extent, Kenyan development reflects the continuing availability of unfarmed arable land and the sizable magnitude of foreign exchange that is generated through tourism (and the substantial growth of an informal urban sector). Indeed, GNP per capita in Kenya increased 2.3 percent per year from 1955-83, in contrast to the experience of the bordering countries of Somalia, Ethiopia, Tanzania, and Uganda, which had growth rates of -0.8 percent, 0.5 percent, -0.9 percent, and -4.4 percent, respectively, over the same period (and 1970-82 population growth rates of 3.1 percent, 2.7 percent, 3.2 percent, and 3.1 percent, respectively).

Although some countries may be able to facilitate labor absorption by bringing additional land under cultivation, others may already be too densely populated to make that a viable option. Examples of such countries include India and Indonesia. In these countries, however, labor absorption can be facilitated by changes in agricultural technology. For example, in the Punjab region of India, the labor-intensive "Green Revolution" has resulted in an expansion of both agricultural output and employment. Similarly, in Indonesia, the traditional rice economy has been transformed by the use of (relatively labor-intensive) high-yielding varieties of rice, and by the growing practices of double- and triple-cropping.

In Brazil, by contrast, where population density is modest, the productivity of agricultural labor was increased by the adoption of more efficient agricultural production techniques rather than by increased land cultivation, thereby releasing labor to other sectors and compounding the absorption problem. In fact, employment in Brazil seems to have kept pace with increased labor supply, although apparently at the expense of real wages, which have fallen over time. The Philippines is another example of a country in which absorption has been achieved at the expense of falling real wages.

In addition to land, oil is another natural resource that can (and has) figured quite prominently in the absorption ability of developing economies. Here, we may cite Indonesia, Venezuela, and Mexico as examples of countries that either export or have the capacity to export oil in international markets. To the extent that oil exports contribute to the generation of foreign exchange, they can provide an important boost to capital formation and the expansion of industrial employment in developing economies. On the other hand, oil dependency can greatly hinder the pace and stability of a country's development. For example, many of the balance-of-payments problems in the Philippines, which have affected economic growth and labor absorption through their effects on domestic capital markets and government monetary and fiscal policies, have been traced to variations in world oil prices.

A final factor conditioning the labor absorption capacity of individual developing economies is governmental policy impacting on the labor market. Earlier, we noted the importance of government-established minimum wages in creating growth-inhibiting distortions in an economy. Here, we mention another government policy aimed directly at increasing labor absorption--public employment programs. One example of a country in which such programs have been heavily relied upon is Egypt. Excluding the military, public employment in Egypt increased at an annual rate of nearly 7 percent between 1966 and 1978. This trend is largely the consequence of the government's establishment of employment guarantees for university graduates (since 1966) and military conscripts (from 1973 to 1976). This policy, which resulted in substantial labor absorption at a time when Egypt was still a classic surplus labor economy (i.e., before the massive emigration of Egyptian labor to the oil-rich Arab countries), appears to be constraining productivity growth under the current circumstances of labor scarcity since government workers have relatively low productivity. This example highlights the point that it is not simply employment that matters, but employment in productive jobs.

Another set of government policies deserving mention are those that relate to the relative price of capital. In an effort to stimulate the growth of industry, a number of developing countries have adopted aggressive fiscal and monetary policies that tend to induce a capital bias in their overall development pattern. For example, Brazil, Indonesia, and the Philippines have all had macroeconomic policies that provided incentives for private companies to borrow from abroad or forced the central government to borrow heavily to cover a deficit. As a consequence, economic conditions in these countries have been highly sensitive to the state of world capital markets, and relatively capital-intensive patterns of development have been induced. In contrast, other developing countries, such as India (and both Brazil and the Philippines in past years), have pursued more conservative monetary and fiscal policies in concert with import substitution strategies designed to impart internal stability to their economic systems and to promote long-term growth and labor absorption. Foreign exchange restrictions, which can be used to depress the importation of capital, can also help to promote labor absorption.

Finally, many developing countries have intervened in agricultural markets, often purchasing output from farmers and providing low-cost food for urban dwellers. These policies can affect the allocation of labor among sectors, rural-urban migration, and success in adjusting to population increases. As yet,

there has been no definitive study of the effects of food price
policy (or capital price policy) on the overall success of
countries in absorbing labor into productive jobs.

CONCLUSIONS AND SPECULATIONS ABOUT THE FUTURE

This review of evidence has shown that developing countries have
faced an enormous increase in population in the past two decades.
Fertility and mortality patterns guarantee a similar large
increase in the future. The experience of the past indicates,
however, that despite population increasing more than the labor
force, and despite inefficient dualistic labor markets due
potentially to government-induced and other imperfections,
developing countries were, on the whole, relatively successful
in improving their economic positions over the period. The
labor markets absorbed a "huge" population increase, with per
worker incomes rising and shifts taking place in the labor force
distribution toward more productive sectors of the economy. The
analysis here has also highlighted the wide range of country
experiences in population growth, in labor market policies
likely to influence "absorption" in modern sectors, and
ultimately in the likely impact of population growth on per
capita incomes. Overall, the experiences of the 1960-80 period
tend to be more supportive of an optimistic than a pessimistic
view of the ability of developing economies to adjust to
population growth.

What about the future? Simply because the developing
economies managed to raise productivity and shift employment into
the service and manufacturing sectors in the 1960-80 period does
not necessarily mean that they will be able to do so in the next
two decades. We consider next the factors likely to make the
absorption of increased population easier and those likely to
make it more difficult in the 1980-2000 period.

To begin with, consider the projected population and labor
force growth rates in Table 14. The figures here show two
advantages compared to the 1960-80 period examined in Table 1.
First, rates of population growth will be smaller than in the
earlier periods: for all low-income developing countries, the
rates of growth fall from 2-3 percent (1960-70) and 1.9 percent
(1970-82) to a projected 1.7 percent. The rate of population
increase also falls for lower and upper middle-income developing
countries. Second, in sharp contrast to the earlier period, the
labor force will increase more rapidly than population in all
types of economies. For the first time in recent years, dependency rates will be getting lower. Hence, smaller increases in
income per worker will be needed to produce any given increase
in income per capita.

On the negative side are the absolute magnitudes of the
increases noted at the outset of the chapter. From 1960 to
1982, labor supply in less developed countries grew by 173
million workers; from 1980 to 2000, the supply will increase by
255 million workers. In lower middle-income developing

TABLE 14   Projected Population and Labor Force Growth Rates
1980-2000, by Income Group

| Type of Economy | Population | Labor Force | Difference |
|---|---|---|---|
| Low-Income Developing | 1.7 | 2.0 | 0.3 |
|    China | 1.0 | 1.6 | 0.6 |
|    India | 1.9 | 2.1 | 0.2 |
|    Other low-income | 2.9 | 3.0 | 0.1 |
| Lower Middle-Income Developing | 2.4 | 2.6 | 0.2 |
| Upper Middle-Income Developing | 2.1 | 2.5 | 0.4 |
| Industrial Market | 0.4 | 0.6 | 0.2 |

Source:  World Bank (1984).

countries, the absolute growth in labor force will rise from 50
million (1960-82) to 84 million (1980-2000), while in upper
middle-income countries, the increase will be from 35 million
(1960-82) to 59 million (1980-2000).[21] To be productive,
these workers must be equipped with both material and human
capital.  In absolute magnitudes, this growth will place great
demands on world capital markets (both public and private) and
thus on world savings behavior.  To the extent that less
developed countries rely on capital flows from more developed
countries, they will, in turn, require greater per capita
investments from those countries.
    In our view, if modern technology is applied to less
developed countries at the same rate as in the past two
decades--which presumably will require both human and physical
capital investments of enormous absolute magnitudes, but of
relative magnitudes comparable to those of the past--Malthusian
disasters will not necessarily be the result of forecasted
population growth.  However, on the basis of past history, the
middle-income developing countries are likely to perform better
in this respect than the low-income countries, some of which may
need considerable help if they are to absorb increased population
while shifting labor to more productive sectors and raising
output per worker.


NOTES


1  By developed countries we mean Western Europe, Australia,
   Japan, Canada, and the United States, as indicated in
   Appendix Table A.2.  Except for countries with mid-1982

populations below one million, high-income oil exporters, and East European nonmarket economies, all other countries are considered less developed, despite the wide range of industrialization and income per capita among them.

2   These figures are taken from the World Development Report 1984 (World Bank, 1984) and from the Population Reference Bureau's 1984 World Population Data Sheet.

3   See Simon (1981) for a presentation of the optimists' point of view; see Coale and Hoover (1958) for a statement of the pessimists' view.

4   For such correlations see Kuznets (1973:43), who reports the rank correlation between the rate of growth of population and per capita product as -.31 for all countries and .11 for all underdeveloped countries.

5   See Standing (1976) for an excellent discussion of this issue; see also Dixon (1982) and Anker (1983) for thorough treatments of the problems involved in measuring the labor force participation of women in developing countries.

6   This simple insight into the dynamic relationship between population and labor force growth was behind some of the main results derived in one of the earliest neoclassical treatments of the relationship between population and economic growth, the classic volume by Coale and Hoover (1958).

7   One can think of individuals choosing to migrate to urban areas in response to fertility or mortality changes that affect the benefits and costs of such migration. See Stark and Bloom (1985) for a review of recent developments in the migration literature. See Williamson (1986) for some discussion of age selectivity in migration.

8   See Durand (1975) for a thorough empirical study of labor force participation rates in less developed economies.

9   See Bloom and Freeman (1986) for a review of this literature and for some new empirical results.

10  See Chenery and Syrquin (1975) for an attempt to characterize "average" patterns of development. Note, however, that Chenery and Syrquin do not focus on deviations from those average patterns, which are substantial, nor do they focus on empirical testing of theoretical relationships between the variables.

11  In this model, the average product of labor in the agricultural sector will, of course, increase somewhat as more labor is drawn into the modern sector. This will tend to raise wages in the modern sector in the simple model outlined here.

12  Further references to theoretical models of dual economies include Jorgenson (1961), Fei and Ranis (1964), and Dixit (1970).

13  This conclusion rests, of course, on the assumption that the savings rate from industrial-sector wages is less than that from profits. If this assumption is reasonable, labor market imperfections in the modern sector will constrain the economy's ability to absorb new labor.

14  According to McNicoll (1984a:197), ". . . there is strong
    evidence of population-induced innovation in some agricul-
    tural settings, but there are cases too where rapid
    population growth has been accompanied by stagnant
    productivity or by labor-saving rather than labor-using
    technical progress."
15  Indeed, at the level of causal empiricism, this theory is
    not inconsistent with the emergence of the urban informal
    sector (see Portes and Benton, 1985).
16  Since much agricultural production in developing countries
    is not exchanged, the World Bank has imputed part of its
    value for many countries.
17  Ideally, we would also analyze the wage effects of rapid
    population growth. Unfortunately, the sketchy and unre-
    liable nature of wage data for most developing countries
    renders such an analysis beyond the scope of this chapter.
    However, the chapter analyzes variations in a kindred
    measure—output per worker—across sectors and over time.
18  See Kuznets (1984) for a detailed analysis of the decline of
    agricultural employment.
19  The material presented in this section draws heavily on the
    studies by Alba (1984), Hansen and Radwan (1982), Inter-
    national Labour Office (1972), Leiserson and World Bank
    (1980), Lluch and Mazumdar (1983), McNicoll (1984b), Paiva
    (1984), Paqueo (1984), Radwan (1984), and Visaria (1984).
20  See Lucas and Stark (1985) for an interesting analysis of
    emigrant remittances.
21  These figures are extracted from World Bank (1984:148 and
    218).

REFERENCES

Alba, F. (1984) Country Case Studies. Mexico: Achievements
    and Limitations in Labor Force Absorption. Paper presented
    at the conference on Population Growth and Labor Absorption
    in the Developing World: 1960-2000, Bellagio, Italy.
Anker, R. (1983) Female labour force activity in developing
    countries: a critique of current definitions and data
    collection methods. International Labour Review 122:709-723.
Berg, E. (1970) Wage structures in less developed countries.
    In A.B. Smith, ed., Wage Policy Issues in Economic Develop-
    ment. London: Macmillan.
Binswanger, H.P. (1979) Induced technical change: evolution of
    thought. In H.P. Binswanger and V.W. Ruttan, eds., Induced
    Innovation: Technology, Institutions, and Development.
    Baltimore, Md.: The Johns Hopkins University Press.
Bloom, D.E., and R.B. Freeman (1986) The Youth Problem: Age or
    Generational Crowding? National Bureau of Economic Research
    Working Paper No. 1837, Cambridge, Mass.
Boserup, E. (1981) Population and Technological Change—A Study
    of Long-Term Trends. Chicago: University of Chicago Press.

142                                                    Bloom and Freeman

Chenery, H., and M. Syrquin (1975)  Patterns of Development,
    1960-70. London: Oxford University Press.
Coale, A.J. (1978)  Population growth and economic development:
    the case of Mexico. Foreign Affairs 56:415-429.
Coale, A.J., and E.M. Hoover (1958)  Population Growth and
    Economic Development in Low-Income Countries. Princeton,
    N.J.: Princeton University Press.
Dixit, A. (1970)  Models of dual economies. Pp. 327-352 in J.A.
    Mirrlees and N.H. Stern, eds., Models of Economic Growth.
    New York: John Wiley.
Dixon, R.B. (1982)  Women in agriculture: counting the labor
    force in developing countries. Population and Development
    Review 8:539-566.
Durand, J.D. (1975)  The Labor Force in Economic Development: A
    Comparison of International Census Statistics: 1946-66.
    Princeton, N.J.: Princeton University Press.
Fei, J.C.H., and G. Ranis (1964)  Development of the Labor
    Surplus Economy. Homewood, Ill.: Irwin.
Gregory, P. (1975)  The impact of institutional factors on urban
    labor markets.  In Studies in Employment and Rural Develop-
    ment. Washington, D.C.: World Bank.
Hansen, B., and S. Radwan (1982)  Employment Opportunities and
    Equity in a Changing Economy: Egypt in the 1980s. Geneva:
    International Labour Office.
Harris, J., and M.P. Todaro (1970)  Migration, unemployment, and
    development: a two-sector analysis. American Economic
    Review 60:126-132.
Hayami, Y., and V.W. Ruttan (1985)  Agricultural Development.
    Baltimore, Md.: The Johns Hopkins University Press.
Heller, P.S., and A.A. Tait (1983)  Government Employment and
    Pay: Some International Comparisons. Occasional Paper No.
    24, International Monetary Fund, Washington, D.C.
Hirschman, A.O. (1958)  The Strategy of Economic Development.
    New Haven, Conn.: Yale University Press.
House, W.J., and H. Rempel (1976)  Impact of unionization on
    negotiated wages in manufacturing sector in Kenya. Oxford
    Bulletin of Economic Statistics 38:111-123.
Instituto Nacional de Estadisticas (1977)  Chile: Anuario
    Estadistico, 1976. Santiago: Instituto Nacional de
    Estadisticas.
International Labour Office (1972)  Employment, Incomes, and
    Equality: A Strategy for Increasing Productive Employment
    in Kenya. Geneva: International Labour Office.
International Labour Office (1975)  Yearbook of Labour Statis-
    tics. Geneva: International Labour Office.
International Labour Office (1981)  Yearbook of Labour Statis-
    tics. Geneva: International Labour Office.
International Labour Office (1984)  Yearbook of Labour Statis-
    tics. Geneva: International Labour Office.
Jorgenson, D.W. (1961)  The development of a dual economy.
    Economic Journal LXXI:309-334.

Krueger, A.O. (1983)  Trade and Employment in Developing
    Countries, 3:  Synthesis and Conclusions.  Chicago:
    University of Chicago Press.
Kuznets, S. (1965)  Economic Growth and Structure: Selected
    Essays.  New York:  Norton.
Kuznets, S. (1973)  Population, Capital, and Growth.  London:
    Heinemann Educational Books.
Kuznets, S. (1984)  The pattern of shift of labor force from
    agriculture 1950-70.  Pp. 44-59 in M. Gersovitz, C.F.
    Diaz-Alejandro, G. Ranis, and M.R. Rosenzweig, eds., The
    Theory and Experience of Economic Development.  London:
    George Allen and Unwin.
Leibenstein, H. (1978)  General X-Efficiency Theory and Economic
    Development.  New York:  Oxford University Press.
Leiserson, M., and World Bank (1980)  Employment and Income
    Distribution in Indonesia.  Washington, D.C.:  World Bank.
Lewis, W.A. (1954)  Economic development with unlimited supplies
    of labour.  Manchester School 22:137-191.
Lewis, W.A. (1958)  Unlimited labour:  further notes.  Manchester
    School 26:1-32.
Lluch, C., and D. Mazumdar (1983)  Wages and Employment in
    Indonesia.  Washington, D.C.:  World Bank.
Lucas, R.E.B., and O. Stark (1985)  Motivations to remit:  the
    case of Botswana.  Journal of Political Economy 93:901-918.
McNicoll, G. (1984a)  Consequences of rapid population growth:
    an overview and assessment.  Population and Development
    Review 10:177-240.
McNicoll, G. (1984b)  Population Dynamics and Labor Absorption
    in Indonesia:  A Case Study.  Paper presented at the confer-
    ence on Population Growth and Labor Absorption in the
    Developing World:  1960-2000, Bellagio, Italy.
Paiva, P. (1984)  Fifty Years of Population Growth and Labor
    Absorption in Brazil:  From 1950-2000.  Paper presented at
    the conference on Population Growth and Labor Absorption in
    the Developing World:  1960-2000, Bellagio, Italy.
Paqueo, V.B. (1984)  Population Growth, Employment and Total
    Factor Productivity Growth:  Problems and Prospects of the
    Philippine Political Economy.  Paper presented at the con-
    ference on Population Growth and Labor Absorption in the
    Developing World:  1960-2000, Bellagio, Italy.
Portes, A., and L. Benton (1984)  Industrial development and
    labor absorption:  a reinterpretation.  Population and
    Development Review 4:589-611.
Radwan, S. (1984)  The Labour Markets in an Open Economy:  Egypt.
    Paper presented at the conference on Population Growth and
    Labor Absorption in the Developing World:  1960-2000,
    Bellagio, Italy.
Ranis, G., and J.C. Fei (1984)  Lewis and the classicists.  Pp.
    31-42 in M. Gersovitz, C.F. Diaz-Alejandro, G. Ranis, and
    M.R. Rosenzweig, eds., The Theory and Experience of Economic
    Development.  London:  George Allen and Unwin.
Sen, A.K. (1968)  Choice of Techniques.  Oxford:  Basil
    Blackwell.

Simon, J. (1981)  The Ultimate Resource.  Princeton, N.J.:
    Princeton University Press.
Squire, L. (1981)  Employment Policy in Developing Countries.
    Washington, D.C.:  World Bank.
Standing, G.M. (1976)  Concepts of Labor Force Participation and
    Underutilisation.  Population and Employment Working Paper
    No. 40, International Labour Office, Geneva.
Standing, G.M. (1978)  Labour Force Participation and Develop-
    ment.  Geneva: International Labour Office.
Standing, G.M., and G. Sheehan, eds. (1978)  Labour Force Parti-
    cipation in Low-Income Countries.  Geneva:  International
    Labour Office.
Stark, O., and D.E. Bloom (1985)  The new economics of labor
    migration.  American Economic Review:  Papers and Proceedings
    75:173-178.
Starr, G. (1981)  Minimum Wage Fixing.  Geneva:  International
    Labour Office.
United Nations (1968-80)  Yearbook of Industrial Statistics.  New
    York:  United Nations.
U.S. Department of Labor (1983)  Handbook of Labor Statistics.
    Washington, D.C.:  U.S. Government Printing Office.
Visaria, P. (1984)  The Growth of Population and Labour Force in
    India:  1961-2001.  Paper presented at the conference on
    Population Growth and Labor Absorption in the Developing
    World:  1960-2000, Bellagio, Italy.
Webb, R.C. (1977)  Wage policy and income distribution in devel-
    oping countries.  In C.R. Frank and R.C. Webb, eds., Income
    Distribution and Growth in the Less Developed Countries.
    Washington, D.C.:  Brookings Institution.
Williamson, J.G. (1986)  Migration and urbanization.  In H.
    Chenery and T.N. Srinivasan, eds., Handbook of Developing
    Economics, forthcoming.
World Bank (1982)  World Development Report 1982.  Oxford:
    Oxford University Press.
World Bank (1983)  World Tables, vol. II.  Social Data.
    Baltimore, Md.:  Johns Hopkins University Press.
World Bank (1984)  World Development Report 1984.  New York:
    Oxford University Press.

APPENDIX TABLE A.1  Developing Countries by Income Group and Geographic Region

|  | Income Group | | |
|---|---|---|---|
| Region | Low-Income Developing Countries | Lower Middle- Income Developing Countries | Upper Middle- Income Developing Countries |
| Africa South of Sahara | Benin<br>Burundi<br>Cent. Afr. Rep.<br>Chad<br>Ethiopia<br>Ghana<br>Guinea<br>Kenya<br>Madagascar<br>Malawi<br>Mali<br>Mozambique<br>Niger<br>Rwanda<br>Sierra Leone<br>Somalia<br>Tanzania<br>Togo<br>Uganda<br>Upper Volta<br>Zaire | Angola<br>Cameroon<br>Congo People's Rep.<br>Ivory Coast<br>Lesotho<br>Liberia<br>Mauritania<br>Nigeria<br>Senegal<br>Sudan<br>Zambia<br>Zimbabwe | South Africa |
| Middle East and North Africa | | Egypt<br>Lebanon<br>Morocco<br>Tunisia<br>Yemen Arab Rep.<br>Yemen, PDR | Algeria<br>Iran<br>Iraq<br>Jordan<br>Syria |
| East Asia and Pacific | China<br>Kampuchea, Dem.<br>Laos, PDR<br>Viet Nam | Indonesia<br>Korea, N.<br>Mongolia<br>Papua New Guinea<br>Philippines<br>Thailand | Hong Kong<br>Korea, S.<br>Malaysia<br>Singapore |
| South Asia | Afghanistan<br>Bangladesh<br>Bhutan<br>Burma<br>India<br>Nepal<br>Pakistan<br>Sri Lanka | | |

Bloom and Freeman

APPENDIX TABLE A.1 (continued)

| | Income Group | | |
| Region | Low-Income Developing Countries | Lower Middle-Income Developing Countries | Upper Middle-Income Developing Countries |
| --- | --- | --- | --- |
| Latin America and Caribbean | Haiti | Bolivia<br>Colombia<br>Costa Rica<br>Cuba<br>Dom. Rep.<br>Ecuador<br>El Salvador<br>Guatemala<br>Honduras<br>Jamaica<br>Nicaragua<br>Paraguay<br>Peru | Argentina<br>Brazil<br>Chile<br>Mexico<br>Panama<br>Trinidad & Tobago<br>Uruguay<br>Venezuela |
| South Europe | | Turkey | Greece<br>Israel<br>Portugal<br>Yugoslavia |

Note: The countries listed in this table reflect the income group and geographic location classification used by the World Bank in its 1984 World Development Report. All of the countries in this table had mid-1982 populations exceeding 1 million persons.

APPENDIX TABLE A.2   Countries with Industrial
Market Economies, by Region

| Region | Countries |
|---|---|
| Pacific | Australia |
| | New Zealand |
| North America | Canada |
| | United States |
| Western Europe | Austria |
| | Belgium |
| | Denmark |
| | Finland |
| | Germany, F.R. |
| | Ireland |
| | Italy |
| | Netherlands |
| | Norway |
| | Spain |
| | Sweden |
| | Switzerland |
| | United Kingdom |
| Asia | Japan |

Note:   The countries listed in this table
reflect the income group classification used
by the World Bank in its 1984 World
Development Report.  All of the countries in
this table had mid-1982 populations exceeding
1 million persons.

# 5
# The Impacts of Urban Population Growth on Urban Labor Markets and the Costs of Urban Service Delivery: A Review

## Mark R. Montgomery

### INTRODUCTION

Few issues in economic development have provoked such concern as the level and nature of less developed country (LDC) urbanization. While almost no one would disagree that urbanization and economic development are closely associated over the long term, there is great diversity of opinion regarding current urbanization patterns. A particular focus of concern is the extent of "overurbanization." The notion of overurbanization, while rarely defined with precision, draws together a number of justifiable fears about city growth: the worry that increases in urban population will outstrip employment opportunities; a concern that urban service levels and the level of the housing stock may fail to keep pace; and a recognition that government policies toward agriculture, in particular, have tended to penalize that sector and may have pushed urban growth rates above their optimal levels. In other words, the overriding concern among policy makers appears to center on the adjustment costs involved in accommodating LDC urbanization. These costs are apt to be large in the best of circumstances, placing special stress on public-sector revenue generation and management skills, and they surely have been made even more difficult to bear as a result of policy distortions that tend to favor urban areas. The intent in this chapter is to assess critically the notion of "overurbanization," with particular focus on the consequences of urban population growth and rural-urban labor transfer for urban employment and public-service delivery costs. The emphasis throughout is on policy options that can minimize the adjustment costs associated with urbanization--though these may still be large--and encourage efficient locational decisions on the part of individuals and firms.

Any discussion of LDC urbanization must begin with a recognition that urban population growth is fueled by high rates of natural increase in urban areas, as well as by rural-to-urban migration. As has been pointed out (United Nations, 1980: Chapter 3), the largest contributor to urban growth rates in developing countries is the rate of natural increase in urban

149

areas: on average, natural increase accounts for some 60.7 percent of total urban growth. LDC urban growth rates are virtually without historical precedent, in large part because of these high rates of natural increase. Policies designed to slow urban growth have generally been aimed at discouraging rural-urban migration; it seems that the central role played by urban natural increase in urban growth has often gone unappreciated. Clearly, concerns about population growth in general and the growth of the total urban population are inextricably linked.

In what follows, an attempt is made to isolate further the impact of population growth rates on proportions urban, on primacy levels, and on the structure of the urban labor force. Although definitive statements are premature at this point, it would appear that the direct impact of population growth in these areas is either weak or ambiguous. Both theory and limited empirical evidence suggest that the economic consequences of urban population growth will vary depending on the nature of market imperfections in an economy and on the special constraints that face the public sector.

In the next section, the simple two-sector model outlined by Corden and Findley (1975) is reviewed as a guide to the discussion in the remainder of the chapter. The emphasis here is on the impact of labor transfer on urban and rural earnings levels and on the role played by differential rates of technological change; the latter, in particular, have been identified as key factors in LDC urbanization in the work of Kelley and Williamson (1984). Simple empirical associations between urbanization, sectoral labor force shares, and per capita income levels are then briefly reviewed; the discussion is based on cross-national data taken from the World Development Report, 1984, supplemented with information from Agarwala's (1983) study of LDC price distortions. Next are three more detailed discussions concerning the economic consequences of rural-to-urban migration for the individual migrant, the consequences of urban population growth for urban labor markets, and, finally, an important but still poorly understood set of issues--the impact of outmigration on rural, sending regions. The next major section of the chapter addresses policy issues involved in the provision of urban services, including public-sector investment in urban service delivery, and urban public finance and administration. The final section turns to broad population distribution policy alternatives; it reviews the available literature on antiaccommodationist schemes designed to deter rural-urban migration, and also considers those employment deconcentration or decentralization policies that aim to divert urban growth from primate cities.

LABOR TRANSFER IN A SIMPLE TWO-SECTOR MODEL

Perhaps the simplest economic framework for considering urbanization is represented by the two-sector model of Figure 1. The economy described here produces two output goods, the prices of

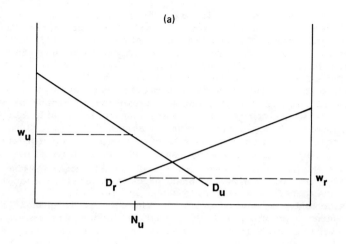

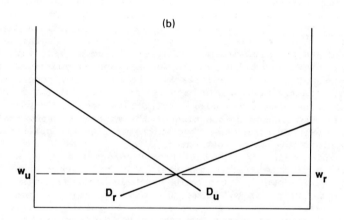

FIGURE 1   Labor Transfer and Wage Equalization

which we will initially assume are fixed in world markets.   The
horizontal axis gives a population's total labor endowment at a
point in time, N; $D_u$ is the demand curve for labor in the
urban sector, and $D_R$ represents the (reversed) demand for
labor in the rural sector.   Figure 1(a) represents an initial
position for the economy; as it is drawn, the urban wage is
given by $w_u$, and the urban labor force by $N_u$.   If $N-N_u$
people remain in agriculture, the agricultural wage is $w_r$.
Such a wage gap could be expected to induce rural-urban migration, and the evidence is overwhelming that it does (Yap, 1977;
Todaro, 1980; Schultz, 1982).   Hence, holding the demand curves
fixed, urbanization (that is, labor transfer) should increase the
wage in agriculture--leaving many of those who remain in the
rural sector better off--and reduce the returns to labor in the

urban economy. In equilibrium, the returns to labor would be
nearly equal in the two sectors, with some persistent differential in wages reflecting higher costs of housing in the urban
sector. Ignoring housing costs, we might represent the equilibrium position as in Figure 1(b).

The model sketched in Figure 1 is a useful benchmark. However, it is oversimplified in a number of respects.

First, if the "small country" assumption on output prices is
violated, then labor transfer out of agriculture will shift the
agricultural supply curve, drive up agricultural prices to a degree that depends on the price elasticity of demand for agricultural products, and therefore shift the demand for labor curve
$D_r$. Just the opposite effects will be at work in the urban
sector. One would suspect that price endogeneity might hasten
the convergence to equilibrium shown in Figure 1.

A second possible objection to the diagram is that it is too
aggregated, and, in particular, that it ignores the existence of
a service sector in rural areas and a very diverse service
sector in urban areas. If, for instance, the removal of labor
from agriculture reduces total agricultural incomes (while presumably increasing the share of income going to wages), then
earnings in rural services might be expected to suffer (Gardner,
1974). In other words, the impact of labor outmigration from
rural areas on rural incomes is likely to be uneven; with fixed
agricultural output prices, landowners and suppliers of rural
services may lose out. Similarly, the arrival of population in
urban areas may stimulate urban service incomes at the same time
that it bids down urban wage levels. The results in both cases
are affected by the composition of the migrant stream, that is,
by the types of employment from which migrants are drawn and the
occupations into which they enter.

A third point of departure from Figure 1 has to do with the
operation of urban factor markets. The notion that urban wages
might be bid down by inmigration has been challenged most vigorously by Harris and Todaro (1970), who suggest that wage levels
in the urban modern sector are rigid. An equally important set
of price rigidities--and one that has been receiving an increasing amount of attention--has to do with government policies
toward agriculture. Agarwala (1983) has gathered statistical
evidence and expert opinion on the underpricing of agriculture
in LDCs; his findings suggest that countries in which agricultural markets are highly distorted do show lower rates of growth
in agricultural output. Such policies keep the gap between
urban and rural earnings levels larger than would otherwise be
the case and serve as an artificial stimulus to migration.

There are a number of dynamic elements missing from the two-
sector model as well. Foremost among these is population growth,
which might be represented as an expansion of the horizontal axis
of the figure. Equally important, perhaps, is the omission of
differential rates of technical change. As Kelley and Williamson
(1984) point out, the importance of technical change in stimulating migration and urbanization depends to a significant degree
on exogeneity in output prices. If agricultural and industrial

output prices are kept fixed, as in the Kelley-Williamson small-country simulations, then a faster rate of (factor-neutral) technical change in urban areas will spur rural-urban migration. When prices are endogenous, however, the shift in the industry supply curve that accompanies technical change will induce some downward movement in industrial prices (to an extent determined by the price elasticities of demand for industrial products), and the influence of technical change on migration will be muted.

Investment flows and differential rates of capital accumulation have been emphasized since the earliest writings on LDC urbanization (e.g., Lewis, 1954). An important element of the "overurbanization" thesis is that, for a variety of reasons, investment funds tend to be diverted toward urban areas and, in particular, toward a country's largest city. It is commonly suggested that underpricing of capital, accompanied by inefficient exchange rate policies, has had much to do with this form of "urban bias." The combined effect would be to keep the urban capital-labor ratio in particular industries higher than would be optimal, and, if investment funds continued to flow to such industries, to shift their demand for labor curves more rapidly than would be the case under an optimal policy. Urban-to-rural remittances constitute another flow of funds worth considering. Stark (1976) argues that such flows lead to rural capital formation, and therefore shift the rural demand for labor curves over time.

In short, the simple two-sector model of Figure 1 can be considered inadequate on a number of counts. It is seriously deficient in its description of urban labor and output markets; in its omission of a service sector in rural areas; and in its treatment of population growth, technological change, and investment flows. In the remainder of the chapter, an attempt is made to sort through some of the evidence on these complex issues.


CONSEQUENCES OF URBANIZATION

This section examines some of the consequences of urbanization. First, the simple associations between urbanization and income levels are reviewed; we then take a more detailed look at the economic consequences of rural-to-urban migration for the individual migrant, the consequences of migration for urban labor markets, and the impact of urbanization on rural welfare.


Simple Associations Between Urbanization and Income Levels

In the discussion, two simple measures of urbanization within developing countries will be examined: the percentage of population classified as urban in 1982, and, of the total urban population, the percentage found in each country's largest city. The latter measure will be referred to as "primacy." Data on both measures, as well as a host of other variables, have been taken from the World Development Report, 1984; in Table 1, means

TABLE 1   Descriptive Statistics for the Full Sample of Developing
Countries

| Basic Indicators | Labor Force |
|---|---|
| Population Size (1982)<br>40.0<br>[1.1, 1008.2] | Percent LF in Agriculture (1960)<br>66.8<br>[8.0, 95.0] |
| Population Growth Rate (1960-70)<br>2.44<br>[0.3, 3.8] | Percent LF in Agriculture (1980)<br>55.0<br>[2.0, 93.0] |
| Population Growth Rate (1970-82)<br>2.50<br>[0.4, 4.9] | Percent LF in Industry (1960)<br>12.9<br>[1.00, 52.0] |
| Land Area<br>799<br>[1, 9561] | Percent LF in Industry (1980)<br>17.4<br>[2.0, 57.0] |
| Per Capita GNP (1982)<br>1239<br>[80, 6840] | Percent LF in Services (1960)<br>20.2<br>[3.0, 69.0] |
| **Urbanization** | Percent LF in Services (1980)<br>27.6<br>[5.0, 62.0] |
| Percent Urban (1960)<br>26.4<br>[2, 100] | **Percent of<br>Government Expenditures (1981)** |
| Percent Urban (1982)<br>37.8<br>[2, 100] | Defense<br>15.0<br>[1.7, 50.4] |
| Growth Rate, Urban Population<br>(1960-70)<br>5.0<br>[1.3, 15.5] | Education<br>14.1<br>[1.9, 30.1] |
| Growth Rate, Urban Population<br>(1970-82)<br>4.7<br>[0.6, 15.4] | Health<br>6.3<br>[1.2, 29.7] |
| Primacy<br>37.0<br>[6.0, 100.0] | Housing/Social Security<br>10.0<br>[0.6, 52.7] |
| Primacy<br>38.1<br>[0.0, 100.0] | Economic Services<br>24.5<br>[3.9, 57.2] |
| | Other<br>32.4<br>[5.5, 69.6] |

TABLE 1 (continued)

---

Total Expenditures (percent of GNP)
26.6
[3.2, 78.4]

Debt

External Debt as a Percentage
of GNP (1982)
39.5
[1.0, 146.5]

---

Note:  Number under each indicator is the mean; numbers in brackets are
ranges.  Excludes high-income oil exporting countries.

Source:  World Bank (1984).

and ranges for these variables are presented for a sample of
developing countries with per capita incomes below $6,840 (U.S.)
in 1982.

Table 2 confirms a long-familiar central tendency in the data
(Mills and Becker, 1983).  There is a positive and curvilinear
association between the proportion of the population that is
urban and income per capita.  Holding income per capita constant,
population growth rates display a mild positive relationship to
proportions urban, as do density levels.  By far the bulk of the
variation in the dependent variable, however, is accounted for
by income per capita.

A number of the models to be reviewed below suggest that LDC
urbanization levels are likely to be strongly influenced by
particular distortions in prices.  Agarwala (1983) has assembled
qualitative evidence on the degree of price distortion within
various sectors for a sample of 31 developing countries.  In
columns 2 and 3 of Table 2, 1982 proportions urban have been
regressed on the full list of his indexes.  DEX is a dummy variable that takes on the value 1 for countries with highly overvalued exchange rates; DPM represents the degree of effective
protection of manufacturing; DAG is the degree of underpricing
in agriculture; DRW is an indicator of wage distortions in manufacturing; DRI indexes countries with low (indeed, negative)
values for real rates of interest; DPT indicates underpricing of
electricity; and DIN is a qualitative index for inflation levels.
These variables are meant to represent the levels of price distortions during the 1970s.

Columns 2 and 3 of Table 2 show that the associations between
these qualitative indexes of market imperfections and the level
of urbanization are mixed.  Results are presented both with and
without controls for income per capita; in either case, only DEX,
the measure of overvaluation in exchange rates, seems to be consistently associated with urbanization.  Note that, in the sample
of 31 countries for which the Agarwala measures are available,

TABLE 2  Proportion Urban, Income per Capita, and Price
Distortions (dependent variable: $U_{1982}$)

| Variable | Regression Specification | | |
| --- | --- | --- | --- |
| | (1) | (2) | (3) |
| Constant | 2.71 | -6.98 | 44.07 |
| (t) | (.48) | (.48) | (2.42) |
| $Y_{1982}$ | $3.1 \times 10^{-2}$ | $4.8 \times 10^{-2}$ | |
| | (10.55) | (3.30) | |
| $Y^2{}_{1982}$ | $-3.9 \times 10^{-6}$ | $-8.7 \times 10^{-6}$ | |
| | (7.31) | (1.69) | |
| Density | 6.47 | -7.41 | -21.75 |
| | (2.50) | (.36) | (.69) |
| Population Growth Rate, 1960-70 | 3.65 | 3.29 | -.29 |
| | (1.76) | (.71) | (.04) |
| DEX | | 16.67 | 24.86 |
| | | (1.82) | (1.77) |
| DPM | | 8.87 | -12.78 |
| | | (1.36) | (1.53) |
| DAG | | .05 | -10.02 |
| | | (.01) | (.98) |
| DRW | | 5.69 | 3.24 |
| | | (1.00) | (.36) |
| DRI | | -3.68 | 23.17 |
| | | (.38) | (1.95) |
| DPT | | -5.19 | -13.52 |
| | | (.92) | (1.60) |
| DIN | | 1.87 | -17.30 |
| | | (.17) | (1.16) |
| $R^2$ | .71 | .81 | .47 |
| N | 81 | 31 | 31 |

the link between population growth rates and urbanization is very
weak.

  Table 3 provides summary regressions on the level of primacy.
Much of the cross-national variation in primacy is left unexplained by our descriptive regressions; there is little here
to suggest that either population growth or price distortions

TABLE 3  Primacy, Income per Capita, and Price Distortions
(dependent variable:  primacy, 1982)

| Variable | Regression Specification | | |
|---|---|---|---|
| | (1) | (2) | (3) |
| Constant | 42.96 | 21.87 | 32.17 |
| (t) | (5.79) | (1.05) | (1.93) |
| $Y_{1982}$ | $1.3 \times 10^{-3}$ | $5.35 \times 10^{-3}$ | |
| | (.75) | (.83) | |
| Density | 11.68 | -25.86 | -27.27 |
| | (3.51) | (.90) | (.95) |
| Population Growth | -1.99 | 2.50 | .95 |
| Rate 1960-70 | (.72) | (.38) | (.15) |
| Area | $-4.1 \times 10^{-3}$ | $-3.8 \times 10^{-3}$ | $-3.6 \times 10^{-3}$ |
| | (3.41) | (1.65) | (1.55) |
| DEX | | -4.83 | -2.43 |
| | | (.37) | (.19) |
| DPM | | 6.86 | 2.82 |
| | | (.76) | (.37) |
| DAG | | 2.87 | .08 |
| | | (.29) | (.01) |
| DRW | | 1.60 | 1.03 |
| | | (.19) | (.13) |
| DRI | | -1.57 | 4.71 |
| | | (.11) | (.41) |
| DPT | | 10.16 | 8.86 |
| | | (1.29) | (1.16) |
| DIN | | 5.85 | .75 |
| | | (.39) | (.06) |
| $R^2$ | .34 | .25 | .23 |
| N | 81 | 31 | 31 |

play a significant role.  Table 4 presents similar findings on
the composition of the labor force.  Again an association between
income per capita and the percentage of the labor force in industry and services is evident.  Among the price distortion measures, only DEX is statistically significant.

TABLE 4   1980 Labor Force Shares, Income per Capita, and Price Distortions

| Variable | Agriculture | | Industry | | Services | |
|---|---|---|---|---|---|---|
| | (1) | (2) | (3) | (4) | (5) | (6) |
| Constant (t) | 86.74 (15.39) | 76.51 (5.71) | 8.79 (3.35) | 13.30 (1.70) | 4.52 (1.05) | 10.19 (.94) |
| $Y_{1982}$ | $-3.1 \times 10^{-2}$ (10.84) | $-4.0 \times 10^{-2}$ (3.01) | $1.0 \times 10^{-2}$ (7.57) | $.9 \times 10^{-2}$ (1.27) | $2.1 \times 10^{-2}$ (9.53) | $3.1 \times 10^{-2}$ (2.84) |
| $Y^2_{1982}$ | $3.3 \times 10^{-6}$ (6.20) | $7.9 \times 10^{-6}$ (1.66) | $-1.0 \times 10^{-6}$ (3.91) | $-1.1 \times 10^{-6}$ (.42) | $-2.3 \times 10^{-6}$ (5.66) | $-6.8 \times 10^{-6}$ (1.75) |
| Density | -1.78 (.70) | -19.13 (1.02) | 3.96 (3.33) | 9.91 (.95) | 2.26 (1.16) | 9.22 (.61) |
| Population Growth Rate 1960-70 | -1.48 (.72) | 3.72 (.87) | -.60 (.62) | -1.79 (.76) | 2.07 (1.32) | -1.92 (.56) |
| DEX | | -23.32 (2.76) | | 7.97 (1.70) | | 15.35 (2.24) |
| DPM | | -3.96 (.66) | | 3.57 (1.07) | | .39 (.08) |
| DAG | | 9.54 (1.49) | | -1.82 (1.07) | | -7.72 (1.49) |
| DRW | | -3.48 (.66) | | -.32 (.11) | | 3.81 (.89) |
| DRI | | -4.53 (.50) | | -.63 (.13) | | 5.16 (.71) |
| DPT | | 7.43 (1.43) | | -.58 (2.00) | | -1.66 (.40) |
| DIN | | 6.82 (.68) | | -1.00 (.18) | | -5.82 (.72) |
| $R^2$ | .76 | .83 | .71 | .67 | .68 | .77 |
| N | 81 | 31 | 81 | 31 | 81 | 31 |

The regressions in Tables 2 through 4 are meant to be des-criptive rather than definitive. Much more work would be re-quired to determine whether population growth, market imperfec-tions, and the interactions between the two affect urbanization. These regressions simply suggest a line of empirical research that might well be pursued further. The sections that follow focus on particular price rigidities and government policies that, many would argue, have made the task of accommodating LDC urban growth especially difficult.

Consequences of Migration at the Individual Level

Since migration decisions are largely motivated by earnings or
wage differentials (see Yap, 1977 and Todaro, 1980 for a review
of the empirical literature), there would seem to be little
ambiguity about the impact of a move on a migrant's well-being.
Indeed, surveys of urban migrants (Yap, 1977) suggest that most
feel themselves to be better off than in their rural areas of
origin. However, this sanguine conclusion must be tempered in
several respects. Lack of information or misperceptions of urban
labor market opportunities or price levels may lead some
individuals to make biased choices concerning migration. Mobility constraints may then strand migrants who find themselves, ex
post, worse off than they were in rural areas. There is some
evidence, for instance, on the existence of communities of the
poor in some LDC cities in which mean earnings levels fall below
those available in agriculture (House, 1984). Finally, to the
extent that rural-to-urban migration is accompanied by open unemployment, job search spells may be longer than prospective
migrants had anticipated. These points deserve some consideration.
    Yap (1977) gathers evidence from a variety of sources
suggesting that the overwhelming majority of migrants find work
either immediately or within 1 to 3 months of arrival. For
instance, in Tanzania, some 80 percent of adult male migrants
found their first job within 3 months of arrival in an urban
area. Garrison's (1982) results for Mexico City show that while
migrants with less than 1 year of residence earn significantly
less than natives, controlling for age and education, the earnings differentials essentially disappear after that. Indeed,
there is an indication that migrants with more than 10 years of
residence may earn more than natives, holding background factors
constant. Garrison also shows that the proportion of migrants
found in informal-sector occupations (those earning less than
$58 [1970 dollars] per month, or involved in personal services,
construction, or trade) falls fairly steadily with length of
residence. As would be expected, women with primary schooling
or less show the least upward mobility.
    Some degree of caution must be used in interpreting these
figures, however, since they represent the experiences of migrants who choose (or are constrained) to remain. Since return
migrants are selected out, the evident improvements in earnings
with duration may be upwardly biased. In addition, it is difficult to control for the cost of living in urban areas, so that
precise comparisons of migrants' earnings levels with those of
their rural counterparts are difficult to make. Nevertheless,
the weight of the evidence suggests that most individual migrants
find themselves better off in economic terms after moving.

The Impact of Rural-Urban Migration on Urban Labor Markets

Perhaps the most pressing set of issues in the urbanization debate involves the impact of urban labor force growth on the conditions of urban employment. Data bearing directly on the subject are still scarce. However, the existing data suggest that
the impact of labor force growth on earnings and urban unemployment is decidedly mixed. This in itself might be a surprising
finding, given the alarmist view--notions of urbanization
accompanied by explosive increases in open unemployment rates--
that is so often encountered in the development literature.
     Before turning to a discussion of the literature, we might
pause to consider whether the consequences of urban labor force
growth for urban employment conditions depend importantly on the
source of that growth; in other words, does it matter whether
the urban labor force grows through migration or through natural
increase? This is an important question for urban policy and an
issue to which remarkably little attention has been devoted.
     At the very least, one would expect there to be composi-
tional differences between the two streams of urban labor market
entrants: a rural-urban migrant may well have fewer years of
education than his native urban counterpart, and in some instances, the sex composition of the migrant stream may be
different from that of urban native entrants. Moreover, both
the skill and sex composition of the migrant stream can vary
with time as conditions in agriculture change (for instance, the
Sahel drought of the early 1970s may have propelled older, less-
skilled migrants into the cities). These compositional differences may be reflected in urban job search strategies. For
instance, a native urban entrant might be in a better position
than the typical rural-urban migrant to choose open unemployment
as a job search strategy; thus, an increase in the urban labor
force produced by native entrants might increase open unemployment rates by more than would a numerically equivalent increase
in rural-urban migration. Finally, migrant job search strategies
and skill acquisition may well depend on whether moves are expected to be temporary or permanent in nature. These are subtle
issues, and they deserve much more detailed consideration than
they have been given in the literature.
     While the literature on labor transfer and urbanization has
moved on from the early Harris-Todaro (1970) model to more sophisticated approaches to the urban economy, this model still
provides us with a convenient point of departure for the consideration of labor market issues. The model divides the urban
labor force into those who work in modern-sector jobs for a fixed
wage $\bar{w}_m$, institutionally set at above market-clearing levels,
and those who are openly unemployed. Since $\bar{w}_m$ is fixed, so is
the number of modern-sector jobs, $\bar{E}_m$; the urban labor force
$L_u$, however, grows (via migration) until expected modern-sector
earnings equal the level of rural earnings:

$$\bar{w}_m \left( \frac{\bar{E}_m}{L_u(*)} \right) = w_r(*) \ ,$$

where $L_u(*)$ and $w_r(*)$ indicate equilibrium levels for these endogenous variables. This expression can be manipulated to produce an implicit expression for open unemployment rates in urban areas:

$$\frac{L_u(*) - \bar{E}_m}{L_u(*)} = 1 - \frac{w_r(*)}{\bar{w}_m} \ .$$

Evidently, in the transition toward equilibrium, one might expect to see rising levels of open unemployment—and, therefore, lost output—accompanying increases in the size of the urban labor force.

Critics of the Harris-Todaro approach (see especially Fields, 1975; Steel, 1978; and Harris and Sabot, 1982) have pointed out that the equilibrium open unemployment rates implied by this model are unrealistically high and have argued (Berry and Sabot, 1984; Mazumdar, 1976) for a reconsideration of the role of unemployment in LDC urban economies. As Mazumdar and Berry have made clear, open unemployment is characteristic of the young and of school leavers, particularly at the secondary level. The incidence of open employment by age and educational attainment suggests that it may be connected to job search during particular life-cycle stages for those individuals whose families are wealthy enough to provide them with support. Open unemployment rates may therefore be imperfect measures of welfare: unemployment can arise from rational job search behavior and may be relatively transitory when viewed from a life-cycle perspective, while its private costs would seem to be borne largely by better-educated individuals and wealthier families.

On the other hand, even if the revisionist view of open unemployment is correct, any exogenous forces or market imperfections that lengthen the periods of search involved in matching individuals to jobs generate output losses for the economy as a whole. One such imperfection, which many have argued is particularly apparent in sub-Saharan Africa, involves the search for secure, public-sector jobs. The predominance of the public sector in modern-sector hiring is an issue which we return to below. The point to be made here is simply that if public-sector pay scales are unresponsive to market conditions, their rigidity will result in real welfare costs, partly evident in the duration of unemployment spells and the overall level of unemployment.

A second point of departure from the early Harris-Todaro view concerns the impact of urbanization on employment conditions outside the modern sector. Fields (1975), using a simple modern sector-informal sector dichotomy, argues that migration and job-search strategies might be considered jointly. Individuals may choose to search for modern-sector jobs full time--that is, while remaining openly unemployed--or to take employment in the informal sector and continue to search, intermittently or with lower efficiency, for modern-sector work. If there are $\bar{E}_m$ modern-sector jobs (each paying $\bar{w}_m$), $U_m$ full-time (unemployed) searchers, and I part-time employed searchers working in the informal sector, then the total number of "searcher equivalents" for modern sector jobs is

$$J_m = U_m + hI ,$$

where $h < 1$ is a parameter reflecting the lower efficiency of job search among informal-sector workers. Field's formulation leads to two equilibrium conditions. The first is reminiscent of Harris-Todaro; for full-time searchers, the expected modern-sector wage must equal rural earnings:

$$\bar{w}_m \left( \frac{\bar{E}_m}{J_m(*) + \bar{E}_m} \right) = w_r(*) ,$$

where, as before, $J_m(*)$ and $w_r(*)$ are equilibrium values. Second, the expected payoff from being unemployed and searching full-time must just equal, in equilibrium, the expected payoff to searching part-time. For part-time searchers, expected earnings are a weighted average of modern-sector wages $\bar{w}_m$ (times the likelihood of landing such a job) and earnings in informal employment $w_I$. The expected payoff to part-time search is

$$\bar{w}_m \cdot h \cdot \frac{\bar{E}_m}{J_m(*) + \bar{E}_m} + w_I(*) \left[ 1-h \cdot \frac{\bar{E}_m}{J_m(*) + \bar{E}_m} \right] .$$

Therefore, when both location and search strategies are in equilibrium, we have a condition that links urban modern-sector earnings, earnings in the informal sector, and rural earnings:

$$\bar{w}_m \cdot h \cdot \frac{\bar{E}_m}{J_m(*) + \bar{E}_m} + w_I(*) \left[ 1-h \cdot \frac{\bar{E}_m}{J_m(*) + \bar{E}_m} \right] = w_r(*) .$$

This last condition is perhaps the most useful one in relating levels of urbanization to earnings in the informal sector. It suggests that, in the transition to equilibrium--that is, as $J_m$ rises and individuals allocate themselves between unemployment and informal-sector employment--earnings levels outside the modern sector will decline. The equilibrium prediction, in fact, is that earnings levels in the urban informal sector should lie below those available in agriculture.

Neither the Fields (1975) nor the Harris-Todaro model addresses population growth directly. Todaro (1969), however, presents a simple dynamic version of his model in which the rate of urban natural increase and the rate of rural-to-urban migration are considered in conjunction with the rate of growth of modern-sector employment. Holding urban modern-sector wages and rural wages constant, the stable, long-run urban unemployment rate is positively related to both urban natural increase and the rate of inmigration; as one would expect, the higher the rate of job creation in the modern sector, the lower the long-run unemployment rate.

Let us now confront these theories with the data. Sabolo (1975) has summarized the trends in the sectoral composition of labor and in open unemployment rates that are coincident with LDC urbanization and urban growth and has projected these to 1990. He divides the labor force into agricultural occupations; a sector comprising manufacturing, mining, energy, and transport; a tertiary sector including services, banking, and financial-sector employment; and a final category representing employment in construction, commerce, and "other" activities. Unfortunately, neither employment nor (apparently) unemployment figures could be broken down by rural/urban location or by sex. The International Labour Organisation (ILO) figures document labor transfer out of agriculture and into the secondary and tertiary sectors, but do not suggest an explosive increase in "informal-sector" service employment (included in the "other" category); both categories of service employment, in fact, appear to rise together. This is just what one finds in the U.N. (1980: Chapter 5) detailed breakdown of trends in urban service employment. Moreover, the findings are consistent with results from other studies (see Mazumdar, 1976) on the employment found by rural-urban migrants. Migrants do not appear to be disproportionately located in informal-sector service jobs or in services relative to manufacturing. While much more detailed research on the question is in order, these aggregate data suggest a gradual transition in the nature of LDC urban service employment; they certainly do not reinforce the view that urbanization in developing countries has been accompanied by enormous increases in low-skill service employment.

The findings on open unemployment rates are equally mixed. Sabolo's data do not show large or systematic increases in LDC unemployment rates over the 1960-73 period. Gregory's (1980) very careful assessment of unemployment trends by country reveals generally erratic changes in unemployment rates and little evidence for clear positive or negative time trends in the data.

Data on the trends in earnings that have accompanied urbanization are exceedingly scarce. One interesting study for the Sahel (Berg, 1976) gives us an idea of the levels of earnings prevalent in the Sahelian countries during a period that covers the Sahelian drought of the early 1970s and the cityward migration that followed. Berg's figures suggest a general decline in the real earnings levels of urban unskilled wage earners over the period in some countries, but not in all of them; the reported

declines seem to have been accentuated during the drought years.
It may be, as suggested above, that an episode such as a severe
drought alters the composition of the rural-urban migrant stream
to include more unskilled migrants than would usually be the
case.

The impression one draws from these data on unemployment and
earnings is that, despite historically unprecedented rates of
urban natural increase and significant inmigration, the conditions of urban employment cannot be shown to have systematically
deteriorated. The picture is, instead, quite mixed. What
factors can account for this? Squire (1981) notes that rates of
growth in modern-sector (manufacturing) employment in LDC economies have often been impressive; granted, that growth may often
occur from a rather small base. As Todaro (1969) points out,
such high rates of growth would tend to reduce urban unemployment
rates even if labor market imperfections remained unaddressed.
Could the growth in the manufacturing sector have spill-over
benefits for the remainder of the urban economy? Here we must
consider both product market linkages between formal- and
informal-sector firms, and issues concerning the demands for
informal-sector products arising from the incomes of modern-
sector employees. Is it possible as well that there is less wage
rigidity in the urban modern sector than many had thought? Let
us consider the last of these issues first.

At one time, it was common to see minimum-wage legislation
identified as the institutional factor that kept modern-sector
wage levels rigid and unresponsive to market forces. Indeed, as
Watanabe (1976) has argued, in the immediate post independence
period in Africa, minimum wage floors were set relatively high
in comparison to average nonagricultural wage levels and may then
have had some influence on open unemployment rates. However, as
Watanabe goes on to show, real minimum wage levels have declined
in most of sub-Saharan Africa since the early post independence
days, and in any case, the coverage and enforcement of the leg-
islated minimum have always been limited. In part this is because governments have grown reluctant to pressure employers to
take actions that might result in cuts in employment.

Trade union pressures have also been identified as a major
source of labor market imperfections, but it is unlikely that
trade union pressures, by themselves, can account for wage
rigidity. In Kenya, for instance, union rights to strike--
certainly the central weapon in direct bargaining with an
employer--have been severely circumscribed over the post
independence period; by the early 1970s, union influences on
wage setting had become largely political pressures, exercised
through government wage councils. House and Rempel (1976) argue
that, within Kenyan manufacturing, the extent of industry unionization has had rather little to do with recent wage bargains,
once firm size and product market concentration are taken into
account.

It has long been apparent that large mining and manufacturing
firms in developing countries have been willing to pay skilled
workers wages that seem to exceed the going rate for those

workers.  Yet high wages for skilled workers are, in part, an
endogenous mechanism for recouping firm-specific training costs.
It seems clear that such wage premia exist (see Fry, 1979, for
an examination of Southern Africa); what is unclear is whether
we should think of wage differentials arising from this source
as reflecting labor market imperfections.  The wage gap necessary
to persuade skilled workers to remain with a firm must surely be
influenced by market conditions and the alternative opportunities
available to those workers.  It is not the existence of a wage
premium that matters in this context, but rather its rigidity.

Several of these arguments point directly or indirectly at
government pay scales and wage-setting mechanisms as perhaps the
key distortionary elements in the modern-sector labor market.
Squire (1981) suggests that wage levels of premiums that represent economically rational efforts to reduce labor turnover in
some private-sector firms may percolate through other sectors of
the economy if they are supported by wage increases for civil
servants.  The influence of public-sector pay scales and the
security of tenure available in some public-sector positions on
modern-sector earnings levels and the duration of unemployment
spells is clearly a subject worthy of further investigation.

To what extent might imperfections in the modern-sector
labor market lead to a spill-over of labor into the informal
sector and a depression of informal-sector incomes?  The Kelley
and Williamson simulations (1984: Chapter 4) suggest that spill-
over effects are important in determining both low-skill service
employment and incomes.  However, recent investigations into the
characteristics of informal-sector occupations imply that there
are product market links between the two sectors that deserve
consideration, and that the informal sector, far from being a
repository for very low-income occupations, may serve in some
circumstances as a training ground for formal-sector employment.

As research on the characteristics of informal-sector employment has accumulated, it has become clear that the term
"informal sector" is inadequate to describe the heterogeneity in
earnings and occupations held outside the identifiably "modern"
sector.  Both Mazumdar (1976) and Squire (1981) note that, while
there is a central tendency for the urban self-employed to earn
less than, say, urban employees in large-scale firms, the two
distributions overlap to a surprising degree.  Not all occupations within the informal sector are subject to free entry
(Sinclair, 1978; House, 1984), so that, given licensing and
other barriers to entry, there are economic rents available in
some occupations and returns to entrepreneurship in others.  In
reviewing a number of ILO studies on the urban informal sector
in Africa, Sethuraman (1977) notes that, for relatively young
job seekers, informal-sector employment may involve periods of
apprenticeship that eventually lead to self-employment in craft
occupations or in other relatively skilled services.

Sethuraman (1977:347) presents the picture of an African
informal sector that is relatively isolated from modern-sector
firms:

In Kumasi . . . direct linkages with formal sector firms
are surprisingly limited, only about 10 per cent of inter
mediate inputs being bought directly from the modern sector.
However, there is a significant strengthening of such linkages as the size of the informal sector firm increases. In
these cases backward linkages with other informal sector
enterprises are also much stronger. . . . [A]t least in the
case of Ghana, linkages take the form of subcontracting to
other informal sector enterprises. For example, certain
aspects of automobile repair, metalwork, and shoe manufacture are subcontracted to more specialized enterprises
with the necessary equipment or skills. This implies a more
efficient use of available capital and other resources. It
also partly explains why the informal sector enterprises
cluster together. Backward linkages with rural areas are
virtually non-existent. Forward linkages are mainly with
individuals, households, and other informal sector enterprises and only to a small extent with the formal sector.
The reasons for this are to be found partly in the pattern
of goods and services produced (mostly consumer oriented)
and partly in the inability of informal sector enterprises
to reach formal sector customers or to turn out high-quality
products.

Note that Sethuraman suggests that agglomeration economies may
be important for enterprises within the informal sector.

House (1984) has investigated the pattern of earnings within
Nairobi's informal sector, focusing in particular on the incomes
accruing to proprietors of informal-sector establishments and the
wage earnings of the sector's employees and apprentices. There
is a surprising degree of heterogeneity in the incomes of proprietors or the self-employed. The mean incomes in furniture and
metal goods manufacture, restaurants, retailing, and vehicle
repair are high relative to those available in other occupations;
this suggests a further division of the informal sector into an
intermediate category and a "residual," very low-income service
sector. House estimates that in his sample (which underrepre-
sents the lowest-income group--hawkers, itinerant traders, and
the like), some 42 percent of proprietor incomes fall below the
minimum wage in the formal sector.

Among the factors that influence proprietor incomes in the
informal sector, one in particular stands out: firms that are
the recipients of subcontracting arrangements--some 23 percent
of the entire sample--generate higher incomes for their proprietors. Most such contracts (about 75 percent) were for supplying
inputs or services to the modern sector; the establishments with
subcontracts were, in general, involved in furniture and metal
goods manufacturing and in vehicle repair.

Proprietors of informal-sector enterprises were not, in
general, recent migrants to Nairobi. Their employees, on the
other hand, tended to be both younger and more recently arrived.
About 50 percent were regular workers, many of whom were family
members; 12 percent were intermittent or casual laborers; and

most of the remaining workers were apprentices, of whom nearly
40 percent received no cash earnings.  Although there are difficulties involved in assessing living standards on the basis of
cash earnings alone when family members and apprentices are concerned, House argues that substantial proportions of informal-
sector employees earn less than the average incomes available in
the rural sector, and that something like 18 percent of informal-
sector proprietors or the self-employed have earnings that fall
below those in agriculture.

The perspective put forward by Fields (1975) and Steel (1978)
would therefore seem to be pertinent to the LDC urban economy.
There is a distinct subsector of the urban economy in which, at
least for the Kenyan case, earnings appear to fall below the mean
incomes available in agriculture.  Some portion of the very low
earners are engaged in job search or in skill acquisition, but
those who remain may form, as House suggests, a community of the
poor.

A comprehensive assessment of the influence of rural-to-urban
migration on urban earnings levels, the sectoral composition of
urban labor, and urban unemployment levels is not yet possible.
Greenwood's (1978) econometric analysis of the impacts of migration at the state level in Mexico is instructive along these
lines; it suggests that if there is a sector within the urban
area that produces consumer-oriented nontradables--much like
Sethuraman's depiction of the African informal sector--then an
influx of population may work to stimulate earnings in the urban
economy as a whole.  Part of the stimulus to informal-sector
earnings would arise from the consumption demands of modern-
sector employees.  However, it is not clear whether or to what
extent informal-sector growth could arise from agglomeration
economies within the informal sector and therefore, in some
sense, be self-generating.

In short, the impact of growth in the urban labor force on
urban employment--whether that growth arises from natural increase or labor transfer--depends on market imperfections,
public-sector policies, the density of product market links between sectors, and the nature of final demands for those goods
and services produced in the informal sector.  It is exceedingly
difficult to isolate the separate influence of the rate of labor
force growth on employment, net of such institutional factors.
We must still presume that very rapid labor force growth cannot
improve conditions in the urban labor market, other things held
constant; unfortunately, the body of evidence on which this
presumption rests remains very slim.

The Impact of Rural Outmigration on Rural Welfare

Having examined the consequences of labor transfer for urban
areas, the receiving regions, one task that remains is to document the impact of outmigration on the sending regions, which
are largely rural.  As important as this issue is, there is still
so little hard information on the rural impact of outmigration

that any definitive statements would be premature at this point.
On the one hand, predictions from simple two-sector models of the
type reviewed earlier suggest that labor transfer out of agriculture should be accompanied by increases in the returns to labor
in agriculture, leaving (presumably) the bulk of the remaining
rural population better off. This position receives some support
in the econometric work of Johnson (1960) and Gardner (1974) on
U.S. farm outmigration. Yet even in these studies, as well as
in Greenwood's (1978) analysis of Mexican internal migration,
there is a recognition that service-related incomes in the rural
sector may decline if there is a loss of population from the
sector; the arrival of population in urban areas may, in turn,
stimulate urban services there and exert a disequalizing influence on the urban-rural income gap. Many observers have pointed
to particular depopulated rural villages, apparently stagnant,
in which the loss of the young and better-educated is keenly
felt. There is a suggestion here of negative externalities
accompanying labor transfer; perhaps, for many villages, any
return flows of remittances prove to be inadequate compensation.

Schuh (1982) reviews the theoretical literature on factor
emigration and provides some empirical illustrations drawn mainly
from U.S. agriculture. His arguments can be summarized briefly
here. The theoretical results turn on two issues: whether agricultural prices should be treated as endogenous or taken as given
(set in world markets); and whether outmigrants take capital with
them, either in the sense of embodied, human capital or in the
removal of (mobile) physical capital.

Given the case in which agricultural prices are determined by
the forces of supply and demand within an LDC economy, and both
labor and capital are mobile, one could argue that labor transfer
out of agriculture would raise both agricultural wage rates and
incomes. A reduction in labor supply would restrict agricultural
output, drive up agricultural prices, and, if the elasticities
of demand for agricultural goods are relatively insensitive to
price, increase agricultural incomes. However, as Schuh (1982:
168) notes:

> . . . abstracting from terms-of-trade effects, the presump-
> tive consequence of more than marginal out-migration is that
> those left behind would be worse off, although the distribu-
> tion of income would improve in the sense that labor's share
> would increase and the returns to labor would rise.

The ambiguous effects of labor transfer on rural incomes suggest
that empirical work on the subject is required to assess the full
impact of outmigration. In an ideal study, data on migration
flows by age, sex, and educational attainment would be linked to
subsequent levels of the rural wage and farm and nonfarm incomes
in regions of origin.

Only Greenwood (1978) has come close to such an ideal study
using LDC data (see Gardner, 1974 for the U.S.), although his
data do not permit a separation of urban from rural income, or
allow rural nonfarm and farm incomes to be distinguished. His

estimates for cross-state migration in Mexico over the 1960-70
period suggest that, in fact, outmigration is not strongly
associated with changes in median earnings levels in the origin
state.  Whether this finding masks effects on wages and other
incomes that work in opposite directions is not clear; neither
is it obvious that such results, drawn from Mexican data, would
necessarily apply elsewhere.

The recent literature on the rural consequences of outmigration contains a growing body of evidence and speculation on
urban-rural remittance flows (see Johnson and Whitelaw, 1974;
Knowles and Anker, 1981).  Both Stark (1976) and Collier and Lal
(1980) have argued that remittances provide a source of capital
to the rural sector that, given the limited penetration of formal
capital markets into rural areas, might not otherwise be available.  These authors go on to suggest that this infusion of funds
leads to increased agricultural investments and a greater willingness to undertake technological change in the agricultural
sector.  In essence, the argument is something like the Lewis
model working partly in reverse: a transfer of labor from rural
to urban areas is accompanied by a flow of capital in the opposite direction, acting to shift the rural demand for labor curve
out over time.

It must be said that the connection between remittance flows
(or the return of "target" migrants, with their accumulated
capital) and investment in agriculture remains a speculative
connection at this point; there is little hard evidence available
beyond impressionistic accounts.  Certainly the survey responses
on the use of remittance funds do not suggest that agricultural
investments are a first priority (Rempel and Lobdell, 1978), although it is not clear whether the availability of remittance
incomes frees other funds for investment purposes.  The "investment" response that appears most often in the surveys has to do
with the use of remittances to finance the education of a
migrant's younger siblings or nephews, that is, with human
capital investments.

Even if remittances do not stimulate rural investment in
agriculture, they may serve to reduce the net variability in
incomes accruing to a rural-based extended family (Stark, 1976).
An extended family receiving remittance income from its migrant
members has at least one source of income that may be more stable
than the incomes available from agriculture.  Remittance transfers could also have an insurance-like function, increasing in
years in which drought or other factors intensify the difficulties in agricultural production.  In either case, employment
conditions in the urban economy may generate spill-over benefits
for families based in the rural sector; remittances may allow
rural-based families to sustain consumption levels in periods in
which agricultural earnings fall.

These arguments, like the ones presented on remittances and
investment, remain speculative; there is little hard evidence to
present.  Nevertheless, they add additional force to an urban
accommodationist argument.  Actions that improve earnings prospects in urban areas may well generate benefits for the rural

sector. If urban earnings improve, the ability of migrants to provide remittances may also improve, and that, at a minimum, might enable such migrants to help sustain consumption levels in their rural families of origin.


POLICY ISSUES

This section reviews some key policy issues related to urbanization in two areas: public-sector investment in urban service delivery, and urban public finance and administration. Broad population distribution policies are discussed in the section that follows.


Public-Sector Investment in Urban Service Delivery

The apprehensions that LDC policy makers clearly feel about urban growth can be traced, at least in part, to the demands such growth can be expected to place on the public sector. The provision of electricity, water supply, waste disposal, transport avenues, and transport modes is crucial to the realization of agglomeration economies in production, and therefore to the economic reason-for-being of urban areas. Such services necessarily involve the public sector, and their provision draws on the funds the public sector is able to mobilize for this purpose. Perhaps the underlying source of policy makers' apprehensions has to do, then, with the institutional constraints limiting the levels of revenue that can currently be generated and managed by the public sector. Revenue instruments and management issues are discussed later; here, we review the literature on urban service delivery, paying special attention to issues of efficient pricing and to options for service provision that may help minimize the strain on public-sector budgets.

Lewis (1977) has argued as follows:

Urbanization is decisive because it is so expensive. . . . The difference turns on infrastructure. Urban housing is much more expensive than rural housing. The proportion of children for whom schooling is provided is always much higher, at the stage where less than 60 percent of children are in school. The town has to mobilize its own hospital service, piped water supplies, bus transportation. . . . It is the fast pace of urbanization that makes a country grow short of capital rather than a dependence on know-how or on managerial expertise.

There would appear to be some support in the aggregate data for Lewis' position. Table 5 shows that the composition of central government expenditures is shifted toward housing and welfare by urbanization, and that changing levels of primacy are associated with increases in the budget share going to education and health. Moreover, Table 6 demonstrates that the ratio of external debt

TABLE 5   Percent Shares of Central Government Expenditures, 1981

| Dependent Variable | Defense | Education | Health | Housing, Welfare | Economic Services | Other |
|---|---|---|---|---|---|---|
| Constant (t) | 22.49 (2.93) | 4.41 (.97) | -2.84 (.82) | 9.77 (1.77) | 25.62 (3.39) | 39.22 (3.74) |
| $Y_{1982}$ | $5.98 \times 10^{-3}$ (2.13) | $.60 \times 10^{-3}$ (.38) | $.66 \times 10^{-3}$ (.55) | $1.05 \times 10^{-3}$ (.54) | $1.55 \times 10^{-3}$ (.57) | $-4.7 \times 10^{-3}$ (1.26) |
| $U_{1982}$ | -.22 (1.67) | -.02 (.24) | .03 (.48) | .27 (2.92) | -.07 (.52) | .06 (.32) |
| Primacy | -.01 (.11) | .12 (2.33) | .11 (2.83) | .07 (1.04) | -.13 (1.38) | -.13 (.94) |
| Density | -1.38 (.23) | .61 (.20) | -1.61 (.69) | -11.55 (2.78) | 4.84 (.85) | 7.33 (.92) |
| Population Growth Rate 1960-70 | -2.00 (.78) | 2.52 (1.74) | 1.63 (1.47) | -5.29 (2.90) | 2.92 (1.16) | .27 (.08) |
| $R^2$ | .13 | .19 | .21 | .54 | .16 | .10 |
| N | 49 | 49 | 49 | 49 | 49 | 49 |

to GNP may be linked to primacy, if not to urbanization as such, suggesting that the costs of financing expenditures in a country's largest city may have something to do with public borrowing.

However, the issues raised by Lewis deserve more detailed attention. We must be careful to distinguish the costs of service provision from the demands for public services that arise naturally with increasing urban incomes; obviously, both cost curves and quantities demanded influence expenditures per capita. In addition, since service quality levels can account for a great deal of variation in average cost curves, we must take account of the range of quality options open to policy makers. Finally, while the "urban bias" discussions often make it seem as though services are provided solely for the benefit of urban consumers, it is important to keep in mind that urban firms use public services as inputs. The provision of water and electricity, in particular, may have direct impacts on production and urban employment.

One of the conclusions to be drawn from the literature is that service quality is an important choice variable from the public sector's point of view, and that it is certainly not efficient to adopt the service standards of Western cities in supplying households and small commercial and industrial users in LDC cities. A second conclusion is that there does not seem to be a compelling justification for government provision of housing construction; there is, for instance, no evidence for economies of scale in construction. However, there remains an important role for governmental action in stimulating private-

TABLE 6   Central Government Expenditures and Public Debt
Relative to GNP

| Variable | Government Expenditures (1981) as a Percentage of GNP | External Public Debt (1982) as a Percentage of GNP |
|---|---|---|
| Constant (t) | 14.92 (2.04) | 13.50 (.96) |
| $Y_{1982}$ | $5.03 \times 10^{-3}$ (2.04) | $-8.20 \times 10^{-3}$ (1.71) |
| $U_{1982}$ | -.07 (.56) | .22 (.91) |
| Primacy | .11 (1.16) | .54 (3.00) |
| Density | -11.16 (1.89) | -11.62 (1.99) |
| Population Growth Rate 1960-70 | 2.07 (.90) | 3.51 (.79) |
| $R^2$ | .16 | .20 |
| N | 60 | 75 |

sector housing investment--through the provision of services (at
appropriate quality levels) to low-income areas, through land
policy and the regularizing of ownership, and through the lifting
of regulations that encumber financial markets and discourage
construction.   The experiences of LDC governments with World
Bank-sponsored  "sites  and  services"  programs  is  instructive
here.   Finally,  in some contrast to Lewis' view, the findings
from World Bank research, particularly in sub-Saharan Africa,
suggest  that  it  is  the  shortage  of  managerial  expertise  and
know-how that makes it particularly difficult to accommodate
urban growth (Cohen, 1982).
     Linn (1983) has assembled a wealth of evidence on the pro-
vision of urban public services and the incidence of slum and
squatter areas.   His figures show that, while service levels are
low  in  the  largest  cities,  services  appear  to  be  even  less
available in secondary cities.   On the basis of detailed "sites
and services" reports from the World Bank's urban-sector work,
it appears that infrastructure provision in African secondary
cities,  in  particular,  often  falls  below  the  minimum  levels
necessary to encourage economies of agglomeration; in many cases,
such cities would appear to be dominated by their large communities of the poor.

Kisumu provides a case in point. This is a relatively rapidly growing secondary city (1974 population of 46,000) located in the midst of Kenya's densely settled, agricultural western region. World Bank estimates are that over 50 percent of households in Kisumu are located in squatter areas (as opposed to roughly a third in Nairobi), and that employment growth in Kisumu has been plagued by severe underinvestment in infrastructure. Yet Kisumu would appear to have potential as an agricultural marketing and services center. Similarly, Francistown, Botswana's second largest city (1975 population 23,000) and the location of earlier (1974) Bank assistance, has roughly 60 percent of its population in squatter settlements, while in Gabarone the figure is closer to 27 percent. The discussion below summarizes some of the general lessons learned in the course of the World Bank-sponsored sites and services programs, with an eye toward the linking of infrastructure policies with employment policies for the urban poor. Six areas are examined--transportation, water supply, sewage disposal, solid waste disposal, electricity, and land policy and housing.


## Transportation

Transportation issues could not be more central in determining whether resources are allocated efficiently within an urban area. A transport system connects one firm to another, thereby affecting the extent to which pecuniary economies are realized. It links workers to firms, influencing both the time and money costs involved in labor force participation. It alters the costs of distributing firm output to local consumers. Finally, a transport system can be the decisive factor in determining whether and to what extent other public services--in particular, water supply and waste disposal--can be provided to certain areas, and in determining the access of both firms and consumers to offsite public services. Transport therefore plays a key role in influencing the allocation of urban resources at a point in time, in providing for the growth of output and employment opportunities over time, and in setting constraints on the optimal pace of urban growth.

Household demand for transport services is a derived demand, based in large part on the location of employment and the housing rent gradient. In general, it appears that the choice of transport mode in trips to and from work is dependent on household income and earnings opportunities. Walking trips are perhaps the only option for the poorest groups in the urban population (Linn, 1983:106). Even in large cities, walking and cycling can account for some 60 percent of all trips (Linn, 1983:91, cites Kinshasa, Dar es Salaam, and Karachi as examples), although as Mills and Song (1979) note for Korea, bus transport becomes an important mode in work trips as incomes improve. One important element of transport costs--time costs--depends both on the choice of mode and on the level of congestion; hence, these costs are at least partly endogenous from the point of view of the urban system as a whole. The time costs involved in work trips may discourage labor force participation among poor and secondary earners and clearly reduce the welfare of the poor.

The demands placed by firms on the urban transport system also deserve consideration. The early Stanford Research Institute (SRI) (1968) study of urban service delivery in India suggests that employment policies directed at the promotion of labor-intensive manufacturing should also take into account the stress on urban roadways and the traffic mix such industries might generate.

What transport policies should LDC governments pursue? There appear to be some expenditure items that can be moved entirely out of public budgets. Linn (1983: 115), drawing on World Bank work in Jakarta, argues that the public sector appears to have no comparative advantage in the provision of bus services. Private bus companies seem to provide efficient service so long as they are not overly regulated, although a role for the public sector might remain in subsidizing private firms to provide service to low-income areas.

There are a number of additional areas involving a regulatory role for the public sector. Congestion costs can be reduced by the use of reserved lanes for buses and bicycles, and by such simple devices as one-way streets and the diversion of through traffic around the already-congested central city areas. The congestion costs generated by private auto traffic--hence due primarily to upper-income groups--can be limited by a system of time-of-day or area license plates or by outright bans on automobiles in certain locations (as in Singapore). The World Bank has estimated that the increase in private automobile ownership has greatly outstripped urban population growth; for Lagos, for instance, the rate of growth for automobile ownership was 15.5 percent over the 1960-70 period, versus 7.9 percent for population growth.

Both efficiency and equity aims can be served by improving the access of the poor to employment. Linn (1983:101) suggests that planners in large cities (where work trips are long) give more attention to pedestrian overpasses, neighborhood walkways, and bicycle paths.

## Water Supply

Water is used both as an input to production (primarily in manufacturing) and for household consumption. With respect to the latter, there are important externalities involved in supplying treated water to households. The World Health Organization suggests that, on a daily basis, some 20-40 liters of treated water per person is necessary to meet minimal sanitation standards and prevent the spread of disease. The proportion of total demand for water that is due to industrial or commercial firms is significant, although the figures cited are certainly imprecise. Warford and Julius (1977) suggest that residential users account for only 40 percent of total consumption in an

East African context, while the World Bank (1980) gives a range
of 40 to 70 percent for residential use.

Household demand for water depends on household income.
Meerman (1979:201-209) shows that, for Malaysia, income effects
are strong at the low end of the income scale and suggests that
household connection fees (often, outside the Malaysian context,
priced well above true connection costs) discourage low-income
consumers. When water is supplied through communal standpipes,
the primary cost from the user's point of view is the opportunity
cost of time spent drawing water or, in cases where access is
difficult, in the fees paid to private water vendors. The time
costs involved in drawing water reduce the hours available for
market work by women and secondary earners; in addition, as noted
in Saunders and Warford (1976:124), water consumption by households that must rely on standpipes often falls well below the
levels necessary to ensure minimum health standards.

Scattered evidence suggests that the average cost curves for
water supply--encompassing production, treatment, storage, and
distribution--are roughly U-shaped with city size, with a great
deal of variation depending on local topography. The greater the
quantity of water required, the more likely that distant, less
accessible sources will be utilized and that pumping will be
required. Such natural limitations surely raise costs as city
size increases. As regards water treatment, it seems clear that
large-scale treatment plants exhibit lower average costs. Perhaps the key issues, however, involve distribution costs. These
depend largely on the length of pipe to be laid (pipe diameter
is less important); the terrain through which pipes are run
(i.e., whether secondary pumping is required to service hilly or
outlying areas); and the number and type of connections, that
is, standpipes or individual household connections.

The level of distribution costs is significantly influenced
by public-sector decisions on service quality levels. Perhaps
the most crucial aspect of investment in urban water supply is
the extent to which low-income residential users can be adequately served by communal standpipes rather than a system of
house connections. Linn (1983:149) points out that the average
cost of an in-house connection is between 75 and 150 percent
higher than that of communal standpipes; moreover, the spacing
between standpipes can have substantial effects on average
costs. Since the savings in distribution costs involved in a
standpipe system are considerable, the position of the World
Bank (1979) is that such systems are to be preferred in
servicing low-income areas; indeed, a standpipe system may be
the only feasible option from a budgetary point of view. The
number and location of standpipes remains important, however,
since standpipes that are too widely spaced may generate time
costs and discourage consumption. Experts at the World Bank
(1980) have also pointed out that in planning to extend service
delivery, it is desirable to plan for an area's ultimate
capacity. It is far more economical to lay one large-diameter
pipe than to lay two smaller pipes sequentially.

Pricing decisions are equally critical in ensuring that water is used efficiently. Metering is usually appropriate for industrial and large-scale commercial consumers; it may not be appropriate for small commercial and domestic users (Saunders and Warford, 1976:123). Standpost systems are, of course, not easily metered, and in general, flat fees for access must be collected from households. Households with connections can be metered (the World Bank has experimented with pricing connection fees at or below cost and with "lifeline" pricing schedules designed to encourage at least minimum consumption); alternatively, charges can be levied on the basis of size of connection, number of household fixtures, and the like (World Bank, 1980:33). Saunders and Warford (1976:176-179) suggest that fees be keyed to the long-run incremental costs of providing service. In general, geographically uniform pricing systems (often the result of a consolidation of regional water boards) do not encourage efficient locational decisions.

## Sewage Disposal

The supply of water and the collection, treatment, and disposal of waste water and sewage are rather closely linked. Not only does the level of water supply influence the need for a disposal system (Rovani [1979] notes that once house connections have been made, the level of daily water flow typically exceeds 100 liters per person and makes a sewage system necessary), but also the nature of the health externalities involved in providing the two services is similar. Moreover, as in the case of water supply, there appear to be a range of low-cost technologies available for sewage systems that have the potential to ease expenditure strains on government budgets.

The major distinction to be drawn here is between waterborne sewage systems--the ones that, in the past, have tended to be favored by LDC urban engineers--and lower-cost technologies, some of which have been developed only recently, often involving separate disposal of excreta and waste water (World Bank, 1980:22). Waterborne systems display collection economies much like those evident in water supply; as regards treatment and disposal, there appear to be technological scale economies in treatment plant size (Linn, 1982:636), although these may not be realized if plants are built sequentially. An obvious but important point concerns water costs: waterborne systems rely on the use of large amounts of water, so that investments in waterborne sewage systems imply some previous commitment to an investment in water supply.

The lower-cost technologies range from pit latrines and communal toilets to vacuum truck cartage, low-cost septic tanks, and sewered aquaprivies. The World Bank's experience with such technologies suggests that they can provide acceptable levels of sanitation within urban areas, at least outside the central business district (CBD); waterborne systems appear to be required only within the CBD (Linn, 1983:149-151; Linn, 1982:636). There are exceptions, of course; in Abidjan, for example, local flooding and seepage conditions make waterborne systems necessary.

The World Bank has identified a series of systems through which developing-country cities might progress, beginning with low-cost technologies outside the CBD and moving gradually toward waterborne systems. One key point is that the low-cost systems typically involve collection of excreta by vacuum trucks; hence, transport avenues giving access to septic tanks or aquaprivies must be provided.

There is virtually no evidence for developing countries on the demands placed on a waste disposal system by industrial and commercial users. Household demands are clearly affected by household income; Meerman (1979) provides some estimates of income effects for flush systems (available to households with piped water) in Malaysia. Charges for waste disposal can be tied to water supply (for metered users) or, as in Malaysia, paid through local tax assessments (Meerman, 1979:211).

## Solid Waste Disposal

The justification for public-sector intervention in the collection of solid waste--beyond providing transport avenues that allow access--appears to be limited. Private-sector collection systems seem to work well in cities like Cairo and Alexandria and can be financed through user charges. On the other hand, there is some justification for a public-sector role in the disposal of solid wastes. Linn (1982:640) suggests that sanitary land fills are often adequate for LDC cities, and that planners should view proposals for capital-intensive composting facilities or incinerators with caution.

## Electricity

Technological economies of scale in electricity generation appear to be substantial, and there is apparently little scope for quality variation or alternative low-cost technologies. On the other hand, as well established as economies of scale are for the U.S. and developed countries, it is somewhat surprising to see that LDC studies do not show similar results (Linn, 1982:639). Electricity costs are sensitive to the distances between demand centers and to the difficulty of the terrain. As a result, average costs for servicing rural or low-density areas are higher than those for urban areas.

A large part of electricity consumption can be traced to industrial and commercial users; in one World Bank sample, these users accounted for over 60 percent of total consumption. Household demands are sensitive to income, as documented in Meerman (1979:188). The most efficient electricity pricing systems, in principle, involve time-of-day or peak-load pricing in addition to regional variation. Unfortunately, sophisticated metering systems are difficult to maintain and are themselves vulnerable

to power outages; therefore, meters are generally economical only
for the larger industrial and commercial users. Residential
users can be charged flat rates and given current-limiting
devices to restrain consumption.


## Land Policy and Housing

The view of the World Bank, developed over the course of a number
of sites and services programs beginning in the early 1970s, is
that the construction of shelters is an activity best carried
out by the private sector, so long as the proper incentives are
in place to encourage housing investment. There are no apparent
economies of scale in construction, and public housing projects
have tended to set quality standards that put the units out of
reach of most of the urban poor. Key incentives include the
availability of services, as discussed above, and, perhaps most
important, security of tenure or land ownership. The dilemma in
housing policy, then, is how best to encourage private investment
in housing when significant portions of the low-income population are illegal squatters or are renting from owners who have
divided lots in violation of zoning laws.

Several conversion schemes have been explored during the
World Bank's sites and services and slum-upgrading programs.
Regularization of ownership rights is perhaps easiest when
squatters occupy publicly owned land; in such cases, ownership
can be granted in return for a payment, as in the World Bank's
Cairo project. Squatters on private land present more difficult
problems. Here the conversion costs are both political and economic; they include meeting owners' objections to public acquisition or expropriation, as well as the financial costs of acquisition. Strain on budgetary resources is lessened if payments
are required of the new owners and if laws permit the public
sector to expropriate land.

Ownership gives a low-income household a foothold in capital
markets, since land can be used as collateral for construction
loans. There is some evidence that public-sector loans for
building materials can encourage investment among middle- and
higher-income groups, and that the lifting of mortgage rate
ceilings and rent control can help the poor by stimulating
overall housing construction.

A persistent difficulty involved in selecting sites to be
upgraded or serviced involves matching locations to employment
opportunities. The importance of judicious choices here was
brought home in one of the earliest sites and services projects--
in Pikine, located outside Dakar. The primary difficulty with
Pikine has been that it is too far from the bulk of employment
opportunities open to the poor in Dakar. The hope was that,
despite the geographic distance involved, the low-income population might find various forms of low-cost transport to and
from work; however, such transport services have never fully
materialized.

In designing policies that cut across various infrastructure sectors, a general principle behind the World Bank's programs has been to employ user charges whenever feasible and to link these as closely as possible to the long-run marginal costs of service provision.  In part, the World Bank's emphasis has been meant to develop local public finance and administration capacities; the issues here are discussed in the next section.  A very real difficulty in applying marginal cost pricing in a sites and services or slum-upgrading program, however, is that very often it is only the poor or project participants who are paying anything close to marginal costs.  Upper-income groups in African cities, for instance, can rely on the long tradition of heavily subsidized public service provision.  The inequities are, of course, obvious to lower-income project participants, and are an important source of tension in efforts to rationalize prices and move public service pricing policies toward more efficient levels.

## Urban Public Finance and Administration

We have already touched on a number of issues related to cost recovery and appropriate pricing schemes for public service delivery.  The intention here is twofold:  to discuss briefly some of the more general revenue instruments available to the public sector; and then to summarize, following Cohen (1982), several of the political and institutional constraints that in Africa and elsewhere have inhibited revenue raising, as well as the implementation of urban infrastructure investments and integrated employment-service provision policies.
An essentially universal aspect of urbanization is that sites near the city center and along transport routes are bid up in value as a city grows.  If urbanization requires substantial investments in infrastructure, it is natural to ask why such expenditures should not be financed out of revenues drawn from property or site taxation.
It is generally agreed (Bahl et al., 1983) that property and land value taxes are underutilized in developing countries, and that, even where such taxes are in place, revenues have not kept pace with growth in the potential urban tax base.  Assessment practices are clearly inadequate in many developing-country cities, partly because of a shortage of trained assessors; difficulties involved in collection; and, in some cases, taxpayer resistance.  Inflation transforms an already difficult assessment task into one that is exceedingly difficult to carry out efficiently or equitably.  Shoup (1979) has identified some additional political considerations that may make the administration of such taxes difficult.  Relatively little commercial real estate in urban areas is owned by foreign firms or large domestic corporations, each of which might be taxed at low political cost.  Instead, one observes that in many LDC cities, it is the important government officials, their families, and other elites who are the major property owners.  For obvious political reasons,

their assets may be nontaxable.  Unfortunately, there is often
very little in the way of middle-class housing or land ownership
to draw upon as an alternate source of tax revenue; as Shoup
(1979:273) puts it, there is a gulf between the "politically
nontaxable mansions and luxury apartments in high-rise structures, on the one hand, and the shanties of the poor that are
not worth trying to tax, on the other."
     Bahl et al. (1983) argue that, for the near term at least,
property taxation cannot be relied upon to produce major new
infusions of revenue.  They suggest that there is at least one
new revenue source, however, that has good potential:  automobile
taxation.  On both revenue-raising and efficiency grounds, a set
of taxes directed at automobile ownership, use, and fuel consumption makes good sense; the equity dimension adds additional force
to the argument.  If retail fuel outlets are government run, as
they very often are, the administrative difficulties involved in
fuel taxation are minimal.
     Perhaps the most vexing long-term problem in urban public
finance and administration, touching on both the revenue side of
urban public finance and the implementation of urban projects
and investment strategies, is the shortage of skilled public-
sector personnel (Cohen, 1982).  While local administrative
capacities are certainly underdeveloped across LDCs, particular
weaknesses are evident in the francophone nations of sub-Saharan
Africa.  For instance, both francophone and anglophone countries
inherited, upon independence, housing authorities that had primarily served the housing needs of the upper-income population
and foreign nationals; similarly, both francophone and anglophone
nations moved, during the 1960s, to replace or supplement these
inherited housing authorities with new bureaucratic structures
devoted to the construction of "low-cost" housing (Cohen, 1982).
The differences between the two lay primarily in the extent of
African involvement--technical staffs and municipal councils--in
the design and execution of housing programs.  As Cohen (1982:30)
notes, "The advantage of the anglophone experience . . . has been
that despite the relatively small number of units built, . . . a
larger pool of trained, experienced local personnel was created."
These early post independence characteristics are still in
evidence (Cohen, 1982:30):

     The anglophone countries have been much more able to
     design and implement projects for low-income households.
     Anglophone institutions appear better staffed with higher
     levels of local competence than their francophone counter-
     parts.  There also appears to be a greater flexibility on
     questions such as infrastructure standards.  The extreme
     centralization of urban policy institutions in francophone
     Africa hinders the development of local responsibility, with
     the result that small issues are elevated to the ministerial
     level much more quickly . . . .

Although many of the sites and services projects have involved
the training of local personnel and efforts to strengthen local

housing authorities, it is not yet clear whether local administrators can carry the effort through as housing and infrastructure programs move beyond the pilot stage.

BROAD POPULATION DISTRIBUTION POLICIES

The arguments of the two preceding sections can be briefly summarized. If urban population growth is to be accommodated, the
areas to which policy makers should turn their attention relate
to the proper division of the public-sector role into service
provision and regulation; efficient pricing; the development of
more flexible, feasible revenue instruments; and the training of
public-sector personnel. The aim of a redirected set of policies
would be to foster agglomeration economies in production, to
arrange service provision so as to reduce the costs of labor
market participation, and to provide services at quality levels
that would take health externalities into account. The sources
of urban population growth--that is, migration and natural
increase--become important in decisions on the balance of
resources to be given to, say, sites and services programs for
new arrivals relative to slum upgrading and in plans for an
efficient progression of service-delivery levels. An explicit
role for population policy would involve reducing urban rates of
natural increase.
     This general approach leaves open the question of whether
the accommodation of urban growth is, in fact, desirable. After
all, as Simmons (1981) and Laquian (1981) have noted, initial
LDC policy responses to the urban growth experienced in the 1960s
tended to involve constraints on population movements and migration disincentives. Whether or not such policies were well
thought through, their popularity suggests that LDC urban policy
makers were--and probably remain--largely unconvinced about the
wisdom (or feasibility) of accommodation. In particular
(Laquian, 1981:101),

> [policies often] took the form of resettling people to rural
> areas or urban peripheries, demolition of shanty towns, cur-
> tailment of services to slum/squatter communities, exclusion
> of migrants from large cities and the enactment of zoning
> codes, minimum housing standards and health regulations that
> sought to protect other city-dwellers from problems created
> by migrants. . . . Planners and administrators thought (and
> hoped) that the "mushrooming" of slum/squatter communities
> would be a temporary phenomenon. They were, therefore,
> reluctant to extend services to those areas.

It is likely that such "closed-city" policies have reflected justifiable fears about the adjustment costs involved in accommodating urban growth. Even if policy makers feel driven to such
extremes, however, there remains the question of whether antiaccommodationist policies can be expected to work. A review of
experiences in a number of LDCs suggests that control-oriented

policies are exceedingly difficult to enforce and require the expenditure of political capital, as well as economic resources.

The examples of Manila and Jakarta are instructive here. In Manila, beginning in 1963, migrants and commuters were required to pay a large fee to enter their children in the school system, while native residents were offered free schooling. The result of this disincentive program was to create a flourishing market in fictitious residence certificates and sworn affidavits, while rural migration to Manila continued unabated. In Jakarta, a similar scheme was put forward in 1970, in which migrants who were out of work 6 months after their arrival were trucked back to their villages of origin. Again, the immediate effect of the policy was to encourage petty corruption and trafficking in identity cards; moreover, most violators apparently returned to Jakarta rather quickly. In the late 1970s, antiaccommodationist policies in Jakarta began to focus on restricting the employment options typically open to new migrants--taxi (betjak) driving, sidewalk vending, scavenging, and the like. Simmons (1981:91) suggests that such employment-based policies may well have deflected migrants elsewhere, but at some cost to the employment opportunities available to the urban poor.

Clearly a regulatory, constraint-based, antiaccommodationist approach can have an impact, but only if it is accompanied by the political will necessary for enforcement. Certainly in South Africa, a tight system of controls on black labor has succeeded in relocating the poor and exporting urban squalor outside city boundaries (Simmons, 1981:91). The system of direct regulations on urbanization pursued in China has also had a measurable effect. However, these are extreme examples; in few other developing countries can such a system of constraints and checks on movement be kept in place.

At best, antiaccommodationist measures of this sort enable municipal governments to slow the urban growth that results from inmigration; they are not effective against high rates of urban natural increase and certainly do not address the underlying issues of employment, public-service delivery, and urban housing. Therefore, an antiaccommodationist stance is one that is not easily maintained over the long term.

There is continuing interest within the policy community in measures that might redirect population to smaller cities. Of course, inherent in any such policy is some notion of what an optimal city size distribution might be. Since decentralization measures typically involve the promotion of employment opportunities outside the largest cities, such policies are apt to be costly and are unlikely to effect large changes in patterns of urban growth over the near term. Therefore, policy makers must be willing to adhere to a particular view of an optimal city size distribution, and to divert resources toward such a goal in the face of what is likely to be slow progress. What, then, is the evidence on the goal itself--the most appropriate distribution of city sizes for a given setting?

While there are certainly empirical regularities in city size distributions across countries, this in itself suggests

little about the optimal pattern to be pursued for any given
LDC. However, the theoretical literature (see Henderson, in
this volume) on localization and urban economies in industry
provides some more specific guidance. The notion that localization economies are exhausted at different points for different
industries suggests that firms in an industry in which localization economies are exhausted only at high levels of industry
employment have an incentive to cluster together and form the
core of the largest cities in the urban hierarchy. Firms in an
industry in which localization economies are quickly exhausted,
on the other hand, have, in the abstract, no particular incentive to form large clusters and might well be found primarily in
smaller cities. In addition, industries that exhibit strong
economies of urbanization, but rather weak localization economies, have an incentive to locate in larger cities. Thus the
concept of localization economies provides one rationale for the
existence of an urban hierarchy and suggests that there may be
limits on the extent to which policy measures can decentralize
certain types of industries. Overlaid on the general pattern
produced by localization and urbanization economies in industry
is the location of "footloose industries" and services.

These incentives arising from localization and urbanization
economies must be balanced against several factors that may exert
equally strong influences on firm behavior: the transport costs
involved in the supply of raw materials and primary inputs and
in shipping final product; land rents and wage levels, which
theory and empirical evidence suggest will tend to decline
outside large urban centers; and, particularly in economies in
which government interventions are pervasive, access to public-
sector decision makers.

Economic theory, therefore, cannot provide a clear statement
about optimal city size distribution. A number of writers have
argued that in the early stages of development, one might expect
to see high levels of primacy. Hamer (1984:13-14) puts the case
well:

> At low levels of income, the development of manufacturing
> activity is likely to be concentrated in relatively few urban
> centers, except for the very simplest artisan and food pro-
> cessing activities. Those urban centers will have some priv-
> ileged resource, such as port facilities; a strategic posi-
> tion along rail or road networks; and/or an important politi-
> cal function. At such locations commercial and financial
> services are relatively well developed and a concentration of
> purchasing power exists. Given the limited size of the
> skilled labor pool, few locations outside big cities could
> hope to assemble a diversified labor market. Finally, indus-
> trial experience is so limited that firms seeking to maximize
> their knowledge of markets and new technology will seek large
> centers. Thus at early stages of development most industries
> act as if urbanization economies associated with sheer city
> size are crucial; city specialization is rare and the inter-
> mediate city system suffers.

Over the longer term, however, rising wages and land costs will
create a market incentive for some firms to relocate in the urban
periphery. If these economic incentives for decentralization are
accompanied by infrastructure policies that begin to funnel investment funds toward promising secondary cities, a less-
centralized urban system may begin to emerge.

The World Bank's experience in Sao Paolo suggests that it
may be difficult for location policies to spur the decentralization process along. One might think that the most natural
starting point for policy would be to encourage firms located in
the central metropolitan area to open branches or to transfer to
new locations, especially given the lower land rents and wage
levels available outside the central metropolitan area. In fact,
a surprisingly small proportion of employment decentralization
in the Sao Paolo region results from either branching or transfers; the bulk arises from stationary expansion of firms already
in place and "births" of new firms. Worries about the availability of public services--particularly electricity and tele-
communications--have tended to discourage firms located in the
Sao Paolo metropolitan area from looking very far into the urban
periphery. Declines in wage levels do not appear to have provided much of an incentive for relocation, while land rents,
which decline more steeply with distance, do emerge as more
significant.

These findings suggest that, once the underlying economic
incentives for decentralization have emerged, LDC governments
might act to make firms aware of such opportunities; Hamer's
(1984) review suggests that urban firms operate under surprisingly limited information about alternative locations. LDC
governments can also provide the necessary infrastructure and
attempt to promote local entrepreneurship and selected local
firms as the key to secondary-city growth. There is certainly
an interim role for the public sector in monitoring the evolution of wages and land rents by location and in developing con-
tingency planning for the relatively rapid provision of services
once the underlying economic incentives point toward particular
secondary cities. The decentralization of government authority,
certainly a slow process in its own right, may help the process
along. It appears, for instance, that countries with a federal
system of government are often those with more decentralization in their city systems, perhaps because local revenue and
administrative capacities tend to be better developed. All
these are policy options for the long term; LDC experience certainly suggests that premature efforts to promote secondary city
alternatives rarely meet with success.


CONCLUSIONS

The theme of this chapter is that the economic consequences of
rural-to-urban migration and natural rates of growth in urban
populations are very much conditioned by imperfections in labor
and product markets, by public-sector policies, and by the

talents on which the public sector can draw. Perhaps the crucial
bottleneck in accommodating urbanization is the shortage of
skilled labor in urban public administration. Without well-
trained personnel, it will be difficult for the public sector to
tap new sources of revenues, to impose an economically rational
system of user charges and use-related taxes, and to attack labor
market imperfections in the modern sector. As long as such
problems remain unaddressed, it should not be surprising to see
LDC urban managers responding to urban growth with policies
that, all too often, combine coercion with inefficiency.

REFERENCES

Agarwala, R. (1983) Price Distortions and Growth in Developing
Countries. World Bank Staff Working Paper No. 575, World
Bank, Washington, D.C.
Bahl, R., D. Holland, and J. Linn (1983) Urban Growth and Local
Taxes in Less Developed Countries. Papers of the East-West
Population Institute, No. 98, East-West Population Center,
Honolulu.
Berg, E. (1976) The Economic Impact of the Drought and Inflation
in the Sahel. Discussion Paper No. 51, Center for Research
on Economic Development, University of Michigan, Ann Arbor.
Berry, R.A., and R. Sabot (1984) Unemployment and economic
development. Economic Development and Cultural Change 33(1):
99-116.
Cohen, M. (1982) The Political Economy of Urban Reform in
Africa. Paper presented at a meeting of the Canadian
Association of African Studies, Toronto.
Collier, P., and D. Lal (1980) Poverty and Growth in Kenya.
World Bank Staff Working Paper No. 389, World Bank,
Washington, D.C.
Corden, W., and R. Findlay (1975) Urban unemployment, inter-
sectoral capital mobility, and development policy. Economica
42:59-78.
Fields, G. (1975) Rural-urban migration, urban unemployment and
underemployment, and job-search activity in LDCs. Journal
of Development Economics 2:165-187.
Fry, J. (1979) A labor turnover model of wage determination in
developing economics. Economic Journal 89:353-369.
Gardner, B. (1974) Farm population decline and the income of
rural families. American Journal of Agricultural Economics
56(3):600-606.
Garrison, H. (1982) Internal migration in Mexico--a test of the
Todaro model. Food Research Institute Studies 18(2):197-214.
Greenwood, M. (1978) An econometric model of internal migration
and regional economic growth in Mexico. Journal of Regional
Studies 8(1):17-31.
Gregory, P. (1980) An assessment of changes in employment
conditions in less developed countries. Economic Development
and Cultural Change 28:673-700.

Hamer, A. (1984) Decentralized Urban Development and Industrial
    Location Behavior in Sao Paulo, Brazil: A Synthesis of
    Research Issues and Conclusions. Discussion Paper UDD-29,
    Water Supply and Urban Development Department, World Bank,
    Washington, D.C..
Harris, J., and R. Sabot (1982) Urban unemployment in LDCs:
    toward a more general search model. In R. Sabot, ed.,
    Migration and the Labor Market in Developing Countries.
    Boulder, Colo.: Westview Press.
Harris, J., and M. Todaro (1970) Migration, unemployment, and
    development: a two-sector analysis. American Economic
    Review 60(1):126-142.
House, W. (1984) Nairobi's informal sector: dynamic entre-
    preneurs or surplus labor? Economic Development and
    Cultural Change 32(2):227-302.
House, W., and H. Rempel (1976) The Impact of Unionization on
    Negotiated Wages in the Manufacturing Sector in Kenya.
    Working Paper No. 37, World Employment Program, International
    Labour Office, Geneva.
Johnson, D.G. (1960) Output and income effects of reducing the
    farm labor force. Journal of Farm Economics 42(4):779-796.
Johnson, G.E., and W.E. Whitelaw (1974) Urban-rural transfers
    in Kenya: an estimated remittances function. Economic
    Development and Cultural Change 22:473-497.
Kelley, A., and J. Williamson (1984) What Drives Third World
    City Growth? Princeton, N.J.: Princeton University Press.
Knowles, J., and R. Anker (1981) An analysis of income transfers
    in a developing country: the case of Kenya. Journal of
    Development Economics 8(2):205-226.
Laquian, A. (1981) Review and evaluation of urban accommoda-
    tionist policies in population redistribution. In United
    Nations Population Distribution Policies in Development
    Planning. Department of International Economic and Social
    Affairs, Population Studies, No. 75. New York: United
    Nations.
Lewis, W.A. (1954) Economic development with unlimited supplies
    of labour. Manchester School of Economic and Social Studies
    22(2):139-191.
Lewis, W.A. (1977) The Evolution of the International Economic
    Order. Discussion Paper No. 74, Research Program in
    Development Studies, Woodrow Wilson School, Princeton
    University.
Linn, J. (1983) Cities in the Developing World: Policies for
    Their Efficient and Equitable Growth. New York: Oxford
    University Press.
Linn, J.F. (1982) The costs of urbanization in developing
    countries. Economic Development and Cultural Change
    30(3):625-648.
Mazumdar, D. (1976) The urban informal sector. World Develop-
    ment 4(8):665-679.
Meerman, J. (1979) Public Expenditure in Malaysia: Who Benefits
    and Why. New York: Oxford University Press.

Mills, E., and C. Becker (1983)  The Relationship Between Urbani-
    zation and Economic Development.  Discussion Paper UDD-1,
    Water Supply and Urban Development Department, World Bank,
    Washington, D.C.
Mills, E., and B. Song (1979)  Urbanization and Urban Problems.
    Cambridge, Mass.:  Harvard University Press.
Rempel, H., and R. Lobdell (1978)  The role of urban to rural
    remittances in rural development.  Journal of Development
    Studies 14(3):324-341.
Rovani, Y.  (1979)  The problems of water supply and waste dis-
    posal.  Finance and Development 16:14-18.
Sabolo, Y.  (1975)  Employment and unemployment, 1960-90.
    International Labour Review 112(6):401-411.
Saunders, R., and J. Warford (1976)  Village Water Supply.
    Baltimore, Md.:  The Johns Hopkins University Press.
Schuh, G.E.  (1982)  Outmigration, rural productivity, and the
    distribution of income.  In R. Sabot, ed., Migration and the
    Labor Market in Developing Countries.  Boulder, Colo.:
    Westview Press.
Schultz, T.P.  (1982)  Lifetime migration within educational
    strata in Venezuela:  estimates of a logistic model.
    Economic Development and Cultural Change 30(3):559-593.
Sethuraman, S.  (1977)  The urban informal sector in Africa.
    International Labour Review (115):343-352.
Shoup, C.  (1979)  The taxation of urban property in less
    developed countries:  a concluding discussion.  In R. Bahl,
    ed., The Taxation of Urban Property in Less Developed
    Countries.  Madison, Wis.:  University of Wisconsin Press.
Simmons, A.  (1981)  A review and evaluation of attempts to
    constrain migration to selected urban centres and regions.
    In United Nations (1981)  Population Distribution Policies
    in Development Planning.  Department of International
    Economic and Social Affairs, Population Studies, No. 75.
    New York:  United Nations.
Sinclair, S.  (1978)  Urbanization and Labor Markets in
    Developing Countries.  New York:  St. Martin's Press.
Squire, L.  (1981)  Employment Policy in Developing
    Countries:  A Survey of Issues and Evidence.  New York:
    Oxford University Press.
Stanford Research Institute (SRI)  (1968)  Cost of Urban
    Infrastructure for Industry as Related to City Size in
    Developing Countries:  India Case Study.  Stanford, Calif:
    Stanford Research Institute.
Stark, O.  (1976)  Rural-to-Urban Migration and Some Economic
    Issues:  A Review Utilizing Findings of Surveys and
    Empirical Studies Covering the 1965-75 Period.  Working
    Paper No. 38, World Employment Program, International Labour
    Office, Geneva.
Steel, W.  (1978)  The Intermediate Sector, Unemployment and the
    Employment-Output Conflict:  A Multi-Sector Model.  World
    Bank Staff Working Paper No. 301, World Bank, Washington,
    D.C.

188                                                      Montgomery

Suits, D. (1984) U.S. Farm Migration: An Application of the Harris-Todaro Model. NUPRI Research Paper No. 12, Nihon University Population Research Institute, Tokyo.

Todaro, M. (1969) A model of labor migration and urban unemployment in less developed countries. American Economic Review 59(1):138-148.

Todaro, M. (1980) International migration in developing countries: a survey. In R. Easterlin, ed., Population and Economic Change in Developing Countries. Chicago: University of Chicago Press.

United Nations (1980) Patterns of urban and rural population growth. Department of International Economic and Social Affairs. Population Studies. No. 68. New York: United Nations.

Warford, J., and D. Julius (1977) The multiple objectives of water rate policy in less developed countries. Water Supply and Management 1:335-342.

Watanabe, S. (1976) Minimum wages in developing countries: myth and reality. International Labour Review 113(3):345-358.

World Bank (1979) World Development Report, 1979. New York: Oxford University Press.

World Bank (1980) Water Supply and Waste Disposal. Washington, D.C.: World Bank.

World Bank (1984) World Development Report, 1984. New York: Oxford University Press.

Yap, L. (1977) The attraction of cities: a review of the migration literature. Journal of Develoment Economics 4(3):239-264.

# 6
## Industrialization and Urbanization: International Experience
## J. Vernon Henderson

INTRODUCTION

This chapter examines urbanization experience in various parts of the world. Based on a variety of scientific papers, it identifies common features of the urban sector across countries. These features include trade relations and production patterns among cities in an economy and their relationships to city size distributions, location of economic activity, and regional development. In the course of the analysis, the relationships among population growth, economic development, urbanization, industrialization, centralization, and urban concentration are examined. In the discussion, the role of population size, or scale, and the various types of economies of scale in production are detailed. The international experience drawn upon consists of both overviews of large samples of countries and more detailed looks at Brazil, Korea, and the United States, as well as some aspects of Japan, India, Taiwan, and the U.S.S.R.

Development and Urbanization

There is a strong relationship between economic development and urbanization. Based on a sample of 111 countries, Renaud (1979) estimated a strong positive statistical relationship between income per capita and the percent of a country's population that is urbanized. This relationship may be seen in a comparison of columns (ii) and (iv) of Table 1: as we move from $250 per capita (e.g., India) to $1,500 (e.g., Turkey, Korea) to $5,000 or more, the percent urbanized increases from about 25 percent to about 50 percent to over 75 percent. Note, however, that even for a very highly developed country such as the United States, a significant proportion (20-25 percent) of the population remains rural and mostly nonagricultural.

---

Parts of this chapter are drawn from an unpublished background paper written for the Ministry of Finance, the People's Republic of China, under the auspices of the World Bank.

TABLE 1   Urbanization and Economic Development[a]

| Country | Per Capita Income (1981$) | Percent Urbanized | | Percent Urban Population Living in Cities Over 500,000[a] | | Annual Growth Rates 1970-81 Urban Pop. Rate/ Total Pop. Rate |
|---|---|---|---|---|---|---|
| | | 1960 | 1981 | 1960 | 1980 | |
| (i) | (ii) | (iii) | (iv) | (v) | (vi) | (vii) |
| India | 260 | 18 | 24 | 26 | 39 | 3.7/2.1 |
| China | 300 | 18 | 21 | n.a. | 51 | |
| Pakistan | 350 | 22 | 29 | 33 | 51 | 4.3/3.0 |
| Indonesia | 530 | 15 | 21 | 34 | 50 | 4.0/2.3 |
| Thailand | 770 | 13 | 15 | 65 | 69 | 3.4/2.5 |
| Nigeria | 870 | 13 | 21 | 22 | 58 | 4.8/2.5 |
| Peru | 1,170 | 40 | 66 | 38 | 44 | 3.5/2.6 |
| Turkey | 1,540 | 30 | 47 | 32 | 42 | 4.1/2.3 |
| Republic of Korea | 1,700 | 28 | 56 | 61 | 77 | 4.3/1.7 |
| Brazil | 2,200 | 46 | 68 | 35 | 52 | 3.9/2.1 |
| Chile | 2,560 | 68 | 81 | 38 | 44 | 2.4/1.7 |
| Yugoslavia | 2,790 | 28 | 43 | 11 | 23 | 2.4/0.9 |
| Venezuela | 4,220 | 67 | 84 | 26 | 44 | 4.2/3.4 |
| Spain | 5,640 | 51 | 75 | 37 | 44 | 2.2/1.1 |
| Italy | 6,960 | 59 | 70 | 46 | 52 | 1.1/0.4 |
| United Kingdom | 9,110 | 86 | 91 | 61 | 55 | 0.3/0.1 |
| Japan | 10,080 | 62 | 79 | 35 | 42 | 2.0/1.1 |
| Canada | 11,400 | 69 | 76 | 31 | 62 | 1.2/1.2 |
| United States | 12,820 | 70 | 77 | 65 | 72 | 1.5/1.0 |
| Fed. Rep. of Germany | 13,450 | 77 | 85 | 48 | 45 | 0.5/0.0 |
| U.S.S.R. | n.a. | 44 | 63 | 21 | 33 | 1.8/0.9 |
| Dem. Rep. of Germany | n.a. | 72 | 77 | 14 | 17 | 0.2/0.2 |
| Average for Lower Middle-Income Countries | 850 | 24 | 33 | 28 | 47 | 4.3/2.6 |
| Average for Upper Middle-Income Countries | 2,490 | 45 | 63 | 38 | 51 | 3.8/2.2 |

[a]In general, the numbers in these columns are not very accurate, so that while they do not give a very accurate picture of levels in 1960 and 1980, they probably do give a credible picture of the proportionate increases in population housed in larger cities.

Sources:  World Bank (1983).  For China in column (vi):  State Statistical Bureau of the Peoples' Republic of China (1981).  For the U.S. in columns (v) and (vi):  U.S. Department of Commerce (1982).

Initially, urbanization is accomplished mostly by rural-urban migration, as is reflected by the relatively rapid urban growth rates in less developed countries (LDCs) in column (vii) of Table 1. Later, urban growth is more through internal growth of the urban population (Squire, 1979; Renaud, 1979). However, it is useful to note, from column (vii) of Table 1, that urban growth rates still exceed general population growth rates in almost all countries, suggesting that rural-urban migration is still occurring in the most developed countries. As documented in Squire (1979), rural-urban migration represents a basic structural change in the economy in which national product patterns shift in favor of goods produced in urban areas, and/or technological development in agriculture reduces the demand for agricultural labor. In both cases, urban wages rise relative to rural wages, drawing the rural population into cities. The reasons for these structural and technological changes in the economy are discussed below.

## Industrialization and Urbanization

While there is a strong relationship between the level of development and urbanization, the link between urbanization and the general level of industrialization appears weaker. If we look at developed countries, the percent of the labor force in manufacturing has increased only mildy over time, despite rapid urbanization. For example, in 1880 the United States was 27 percent urbanized, with 19 percent of its labor force in manufacturing; by 1970 it was 73 percent urbanized, but the percent of the labor force in manufacturing had risen to only 25 percent (Bureau of the Census, 1976). Similarly, if we look at current middle-income countries worldwide, with their rapid urbanization since 1950, the average proportion of their labor force in manufacturing has risen only from 14 to 19 percent (Squire, 1979).

In almost all these cases, what has happened most dramatically is a shift in the composition of the manufacturing labor force from nondurable (e.g., textiles and food processing) to durable (e.g., metals, machinery) goods production. Table 2 shows that, for the United States and Korea for relevant time periods, using both general and specific industrial composition comparisons, there have been dramatic drops in the ratio of workers engaged in traditional manufacturing (textiles, food processing) to those engaged in heavy manufacturing (metals, machinery) as populations have moved from rural to urban areas. This suggests that urbanization is more closely linked with industrial composition than industrialization per se. These notions are explored further below.

There is also an idea that, with changes in manufacturing technology over time, effective utilization of the newer technologies has required greater urbanization. Sophisticated manufacturing techniques can require many workers with very diverse specialized skills. To find these employees, firms may need to locate in large urban areas with their larger, more

TABLE 2   Industrial Composition and Urbanization

| Country | Percent Urbanized | Ratio of Textile Workers to Iron and Steel Workers |
|---|---|---|
| United States | | |
| 1880 | 27 | 1.30 |
| 1960 | 70 | 0.56 |
| | | Ratio of Nondurable Goods to Durable Goods Workers |
| United States | | |
| 1940 | 56 | 1.20 |
| 1970 | 73 | 0.73 |
| | | Ratio of Workers in Textile and Food Processing to Workers in Metals and Machinery |
| Korea | | |
| 1966 | 35 | 2.7 |
| 1978 | 55 | 1.5 |

diversely skilled labor markets. Hand-in-hand with this idea is the notion that rates of change in technology have speeded up over time, and that the speed at which firms find out about and adopt the new technologies is affected by whether or not they locate in urbanized areas.

This section has so far addressed developed and middle income countries. The data for current low-income countries raise an unanswered question. Historically, these countries generally have had a much lower proportion (under 10 percent) of their labor force in manufacturing than have countries and middle-income countries over the last 40 years, perhaps, as will be suggested below, because of their low rates of literacy and educational attainment. While it appears that development for these countries will require greater industrialization and up-grading of their labor forces, what is unclear is whether that process will require extensive concentrated urbanization in the near future. The answer appears to depend on the nature of the industrialization involved.

We should note, then, that there is a link between urbanization and nonmanufacturing labor force activity. First, and obviously, the percent of the labor force in agriculture drops

precipitously.    Second,   service   activity   rises   substantially.
For  example,   in  the  United  States,  on  the  basis  of  industry
divisions,  there was  a  rise in  service employment  (wholesale and
retail  trade,  finance,  insurance,  real  estate,  and  personal
services)  from 30 to 43 percent of the labor force between 1900
and 1970  (Bureau of  the Census,  1976).   Similarly,  for middle-
income countries,  service industry employment rose from 14 to 19
percent  of the   labor force between 1950 and 1970  (Squire, 1979).
This rise in service activity is more pronounced if one looks at
the division of labor on an occupational basis, shifting within
manufacturing activities  from blue collar  work to  white collar
technical and clerical work.   For example,  in the United States
in  1900,   service   (service,   sales,   clerical)   workers  and  professional  and technical  workers accounted  for 17  percent and 4
percent of the labor force, respectively; by 1970, these numbers
had  risen to  38 percent and 14  percent, respectively  (Bureau of
the Census, 1976).


Urban Concentration and Urbanization

In general,  urban concentration  is  weakly  associated with the
extent of  urbanization.   Concentration  reflects  the  extent  to
which the urban population is housed mostly in one or two urban
areas, as opposed to many.  The relationship that exists suggests
that   as   urbanization   increases,   urban   concentration   falls.
Although as a national urban population grows, most individual
urban areas tend to grow as well, the number of urban areas grows
more rapidly,  so that  the share  of any  one urban  area in  the
national urban population falls (Henderson, 1980).   However, it
is important to note that this does not preclude the widespread
phenomenon  in   which,   as   urbanization   increases,   a   higher
proportion of  the urban population is housed in  (an increasing
number of) relatively larger urban areas.  That fact is reflected
in Table 1 in a comparison of columns (iii) and (iv) with columns
(v) and (vi).   Although these relationships between urbanization
and urban concentration exist (explored below), urban concentration is more closely associated with industrial composition, the
country's system of government, the availability of inhabitable
land,  and  the  nature  of  the  national  transportation  system.
Also  explored  is  the  fact  that  in  smaller  fast-developing
countries, urban concentration sometimes increases rapidly with
urbanization for, say, two decades and then drops off.


Issues Explored in This Chapter

This  chapter  explores  the  links  between  industrialization,
urbanization, national population size, and urban concentration
from two perspectives.
     First, by examining both large countries that currently have
a relatively stable system of cities and the basic concepts about
city system, this chapter explores the relationship between what

a country produces, and urban concentration and urbanization.
It also examines the extent of spatial dispersion of urban areas
and populations to see why in some countries large urban areas
are spread throughout the country, while in others they are
clustered in small areas, such as a national capital region
containing the capital and a set of satellite cities.

Second, by examining some rapidly developing countries, the
chapter explores why some countries have experienced initial
rapid concentration of the urbanized population into one or two
urban areas, followed by deconcentration. Both the fact of
deconcentration and its encouragement by widespread policies in
many of these countries today may indicate that the initial
levels of concentration were unnecessary. In any case, deconcentration is examined, as well as the successes and failures of
various policies encouraging it. In the process, this chapter
uncovers critical aspects of both the concentration and
deconcentration processes.

NATIONAL OUTPUT PATTERNS, URBAN AREA SIZE DISTRIBUTION, AND
SPATIAL DISPERSION OF THE URBAN POPULATION

There is a natural economic relationship between national
production patterns, urbanization, and the size distribution of
urban areas. The first part of this section explores this
relationship. The second part explores the determinants of how
urban areas are spatially distributed--whether clustered close
together or spatially dispersed throughout the country. The
third part analyzes the conditions that must obtain in a country
for the relationship between production patterns and urban concentration to be a strong one and suggests types of government
policies that can affect this relationship.

National Production Patterns and Urban Concentration

General Patterns

As a general pattern, if we look across the system of cities in
a country, as urban sizes increase, the share of manufacturing
in local employment increases slowly, reaches a maximum, and
then declines. In contrast, the share of services appears to
rise indefinitely as we move to larger and larger urban areas.
These relationships are postulated as holding generally in most
countries by Richardson (1977) and are specifically detailed for
Japan (Renaud, 1979), Korea (Renaud, 1979), and the United States
(Henderson, 1983). For a more detailed industrial breakdown, the
latter study investigates these relationships for the United
States in 1970 for urban areas of over 50,000, with urban area
defined as the central city and its suburbs. The study finds
that the share of heavy manufacturing is constant or declines
weakly with urban area population, while the share of light
manufacturing weakly increases up to an urban area population of

5 million. In contrast, the relationships for high-tech manufacturing and for modern services (professional activities, business services, finance, insurance, real estate, etc.) are much stronger and sharper. High-tech manufacturing is highly concentrated in urban areas over 1 million but under 6 or 7 million. Shares of modern services all experience rapid rates of increase with urban area populations throughout most of the relevant size range of urban areas.

## Determinants of the General Patterns

What underlies these patterns? For manufacturing, there has been a detailed examination of hypotheses that would explain these patterns for two large countries—the United States (Bergsman et al., 1972, 1975; Sveikauskas, 1975; Henderson, 1985a) and Brazil (Hamer, 1983; Henderson, 1982b). Several facts emerge from these examinations. First, smaller and medium-sized urban areas tend to be highly specialized in their industrial production patterns (Henderson, 1985a, 1982b). About half of the 243 U.S. urban areas of over 50,000 in 1970 could be classified as being specialized in auto production, aircraft, shipbuilding, steel, industrial machinery, communication equipment, petrochemicals, textiles, apparel, leather products, pulp and paper, or food processing. The other half of the urban areas were nonindustrialized state capitals, college towns, or agriculture service centers (specialized in warehousing, business, and transport services), or were very large diversified metropolitan areas. A partial classification of U.S. urban areas for 1970 is reported in Table 3. For Brazil (Table 4), the pattern is very similar, although not surprisingly, there are relatively more urban areas specialized in textiles and food processing and relatively fewer in transport equipment, machinery, and petrochemicals.

It should be noted that specialization in this context is very much a relative concept. Much of a city's labor force is engaged in nonexport service and retail activity; at most, 40 percent of the labor force will be engaged in some type of export activity. Typically, specialization is defined on the basis of 10-20 percent of the city's labor force being engaged in a particular manufacturing or service activity, perhaps another 10-20 percent being involved in diverse other activities, and many support activities being carried out for the specialized industry. Other patterns are possible. For example, an industry typically employing males (iron and steel) is sometimes complemented by an industry likely to employ females (textiles).

Specialization can also be viewed from another perspective. In Brazil, for any one of most three- and four-digit manufacturing industries, there appear to be three sets of urban areas: the first, typically containing well over 50 percent of all urban areas, has absolutely no employment in that industry; the second, typically containing 35-45 percent of all urban areas, has minimal employment (under 150 workers) in that industry, usually

TABLE 3   Urban Specialization in the United States

| Auto | Pulp and Paper | Steel |
|---|---|---|
| Bay City, MI (13%) | Appleton/Oshkosh, WI (13%) | Birmingham, AL (8%) |
| Cleveland, OH | Green Bay, WI (11%) | Gasden, AL (11%) |
| Detroit, MI (17%) | Mobile, AL | Gary/Hammond/ |
| Flint, MI (36%) | Monroe, LA | East Chicago, IN (26%) |
| Jackson, MI (7%) | Portland, ME | Huntington/Ashland, |
| Kenoska, WI (16%) | Savannah, GA | WVA/KY/OH (7%) |
| Lansing, MI (15%) | | Johnstown, PA (13%) |
| Muncie, IN (13%) | Shipbuilding | Pittsburg, PA |
| Saginaw, MI (17%) | | Pueblo, CO (8%) |
| South Bend, IN (6%) | Charleston, SC (7%) | Steubenville/Weirton, |
| Springfield, OH (9%) | New London/Groton/Norwich, | OH/WWA (29%) |
| Toledo, OH/MI (8%) | CT (12%) | Wheeling, WVA/OH (7%) |
| | Newport News/Hampton, VA | |
| Textiles | (17%) | Leather Products |
| (excluding apparel) | Vallejo/Napa, CA (10%) | |
| | | Brockton, MA (6%) |
| Ashville, NC | Apparel | Lewiston/Auburn, ME |
| Augusta, GA (10%) | | Manchester, NH |
| Chattanooga, TN/GA (11%) | Allentown/Bethlehem/ | |
| Columbus, GA | Easton, PA/NJ (9%) | Petrochemicals |
| Greenville, SC (18%) | Atlantic City, NJ | |
| Wilmington, NC (7%) | El Paso, TX | Baton Rogue, LA (10%+) |
| | Fall River, MA/RI (16%) | Beaumont/Port Arthur/ |
| Food Processing | New Bedford, MA (13%) | Orange, TX (18%+) |
| (excluding agriculture, | Scranton, PA (13%) | Galveston/Texas City, |
| fisheries, and whole- | Wilkes-Barre/Hazelton, PA | TX (11%+) |
| saling) | | Lake Charles, LA (12%+) |
| | College/State Capital Towns | |
| Brownsville/Harlington/ | | Service Centers |
| San Benito, TX | Austin, TX | |
| McAllen/Phan/Edinburg, TX | Normal-Bloomington, IL | Amarillo, TX |
| Modesto, CA | Bryant/College Station, TX | Billings, MT |
| Salinas/Monterey, CA | Champaign-Urbana, IL | Duluth/Superior, MN |
| Stockton, CA (5%) | Columbia, MO | Little Rock/North |
| | Columbus, OH | Little Rock, AR |
| Aircraft | Durham, NC | Omaha, NB |
| | Fargo/Moorhead, ND/MN | Spokane, WA |
| Anaheim/Santa Ana/Garden | Gainesville, FL | Springfield, MA |
| Grove, CA (5%) | Lafayette, LA | |
| Bridgeport, CT (7%) | Lafayette/W. Lafayette, IN | Diverse Manufacturing |
| Fort Worth, TX (13%) | Lexington, KY | |
| Hartford, CT (11%) | Lubbock, TX | Dallas, TX |
| Seattle/Everett, WA (10%) | Madison, WI | Newark, NJ |
| Wichita, KS (14%) | Raleigh, NC | Philadelphia, PA |
| | Reno, NV | Phoenix, AZ |
| Radio, Television, and | Santa Barbara, CA | Syracuse, NY |
| Communication Equipment | Tallahassee, FL | |
| | Terre Haute, IN | Industrial Machinery |
| Binghamton, NY/PA (7%) | Tucson, AZ | |
| Cedar Rapids, IA | Tuscaloosa, AL | Bristol, CT (10%) |
| Lawrence/Haverhill, | | Canton, OH (6%) |
| MA/NH (7%) | | LaCrosse, WI (11%) |
| Nashua, NY (8%) | | New Britain, CT (10%) |

Notes:  This grouping of urban areas is based on extensive cluster analysis as reported in Henderson (1983).  The criterion used in reporting these urban areas is very strict; a looser criterion increases the number of urban areas in each category.  Where available, employment fractions are reported in parentheses.
    To do the cluster analysis, a matrix was formed showing the fraction of employment of each of 243 standard metropolitan statistical areas (SMSAs) in 229 industries (based on 1,270 of the sixth count of the 1970 population census). (SMSAs incorporate a central city and its suburbs, including rural population;

involved in repair and service activities; the third, typically
containing 5-10 percent of all urban areas, has extensive
employment in that industry, which is often its industry of
specialization. The numbers for different industries are given
in Table 4.

Similar detailed industrial data for the United States have
not been released. However, from the population census it
appears that similar patterns exist. Table 5 presents the
numbers for a variety of U.S. industries that may conform to the
hypothesized pattern, although these numbers are not so precise
and are based on how household members categorize the industrial activities at their work place. The numbers indicate two
patterns. First, most standard metropolitan statistical areas
(SMSAs) have small levels of employment in different industries.
(Given that the numbers are from the population census, we cannot distinguish between small and zero employment.) Second, the
numbers indicate that a few SMSAs have very high concentrations
of employment for each particular industry.

The fact that specialized production results in different
types of urban areas has important implications for their size
distribution. The different types of specialized urban areas
appear to fall into different size categories. However, this is
a weak statistical relationship, suggesting that the forces
determining an urban area's size are varied and extremely
complex (as discussed below). For example, in Brazil, urban
areas specialized in textiles and ceramics tend to be smaller
than those specialized in iron and steel production, while the
latter in turn tend to be smaller than those specialized in
transport equipment or machinery (Henderson, 1985c).

These patterns of specialization form a direct link between
national output patterns and urban area size distributions.
National output patterns are determined by a country's overall
natural resources, consumption patterns, trade relationships,
and governmental policies. These patterns then imply a city
system, broken into different types of cities specialized in the

TABLE 3 (continued)

---

approximately 55 percent of all people in SMSAs live in suburbs.) From that
matrix, a 243 x 243 symmetric matrix of simple correlation coefficients between
pairs of columns of employment fractions for each pair of SMSAs was formed. The
correlation coefficients measure the degree of similarity or dissimilarity (for
negative coefficients) between the employment patterns of each pair of SMSAs.
The primitive cluster algorithm picks the highest correlation coefficient and
combines those two SMSAs, reducing the rows and columns of the matrix by one.
In terms of the correlation between the combined SMSAs and any remaining SMSA,
the algorithm picks either the highest or lowest of the pair of coefficients
between that remaining SMSA and the original SMSAs that were combined. The
results in this table are based on retaining the lowest. For the new 242 x
242 matrix, the algorithm then repeats itself, picking the highest correlation
coefficient and combining two SMSAs to be the start of a (probably) new cluster.
The results in this table are based on the correlation coefficient for the last
SMSA added of .6.

TABLE 4   Employment Concentrations in Southern Brazil; Number of Cities of
Various Employment Intervals

| | Employment Intervals | | | | |
|---|---|---|---|---|---|
| | Out of All 126 Urban Areas | | | Out of 26 Urban Areas with Populations of 100,000 to 500,000 | Out of 63 Urban Areas Under 50,000 Population |
| Industry | 0 | 1-150 | 3,000+ | 2,000+ | 500+ |
| Ceramics (tile, bricks) | 54 | 52 | 5 | 1 | 2 |
| Glass and crystal | 96 | 22 | 2 | 0 | 0 |
| Iron and steel | 45 | 49 | 6 | 4 | 2 |
| Engines and turbines | 82 | 34 | 1 | 0 | 1 |
| Ventilation and refrigeration equipment | 56 | 58 | 3 | 1 | 0 |
| Machine tools and industrial equipment | 58 | 47 | 2 | 1 | 0 |
| Agricultural machinery | 53 | 55 | 1 | 0 | 0 |
| Electrical equipment for households (e.g., toasters) | 94 | 28 | 1 | 0 | 0 |
| Communications equipment (e.g., radios, TV) | 85 | 34 | 2 | 0 | 0 |
| Accessories for autos | 24 | 82 | 2 | 3 | 0 |
| Artificial fibers | 116 | 4 | 1 | 1 | 0 |
| Spinning and weaving of natural fibers | 62 | 15 | 6 | 4 | 11 |
| Spinning and weaving of artificial fibers | 105 | 8 | 3 | 1 | 2 |
| Finishing of cloth: spinning | 88 | 17 | 2 | 0 | 2 |
| Sugar | 84 | 28 | 1 | 1 | 1 |
| Toys | 95 | 29 | 1 | 0 | 0 |
| Shoes | 28 | 80 | 4 | 1 | 0 |

Note:   This table is based on uncensored precise counts from the 1970
industrial census of Brazil, covering all firms of all sizes (down to one
employee) for three-and four-digit industries. The numbers shown refer to a
region with a total urban population of under 35 million.

production of different goods, with the numbers of each type
depending on the levels of national output of the  various goods.
The size distribution of cities then depends on the numbers of
each type of city of differing average size required to meet
overall national production patterns.

If we compare different economies at a point in time as
production patterns shift away from traditional industries (e.g.,
natural fiber textiles, warehousing and transport for agricultural output, food processing, retail and personal services for
farm communities, and ceramics) toward heavy machinery and

TABLE 5   Employment Concentration in U.S. Metropolitan Areas in 1970

| | Employment Intervals | | | | |
| | No. of SMSAs in the Employment Interval out of 210 SMSAs with Populations from 50,000 to 1 Million | | | | Out of 33 SMSAs Over 1 Million |
| Industry | <250 | 2,000-5,000 | 5,000+ | 10,000+ | 10,000+ |
|---|---|---|---|---|---|
| Blast furnaces, steel works, rolling and finishing mills | 168 | 7 | 10 | 6 | 7 |
| Cutlery, hand tools, and other hardware | 164 | 3 | 1 | 0 | 0 |
| Metal stamping | 175 | 3 | 0 | 0 | 2 |
| Engines and turbines | 190 | 1 | 1 | 0 | 1 |
| Farm machinery and equipment | 185 | 3 | 2 | 1 | 0 |
| Construction and materials handling equipment | 151 | 9 | 1 | 0 | 4 |
| Electronic computing | 183 | 3 | 2 | 0 | 3 |
| Household appliances | 177 | 6 | 3 | 2 | 1 |
| Motor vehicles and equipment | 130 | 16 | 17 | 8 | 13 |
| Aircraft and parts | 143 | 12 | 9 | 4 | 11 |
| Shipbuilding | 171 | 4 | 6 | 2 | 2 |
| Photographic equipment and supplies | 206 | 2 | 1 | 1 | 0 |
| Tobacco manufacturing | 193 | 3 | 3 | 1 | 0 |
| Meat products | 133 | 7 | 0 | 0 | 0 |
| Canning and preserving | 167 | 5 | 0 | 0 | 0 |
| Knitting mills, textiles | 181 | 4 | 2 | 1 | 1 |
| Yarn, thread, and fabric mills | 145 | 8 | 6 | 3 | 1 |
| Apparel and accessories | 85 | 16 | 15 | 4 | 9 |
| Pulp, paper, and paper board products | 147 | 6 | 3 | 0 | 0 |
| Industrial chemicals | 153 | 4 | 3 | 0 | 1 |
| Rubber products | 151 | 12 | 2 | 1 | 0 |
| Footwear | 178 | 9 | 1 | 0 | 0 |

Source:   1970 Population Census, Sixth Count, Table 1270.

transport industries, we can expect to see a shift from smaller to medium-sized cities. Moreover, as discussed below, with a shift from general manufacturing into modern services or high-tech manufacturing, we might expect another shift from medium- to large-sized urban areas.

Note that which particular cities grow from smaller to larger
depends on which locations are better endowed with the amenities
relevant to expanding manufacturing industries (e.g., access to
natural resources for iron and steel). That is, a city's size
is determined primarily by which type of industry it attracts.
In turn, which type of industry it attracts depends in part on
whether its natural amenities are attractive to that type of
industry. Of course, in a more generalized context, some cities
may be more efficient at carrying out investments in the urban
infrastructure that are attractive to particular industries. In
short, the question of which particular cities end up with which
particular industries is a complex one that has not been
extensively researched. However, that question is not central
to the issues here; our concern is with patterns of urbanization,
not why, in a particular context, city A ended up with the steel
industry and city B the textile industry.

It is important to understand the reasons for industrial
specialization by urban areas, for the size differences across
urban areas, and for the service orientation of large metropolitan areas. We now briefly explore these reasons, which have to
do primarily with the nature of the economies of scale in production that give us population agglomerations in the first
place. Greater scale of economic activities in cities enhances
productivity within an industry by encouraging "communications"
among firms. Those communications speed up the adoption of new
or existing technological innovations and the reaction to
changing national and international market conditions through
the following: labor market economies for workers and firms
searching, respectively, for specific jobs and specific skill
combinations; greater opportunities for specialization in firm
(and worker) activities; and scale economies in the provision of
intermediate common inputs (docking facilities, warehousing,
power, etc.). The question is whether these scale economies
affecting firms in a specific industry arise from its own size
or from more general urban area size. Is the incubator the
industry itself or the city? This is the critical question. We
first examine it for manufacturing industries, then explore how
it relates to the issue of scale economies at a national level,
and then examine it for traditional service industries.

Scale Economies in Manufacturing. For both Brazil and the
United States, for almost all manufacturing industries, economies
of scale are estimated to arise solely from the benefits of increased local industry size, not urban area size. Scale economies of the industry type are called "localization" economies,
while those based on urban area scale are called "urbanization"
economies. The existence of localization economies only holds
particularly for primary metals, electrical and nonelectrical
machinery, transport equipment, petrochemicals, pulp and paper,
leather products, and wood products. The extent of localization
economies for apparel, textiles, and food processing in Brazil
is weaker, which could suggest weak benefits from agglomerating
employment in these industries as opposed to their being in

small towns (rural areas); however, this result may also reflect statistical problems in estimation (see Table 6, footnote c). Those industries in Table 6 exhibiting localization economies tend to produce standardized products that are exported from the city around the country and internationally. Because the products are standardized, it is not so important for the cities involved to be new centers of innovation. Rather, they benefit from large plant sizes with large assembly lines (e.g., transport equipment) and/or from large own-industry concentrations drawing on a common labor market (e.g., pulp and paper, wood products, textiles).

Results for scale economies on which the above statements are based are reported in Table 6. They are based on production functions of the form

$$Y = g(\vec{s})\ Y(\vec{K})\ ,$$

where $Y(\bullet)$ is the firm's own constant returns to scale technology for a vector of inputs $\vec{K}$. $g(\vec{s})$ is a Hicks' neutral external shift factor whose arguments are scale and technology measures specific to an industry in an urban area. After considerable investigation, scale effects were specified to take the form

$$g(\bullet) = e^{\gamma/L}\ N^{\epsilon_N} \quad \text{or} \quad \log g(\bullet) = \gamma/L + \epsilon_N \log N\ ,$$

where L is own-industry employment in an urban area and N the population of the area. $\epsilon_N$ is the elasticity of scale effects with respect to population increases. For own-industry employment, the corresponding expression is

$$\epsilon_L = d\log Y/d\log L = \gamma/L\ .$$

The interpretation of the $\epsilon_L$ and $\epsilon_N$ elasticities is that a 1 percent increase in L or N, respectively, leads to a $\epsilon_L$ or $\epsilon_N$ percent increase in the output of any firm in the industry in the urban area, holding firm inputs fixed. $\epsilon_L$ is specified as a declining elasticity.

Scale economics were estimated based on both production function and productivity specifications, controlling for industry inputs (or input prices for dual specifications) and industry labor force quality. The assumptions of Hicks' neutrality, constant returns to scale to firm's own technology, and a declining $\epsilon_L$ were all tested and strongly supported. Specification tests were conducted to test for endogeneity of explanatory variables, and two-stage estimates were examined. The primary results on $\gamma$ and $\epsilon_N$ coeffieients are reported in Table 6, along with their t-statistics and sample calculations of $\epsilon_L$ evaluated at 1,000 local own-industry employees. As stated above, the evidence for the existence of only localization economies in standardized manufacturing is very strong. Sign patterns for localization economies are consistent and the coefficients generally statistically strong; sign patterns for urbanization economies are mixed and the coefficients generally statistically weak.

TABLE 6  Economy-of-Scale Parameters

| Localization Economies | United States | | | Brazil | | |
|---|---|---|---|---|---|---|
| | $\gamma$ | $\epsilon_N$ | $\epsilon_L$(at L=1000) | $\gamma$ | $\epsilon_N$d | $\epsilon_L$(L=1000) |
| Nonelectrical Machinery | -67.3 (2.56) | .033 (.20) | .07 | -43.7 (2.71) | 0 | .04 |
| Electrical Machinery | -180.7 (2.87) | .022 (1.07) | .11 | n.a. | n.a. | n.a. |
| Primary Metals[a] | -120.1 (2.12) | .073 (1.78) | .12 | -93.7 (1.94) | 0 | .09 |
| Petrochemicals[b] | -222.6 (2.50) | -.302 (3.26) | .22 | -103.7 (2.59) | .084 (1.28) | .10 |
| Pulp and Paper | -46.0 (2.15) | -.021 (1.27) | .05 | -65.2 (1.51) | 0 | .07 |
| Textiles[c] | -164.8 (1.25) | -.070 (1.36) | .16 | -57.8 (1.57) | 0 | .06 |
| Apparel[c] | -222.6 (2.23) | .050 (.88) | .22 | -22.8 (.92) | 0 | .02 |
| Food Processing[c] | -206.3 (2.11) | -.047 (1.09) | .21 | -21.6 (.78) | -.038 (.76) | .02 |

Source:  Henderson (1985b:Table 1).

[a]For Brazil, this includes only iron and steel.
[b]For Brazil, this includes all chemicals.
[c]For the United States, based on specification test results, these equations were estimated by 2SLS, dramatically changing the results. Unfortunately, for Brazil 2SLS estimation was not possible because of a lack of reliable instruments. (2SLS work for Brazil implausibly strengthened the results.)
[d]Equations for Brazil were reestimated without the N term if both the coefficient was less than .03 and its t-statistic was less than 0.75.

On the other hand, Henderson (1985a) reports that ubiquitous industries, many of whose products are locally consumed, such as fabricated metals (e.g., cans, cutlery, hand tools, plumbing fixtures, structure of metal products, stampings) and nonmetallic minerals (e.g., cement, glass), exhibit little or no scale effects. These goods tend to be nontraded across cities because the benefits of agglomerating production do not outweigh the trade costs of transporting the goods between cities. Further, volatile consumer-oriented industries, such as publishing, appear to benefit more from increases in urban area sizes than from own-industry size per se.

Why are industries that exhibit localization economies found in smaller and medium-sized specialized urban areas? First, from an efficiency point of view, there is the notion that increases in population agglomeration are beneficial only on the production side. On the consumption side, per person costs of housing and commuting generally rise continously with city size; certain aspects of quality of life (pollution, congestion, crime) decline continuously; and scale benefits in providing public utilities are quickly exhausted (Hirsch, 1973). While these notions are subject to some challenge (they are explored in detail above), the general conclusion can be reached that, from the consumption side, beyond some relatively small size, increases in urban area size are costly.

Thus, the efficiency basis for increasing city sizes lies on the production side. For any city size, industrial efficiency is maximized by the relative specialization of that part of the urban area's labor force not engaged in producing housing, local public services, local retail and personal services, etc. Specialization maximizes the exploitation of scale effects within an urban area's export industry, while diversification dissipates scale effects for any one industry by spreading employment over many industries.

The extent of these scale effects both peters out in any industry and differs by type of industry. These facts suggest that, given the rising per resident consumption costs of increasing city size, efficient increases in urban area sizes are limited, and the efficient size of an urban area will vary with the industry in which it specializes, as well as other considerations.

Implications of the Results for the General Analysis of Scale in an Economy. People have raised issues related to economies of various kinds at a national level--economies of national population density, economies of national size, economies of scope, and so on--in an attempt to determine whether national population size is related to economic efficiency. The results and analyses reported here bear on these issues.

First, for efficiency internal to a manufacturing industry, density is generally not important. High densities that people actually experience are achieved in all economies by city formation. They can be increased if it becomes efficient to do so by greater clustering of production centers into metropolitan areas. Controlling for intracity or metropolitan area densities, higher national population densities mean only that there are fewer open spaces between cities. Moreover, if one views economies as having fixed endowments of potential urban sites of varying qualities (for example, access to water transportation and to natural recreation amenities), as the number of cities grows in any economy and national "density" increases, cities form on increasingly inferior-quality manufacturing sites. In summary, it is difficult to conceive of how increases in national density per se can be internally beneficial to industries. An exception might be tiny countries that cannot support even one large metropolitan area. Note, however, that increases in national population density can impact favorably the average costs of infrastructure investment. Intercity road systems may be cheaper on a per capita basis if there are more people to use them. We comment on this later.

Second, the lack of evidence of urbanization economies in standardized manufacturing at the local level is evidence that, for these industries, agglomeration at a national level is also irrelevant. The very nature of scale economies (involving close spatial proximity for communications and specialization in tasks) means that if these do not exist for an industry in its local environs, they will not exist for it outside its environs. Scale economies appear to depend generally on local own-industry employment and are effectively exhausted within cities, implying that there is no advantage to greater national scale (e.g., more cities doing the same thing). However, there may be economies of scope at a national level. Larger national economies may produce a broader range of products in a broad range of types of cities; small economies may not have the scale to produce a full range of products, in particular a full range of efficient-sized cities. Producing a broader range of products may foster economies of scope, in which, as the range of products increases, the possibilities for technological "trade" and development within a country across industries are enhanced.

Traditional Service Industries. We return to the analysis of urban scale economies and specialization to examine the service sector. The situation for cities specialized in traditional service industries--higher education; state/provincial government; transport and warehousing; and personal, repair, and retail services for farmers--is similar to that for cities specialized in manufacturing. We know that many urban areas over 50,000 and many more cities under 50,000 are specialized in these activities. We presume specialization occurs as for manufacturing because of localization economies, although the relationships may be more complex. A college urban area will support a variety of education-related activities, such as commercial research and testing, research hospitals, educational computer soft-ware, and some instrument manufacturing. An urban area specialized in warehousing and transportation can be a transport head for the collection of agricultural produce (e.g., grains) or a node for the wholesale distribution of manufactured products for retailing in smaller towns. Despite these patterns, there is no statistical work estimating localization economies in the service sector; however, for personal, repair, and retail services for farmers, there is a massive literature detailing the patterns observed in different areas at different points in time.

This literature describes hierarchies of the smaller towns and cities in an economy whose primary purpose is to provide personal, repair, and retail services (no manufacturing) to rural areas. The smallest cities in the hierarchy offer the fewest and most ubiquitous services; as we ascend the hierarchy in terms of city population, the number of services offered cumulates until the largest city in the hierarchy (which in itself is quite small, say, under 50,000, in absolute terms) produces the whole range of traditional services. As regards the range of services, Berry (1968), looking at U.S. rural areas of

30 years (or more) ago, suggests that the smaller towns in the hierarchy will offer banking, food retailing, repair, farm machinery retailing, and physician and religious services; the next larger sets of towns will additionally offer furniture and drug retailing, and then dry cleaning and legal services; and the largest sets of towns will add hopital and apparel retailing services.

While town sizes are in part limited by the factors discussed for manufacturing (scale economies in production versus diseconomies in consumer and commuting activities), there is an additional dominant consideration: the cost of delivering these services and retail goods from the towns to people in the rural areas. This cost limits the market area spatially and the extent of sales of any good from any town. Towns producing low-scale economy, expensive-to-transport goods or services, or selling to a low-density rural area, will tend to be smaller.

## Some Qualifications

It is critical to note that the links we have stressed between industrial specialization of a city and city size and between national output patterns and the size composition of cities are rough. We explore the roughness of each of these links in turn.

First, while on average, efficient city size is directly linked to internal industrial composition, in practice the link for a specific city is weak (Henderson, 1985b and 1985c). City size is strongly affected by consumption considerations and geographic characteristics such as the following: public service levels, qualities, and taxes; quality-of-life measures, such as crime rates and pollution levels; natural amenities, such as weather conditions, which affect everything from heating costs to health to pollution dispersion; and geological formations affecting the city's shape and transport system. These conditions also affect the desire of high-skill relative to low-skill people to live in the city, and that skill variation itself will affect the precise production techniques chosen and the composition of support industries for a base industry. In short, each city's attributes are unique and its efficient size different. Unfortunately, statistical measures of the relationships involved are subject to error and lack of data; in complex models, there is even difficulty in specifying the conditions describing efficient city size. Moreover, simple simulation work indicates that small variations in the key characteristics of a city can produce large variations in city size without affecting the welfare of residents. In estimation, the lower and upper bounds of the interval in which efficient size is estimated to lie can vary by severalfold. In summary, it is impossible for a planner to specify accurately the efficient size of a given city since that efficient size evolves over time (see Tolley et al., 1979; Yezer and Goldfarb, 1982; Henderson, 1980, 1985b; Segal, 1976).

Second, it is true that there is a relationship between the
industrial composition of national output and the size distribution of cities that results because many smaller and medium-
sized cities tend to specialize in industrial production, and
each type of city on average has a different size. However, it
must be recognized that on an absolute basis, much industrial
production occurs in large metropolitan areas (e.g.,
Philadelphia, Chicago, Detroit, and Newark), and that even some
not-so-large metropolitan areas have diverse manufacturing bases
(e.g., Buffalo, Phoenix, Syracuse, and Dallas). Part of this is
an historical phenomenon, with population clustering around a
resource-based core city, a phenomenon explored below. However,
much of this fact probably involves complex interrelationships
among specific industries identified at a very detailed level
(i.e., looking at four- or five-digit industries rather than
two- or three-digit); we have only just started to study these
interrelationships (see Bergsman et al., 1972, 1975), and the
data are very limited (e.g., censored in the United States
because of disclosure problems).

The analysis so far has applied only to manufacturing and
traditional service industries. We also need to consider modern
service industries, such as finance, entertainment, insurance,
and specialized health care, as well as high-technology manufacturing and components of the publishing and apparel industries. Because these industries are often concentrated in large,
diverse metropolitan areas, they must experience economies mostly
from urban size, rather than just own-industry size. Moreover,
these urbanization economies may arise from the complex interaction of various service industries, diverse labor markets,
large local consumer markets for testing products, and the
diverse environment for firms engaged in product development and
innovation. This is an area in which research is almost
nonexistent.

The relationship between urban area size, urban concentration, and the proportion of the labor force engaged in professional, technical, business service, financial clerical, and
related occupations can be illustrated. In the United States,
the proportion of the urban population living in urbanized areas
over 1 million rose from 39 percent to 47 percent (mostly by
expansion of the number of urban areas over 1 million) between
1950 and 1970 as service occupations expanded and blue collar
occupations declined (from 46 percent of the labor force to 33
percent). More generally, for a sample of 34 countries,
Henderson (1980) finds a positive relationship between measures
of national urban concentration in larger versus smaller urban
areas and the national ratio of service to manufacturing employment, holding other characteristics of countries constant.


Spatial Dispersion of Urban Activity: Centralization and
Concentration

So far, we have discussed urban concentration, or the extent to
which the urban population is housed in larger as opposed to

smaller urban areas. There is also, however, the issue of
centralization--the extent to which these urban areas, large or
small, are spread throughout the country as opposed to being
clustered together in a few small pockets, for example, on the
coast or around a national capital. There are two interrelated
conceptual frameworks used to analyze this question: one deals
with the notion of regions and regional comparative advantage,
and the other with location theory and the location of natural
resources.

In the first of these frameworks, the interregional mobility
of the population is assumed to be very limited, and regional
output composition is assumed to depend on comparative advantage
and relative regional endowments of labor and resources (Borts
and Stein, 1964). In the second framework, the interregional
mobility is assumed to be potentially high for a "reasonable"
proportion (10-35 percent?) of the population. Regional comparative advantage in production then becomes based on natural
resource endowments, and regional populations depend on the
labor force needed to utilize those endowments given national
production patterns. Historically, work on the United States
(Williamson, 1977; Henderson, 1980) or Peru (Thomas, 1978), and
on developing countries generally (Squire, 1979), suggests that
labor is in fact highly mobile, with different skill groups
moving rapidly across regions to equalize real wages across
regions for each group. Such mobility may still produce large
differences in regional per capita incomes. These differences
do not necessarily reflect inequities or inefficiencies, but
simply differences in the skill composition of the labor force,
labor force participation, and costs-of-living. In the analysis
to follow, we tend to adhere to the more modern approach and
assume interregional labor mobility. However, for a large
country, we could first divide it into several main regions with
limited interregional mobility, and then subdivide the regions,
assuming potentially extensive mobility across subdivisions; our
analysis would then focus on activity within a main region.

We will start by briefly outlining the determinants of
whether urban production in an economy tends to be highly
centralized into one (sub)region, as opposed to being spread out
across various (sub)regions. The analysis here examines economies with sufficient urban population to support a large system
of cities; later, we will examine situations where this may not
be the case. Our examination of these determinants is brief
simply because population dispersion is very much a function of
each economy's unique geographic features.

Urban areas generally tend to cluster together to reduce the
transport and communications costs of trade among themselves.
However, natural resources used in production are generally
spatially dispersed, whether they be fertile agricultural land;
natural harbors for ports; deposits of iron, coal, oil, lime-
stone, etc.; or forested lands for timber, pulp, and paper.
Transport cost efficiencies indicate that urban areas engaged in
weight-reducing, resource-using production, such as primary
metals, heavy machinery, wood products, and food processing, will

be spread throughout the economy near the resources they utilize. This also has the advantage that some of the most polluting production (e.g., iron and steel) often occurs in smaller urban areas, away from major population centers. Moreover, some footloose production that may not be especially weight-reducing but is highly standardized may be very sensitive to cheap power, land, and labor in its location choices. For this reason, textiles and some other light manufacturing may also be somewhat spatially dispersed--staying near major urban markets, but far enough away to avoid being affected by the high wage and land costs in those markets. Because much footloose production will want to cluster very near large cities to remain sensitive to market and technological changes, we can expect to see large core urban areas engaged, say, in resource-oriented production (e.g., a port, food processing center, or heavy manufacturing center); these areas will be surrounded by footloose cities, or satellites, clustered there for access to the market in the core urban areas, as well as to each others' markets.

We should note that the phenomenon of clustering of urban areas often presents a problem in defining what an urban or metropolitan area is. For example, there are several definitions of the New York urban area, starting from its five central boroughs and expanding west and north to incorporate outlying urbanized areas; the population range of these definitions goes from 7.5 million up to 18 million or even more. Historically, as New York City's economy expanded, its labor and housing markets essentially overran outlying, previously independent urban areas (such as Newark and Patterson). Thus, while the core urban area may be service- and commerce-oriented, including a market-oriented apparel industry, it has incorporated a diverse set of heavier manufacturing industries. The same problem exists in examining, for example, Chicago: if we look at the core urban area or at that area plus the parts of the State of Indiana it has incorporated, we get a different picture of its industrial base.

Given these notions, regardless of how we interpret spatial patterns of clustering, we can state that the extent of urban centralization depends on the centralization of natural resources. If an economy has little in the way of fertile land and natural resources, its urban areas may be clustered around one or two ports that import its resources and export its products (e.g., Korea, with the national capital Seoul using Inchon as its port). On the other hand, if a country has rich inland deposits of iron, coal, forests, fertile land, and so on, it will have major inland metropolitan areas and sets of manufacturing and agricultural service cities (e.g., the United Kingdom, Brazil, and the United States).

The ability of urban areas to spread out can be particularly limited by the extent of inhabitable land. Fuchs and Street (1980) point this out for Taiwan. That country has an urbanized economy (65 percent of the population), with a rich agricultural base and a diverse manufacturing sector that expanded from 11 percent to 28 percent of the work force between 1952 and 1976. Given its diverse economy and rich agricultural food-processing base, its degree of urban concentration is very low compared to, say, that of Korea or Japan (Renaud, 1979), and its population is distributed among a number of well-developed urban areas interconnected by rails and highways. However, because it has relatively little inhabitable land (23 percent plains land), its urban areas are forced onto a small ribbon of land along the western side of the island. The negative environmental impact of this inability to disperse its urban areas spatially is the focus of much concern (Fuchs and Street, 1980).

## Government Policies Affecting Centralization and Concentration

Although a country's geographic features greatly influence the spatial dispersion of its urban population, its government's policies are also critically important. This is illustrated below in an examination of a number of key policy areas. First, it may be noted that some believe various government policies in many countries have inadvertently led to overconcentration and centralization of the urban population. Some countries that hold this view have recently enacted explicit policies intended to offset these biases, and to encourage decentralization and deconcentration (e.g., Brazil, Korea, and Egypt).

### Transportation Policies

A country's transportation policies critically affect centralization and concentration. Obviously, a country cannot effectively exploit its hinterland resources if it does not have an effective rail, water, or highway trucking system to get those resources to producers, and goods to national population centers and ports for export. However, more than resource exploitation is involved here. An effective transport system integrates an economy so that the hinterland can develop a full system of cities, producing lighter as well as heavier manufacturing products. Such a system means that footloose producers can cluster near inland users of natural resources or sources of cheap power, labor, and land and still have access to coastal and international markets.

The critical role of transport development in decentralization in the United States has been studied systematically by economic historians (Fogel, 1964). In currently developing areas, such as southern Brazil, that have invested in a modern highway system, one can now find, in addition to traditional textiles and food processing, the most sophisticated, modern light manufacturing production occurring deep in the hinterland in rapidly growing urban areas (e.g., Ribeirao Preto, Sao Jose do Rio Preto, and Aracatuba in the interior of the state of Sao Paulo). Of course, the Amazon area of Brazil illustrates the fact that building transport access to hinterlands is not sufficient to ensure development; also required are the resources to be exploited and people currently living there or willing to do

so. Moreover, the extension of transport facilities into
isolated areas can hurt certain local industries at the same
time that it helps the overall local economy: some industries
that produce goods only for local consumption may find that
transport improvements lower the barriers to trade and bring in
competing goods from the outside.

Recent research on transportation and spatial development
has been focused on the issue of urban concentration. Studies
have looked at Korea (Kwon, 1981; Song and Choe, 1981; Lee,
1982a), at Colombia (Lee, 1982b), at Brazil (Townroe, 1981), and
at the United States (Hekman, 1982). Most of this work has been
focused on the determinants of the deconcentration of manufacturing industries already in metropolitan areas, or on when and
what industries are willing to move out of major metropolitan
areas into outlying areas. The discussion later will focus on a
specific example; however, some general conclusions can be
stated. Critical in firms' decisions to deconcentrate is the
fact that the new location has excellent access to major markets;
the difference between road access of 1/2 hour and 1 1/2 hours
to a major population center will determine which outlying cities
will attract manufacturing (Song and Choe, 1982; Townroe, 1981;
Lee, 1982b). Firms that do deconcentrate tend to be larger (Lee,
1982b) and to produce standardized (e.g., brand name) products.
However, it is only the firms' production activities that decentralize; the headquarters often remain in large metropolitan
areas to engage in administrative, financial, and certain sales
activity (Hekman, 1982). Of all the location aspects involved,
access to markets may be the most critical factor in whether a
given location will attract industry.


High-Skill Labor

Numerous studies have focused on the fact that rapid growth in
efficient manufacturing production in a region or a country
simply cannot occur without the presence of reasonable numbers
of highly skilled workers. There are general studies, with
calculations of the very high rates of return to education in
developing compared to developed countries (see Squire, 1979 for
a review). There is also Ramos' (1970) work on Latin America,
linking the high rates of manufacturing output growth between
1960 and 1970 to growth in labor force quality, not growth in
employment.

Corresponding to these notions is work on production technology in both the United States and Brazil (Henderson, 1983,
1985a), which indicates that high- and low-skill workers are very
poor substitutes in the production of such manufactured products
as iron and steel, agricultural machinery, transport equipment,
textiles, leather products, ceramics, electrical machinery, and
nonagricultural machinery, for which the skill division is based
on educational attainment. The partial elasticities of substitution are reported in Table 7 for a sample of three-digit
Brazilian industries. $L_H$ is the elasticity of substitution

between high-skill (primary school or more) and low-skill labor. These elasticities are all under .16 and most are negative, indicating a relationship of complementarity, rather than substitutability. $_{LK}$ and $_{HK}$ are the elasticities of substitution between the two types of labor and capital; they all lie in the range of .67 to 1.41, which is conventional.

These facts have strong implications for urban development. Poor substitutability means that efficient skill mixes in production are not very flexible; further, as manufacturing industries develop in smaller urban areas, they cannot employ only local low-skill workers and do without high-skill workers. Although the skill mix in production in any one industry may not be flexible, the high-skill usage of some industries (primary metals and machinery) is much greater than that of some others (textiles, apparel, ceramics, leather products). Nevertheless, for manufacturing production to be decentralized and deconcentrated, so must high-skill labor.

Given the skilled labor force needed nationally to support a widespread manufacturing base, decentralization and deconcentration of industry and high-skill labor go hand in hand. The complication is that in developing countries, high-skill relative to low-skill labor seems to have a strong desire to live in larger as opposed to smaller urban areas, and there is a very strong correlation between city size and the skill composition of the labor force. Apart from job opportunities, work on Korea (Kwon, 1981) and Brazil (Hamer, 1983; Henderson, 1985c) suggests that for high-skill workers, a key variable in their choice of residential location is the quality of the school system for their children. Post-grade school educational quality in smaller urban areas in Brazil is notoriously bad or nonexistent, and even grade school education in many places is nonexistent or of very low quality (World Bank, 1979). Both Henderson's (1985c) work on Southern Brazil in general and the German government's work on the state of Minas Gerais in southern Brazil suggest that a key to attracting high-skill labor to decentralized locations

TABLE 7  Complementarity of High-Skill and Low-Skill Labor in Brazilian Manufacturing

| Partial Elasticities of Substitution | Iron and Steel | Agricultural Machinery | Auto Accessories | Chemicals | Ceramics | Shoes |
|---|---|---|---|---|---|---|
| $\sigma_{LH}$ | -.24 | -.40 | -.27 | -1.12 | .04 | .16 |
| $\sigma_{LK}$ | 1.13 | .67 | 1.27 | .79 | .88 | .85 |
| $\sigma_{HK}$ | 1.16 | .69 | .96 | 1.41 | 1.29 | 1.04 |

Source:  Henderson (1985a:Table 1).

is having a good-quality educational system. Researchers examining Korea (e.g., Kwon, 1981) indicate the same findings.

Work on the United States (Getz and Huang, 1978; Smith, 1978; Henderson, 1982a) suggests that high-skill people are simply much more amenity-oriented in general than low-skill people, placing a high value on good retailing and personal and local public services, as well as a clean, safe environment. To the extent that smaller cities in developing countries cannot offer sophisticated retailing and public services, accounting for cost-of-living differences across cities of different sizes, smaller cities have greater difficulty attracting high-skill workers.

In summary, a key to having decentralized manufacturing is having decentralized high-skill labor. In an economy where people are free to move, one key to inducing high-skill labor to decentralize is having decentralized high-quality local public services. The question for local public services, and to some extent for transportation, is what determines whether local public services are decentralized. We turn to this momentarily.

## Public Services for Industries

While we have emphasized the need for decentralized amenities to decentralize high-skill labor for industry, it must be recognized that in developing countries, industries themselves are often the biggest users of public utilities such as water, electricity, and telephones, often accounting for well over 50 percent of their use (Linn, 1979a). Obviously, if even almost entirely low-skill industries are to decentralize, beyond transportation access, public utilities must be decentralized. Firms in theory can (and sometimes do) provide their own water and electrical service; however, there are sufficient scale economies involved in providing these services (Nerlove, 1965; Hirsch, 1973) that, even for large plants, the scale of the utilities is so relatively small that the unit cost of service becomes very high. In Brazil, based on the experience of low-quality service in the 1960s, most firms surveyed that are deconcentrating from Grande Sao Paulo cite access to reliable utilities as one of their primary concerns (Townroe, 1981). In general, we again face the question of what determines whether services are decentralized, a topic to which we now turn.

## Centralization of Government Services

There is a notion that in most countries where government decision making is highly centralized, the provision of public services is spatially biased toward having much higher-quality services in the national capital and major metropolitan areas. In contrast, in federal systems of government, where the states or provinces have a reasonable degree of fiscal autonomy, public services are provided much more uniformly across urban areas. The reasoning is simple: people working in a highly centralized

government will be biased toward providing services in the
(national capital) area where they live and may be insensitive
to the needs and concerns of outlying areas; when taxation
powers and expenditure decision making are decentralized in a
federal system, the regional governments will respond to
regional needs, and regional cities can develop. In empirical
work on urban concentration in 34 countries, Henderson (1980)
finds that the most important determinant of national urban
concentration is whether a country is federalized or not (or
alternatively the ratio of state and local government
expenditures to all government expenditures).

It may also be noted that in a highly centralized system of
government, apart from public service provision, firms may feel
a strong need to locate near the national capital to be able to
lobby effectively and cut through the red tape of bureaucratic
decision making. Kwon (1981) and Nam and Ro (1981) suggest that
this is a problem for Korea, where many firms are unwilling to
decentralize from Seoul and lose their access to the central
bureaucracy.

Even in a decentralized, deconcentrated country with a
federalized system of government, such as Brazil, the central
government can still have a strong influence on locational
patterns. The particular illustration is the high level of
industrialization of the metropolitan area of Sao Paulo (GSP)
(Henderson, 1982b; Hamer, 1983). Relative to similar-sized
American urban areas such as New York, Los Angeles, and Chicago,
GSP has an incredible concentration of heavy industry. For
example, GSP and the combined three U.S. urban areas both account
for 20 percent of their respective country's urban populations;
however, GSP accounts for about 40 percent of Brazil's steel production, 72 percent of transport, and most petrochemicals, while
the three combined U.S. urban areas account for only 11 percent
of all primary metals and very small proportions of transport and
petrochemicals.

For Brazil, there seems to be no efficiency basis for this
concentration: these industries do not benefit from generalized
urbanization economies, they contribute to the extremely bad
environmental conditions in GSP, and they are forced to pay the
very high prevailing wages and land rents. For the latter
reason, one would not expect such firms to choose to locate in
GSP voluntarily. However, it is possible to explain why they
are there and how they survive. The iron and steel industry is
currently 50 percent state-owned. The state forced that
industry's initial (late 1940s) and a large proportion of its
new operations to locate along the short Rio de Janeiro—GSP
axis, and also appears to have acquired old iron and steel works
in GSP as they fell into receivership (Baer, 1969). Currently,
therefore, the state-owned production is located in GSP, while
private production has chosen more efficient interior locations
(where there are raw materials) in the state of Minas Gerais.
The state-owned industries may survive in GSP because they do not
have to pay the competitive cost of capital and can earn very low
returns on their investments. Similarly, the petrochemical

industry in GSP appears to be largely state-owned. Finally, the auto transport industry in GSP is foreign-owned, but is constrained in its location choices by the central government. Thus, one gets a general picture of government-owned or highly influenced firms being forced into or very near the large metropolitan areas of GSP and Rio de Janeiro, while private producers who are unconstrained choose locations in smaller urban areas.

Why has Brazil displayed this bias toward locating heavy and polluting manufacturing industries in the largest urban areas? While individual government officials may have profited privately from these location constraints, Brazilian officials seem to believe strongly in the existence of widespread urbanization economies for all industries, whether or not they produce standardized products or interact with other industries (Hamer, 1983; Henderson, 1982b). The existence of this belief is reflected in the operation of the part of the capital market controlled by the state-owned banking system. Informal information suggests that the part of the money flowing into the banking system that is used for long-term loans often goes only to very large firms (e.g., 1,000+ employees in highly central locations). This suggests in turn that much of the capital for decentralized private industrial development has come from the original large land-holding families, who have their own capital resources. This hypothesis is consistent with the general story of how the state of Sao Paulo industrialized (prior to the development of state capitalism) (see Katzman, 1977).

This strong and we believe incorrect view that, for efficiency, manufacturing enterprises must locate in large metropolitan areas appears to have prevailed in other countries as well, such as Japan (Mera, 1975) and Korea (Kwon, 1981). However, not all highly centralized systems have a centralization bias. A good example is the U.S.S.R.

It is hypothesized that by maintaining a very labor-intensive agricultural sector and a highly capital-intensive industrial sector, the U.S.S.R. has been able to restrict urban concentration severely (Renaud, 1979). It has enhanced this restriction by maintaining a rough rural-small city-large city wage parity regardless of productivity and by not improving the quality of public services in large cities, so that the incentives for legal or illegal migration into larger cities have been mostly eliminated (Renaud, 1979). Clearly, however, like concentration, deconcentration can be overdone. The costs of having wages unconnected to productivity, of having a low-productivity agricultural sector, and of over-capitalizing industrial production are the subject of much analysis and discussion (e.g., Wellisz, 1964).

THE DYNAMICS OF CONCENTRATION AND DECONCENTRATION

This section examines urban concentration and deconcentration in rapidly developing countries. The issue focused on is the costs

and benefits of encouraging the deconcentration of resources out
of major metropolitan areas into nearby cities.


## Urban Concentration and Deconcentration

The discussion above presents basic notions about the ways
existing patterns of urban (de)concentration and (de)central-
ization in a country can be related to the composition of
national production and the spatial distribution of public
services and transport systems.  It also addresses long-term
changes in urban concentration in a developed country such as
the United States.  What has not been specifically examined are
the rapid changes in urban concentration in some rapidly developing countries, such as Japan and Korea.  There has been a
general mild worldwide increase in urban concentration, which
may be related to the relative expansion of the service sector
and changes in the composition of the manufacturing sector in
many economies; however, in countries that experienced very rapid
increases in concentration between 1950 and 1970, the 1970s saw
a sharp drop in the rate of increase in concentration, or even a
decline in concentration.  Mera (1978) focuses on this for Japan
and Korea.
   Mera (1978) suggests that a natural process is at work here.
In the initial stages of the development of modern manufacturing,
concentration of the activity in one or two major urban areas
enhances an incubator process.  In this process, firms are dis-
covering what levels of technology (existing abroad) are appropriate to the skills available in the labor force, and what
markets are available nationally and particularly internationally
for which goods.  At this stage of development, in essence there
are urbanization economies available to all industries that make
it worthwhile for them to locate in large urban areas with their
high wage and land costs.  These economies may be enhanced if
skilled labor is very scarce, so that the country can support
only one or two large diverse urban labor markets.  Mera (1978)
and Kwon (1981) then go on to suggest that there is a natural
reversal to this process.  This reversal occurs for two reasons:
because overtime production becomes standardized, and firms can
move out of the incubator to outlying areas where land is
cheaper; and because the quality of life declines and the cost
of living rises sufficiently in the main metropolitan areas so
that economic activity is driven to secondary locations.


## The Initial Concentrations

While people now recognize that deconcentration is occurring and
believe that it is desirable, this view did not always exist.
Until the last 10 years or so, there was a strong belief in the
benefits of overall urban concentration, and also a perception
that spatially concentrated investments in social overhead
capital were much more efficient than deconcentrated investments

(Mera, 1975). These beliefs may account in part for policies
that may have attracted excessive numbers of people to large
metropolitan areas from smaller urban and rural areas. Several
such policies may be noted. For example, there appear to be
spatial biases in public investments toward the largest
metropolitan areas in Brazil and Japan; in the latter case,
government investment per capita was about 45 percent higher in
the three largest cities as compared to the average for other
highly urbanized areas (Mera, 1975:21). Moreover, the strong
general urban-rural bias in the provision of basic social
services in many developing countries is well documented
(Squire, 1979; Linn, 1979).

Other spatial policies encouraging urbanization and urban
concentration should be mentioned. In many countries, including
Korea (Renaud, 1979), there is the notion that agricultural
development has been deemphasized both by underinvestment in
research and development in agriculture (Evenson and Kisler,
1975), and by trade protection and capital market policies
favoring urban industries (Squire, 1979). A result is that
incomes in agriculture relative to those in urban areas have
fallen, encouraging rural outmigration. There is very strong
evidence (see Squire, 1979, for a review) that rural migration
is very sensitive to wage differentials. For example, the
slowing of rural-urban migration in Korea in the early 1970s has
been related to an agricultural income policy that at least
temporarily eliminated the rural-urban income gap (Song and
Choe, 1982; Mera, 1978).

Moreover, government policies that specifically discriminate
against agriculture and traditional manufacturing in favor of
modern manufacturing distort development patterns. The welfare
costs of resource misallocation that results from inhibiting
some industries while artificially encouraging others are well
known. Little et al. (1970), Barret (1972), and Reboucas (1974)
document these misallocations and show for a wide variety of
countries that protected industries have very low net value
added and social rates of return to investment. In contrast are
the extremely high rates of return to investment in agricultural
research and development documented for countries such as India
(Evenson and Kisler, 1975) and estimated for investments in the
diffusion of technical information for agriculture in Japan
(Harker, 1979; see also Renaud, 1979, on Korea).


The Costs of Urban Concentration

While much of the literature of 10-20 years ago emphasized the
benefits of urban concentration, the more recent literature has
emphasized and documented the costs. Two types of costs are
emphasized--social overhead capital (SOC) and environmental.

Research shows that there have been very high returns to
manufacturing from investment in relevant SOC in the United
States and Japan (Mera, 1975). However, the productivity
benefits of spatially concentrating SOC investments appear to be

weak (Mera, 1975:Table 4.16), suggesting that high returns to SOC investments per employee may occur almost equally well in smaller cities. Then a basic question is how the costs of public service provision vary with city size; the data on this are not encouraging.

The costs of road provision and commuting costs per resident rise dramatically with urban area population. For example, Zahavi (1976), looking at data for a variety of countries, suggests that in moving from an urban area population of 1 million to 8 million, per person trip distances can be expected to rise by at least 65 percent; trip times rise even more; and per person road provision, even in a moderately motorized situation (5 cars per 100 residents), can be expected to rise 350 percent.

For public utilities (water, electricity, and waste disposal), while there are economies of scale, even in the best of conditions, these economies are completely exhausted by an urban populations of 1/2 million (Hirsch, 1973; Nerlove, 1965). Moreover, there is some confusion surrounding this issue (Linn, 1979): these scale economies refer to the operation of large systems built from scratch; most expansion of public utilities involves adding onto existing systems. For electricity, the expansions then involve building smaller-scale plants; for water and waste disposal, if the capacity of existing systems is already strained, adding on extensions either involves a drop in quality of service or the extremely expensive operation of tearing up old systems. This suggests first that the long-run costs of supplying public utilities to 250,000 new users in a large metropolitan area can exceed the long-run costs of supplying public utilities to the 250,000 recent residents of a new medium-sized urban area. Second, there are indications that per person costs fall with population density because fewer feet of pipes and power lines are required per resident; however, if population density rises rapidly in a city, the capacity of existing systems may be overburdened, again leading to declines in quality of service or costly overhauling of the system. Third, providing, for example, waste disposal by standardized large-city technology in smaller cities can be very expensive; however, the requirements for this utility may decline with city size, and less expensive technologies (pit latrines or septic units) can be used (Linn, 1979 argues that in many cases, they could well be used in larger cities also).

The second type of costs associated with increases in urban area size are environmental, including such social costs as congestion and crime. For a manufacturing firm, part of the true costs of its production are the damages and unpleasantness it imposes on others through pollution emissions. Since dumping emissions into the environment typically costs the firm nothing, the firm is likely to impose excessive damages on others by, for example, using more-polluting rather than less-polluting inputs (e.g., soft versus hard coal). In the absence of effective policies regulating these emissions, it is tempting to conclude that urban area populations are best limited so as to limit the

218                                                            Henderson

number of firms contributing to a poor environment in any
location. However, in many circumstances such a conclusion can
be unwarranted. In many LDCs, the worst of the environmental
problems in very large urban areas arise because heavy polluting
industries are forced into large metropolitan areas, when in
fact they would be best off, apart from environmental considerations, locating in currently smaller cities in the hinterlands
where raw materials are found. The solution, then, is not to
limit the size of large urban areas, but to allow heavy industry
to relocate, perhaps inducing some population relocation as well.


Deconcentration Policies for Seoul, Korea

Korea has relatively strong policies designed to encourage industries in Seoul to move from the main urban area to surrounding
cities and towns. By examining which deconcentration policies
are effective, one can start to determine which considerations
are critical to the successful development of satellite cities
surrounding a metropolitan area. We use the example of Seoul,
Korea because it is the only country having implemented a strong
deconcentration policy on which research has been done. We first
describe the situation in Korea; then examine its deconcentration
policies; and finally draw some conclusions about which policies
best prevent undesired concentration or, alternatively, best
promote desired deconcentration.

        Korea has two main regions of industrial concentration and
growth--the national capital region in the North (West) and the
South (East) region around Busan, although all provinces are
fairly well urbanized. Currently (1975-80), the populations of
the urban area of Seoul and of the entire national capital region
are both growing at only 4 percent a year, while major Southern
urban areas, such as Ulsam (9.7 percent), Pohang (9.3 percent),
and Busan (5.3 percent), are growing more rapidly (for 1970-80).
Within the national capital region, however, some smaller and
medium-sized cities are growing at very high rates (10-15
percent), and there is rural-urban migration.

        There appears to be a process of both decentralization and
deconcentration from the Seoul urban area. Seoul's rate of
growth of manufacturing employment from 1973-78 averaged 5.6
percent, but its share in national manufacturing employment fell
from 34 to 25 percent. In contrast, in terms of decentralization
to the South, the growth rates of manufacturing in Busan and its
province were 12.9 percent and 15.6 percent, respectively, for
1973-78, with their shares rising modestly. In terms of deconcentration, the manufacturing growth rate in the national capital
region other than the Seoul urban area for 1973-78 was 23.6
percent, while its share in manufacturing employment rose from
14.1 percent to 22.9 percent. Thus, while decentralization to
the relatively resource-rich Southern part of Korea is occurring,
the pervasive phenomenon is deconcentration from the Seoul urban
area to the outlying parts of the national capital region.

More specifically, if we divide the national capital region into five rings between 1973 and 1980, the Central Business District had a negative manufacturing employment growth rate (-7.6 percent per year), the next ring a zero growth rate, and the third and final ring within the Seoul urban area an 11 percent growth rate, while the two rings outside the urban area had growth rates of 22 percent and 34 percent. While existing (mature) firms within Seoul are growing, there is strong out-migration, and the outlying regions are experiencing both high rates of births of firms and mature growth. Almost all relocating firms remain in the national capital region, although the Southeast region experiences high birth rates of new firms.

Why has this deconcentration occurred? Kwon (1981) and Song and Choe (1982) indicate that the firms most willing to move are large ones (especially in machinery and metals) producing brand name or standardized products. They are looking for cheap land and labor, and want to avoid the highly congested Seoul area, given that incubator effects and urbanization economies may have dissipated over time for their activities.

To enhance this natural process of deconcentration, the central government has instituted a number of policies, including tax and credit incentives, the building of industrial sites, a prohibition against new firms choosing Seoul locations, and relocation orders for existing firms to move out of Seoul. It appears that the latter, which have been given to 3,000 firms (1976-80), are not effective. First, while firms initially complied, the compliance rate has dropped to under 40 percent (Song and Choe, 1981). Second, a small percentage of mover-firms indicate that relocation orders benefited them (Song and Choe, 1981); that is, relocators were mostly firms who were planning, or at least willing, to move anyway. The tax and credit incentives are very substantial, and many firms take advantage of them. However, the primary impact of the incentives appears to be not on the decision to move (Song and Choe, 1981), but on the over-use of capital relative to other factors. Murray (1983) argues that the incentives have grossly distorted the use of capital by relocating firms.

Similarly, the widespread building of industrial sites is viewed negatively by various researchers (Renaud, 1979; Song and Choe, 1981; Murray, 1983). It is not that there is anything wrong with the sites per se; it is just that without certain features, they are not utilized. The targeted satellite city of Banweol in the national capital region is used to illustrate the problems involved. Banweol had 1,000 industrial sites prepared in 1977; only about 200 have been filled to date. There appear to be two reasons for this dismal performance. First, compared to the growing satellite cities of Seoul, Banweol has poor access to Seoul (1 1/2 hours by road, compared to 20-30 minutes for the satellite cities). Access to Seoul is viewed as being critical, not just for the marketing of goods, but also for access to service industries, the central bureaucracy, and specialized high-skill workers. Second, it appears that in planning, the central government did not develop good-quality public services

in Banweol, and it is therefore difficult to get skilled workers
to live there.  In fact, only 46 percent of Banweol's workers
live there, with 70 percent of the rest commuting the 1 1/2
hours each way from Seoul (Song and Choe, 1981).  Even industrial
services are limited; for example, industrial users of water must
buy and pay high rates for residential-quality water.  Firms that
have moved to Banweol also complain about the red tape involved
in their interactions with the relocation authorities.  In contrast is the fastest-growing satellite city of Seoul, Bucheon,
whose distinctive features are rapid access to Seoul and local
fiscal autonomy.  With a good tax base, Bucheon provides its own
local public services; it is apparently well planned by its own
population and not dependent on the sometimes haphazard decisions
of central government bureaucrats.  However, it must also be
added that there are fast-growing, government-targeted satellite
cities (e.g., Anyang and Gumi).

In summary, the most effective deconcentration policies
provide deconcentrated urban sites that have good access to
central markets, have the good-quality local public services
demanded by high-skill workers, have sufficient local autonomy
in providing industrial residential services to be responsive to
the particular needs of workers and firms that move there, and
are not snared in central government red tape.

There is an entirely different issue involved in the Seoul
deconcentration policies--the tradeoff with decentralization.
There is a suspicion that, with the focus so much on deconcentration policies in the national capital region, decentralization to the South and other regions has been slowed.  While the
South is an attractive growth area, given its resources and
harbors, the transport network about Busan appears to be much
more limited (Song and Choe, 1981: maps 4 and 6).  Moreover, by
apparently focusing policy implementation on satellite cities
around Seoul, the government may have attracted more local rural
population and extra-provincial migration to the urbanized
national capital region than might otherwise have occurred.  In
the absence of the deconcentration focus, these migrants and new
firms might have tended to choose locations outside the national
capital region.  The danger of focusing on satellite cities is
twofold.  First, the central city may eventually overrun the
satellites, so that the whole area becomes one massive, highly
congested agglomeration, although that tendency can be inhibited
by imposing greenbelts around cities.  Second, the whole area
may attract much more population than is intended; while the
satellites encourage deconcentration, they may also attract
significant numbers of migrants from beyond the region.


CONCLUSIONS

There is a strong link  between urbanization and economic growth.
While this link is complex, a central feature is that national
production patterns and urbanization are directly related.
Certain types of manufacturing and service goods are subject to

economies of scale in production; for example, their efficient production requires spatial agglomerations of people, that is, cities. As an economy develops, it tends to shift national production patterns toward those types of goods most efficiently produced in significant-sized cities. Moreover, the particular mix of manufacturing and service production affects the size distribution of cities. Because of the nature of scale economies, efficient production for many industries occurs in specialized cities, so that there are many types of cities, categorized by the industrial production in which they specialize. Each type of city has a different efficient size, depending on the precise extent of scale economies for that industrial good. Thus an economy relatively specialized in goods produced in large cities will have a higher degree of urban concentration.

The link between urbanization and economic growth is strongly affected by government policies, which tend to affect the character of the urbanization process. In particular, it appears that many government policies encourage overconcentration and centralization. An illustration is the distribution of public services, with, for example, good intermediate and upper-level schooling available only in certain key cities. Another illustration is the heavy subsidization of urban utilities in only one or two cities (e.g., Mexico). A third is constraints on state-owned industries to locate only in a few key cities. Overconcentration has direct economic costs, but it also has social costs. For example, traditional social structure and cultural institutions may erode much more quickly in large metropolises. If much of urbanization can be achieved with less upheaval in smaller cities, greater social stability may result.


REFERENCES

Baer, W. (1969)  The Development of the Brazilian Steel Industry.
    Nashville, Tenn.: Vanderbilt University Press.
Barrett, R.N. (1972)  The Brazilian Foreign Exchange Auction
    System. Unpublished Ph.D. dissertation, University of
    Wisconsin.
Bergsman, J., P. Greenston, and R. Healy (1972)  The agglomer-
    ation process in urban growth. Urban Studies 9(3):263-288.
Bergsman, J., P. Greenston, and R. Healy (1975)  A classification
    of economic activities based on location patterns. Journal
    of Urban Economics 2:1-28.
Berry, B. (1968)  Geography of Market Centers and Retail Distri-
    bution. Englewood Cliffs, N.J.: Prentice-Hall.
Borts, G., and J. Stein (1964)  Economic Growth in a Free Market.
    New York: Columbia University Press.
Bureau of the Census (1976)  Historical Statistics of the U.S.A.,
    Colonial Times to 1970, Part 1. Washington, D.C.: U.S.
    Department of Commerce.
Evenson, R., and Y. Kisler (1975)  Agricultural Research and
    Productivity. New Haven, Conn.: Yale University Press.

Fogel, R. (1964)   Railroads and American Economic Growth.
Baltimore, Md.: The Johns Hopkins Press.

Fuchs, R.L., and J.M. Street (1980)   Land constraints and
development planning in Taiwan. Journal of Developing Areas
14:313-326.

Getz, M., and Y. Huang (1978)   Consumer revealed preferences for
environmental goods. Review of Economics and Statistics 60:
449-458.

Hamer, A. (1983)   Decentralized Urban Development and Industrial
Location Behavior in Sao Paulo, Brazil. Working paper, World
Bank, Washington, D.C.

Harker, B.R. (1979)   Education, Communication and Agricultural
Change: A Study of Japanese Farmers. Unpublished Ph.D.
dissertation, University of Chicago.

Hekman, J. (1982)   Branch Plant Location and the Product Cycle
in Computer Manufacturing. Working paper, University of
North Carolina.

Henderson, J.V. (1980)   A Framework for International Comparisons
of Systems of Cities. Working paper, World Bank, Washington,
D.C.

Henderson, J.V. (1982a)   Evaluating consumer amenities and interregional welfare differences. Journal of Urban Economics
11:32-59.

Henderson, J.V. (1982b)   Urban Economies of Scale in Brazil.
Working paper, World Bank, Washington, D.C.

Henderson, J.V. (1983)   Industrial bases and city sizes.
American Economic Review 73:164-168.

Henderson, J.V. (1985a)   Efficiency of resource usage and city
size. Journal of Urban Economics (in press).

Henderson, J.V. (1985b)   Population composition of cities:
restructuring the Tiebout model. Journal of Public
Economics  27(2):131-156.

Henderson, J.V. (1985c)   Urbanization in a developing country:
city size and population composition. Journal of Development
Economics (forthcoming).

Hirsch, W.Z. (1973)   Urban Economic Analysis. New York:
McGraw-Hill.

Katzman, M. (1977)   Cities and Frontiers in Brazil: Regional
Dimensions of Economic Development. Cambridge, Mass.:
Harvard University Press.

Kwon, W.Y. (1981)   A study of the economic impact of industrial
relocation: the case of Seoul. Urban Studies 18:73-90.

Lee, K.S. (1982a)   A model of intra-urban location. Journal of
Urban Economics 12:263-279.

Lee, K.S. (1982b)   Changing Location Patterns of Manufacturing
Employment in the Seoul Region: A Summary Report. Mimeo,
World Bank, Washington, D.C.

Linn, J.F. (1979)   Policies for Efficient and Equitable Growth
of Cities in Developing Countries. Working Paper No. 342,
World Bank, Washington, D.C.

Little, I.M.D., I.M. David, T. Scitovsky, and M. Scott (1970)
Industry and Trade in Some Developing Countries. Oxford,
England: Oxford University Press.

Mera, K. (1978)  Income Distribution and Regional Development.
   Tokyo:  Tokyo University Press.
Murray, M.D. (1983)  An Illustration of Analytical Tools and
   Their Transferrability to Other Cities.  Mimeo, World Bank,
   Washington, D.C.
Nam, D.W., and K.K. Ro (1981)  Population research and population
   policy in Korea in the 1970s.  Population and Development
   Review 7:651-669.
Nerlove, M. (1965)  Estimation and Identification of Cobb-Douglas
   Production Functions.  Amsterdam:  North-Holland.
Ramos, J.R. (1970)  Labor and Development in Latin America.  New
   York:  Columbia University Press.
Reboucas, O.E. (1974)  Interregional Effects of Economic
   Policies.  Unpublished Ph.D. dissertation, Harvard
   University.
Renaud, B. (1979)  National Urbanization Policies in Developing
   Countries.  Working Paper No. 347, World Bank, Washington,
   D.C.
Richardson, H.W. (1977)  City Size and National Spatial
   Strategies in Developing Countries.  Working Paper No. 252,
   World Bank, Washington, D.C.
Segal, D. (1976)  Are there returns to scale in city size.
   Review of Economics and Statistics 63:339-350.
Smith, B. (1978)  Measuring the value of urban amenities.
   Journal of Urban Economics 5:370-387.
Song, B.N., and S.C. Choe (1981)  Review of Urban Trends in
   Korea.  Working paper, World Bank, Washington, D.C.
Song, B.N., and S.C. Choe (1982)  An Evaluation of Industrial
   Location Policies for Urban Deconcentration in Seoul
   Region.  Working paper, World Bank, Washington, D.C.
Squire, L. (1979)  Labor Force, Employment and Labor Markets in
   the Course of Economic Development.  Working Paper No. 336,
   World Bank, Washington, D.C.
State Statistical Bureau of the People's Republic of China (1981)
   Statistical Yearbook of China.  Hong Kong:  Economic
   Information and Agency.
Sveikauskas, L. (1975)  The productivity of cities.  Quarterly
   Journal of Economics 89:393-413.
Thomas, V. (1978)  The Measurement of Spatial Differences in
   Poverty:  The Case of Peru.  Working Paper No. 273, World
   Bank, Washington, D.C.
Tolley, G., P. Graves, and J. Gardner (1979)  Urban Growth
   Policy in a Market Economy.  New York:  Academic Press.
Townroe, P. (1981)  Location Factors for Industrial Decentra-
   lization from Metropolitan Sao Paulo.  Working paper, World
   Bank, Washington, D.C.
U.S. Department of Commerce (1982)  U.S. City and County Data
   Book.  Washington, D.C.  U.S. Department of Commerce.
Wellisz, S. (1964)  The Economics of the Soviet Bloc.  New York:
   McGraw-Hill.
Williamson, J.G. (1977)  Unbalanced Growth, Inequality and
   Regional Development:  Some Lessons from American History.
   Mimeo, University of Wisconsin.

World Bank (1979)  Brazil:  Human Resources Special Report.
    Washington, D.C.:  World Bank.
World Bank (1983)  World Development Report 1983.  Washington,
    D.C.:  World Bank.
Yap, L. (1977)  The attraction of cities:  a review of the
    migration literature.  Journal of Development Economics
    4:239-264.
Yezer, A., and R. Goldfarb (1982)  An indirect test of efficient
    city size.  Journal of Urban Economics 5:46-65.
Zahavi, Y. (1976)  Travel Characteristics in Cities of Developing
    and Developed Countries.  Working Paper No. 230, World Bank,
    Washington, D.C.

# 7
# Population and Technical Change in the Manufacturing Sector of Developing Countries

Jeffrey James

## INTRODUCTION

The literature on the impact of population on technical change in developing countries has been overwhelmingly concerned with the agricultural sector of these countries.[1] Seldom have authors questioned the applicability of theories formulated specifically for this sector to other areas of the economy--most notably manufacturing. At the same time, those concerned with the analysis of technical change in manufacturing have not paid much specific attention to the role of population in the process by which this change is generated. As a result, we know relatively little about the impact of population on the rate and direction of technical change in manufacturing. The purpose of this chapter is, accordingly, to try to fill this gap in our knowledge. The chapter contends that the impact of population on technical change in the manufacturing sector of contemporary developing countries needs to be sharply distinguished from two other phenomena: the impact of population on technical change in the manufacturing sector during the comparable stage of development within the now developed countries, and that impact in the agricultural sector of developing countries. These differential impacts are shown to derive from a combination of the historical conditions of latecomer industrialization (particularly those associated with a pronounced degree of technological dependency), the role and size of manufacturing in the overall economy, and particular development policies pursued in the post-war period. For purposes of analyzing these relationships, this chapter adopts a comparative historical perspective described briefly in the next section below. This is followed by a discussion of the mechanisms through which population variables transmit an impact

The author is indebted to the Working Group on Population Growth and Economic Development of the Committee on Population for comments on an earlier draft and to Frances Stewart for kindly sharing her ideas on this subject. Prasannan Parthasarathi provided research assistance of a very high order.

on technical change in manufacturing. The chapter ends with a
summary and conclusions.


A COMPARATIVE HISTORICAL PERSPECTIVE

In the search for a unidirectional relationship between population and technical change, the relevance of the impact of specific (historical, sectoral, and macro-policy) factors on this
relationship is often ignored. This comes about, for example,
through the choice of a unit of analysis that is highly aggregated. Thus, in one recent paper (Simon and Steinmann, 1984:
169), "The more-developed world as a whole" is taken to be "the
appropriate unit of analysis . . . individual countries are used
in empirical studies we refer to only because of their convenience as research observations and for thought experiments."
Another example is the specification of a set of relationships
that is purported to apply over long periods of time in a particular country. Julian Simon's (1977:23-24) simulation model for
developing countries, for instance, is described as being "appropriate both to the pre-industrial stage and to the industrial-
izing stage."
      The view taken here, however, is that this failure to vary
the analysis of the impact of population on technical change
according to the particular circumstances of each nation is no
help to the policy maker who must formulate specific policies,
and who can take neither historical experience nor experience
from other sectors and countries as a secure basis for conducting
this task. Indeed, the impact of population on technical change
in the manufacturing sector may vary not only from that in earlier historical periods (in the same sector of the now developed
countries) and from that in agriculture, but also among different
developing countries that pursue alternative economic strategies
with a contrasting set of associated macro-policies. What is required, therefore, is an approach sensitive to variations in the
conditions under which the impact of population on technical
change is to be transmitted. Some of the most important of these
variations are shown in Table 1.
      The historically distinctive dimension of latecomer indus-
trialization is schematically reflected in the first two rows of
the matrix, showing, respectively, the associated greater dependence on imports of technology and more marked economies of
scale, as opposed to both comparable historical experience in
the manufacturing sector and experience in the agricultural
sector in the contemporary developing countries. The sectoral
differentiation is captured through the implication of the small
numbers employed in the manufacturing relative to the agricultural sector in the developing countries, and the policy variables are those relating to factor prices and the degree of
competition. The rest of this chapter will examine how the interaction among these distinguishing features produces correspondingly distinctive impacts of population on technical change
in manufacturing. The focus will be on the four mechanisms

TABLE 1  The Impact of Population Growth on Technical Change:  The Distinguishing Features of Latecomer Industrialization

| Variable | Sector | | |
|---|---|---|---|
| | Manufacturing in Contemporary Developing Countries | Manufacturing in Industrial Revolution | Agriculture in Contemporary Developing Countries |
| Imports of New Processes and Products | Dominant source of technical change | Unimportant in Britain; more important in early-follower countries where formed basis of adaptive innovations | Minor compared to the manufacturing sector |
| Economies of Scale | Dominant feature of techno-logical shelf on which developing countries most rely | Not much in evidence until about 1870[a] | Unimportant |
| Contribution of Sector to Total Employment | In about 1970, percentage of male working population occupied in manufacturing ranged from less than 10% in most Afro-Asian countries to about 20% in the more developed Latin American countries[b] | "Because there are no statistics, the precise percentage of the working population employed in manufacturing during the very early phase of industrialization in the developed countries cannot be determined.  Nevertheless it can be assumed from extrapolations and some fragmentary figures, that at the moment of 'take off' the percentage was between 10 and 12%"[c] | For the mid-1970s, agriculture occupied between 65 and 75% of the total active population[d] |
| Factor Prices | Highly distorted in most cases | Sensitive to factor endowment | Sensitive to factor endowment |
| Degree of Competition | Low, mostly oligopolistic or monopolistic | Intense | Intense |

Sources:
[a]Mokyr (1977).
[b]Bairoch (1975:Table 22).
[c]Bairoch (1975:80).
[d]Bairoch (1975:13).

227

through which these impacts are transmitted: (1) the dampened inducement to innovate; (2) the permissive effect of scale economies; (3) population density, urban concentration, and infrastructural investment; and (4) population size, the domestic capital goods sector, and indigenous technical change. The term technical change is used here to include changes in technology as well as in products, and the focus of the discussion will be on the large-scale or organized component of the manufacturing sector, in which most such changes have occurred.[2]

## MECHANISMS FOR THE IMPACT OF POPULATION ON TECHNICAL CHANGE IN MANUFACTURING

### The Dampened Inducement to Innovate

As indicated in Table 1, unlike agriculture, manufacturing in most developing countries comprises a small proportion of total employment. This proportion, according to Bairoch's fragmentary data, also shown in the table, appears (on average) to be of the same order of magnitude as that which obtained during the very early phases of industrialization in the now developed countries.[3] As a result, even rapid growth of this sector implies only a very modest increase in the demand for labor; a corollary is that high rates of population growth may not be necessary to ensure an abundant supply of labor for producers in manufacturing. In fact, labor abundance may be consistent with only a modest rate of growth in population; Lewis (1979:219) has pointed this out in relation to the historical experience of the European economies, where "in the second half of the nineteenth century European populations were growing at just over one per cent per annum, and this rate created an abundance of labour in most of them." The abundance of labor in most contemporary developing countries, in contrast, is associated with very much more rapid rates of population growth (which, over the period 1950 to 1970, for example, averaged 1.7 percent per annum) (Squire, 1981).

### Distinctive Historical Patterns

During the Industrial Revolution in Great Britain and most of the early-follower countries, the pattern of technical change in the manufacturing sector appears to have responded sensitively to the condition of a relative abundance of labor. However, a quite different response has been evoked in the post-war developing world, as indicated by two related pieces of evidence.

The first has to do with comparative rates of productivity growth. Table 2 shows recent rates of labor productivity growth for the developing countries as a group, and compares these rates with the magnitudes for two periods from the history of the now developed countries. Though considerable in relation to both these latter estimates, the developing country performance is

TABLE 2  A Crude Historical Comparison of Rates of Industrial
Productivity Growth

| Country | Period | Growth Rate in Industrial Productivity (percent p.a.) |
|---|---|---|
| Contemporary Developing Countries | | |
| Sample of countries from Table 3 | 1960-70 | 3.81 |
| All developing countries, excluding those with a population of less than 20 million in 1976[a] | 1960-70 | 4.6 |
| The Historical Experience of Developed Countries | | |
| Britain[b] | 1780-1860 | 0.65 |
| Developed countries | 1880-1900 | 2.0 |

[a]Excluding Brazil, Vietnam, and Zaire.
[b]Refers to nonagricultural sectors.

Sources: For the contemporary developing countries, Table 3 and
Squire, (1981). For the historical experience of the now developed
countries, McCloskey (1981:114); Squire (1981).

especially pronounced when compared to the earlier period, a time
when Britain was at a stage of development more nearly comparable
to that of the "typical" developing country in the 1960s.
    The second piece of evidence concerns the differential rates
of growth of capital per head with which the rates of productivity growth shown in Table 2 were associated. The comparative
data available in this regard (though they, like the data shown
in the table, are subject to major problems of measurement) point
to a degree of distinctiveness in the developing country experience that is no less striking.
    Recent evidence for the period of the Industrial Revolution
in Britain up to 1830 suggests that capital and labor grew at
more or less the same rate. "Labor-intensive technical changes
must have been about as powerful as labor-saving ones in their
effects, so that up to about 1830 the direction of technical
change was neutral as between capital and labor" (von Tunzelmann,
1981:158). In the manufacturing sector, in particular, "very
sketchy evidence suggests that capital and labor grew at identical rates of about 2 1/2 percent during the early part of the
nineteenth century" (von Tunzelmann, 1981:159). That is to say,
technical change during this period resulted in the proportional
expansion of employment creation and capital accumulation that
is implicitly envisaged in the well-known model of development

proposed in 1954 in Lewis. In the early-follower European
countries, too, there appear to have been concerted and systematic efforts to adapt technologies to the labor abundance that,
as noted above, existed in spite of only relatively modest rates
of population growth. Landes (1965:116) has described these
efforts (the effect of which was to exert a restraining influence
on the growth of capital per man) in the following terms:

> In Europe the follower countries made the most of their cheap
> manpower by building more rudimentary but less expensive
> equipment, buying second-hand machines whenever possible, and
> concentrating on the more labor-intensive branches or stages
> of manufacture. Not until the last third of the century did
> the Continental economies conform to the usual theoretical
> model and avail themselves of the opportunity to adopt the
> latest techniques; and even then they maintained a larger
> working force per unit of production . . . than Britain or
> the United States. In addition, they tended to be prodigal
> in their use of labor to manipulate or move materials and
> goods . . . . Finally, the Continental mills, like the early
> British factories, worked their equipment as long and hard
> as possible.

In contrast, fragmentary data for particular developing countries show that the ratio of capital per man has risen rapidly
over a wide range of manufacturing industries.[4] For a group of
mostly Latin American countries, for instance, Baer and Herve
(1966:90-92) conclude that "mechanization has taken place across
the board. Not only was there an increase in industries which
by their very nature are capital-intensive (such as chemicals,
metal products, etc.), but the installed per capita power capacity or electricity consumption per capita has rapidly increased
in the more traditional industries." Similarly, in the case of
Puerto Rico, Reynolds and Gregory (1965:90-91) found that "substantial increases have occurred in the ratio of capital to labor
within individual manufacturing industries." In fact, they found
a doubling of this ratio for all reporting firms over the period
between 1954 and 1961. Gouverneur's (1971) data for a sample of
industrial firms in the Congo show much the same pattern.
    From the fragmentary evidence available, it is not possible
to estimate the degree to which these pronounced tendencies to
capital deepening--as opposed to other factors, such as learning
effects--have caused the rapid rates of growth of productivity
noted above. Nevertheless, both sets of time-series data are
consistent with the evidence for widespread imports of technology from developed countries, where, in the condition of growing
labor scarcity, similar patterns of change had emerged. At the
micro level, the tendency toward importing technological change
from the developed countries has been documented by Gouverneur
(1971:124), whose comparison of firms in Belgium with those in
the Congo concludes that "the labor coefficient, capital coefficient, and capital-labor ratio of a firm in a less-developed
country generally change in the same direction as those of a

comparable firm in an advanced country.  But similar conclusions about the <u>direction</u> of the changes do not imply similar <u>levels</u> of the coefficients in the two countries at the various times nor a constant difference between these levels."  At the macro level, the tendency for technological change in the developing countries to advance in the same direction as that in the developed world follows from the pronounced degree of technological dependency of the former on the latter.  The extent of this dependency is indicated by the global concentration of R&D and researchers in the rich countries, the balance of trade in machinery and transport equipment, and payments for transfers of technology (Stewart, 1977).

If the technological dependence associated with latecomer industrialization is evidently part of the explanation for the historically distinctive pattern of technical change in the developing countries, it is clearly also only part of a more complex story.  For what still needs to be explained is why an alternative pattern of technical change more appropriate to the factor endowments of these countries was not evoked in the manner posited by the theory of induced innovation.[5]  This theory--which focuses principally on the effect of prices in inducing technical change--has been shown to have considerable explanatory power in the context of innovations in the agricultural sector of developing and developed countries (see Binswanger and Ruttan, 1978; Hayami and Ruttan, Chapter 3 in this volume).  The direction of technical change described above in relation to the Industrial Revolution also seems to have conformed in a rough way with the theory's predictions.  What, then, has so forcefully arrested the inducement mechanism in the contemporary industrial experience of the Third World?

Part of the explanation would seem to lie on the side of supply, that is, in the ability of the local technological system to respond effectively and continuously to any demands for indigenous innovations that are induced (the supply response may of course involve various adaptations of existing techniques, as well as the generation of entirely new ones).  It is difficult to specify exactly what is required for this capability since it is in part organizational and in part a function of scientific, engineering, and technical skills.  Nevertheless, however this capability is measured, what is clear is that developing countries will surely differ widely in the degree to which they possess it, and that this variation influences the degree of local technical change that can be induced in a manner comparable to the experience of the early-follower countries such as the United States and Germany.[6]  The possibilities for generating own-technology tend to be much greater in very large countries, for example, than in small ones.  (This question is discussed in more detail below in the context of the relationship between the domestic capital goods sector and population size.)

Even where a supply-side capacity for locally induced innovation exists, however, it must be matched by a corresponding pressure on the side of demand.  In the majority of developing countries, the conditions required for this pressure to be effective

are mostly absent; this may be demonstrated with the aid of a
very simple diagram,7 as illustrated below.

## Conditions for Locally Induced Innovation

What we are concerned to specify here, as depicted in Figure 1,
is the following:  the conditions that will induce a firm (which
is initially at point A) to search for new techniques in the
south-easterly direction (C), which is appropriate to the condition of labor abundance, rather than in the (north-westerly)
labor-saving direction (B) taken by most innovations in the developed countries (where B & C represent biased technical change
in the Hicksian sense, which does not require that the absolute
amount of both factors per unit of output be reduced).  These
conditions relate to information, factor prices, cost minimization, and products must obtain.

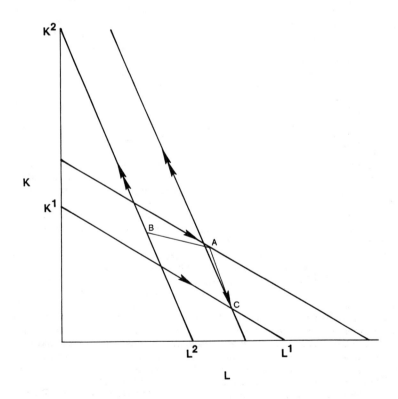

FIGURE 1   The Requirements for an Effective Demand for Locally
Induced Innovations

## Information

The information available to decision makers influences their perception of the probability of success from searching in one direction rather than another (it may even influence their estimation of the probable payoffs). In general, information flows to developing countries are such as to discourage search in the direction of C and make B appear to be the more promising avenue. One major source of this bias is that innovations emanating from developed countries are heavily promoted (by, for example, consultants and machinery salesmen) relative to more labor-using alternatives.[8] Information biases also arise from professional predilections that favor modernity and eschew the more dated. A very good illustration of this type of bias was revealed in a recent World Bank Report (Kalbermatten et al., 1980:25) on water supply and sanitation technologies, which observed that "many nonconventional technologies are being utilized around the world, but there is a real dearth of detailed information about them . . . . With few engineers aware of the range of sanitation technologies available, it is not surprising that even fewer planners and administrators had knowledge of them. This lack of knowledge ften resulted in terms of reference for sanitation studies that called only for the examination of various configurations of sewerage systems."

## Factor Prices

If search in the socially appropriate direction (C) is to be induced, factor prices need to be such that movement in this direction is privately profitable. This will be the case in Figure 1 when relative factor prices are represented by the budget line $K^1L^1$, since movement in the south-easterly direction then produces more of a reduction in costs than an equivalent movement in the north-westerly direction; however, when the budget line has the slope $K^2L^2$, the converse is true, and search in the socially desirable direction will then to this extent be discouraged.

There is no doubt that in most developing countries, factor prices in the manufacturing sector are highly distorted, nor is there any reason to deny that these distortions exert some influence in this direction. However, there is growing evidence to suggest that this focus has been considerably overdone, and that other influences on the demand side are equally, if not probably, more important explanations of the muted role of the induced innovation mechanism. The essential point is that the decisive role of factor prices in the theory of induced innovation--and indeed in traditional micro-theory in general--derives from a number of assumptions that have strictly limited validity in the context with which we are concerned in this chapter. One of the most important of these assumptions is that of cost-minimizing behavior by firms.

## Cost Minimization

The idea that firms seek to minimize costs may well be a good description not only of what currently takes place in agriculture (where competition is usually intense), but also of what occurred in industry during the nineteenth century, when as Dobb (1958:23) has pointed out, "free trade and free competition were the watchwords of the hour," and each businessman was under constant pressure to cheapen his product. However, the idea does not seem to apply over a wide range of manufacturing activity in the contemporary developing countries.[9] To this extent, factor prices cease to be the driving force of the inducement mechanism; instead, in the highly noncompetitive environment that usually exists in the manufacturing sector, a different set of forces becomes dominant.

In large part, the high degree of industrial concentration, which, according to Merhav (1969:44-47), "is as high, if not higher as in the advanced countries" is the consequence of policies, pursued in the name of the strategy of import substitution, that afford a considerable amount of effective protection to local producers. Freed thus of the strictures of cost minimization for survival, firms producing final goods turn to the satisfaction of other goals. These goals actively seem to steer the search for new technologies in a north-westerly (developed country) direction, irrespective of the slope of the budget line of factor costs. At the same time, moreover, local producers of capital goods tend to be discouraged by the protective policies insofar as these permit the free entry of foreign capital goods and thereby tend to weaken also the supply side of the requirements for the induced innovation mechanism (see Ranis, 1984).

One of the alternate goals pursued is expressed in the concept of "engineering man," who, unlike "economic man," does not seek to minimize costs (Wells, 1974). Instead, he has among his main objectives a desire to manage machines rather than workers, a desire to produce the highest possible quality product, and a preference for using sophisticated machinery that appeals to his sense of "aesthetics." All of these preferences incline "engineering man" to favor increasingly sophisticated, automated technology.

Another goal that has been proposed, mainly to explain the behavior of state-owned enterprises in developing countries, is expressed in the notion of "bureaucratic man."[10] The main idea here is that the incentive system in these enterprises (which are mostly highly sheltered from competitive forces) is such that it rewards managers not for cost reductions, but rather for rapid output growth (which will help meet what often seems to be the dominant policy goal in industry of substituting for imports in as short a period of time as possible). Constrained as he normally is in meeting this goal by a scarcity of foreign exchange, the manager turns toward large-scale turnkey projects embodying sophisticated technology that tend best to meet the requirements of rapidly raising finance and ensuring rapid delivery and construction.

A distinction must be made between the two hypotheses described above and the models of satisficing and X-inefficient
behavior that are associated, respectively, with Simon (1982) and
Leibenstein (1978). The two latter approaches--in contrast to
the former--have implications for the extent of search rather
than its direction. That is, whereas the engineering and bureaucratic man notions have specific directional implications for the
search behavior of the firm under noncompetitive conditions,
satisficing and X-inefficiency are concerned with decision
procedures that, under the same circumstances, involve a lesser
degree of search than would be associated with an optimizing
procedure. However, given the biased nature of the information
that comes in to the firm (as described above), it seems reasonable to suggest that the little search undertaken will again
tend to be in a direction other than (and often opposite from)
what is required by the demand side of the induced innovation
mechanism. Morley and Smith's (1977) study of the search behavior of multinational subsidiaries in Brazil provides some
interesting support for this view. They show that in the highly
protected environment in which these firms operate, satisfactory
profits and other goals can be realized without the need for
extensive search; in fact, can often be met by use of the known
and familiar techniques that originated from within the firm
itself.


## Products

Perhaps because it was originally formulated specifically to explain technical change in agriculture, the focus of the induced
innovation approach on the role of factor prices entirely ignores
the changes in products that almost invariably accompany movements away from A (in Figure 1) in the case of manufacturing industry. The nature of these changes, moreover, is likely to vary
systematically according to whether the direction of search is
toward B or C.
    Using a Lancasterian characteristics approach to conceptual-
ize product quality, Stewart (1977) was the first to show that
this systematic variation has to be understood in the dynamic/
historical context of the industrialized countries. Since almost
all new products are developed in and for these societies, whose
members on average enjoy rising living standards, it follows that
product designs come to acquire an increasingly high proportion
of "high-income" characteristics over time; partly as a result,
the techniques required to produce them become increasingly
capital-intensive and large-scale. What evolves, consequently,
is a close relationship over time between products (defined as
bundles of characteristics) and the nature of production technology (though this generally close relationship does not exclude
exceptional cases in which luxury labor-intensive goods, such as
"Persian" carpets and "Meerschaum" pipes, are purchased by the
richer members of society). The closeness of this relationship,
in turn, means that once the product is chosen and is closely

specified in terms of its embodied characteristics, the range of
available technologies often becomes very narrow, and in the
limit approaches one.

Therefore, far from each point in Figure 1 representing the
identical product (as is implicitly assumed in the underlying
micro model of the theory of induced innovation), in Stewart's
approach it becomes more realistic to posit not only that each
such point is associated with a different product, but also that
the direction of causality tends to run from the latter to the
former. Figure 2 (with arrows indicating the direction of causality) shows the amendment to the original diagram that is needed
to incorporate the notion of product variations.

Thus to the extent that there are forces in the economy
favoring "high-income," developed-country types of products (such
as B, which embodies a relatively high proportion of "high-
income" characteristics), these forces will exert a powerful
countervailing influence against search in the direction of C
(even if this type of search is encouraged by a favorable set of
factor prices). In many developing countries, the highly unequal
distribution of income provides a major source of such influence,
for it is then primarily the income and tastes of the affluent
minority that dictate the direction of change in product characteristics. Moreover, because these tastes tend to mirror closely
those obtaining in the developed countries, the pattern of change
in technology becomes merely derivative of this change in products, a process that seems to characterize accurately the industrial situation in India. There,only a "handful million out of
the country's 600 million" constitutes the "target group for
market research, product development, advertising, and sales
promotion of the organised industry's branded products. This
concentration is sharply reflected in the rapid growth of the
superfine and synthetic textiles industry together with the
sluggishness in the ordinary--especially coarse--cotton textiles
industry. Indeed the employment, and hence spread of purchasing
power, in the textiles industry has declined with the use of
sophisticated technology associated with the new pattern of
textile production" (Economic and Political Weekly, 1978:65).

Apart from the degree of inequality in income distribution,
it is the foreign trading pattern of a developing country that
seems primarily to determine the degree of pressure from the
product side to search in one direction rather than the other.
What is important is not simply the trade pattern between devel-
oped- and developing-country markets--with an orientation to the
former tending to impart product pressure for search in a north-
westerly direction--but also the particular market within these
countries that the manufactured exports are designed to
serve.[11] In developing countries with a highly unequal income
distribution, for example, the factor intensity of exports to the
richest groups in these countries will be constrained to much the
same degree as exports to developed countries. By the same
token, however, the constraint on labor intensity that is imposed
by the high average incomes in the rich countries may be eased
by exports to the less affluent segments of these societies.

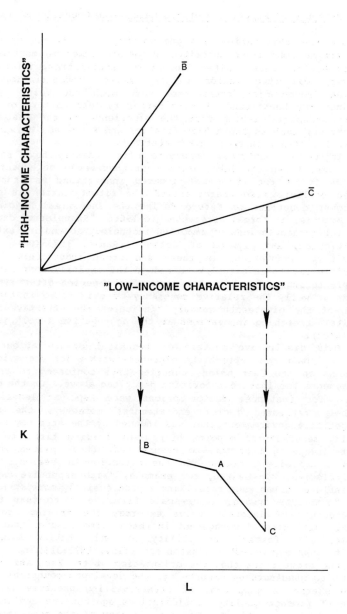

FIGURE 2   Products and the Direction of Search

## The Exceptional Experience of the East Asian Countries

To a degree that varies from one country to another, the supply and demand conditions described above are unmet in most of the Third World, where limited innovatory capabilities, information biases, distorted factor prices, market concentration, and skewed income distribution are very much the rule. It is against the background of this rather typical pattern of late-comer industrialization that the experience of the East Asian countries, such as Japan historically, and Korea and Taiwan more recently, stands in such marked contrast.

In these countries, innovations in industry have for the most part taken the labor-using form that would be expected on the basis of the theory of induced innovation, and that, as noted earlier, also characterized the situation in the early-follower countries of Europe during the Industrial Revolution. For example, in Korea, after the mid-1960s, "Examples of capital-stretching adaptations of imported technology abound in textiles, electronics, and plywood production" (Ranis, 1973:402). As a result of innovations in these and other industries, it was possible for Korea actually to reduce the capital/labor ratio in manufacturing as a whole for part of the period after 1964; in Japan as well, the relative constancy of this ratio in the last part of the nineteenth century "indicates the effectiveness of capital-stretching innovations at the aggregative level" (Ranis, 1973:402).

This distinctive pattern of technical change appears, at least in part, to reflect the closeness with which economic con-ditions in the East Asian countries have conformed to the re-quirements for induced innovation described above. On the demand side, for instance, factor prices were kept at levels that closely reflected factor endowments; moreover, the highly competitive environment that was induced by the strategy of pro-moting manufactured exports helped--by forcing firms to adopt cost-minimizing behavior--to ensure that these prices were in fact a decisive influence in the direction of search for new technologies. In Taiwan, for example, "With expensive capital, noninflated urban wage rates, and a progressively more open econ-omy from 1959 onward, large-scale firms began to turn to the manufacture of labor-intensive exports; the driving organiza-tional abilities of management in these firms insured that every commercially feasible possibility for substituting labor for capital was exploited" (Johnston and Kilby, 1975:315).

One might think that the orientation of the East Asian coun-tries to manufactured exports (to the developed countries) would have exerted a good deal of countervailing pressure from the side of product quality considerations against the evolution of labor-using innovations. However, in many of the most important export industries, such as textiles, garments, and plywood, the products of these countries appear to have competed principally upon the basis of price rather than product-differentiating inno-vations;[12] put another way, they have competed among people "too poor to be concerned with brand names" (see Chenery and

Keesing, 1979:25). In other industries, a reduction in the
demands imposed by product quality considerations was achieved
by exports to the less exacting markets of other developing
countries. Amsden (1977:219) has shown, for example, how the
export of a lower-quality hand tool to Hong Kong and Southeast
Asia "suited the factor endowments prevailing in Taiwan at the
time." A similar observation has been made for firms exporting
simpler, cheaper machinery from Hong Kong for "what, in effect
was a different, lower-income market" (Fransman, 1984b:311).

If the trading patterns of the East Asian countries were at
least not unfavorable to the inducement of appropriate, labor-
using innovations, the same could also be said of the domestic
product demands. The latter, based as they were on the relatively egalitarian income distribution that prevailed in these
countries (Chenery et al., 1974) were presumably to this extent
devoid of the type of countervailing pressure that, as noted
above, tends to be associated with a more highly uneven pattern
of income distribution. To these apparently favorable circumstances on the demand side was generally added enough of an
indigenous technological capability to evoke an effective response on the side of supply. Much of this response, it is
worth noting, included both alterations in the manner of use of
imported equipment with respect, for example, to its speed and
intensity of operation, and additions to the labor engaged in
activities peripheral to the main process (such as handling and
packaging) (Ranis, 1973).

The generally labor-using pattern of technical change that
resulted from these "induced innovations" in manufacturing is so
strikingly different from the "stylized facts" of post-war industrialization in the Third World that one might have expected a
variety of direct country comparisons at the sectoral level to
have been produced in an effort to acquire a more detailed understanding of the distinguishing aspects of the East Asian experience. Surprisingly, however, there has been very little systematic micro-comparative work of this kind. Nevertheless, the
pieces of evidence that do exist throw some particularly interesting light on the much more macro-oriented explanations offered
in the earlier discussion.

Consider first a comparison of textile-machinery production
in Korea and India (Pack, 1981:239):

Both countries have a fairly substantial capacity to produce
textile machinery, with India's spanning a broader spectrum
from spinning to finishing. Korea produces semi-automatic
and simple looms; the principal Indian firms manufacture
modern labor-saving equipment. This discrepancy can be
plausibly attributed to the protected position of Indian
textile producers, whereas the Korean textile industry has
been export-oriented from its inception. Although there is
limited pressure on Indian producers to reduce costs by
using more labor-intensive equipment, the pressure is greater
on Korean producers, who in turn demand labor-intensive
equipment.

In a detailed analysis of causes for the difference in the technological development of the textile industry in India and Japan in the late nineteenth and early twentieth centuries, Ranis and Saxonhouse (1983) sought to explain why, despite similarities with respect to labor abundance, relative factor prices, and degree of protection, the latter country was able, to a far greater extent than the former, to make labor-using adaptations to the same initial imports of technology. They attribute this differential technological performance to differences in the institutional/organizational environment in the two countries. These differences centered, first, on the nature of managers' incentives to innovate. In India, for example, "the failure to link commissions to profits, if not positively perverse in its effects, undoubtedly reduced the incentive to pursue the search for innovations intensively" (Ranis and Saxonhouse, 1983:21). Second, Ranis and Saxonhouse point to institutional differences that resulted in the fact that "Indian managers clearly were not as effectively presented with information and advice on available technology choices as were their Japanese counterparts." Third, whereas the "appropriateness" of consumer preference patterns in Japan (apparently because of the strength of their resistance to international demonstration effects and to fortuitous climatic factors) helped to promote the move to labor-using technical change, "the preference of Indian consumers for finer count yarn products, signalled through the market, was certainly one factor leading to the . . . delayed introduction of rings in India" (Ranis and Saxonhouse, 1983:24).

Limited though they are, these micro insights do lend some degree of support to the attempt made above to identify the macro-economic factors that discriminate the successful operation of the induced innovation mechanism in the East Asian countries from the more typical pattern of industrial technical change in the Third World, which appears to be more or less entirely disassociated from the prevailing factor endownments.

## The Permissive Effect of Scale Economies

Whereas the previous section was concerned mainly with the influence of population growth on the direction of technical change, other theories have focused instead on the extent to which the latter is influenced by the former. The view that the outcome of this relationship is favorable from the point of view of growth in productivity is associated mainly with Simon (1977). This view rests not only on the nature and strength of the connection posited between population growth and economies of scale, but also on the assumed empirical significance of the latter.

During the Industrial Revolution, scale economies in manufacturing do not appear to have been at all widespread (nor for that matter are they of much importance in contemporary nonindustrial activities). Indeed, Mokyr (1977:995) has recently argued that "it is not an easy task to substantiate the case for increasing returns in manufacturing anywhere before, say, 1870."[13] Since then, in conjunction with rising average incomes, increasingly sophisticated products, and a continual rise in capital per man, it is clear that scale has become of major importance in many lines of manufacturing in the rich countries (see, for example, Pratten, 1971). However, the degree to which population growth in the poor countries (by expanding market size) is important to the capture of these economies, as well as the welfare effects of any such relationship, is much less clear.

Economies of scale in manufacturing tend to occur in large, discontinuous jumps. To this extent, differences in population growth rates of 1 or 2 percent over a period of 10 or even 20 years are unlikely to make much difference. A data set for 45 developing countries over the period 1960 to 1970 (see Table 3) confirms this expectation: the population growth variable (with an estimated coefficient value of unity) was not a statistically significant determinant of the variations in industrial productivity growth.[14] Moreover, the fact that the change in per capita income (which varies far more widely across the sample than the change in population) does show significance[15] suggests that this variable may be a more important influence on market size than population growth over a period of this length (though, of course, the causality may also run from the change in productivity to that in income).

Even in the comparison between small and large populations (which over time of course involves very much longer periods), any simple view of the relationship between population and scale seems unwarranted. This is because, as we saw to be the case also with the theory of induced innovation, the actual outcome is strongly conditioned by a variety of economic policies.

The influence of policies that directly or indirectly determine the distribution of income derives from the above-mentioned tendency for larger-scale production to be associated over time with growing sophistication of products. The latter has as a corollary a tendency for earlier, less sophisticated goods to be produced with a lesser degree of scale economies. A systematic association of this kind therefore reflects the historical tendency for technological developments to occur overwhelmingly in and for the developed countries, rather than any inherent characteristics of technology itself. Further, to the extent that it exists, the hypothesized relationship means that the realization of scale economies in a developing country of given size and average income depends on the way income is distributed, because it is this (together with other influences on consumer tastes) that will determine the degree of demand for products of different "vintages."

At one extreme, "where income is more or less evenly distributed over broad segments of the population, the result is large markets for comparatively simple goods" (Johnston and Kilby, 1975:304). This pattern will be reflected partly in the prominence of particular categories of manufactures (such as textiles, footwear, and furniture), and partly perhaps also in shifts within these categories toward simpler product varieties.[16]

TABLE 3  Population Variables, Per Capita Income, and Productivity Growth

| Country | Industrial Productivity Growth 1960-70 | Per Capita Income Growth 1960-70 | Population Growth 1960-70 | Population Size 1965 (in millions) | Population Density 1965 | Agricultural Productivity Growth 1960-70 |
|---|---|---|---|---|---|---|
| **Africa** | | | | | | |
| Ethiopia | 2.72 | 2.8 | 2.4 | 22.7 | 18.6 | 0.62 |
| Somalia | -1.15 | -1.1 | 2.8 | 2.5 | 3.9 | -1.89 |
| Central African Rep. | 0.79 | -- | 1.9 | 1.43 | 2.3 | -0.61 |
| Niger | 6.72 | -2.0 | 3.4 | 3.51 | 2.8 | 1.04 |
| Senegal | 0.69 | -- | 2.3 | 3.49 | 17.8 | 1.58 |
| Mauritania | 9.55 | -- | 2.3 | 1.05 | 1.0 | 0.08 |
| Egypt | -1.34 | 1.7 | 2.5 | 29.39 | 29.4 | 1.4 |
| Morocco | 0.13 | 1.0 | 2.6 | 13.32 | 29.8 | 3.93 |
| Nigeria | 9.95 | 0.1 | 2.5 | 48.68 | 52.7 | -0.89 |
| People's Rep. of Congo | 3.19 | -- | 2.4 | 0.84 | 2.5 | 2.23 |
| Ivory Coast | 7.29 | 4.5 | 3.8 | 3.84 | 11.9 | 2.79 |
| Tunisia | 5.7 | 0.5 | 2.0 | 4.72a | 28.8a | 2.58 |
| Algeria | 8.48 | 1.7 | 2.4 | 11.92 | 5.0 | -0.2 |
| **Asia** | | | | | | |
| Bangladesh | 4.95 | -- | 2.5 | 59.68 | 414.4 | 0.44 |
| Burma | -1.48 | -- | 2.2 | 24.73 | 36.5 | 4.35 |
| India | 1.9 | 1.2 | 2.3 | 474.87 | 144.4 | 0.85 |
| People's Rep. of China | 6.92 | -- | 2.3 | 707.14 | 74.0 | 1.21 |
| Sri Lanka | 3.78 | 1.5 | 2.4 | 11.16 | 169.1 | 1.08 |
| Pakistan | 7.66 | -- | 2.8 | 54.25 | 67.5 | 3.4 |
| Indonesia | 1.41 | 1.0 | 2.1 | 104.88 | 54.7 | 1.74 |
| Thailand | 6.58 | 4.9 | 3.0 | 28.50b | 55.4b | 4.02 |
| Philippines | 3.26 | 2.9 | 3.0 | 31.77 | 105.9 | 3.43 |

| Country | Col 1 | Col 2 | Col 3 | Col 4 | Col 5 | Col 6 |
|---|---|---|---|---|---|---|
| Turkey | 6.86 | 3.9 | 2.5 | 31.15 | 39.9 | 2.73 |
| South Korea | 6.04 | 6.8 | 2.6 | 26.90[b] | 274.5[b] | 4.2 |
| Iran | 8.92 | 5.4 | 3.0 | 24.81 | 15.1 | 3.53 |
| Iraq | -0.05 | 2.5 | 3.2 | 8.05 | 18.5 | 4.2 |
| Singapore | 6.87 | -- | 2.4 | 1.86 | 18.6 | 9.04 |
| Lebanon | 1.38 | -- | 2.9 | 2.41 | 241.0 | 9.95 |
| **Latin America** | | | | | | |
| Bolivia | 2.56 | 2.5 | 2.4 | 4.33 | 3.9 | 1.86 |
| Honduras | 0.85 | 1.8 | 3.1 | 2.18 | 19.5 | 2.44 |
| El Salvador | 4.29 | 1.7 | 2.9 | 2.93 | 139.5 | 1.08 |
| Nicaragua | 8.14 | 2.8 | 2.6 | 1.66 | 12.8 | 7.22 |
| Guatemala | 3.25 | 2.0 | 3.0 | 4.44 | 40.7 | 2.63 |
| Peru | 2.58 | 1.4 | 2.9 | 11.65 | 9.1 | 3.21 |
| Jamaica | 4.03 | -- | 1.4 | 1.74[c] | 158.2[c] | 3.61 |
| Dominican Republic | 2.00 | 0.5 | 2.9 | 3.52 | 71.8 | 0.35 |
| Colombia | 2.07 | 1.7 | 3.0 | 18.04 | 15.8 | 3.59 |
| Costa Rica | 4.85 | 3.2 | 3.4 | 1.49 | 29.2 | 4.2 |
| Panama | 5.39 | 4.2 | 2.9 | 1.23 | 16.0 | 4.47 |
| Mexico | 4.99 | 3.7 | 3.3 | 39.49[b] | 20.0[b] | 3.73 |
| Argentina | 5.7 | 2.5 | 1.4 | 21.49 | 7.8 | 2.53 |
| Chile | 3.82 | 1.6 | 2.1 | 8.02[b] | 10.6[b] | 3.98 |
| Uruguay | -0.31 | -0.4 | 1.0 | 2.71 | 15.4 | 3.89 |
| Venezuela | 1.03 | 2.3 | 3.4 | 8.72 | 9.6 | 6.53 |
| Haiti | -1.47 | -0.9 | 1.6 | 4.40 | 157.1 | -0.42 |

[a]Refers to 1966.
[b]Refers to 1963.
[c]Refers to 1964.

Sources:
Column 1:  World Bank (1983:Table 2) and International Labour Organisation (1977).
Column 2:  Morawetz (1974:Table 1).
Column 3:  World Bank (1983:Table 1).
Column 4:  United Nations Demographic Yearbook (various years).
Column 5:  United Nations Demographic Yearbook (various years) and World Bank (1983:Table 1).
Column 6:  World Bank (1983:Table 2).

Both these tendencies limit the degree to which the scale economies associated with the most modern Western products and processes can be realized. For many of these products, it will be the case that "whatever the cost and price reductions achieved by a more elaborate division of labor . . . such cheapening may still be insufficient to attract demand by low-income consuming units. This obtains even if market size is increased by the multiplication of the number of such units" (Amsden, 1977:219). In contrast, where the distribution of income is highly skewed, the demand for manufactures on the part of the high-income minority comes to approximate the rich country pattern favoring consumer durable goods, many of which exhibit marked scale economies in production.

However, even in circumstances where a demand for consumer durables is created in this way, it is the market structure that determines the extent to which a particular product will be able to realize scale economies. As Little et al. (1970:153) have observed, "even where in developing countries an industry with clear economies of scale is newly established, very often there are too many plants for such economies to be adequately realized. This has been as much due to government policy as to anything else" (emphasis added). Consider, for example, what has occurred in the Argentinian automobile industry: "High tariff structure has resulted in small-scale, inefficient vehicle manufacturers and automotive parts suppliers. Clearly too many producers were manufacturing too many models for a market the size of Argentina's. Small-scale production inevitably has meant higher capital-output ratios and low efficiency in capital resource utilization" (Baranson, 1969:86). In contrast, other countries, such as Brazil and India, have fewer models, and from this point of view are able to reduce the problems of inefficiency that Argentina has encountered.

Just as the influence of policy with respect to market structure is thus seen to drive a wedge between population size and economies of scale, so, too, does the policy stance that is taken toward foreign trade. In many developing countries where policies of import substitution have been pursued, exports of manufactured goods have been discouraged by an overvalued exchange rate and by the more profitable opportunities in the protected domestic market. To this extent, the advantages of scale have been confined to those achievable within the local market. Certain other countries, in contrast, through the active pursuit of policies designed to encourage exports, have been able to acquire the potential for scale economies inherent in much larger countries. The findings reported by Gillis et al. (1983: 544) with regard to the economic features of countries at per capita income levels of 350 and 1,300 U.S. dollars (in 1978 prices) tend to bear this out. They conclude that, "in making this transition [from the lower to the higher income level] size appears to be less important than resource endowment and development strategy. Small countries oriented towards exports of manufactures--such as Chile, Kenya, Taiwan, Belgium or Norway-- have characteristics very much like those of large countries at both levels of income."

For this reason, and the others given above, the relationship between population size and economies of scale may frequently be rather weak and sometimes nonexistent. However, even if this were not the case and the connection between them were much stronger, the resulting welfare effects are deserving of much more serious consideration than Simon, for one, has chosen to accord them. In many of his writings, Simon tends to adopt an analytical perspective that minimizes the historically distinctive aspects of latecomer industrialization. A particularly clear illustration of this tendency is to be found in his point of view that "because of the economic interrelatedness of all modern countries, we should think about the population and productivity growth of the developed world--or indeed of the world as a whole--rather than think about any particular country" (Simon, 1981:102). Perhaps largely on account of this view, Simon is led to ignore the differential welfare effects of scale economies in developing as opposed to developed countries, and to focus in both exclusively on the growth of per capita income.[17] In contrast, it seems that it is precisely the "interrelatedness" between countries, and in particular the dependence of the developing countries on the technologies developed in and for the rich countries, that suggest the need to analyze the impact of scale economies in the former in other terms than merely the growth of per capita income. For though these technologies are usually highly productive (affording high wages to those they employ), they are in numerous other respects highly inappropriate to the circumstances in the developing countries in which they are applied.

We have already had occasion to note, for example, the pronounced tendency to industrial concentration in the developing countries; this tendency, at least in part, is the inevitable consequence of the need to "make room" in these markets for the relatively large scale with which most technologies imported from the industrialized countries are associated. However, by far the most widely acknowledged consequences of inappropriateness are the result of the high and rising capital intensity of these technologies. In particular, "poor countries obtaining technology (unmodified) from rich countries . . . receive technology whose cost is in line with the resources of the advanced countries, not with what they can afford. To the extent that they do spend their resources on advanced country technology, their limited investment resources will mean that only a fraction of their labor force can be equipped . . . a dualistic form of development is an inevitable result of adopting advanced country technology without major modification" (Stewart, 1974: 88). Nowhere are the manifestations of this dualism more evident than in Brazil: "The aggregate, that is, average, income levels disguise the dual character of the Brazilian economy. The rapid and impressive industrialization and economic progress has been concentrated both geographically and socially. Large geographic areas and segments of the population, consisting mostly of the rural poor, have simply been bypassed by the growth of the modern sector" (Tyler, 1981:2).

What has been argued in this section, then, is that insofar
as a larger population size does expand the market (which is by
no means universally the case), its role is essentially permis-
sive--allowing the scale advantages of technology imports to be
realized on the one hand, but requiring the developing country
to suffer from the distinctly inegalitarian consequences of these
imports on the other.  This permissive role of population needs
to be distinguished from the manner of its (more "active") influence under the induced innovation theory, namely, to produce a
different--and from the standpoint of factor endowments and
equality in income distribution a more appropriate--pattern of
technical change than that implied by the continued, and
passive, reliance on (unmodified) imports of technology.


Population Density, Urban Concentration and Infrastructural
Investment

In the previous section, we examined arguments relating population growth and size to economies of scale through the effect of
an enlarged market.  An additional mechanism, proposed by both
Simon and Boserup, operates through the allegedly favorable impact of population density on infrastructural investment.  In
particular, a more dense population is said to make profitable
"many major social investments that would not otherwise be
profitable (e.g., railroads, irrigation systems, ports)" (Simon,
1977:36).  Indeed, for Boserup (1981:129), this is the "main
advantage" of a dense population.
    Both authors adduce cross-country evidence in support of this
hypothesis.  Boserup (1981) shows that there is a positive correlation between population density and the extensiveness of a
country's transport networks.  Simon and Gobin (1980) use a set
of U.N. and World Bank data to show that density has a statistically significant effect on the rate of a developing economy's
productivity growth for the period 1969-70.  These results,
however, are at the level of the economy as a whole; when they
are disaggregated by sector, a disparate pattern emerges, confirming once again the need to make a distinction between manufacturing and other economic activities in considering the impact
of population growth on technical change.  On the basis of a
sample that is similar in size and composition to Simon and
Gobin's (see Table 3) and for the same period (1960-70), the
population density variable was correlated separately with growth
rates of productivity in agriculture and industry.  What emerged
was a significant relation only with respect to the agricultural
sector[18] (a finding that is still consistent with the significant result for the economy as a whole, since this sector normally constitutes a large fraction of the latter).
    To explain these sectorally disaggregated findings, it is
necessary first to distinguish between the overall density of
population and its spatial distribution, with respect, in particular, to the distribution between rural and urban areas.  As
Renaud (1981) has pointed out, urban concentration depends on

many things other than (or in addition to) population density,
such as government policy toward industry and agriculture (which
often provides strong incentives for firms to locate in the main
urban region), and location decisions affecting the distribution
of manufacturing and hence service activities among cities.   In
fact, density is in general likely to bear only slightly, if at
all, on the degree of urban concentration.  Moreover, it is on
the latter and not the former that the profitability, through
scale economies, of much infrastructure for industry depends.[19]
One study of urban infrastructure in India, for example, showed
that "in a town of 50,000, infrastructure for industry costs 13
percent more than in a city of one million, allowing for both
capital and recurrent costs.  No measurements were made for
larger cities, in which economies of scale are evidently exhausted and congestion may well raise the unit cost of infrastructure" (Gillis et al., 1983:555).  The total scale effects arising
from the provision of infrastructure to industry are thus likely
to depend not only on the extent to which population is concentrated in urban, rather than rural locations, but also on the
dispersal of the urban population among cities of different
sizes.  It is evidently only to the agricultural sector that
overall population density has relevance in the determination of
infrastructural economies of scale.


Population Size, the Domestic Capital Goods Sector, and
Indigenous Technical Change

Discussion above focused on the nature of the relationship between population size and economies of scale, and on the view
that the outcome of this relationship has favorable implications
for the rate of productivity growth in the manufacturing sector
of developing countries.  This section examines the possibility
that population size may alternatively, or additionally, have
implications for the direction of technical change that is taken
in this sector.  This possibility is based on two points:  first,
the notion that very large countries possess, to a greater degree
than small countries, the ability to generate local technological
development; and second, the condition that this capability will
be used to generate a more appropriate pattern of change in technology (in the sense defined earlier) than is possible through
the alternative policy of importing new techniques over time, to
which small countries (on this view) are confined.
     The first strand of this argument--that concerning differen-
tial technological capabilities--can be defended on the grounds
that the existence of a well developed capital goods sector is a
necessary condition for the emergence of local technological
activity, and that this condition is more likely to be met in
large than in small countries.  Support for both these views can
be found.  Indeed, with respect to the former, "there is a wide
consensus on the importance of an indigenous capital goods sector
for facilitating indigenous technological change" (Fransman,
1984a:24).  In support of the latter view, there is evidence that

at given levels of per capita income, some small countries have
a distinct tendency to be less involved in the production of
consumer durables and producer goods than large countries (Gillis
et al., 1983:543).

If the proposition that large countries have a greater capacity to generate local technological developments appears thus
to be defensible, there is disappointingly little evidence that
this capacity has been systematically used to effect appropriate
types of innovations. On the contrary, according to Little
(1982:243), "most of the capital goods now made in developing
countries are copies of those available abroad. From the point
of view of 'appropriateness,' the country is just as 'technologically dependent' if its own capital goods industry turns out
copies. The fact that there are a number of examples where research has shown this not to be the case only proves the rule."

India is a particularly clear example of a large country to
which Little's criticism applies with some force. On the one
hand, one can point to several innovations in this country that
have become justly celebrated examples of appropriate technical
change. The development of the Swaraj tractor as a (commercially
successful) labor-using alternative to imported brands is one
such example (Morehouse, 1982), and the recent improvement in
small-scale open pan sulphitation sugar technology is another
(Kaplinsky, 1983). However, when viewed against overall charac-
terizations of developments in the capital goods sector, examples
such as these appear very much to be exceptional. For though
"one might think that India would have an advantage in products
based on indigenous development in 'intermediate technology'"
(Frankena, 1974:263), during the 1960s "there were few efforts
to develop indigenous designs rather than rely on foreign
collaboration and few adaptations and improvements of the foreign
designs which were used. This was true even for large firms with
more than a decade of production experience and in major industries such as stationary diesel engines and cotton textile machinery" (Frankena, 1974:256). Partly as a consequence of this
type of orientation of its capital goods sector, "India has one
of the most capital-demanding industrial developments in the
world" (Little, 1982:243).

An explanation of the Indian experience has necessarily to
be sought in the failure of forces on the demand side to induce
a more appropriate pattern of technical change from the capability that evidently existed on the side of supply. At a very
general level, this failure may have arisen from the fact that
the rationale underlying the development of the capital goods
sector was "the Mahalanobis one of a rapid build-up in capacity,
rather than any idea of generating appropriate technical change"
(Stewart, 1977:153). At a much more specific level, Frankena
(1974) has tried to show how the failure to adapt product designs
to local conditions in the 1960s was a direct consequence of the
prevailing industrial and trade policies, which, among other
effects, reduced the demands of firms for these types of
adaptations.

What the experience of India thus emphasizes is that circumstances bearing on the demand for new techniques can serve to undermine the potential of countries with a large population for escape from the imperatives of technological dependency.[20] Conversely, if demand conditons in a small country are in this sense favorable, the inherent difficulties of responding to these pressures that are imposed by limitations of supply can be ameliorated in two ways: by the selective import of suitable techniques from large countries (as when, for example, Tanzania imports textile machinery from China), and by the pooling of technological developments with neighboring countries. Therefore, just as we saw to be true of the relationship between population size and economies of scale, the nexus between the former and the appropriateness of technical change in manufacturing admits of no easy generalizations.


SUMMARY AND CONCLUSIONS

This chapter has examined the four mechanisms through which population variables transmit an influence on technical change in manufacturing, and in none was any simple relationship found to exist. This lack of unidirectionality is reflected partly in the absence of significant correlations between the population variables and cross-country data for productivity growth, and partly in the highly disparate degree of success with which the induced innovation mechanism has recently operated in most developing countries, compared to both the contemporary East Asian experience and the historical experience of the Industrial Revolution. It therefore becomes necessary to postulate a more complex set of relationships, and in particular, to identify the circumstances in which population variables do exert an influence in the direction that is posited by each causal mechanism. In the analysis above, a variety of such conditioning factors are discussed. These are shown in the summary form of Table 4, which also indicates the developmental impact that can be expected when the configuration of these factors is conducive to the operation of each particular causal mechanism.


NOTES

1   Both the induced innovation approach and Boserup's theory, for example, were initially formulated in relation specifically to agriculture. See, respectively, Binswanger and Ruttan (1978) and Boserup (1965).

2   In the absence of total factor productivity data in manufacturing across developing countries, growth in average labor productivity is used in the empirical sections of the chapter as a crude measure of the change in technology.

TABLE 4  A Summary of Conditioning Factors on Development and Their Impact

| Population Variable | Causal Mechanism | Conditioning Factors | Main Impact on | Impact on Degree of Inequality in Income Distribution |
|---|---|---|---|---|
| Growth Rate/Size | Labor supply/ induced innovation | Demand: information, product characteristics, managerial incentives, degree of competition, factor prices, trade policy Supply: technological capability (scientific, organizational, and technical) | The direction of technical change (toward the use of labor) | Probably favorable because employment creation is an important way of reducing income inequality |
| Growth Rate/Size | Economies of scale from market size | Per capita income, trade patterns, income distribution/tastes, market structure | Productivity growth | Probably unfavorable (especially if it is permissive of the most modern imports of technology) because of the creation of dualism |
| Density | Economies of scale from infra- structural investment | Concentration of the population in urban areas and in cities of different sizes | Productivity growth | Uncertain |
| Size | The enhanced capability to produce domestic capital goods and scientific knowledge for indigenous innovations | Those bearing on the demand for appropriate local innovations, mostly a function of overall development strategy | The direction of technical change (toward the use of labor) | Probably favorable because employment creation is an important way of reducing income inequality |

3   Manufacturing's contribution to total output is, of course, generally much greater. In 1982, for example, this sector contributed 14 percent and 20 percent to GDP in the low- and medium-income developing countries, respectively. See World Bank (1984).

4   This and the following paragraph draw on Chapter 3 in Stewart (1977).

5   It should be noted, however, that the differential rates of labor productivity growth in the contemporary Third World vis-a-vis the historical experience of the developed countries (which we are taking to reflect underlying technological differences) cannot alone be used as a guide to differences in the amount of employment created in the two periods, and hence to the degree of conformity of the technologies to prevailing factor endowments. One reason is that employment growth is a product of output growth as well as the change in the productivity of labor, and the former may itself depend on the latter. Insofar as the output growth achieved in the recent experience of the developing countries was in fact higher than that attained during the historical experience of the now developed countries because of the differential rates of productivity growth, the degree of inappropriateness of the technical change that occurred in the former period will be less than that described in the text. (On the magnitude of the different rates of output growth for the developing and developed countries, see Squire, 1981.) Another factor that ought ideally to be taken into account is the inter-industry linkage effect of output expansion (i.e., the indirect employment effect). Stern and Lewis (1980) show how the magnitude of this indirect effect varies according to the type of industry and stage of development of the developing country.

6   For a discussion of the determinants of the indigenous technological capabilities possessed historically by these and other now developed countries, see Ranis (1984).

7   This diagram is based on Figure 4.1 in Bruton (1985). The analysis based on the diagram is similar to that in Stewart (1977).

8   "Businesses that could fill the gaps in knowledge and supply the appropriate equipment are largely absent: domestic capital-goods producers, agents of used-equipment dealers, and representatives of producers of appropriate capital goods in developed countries" (Pack, 1982:32).

9   Lecraw's (1979) study of 400 manufacturing firms in Thailand, for example, found that many of the firms failed to choose cost-minimizing techniques. In this paper, Lecraw cites similar findings from numerous other case studies.

10  This hypothesis is due to Williams (1979); see also James (1983).

11  For a full discussion, see Stewart (n.d.); also see Krueger (1978).

12  The products in these three industries "are either quite
    highly standardised (plywood, for example) or differen-
    tiated in technologically minor respects and not greatly
    dependent on brand recognition for purchaser acceptance
    (textiles and apparel, for example)" (Dahlman and Westphal,
    1982).

13  Though also skeptical of the existence of technological
    economies of scale over this period, von Tunzelmann (1981:
    144) notes that there may nevertheless have been economies
    of scale of an organizational kind that were created by a
    rising population "in the transport and marketing of goods,
    and possibly within the 'putting-out' or domestic system of
    production, because of the need for more efficient organisa-
    tion to deal with a larger number of domestic workers."

14  The estimated equation is

$$y = 1.17 + 1.04x \qquad R^2 = 0.034, \quad N = 45 ,$$
$$\phantom{y = }(0.52) \; (1.23)$$

    where y = industrial productivity growth from 1960 to 1970
    and x = population growth rate from 1960 to 1970 (t-ratios
    in parentheses).

15  Adding the change in per capita income from 1960 to 1970 (z)
    to the equation in the previous footnote gives (with
    t-ratios in parentheses)

$$y = 1.42 + .34x + .68z \qquad R^2 = 0.19, \quad N = 34 .$$
$$\phantom{y = }(0.61) \; (0.38) \; (2.40)$$

    It should be noted that the sample size in this case is
    somewhat smaller than that on which the previous equation
    is based.

16  Evidence in support of this view for a particular industry
    in India is given in James (1980).

17  In his 1977 study, Simon specifically states, "The subject
    of this book is the over-all economic level. No attention
    is given to the effects of population growth upon income
    distribution, either as a variable of interest in itself or
    as a force that might affect the level of economic activity"
    (Simon, 1977:42).

18  For agriculture, the relation is given by

$$y = 2.37 + 0.0034x \qquad R^2 = 0.16, \quad N = 45 ,$$
$$\phantom{y = }(6.67) \; (2.82)$$

    where y = agricultural productivity growth between 1960 and
    1970 and  x = population density in 1965.
    For the industrial sector, the estimated equation is

$$y = 3.70 + 0.0015x \qquad R^2 = 0.018, \quad N = 45 ,$$
$$\phantom{y = }(7.2) \; (0.89)$$

where y = industrial productivity growth between 1960 and
1970 and x = population density in 1965.   (In both cases,
t-ratios are shown in parentheses.)

19   The efficiency of certain marketing services, however, may
depend on density rather than urban concentration.

20   An argument along similar lines can be made to challenge
the relevance of much of the extra scientific knowledge
that a large country may be able to produce (in comparison
with a small one).  In the literature on science and technology in developing countries, this type of argument has
focused on the concept of "marginalization," which has
"played a considerable part in explanations of the apparent
ineffectiveness of science and technology institutions in
developing countries in producing relevant innovations. . .
The starting point is the observation that social and economic factors in the developing countries generally do not
produce much demand for local science and technology. . . .
It then is argued, because of the lack of social and
economic pressures, that activities in science and technology become inward-looking in the sense that the predominant,
if not the only, criteria of success in these activities
become scientific and technical.  Criteria of social usefulness and economic welfare do not come into the question"
(Cooper, 1982:10-11).  The ideas embodied in the concept of
"marginalization" ought thus to somewhat dampen the enthus-
iasm with which writers such as Simon have pursued the idea
that "a larger population implies a larger amount of knowledge being created, all else being equal.  This is the
straightforward result of there being more people to have
new ideas" (Simon, 1981:210).

REFERENCES

Amsden, A.H. (1977)  The division of labor is limited by the type
    of market:  the case of the Taiwanese machine tool industry.
    World Development 5(3):217-233.
Baer, W., and M. Herve (1966)  Employment and industrialisation
    in developing countries.  Quarterly Journal of Economics
    LXXX(1):90-92.
Bairoch, P. (1975)  The Economic Development of the Third World
    Since 1900.  Berkeley, Calif.:  University of California
    Press.
Baranson, J. (1969)  Industrial Technologies for Developing
    Economies.  New York:  Praeger.
Binswanger, H.P., and V.W. Ruttan (1978)  Induced Innovation.
    Baltimore, Md.:  The Johns Hopkins University Press.
Boserup, E. (1965)  The Conditions of Agricultural Growth.
    London:  Allen and Unwin.
Boserup, E. (1981)  Population and Technological Change.
    Chicago:  University of Chicago Press.
Bruton, H. (1985)  On the production of a national technology.
    In J. James and S. Watanabe, eds., Technology, Institutions,
    and Government Policies.  London:  Macmillan.

254                                                              James

Chenery, H., and D. Keesing (1979) The Changing Composition of Developing Country Exports. World Bank Staff Working Paper No. 314, World Bank, Washington, D.C.

Chenery, H., M. Ahluwalia, C. Bell, J. Duloy, and R. Jolly (1974) Redistribution with Growth. Oxford: Oxford University Press.

Cooper, C. (1982) Policy Interventions for Technological Innovation in Developing Countries. World Bank Staff Working Paper No. 441, World Bank, Washington, D.C.

Dahlman, C., and L. Westphal (1982) Technological effort in industrial development--an interpretive survey of recent research. In F. Stewart and J. James, eds., The Economics of New Technology in Developing Countries. London: Francis Pinter.

Dobb, M. (1958) Capitalism Yesterday and Today. London: Lawrence and Wishart.

Economic and Political Weekly (1978) Review of Management. August.

Frankena, M. (1974) The industrial and trade control regime and product designs in India. Economic Development and Cultural Change 22(2):249-264.

Fransman, M. (1984a) Introduction. In M. Fransman and K. King, eds., Technological Capability in the Third World. New York: St. Martin's Press.

Fransman, M. (1984b) Some hypotheses regarding indigenous technological capability and the case of machine production in Hong Kong. In M. Fransman and K. King, eds., Technological Capability in the Third World. New York: St. Martin's Press.

Gillis, M., D.H. Perkins, M. Roemer, and D.R. Snodgrass (1983) Economics of Development. New York: W.W. Norton.

Gouverneur, J. (1971) Productivity and Factor Proportions in Less Developed Countries. Oxford: Clarendon Press.

James, J. (1980) The employment effects of an income redistribution: a test for aggregation bias in the Indian sugar processing industry. Journal of Development Economics 7(2):175-189.

James, J. (1983) Bureaucratic Engineering and Economic Men: Decision-Making for Technology in Tanzania's State-Owned Enterprises. World Employment Programme Working Paper, International Labour Organisation, Geneva.

Johnston, B.F., and P. Kilby (1975) Agricultural and Structural Transformation. Oxford: Oxford University Press.

Kalbermatten, J.M., D.S. Julius, and C.G. Gunnerson (1980) Appropriate Technology for Water Supply and Sanitation. Washington, D.C.: World Bank.

Kaplinsky, R. (1983) Sugar Processing: The Development of a Third-World Technology. London: Intermediate Technology Publications.

Krueger, A.O. (1978) Alternative trade strategies and employment in LDCs. American Economic Review 68(2):270-274.

Landes, D.S. (1965) Japan and Europe: contrasts in industrialization. In W.W. Lockwood, ed., The State and Economic Enterprise in Japan. Princeton, N.J.: Princeton University Press.

Change in the Manufacturing Sector                              255

Lecraw, D. (1979)   Choice of technology in low-wage countries:
    a non-neoclassical approach.   The Quarterly Journal of
    Economics 93(4):631-654.
Leibenstein, H. (1978)   General X-Efficiency Theory and Economic
    Development.   Oxford: Oxford University Press.
Lewis, W.A. (1954)   Economic development with unlimited supplies
    of labor.   The Manchester School XXII (2):139-191.
Lewis, W.A. (1979)   The dual economy revisited.   The Manchester
    School XLVII (3):211-229.
Little, I.M.D. (1982)   Economic Development.   New York:   Basic
    Books.
Little, I., T. Scitovsky, and M. Scott (1970)   Industry and Trade
    in Some Developing Countries.   London: Oxford University
    Press.
McCloskey, D.N. (1981)   The Industrial Revolution 1780-1860:
    a survey.   In R. Floud and D. McCloskey, eds., The Economic
    History of Britain Since 1700, Vol. 1, 1700-1860.
    Cambridge, England:   Cambridge University Press.
Merhav, M. (1969)   Technological Dependence, Monopoly, and
    Growth.   Oxford:   Pergamon Press.
Mokyr, J. (1977)   Demand vs. supply in the industrial revolution.
    Journal of Economic History 37(4):981-1008.
Morawetz, D. (1974)   Employment implications of industrializa-
    tion:   a survey.   Economic Journal 84:491-542.
Morehouse, W. (1982)   Opening Pandora's Box:   technology and
    social performance in the Indian tractor industry.   In F.
    Stewart and J. James, eds., The Economics of New Technology
    in Developing Countries.   London:   Frances Pinter.
Morley, S.A., and G.W. Smith (1977)   Limited search and the
    technological choices of multinational firms in Brazil.
    Quarterly Journal of Economics XCI(2):263-287.
Pack H. (1981)   Fostering the capital goods sector in LDCs.
    World Development 9(3):227-250.
Pack, H. (1982)   Aggregate implications of factor substitution in
    industrial processes.   Journal of Development Economics
    11(1):1-37.
Pratten, C.F. (1971)   Economies of Scale in Manufacturing
    Industry.   Cambridge, England:   Cambridge University Press.
Ranis, G. (1973)   Industrial sector labor absorption.   Economic
    Development and Cultural Change 21(3):387-408.
Ranis, G. (1984)   Determinants and consequences of indigenous
    technological activity.   In M. Fransman and K. King, eds.,
    Technological Capability in the Third World.   New York:   St.
    Martin's Press.
Ranis, G., and G. Saxonhouse (1983)   International and domestic
    determinants of technology choice by the less developed
    countries.   In B. Lucas and S. Freedman, eds., Technology
    Choice and Change in Developing Countries:   Internal and
    External Constraints.   Dublin:   Tycooly International.
Renaud, B. (1981)   National Urbanization Policy in Developing
    Countries.   Oxford:   Oxford University Press.
Reynolds, L.G., and P. Gregory (1965)   Wages, Productivity, and
    Industrialization in Puerto Rico.   Homewood, Ill.:   Richard
    D. Irwin.

Simon, H.A. (1982)  Models of Bounded Rationality.  Cambridge,
    Mass.:  M.I.T. Press.
Simon, J.L. (1977)  The Economics of Population Growth.
    Princeton, N.J.:  Princeton University Press.
Simon J.L. (1981)  The Ultimate Resource.  Princeton, N.J.:
    Princeton University Press.
Simon, J.L., and R. Gobin (1980)  The relationship between popu-
    lation and economic growth in LDCs.  Population Economics
    2:215-234.
Simon, J.L., and G. Steinmann (1984)  The economic implications
    of learning-by-doing for population size and growth.
    European Economic Review 26(1-2):167-185.
Squire, L. (1981)  Employment Policy:  A Survey of Issues and
    Evidence in Developing Countries.  Oxford:  Oxford
    University Press.
Stern, J.J., and J.D. Lewis (1980)  Employment Patterns and
    Income Growth.  World Bank Staff Working Paper No. 419,
    World Bank, Washington, D.C.
Stewart, F. (n.d.)  Recent Theories of International Trade:  Some
    Implications for the South.  Unpublished report, Queen
    Elizabeth House, Oxford, England.
Stewart, F. (1974)  Technology and employment in LDCs.  In E.
    Edwards, ed., Employment in Developing Countries.  New
    York:  Columbia University Press.
Stewart, F. (1977)  Technology and Underdevelopment.  London:
    Macmillan.
Stewart, F. (1985)  Macro-policies for appropriate technology:
    an introductory classification.  In J. James and S. Watanabe,
    eds., Technology, Institutions, and Government Policies.
    London:  Macmillan.
Tyler, W.G. (1981)  The Brazilian Industrial Economy.  Lexington,
    Mass.:  D.C. Heath.
United Nations (various years)  Demographic Yearbook.  New York:
    United Nations.
von Tunzelmann, G.N. (1981)  Technical progress during the Indus-
    trial Revolution.  In R. Floud and D. McCloskey, eds., The
    Economic History of Britain Since 1700, Vol. 1, 1700-1860.
    Cambridge, England:  Cambridge University Press.
Wells, L.T. (1974)  Economic man and engineering man:  choice of
    technology in a low-wage country.  In C.P. Timmer et al., The
    Choice of Technology in Developing Countries (Some Cautionary
    Tales).  Cambridge, Mass.:  Harvard University Center for
    International Affairs.
Williams, D. (1979)  National planning and the choice of technol-
    ogy.  In K.S. Kim, R.B. Mabele, and M.J. Schultheis, eds.,
    Papers on the Political Economy of Tanzania.  London:
    Heinemann.
World Bank (1983)  World Development Report 1983.  Washington,
    D.C.:  World Bank.
World Bank (1984)  World Development Report 1984.  Washington,
    D.C.:  World Bank.

# III.  Natural Resources

# 8
## Natural Resource Scarcity: A Global Survey
F. Landis MacKellar
Daniel R. Vining, Jr.

## INTRODUCTION

Resource scarcity has been a perennial issue (Pavitt, 1973). A number of well-publicized, but inaccurate, projections of impending crises have been made through the years: by Malthus (1798) in the case of food; Jevons (1865) in the case of energy; and Leith (1935) in the case of minerals, for instance. In recent years, the pessimistic baseline scenarios presented by the Limits to Growth study (Meadows et al., 1974; hereafter Limits) and the Global 2000 Report to the President (U.S. Department of State and Council on Environmental Quality, 1980; hereafter Global 2000) have elicited heated debate.

This chapter is a broad review, at the global level, of recent scarcity trends for a spectrum of important natural resources: energy (mostly conventional crude petroleum, with brief references to unconventional oil and other energy sources); food (mostly agricultural resources, with a short comment on fish); forest resources; and species. These sections may be read independently by readers interested in a particular resource. Nonfuel minerals and the quality of the environment are beyond the scope of this chapter. For each resource, the authors ask whether the evidence suggests, on balance, that supply-side con-

This chapter has profited substantially from the comments of a number of readers. Among these are Pierre Crosson, Herman Daly, Lincoln Day, Riley Dunlap, Garrett Hardin, Gale Johnson, Robert Kaufman, Gerhard Lenski, Geoffrey McNicoll, Dennis Meadows, Peter Odell, Samuel Preston, Edward Renshaw, Julian Simon, Kerry Smith, Fritz Steiner, Karl Weber III, and James Zucchetto. It has not been possible to incorporate all of their suggestions, and the authors take responsibility for remaining flaws. In the early stages of this project, research assistance on the subjects of oil and forests was provided by Dah-Lih Wang and James Hartzell, respectively. We thank Wharton Econometric Forecasting Associates, Philadelphia, Pennsylvania, for making available some of the data employed here.

straints will be serious in the next generation; if so, appropriate policy responses are briefly described.  The conclusions
reached are mainly mixed:  neither extreme position in the current policy debate is endorsed.  Some resources are becoming more
scarce, while others are not; selective policy responses are indicated, but no broad reordering of priorities is necessary.


MEASURING SCARCITY


A resource is economically scarce when the total cost of obtaining it, including opportunity costs and the present value of
costs imposed on future generations, is high.  Despite this
straightforward definition, it is difficult to design adequate
scarcity measures.  Since the pioneering work of Barnett and
Morse (1963), economists have usually chosen real unit extraction
costs and relative resource price as scarcity indexes.  Less commonly used measures include marginal user cost (scarcity rent for
the resource in situ) and marginal discovery cost.  In addition
to these price measures, many quantity measures have also been
employed:  reserves, reserves-to-production ratios, consumption,
and so on.
        There is no reason to think that any one scarcity measure,
used in isolation, can serve as an accurate basis for policy
decisions (MacKellar and Vining, 1986a).  For example, all quantity measures, and unit extraction cost as well, fail to capture
fully the supply-demand interaction which is at the heart of
economic scarcity.  Relative price is frequently biased by government controls, monopoly rents, and so on.  None of the measures reliably measure the costs of environmental degradation
caused by resource extraction and consumption.
        Given these ambiguities, it is perhaps not surprising that
the scarcity debate has revealed deep divisions within the
academic community.  We have reviewed this debate elsewhere
(MacKellar and Vining, 1986b).  The counterpart to the academic
debate has been a radical swing in U.S. public policy, from the
"limits to growth" theme of the 1970s to the "limitless growth"
theme of the present Administration.
        At this juncture, the authors believe that the time is ripe
for a nonpartisan review of the empirical evidence.  This will,
of necessity, be broad rather than deep, and its main task will
be simply the presentation of consistent postwar time series for
a spectrum of global resource scarcity measures.  The time frame
adopted will be flexible; however, the period of greatest concern
will be roughly 1950-2025.  The authors, with some regret, do not
address the important question of whether we will run out of some
resources in the very long term.  Their rationale for this is
that the focus of the current policy debate is not very long-term
resource availability, but rather the proposition that a crisis
is unfolding right now, before our eyes.  The resource surveys
presented below tend to emphasize the supply side, and, in particular, do not treat questions of resource-saving technical
change in the detail these questions deserve.  If the treatment

of resource demand had been expanded, each section in this chapter would have turned into a chapter in its own right.   Finally,
this survey will not treat the critical question of whether environmental quality is being seriously degraded (for the interested reader, a good starting point is Baumol and Oates,
1984).  Although this is a vital resource issue, space limitations dictate its exclusion here.

     As noted above, all of the commonly employed measures of
resource scarcity are deficient in one way or another.  Nevertheless, they represent the only available tools of empirical
analysis in this area.  Furthermore, the power of these imperfect
tools is enhanced if we look at many of the measures before
drawing conclusions.  In this survey, emphasis is placed on real
resource prices and physical measures.  The unit extraction cost,
scarcity rent, and marginal discovery cost measures have not been
consistently employed here because of the great difficulty involved in assembling global time series.

     Finally, throughout this chapter the authors have relied on
tabular and graphical presentation as a means of analysis; in
defense of these informal approaches, they suggest that policy
action on the resource front is likely only in the face of unambiguous, easily grasped evidence.  Details on the construction
of data series presented graphically are contained in the notes
and sources of the figures.


ENERGY

Energy is a key resource.  Since it can be employed to manufacture and extract scarce materials from abundant ones (Goeller
and Weinberg, 1978; Skinner, 1976:267), its scarcity is frequently the basis for that of other resources.  It is an essential input to food production (Cook 1977:1-4; Steinhart and
Steinhart, 1974; Whittlesey and Lee, 1976), manufacturing, and
transportation.

     The availability and price of energy are closely related to
the  long-term  structural  evolution  of  economic  activity
(Cleveland  et  al.,  1984;  Darmstadter  et  al.,  1971:69-74;
Steinhart and Steinhart, 1974:310); for instance, the Industrial
Revolution in late eighteenth-century Britain has been interpreted as an adaptive reaction to the shortage of biomass energy
(Thomas, 1980).  Hamilton (1983a, especially 229, Figure 1) has
noted that seven of the eight postwar U.S. recessions were pre-
ceded by a sharp energy price increase, and Sheehan and Kelly
(1983) have demonstrated that between 1956 and 1980, increases
in oil prices were related to subsequent increases in the U.S.
wholesale price index.  Taking an extremely long view, Fischer
(1980:100) has asserted that in each of the four major inflationary waves since the thirteenth century, the pressure of
population against energy (and agricultural) resources was the
prime mover.

     Energy  consumption  is  conventionally  defined  as  either
commercial or noncommercial, the latter consisting of fuelwood,

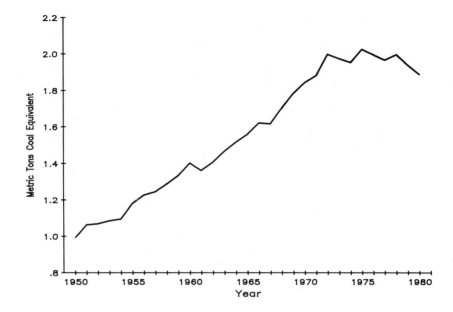

FIGURE 1  World Commercial Energy Consumption Per Capita

Note:  Extrapolated using compound growth rates calculated from
data points for years shown.

Sources:  1978-81 from United Nations (1981:3, Table 1); 1970-77
from United Nations (1977:3, Table 1); 1950-69 from United
Nations (1976:3, Table 1); population from United Nations (1979/
80:2, Table 1).

animal dung, and crop residue consumption in the less developed
countries (LDCs).  In East and West Africa, for instance, biomass
energy comprises virtually all of rural and more than half of
urban energy consumption (Anderson and Fishwick, 1984:11-12,
especially Table 2.1).  However, since problems relating to the
biomass energy resource are better discussed in the context of
the deforestation debate, this section is limited to questions
of commercial energy production and consumption.

The output elasticity of commercial energy consumption was
roughly unity for the world as a whole between 1950 and 1965 (see
Table 1).  The period between the end of World War II and the
1973-74 oil shock was one of especially rapid growth in energy
consumption (see Figure 1), calculated by Rosing and Odell (1983:
2-5 and 6, Figure 1) to have been 5 percent per annum, as opposed
to the long-term trend of 2 percent.  Fuel power was rapidly sub-

TABLE 1   Energy-GNP Elasticities, by Region, 1950-65

| Region | Elasticity |
|--------|-----------|
| North America | 0.84 |
| Western Europe | 0.92 |
| USSR and Eastern Europe | 1.23 |
| Oceania | 1.19 |
| Africa | 1.23 |
| Latin America | 1.55 |
| Asia (excluding China) | 1.32 |
| China | 2.48 |
| World | 1.06 |

Source:  Darmstadter et al. (1971:37, Table 17).


stituted for human, animal, and water power in production processes; for instance, between 1915-19 and 1977-81, the number of
labor hours per 100 bushels of wheat in American agriculture fell
from 98 to 8 (U.S. Department of Agriculture, 1982a:411, Table
592; see also Steinhart and Steinhart, 1974:310, Figure 3).   In
all phases of production and consumption, there was a move from
natural materials to energy-intensive synthetics.   These years
also saw rapid modernization in the developing and centrally
planned economies (CPEs), a process almost synonymous, in its
earlier stages, with the shift to a more energy-intensive output
basket and production technology (Slade, 1986, especially Figure
3).
     As world production became more energy-intensive, the energy
consumption basket shifted from coal to oil, as illustrated in
Table 2.   In addition to attractions on the demand side--oil is


TABLE 2   Composition of World Commercial Energy Proauction
(in percent)

| Energy Source | 1929 | 1950 | 1965 | 1970 | 1975 | 1981 |
|---------------|------|------|------|------|------|------|
| Solid Fuels | 77.8 | 59.2 | 40.5 | 30.6 | 28.4 | 29.0 |
| Liquid Fuels | 17.2 | 29.9 | 41.4 | 48.6 | 49.3 | 46.5 |
| Natural Gas | 4.2 | 9.3 | 16.1 | 18.6 | 19.5 | 20.9 |
| Hydroelectric | 0.8 | 1.6 | 2.0 | 2.2 | 2.8 | 3.5 |

Sources:  1929-65:  Darmstadter et al. (1971:21, Table 8).
          1970-81:  United Nations (1981:2, Table 1).

easy to convert into end-use fuels, easy to transport, and clean-
burning--supply-side factors also favored oil (Rosing and Odell,
1983:3). Demand was stimulated by a falling real price (see
Figure 2), the result of the coming on-stream of vast new reserves in the Middle East. World reserves rose steadily, as
illustrated in Figure 3. The world reserves-to-production (R/P)
ratio climbed rapidly in the 1950s, when major Middle Eastern
reserves were developed. In Table 3, it may be seen that between
1950 and 1970, the Middle East accounted for almost two-thirds of
the global increment to reserves.

So many factors were at work that the proximate cause of the
1973-74 price explosion (see Figure 2) may never be known with
certainty (Hamilton, 1983b:30; Rosing and Odell, 1983:4).1 It
is clear, however, that had slack non-OPEC capacity been available at the margin, OPEC could never have made the price hike
stick. At the time of the crisis, conventional economic opinion
held that two developments could be expected. First, the higher
price of oil would encourage substitution toward other energy

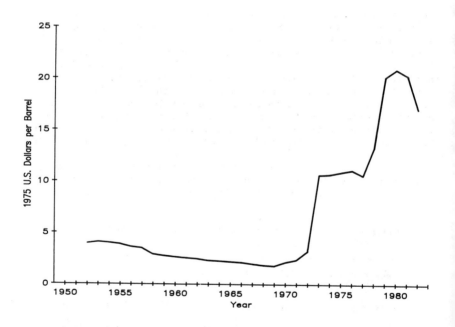

FIGURE 2   Price of Saudi Arabian Crude Oil

Note:   Deflated by U.S. GDP deflator from Wharton Econometric
Forecasting Associates.

Source:   International Monetary Fund (1983:89-91).

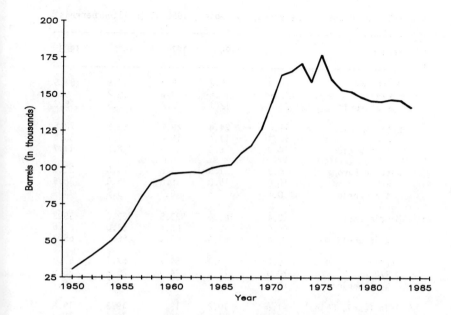

FIGURE 3   World Oil Reserves Per Capita

Note:   Population as in Figure 1

Sources:   1950-80 from American Petroleum Institute (1984: Section 2, Table 1); 1984 from World Oil (1983).

sources and conservation of energy in general.  Second, the profits suddenly to be made in oil would elicit exploration that
would dramatically expand reserves.  The incentive to explore
would be especially strong in non-OPEC countries, where producers
could, in effect, sell as much oil as they could pump out of the
ground at a price only marginally lower than the OPEC benchmark.
As new producers made inroads on OPEC's market share, the cartel
would crumble and finally disintegrate.  Once again, oil would
sell at a price only slightly in excess of the unit extraction
cost.
    Economists' predictions on the demand side have been amply
realized.  Figure 1 shows that world per capita commercial energy
consumption has declined since the mid-1970s.  Deep structural
shifts have occurred in the relationship between economic activity and energy consumption (Lin, 1984:786-802; Organization for
Economic Cooperation and Development (OECD), 1982:79-103 and 155-
159; Brown, 1984a; Choe et al., 1981:16-23).  The energy consumption data employed to construct Figure 1, combined with global

266                                        MacKellar and Vining

TABLE 3   Crude Oil Reserves, by Region, 1950-83 (billion barrels)

| Region | 1950 | 1960 | 1970 | 1980 | 1983 |
|---|---|---|---|---|---|
| North America | 25.8 | 35.2 | 38.3 | 33.9 | 34.9 |
| R/Pa | 12.9 | 12.6 | 9.6 | 9.2 | 9.5 |
| % of world | 33.7 | 12.1 | 7.2 | 5.3 | 5.2 |
| Latin America | 11.4 | 24.4 | 29.2 | 56.5 | 78.5 |
| R/P | 16.3 | 17.4 | 15.4 | 27.7 | 35.5 |
| % of world | 14.9 | 8.4 | 5.5 | 8.8 | 11.7 |
| Western Europe | 0.3 | 1.5 | 1.8 | 23.5 | 22.9 |
| R/P | 10.0 | 15.0 | 18.0 | 26.3 | 18.5 |
| % of world | 0.4 | 0.5 | 0.3 | 3.7 | 3.4 |
| Middle East | 32.4 | 181.4 | 333.5 | 362.0 | 369.3 |
| R/P | 54.0 | 95.5 | 65.4 | 54.0 | 87.6 |
| % of world | 42.4 | 62.6 | 62.9 | 56.4 | 55.3 |
| Africa | 0.2 | 7.3 | 54.7 | 57.1 | 57.8 |
| R/P | 10.0 | 73.0 | 24.9 | 25.6 | 35.9 |
| % of world | 0.3 | 2.5 | 10.3 | 8.5 | 8.7 |
| Asia (excl. China) | 1.6 | 10.2 | 13.1 | 19.3 | 19.8 |
| R/P | 17.8 | 51.0 | 26.2 | 18.4 | 19.3 |
| % of world | 2.1 | 3.5 | 2.5 | 3.0 | 3.0 |
| Centrally Planned Economies | 4.7 | 30.0 | 60.0 | 90.0 | 85.1 |
| R/P | 15.7 | 25.0 | 20.7 | 17.3 | 16.1 |
| % of world | 6.2 | 10.3 | 11.3 | 14.0 | 12.7 |
| World | 76.5 | 290.0 | 530.5 | 642.2 | 668.3 |
| R/P | 17.9 | 37.7 | 31.8 | 29.5 | 34.7 |

Note:  Reserves as of 1 January.

aR/P:  reserves-to-production ratio.

Source:  American Petroleum Institute (1984:Section II, Table 1 and Section IV, Table 1a).

activity data from the World Economic Service of Wharton Econometric Forecasting Associates, indicate that the world energy-output elasticity dropped from 1.15 in the period 1965-73 (Darmstadter et al., 1971, place it at 1.06 between 1950 and 1965) to only 0.44 in the period 1974-81. Lin (1984:792-793, Table 7) calculates that between 1963-73 and 1973-78, the energy-output elasticity in the industrial countries declined from 1.00 to 0.16, whereas in the oil-importing LDCs, it dropped only from 1.34 to 1.15. The world energy basket, which can be seen in Table 2 to have shifted uninterruptedly toward oil between 1929 and 1975, reversed the trend between the latter year and 1981.

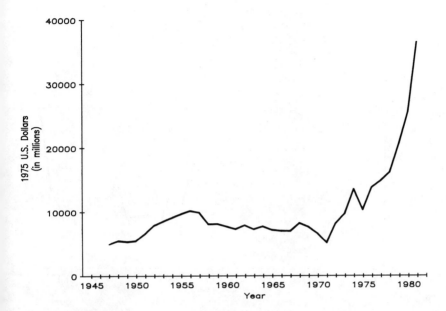

FIGURE 4   U.S. Exploration and Development Expenditures

Note:  Deflated as in Figure 2.

Source:  American Petroleum Institute (1984:Section 5, Table 9a).

Predictions that higher prices would stimulate exploration
were also confirmed.  In the 1950s and 1960s, the expenditure of
major oil companies on U.S. exploration and development stagnated
in real terms (see Figure 4).  World geophysical exploration--
the seismic prospecting that precedes exploratory drilling--
declined steadily (see Figure 5).  Two reasons may be deduced
for these trends:  first, little exploratory effort was required
to bring on-stream plentiful reserves in the Middle East; and
second, the real price of oil, and hence the unit value of reserves, was falling.  Indeed, more than half of capital investment in the oil industry during these decades went into more
lucrative downstream activities such as transportation, refining,
and retailing (Choe et al., 1981:39).  As Figures 4 and 5 demonstrate, the 1973-74 price hike reversed both trends, although
there was a significant lag before world geophysical exploration
picked up.  The added exploratory effort was initially concentrated in industrial countries, which had already been heavily
explored.  Exploratory well completions in non-OPEC LDCs stagnated in the years immediately following the price hike, but

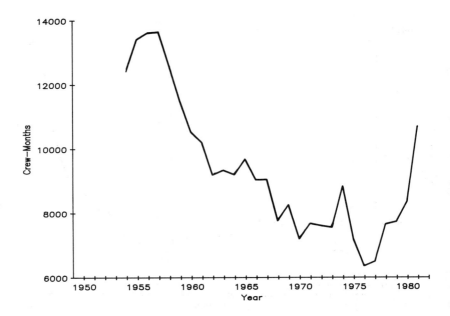

FIGURE 5   World Geophysical Exploration

Note: Excluding centrally planned economies.

Source:   American Petroleum Institute (1984:Section 3, Table 4).

surged after 1979 (see Table 4, where the column labeled "Other"
corresponds almost exactly to the non-OPEC LDC aggregate).
   The result of these exploratory efforts has been a significant shift in the world distribution of oil production.  Between
1972 and 1982, OPEC production fell from 51 to 35 percent of the
world total, and it is smaller today (Basile and de la
Grandville, 1984:104, Table I).  Oil production within the OECD
increased from 13.6 to 15.3 million barrels per day (mbd), major
non-OPEC LDC producers (those producing over 0.2 mbd) increased
production from 0.4 to 6.7 mbd, and marginal LDC producers raised
production from 1.1 to 1.3 mbd.  Since world noncentrally planned
economy production fell by 2.4 mbd, from 43.8 mbd in 1972 to 41.4
mbd in 1982, these increments to non-OPEC production forced the
cartel to reduce its output from 26.8 mbd (it peaked at 31.8 mbd
in 1977) to 19.4 mbd; it is currently running around 18 mbd.
OPEC no longer sets the price of oil; it is set, rather, on the
free market, where many economists predicted all along that it
would eventually be set.

TABLE 4   Noncommunist World Oil Well Completions
(in 1,000s)

| Year | U.S., Canada, Europe | OPEC | Other | Total |
|---|---|---|---|---|
| 1970 | 32.9 | 1.4 | 2.1 | 36.5 |
| 1971 | 39.9 | 1.6 | 2.3 | 34.8 |
| 1972 | 32.8 | 1.5 | 2.2 | 36.5 |
| 1973 | 32.6 | 1.7 | 2.1 | 36.6 |
| 1974 | 37.6 | 2.1 | 2.1 | 41.8 |
| 1975 | 43.9 | 1.7 | 2.1 | 47.8 |
| 1976 | 48.2 | 1.7 | 2.2 | 52.1 |
| 1977 | 53.3 | 1.5 | 2.5 | 57.4 |
| 1978 | 56.3 | 2.0 | 2.9 | 61.2 |
| 1979 | 59.4 | 2.5 | 5.4 | 67.3 |
| 1980 | 72.3 | 3.0 | 7.0 | 82.3 |
| 1981 | 88.6 | 3.2 | 7.3 | 99.1 |
| 1982 | 95.6 | 2.4 | 4.3 | 102.3 |

Notes:  Data for Iraq are unavailable for 1977 and
1978.  1979-81 data are reported to be incomplete.
"Other" corresponds to non-OPEC LDCs and developed
Oceania.

Source:  American Petroleum Institute (1984:Section
3, Table 12).

Despite this change in the locus of production, the reserves picture has changed remarkably little.  The world reserves-to-production (R/P) ratio, as seen in Figure 6, has remained in the range of 30-40 years.  World reserves, shown on a per capita basis in Figure 3, have actually declined in the post-oil shock period.  In the last several years, some spectacular and costly busts have been recorded in areas once regarded as quite promising by petroleum geologists (Economist, 1984d).

Despite a decade of intense non-OPEC exploration and development, the decline in OPEC's share of world reserves has been remarkably small (see Figure 7).  Given limited reserve accretions and high production, the non-OPEC R/P ratio, 17.6 on 1 January 1983, is low, especially when compared to the OPEC R/P of about 75 at the same time.  For OECD members, the ratio was 12.6; for non-OPEC LDC producers, it was 33.6; and for CPEs, it was estimated to be 15.7 (Basile and de la Grandville, 1984:109, Table VI).  Excluding Mexico, with by far the largest reserve base outside of OPEC, the non-OPEC LDC R/P ratio was 21 and the total non-OPEC ratio 14.9.

The sluggish reaction of oil reserves to the OPEC phenomenon requires explanation.  One must conclude that unless reserves are being underreported on a grand scale, economists correctly anticipated the supply response of oil companies, but overestimated the success of exploratory efforts.  This suggests that they

FIGURE 6    World Oil Reserves:    Production Ratio

Note:    Calculated from reserves data as in Figure 3 and
production data from same source.

Sources:    See Figure 3.


overlooked   the   geological   parameters   of   the   supply   process.
What, then, are these parameters?
     Even at current depressed production levels, the additions to
reserves  required  to  keep  R/P  and  per  capita  reserves  from
falling are very large.   Furthermore, the accumulation of oil in
a commercially viable pool is the outcome of a complex and unstable sequence of geological developments; it is thus a statistically rare event (Nehring, 1982:180 and 182).   A consensus has
emerged among geologists in the public, corporate, and academic
sectors that ultimate world recovery of crude oil from conventional sources will be on the order of 2000 billion barrels.   At
the production levels that prevailed during the 1970s, this implies ultimate resource exhaustion in about 70 years; most depletion scenarios associated with the 2000 billion barrels estimate
show  global  production  peaking  in  1990-2020  and  falling  off
steadily  to  zero  around  2100  (for  instance,  OECD,  1982:215;
Hubbert, 1977:644).   The 2000 billion barrel estimate is supported by two different statistical approaches.

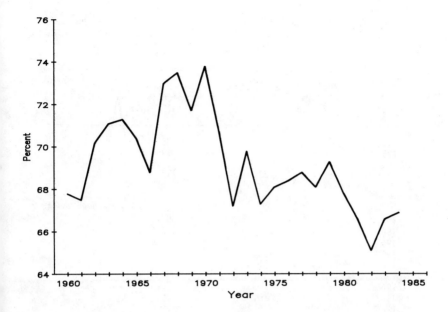

FIGURE 7   OPEC Reserves : World Oil Reserves

Note:   Calculated from sources cited in Figure 3


     The geological-probabilistic approach is best exemplified by
Nehring's survey (1982; see also Nehring, 1978) of world oil deposits.  It cannot be overemphasized, runs this argument, that
the distribution of oil occurrence is highly skewed; most oil
occurs in large provinces and within a province in the largest
fields.  Over half of all oil discovered before 1980, for instance, was found in the Arabian-Iranian megaprovince, which
contained 626 billion barrels upon discovery.  Over half of the
oil discovered in the Arabian-Iranian province was in its 10
largest fields (Nehring, 1982:186, Table 4).  Of the estimated
30,000 fields producing oil and gas worldwide, fewer than 300
account for 75 percent of world output, and only 35 produce 55
percent of the total (OECD, 1982:208).
     As a result of the skewed distribution of oil deposits, the
difficulty of obtaining new reserves has steadily increased.
Fisher (1981:109, Table 4.6) presents time-series data indicating
that between 1946 and 1971, real average unit costs for discover-
ing oil and gas in the United States grew at a compound rate of
5.7 percent per year.  Data series in Table 5 demonstrate that
real oil and gas well-drilling costs decreased in the United
States until the mid-1960s, but have been on the rise ever since.

TABLE 5   Real Well-Drilling Costs in the U.S., by Type of Well

| Year | Onshore | | Offshore | |
|---|---|---|---|---|
| | Per Well (1,000s 1975 U.S.$) | Per Foot (1975 U.S.$) | Per Well (1,000s 1975 U.S.$) | Per Foot (1975 U.S.$) |
| 1953 | 106.2 | 26.41 | 638.3 | 66.86 |
| 1955 | 90.8 | 22.79 | 799.6 | 83.60 |
| 1956 | 94.4 | 23.51 | 831.7 | 86.73 |
| 1959 | 93.7 | 22.91 | 713.4 | 71.40 |
| Average | 96.3 | 23.91 | 745.8 | 77.15 |
| 1960 | 93.1 | 22.45 | 706.5 | 67.77 |
| 1961 | 90.7 | 21.78 | 692.5 | 68.97 |
| 1962 | 95.2 | 22.12 | 637.0 | 62.42 |
| 1963 | 85.9 | 20.37 | 650.0 | 62.53 |
| 1964 | 84.1 | 20.02 | 621.0 | 60.69 |
| 1965 | 86.6 | 19.90 | 698.1 | 66.48 |
| 1966 | 89.8 | 20.54 | 772.6 | 73.36 |
| 1967 | 88.8 | 20.43 | 715.3 | 75.58 |
| 1968 | 94.0 | 20.35 | 769.8 | 80.66 |
| 1969 | 99.6 | 20.57 | 810.6 | 82.87 |
| Average | 89.8 | 19.85 | 707.3 | 70.13 |
| 1970 | 104.3 | 21.50 | 778.1 | 80.41 |
| 1971 | 100.3 | 20.96 | 774.8 | 76.04 |
| 1972 | 107.8 | 21.86 | 801.1 | 79.55 |
| 1973 | 113.0 | 23.14 | 774.4 | 82.32 |
| 1974 | 131.5 | 28.08 | 895.3 | 100.39 |
| 1975 | 150.2 | 32.15 | 1142.2 | 120.02 |
| 1976 | 150.1 | 32.60 | 1363.9 | 142.81 |
| 1977 | 166.6 | 35.30 | 1517.8 | 160.35 |
| 1978 | 192.8 | 40.06 | 1800.3 | 183.31 |
| 1979 | 209.7 | 44.02 | 1959.4 | 199.23 |
| Average | 142.6 | 29.97 | 1180.4 | 122.44 |
| 1980 | 220.0 | 47.15 | 2132.5 | 216.95 |
| 1981 | 252.8 | 53.57 | 2424.2 | 248.10 |
| 1982 | 269.0 | 58.12 | 2555.3 | 257.33 |
| Average | 247.3 | 52.95 | 2370.7 | 240.79 |

Note:  Deflated by U.S. GDP deflator from Wharton Econometrics. Includes oil wells, gas wells, and dry holes.

Source:  American Petroleum Institute (1984:Section III, Table 11).

The sharp cost increase in the wake of the first oil shock under-
scores that oil exploration and recovery are themselves energy-
intensive processes. The percentage of new oil field discoveries
subsequently proven to be of significant size has steadily declined, as illustrated for the U.S. case by data in Table 6.
Although exploratory activity in the developing and centrally
planned economies has not been as intense as in other regions

TABLE 6   Percent of New Oil Field Discoveries in U.S.
Proved After 6 Years to be of Significant Size

| Year | Percent |
|------|---------|
| 1947 | 2.20 |
| 1948 | 1.76 |
| 1949 | 2.05 |
| 1950 | 1.88 |
| 1951 | 1.42 |
| 1952 | 1.32 |
| 1953 | 1.69 |
| 1954 | 1.41 |
| 1955 | 1.49 |
| 1956 | 1.14 |
| 1957 | 0.95 |
| 1958 | 1.56 |
| 1959 | 0.84 |
| Average | 1.52 |
| 1960 | 0.60 |
| 1961 | 0.75 |
| 1962 | 0.71 |
| 1963 | 0.78 |
| 1964 | 0.91 |
| 1965 | 0.73 |
| 1966 | 0.76 |
| 1967 | 0.87 |
| 1968 | 0.90 |
| 1969 | 0.81 |
| 1970 | 1.18 |
| Average | 0.82 |
| 1971 | 0.60 |
| 1972 | 1.02 |
| 1973 | 0.56 |
| 1974 | 0.65 |
| 1975 | 0.84 |
| 1976 | 0.77 |
| Average | 0.74 |

Note: Fields are considered significant if they contain
1 million barrels of oil or more.

Source:  American Petroleum Industry (1984: Section III,
Table 6a).

(Grossling, 1977), continues the argument, world exploration is sufficiently advanced to estimate the number of provinces remaining to be found. In already-known provinces, although significant upward revisions are occasionally made, as recently in the case of the North Sea (Lawson, 1984), future productivity may be accurately assessed. Proceeding across the major geological regions of the world, it is possible, therefore, to make a fairly accurate geological assessment of resource potential. Nehring (1982) estimates that ultimate conventional crude oil recovery will be between 1600 and 2400 billion barrels. The latter estimate assumes that recovery rates will increase from the current 25-30 percent of original oil-in-place to 55-60 percent, an assumption at the upper bound of the expert consensus (OECD, 1982:209-210).

The main competing method for estimating world oil resources is the extrapolation procedure of Hubbert (1962:50-94). In the language of stock market analysts, this might be called a "technical" method as opposed to the "fundamental" geological-probabilistic method. Hubbert assumes that discoveries of crude oil reserves ($dQd/dt$, where $Qd$ is cumulative discoveries to date) follow a bell-shaped curve, rising rapidly as easily found deposits come to light, then peaking and declining as exploration becomes more advanced. This is illustrated in Figure 8. He also assumes a fixed lag, estimated to be around 20 years at the global level, between the time that a barrel of oil is added to reserves and the time it is extracted. From these assumptions, the curves in Figure 8 may be traced out. Cumulative discovery and cumulative production ($Qp$) follow logistic curves to a common asymptote at the level of ultimate resource recovery. The model is estimated by fitting a curve to cumulative discovery, experimenting with different levels of ultimate recovery until the closest fit is obtained.

On its face, this model is naive, but it has borne the test of time well. The U.S. oil production forecast made by Hubbert in 1962, especially the then-controversial peak around 1970, has proven highly accurate (Renshaw and Renshaw, 1980). Hubbert has been criticized for a lack of statistical rigor (Pensak, 1978; Wiorkowski, 1981), but in fact, the model is extremely robust to changes in curve specification and estimation (Mayer et al., 1979).

In 1962, Hubbert estimated ultimate world recovery at 1250 billion barrels (Hubbert, 1962:74, Table 6); in a subsequent reassessment, he raised the estimate to roughly 2000 billion barrels (Hubbert, 1977). In both cases, the production curves associated with the projections peak around the turn of the century. It is largely acceptance of the Hubbert estimate that has reduced the variation among industry experts' assessments of ultimate recovery; most of these now fall within a very narrow range.

Dissenting views (Odell, 1982, 1984; Rosing and Odell, 1983) hold that the world oil industry has failed to look wholeheartedly for additional reserves, and that demand growth will be much slower in the future than in recent decades. Assuming ulti-

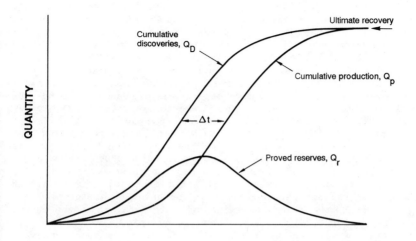

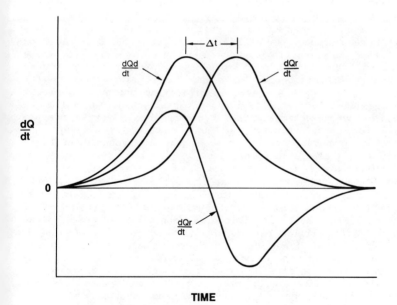

FIGURE 8    The Hubbert Model

Source:    Cook (1967:6)

mate recovery of 3000 billion barrels of conventional oil, no
production of unconventional oil, and 2.6 percent per year demand
growth (as opposed to the 5 percent growth implicitly extrapolated in the Hubbert procedure), Rosing and Odell (1983:24) have
projected that world production will not peak until almost 2020.
    Even in this optimistic scenario, then, conventional oil pro-
duction will start to decline early in the next century. Will
unconventional crude oil sources--shale oil and tar sands--be
able to take up the slack? These resources are far from competitive today, but may become economical to exploit as the price of
oil rises. Global 2000 (pp. 199-200) estimated that about 190
billion barrels of shale oil and 250-285 billion barrels of oil
from tar sands were marginally recoverable in 1980. The OECD was
quite pessimistic about the potential for these sources in 1982
(OECD, 1982:212).2 Given annual world crude oil demand growth
of only 1 percent per year between now and 2050 (which implies,
given the likely long-term economic growth path, an energy-output
elasticity of 0.25-0.50 over this interval), oil consumption at
mid-century will be about 40 billion barrels per year. Conventional oil reserves will, even in an optimistic view, be of
little importance by that time. If 1000 billion barrels of unconventional crude is economically recoverable by mid-century,
three to four times the amount currently estimated to be (marginally) recoverable, we will still be facing an R/P ratio of
25. Furthermore, barring technical advances, energy from these
sources will be significantly more expensive than the energy we
now consume. Contributing to higher real prices will be the
lower net energy gain achieved in exploiting unconventional oil
resources (Cleveland et al., 1984, especially 894, Table 1). In
conclusion, unconventional crude petroleum has a very large potential for contributing to a "soft landing" as we make the
transition to nonoil energy sources, but it probably will not
provide a long-term answer in and of itself.
    Coal resources are vast relative to current utilization--
Beckmann (1984a:428) reports that the world R/P ratio is around
200--and will probably play a large part in future energy production (Ford Foundation, 1979:277-408). At 660 billion tons,
economically recoverable coal reserves contain energy equivalent
to around 2500 billion barrels of oil, and total resources-in-
place are over 10 times greater than economically recoverable
resources. However, the environmental implications of increasing
coal consumption--on-site environmental degradation, water pollution, air pollution, acid precipitation, and carbon dioxide
buildup in the atmosphere--are serious, and the costs of abatement are high (Beckmann, 1984a:432-433).
    Natural gas reserves, which unlike conventional oil reserves
have grown steadily on a per capita basis since record keeping on
a worldwide basis began in 1967, are also significant (see Figure
9). Hubbert (1977:640, Table XIX-5) has estimated world ultimate
recovery of conventional natural gas at 10,000 trillion cubic
feet, which translates in energy-equivalent terms into about 1800
billion barrels of oil. The main drawbacks with gas are that it
is a localized resource (between them, the Soviet Union and the

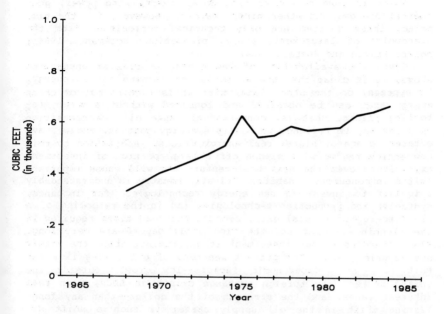

FIGURE 9   World Natural Gas Reserves Per Capita

Source:   American Petroleum Institute (1984:Section 13, Table 1).

Middle East account for well over half of known gas reserves) and
is costly to transport.

Biomass energy, mostly from fuelwood, is of limited potential
given the apparent crisis in the world forests (Gamser, 1980; a
more optimistic view is given by Flavin and Postel, 1984:140-145;
see detailed discussion below).  However, its contribution could
be increased given investment in plantation silviculture (Sedjo
and Clawson, 1984) and household-level agro-forestry (Anderson
and Fishwick, 1984).

Nuclear power offers an apparently cheap source of energy,
but opinion is sharply divided on its safety and on whether less
capital-intensive energy technologies are preferable (B. Cohen,
1984; K. Cohen, 1984; Flavin, 1984).   In the final analysis,
expert views may be irrelevant. Public opinion, perhaps dis-
playing the fickleness discussed by Ashby (1976, 1979; see B.
Cohen, 1984 for the argument that the public grossly exaggerates
nuclear power risks), has become stubbornly fixed against this
power source.  While taking no stand in the nuclear power debate,
the authors submit that only sharp increases in the real price
of electricity would bring about public acceptance of nuclear
technology.

There is some potential from solar power, wind power, geo-
thermal energy, and other minor sources. However, for the time
being, these sources are only technical curiosities from the
standpoint of large-scale energy production (Beckmann, 1984b;
contra Flavin and Postel, 1984).

Given the availability of new energy sources as enumerated
above, it is clear that the world is not running out of energy.
It appears, on the other hand, that it is running out of cheap
energy that can be obtained and consumed without a major retooling effort, that is, conventional crude oil. A transition
is under way to reliance on multiple energy sources, and we have
entered an age of higher real energy prices. Adaptation to this
new energy regime will siphon off a large portion of investment
expenditure over the next half-century and will cause important
shifts in consumption habits. Private industry is understandably
reluctant to invest in new energy technologies (for instance,
synfuels) and production technologies (as in the retooling of a
plant to run on natural gas), because the lead times required in
the planning process and the time until payoff are very long.
Also retarding energy investment is uncertainty about the future
energy price path. The present weakness of oil prices is a result more of macroeconomic factors--low growth outside the
United States, the foreign exchange crisis in LDCs, high real
interest rates, and the strength of the dollar--than any long-
lasting shift in the oil supply curve; if such a shift has
indeed taken place, it should show up more clearly in reserve
statistics. In early 1986, Saudi Arabian policy makers en-
gineered a world oil glut to drive the price of oil into the low
teens. All indications are that prices will fairly soon return
to the high teens, or even break into the twenties again. Nevertheless, low oil prices are discouraging investment that should
be undertaken now, not later. The authors conclude that government should adopt an active policy stance in encouraging an orderly transition away from dependence on conventional crude oil.

It is important to remember that there have been two energy
revolutions already: the switch from wood to coal and the switch
from coal to oil. During these transitions, with their attendant
social and economic dislocation, aggregate social welfare, measured by any reasonable index, continued to rise. However, there
is an important difference in this transition: for the first
time, we are shifting to energy sources that, in terms of net
energy gain and the efficiency with which they can be converted
into work, are inferior to the presently favored source
(Cleveland et al., 1984). The technical and scientific tools at
our disposal are an order of magnitude more powerful than they
were during the previous two transitions, and therefore to assume
that the world must fare worse in the present transition is to
be pessimistic. On the other hand, to argue that the best energy
policy is that which is most laissez-faire is, in our view,
misguided.

FOOD

Agricultural Resources

Trends in Production and Price

History indicates that world per capita food output is increasing
(see Figure 10).  Despite occasional downturns, food output as
indexed by the United Nations Food and Agriculture Organization
(UNFAO) has grown, on average, about 1 percent faster than population in the postwar period.  Figure 11, based on statistics
from the U.S. Department of Agriculture (USDA) indicates a similarly optimistic trend in the case of grains (wheat, coarse
grains such as corn, and rice).  Researchers disagree on whether
the variability of world production, measured by the coefficient
of variation, has increased over time (Barr, 1981:1088 and footnote 9; versus Donaldson, 1984:188); there is no disagreement,
however, that the trend has been unmistakably upward.  Area har-

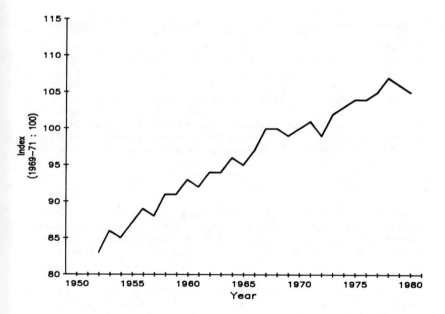

FIGURE 10   FAO Per Capita Food Index

Sources:  1969-80 from UNFAO (1980a:79, Table 6); 1966-68 from
UNFAO (1977:77, Table 6); 1961-65 extrapolated back using UNFAO
(1972a:31, Table 9); 1952-60 extrapolated back using UNFAO
(1967:26, Table 88).

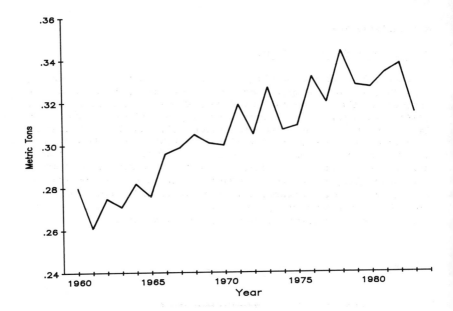

FIGURE 11   World Total Grain Output Per Capita

Note:   Calendar year on the graph corresponds to the world
marketing year, i.e., 1960 is marketing year 1960-61, etc.
1984-84 preliminary.   Populations as in Figure 1.

Source:   U.S. Department of Agriculture (1984:28).


vested and yield per hectare, shown in Figures 12 and 13, have
generally increased during the past quarter-century.   At least
through 1980, there is no evidence in U.S. agriculture that a
"yield plateau" has been reached or that gains in total productivity are slackening (Johnson, 1984:101-103; Swanson and Heady,
1984:211-215).
     Of particular note in these graphs is the effect of the 1973
"wheat shock," when Soviet wheat purchases following several
years of poor harvests caused all world grain prices to rise
sharply relative to the U.S. GDP deflator (see Figure 14).   World
plantings responded immediately to the price stimulus and have
remained high relative to their pre-1974 levels, even though real
grain prices have in recent years been no higher than they were
in the 1950s and 1960s.   Lower grain yields in 1974 must be
partly attributed to the bringing of marginal land into production in the face of higher grain prices; however, as Figure 13
makes clear, yields quickly returned to the path of steady improvement they followed in previous decades.

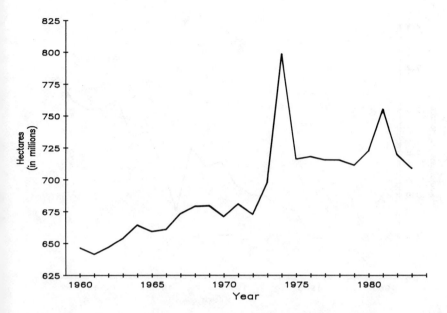

FIGURE 12   World Grain:   Area Harvested

Source:   U.S. Department of Agriculture (1984).


     Longer-term trends in grain production also give little cause
for alarm.   Table 7, based on data assembled from the USDA annual
Agricultural Statistics, contains decadal average wheat production, area harvested, and yield by major world region for the
period 1930-39 to 1970-79.[3]   Wheat is not, of course, the only
critical food crop, but it is the most important one in terms of
human caloric consumption.   Furthermore, long-term trends in
wheat culture are good indicators of developments throughout the
critical grain and oilseed complex.
     Three major facts may be observed in Table 7.   First, in most
regions, higher yield, rather than expanded area, is to be
thanked for increased wheat production; at the global level,
yield improvement accounted for almost 60 percent of the increment to annual average production between 1930-39 and 1970-79.
Second, yield improvement has been an almost entirely postwar
phenomenon.   Finally, interregional yield disparities have increased with time:   in the 1930s, the most advanced region,
Western Europe, enjoyed wheat yields 2.2 times those in Africa,
the least productive region;   by the 1970s, this factor had
steadily increased to over 3.

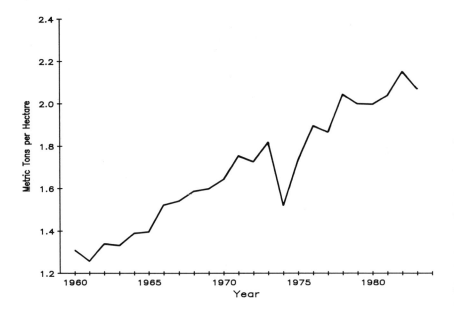

FIGURE 13   World Grain:   Yield

Source:   Calculated from data in Figures 11 and 12.


This regional diversity in yield improvements, when combined
with wide variation in population growth rates, has caused
significant divergence in regional per capita food production
growth.   Food production in the developing countries as a group
has barely kept pace with population growth.   Mellor and Johnston
(1984:535, Table 1) report, for instance, that the increase in
global per capita food production between 1961 and 1977 is almost
entirely attributable to progress in the developed countries,
including the USSR and the centrally planned economies of Eastern
Europe.   Employing the data in Table 7, we calculate that between
1930-39 and 1970-79, developed countries, defined in the same way
as Mellor and Johnston's aggregate, accounted for 71 percent of
the increment to world output, far in excess of their contribution to world population increase.
    What has depressed production in the developing countries,
and how may this problem be addressed?   Simply increasing price
incentives for farmers will not, in and of itself, suffice to end
the food production difficulties that have been experienced in
the developing countries, especially in Africa (Mellor and
Johnston, 1984:542; Eicher, 1984 on the need for a multidimen-
sional response to the African food crisis).4   On the other

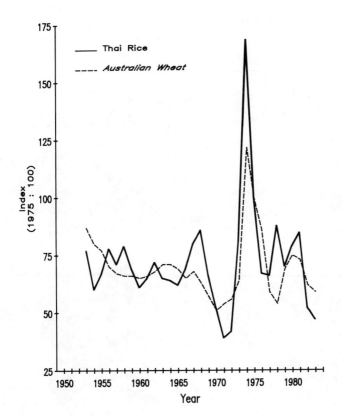

FIGURE 14   World Grain:   Price Indexes

Note:   Deflated as in Figure 1.

Source:   International Monetary Fund (1983).


hand, distortions are among the most important price disincentives to production (G.T. Brown, 1978; Pereira, 1978:25; Bale
and Southworth, 1982:37; Bale and Duncan, 1983a:247; the supply
response to higher prices is documented in Behrman, 1968).
Regrettably, the supply response of LDC farmers is largely a
long-run one.   Mellor and Johnston (1984:541) cite research
placing the short-run price elasticity of supply at only 0.1-0.2.
In the cost-benefit calculus of LDC policy makers, the near-term
benefits of cheap food all too often exceed the heavily discounted benefits of adequate food supplies in the longer term.

TABLE 7   World Wheat Output, Area Harvested, and Yield, by Region
(decadal annual average)

| Region | 1930-39 | 1940-49 | 1950-59 | 1960-69 | 1970-79 |
|---|---|---|---|---|---|
| **North America** | | | | | |
| Output | 29.7 | 40.1 | 44.4 | 57.3 | 68.7 |
| Area | 33.5 | 37.4 | 33.5 | 31.9 | 33.6 |
| Yield | 0.89 | 1.07 | 1.33 | 1.80 | 2.04 |
| **South America** | | | | | |
| Output | 7.8 | 7.6 | 8.6 | 9.3 | 10.8 |
| Area | 8.6 | 7.0 | 7.4 | 7.3 | 8.5 |
| Yield | 0.91 | 1.09 | 1.16 | 1.27 | 1.27 |
| **Western Europe** | | | | | |
| Output | 30.4 | 25.8a | 33.5 | 44.3 | 51.5 |
| Area | 20.1 | 19.3 | 18.7 | 17.9 | 16.2 |
| Yield | 1.51 | 1.34 | 1.79 | 2.47 | 3.18 |
| **Eastern Europe** | | | | | |
| Output | 11.7 | 8.6a | 14.2 | 23.1 | 31.0 |
| Area | 10.2 | 7.5 | 10.3 | 10.4 | 11.8 |
| Yield | 1.15 | 1.15 | 1.38 | 2.22 | 2.63 |
| **USSR** | | | | | |
| Output | 28.8 | 24.1a | 42.9 | 63.7 | 92.7 |
| Area | 38.6 | 33.2 | 54.7 | 66.6 | 61.5 |
| Yield | 0.75 | 0.73 | 0.78 | 0.96 | 1.51 |
| **Asia (excl. China)** | | | | | |
| Output | 18.6 | 19.3 | 27.0b | 34.1 | 53.6 |
| Area | 24.0 | 24.3 | 31.8 | 34.4 | 45.9 |
| Yield | 0.78 | 0.79 | 0.85 | 1.0 | 1.17 |
| **China** | | | | | |
| Output | 22.4 | 22.7 | 23.9b | 21.9 | 41.9 |
| Area | 19.3 | 21.0 | 26.5 | 27.5 | 26.5 |
| Yield | 1.16 | 1.08 | 0.90 | 0.80 | 1.58 |
| **Africa** | | | | | |
| Output | 3.8 | 3.6 | 5.2 | 6.3 | 8.7 |
| Area | 5.4 | 5.8 | 5.8 | 7.4 | 8.7 |
| Yield | 0.70 | 0.62 | 0.76 | 0.85 | 1.00 |
| **Oceania** | | | | | |
| Output | 5.0 | 4.1 | 4.9 | 10.6 | 11.7 |
| Area | 5.8 | 4.7 | 4.2 | 8.3 | 8.9 |
| Yield | 0.86 | 0.87 | 1.17 | 1.28 | 1.31 |
| **Discrepancy** | | | | | |
| Output | 0.2 | 2.4 | -1.5 | 3.5 | 0.0 |
| Area | 0.4 | 0.4 | -3.2 | -0.2 | -2.3 |

TABLE 7 (continued)

| Region | 1930-39 | 1940-49 | 1950-59 | 1960-69 | 1970-79 |
|---|---|---|---|---|---|
| World Total | | | | | |
| Output | 158.4 | 158.3 | 203.1 | 274.1 | 370.6 |
| Area | 165.9 | 160.6 | 190.7 | 211.5 | 219.3 |
| Yield | 0.95 | 0.99 | 1.07 | 1.30 | 1.69 |

Notes: output: million metric tons; area: million hectares; yield: metric tons per hectare; na: not available.

a1944-49 only.
b1955-59 only.

Source: All data from the U.S. Department of Agriculture (1936-1982). Details of time series construction available from authors.

The modal form of price distortion in developing countries is the fixing of farmgate prices at unremunerative levels. In doing so, national authorities reduce the food prices paid by the politically potent urban population, but at the cost of reducing farmers' incentive to produce in excess of personal consumption needs. Another important factor is the overvaluation of exchange rates, which stifles agricultural production by encouraging dependence on imported food. Weak consumer demand, a factor whose importance is difficult to assess, also sometimes limits food production. Demand for food can be constrained not only by generalized macroeconomic malaise, such as that which has resulted form the recent balance-of-payments crisis in developing countries, but also by an income distribution highly skewed in favor of the urban elite (Bale and Southworth, 1982:28).

Turning from long-term output trends to long-term price trends, real U.S. agricultural producer prices during the twentieth century are plotted in Figure 15 (see Johnson, 1984:78-93 for a more comprehensive presentation of long-term price trends). The period between the bottoming-out of the Great Depression and the end of the inflationary interlude that followed World War II stands out as one of increasing real prices, as does the period immediately following the "wheat shock;" however, the general trend in this century has clearly been toward lower real prices. Movements in farmgate prices have been approximated by changes in a broader indicator of food scarcity--the real price of food to urban consumers (see Figure 16). That the price of food on the urban supermarket shelf has not fallen off as rapidly following the "wheat shock" as have farmgate prices is to be explained by the fact that retail prices are not nearly as cyclically sensitive as farmgate prices: note that the range of price variation in Figure 16 is much narrower than in Figure 15 (we are indebted to D. Gale Johnson for pointing this out to us).

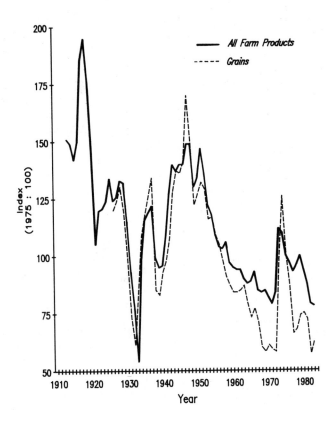

FIGURE 15  U.S. Agricultural Producer Prices

Note:  Deflated as in Figure 2.

Source:  Wharton Econometric Forecasting Associates


    The method of argument employed above--pointing to largely
favorable trends over recent decades--has also been employed by
Johnson (1984), Grigg (1983), and, of course, Simon (1981a:14-
16). It has not, however, found universal acceptance. Some
researchers (e.g., Brown, 1984b:175-178; Gillman, 1981:76-78;
Barr, 1981:1088, Table 1; Mellor and Johnston, 1984:534-536 and
especially Table 2) have identified a progressive slowdown in the
rate at which world agricultural output has grown. Such second-
derivative trends are, however, less than compelling. Agricultural production is volatile from year to year; that is, it is

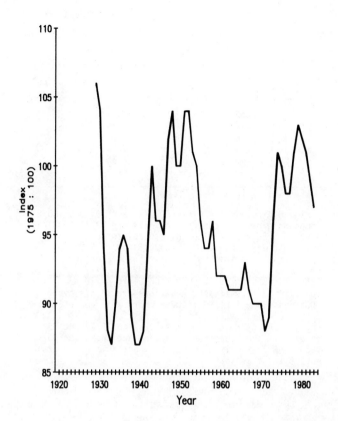

FIGURE 16   Price of Food to U.S. Urban Consumers

Note:   Deflated as in Figure 2.

Sources:   1934-69 from U.S. Department of Agriculture (1972:696, Table 816); 1970-79 from U.S. Department of Agriculture (1982:523, Table 721).

very "spikey" when plotted against time. Moreover, production estimates for the last 3 to 5 years are subject to significant revision by the responsible statistical agencies. For these reasons, conclusions about the second derivative may depend substantively on which data series is employed, which bounding years are chosen in the computation of growth rates, whether compound or average annual growth rates are calculated, whether the data series has been smoothed by taking a moving average,

TABLE 8   Growth in World Grain Output:   Some Comparisons

| | Annual Percent Change | |
|---|---|---|
| Growth Rate[a] | "Golden Age" | "Slowing of Gains" |
| 1 | 2.68 | 2.71 |
| 2 | 3.18 | 2.04 |
| 3 | 2.76 | 2.83 |
| 4 | 3.21 | 2.82 |
| 5 | 3.40 | 2.85 |
| 6 | 3.35 | 2.50 |

a:
1:  Compound growth rate 60/61 to 70/71 and 70/71 to 80/81.
2:  Compound growth rate 60/61 to 73/74 and 73/74 to 81/82.
3:  Average growth rate 61/62 over 60/61 to 70/71 over
    69/70 and 71/72 over 70/71 to 80/81 over 79/80.
4:  Data series smoothed by 3-year running average;
    compound growth rate 61/62 to 71/72 and 71/72 to 79/80.
5:  Regressions using data points 60/61 to 69/70 and 71/72
    to 80/81.  The estimated equations are ln x = 6.656 +
    .034+ and ln x = 6.993 + .028+ where x is world grain
    output and t is year.
6:  Regressions using data points 60/61 to 72/73 and 73/74
    to 81/82.  The estimated equations are ln x = 6.663 +
    .033+ and ln x = 7.087 + 0.025+ where x is world grain
    output and t is year.

and so on.  In addition, the measurement errors committed in
estimating agricultural output at the international level are
relatively large.  One must conclude, therefore, that the confidence interval on a given estimate of the rate of change in the
rate of change, like that on a given estimate of the coefficient
of variation (discussed above), is wide.

This is illustrated in Table 8, where various methods have
been used to infer the annual growth of world grain output in
the 1960s ("Golden Age") and 1970s ("Slowing of Gains").  The
compound annual growth rates numbered 1 through 4 vary rather
widely, and while in two cases (2 and 4), the "slowing of gains"
hypothesis is supported, in two others (1 and 3), it is rejected.
Gillman (1981:77) has suggested that such ambiguities may be
resolved by the use of regression techniques to fit trend lines.
This approach is probably better, but there remains the question
of what regression model to fit, and regression coefficients are
themselves somewhat sensitive to decisions such as those enumerated above.  The semi-log regression results in Table 8 support
the "slowing of gains" hypothesis, but the differences in growth
rates are not, in the authors' view, large enough to negate the
impression gained through a look at Figures 10 and 11.

Constraints on Production

Land Quality. The generally favorable trend in aggregate statistics is remarkable because there are reasons to believe that world agriculture should, like an aging athlete, be training harder just to turn in the same performance. The Ricardian nightmare, in which ever-larger amounts of capital are required to eke food from progressively less desirable land, was an important source of collapse in Limits (Meadows et al., 1974:126-128) and has received extensive attention lately. Brown (1978:28) and Crosson (1982:257-258) have both identified signs of this process at work in the United States during the 1970s. Expert opinion is, however, divided. The USDA's Lee (1978:17) found that the quality of land under the plow improved between 1967 and 1975, and Dideriksen et al. (1981:22) found a longer-term improvement in land quality over the period 1950-77. The latter study did, however, conclude that movement to marginal land would occur in the last quarter of this century, although this projection may be pessimistic in light of the authors' acceptance of an extremely high estimate of cropland loss to nonagricultural uses. International evidence of the Ricardian process at work is either anecdotal (e.g., Brown, 1978:30-32) or subject to even more debate than is evidence from the United States.

Land Availability. A related problem, shortage of arable land, was reportedly behind the pessimism of the Global 2000 baseline agricultural scenario (Gillman, 1981:77-78). (It is argued below that the Global 2000 staff's pessimistic assumptions regarding fertilizer application in LDCs also contributed to their gloomy agricultural forecast.) The 1979 National Agricultural Lands Study (NALS) (U.S. Department of Agriculture, 1979) concluded that 3 million acres per year of farmland was converted to nonagricultural uses in the United States between 1967 and 1975-77; this is the estimate accepted by Dideriksen et al. (1981). Conversion at this rate would very rapidly deplete America's cropland base, and for that reason, what has been dubbed "The Statistic" was subjected to minute scrutiny (Vining, 1982). Most researchers have concluded that NALS greatly overestimated the rate of conversion (See Vining, 1982:113 and Hart, 1984:242-244 for references to major contributions). The present deflation of prime farmland prices in the United States, which figures prominently among the causes of the farmbelt depression, argues eloquently against the hypothesis that agricultural land, even prime farmland, is becoming increasingly scarce. Finally, within absolute constraints that are far from being reached, farmland is not fixed in absolute supply, but responds to price signals (Simon, 1980:2-3), as in the case of the area planted in wheat in 1974. There appears to be an ample extensive margin available for use in the critical U.S. farmbelt, even if restrictions are placed on the erosiveness of new land brought under the plow (Amos and Timmons, 1983; Swanson and Heady, 1984:217-218).

The cropland availability picture outside the United States
is less clear.  Regarding the critical LDCs, it is important to
realize that it is not area per se that is the critical concept.
The number of crop rotations possible, the scope for irrigation,
the availability of appropriate seeds, and other variables are
equally important.  Revelle (1984) summarizes FAO research that
concluded that the world agricultural land base has, under ideal
conditions, a near-astronomical carrying capacity.  For instance,
in Africa, state—of-the—art agricultural cultivation could support 10 billion persons, and even under pessimistic farming conditions, enough land exists to feed 1.5 billion persons.  Under
the U.N. medium variant population projection, African population
will not reach this level until 2025.  The theoretical carrying
capacity of the world land base is, of course, a highly ideal-
ized, abstract concept.  However, there is ample evidence that
land tenure systems, the intensity of cultivation, and the level
of inputs to agriculture all respond flexibly (albeit only over
the long term in some cases) to demand for food and fiber (see
Binswanger and Pingali, 1984 for the case of traditional African
agriculture).  Therefore, figures such as those proffered by FAO
tend to dispel the fear that a global crisis of agricultural land
availability is upon us.


Erosion.  It has long been believed that the most serious
physiocratic problem in United States, and probably world, agriculture is soil erosion (Crosson and Bruebaker, 1982; Brown,
1984c).  Erosion has both on-farm and off-farm effects.  On-farm,
it reduces the productivity of agricultural land; that is, unless
compensatory inputs such as fertilizer are employed, eroded land
will be less fertile than it originally was.  Off-farm, eroded
soil usually comes to rest in rivers and reservoirs.  This reduces the recreational value of the water bodies involved; more
important, it reduces their suitability for navigation, irrigation, and the generation of hydroelectric power.
    Surveys have unanimously concluded that in the United States,
many regions undergo erosion in excess of topsoil formation
(Pimentel et al., 1976:150-151; Larson et al., 1983).  Assembling
the evidence on erosion outside the United States, Brown (1984c:
61-62) has estimated that the world topsoil resource is being
depleted at a rate of 0.7 percent per year.  Crosson (1983) has
examined what little there is of hard evidence on erosion in
major LDC river basins and concluded that, indeed, the volume of
soil loss is high.
    Erosion in the United States is associated with progressively
higher intensity of land use, which can be attributed, in turn,
to export sales (Crosson, 1982:255-256) and federal subsidization
of overplanting (Bovard, 1984; the 1985 Farm Bill attempts to
correct this bias).  In developing countries, less is known about
the etiology of the problem, and causes no doubt differ from region to region.  Among these are population pressure on the land,
use of inappropriate farming methods, overgrazing, and deforestation (Repetto, 1985 for the case of Java; Brown and Wolf, 1985:
37-45 for Africa).

A fundamental aspect of the erosion problem, one which probably applies throughout the world, is that while the means of erosion control exist, the expected gain as reckoned in the farmer's cost-benefit calculus is frequently negative (Brown 1984c: 67-69; Pimentel et. al., 1976:152-153; Swanson and Heady, 1984: 209-211). Does the private discount rate applied by the farmer exceed the social discount rate? If so, then public policy should be active, offering subsidies, tax-breaks, and so on to cooperative farmers, or even coercive, imposing legal penalties on recalcitrant ones (Crosson, 1982:277-282). However, economists have been reluctant to declare, at least regarding the on-farm effects of erosion, that there has been such a market failure. McConnell (1983) has presented a theoretical model suggesting that, insofar as on-farm effects are concerned, observed rates of erosion may well be socially optimal.

Indeed, recent empirical work has given strong support to a "new wave" view that on-farm erosion costs are probably not a critical social problem. Crosson (1984b) has calculated that, under mainstream assumptions, the present value of the future U.S. farm output that will be foregone because of erosion is surprisingly low--an order of magnitude less, for instance, than the U.S. federal budget or external trade deficits of recent years. Some aspects of the calculation are open to controversy-- whether the discount rate employed should not be extremely low, whether yields on eroded land are not inherently unstable, whether imposing even slightly reduced productivity on future generations is ethically defensible, whether the supplies and costs of compensatory inputs (such as energy) have been adequately considered, and so on. However, that the cost-benefit analysis so firmly rejects the familiar "erosion crisis" model is provocative, and this research may well have redefined the economic debate over erosion for the next few years.

Significantly, far from concluding that erosion is a "nonproblem," Crosson's research led to the conclusion that the off-farm costs of erosion are extremely high, many times greater than the on-farm costs. Since the former costs are entirely external to farmers' cost-benefit calculus, the "new wave" view appears to suggest heavy application of the sorts of remedies to market failure enumerated above.

In conclusion, most expert observers agree that erosion is a serious problem. However, their opinion appears to be shifting in favor of the proposition that the greatest damage caused by erosion is not to food production. It is surely safe to assume that expert opinion is in flux, and to discount the impact of erosion on food supply accordingly.

Other Constraints. The "slowing of gains" model is compelling not only because of pressures on the land, erosion prominent among them, but also because it is tempting to project diminishing returns to the yield-enhancing measures that have been implemented in recent decades. Diminishing returns do not, however, appear to be a serious problem for the near future. In

the United States, rapid expansion in irrigated cropland, encouraged by access to cheap water, has underwritten the availability
of abundant supplies of cheap meat (Batie and Healy, 1983:47).
In the past decade, however, energy price increases have sharply
raised irrigation costs, forcing a reduction of irrigated acreage
in some locales (Brown, 1981:1000-1001; Postel, 1985:52) and
making further irrigation development prohibitively expensive in
others (Whittlesey et al., 1981 for the case of the Pacific
Northwest). Yet despite these developments, and although a slowdown in the growth of irrigated acreage is widely anticipated,
experts do not believe that water shortage will be a binding
constraint on U.S. agriculture, especially given opportunities
for improved efficiency in irrigation (Castle, 1982:814-815).
Two problems appear to be serious: inefficiencies resulting
from the patchwork of federal, state, and local agencies having
authority over water usage, and the deeply ingrained tendency to
regard water as a free good.

Irrigation has also been a source of improved productivity
abroad, especially in the developing countries. At present,
salinization and waterlogging on irrigated land are seriously
reducing yields in some regions (Postel, 1985:55-56). While
large capital expenditures would be required, the reclamation of
such land through the installation of proper drainage systems is
a potential source of added food supply. On a global level, the
potential for increasing the efficiency of water usage is tremendous (Postel, 1985:62-72), and a range of policy tools is available (O'Mara, 1984). Gilbert White (1984) concludes his survey
of the world water situation by asserting that although current
exploitation is grossly inefficient, the probability that the
world will run out of water to sustain itself is zero.

The case of fertilization is similar to that of irrigation.
In the United States, higher energy prices and the fact that much
land is already optimally fertilized both imply that fertilization will not raise yields as rapidly in the future as it has in
the past (Crosson, 1982:259). In the developing countries, on
the other hand, fertilizer application lags far behind its level
in the industrial world, and Falcon (1984:184) has asserted that
poor policy regarding fertilizer usage in developing countries
may have been "the most consistent and costly food policy mistake
of the past ten years." Simple sensitivity analysis of statistics presented in Global 2000 (pp. 91-101) indicates that if, in
the baseline agricultural scenario, a more optimistic view had
been taken on fertilization in the LDCs, the global "slowing of
gains" effect would have virtually disappeared.

Brown (1984b:179) has correctly observed that the world incremental grain-fertilizer response ratio has steadily fallen in
the postwar period; however, he does not point out that this has
occurred largely because land in the developed countries has
approached its optimal level of fertilization. The response to
fertilization in the developing countries, where most future
food demand increases will occur (Crosson, 1984a:4-5 and 20-21),
will be dramatic. (This is not to say, of course, that heavy
fertilizer application is indicated across the entire range of

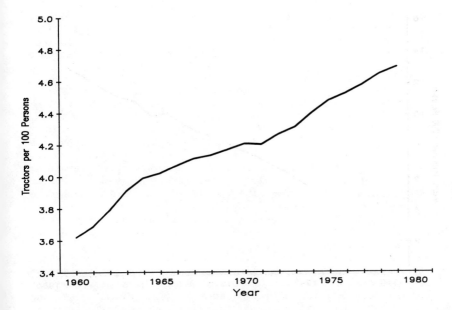

FIGURE 17   World Tractor Utilization Per Capita

Note:   Population as in Figure 1.

Sources:   1973-80 from United Nations (1980/81:539, Table 98);
1972 from United Nations (1979/80:101, Table 25); 1960-71 from
United Nations (1973:97, Table 25).

LDC ecological and labor market conditions; Lincoln Day has
cautioned us on this point.)   Data through 1980 (see Figures 17
and 18) show that two indicators of capital intensity in world
agriculture--fertilizer application and tractor utilization per
capita--were unaffected by the 1973-74 oil shock; Brown and Wolf
(1985:59) present a graph indicating that fertilizer application
in Africa grew unabated through 1982.

On the world level, Brown (1984b:178 and 1985a:30-31) asserts
that fertilizer consumption has faltered in the wake of the 1980
oil shock.   However, any such downturn is surely more the result
of the farmbelt crisis and the unprecedented LDC economic crisis
than of the oil shock per se.   Therefore, to project a pessimistic 1981-84 global trend into the future is to make heroically
somber assumptions.   Analyzing data through 1980, Bale and Duncan
(1983b:29) reached highly optimistic conclusions regarding the
potential for yield improvement in the developing countries.   If
the present foreign exchange crisis in the LDCs does not irrevo-

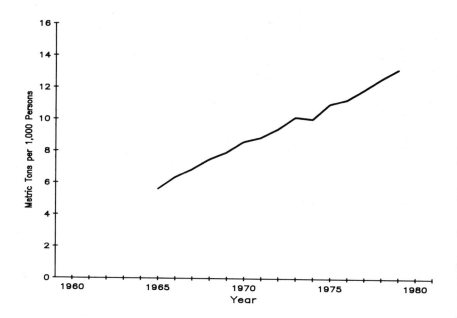

FIGURE 18   World Nitrogenous Fertilizer Application Per Capita

Notes:  Fertilizer-year 1965-66 corresponds to calendar year
1965, and so on.  Population as in Figure 1.

Sources:  1973-80 from United Nations (1980/81:545, Table 100);
1965-72 from United Nations (1973:513, Table 167).

cably set back agricultural modernization, and if returns to
farmers are improved by appropriate policy actions, the yield
disparities that increased between the 1920s and 1970s (see Table
7) will be diminished.  On the other hand, there will indeed be
reason for concern if international trade and capital flows do
not recover sufficiently to allow LDCs to resume importing fertilizer, oil, and capital equipment; or alternatively, if LDC
policy makers persist in antirural, cheap food policies.  However, such a scenario is better considered as a pessimistic
alternative than as a most-likely outcome.

     Will rising energy costs boost food costs as well?  There
are two bases for concern.  First, many of the yield-enhancing
technologies--fertilization, use of heavy machinery, irrigation,
and so on--are energy-intensive.  Second, the use of agricultural
inputs to produce biomass energy (for instance, the diversion of
corn to alcohol production) might directly reduce food availability (we are indebted to Edward Renshaw for reminding us of
this).

Whittlesey and Lee (1976) examined direct energy inputs into the production and consumption of 18 food products produced in the State of Washington. (Direct energy inputs include, for instance, the gasoline consumed by a tractor, but do not include the energy used to manufacture the tractor.) They calculated that a 100 percent increase in all energy input prices would increase the cost of placing food on the table--producing, processing, transporting, storing, retailing, home-refrigerating, and cooking--by only about 5 percent. The retail price of food would increase more, as entrepreneurs along the chain raised markups to cover their rising costs of doing business in a high energy price environment; on the other hand, most consumers nominal income would also rise substantially in the inflationary environment. We conclude that the rising real energy prices anticipated earlier in this chapter will not be the most critical problem in the world food system during the next half-century or so.


## Sources of Instability in the World Food System

Over the last 30 years, world agriculture has enjoyed ideal weather conditions, and there is presently a consensus among climatologists that significant climate change is likely over the next 50 years (National Research Council, 1983; National Defense University, 1979; see also Global 2000:52-65). There is a large body of opinion that the observed rising atmospheric concentration of carbon dioxide, caused by combustion of fossil fuels and deforestation, will, all else being equal, cause a global warming (Firor and Portney, 1982:180-192; Hansen et al., 1981; National Research Council, 1983; Clark, 1982; Perry, 1984; WGBH-Boston, 1983). Even though the mean of the probability distribution of temperatures might move only slightly to the right, the number of extreme "degree days" observed in an average year might increase by an order of magnitude because the probability mass in the right-hand tail of the distribution would increase many times. In addition, world precipitation patterns and the distribution of water resources for irrigation would change dramatically (Revelle, 1984:199-200).

It has been impossible to document the warming effect empirically because all else has not been equal, and because the variance of weather conditions is high (Landsberg, 1984). A minority view holds that the effects of rising carbon dioxide concentration are largely unpredictable (Idso, 1984). Precise effects on agriculture will be sensitive to the accompanying changes in precipitation levels and water availability. Production could shift markedly away from the North American and Russian agricultural complexes (Butzer, 1980). The difficulty of predicting effects on agriculture becomes even greater when account is taken of the biological effects, many of them highly favorable, of increased carbon dioxide concentrations on plant growth and agriculture (Idso, 1984:22; Revelle, 1984:198); see also the citations of both upside and downside views in Crosson,

1984a:8). In considering how the long-term agricultural outlook should reflect current understanding of the "$CO_2$ Crisis;" Crosson (1984a:10) could conclude nothing more definite than that the problem compounds other uncertainties.

A nearer-term cause for concern is that the world food system is in jeopardy of being disrupted by a sharp and sustained downturn in North American farm output. While North American grain does not now account for a much larger proportion of world output than in the past (see, for instance, Table 7 in the case of wheat), North America is the vital swing producer whose stocks and idle capacity, in the form of untilled land, meet world demand at the margin. Between the 1960-61 and 1970-71 crop years, added North American exports of wheat, coarse grains, and rice accounted for 3.3 percent of the increment to world grain utilization; between 1970-71 and 1983-84, the North American contribution was 14.2 percent (authors' calculations from U.S. Department of Agriculture, 1984:25-29).

It is North American farmers who have made good the shortfall in developing country production: rising food consumption in these countries (as an aggregate) has been made possible only by their increasing net food imports from 1.5 percent to 5 percent of domestic production between the mid-1950s and mid-1970s (Mellor and Johnston, 1984:537). Perhaps contrary to popular opinion, however, it is not the very poorest countries of the world that have come to depend on North American grain; in fact, food imports into the low-income developing countries have actually declined on a per capita basis since 1970 (Economist, 1984b; Donaldson, 1984:190-191). Rather, it is the rapidly modernizing middle- and high-income LDCs whose imports have grown dramatically. To some extent, this is simply because in these relatively successful countries, the balance of payments has been favorable enough to permit the sorts of price and exchange rate distortions enumerated above (Nigeria, until recently, being an example). More to the point, it has been in these countries that food demand, especially for highly grain-intensive meat and poultry products, has been strong (Mellor and Johnston, 1984:540-541). In some countries, particularly those of the East Asian rim, increased food imports have also been a natural consequence of growth in the tremendously successful manufacturing sector, which has occurred at some expense to the traditional rural sector.

Also contributing to the growing importance of North American grain was a decisive shift in the net trade position of Eastern Europe and the USSR. In the 1930s, this region was a net grain exporter, but by the 1970s, because of Soviet policy decisions, it had become a large-scale net importer (Brown, 1981:998, Table 3; Brown, 1984c:183, Table 10-4).

Conventional economic analysis would defend increasing world reliance on traded grain (see Figure 19) because free trade maximizes system-wide efficiency (Donaldson, 1984). The same point would be made about the progressively lower level of stocks relative to utilization (see Figure 20), a phenomenon that has occurred as countries have increasingly met unexpected supply short-

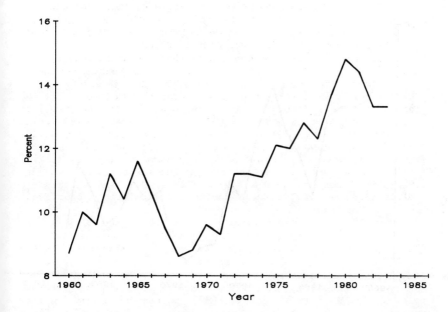

FIGURE 19   World Grain:   Trade : Utilization

Source:   U.S. Department of Agriculture (1984).


falls by importing grain rather than drawing down stocks. However, maximizing efficiency does not go hand-in-hand with minimizing risk; indeed, these are frequently conflicting goals. A major disruption of North American grain production, persisting over several growing seasons, would strain world stocks and the food system's capacity to divert grain from feed usage.

These sources of added instability are mitigated, however, by other developments in the world food system. The expansion of futures and options markets, which allow risks of adverse harvests to be placed on the willing shoulders of speculators, is one such development. More important are the improved storage, distribution, and communication systems that have led to an almost certain reduction in deaths from famine over the course of the last century (Simon, 1981c:60-64; the instances cited by Brown [1984c:188-189] pale in comparison with the disasters of the nineteenth and early twentieth centuries). Unprecedented sums are being spent on research and development related to LDC agriculture, and for the first time there is explicit recognition by most (though regrettably still not enough) LDC policy makers that agriculture has been given insufficient priority. Finally, improvements in agricultural information systems and methods of

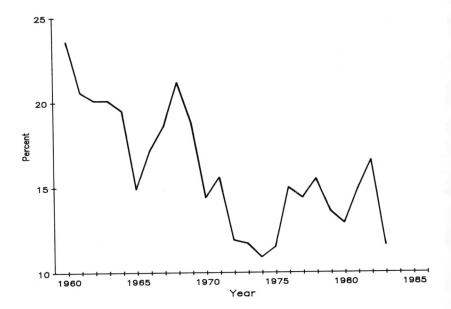

FIGURE 20   World Grain:   Stocks : Utilization

Source:   U.S. Department of Agriculture (1984).


forecasting agricultural supply and demand cannot be underestimated.  Thanks  to  these  improvements,  as  well  as  progress  in
weather  forecasting  methods,  policy  makers,  technical  experts,
and  market  participants  are  less  susceptible  today  to  sudden
surprises  than  was  the  case  even  a  decade  ago  (Donaldson, 1984:
189).
      Passing  reference  should  be  made  to  the  recent  African
famine.  This  has  been  partially  caused  by  erosion,  which  is,  in
some  regions,  related  to  deforestation  and  the  subsequent  diversion  of  animal  dung  and  crop  residues  into  energy  uses.  On  the
other  hand,  ecological  degradation  has  not,  at  least  throughout
the  continent,  been  a  prime  mover  in  the  crisis.   Persistent
"urban  bias"  in  policy  decisions  over  recent  decades  led  to  the
deterioration  of  food  supply  capacity,  and  this  deterioration
has  combined  with  poor  weather  conditions  to  trigger  the  crisis.
The  latter  cannot,  on  the  basis  of  evidence  to  date,  be  confi-
dently  ascribed  to  man-induced  climatic  change  (although  see
Brown  and  Wolf, 1985:19-29 for  a  discussion  largely  sympathetic
to  the  hypothesis  of  climatic  change  caused  by  population  pressure).  In  any  probability  process  in  which  the  number  of  trials
is  very  large,  "runs"  even  of  phenomena  whose  probability  of

occurrence on a given trial is small will not be uncommon.
Furthermore, there exists strong positive autocorrelation in
many climatic variables (Mandelbrot and Wallis, 1968). Finally,
the human and institutional side of the African disaster cannot
be overemphasized. It is instructive to contrast the mitigation
of the effects of the drought that was accomplished in Zimbabwe,
blessed with an adequate agricultural infrastructure and an
effective policy establishment (Waldmeir, 1985), and the debacle
in Ethiopia, which has, at present, neither.


## Conclusion

To conclude this review, while analytical models offer compelling
reasons why agriculture should be approaching limits to growth,
the empirical record fails to substantiate these developments.
The recent "slowing of gains," if it exists, is too slight to
merit great concern, and there is no consensus on whether the
variability of world production is increasing. An expert consensus is similarly lacking that movement to marginal land and loss
of farmland to urban uses are serious problems. Problems associated with irrigation are impeding production in many areas, but
the means of addressing these problems are well understood.
Given the scope for progress in developing countries, particularly greater fertilizer application, it cannot be said that
limits to global yield improvement have been approached. While
erosion may have reached crisis proportions in many countries,
experts cannot agree that the effect on food output is critical.
Energy prices have the potential to raise the cost of producing
food, but it is not clear that even sharp energy price increases
would seriously erode most consumers' food buying power.

Several problems do stand out. One is the instability posed
by the importance of North America as a swing producer in world
agriculture. Climatic change, while its effects are largely
speculative at present, is a source of concern as well. Finally,
since future increments to world food demand will be concentrated
in the LDCs, it is critical that these countries return to a
rapid growth path. If they do not, consumer demand for food will
languish in these countries, domestic savings will be insufficient to finance agricultural investment, and the balance of
payments will be too weak to permit the import of agricultural
inputs and technology.


## Fish

In the interest of brevity, only passing reference will be made
in this chapter to the fishery resource, in part because its
relative importance in the world's food system is rather small
(fish account for about one-quarter of world animal-protein consumption), and in part because there is little empirical literature on this resource (there is a small growth industry, on the
other hand, in theoretical fishery models, e.g., Peterson and
Fisher, 1977).

Fisheries (along with water, discussed above) provide a classic example of what Hardin called "the tragedy of the commons," referring to the fact that when a resource is held in common and openly accessible, it is in every producer's interest to overexploit it (Hardin, 1968). Since no individual holds title to the fishery resource, no one pays attention to its present value--the quantity that reflects the cost, in terms of lost future catch, of overfishing in the present period (Peterson and Fisher, 1977:688-690). With the maximization of current profit the sole criterion, fishermen will enter until average profits are driven to zero and, quite possibly, the fishery is exhausted. An instance in which this appears to have happened is the failure of the Peruvian anchovy fishery in 1972 (Anderson, 1982:154-159; this is not a universally accepted explanation for the incident, however). Between 1975 and 1980, catastrophic drops were also experienced in catches of North Sea herring, Northwest Atlantic cod, and South African pilchards; all of these are major components of the world catch (Economist, 1984c; see also Brown, 1985b:76-81 for a survey of overfishing). Based on the time series they have examined, the authors conclude that, given prevailing tastes and fishing practices, and in the absence of a sustained development effort, the world per capita catch cannot return, in the next few decades, to the rapid growth path (about 4 percent per year; see Figure 21) of 1950-70 (see also Anderson, 1982:152-154).

As shown in Figure 21, the world per capita catch of all fish declined during the 1970s. The most dramatic decline was in the catch of fish for nonhuman consumption (mostly animal feed), and is directly related to the collapse of the Peruvian anchovy fishery (we are grateful to D. Gale Johnson for urging us to disaggregate the total catch by end-use). However, even the human consumption component has fallen below its long-term trend since the mid-1970s. This conclusion is slightly more pessimistic than that reached by Wise (1984, especially 123 and 115, Table 3.2). It is clear, however, that the world per capita catch is not growing significantly, in sharp contrast to its rapid increase in the 1950s and 1960s. When combined with the population data series used in this chapter, the Wise fish data themselves indicate that the world catch has failed to reattain its pre-1972 peak, and that while a recovery of sorts may be occurring, it is a meager one. Data presented by Brown (1985b:74, Table 4.1) also indicate virtually zero per capita growth. The slowdown here is much more distinct than that discussed above in the case of world agriculture.

There is no disagreement on real price trends. The U.S. consumer price of fish products, a good proxy for the global level of fish prices, has increased at an accelerating rate relative to the price of all goods and services in the postwar period (see Figure 22). Confusingly, though, the real price of industrial fishmeal has not tended to increase over the long term (authors' calculations from International Monetary Fund, 1983:88-89). Perhaps in the case of fishmeal, as opposed to fish for human consumption, cheaper, alternative fish sources have been found.

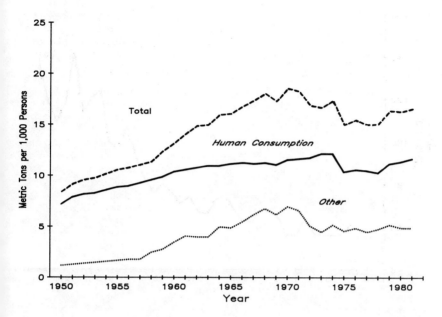

FIGURE 21   World Fish Catch Per Capita

Note:   Population as in Figure 1.

Sources:   1977-81 from UNFAO (1981:Table A1-1); 1976 from UNFAO
(1980c:Table A1-1); 1975 from UNFAO (1979:Table A1-1); 1970-74
from UNFAO (1978:Table A1-1); previous years from UNFAO
(1970-74).

Although policy measures for the efficient management of
fisheries are well understood, experience suggests it is unlikely
that cooperative agreements extending these measures to international waters will be successfully implemented.   In fisheries
that were brought entirely under one national jurisdiction by
the extension of the Exclusive Economic Zone (EEZ) to 200 miles,
an impressive replenishment of fish stocks has been accomplished
(Sullivan, 1984:17).   However, in the far more common case of
joint stocks, that is, a fishery extending over several EEZs, recorded catches have continued to exceed greatly the recommendations of international fishing bodies.
   This is not to say that the world is running out of fish, or
even that no expansion of output is possible.   The UNFAO has
estimated that adequate investment expenditure could raise the
catch from the current 70-80 million metric tons to 130 million
within 20 years (Economist, 1984c); Brown (1985b:95-96) cites

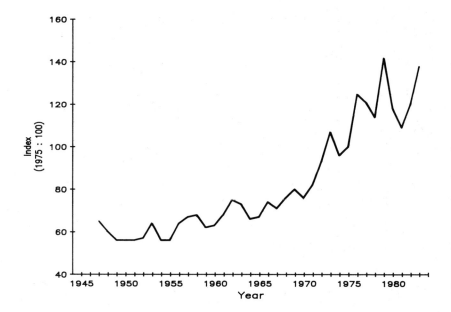

FIGURE 22  U.S. Consumer Price of Fish Products

Notes:  Delfated as in Figure 2.

Sources:  Bureau of Labor Statistics producer price, Wharton
Econometric Forecasting Associates.


another FAO study whose baseline scenario foresees the world
catch's rising to 93 million metric tons.  Wise (1984:119) cites
further sources indicating that with proper management and investment, the catch of conventional species may be increased to
100-120 million metric tons by the end of the century, and other
sources who feel that this is an overly cautious estimate.
Taking, perhaps somewhat arbitrarily, 100 and 120 million tons
as the bounds of the mainstream baseline view, the implied
annual growth projection is roughly 1.5-2.5 percent per year.
This will make for some increase in per capita fish availability;
however, it is much slower than the per capita growth experienced
during the first two decades of the postwar era.  Given the importance of energy costs in fishing, the authors' view that real
energy prices will continue to grow, and the long-term trend
observed in Figure 22, there is little reason not to project
further increases in real fish prices.
      This latter pessimistic picture could be changed by several
factors.  Nontraditional fish products, such as Antarctic krill,

squid, plankton, and so on, have tremendous potential.  There is
far too much spoilage and waste in present fishing practices.
Aquaculture--raising fish in controlled environments like crops--
is already being practiced in many parts of the world and its
contribution could be significantly increased.  Estimates of what
the world fishery resource could yield under absolutely ideal
conditions range all the way up into the billions of metric tons
(Wise, 1984:119).  However, a significant improvement would call
for a major investment effort, and that effort is unlikely to
take place unless it is elicited by continued, and perhaps accelerated, increases in real fish prices.


FOREST RESOURCES


Tropical Moist Forests

Since temperate-region forests appear to be stable (Sedjo and
Clawson, 1984:146-147 and Table 4.7), concern over world forest
resources is focused on forests in the LDCs, and particularly on
the tropical moist forests (TMFs).  (An exception to this is, of
course, the problem of acid rain, which we discuss subsequently.)
Tropical moist forests are located mostly in Bolivia, Brazil,
Colombia, Peru, and Venezuela in Latin America; Indonesia and
Malaysia in Southeast Asia; and Gabon and Zaire in Africa (Myers,
1980:5).  Forests in LDCs account for 22 percent of world softwood (coniferous species) production and 83 percent of hardwood
(nonconiferous species) production (Sedjo and Clawson, 1984:146,
Table 4.5).  These figures include estimates of fuelwood production.  If fuelwood is excluded to arrive at estimates of industrial wood production, LDC forests account for 12 and 50 percent
of softwood and hardwood production, respectively (Sedjo and
Clawson, 1984:146, Table 4.6).  As will be discussed at some
length presently, the TMF component of LDC forest area is the
habitat of a large portion of all species.
    Only four major surveys of the world forest resource have
been conducted.  The basic source for the first two is the land
use reporting system of the UNFAO, in which national agencies
submit annual estimates of forest cover.  Persson (1974) concludes in his research that for over 40 percent of the area
studied, FAO forest cover statistics could not be regarded as
accurate to within even plus or minus 40 percent.  Sommer (1976)
also used the FAO statistics and commented on the caution with
which they should be approached.  He concluded that 11 million
hectares of TMF forest cover was disappearing per year during
the mid-1970s, an annual rate of about 1 percent.  FAO data on
the percent of land area classified as forest and woodland, presented in Table 9, appear to confirm the shrinkage of forest
cover in the regions of concern.  However, in light of the large
inaccuracies found by experts, such as those cited above, no firm
conclusion can be reached on this evidence.

TABLE 9  Forests and Woodland as Percent of Land Area, by Region

| Area | 1970 | 1974 | 1977 | 1980 |
|------|------|------|------|------|
| North America | 31.8 | 31.9 | 31.9 | 31.6 |
| South America | 55.1 | 54.3 | 53.6 | 52.9 |
| Central America | 26.4 | 25.4 | 24.5 | 23.6 |
| Europe | 30.8 | 31.4 | 31.7 | 31.8 |
| Asia | 20.0 | 19.9 | 19.8 | 19.8 |
| Afria | 24.0 | 23.6 | 23.3 | 22.9 |
| Oceania | 21.4 | 21.4 | 17.8 | 17.8 |
| Industrial Countries | 28.9 | 29.0 | 28.1 | 27.9 |
| LDCs | 33.2 | 32.7 | 32.3 | 31.8 |
| Centrally Planned Economies | 31.4 | 31.5 | 31.6 | 31.6 |

Source: UNFAO (1980a:45-46, Table 1).

Under the auspices of the National Academy of Sciences, Myers (1980) carried out an ambitious survey of TMFs that supplemented data from the FAO with responses from a survey of officials in affected countries and independent experts. Based on this research, he concluded that an annual TMF deforestation on the order of 20 million hectares, about 2 percent of the resource base, was indicated. The seriousness of the problem, found Myers, varied significantly across countries, with some (such as Zaire) only mildly affected and others (for instance, Ivory Coast) apparently certain to lose all their forest cover by the end of the century. Myers concluded that by far the most important cause of deforestation was increasing intensity of agricultural practices because of population pressure on the land. The greater importance of clearing for farming, as opposed to fuelwood gathering, has been documented in the case of a Nepali village by Bajracharya (1983).

Global 2000 relied on the work of Sommer and Persson and its own survey of U.S. embassy officials to project deforestation in LDCs of 20 million hectares per year between 1980 and 2000 (Global 2000:117, 126), an annual rate of 1.8 percent. This is a pessimistic view, but one not devoid of a credible analytical basis, contra Simon (1981b:83-84). LDC deforestation is an area in which accurate long-term trend data, the essential grist for Simon's mill (1981a:16-17), are unavailable.

The most recent survey of forests in LDCs (UNFAO and United Nations Environment Programme [UNEP], 1981a, 1981b, 1981c; see also Lanly, 1982) is notable for its emphasis on reducing definitional inconsistencies across countries. It supplemented data from government sources with LANDSAT survey photographs, interviews with responsible national officials, unofficial information, and so on. While the level of inaccuracy is probably still

high, the UNFAO-UNEP project is by far the most authoritative
treatment of the problem to appear so far. It concluded that 7.1
million hectares of closed tropical forest cover disappeared each
year between 1976 and 1980, a deforestation rate of 0.60 percent
per year (0.64 percent in Latin America, 0.61 percent in Africa,
and 0.60 percent in Asia). This represents a significant downward revision of the Myers estimate.

The revision is not unexplainable. First, Myers defined deforestation as conversion of TMF cover to any other use, including productively managed forest; UNFAO-UNEP, on the other hand,
limited the definition to include only forest areas converted to
nonforest uses. Second, Myers' global deforestation estimate was
not calculated on the basis of his country-by-country survey,
since not enough countries were covered to make a global estimate
possible. Rather, he based the 20 million hectare figure on a
"back of the envelope" calculation involving assumptions about
the number of shifting cultivators living in TMFs and their
annual land needs. It would be inappropriate to view the UNFAO-
UNEP study as a repudiation of Myers' early work; rather, it
represents an expansion and refinement of the earlier research.

UNFAO-UNEP made a careful distinction between deforestation,
which admits a strong likelihood of eventual regeneration, and
degradation, in which the TMF ecosystem has been so severely disrupted that regeneration is unlikely. No explicit numerical
estimate was made for the extent of degradation, the far more
serious problem; on the other hand, it is clear that this problem
is not uncommon in many regions. A distinction was also made between open and closed forest and several categories of usage--
undisturbed, productively managed, fallow, and so on. In an
important finding, especially because of its implications for
the species loss debate (see below), UNFAO-UNEP concluded that
undisturbed, virgin forest cover is being lost at a rate of only
0.27 percent per year, whereas already-disturbed secondary forest
land is being deforested at a rate of 2.06 percent per year
(Lanly, 1982, cited in Sedjo and Clawson, 1984).

Allen and Barnes (1985:164) have recently reviewed the Myers
and UNFAO-UNEP studies, and also examined changes in forest cover
estimated only from the UNFAO land use data. They conclude as
follows:

Despite the definitional problems, we found a surprising
amount of agreement among estimates of deforestation on a
country by country basis and much similarity in the rank
ordering of countries according to their rates of deforestation. Furthermore, the results of a cross-national
analysis of the causes of deforestation in developing
countries generally confirm the most frequently cited causes
of deforestation.

Supplementing these global surveys are local-area studies.
For instance, Anderson and Fishwick (1984:15, Table 2.3) cite
World Bank staff research indicating that in many African coun-
tries, fuelwood consumption greatly exceeds the maximum sustain-

able yield of the growing stock (not all of these results pertain
to TMFs). Bajracharya (1983) has examined the process of deforestation in Nepal, and Caulfield (1985) has made a major journal-
istic contribution from Central America. Based on these and
other field reports, no one doubts that deforestation and outright degradation have reached crisis proportions in some regions. Unfortunately, such research, however well conducted,
does not help much in addressing the question of whether tropical
deforestation is a generalized crisis across the tropics.


Temperate Region Forests

Despite the fact that forest cover in North America and Europe
has been fairly stable in recent decades (see Table 9), there
has been an increase in concern over the viability of industrial-
country forest resources. There is strong evidence that over the
last 30 years, acid precipitation, resulting from sulfur dioxide
and nitrogen oxide emissions, has severely damaged many forests
(Postel, 1984; Torrens, 1984; Likens, 1984; Economist, 1984a).
Some European forests, especially in Germany, may fairly be said
to have been devastated (Torrens, 1984, especially cover photo-
graph). Damage to forests in some Northeastern areas of the
United States has been very serious and rapid, and there is now
evidence that the effects of acid rain are being felt in other
regions as well (Shabecoff, 1985), among them the Southeast,
where critical commercial forests are located. Ambitious and
expensive efforts to reduce pollutant emissions have received
enthusiastic support in some political circles, but the ecology
of affected forests is so complex, and the possible sources of
insult so varied, that it is difficult to pin down exactly how
the damage is being done (Singer, 1984a, 1984b; Torrens, 1984:
9-12, Economist, 1984a; Katzenstein, 1984). In Germany, for
instance, what was once thought to be a straightforward problem
of acid rain proper is increasingly identified as a complex of
problems--acid rain, ozone, soil acidification, climate, and
plant pathogens (Blank, 1985). Because of the complex nature of
the problem, the cost-effectiveness of emission reduction is a
subject of heated debate among experts.


Implications

Deforestation has four implications: climatic change, species
loss, the shortage of industrial wood products, and increased
soil erosion. In all of these cases, it is the loss of forest
area in LDCs which is of greatest concern. That deforestation
worsens erosion is not in question, and since erosion has already
been previously discussed, this subject will not be pursued here.
The connection between deforestation and climatic change will be
alluded to only briefly, because no expert consensus exists on
this subject. It has been asserted that when trees are cut down
in the tropics, the carbon dioxide released when they are burned

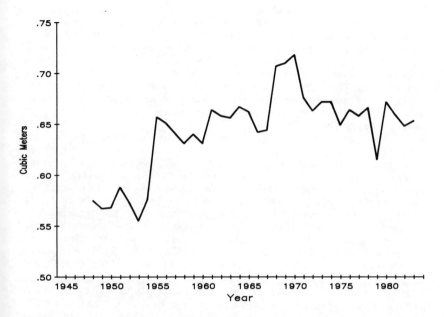

FIGURE 23   World Roundwood Production Per Capita

Note:   Population as in Figure 1.

Source:   1972-83 from UNFAO (1983:64).   Previous years from
UNFAO (1958-82).

or when they rot is a significant contributor to atmospheric carbon dioxide buildup (Woodwell et al., 1983).   Clark et al. (1982:
4; cited in Sedjo and Clawson, 1984:164), on the other hand, deny
that deforestation will contribute significantly to future carbon
dioxide buildup.

This brings us to the problem of forest product availability.
Brown (1979:9, Table 1) has identified a sustained downturn in
world per capita forest product consumption as a cause for concern.   This is illustrated in Figure 23, in which we observe
that, like per capita fish consumption, per capita roundwood[5]
production faltered in the early 1970s, and has failed to return
to its previous peak level.   Looking at Figures 21 and 23, however, it is fair to say that the deterioration in world wood
production is less pronounced than in the case of fish.   It is
to be noted that world wood production statistics, like forest
cover statistics, are from the FAO reporting system; substantial
revisions of history are common, and errors are no doubt large.

308                                    MacKellar and Vining

It is difficult to obtain data series on world wood consumption by product.  A few indicators--world per capita production,
on a decadal annual average basis, of total roundwood, wood
panels (including plywood), and wood pulp--are presented in Table
10.  Consistent with Figure 23, the data in Table 10 indicate
little increase in per capita roundwood production between the
1960s and 1970s.  Per capita production of wood panels increased
markedly in percentage terms, but from an extremely small base.
Wood pulp production grew quite briskly, by 1.5 percent per year
in per capita terms.
It is not entirely arbitrary to split roundwood production
into "traditional" and "modern" end-use product groups.  The former group includes lumber, fuelwood, and miscellaneous industrial
products (fenceposts, barrels, and the like), while the latter
group comprises wood pulp and the plywood-veneer product/wood
panel product complex.  Following this scheme, the data in Table
10 lead us to conclude, in a rough way, that world modern-product
production is expanding much more rapidly than traditional-
product production.  Statistics from developed countries, such
as those from the United States examined shortly, bear this out.
Contra Brown, it is not immediately clear that sluggishness
in world total roundwood consumption is to be taken as an adverse
trend.  Is wood consumption flat because supply scarcity is leading to higher prices, or because consumers prefer the superior
alternative materials that have become available?  If both processes are at work, which is more important?  Which components
of the wood product mix are to blame for the slow growth of the
roundwood aggregate, and in which regions are adverse trends
occurring?  These questions are difficult to resolve because of

TABLE 10  World Wood Production (decadal annual
average)

|  | 1961-70 | 1971-80 |
|---|---|---|
| Total Roundwood (cubic feet per capita) | 23.6 | 24.9 |
| Wood Panels (cubic feet per capita) | 0.5 | 0.8 |
| Wood Pulp (kilograms per capita) | 24.4 | 28.3 |

Note:  Population statistics source is discussed
in the note on data sources in Figure 1.

Sources:  Roundwood production: UNFAO (1980b:69-70;
1972b:3-4).  Wood panels production: UNFAO (1980b:
213-214; 1972b:155-156).  Wood pulp production:
UNFAO (1980b:268; 1972b:212).

the scarcity of reliable international production and consumption data. The excellent statistical evidence available on the U.S. wood industry, however, tends to suggest that the outlook for world wood is somewhat pessimistic. Long-term price trends, in particular, are disheartening.

The timber industry is unique in that in situ rent per unit resource is quite easily observable, and this scarcity index unambigiously indicates growing economic scarcity. Stumpage prices--the fees paid per tree felled to owners of timber stands--have consistently increased in real terms since the 1920s (Gregory, 1972:118, Figure 6-12 for 1920-71). Thus, stumpage prices of the major softwood species sold from U.S. national forests--Douglas fir, southern pine, ponderosa pine, and western hemlock--rose in real terms at rates of 7.6, 2.5, 5.3, and 12.9 percent per year, respectively, between 1950 and 1979 (U.S. Department of Agriculture, 1981a:21, Table 16; western hemlock data series is for the period 1958-79). Hardwood stumpage prices, by contrast, have remained stable, but hardwood is of much less commercial importance. In 1979, apparent per capita consumption (production minus net exports) of softwood in the United States, at 180 boardfeet, was over five times that of hardwood, at 33 boardfeet (U.S. Department of Agriculture, 1981a: 45, Table 31).

Movements in long-term real producer price (Bureau of Labor Statistics producer prices deflated by the U.S. GDP deflator) are plotted in Figures 24 and 25. In Figure 24, the long-term upward trends in real lumber prices and the deflated all-wood products aggregate index generally support the hypothesis of increasing economic scarcity. (The decline in the 1950s and 1960s represents a return to long-term trend after the postwar primary commodity boom.) Plywood, however, represents a contrary trend. Although price data are available only since 1947, both plywood and pulpwood have enjoyed constant or decreasing production costs over the long term (Gregory, 1972:121-147).

The trend of worsening overall forest-product scarcity would be more strongly indicated if the plotted time series extended back into the nineteenth century. Sedjo and Clawson (1984:133-137, Table 4.1) present data series indicating that between 1870 and 1972, the real price of forest products increased at an annual compound rate of 0.6 percent per year. The observation for 1870 is, in fact, an outlier on the upside of trend, and the compound rate of growth between 1871 and 1972 was a much more rapid 1.1 percent.

Figure 25 illustrates real producer price trends in two main components of the paper industry. The price of woodpulp, the essential raw material of the industry, has moved roughly in concert with the prices of all wood products plotted in Figure 24. The real price of paper, the main end use of woodpulp, has, nonetheless, remained quite flat since the 1920s. There have clearly been major gains in processing efficiency in the paper industry.

Developments on the demand side, to the extent that they can be inferred from observed consumption trends, are consistent

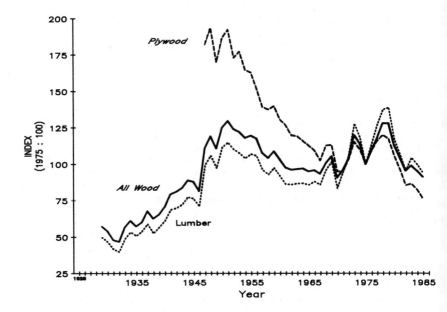

FIGURE 24   U.S. Real Producer Prices of Lumber, Plywood, and All
Wood Products

Note:   Deflated as in Figure 2.

Sources:   U.S. Bureau of Labor Statistics producer prices;
Wharton Econometric Forecasting Associates.

with the hypothesis of growing economic scarcity for lumber and
decreasing scarcity for pulp products and plywood. As shown in
Table 11, U.S. consumption of lumber, fuelwood, and miscellaneous
industrial products has fallen dramatically in per capita terms
during this century. Decreasing demand for lumber and miscellaneous industrial products is consistent with the observed increases in relative prices (a data series on the real price of
miscellaneous products is given by Sedjo and Clawson, 1984:134-
137, Table 4.1). By the same token, per capita consumption of
plywood and veneer products, consistent with declining producer
prices in this sector, has markedly increased during this century. Demand for these products has been further stimulated by
rising lumber prices, which have encouraged their substitution
for lumber in construction.
      Secular demand shifts independent of price movements have
also played a role in causing observed changes in consumption.
Many of the materials that have been substituted for wood in

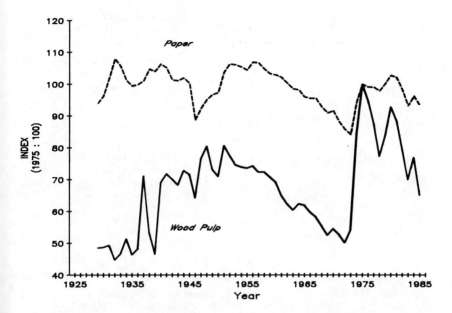

FIGURE 25   U.S. Real Producer Prices of Paper and Woodpulp

Note:   Deflated as in Figure 2.

Sources:   U.S. Bureau of Labor Statistics producer prices;
Wharton Econometric Forecasting Associates.

energy production, construction, and other industrial uses
possess superior physical characteristics. Similarly, more than
falling paper prices can be thanked for the observed growth of
per capita woodpulp consumption: this demand curve has shifted
out as a result of the explosion in demand for printed material
caused by the information revolution. In a study of this scope,
regrettably, we cannot quantify the contribution of such secular
demand shifts to the observed changes in consumption.

The supply and demand considerations sketched above have led
experts at the USDA Forest Service to make a pessimistic recent
assessment of the U.S. wood outlook (U.S. Department of Agriculture, 1982b; the references that follow are to conclusions from
this study summarized in U.S. Department of Agriculture, 1981b).
Econometric model simulation results indicated that softwood
stumpage price increases on the order of 2-4 percent per year in
real terms (U.S. Department of Agriculture, 1981b:247-250) would
occur over the interval 1980 to 2030. Thanks to these price increases, the equilibrium level of softwood timber demand was pro-

TABLE 11  U.S. per Capita Consumption of Wood Products (decadal annual
average; cubic feet roundwood equivalent)

| Wood Product | 1900-09 | 1910-19 | 1920-29 | 1930-30 | 1940-49 | 1950-59 | 1960-69 | 1970-79 |
|---|---|---|---|---|---|---|---|---|
| Lumber | 76.7 | 60.9 | 49.4 | 27.4 | 38.3 | 36.8 | 31.3 | 30.8 |
| Plywood and Veneer | 0.4 | 0.9 | 1.1 | 1.2 | 2.9 | 3.2 | 5.4 | 6.8 |
| Pulp | 3.1 | 4.5 | ʼ 7.0 | 8.3 | 12.7 | 17.5 | 19.3 | 20.9 |
| Other | 20.6 | 19.8 | 13.9 | 7.5 | 6.5 | 3.9 | 2.7 | 1.9 |
| Total Industrial | 100.7 | 86.1 | 71.4 | 44.4 | 60.4 | 61.4 | 58.7 | 60.4 |
| Fuelwood | 51.0 | 41.1 | 30.5 | 35.0 | 21.5 | 11.1 | 5.0 | 2.7 |
| Total | 151.7 | 127.2 | 101.9 | 79.4 | 81.9 | 72.5 | 63.7 | 63.1 |

Sources:  1950-59 to 1970-79 from U.S. Department of Agriculture (1981a:
11, Table 7).  1900-09 to 1940-49 from U.S. Department of Agriculture
(1981b:28-29, Table 3).

jected to grow by only 0.8 percent per year between 1976 and
2000, implying little increase in per capita terms (U.S. Department of Agriculture, 1981b:248-249).  The hardwood situation was
less pessimistic:  real stumpage price increases were more moderate than in the case of softwoods, and demand for hardwood timber
was projected to grow by 2.1 percent per year.
     Critics of these forecasts maintain that the Forest Service
has consistently underestimated the long-term responsiveness of
timber supply to rising real price, leading to an overly pessimistic outlook (Sedjo and Clawson, 1984:142; Office of Technology Assessment, 1983, especially 88-93).  The uncertainties on
both the demand and supply sides are well summarized by Haynes
and Adams (1983:1002-1004); these were the two researchers
primarily responsible for the Forest Service simulations.
     Despite uncertainties, however, the forecast of rising real
prices seems robust.  Employing the Forest Service econometric
model, Haynes and Adams (1983:1004-1007) have done sensitivity
analyses indicating that only a rather potent (and possibly
inconsistent) combination of "upside" alternative exogenous
assumptions can alter the result of rising real stumpage prices.
     Several world-level forecasts are available.  Between 1980
and 2000, UNFAO expects world consumption of fuelwood to grow by
0.8-3.1 percent per year, industrial roundwood by 2.2-2.9 percent
per year, sawnwood by 1.2-1.8 percent per year, panels by 2.6-6.2
percent per year, and paper by 3.8-4.5 percent per year (UNFAO
Forestry Department, 1985:13).  The range of variation between

the optimistic and pessimistic scenarios is quite wide, and at
least in the summary presentation consulted by the authors, the
critical question of price was not discussed at length. The
World Bank, in a partial equilibrium analysis, concluded that if
real wood prices remain constant, world demand for wood products
will grow by 2.6 percent per year between 1976 and 2025; with
account taken of recycling and wood residue use, actual forest
removals would grow at 2.5 percent per year (citation in Gammie,
1981:66-67). Under this constant price assumption, the Bank
identified a supply gap equal to 8.1 percent of ex ante demand
in 2025, implying that actual wood consumption is more likely to
grow in the 1-2 percent range. This implies no significant
growth in per capita terms. Writing from an industry perspective, Gammie (1981) adopted what can accurately be termed a
somber view of the world timber supply-demand balance.

Extrapolating the few international price data that are
available tends to indicate that rising prices in the United
States will be replicated elsewhere. In Table 12, the U.N. index
of world forest product prices and several representative price
series from the International Monetary Fund (1983) International
Financial Statistics are presented. Only in the case of Swedish
woodpulp have prices tended not to increase in real terms over
the last quarter century.

TABLE 12  International Wood Product Prices (five-year averages)

| Wood Product | 1955-59 | 1960-64 | 1965-69 | 1970-74 | 1975-79 | 1980-83 |
|---|---|---|---|---|---|---|
| Swedish Woodpulp (1975 $/metric ton) | 295 | 239 | 213 | 248 | 329 | 281 |
| Philippine Logs (1975 $/cubic meter) | n.a. | 60 | 60 | 68 | 87 | 99 |
| Philippine Plywood (1975 ¢/sheet) | n.a. | n.a. | 119 | 153 | 154 | 157 |
| Malaysian Sawnwood (1975 $/cubic meter) | n.a. | 137 | 128 | 146 | 179 | 206 |
| U.N. Index of World Forest Product Prices (1975 : 100) | n.a. | 76 | 71 | 84 | 110 | 107 |

Notes: All prices and the U.N. index have been deflated by the U.S.
GDP deflator in the Wharton Econometrics national accounts database.
n.a. indicates not available.

Sources: Swedish woodpulp, Philippine logs, Philippine plywood, and
Malaysian sawnwood prices from International Monetary Fund (1983:
88-91). U.N. forest products index from United Nations (various
issues).

Conclusions

This survey indicates that some pessimism regarding the world
wood outlook is justified. Adverse price developments have been
observed during recent decades, and there is little reason to
think that real prices will stop rising. Forest cover loss in
the LDCs, while very difficult to quantify exactly, is evidently
significant. The FAO-UNEP study estimates a 0.6 percent deforestation rate in the tropics; at this rate, over one-quarter of
the forest cover now standing in these regions will be lost over
the next half-century. The same study concludes that at present
loss rates, 12-13 percent of currently undisturbed tropical
forest area will be deforested in the next 50 years, and presumably much more will move into the disturbed, but not deforested,
category. More reliable evidence on the all-important degradation phenomenon is urgently needed. Local area studies in
Africa, Asia, and Latin America tell us that degradation is an
ecological crisis in many isolated locales, but we are not able
to make a broader judgment. Industrial-country forest loss
attributable to the nebulous complex of factors that have come
to be known as "acid rain" is clearly at the crisis stage at
some places in Europe, and has become a serious problem in the
United States as well.

One of the most exciting possibilities for alleviating world
forest and wood problems is silviculture, also sometimes called
"plantation forestry." Sedjo and Clawson (1984:132) flatly
state, "Forestry today is experiencing a transition similar to
that experienced two or three millenia ago in agriculture." The
productivity of managed forests is indeed striking (Sedjo and
Clawson, 1984:152-155). It is estimated, for instance, that if
only 3.5-7.0 percent of global closed forest were managed, the
sustained yield output would suffice to meet the entire world's
projected requirement for industrial roundwood in 2000. The
process of transition from our current "foraging" to silviculture
has even been examined within the context of an optimal control
model (Sedjo and Lyon, 1983). However, it is clear that the
transition from present practices to silviculture cannot occur
unless producers are encouraged by continued increases in real
stumpage prices and, by extension, wood product prices. No
rational entrepreneur will dedicate funds to silviculture unless
the present value of planting, nurturing, and harvesting costs
(discounted over 20-40 years) is exceeded by the present value
of the price of the resulting wood.

Several policy actions seem indicated in the present circumstances. One, needless to say, is strong support for research
on the viability of the forest resource, especially the problems
of TMF degradation and acid rain. Another is action to design
and implement decentralized, local programs in LDCs to alleviate
the impact of gross degradation of forest resources where it has
occurred. Anderson and Fishwick (1984), for instance, have proposed a cost-effective program of household-level agro-forestry
to combat deforestation in Africa. Where plantation forestry
seems viable, governments should supply or encourage research

and development, if it can be convincingly demonstrated that the private sector is investing insufficiently. Finally, governments should recognize that efficient utilization of the forest resource, like that of the fishery and groundwater resources, depends on assigning well-defined property rights. The transition to modern, commercial agriculture could not have been made without the enclosure of agricultural lands, and a modern-day enclosure movement will surely be necessary if a transition to scientifically managed plantation forestry is to occur.


SPECIES LOSS

Genetic diversity is a natural resource in several senses. We are most familiar with the species resource in the context of wildlife preservation. Many persons derive utility from the mere existence of certain species, most commonly large mammals, even though they themselves have no opportunity for observing those species. Others are hunters, or consumers of the recreation services offered by wildlife preserves and parks. However, to this "traditional" view of the species resource must be added a more fundamental aspect: plant and animal species are critical resources for agriculture, medicine, and science, and any significant loss of genetic diversity is therefore a serious resource problem.

The problem of species loss, closely related to that of TMF deforestation, is characterized by such great uncertainty that any ad hoc government policy response is unlikely. Estimates of the number of species extant vary by orders of magnitude, but various educated rules of thumb lead to estimates of 3-10 million (Harwood, 1982). TMFs provide the habitat for many and possibly most of these, but without an explicit functional link between deforestation and species loss, virtually any extinction rate can be inferred for the present and projected for the future (Simon and Wildavsky, 1984:175). This is clear from the model of Lovejoy, who made the frightening prediction in Global 2000 that by the end of the century, up to 20 percent of all species living in 1980 could be extinct (Global 2000:331). As illustrated in Figure 26, Lovejoy assumes that at 0 percent TMF cover loss, 0 percent of the species residing in TMFs are extinguished, and at 100 percent loss, 95 percent of such species disappear. Depending on the joint spatial distribution of species and disruptive activities across TMF areas, different curves may be used to map forest cover loss into species loss.

Unfortunately, although the micro-ecological processes by which changes in the TMF environment cause species to disappear from a given location are fairly well understood (Caulfield, 1985), little information is available for estimating the shape of Lovejoy's curve. An ambitious study now under way in Brazil, in which species diversity will be tracked over 30 years in reserves ranging from 1 to 10,000 hectares, will greatly reduce ignorance in this area (Lewin, 1984:611). Already, less than 5 years into the project, species disappearance results from the 1- and 10-hectare plots are providing useful insights.

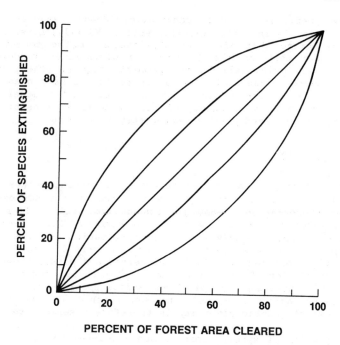

FIGURE 26   The Lovejoy Model

Source:   Global 2000 (329).


     Thanks to the diversity of the TMF resource, some hypotheses
will be difficult to test.   For instance, even the mild distur-
bance of hitherto-untouched forest areas might have more serious
consequences for species loss than would the outright degradation
of large open forest areas because biotic diversity is at its
greatest in the former areas.   If this is true, the FAO-UNEP
finding that undisturbed areas are being deforested less rapidly
than secondary areas is encouraging.   However, if genetic diversity is very heavily concentrated in undisturbed areas, then the
effect of losing 13 percent of such areas over the next half-
century, the loss implied by extrapolating the FAO-UNEP conclusions, might be quite serious.   This 13 percent, moreover, does
not include the undisturbed area converted to disturbed, but not
deforested, area.   When this transition takes place, how much of
the original genetic diversity is preserved?
     The cost-benefit calculus of species extinction is far from
established.   With regard to a known species, it is relatively
simple, at least in theory, to establish a point at which the
benefits of extinction outweigh the opportunity costs of preservation (Clark, 1973).   Such calculations are difficult, however,
in the case of the large-scale extinction of yet-unknown species.

The "lowest" species may make a disproportionate contribution to
science, agriculture, and medicine (Harrington and Fisher, 1982:
118-122), and it is difficult to come to grips with the present
value, in evolutionary terms, of thousands of thus-far uncata-
logued species. The fact that no market exists for most species
tends to suggest that wasteful overexploitation is likely to
occur.

What is clear is that if species loss of the sort documented
locally in the tropics is a general phenomenon, a calamity may
truly be said to exist. In the authors' opinion, Simon and
Wildavsky (1984:180) miss the mark when they assert "The
extinction of some species is an essential precondition of the
development of newer and better versions. . . . The argument
against extinction is not a position in favor of variety but
rather in favor of old variety compared to new." Implicitly,
they seem to conceive of species conservation as a problem of
optimal wildlife herd management. However, what is occurring
now may be qualitatively and quantitatively different from
previous extinctions.

First, a net loss of genetic diversity, as measured simply
by the number of species extant, may be occurring; this, so far
as we know, would be an entirely new and unfavorable phenomenon.
Second, the great majority of extinctions in the past occurred
to species with maladaptive characteristics, species that simply
fell behind in the forced march of evolution. While human intervention was sometimes the culprit (in the case of the dodo, for
instance), this was surely an exception, not the rule. In the
present circumstance, what may be occurring--the wholesale
extinction, through human intervention, of otherwise hardy
species--is quite different.

The ex situ preservation of genetic diversity, for instance,
in germplasm banks and zoos, has some promise but is no panacea
(Simon and Wildavsky, 1984:180; Sedjo and Clawson, 1984:163-164).
The same may be said of the proposal to set aside "species
reserves" in TMFs. Genetic engineering is another field that
might be used to mitigate some of the problems caused by species
loss. All in all, though, species loss is a possibly massive
problem with no apparent solution. Among the resource questions
examined in this survey, none cries out more loudly for immediate
research across a broad front.


CONCLUSIONS


Are natural resources becoming more scarce? Are conservation and
population-control policies called for? We have seen in this
chapter that a sweeping generalization is not appropriate for
answering these questions. First, we have noted that all scarcity indexes are deeply flawed; the analytical tools at our
disposal are very blunt. There is hope that a review of many
scarcity measures, conducted at a global level and in the context of a broad research design, may yield accurate conclusions.
However, there is every reason to believe that when used in iso-

lation, conventional scarcity measures are unreliable tools for forecasting and policy analysis.

This survey has concluded that the era of cheap, plentiful oil is coming to an end. A transition will have to be made, during the next century, to inherently less desirable sources of energy--dirtier, more difficult to extract and transport, and less efficient in end use. While striking technical progress is always a possibility, it is more likely that deep changes in the structure of the world economy will be necessary to maintain the level of energy-derived amenity to which we have become accustomed. However, the success of past energy transitions, combined with the wealth of technical resources at our disposal, gives reason to hope that the present shift, while painful, need not impede human progress in any fundamental way. To the extent that public policy measures can encourage energy conservation and, where appropriate, the movement to alternative energy sources, they should be applied. Unfortunately, the central aspect of the new energy picture will, we believe, be higher real energy prices. Cheap-energy policies, which cushion consumers but impede private-sector energy resource development, are counterproductive, yet they have had an irresistible political appeal.

In the case of agriculture, most trends were found to be encouraging. Despite the many problems that need to be addressed, nothing in our survey makes the "food crisis" model an attractive basis for policy decisions. The greatest challenge to policy makers in this area, we believe, is increasing LDC agricultural productivity, and the best way to work towards this is to restore these countries to macroeconomic health. In many LDCs, rapid productivity growth cannot occur in the absence of imported agricultural inputs, and these imports will not be possible in a sluggish world economy. In virtually all LDCs, a prerequisite to revitalizing agriculture is improving farmers' terms of trade vis a vis city dwellers, a distributional shift few policy makers will undertake if the economy as a whole is not growing briskly.

The case of world fisheries is rather more pessimistic than that of agriculture. While output can probably be expanded further, it does not appear that the rapid growth path of 1950-70 can be reattained in the next few decades, at least without a costly development program. Where possible, government action should mitigate the overfishing that results from open access to the resource. International policing of open-water fishing is needed, but it is not likely that the necessary cooperation will be forthcoming. The conclusion that fish are becoming more scarce and will probably continue to do so is therefore indicated.

In the case of forest resources, since further research is necessary to improve the quality of available data, all conclusions are subject to qualification. Anecdotal evidence and recent surveys unanimously support the conclusion that the deforestation and degradation of LDC forest resources, and the TMF resource in particular, are serious problems. In some locations, the problem can accurately be described as a crisis. While the

extent of deforestation as a generalized phenomenon in the
tropics now appears to be less than was formerly thought, estimated deforestation rates are still high enough to merit concern
and policy action. In the interest of efficiency, such actions
should address deforestation problems at the local level. Evidence has also emerged that forests in the industrial countries
are being adversely affected by factors that have come to be
loosely called "acid rain." The precise mechanism at work is
not understood; however, in locations that have been intensively
studied, deterioration has been rapid and serious. Experts do
not agree on the efficacy of the expensive abatement procedures
that are presently under consideration. Certainly in the United
States, and probably in the world as a whole, wood products have
become more expensive in real terms over the long term. This
worsening of economic scarcity has occurred despite the fact that
numerous substitutes have been developed. It is likely that the
economic scarcity of wood products will continue to increase, although managed plantation forestry may alleviate scarcity in the
very long term.

Finally, species loss, another component of the forest resources debate, is surrounded by great uncertainty. However,
this problem is of such potential gravity that additional research is urgently needed.


NOTES

1   In this and subsequent figures, all prices and price indexes
    are U.S. dollar denominated and have been deflated by the
    U.S. gross domestic product (GDP) deflator (1975 : 100). We
    have discussed elsewhere the rationale for this method of
    calculating real resource prices (MacKellar and Vining,
    1986a).

2   Note that these estimates are highly sensitive to the price
    of oil, and have been falling for several years as oil prices
    have dropped.

3   In this and many other subsequent tables, decadal and,
    occasionally, quinquennial averages are employed to "smooth"
    inherently volatile data series.

4   The secular decline in African per capita production of
    subsistence staple crops such as millet, sorghum, and tubers
    is not accurately reflected in the wheat data in Table 7.

5   Roundwood includes fuelwood, sawlogs, wood designated for
    pulping and plywood production, and wood used for miscel-
    laneous purposes; it is the broadest measure of global
    forest product output.

REFERENCES

Allen, J.C., and D.F. Barnes (1985)   The causes of deforestation
     in developing countries.   Annals of the Association of
     American Geographers 75(2):163-184.
American Petroleum Institute (1984)   Basic Petroleum Data Book
     4(1).   Washington, D.C.:   American Petroleum Institute.
Amos, O.M., Jr., and J.F. Timmons (1983)   Iowa crop production
     and soil erosion with cropland expansion.   American Journal
     of Agricultural Economics 65(3):486-492.
Anderson, D., and R. Fishwick (1984)   Fuelwood Consumption and
     Deforestation in African Countries.   World Bank Staff
     Working Paper No. 704, World Bank, Washington, D.C.
Anderson, L.W. (1982)   Marine fisheries.   Pp. 149-178 in P.R.
     Protney, ed., Current Issues in Natural Resource Policy.
     Washington, D.C.:   Resources for the Future.
Ashby, E. (1976)   Protection of the environment:   the human
     dimension.   Proceedings of the Royal Society of Medicine
     69:721-730.
Ashby, E. (1979)   Reflections on the costs and benefits of
     environmental pollution.   Perspectives in Biology and
     Medicine 23(1):7-24.
Bajracharya, D. (1983)   Fuel, food, or forest?   Dilemmas in a
     Nepali village.   World Development 11(12):1057-1074.
Bale, M.D., and R.C. Duncan (1983a)   Food prospects in the
     developing countries:   a qualified optimistic view.
     American Economic Review 73(2):244-248.
Bale, M.D., and R.C. Duncan (1983b)   Prospects for Food Produc-
     tion and Consumption in Developing Countries.   World Bank
     Staff Working Papers No. 596, World Bank, Washington, D.C.
Bale, M.D., and V.R. Southworth (1982)   World agricultural trade
     and food security:   emerging patterns and policy directions.
     Wisconsin International Law Journal 1:24-41.
Barnett, J.J., and C. Morse (1963)   Scarcity and Growth.
     Baltimore, Md.:   The Johns Hopkins University Press.
Barr, T.N. (1981)   The world food situation and global grain
     prospects.   Science 214(4525):1087-1095.
Basile, P.S., and B. de la Grandville (1984)   The evolution and
     role of non-O.P.E.C. production in the international oil
     market.   Natural Resources Forum 8(2):45-53.
Batie, S.S., and R.G. Healy (1983)   The future of American
     agriculture.   Scientific American 248(2):45-53.
Baumol, W.J., and W.E. Oates (1984)   Long-run trends in environ-
     mental quality.   Pp. 439-475 in J. Simon and H. Kahn, eds.,
     The Resourceful Earth.   New York:   Basil Blackwell.
Beckmann, P. (1984a)   Coal.   Pp. 428-438 in J. Simon and H. Kahn,
     eds., The Resourceful Earth.   New York:   Basil Blackwell.
Beckmann, P. (1984b)   Solar energy and other "alternative" energy
     sources.   Pp. 415-427 in J. Simon and H. Kahn, eds., The
     Resourceful Earth.   New York:   Basil Blackwell.
Behrman, J. (1968)   Supply Response in Underdeveloped Agricul-
     ture.   Amsterdam:   North Holland.

Binswanger, H.P., and P.L. Pingali (1984)   The Evolution of
    Farming Systems and Agricultural Technology in Sub-Saharan
    Africa. Report No. ARU 23, Research Unit, Agriculture and
    Rural Development Department, World Bank, Washington, D.C.
Blank, L.W. (1985)   A new type of forest decline in Germany.
    Nature 314:311-314.
Bovard, J. (1984)   Uncle Sam, super-sodbuster. Wall Street
    Journal, 21 September.
Brown, G.T. (1978)   Agricultural pricing policies in developing
    countries. Pp. 84-113 in T.W. Schultz, ed., Distortions of
    Agricultural Incentives. Bloomington, Indiana:  Indiana
    University Press.
Brown, L.R. (1978)   The Worldwide Loss of Cropland. Washington,
    D.C.:  Worldwatch Institute.
Brown, L.R. (1979)   Resource Trends and Population Policy:  A
    Time for Reassessment. Washington, D.C.:  Worldwatch
    Institute.
Brown, L.R. (1981)   World population growth, soil erosion, and
    food security. Science 124(4524):995-1002.
Brown, L.R. (1984a)   Reducing dependence on oil. Pp. 35-52 in
    L.R. Brown, et al., eds., State of the World 1984. New
    York:  W.W. Norton.
Brown, L.R. (1984b)   Securing food supplies. Pp. 175-193 in L.R.
    Brown, et al., eds., State of the World 1984. New York:
    W.W. Norton.
Brown, L.R. (1984c)   Conserving soils. Pp. 53-73 in L.R. Brown
    et al., eds., State of the World 1984. New York:  W.W.
    Norton.
Brown, L.R. (1985a)   Reducing hunger. Pp. 23-41 in L.R. Brown et
    al., eds., State of the World 1985. New York:  W.W. Norton.
Brown, L.R. (1985b)   Maintaining world fisheries. Pp. 73-96 in
    L.R. Brown et al., eds., State of the World 1985. New
    York:  W.W. Norton.
Brown, L.R., and E.C. Wolf (1985)   Soil Erosion:  Quiet Crisis in
    the World Economy. Worldwatch Paper No. 60. Washington,
    D.C.:  Worldwatch Institute.
Brown, L.R., W. Chandler, C. Flavin, C. Pollack, S. Postel, L.
    Starke, and E. Wolf (1985)   State of the World, 1985. New
    York:  W.W. Norton.
Butzer, K. (1980)   Adaptation to global environmental change.
    Professional Geographer 32(3):269-278.
Castle, E.N. (1982)   Agriculture and natural resource adequacy.
    American Journal of Agricultural Economics 64(5):811-820.
Caulfield, C. (1985)   The rain forests. The New Yorker. 14
    January, 41-101.
Choe, B.J., A. Lambertini, and P. Pollak (1981)   Global Energy
    Prospects. World Bank Staff Working Paper No. 489, World
    Bank, Washington, D.C.
Clark, C.W. (1973)   Profit maximization and the extinction of
    animal species. Journal of Political Economy 81(4):950-961.
Clark, W.C., ed. (1982)   Carbon Dioxide Review 1982. New York:
    Oxford University Press.

Clark, W.C., K.H. Cook, G. Marland, A.M. Weinberg, R.M. Rotty,
     P.R. Ball, and C.L. Cooper (1982)  The carbon dioxide
     question:  perspectives for 1982.  P. 4 in W.C. Clark, ed.,
     Carbon Dioxide Review 1982.  New York:  Oxford University
     Press.
Cleveland, C.J., R. Costanza, C.A.S. Hall, and R. Kaufman (1984)
     Energy and the U.S. economy:  a biophysical perspective.
     Science 255(4665):890-897.
Cohen, B. (1984)  The hazards of nuclear power.  Pp. 454-564 in
     J.L. Simon and H. Kahn, eds., The Resourceful Earth.  New
     York:  Basil Blackwell.
Cohen, K. (1984)  Nuclear power.  Pp. 387-414 in J. Simon and H.
     Kahn, eds., The Resourceful Earth.  New York:  Basil
     Blackwell.
Cook, E. (1977)  Energy:  the ultimate resource?  Resource Papers
     for College Geography, No. 77-4.  Washington, D.C.:
     Association of American Geographers.
Crosson, P.R. (1982)  Agricultural land.  Pp. 253-282 in P.R.
     Portney, ed., Current Issues in Natural Resource Policy.
     Washington, D.C.:  Resources for the Future.
Crosson, P.R. (1983)  Soil Erosion in Developing Countries:
     Amounts, Consequences, and Policies.  Working Paper No. 21,
     Center for Resource Policy Studies, University of Wisconsin,
     Madison, Wisconsin.
Crosson, P.R. (1984a)  Agricultural Development.  Paper prepared
     for the International Institute for Applied Systems Analysis
     (IIASA) Conference on Sustainable Development of the
     Biosphere, Laxenburg, Austria.
Crosson, P.R. (1984b)  National Costs of Erosion Effects on
     Productivity.  Unpublished manuscript, Resources for the
     Future, Washington, D.C.
Crosson, P.R., and S. Bruebaker (1982)  Resource and Environ-
     mental Effects of U.S. Agriculture.  Washington, D.C.:
     Resources for the Future.
Darmstadter, J., P.D. Teitelbaum, and J.G. Polach (1971)  Energy
     in the World Economy.  Baltimore, Md.:  The Johns Hopkins
     University Press.
Dideriksen, R., A.R. Hidlebaugh, and K.O. Schmude (1981)  Trends
     in agricultural land use.  Pp. 13-47 in M. Schnepf, ed.,
     Farmland, Food, and the Future.  Arkeny, Iowa:  Soil
     Conservation Society of America.
Donaldson, G. (1984)  Food security and the role of the grain
     trade.  American Journal of Agricultural Economics
     66(2):188-193.
Economist (1984a)  Raining acid on trees.  Economist 24 March
     82-83.
Economist (1984b)  A sunshine breakfast in grown abroad.
     Economist 26 May 73.
Economist (1984c)  World fishing flounders.  Economist 23 June
     70-71.
Economist (1984d)  Big oil's wildcats are turning into tamecats.
     Economist 25 August 55-56.

Eicher, C.K. (1984) Facing up to Africa's food crisis. Pp. 453-
479 in C.K. Eicher and M. Staatz, eds., Agricultural Develop-
ment in the Third World. Baltimore, Md.: The Johns Hopkins
University Press.
Falcon, W.P. (1984) Recent food policy lessons from developing
countries. American Journal of Agricultural Economics
66(2):180-187.
Firor, J.W., and P.R. Portney (1982) The global climate. Pp.
179-215 in P.R. Portney, ed., Current Issues in Natural
Resource Policy. Washington, D.C.: Resources for the
Future.
Fischer, D.H. (1980) Chronic inflation: the long view. The
Journal of the Institute for Socioeconomic Studies 5(3):
81-103.
Fisher, A.C. (1981) Resource Environmental Economics. New York:
Cambridge University Press.
Flavin, C. (1984) Reassessing the economics of nuclear power.
Pp. 115-135 in L.R. Brown et al., eds., State of the World
1984. New York: W.W. Norton.
Flavin, C., and S. Postel (1984) Developing renewable energy.
Pp. 136-174 in L.R. Brown et al., eds., State of the World
1984. New York: W.W. Norton
Ford Foundation (1979) Energy: The Next Twenty Years.
Cambridge, Mass.: Ballinger
Gammie, J.I. (1981) World Timber to the Year 2000. London:
Economist Intelligence Unit.
Gamser, M.S. (1980) The forest resource and rural energy
development. World Development 8:769-780.
Gillman, K. (1981) Julian Simon's cracked crystal ball. The
Public Interest 65:71-80.
Goeller, H.E., and A.M. Weinberg (1978) The age of substituti-
bility. American Economic Review 68(4):1-11.
Gregory, G.R. (1972) Forest Resource Economics. New York: The
Ronald Press Company.
Grigg, D. (1983) The growth of world food output and population
1950-80. Geography 68:301-306.
Grossling, B.F. (1977) A critical survey of world petroleum
opportunities. Pp. 645-658 in U.S. Congressional Research
Service, ed., Project Interdependence: U.S. and World
Energy Outlook Through 1990. Washington, D.C.: U.S
Government Printing Office.
Hamilton, J.D. (1983a) Oil and the macroeconomy since World
War II. Journal of Political Economy 91(2):228-248.
Hamilton, J.D. (1983b) A Brief Postwar History of Oil Prices and
the U.S. Economy. Unpublished manuscript.
Hansen, J., D. Johnson, A. Lacis, S. Lebedeff, P. Lee, D. Rind,
and G. Russell (1981) Climate impact of increasing atmos-
pheric carbon dioxide. Science 213(4511):957-966.
Hardin, G. (1968) The tragedy of the commons. Science 162
(3859):13-18.

Harrington, W., and A.C. Fisher (1982) Endangered speices. Pp. 117-148 in P.R. Portney, ed., Current Issues in Natural Resource Policy. Washington, D.C.: Resources for the Future.

Harwood, M. (1982) Math of extinction. Audubon 84:18-20.

Hart, J.F. (1984) Cropland changes in the United States, 1944-78. Pp. 224-249 in J.L. Simon and H. Kahn, eds., The Resourceful Earth. New York: Basil Blackwell.

Haynes, R.W., and D.M. Adams (1983) Changing perceptions of the U.S. forest sector: implications for the RPA timber assessment. American Journal of Agricultural Economics 65(5):1002-1009.

Hubbert, M.K. (1962) Energy Resources: A Report to the Committee on Natural Resources. National Research Council, Washington, D.C.

Hubbert, M.K. (1977) World oil and natural gas reserves and resources. Pp. 632-644 in U.S. Congressional Research Service, ed., Project Interdependence: U.S. and World Energy Outlook Through 1990. Washington, D.C.: U.S. Government Printing Office.

Idso, S. (1984) The case for carbon dioxide. Journal of Environmental Science 27(3):19-22.

International Monetary Fund (1983) International Financial Statistics. 1983 Yearbook. Washington, D.C.: International Monetary Fund.

Jevons, W.S. (1865). The Coal Question. London: Macmillan.

Johnson, D.G. (1984) World food and agriculture. Pp. 67-112 in J.L. Simon and H. Kahn, eds., The Resourceful Earth. New York: Basil Blackwell.

Katzenstein, A.W. (1984) Is industry poisoning the forest? Acidity is not the major factor. Wall Street Journal 28 June.

Landsberg, H.E. (1984) Global climate trends. Pp. 272-315 in J.L. Simon and H. Kahn, eds., The Resourceful Earth. New York: Basil Blackwell.

Lanly, J.P. (1982) Tropical Forest Resources. UNFAO Forestry Paper Number 30, United Nations Food and Agriculture Organization, Rome.

Larson, W.E., F.J. Pierce, and R.H. Dowdy (1983) The threat of soil erosion to long-term crop production. Science 219(4584):458-465.

Lawson, D. (1984) The "monte carlo" assessments. Financial Times 30 May.

Lee, L. (1978) A Perspective on Cropland Availability. Agricultural Economic Report No. 406, Economics, Statistics, and Cooperative Services, U.S. Department of Agriculture. Washington, D.C.: U.S. Government Printing Office.

Leith, C.K. (1935) Conservation of minerals. Science 82(2119) 109-117.

Lewin, R. (1984) Parks: how big is big enough? Science 225 (4662):611-612.

Likens, G.E. (1984) Is industry poisoning the forests? We must take prompt action. Wall Street Journal 28 June.

Lin, C. (1984)  Global patterns of energy consumption before and
    after the 1974 oil crisis.  Economic Development and Cultural
    Change 32(3):781-802.
MacKellar, F.L., and D.R. Vining (1986a)  Measuring Natural
    Resource Scarcity.  Unpublished manuscript, City University
    of New York.
MacKellar, F.L., and D.R. Vining (1986b)  Where Do We Stand in
    the National Resources Scarcity Debate?  Unpublished
    manuscript, City University of New York.
Malthus, T. (1798)  First Essay on Population.
Mandelbrot, B.B., and J.R. Wallis (1968)  Noah, Joseph, and
    operational hydrology.  Water Resources Research 4(5):909-
    917.
Mayer, L.S., B. Silverman, S.L. Zeger, and A.G. Bruce (1979)
    Modeling the Rates of Domestic Crude Oil Discovery and
    Production.  Resource Estimation and Validation Project,
    Departments of Statistics and Geology.  Princeton, N.J.:
    Princeton University.
McConnell, K.E. (1983)  An economic model of soil conservation.
    American Journal of Agricultural Economics 65(1):83-89.
Meadows, D.H., D.L. Meadows, J. Randers, and W.W. Behrens III
    (1974)  The Limits to Growth.  New York:  Universe Books.
Mellor, J.W., and B.F. Johnston (1984)  The world food equation:
    interrelations among development, employment, and food
    consumption.  Journal of Economic Literature 22:531-574.
Myers, N. (1980)  Conversion of Tropical Moist Forests.
    Washington, D.C.:  National Academy of Sciences.
National Defense University (1979)  Climate Change to the Year
    2000: A Survey of Expert Opinion.  Washington, D.C.:  U.S.
    Government Printing Office.
National Research Council (1983)  Changing Climate.  Report of
    the Carbon Dioxide Assessment Committee.  Washington, D.C.:
    National Academy Press.
Nehring, R. (1978)  Giant Oil Fields and World Oil Resources.
    Santa Monica, Calif.:  Rand Corporation.
Nehring, R. (1982)  Prospects for conventional world oil
    resources.  Annual Review of Energy 7:175-200.
Odell, P.R. (1982)  New Geopolitics of International Energy:
    Towards a System of World Oil Regions.  Paper presented at
    the 4th Annual International Conference of the International
    Association of Energy Economists, Cambridge, England.
Odell, P.R. (1984)  Outlook for the international oil market and
    options for OPEC.  Energy Policy 12(1):5-12.
Office of Technology Assessment (1983)  Wood Use: U.S.
    Competitiveness and Technology.  Project OTA-ITE-210.
    Washington, D.C.:  U.S. Congress Office of Technology
    Assessment.
O'Mara, G.T. (1984)  Issues in the Efficient Use of Surface and
    Groundwater in Irrigation.  World Bank Staff Working Paper
    No. 707, World Bank, Washington, D.C.
Organization for Economic Cooperation and Development (1982)
    World Energy Outlook.  Paris:  Organization for Economic
    Cooperation and Development.

Pavitt, K.L.R. (1973) Malthus and other economists: some doom-
days revisited. Pp. 137-158 in H.S.D. Cole et al., eds.,
Models of Doom: A Critique of the Limits to Growth. New
York: Universe Books.
Pensak, M. (1978) A Statistical Examination of United States Oil
Production Forecasting. Unpublished thesis, Department of
Statistics, Princeton University.
Pereira, C. (1978) The changing patterns of constraints on food
production in the third world. Pp. 24-34 in T.W. Schultz,
ed., Distortions of Agricultural Incentives. Bloomington,
Indiana: Indiana University Press.
Perry, J.S. (1984) Much ado about C02. Nature 311:681-682.
Persson, R. (1974) World Forest Resources. Department of Forest
Survey Research Notes No. 17, Royal College of Forestry,
Stockholm.
Peterson, F., and A. Fisher (1977) The exploitation of extrac-
tive resources--a survey. The Economic Journal 87(348):
681-721.
Pimentel, D., E.C. Terhune, R. Dyson-Hudson, S. Rechereau, R.
Samis, E.A. Smith, D. Denman, D. Reifschneider, and M.
Shepard (1976) Land degradation: effects on food and
energy resources. Science 194(4261):149-155.
Postel, S. (1984) Air Pollution, Acid Rain, and the Future of
Forests. Worldwatch Paper No. 58. Washington, D.C.:
Worldwatch Institute.
Postel, S. (1985) Managing freshwater supplies. Pp. 42-72 in
L.R. Brown et al., eds., State of the World 1985. New
York: W.W. Norton.
Renshaw, E., and P.F. Renshaw (1980) U.S. oil discovery and
production: the projections of M. King Hubbert. Futures
12(1):58-66.
Repetto, R. (1985) Soil Loss and Population Pressure on Java.
Paper presented at the Annual Meeting of the Population
Association of America, Boston.
Revelle, R. (1984) The world supply of agricultural land. Pp.
184-201 in J.L. Simon and H. Kahn, eds., The Ultimate
Resource. New York: Basil Blackwell.
Rosing, K.E., and P.R. Odell (1983) The Future of Oil: A Re-
Evaluation. Paper 83-1a, Center for International Energy
Studies, Erasmus University, Rotterdam.
Sedjo, R.A., and M. Clawson (1984) Global forests. Pp. 128-170
in J.L. Simon and H. Kahn, eds., The Resourceful Earth. New
York: Basil Blackwell.
Sedjo, R.A., and K.S. Lyon (1983) Long-term forest resources
trade, global timber supply, and intertemporal comparative
advantage. American Journal of Agricultural Economics
65(5):1010:1020.
Shabecoff, P. (1985) Acid rain attacks environment beyond
Northeast. New York Times 29 January.
Sheehan, R.G., and N. Kelly (1983) Oil prices and world
inflation. Journal of Economics and Business 35:235-238.
Simon, J.L. (1980) Are we losing ground? Illinois Business
Review 37(30):1-6.

Simon, J.L. (1981a)  Global confusion, 1980:  a hard look at the
    Global 2000 report.  The Public Interest (62):3-20.
Simon, J.L. (1981b)  False bad news is truly bad news.  The
    Public Interest (65):80-89.
Simon, J.L. (1981c)  The Ulitmate Resource.  Princeton, N.J.:
    Princeton University Press.
Simon, J.L., and A. Wildavsky (1984)  On species loss, the
    absence of data, and risks to humanity.  Pp. 171-183 in J.L.
    Simon and H. Kahn, eds., The Resourceful Earth.  New York:
    Basil Blackwell.
Singer, F. (1984a)  Acid rain.  Policy Review 27:56-58.
Singer, F. (1984b)  Reply.  Policy Review 28:9-10.
Skinner, B.J. (1976)  A second iron age ahead?  American
    Scientist 64(3):258-269.
Sommer, A. (1976)  Attempt at an assessment of the world's
    tropical moist forests.  Unasylva 28(112-113):5-24.
Steinhart, J.S., and C.E. Steinhart (1974)  Energy use in the
    U.S. food system.  Science 184(4134):307-316.
Sullivan, K. (1984)  Overfishing and the new law of the sea.
    O.E.C.D. Observer 129:16-18.
Swanson, E.R., and E.O. Heady (1984)  Soil erosion in the United
    States.  Pp. 202-223 in J.L. Simon and H. Kahn, eds., The
    Resourceful Earth.  New York:  Basil Blackwell.
Thomas, B. (1980)  Towards an energy interpretation of the
    industrial revolution.  Atlantic Economic Journal 8(1):1-15.
Thompson, L.M. (1969)  Weather and technology in the production
    of wheat in the United States.  Journal of Soil and Water
    Conservation 24(6):219-224.
Torrens, I. (1984)  What goes up must come down:  the acid rain
    problem.  O.E.C.D. Observer 129:9-15.
United Nations (various years)  Monthly Bulletin of Statistics.
    New York:  United Nations.
United Nations (1970-1980)  Statistical Yearbook.  New York:
    United Nations.
United Nations (1973)  Statistical Yearbook.  New York:  United
    Nations.
United Nations (1976)  World Energy Supplies 1950-74.
    Statistical Papers, Series J, No. 19.  New York:  United
    Nations.
United Nations (1977)  World Energy Supplies 1972-76.
    Statistical Papers, Series J, No. 21.  New York:  United
    Nations.
United Nations (1979-1980)  Statistical Yearbook.  New York:
    United Nations.
United Nations (1980-1981)  Statistical Yearbook.  New York:
    United Nations.
United Nations (1981)  Yearbook of World Energy Statistics.  New
    York:  United Nations.
United Nations Food and Agriculture Organization (1958-82)
    Yearbook of Forest Products.  New York:  United Nations.
United Nations Food and Agriculture Organization (1967)
    Production Yearbook, Vol. 21.  New York:  United Nations.

United Nations Food and Agriculture Organization (1970-1974)
   Yearbook of Fishing Statistics, Vol. 31-39. New York:
   United Nations.
United Nations Food and Agriculture Organization (1972a)
   Production Yearbook, Vol. 26. New York: United Nations.
United Nations Food and Agriculture Organization (1972b)
   Yearbook of Forest Productions. New York: United Nations.
United Nations Food and Agriculture Organization (1977)
   Production Yearbook, Vol. 31. New York: United Nations.
United Nations Food and Agriculture Organization (1978)
   Yearbook of Fishing Statistics, Vol. 47. New York: United
   Nations.
United Nations Food and Agriculture Organization (1979)
   Yearbook of Fishing Statistics, Vol. 49. New York: United
   Nations.
United Nations Food and Agriculture Organization (1980a)
   Production Yearbook, Vol. 31. New York: United Nations.
United Nations Food and Agriculture Organization (1980b)
   Yearbook of Forest Products. New York: United Nations.
United Nations Food and Agriculture Organization (1980c)
   Yearbook of Fishing Statistics, Vol. 51. New York: United
   Nations.
United Nations Food and Agriculture Organization (1981)
   Yearbook of Fishing Statistics, Vol. 53. New York: United
   Nations.
United Nations Food and Agriculture Organization (1983)
   Yearbook of Forest Products. New York: United Nations.
United Nations Food and Agriculture Organization, Forestry
   Department (1985) A world perspective: forestry beyond
   2000. Unasylva 37(1):7-16.
United Nations Food and Agriculture Organization and United
   Nations Environment Programme (1981a) Tropical Forest
   Resources Assessment Project (in the context of Global
   Environmental Monitoring System): Tropical Africa. Rome:
   United Nations Food and Agriculture Organization.
United Nations Food and Agriculture Organization and United
   Nations Environment Programme (1981b) Topical Forest
   Resources Assessment Project (in the Context of Global
   Environmental Monitoring System): Tropical Asia. Rome:
   United Nations Food and Agriculture Organization.
United Nations Food and Agriculture Organization and United
   Nations Environment Programme (1981c) Tropical Forest
   Resources Assessment Project (in the context of Global
   Environmental Monitoring System): Latin America. Rome:
   United Nations Food and Agriculture Organization.
U.S. Department of Agriculture (1936-1982) Agricultural
   Statistics. Washington, D.C.: U.S. Government Printing
   Office.
U.S. Department of Agriculture (1979) National Agricultural
   Lands Study. Washington, D.C.: U.S. Government Printing
   Office.

U.S. Department of Agriculture (1981a)   U.S. Timber Production,
Trade, Consumption, and Price Statistics 1950-80.  Forest
Service Miscellaneous Publication No. 1408.  Washington,
D.C.:  U.S. Government Printing Office.

U.S. Department of Agriculture (1981b)   An Assessment of the
Forest and Range Land Situation in the United States.
Forest Resource Report No. 22.  Washington, D.C.:  U.S.
Government Printing Office.

U.S. Department of Agriculture (1982a)   Agricultural Statistics.
Washington, D.C.:  U.S. Government Printing Office.

U.S. Department of Agriculture (1982b)   An Analysis of the Timber
Situation in the United States, 1952-2030.  Forest Resource
Report No. 29.  Washington, D.C.:  U.S. Government Printing
Office.

U.S. Department of Agriculture (1984)   Foreign Agricultural
Circular Grains.  U.S.D.A. Publication FG-6-84.  Washington,
D.C.:  U.S. Government Printing Office.

U.S. Department of State and Council on Environmental
Quality (1980)   The Global 2000 Report to the President,
Vol. 2.  Washington, D.C.:  U.S. Government Printing Office.

Vining, D. (1982)   The future of American agriculture.  American
Planning Association Journal 48(1):112-115.

Waldmeir, P. (1985)   The lessons of Zimbabwe.  Financial Times 7
May.

WGBH-Boston (1983)   The Climate Crisis.  Transcript of NOVA,
episode 1019, 20 December.

White, G.A. (1984)   Water resource adequacy:  illusion and
reality.  Pp. 250-266 in J.L. Simon and H. Kahn, eds., The
Resourceful Earth.  New York:  Basil Blackwell.

Whittlesey, N.K., and C. Lee (1976)   Impacts of Energy Price
Changes on Food Prices.  Bulletin 822, College of
Agriculture Research Center.  Pullman, Wash.:  University of
Washington.

Whittlesey, N.K., J.R. Buteau, W.R. Butcher, and D. Walker (1981)
Energy Tradeoffs and Economic Feasibility of Irrigation
Development in the Pacific Northwest.  Bulletin 0896,
College of Agriculture Research Center.  Pullman, Wash.:
University of Washington.

Wiorkowski, J.J. (1981)   Estimating volumes of remaining fossil
fuel resources:  a critical review.  Journal of the American
Statistical Association 76(375):534-547.

Wise, J. (1984)   The future of food from the sea.  Pp. 113-127 in
J.L. Simon and H. Kahn, eds., The Resourceful Earth.  New
York:  Basil Blackwell.

Woodwell, G.M., J.E. Hobbie, R.A. Houghton, J.M. Melillo, B.
Moore, B.J. Peterson, and G.R. Shaver (1983)   Global
deforestation:  contribution to atmospheric carbon dioxide.
Science 222(4528):1081-1088.

World Oil (1983)   Oil and Gas Journal.  Tulsa, Okla.:  Penn Well
Publishing Co.

# 9
## Natural Resources, Population Growth, and Economic Well-Being
### Margaret E. Slade

INTRODUCTION

The idea that scarce natural resources can (and eventually will) constrain the growth of population and of economic well-being has been analyzed and debated for centuries. Historically, economists and political philosophers have taken positions of both pessimism and optimism about man's ability to overcome the constraints imposed by finite stocks of resources.

The early nineteenth-century classical economists, such as Malthus and Ricardo, forecast dire consequences of population growth and, as a result, earned the profession the name of the "dismal" science. Implicit in their view is the idea that population and per capita income determine resource consumption; price is not well integrated into their analysis.

In contrast, the neoclassical economists of the late nineteenth century, such as Walras and Marshall, were not particularly concerned with natural resources, which they considered just another factor of production. The idea that price would equate supply and demand for any factor was partially responsible for the decline in interest in resources as a constraint to growth.

Today's economists also line up on both sides of this debate. Contemporary neoclassical economists, such as Solow (1974) and Stiglitz (1979), emphasize that technical progress and substitution diminish resource scarcity; contemporary Malthusians, such as Georgescue-Roegen (1976) and Daly (1977), stress physical laws that constrain progress and substitutability.

This chapter summarizes the salient issues involved in the controversy. The debate is by no means closed, and many unsolved problems remain. For this reason, while theoretical findings are

This survey was commissioned by the National Research Council's Committee on Population. The views expressed, however, are the author's and not those of the Committee. I would like to thank Anthony Fisher, Ronald Lee, Landis MacKellar, Richard Parks, and Robert Repetto for helpful comments on an earlier draft.

discussed here and empirical evidence bearing on the subject is
marshaled, no definitive answers are given. Many of the conclusions reached are the author's personal views, which are of
course not universal.

In the debate, the term "natural resources" has been defined
in many ways. Some choose a narrow focus and limit themselves
to mineral resources, such as crude petroleum and iron ore.
Others, however, adopt a broader definition that includes renewable and environmental resources, such as forests, fish, air,
and water. This chapter is based on the broad definition; that
is, the term natural resources encompasses all the original
elements that comprise the earth's natural endownment.[1] The
chapter does not, however, emphasize agricultural land, which is
covered elsewhere in this volume (Binswanger and Pingali; Ruttan
and Hayami).

Some questions need not be asked or answered. For example,
it is obvious that there are ultimate limits to population size
and to economic production on a finite planet. More important,
however, are the following questions:

- Which problems will emerge in the forecastable future
  (the next 50 years, for example)?

- Which resources are most apt to be constraining?

- Which economies (underdeveloped, developing, or
  developed) are most apt to be constrained?

This chapter provides tentative answers to these questions.

As natural-resource commodities become increasingly scarce,
it is forecast that their prices will rise. The consequences of
higher prices that are often cited as potential solutions to the
scarcity problem include the following:

- increased exploratory effort, resulting in the discovery
  of previously unknown reserves;

- the substitution of abundant for scarce resources in
  production and consumption; and

- technical progress of the resource-saving variety.

The extent to which these tendencies are actually observed is
also discussed in this chapter.

On the other hand, many resources are unpriced and commonly
owned. For these commodities, the price system cannot be
expected to provide signals, and political agencies must inter-
vene to supply appropriate incentives. Whether these incentives
exist today is also considered here.

The outline of this chapter is as follows. In the next
section, the economic theory of growth with natural resources is
summarized. For both nonrenewable and common-property resources,
a basic model is established, the effects of population growth

on the model predictions are discussed, and the efficiency properties of a market solution are analyzed. In the third section,
many of the problems encountered when one attempts to apply
theoretical models to real-world situations are described, with
particular emphasis on measurement problems. The fourth section
contains more detailed analyses of particular problems: first,
the energy-gross national product (GNP) relationship, and second,
the destruction of tropical forests. The next section addresses
policy issues such as income distribution, international cooperation, and incentive structures. A final section summarizes and
concludes.


THE ECONOMIC THEORY OF GROWTH WITH NATURAL RESOURCES

There are many classification schemes for natural-resource
commodities. One such scheme classifies a resource as nonrenewable if the process that generates it is long, and renewable if
the process is short. For example, although most harvested crops
can be replenished within a year, the geologic processes that
produce minerals take so long that we can for all practical
purposes regard the stock of minerals in the earth's crust as
fixed. Another scheme classifies resources as common property
if their property rights are ill defined, and as public or
private property if property rights are easy to determine and
enforce. For example, whereas most mineral ores are owned by
governments or private mining companies, no one has exclusive
rights to the earth's oceans and atmosphere.
   This chapter addresses nonrenewable and common-propety
resources. Although this division is neither exhaustive nor
mutually exclusive, these two categories are the sources of the
principal problems faced by growing populations. By contrast,
the problems posed by privately owned renewable resources are of
a lesser magnitude.


Nonrenewable Resources

In this section, a simple model of economic growth with exhaustible resources is set up, the way in which population growth
affects the model predictions is considered, and the likelihood
of a free-market system achieving a desirable outcome is
analyzed.
   For simplicity, assume that there is a fixed stock of a
homogeneous resource commodity. Let $S_t$ denote the size of the
stock in period t, where $S_0$ is known in advance to equal $\bar{S}$.
The flow of extraction R from the stock S is used in
production. By assumption,

$$\int_0^\infty R_t dt \leq \bar{S} \; ; \tag{1}$$

that is, the cumulative flow is limited by the finite stock.

Recycling is not explicitly considered. If recycling is perfect (100 percent), the resource is not exhaustible. Suppose instead that some fraction $\delta$ is available for reuse, where $0 \leq \delta < 1$. Then the rate of change of the stock, $\dot{S}_t$, is not equal to $-R_t$ but is instead

$$\dot{S}_t = - R_t + \delta R_t = - (1 - \delta)R_t , \qquad (2)$$

and equation (1) becomes

$$\int_0^\infty (1 - \delta)R_t \, dt \leq \bar{S}$$

or

$$\int_0^\infty R_t \, dt \leq 1/(1 - \delta) \, \bar{S} . \qquad (3)$$

The effect of recycling is thus equivalent to an increase in the initial endownment by a factor of $1/(1 - \delta)$. The analysis, however, is the same.

R is used in production with other inputs K and L. L denotes the size of the labor force, which is temporarily assumed to be fixed at a level $\bar{L}$.[2]

K denotes a stock of man-made goods that are used in production, the economy's stock of capital. For simplicity, assume that K does not depreciate. That is, we consider the most optimistic case. If consumption is seen to be limited under this assumption, it is surely limited when capital depreciates.

The three inputs together produce a homogeneous output Q, which can be consumed or invested. Thus

$$Q_t = \dot{K}_t + C_t , \qquad (4)$$

where $\dot{K}_t$ is investment, $I_t$, and $C_t$ are aggregate consumption.

We are interested in the production possibilities for an economy as a whole, which is assumed to be closed (no trade). Assume that these possibilities can be summarized by a constant-returns-to-scale aggregate-production function that is twice differentiable,[3]

$$Q_t = F(K_t, R_t, L, t) . \qquad (5)$$

Time, t, is included as an argument of the production function to allow for the possibility of technical change.

The objective is to choose time paths for extraction R and consumption C so as to maximize the present value of the utility U of consumption,

$$\max_{R_t, C_t} \int_0^\infty e^{-rt} U(C_t) \, dt , \qquad (6)$$

subject to the initial conditions $\bar{K}_0 = \bar{K}$, $S_0 = \bar{S}$, and $L = \bar{L}$ and the constraints (1) and (4). In equation (6), r is the social rate of time preference.[4]

Many authors have considered such a problem, usually making some assumptions about the functional forms of F and U (e.g., Dasgupta and Heal, 1974; Solow, 1974; Stiglitz, 1974). The discussion here most closely follows Dasgupta and Heal (1979). The principal findings can be summarized as follows.

The elasticity of substitution between K and R is a crucial factor in the analysis. $\sigma$ is defined as the percent change in the K-R usage ratio due to a percent change in their price ratio,[5]

$$\sigma = d \ln(K/R)/d \ln(P_R/P_K) , \qquad (7)$$

where ln denotes the natural logarithm and $P_i$ is the price of factor i. $\sigma$ is thus a summary measure of the ease with which man-made goods can be substituted for the exhaustible resource in the production of Q.

With a constant-elasticity-of-substitution (CES) production function (Arrow et al., 1961) and no technical change, if is strictly greater than one, the finite resource does not limit sustained consumption.[6] The reason for this is that substitution possibilities are abundant and output can be produced with no R. In contrast, if $\sigma$ is less than one, output must eventually decline to zero. In this case, there are severe limits to substitution possibilities that cannot be overcome by capital accumulation.

The interesting case is therefore the case where $\sigma$ is equal to one--the Cobb-Douglas case with production function

$$Q_t = \alpha K_t^{\alpha_1} R_t^{\alpha_2} L^{\alpha_3}, \qquad \alpha_1 + \alpha_2 + \alpha_3 = 1 ,$$

or

$$Q_t/L = \alpha(K_t/L)^{\alpha_1}(R_t/L)^{\alpha_2} , \qquad \alpha_1 + \alpha_2 < 1 . \qquad (8)$$

In this case, the relative size of the parameters $\alpha_1$ and $\alpha_2$ is the crucial factor. If $\alpha_1 > \alpha_2$, capital is sufficiently important in production to allow for a permanently maintainable consumption level; if, however, the reverse is true, consumption must eventually fall to zero.

Finally, if there is a strictly positive rate of resource-augmenting technical progress, sustained consumption is possible regardless of substitution possibilities. Technical progress is said to be resource-augmenting if the production function can be written as

$$Q_t = F(K_t, a(t) R_t, L) , \qquad (9)$$

with da/dt > 0. If the rate of resource-augmenting technical progress is constant, we denote it by $\lambda$ .

There are thus simple conditions on the K-R elasticity of substitution $\sigma$, the capital and resource shares in total cost $\alpha_1$ and $\alpha_2$, and the resource-augmenting rate of technical change $\lambda$ that indicate whether consumption can be maintained indefinitely. Although it might be thought an easy matter to

check these conditions, the problems involved are indeed
sizable; these problems are discussed in the next section.
     Thus far it has been assumed that population is fixed at a
level $\bar{L}$. We now consider what happens when the population
increases to a level $\tilde{L} > \bar{L}$. It is clear from equation (8) that,
with the same K and R, per capita consumption falls. Eventually,
the increased number of workers can produce a larger capital
stock; the resource stock, in contrast, cannot be augmented. It
would therefore require a more than proportional increase in the
capital stock just to maintain per capita consumption at the old
level. Population increases are therefore most likely to lead to
a fall in the sustainable level of per capita consumption.
     Finally, the optimality properties of a market solution are
considered. This is an important issue because most mineral resources are produced and consumed by market economies. The first
theorem in welfare economics holds that under certain conditions,
the competitive solution is Pareto optimal (see, for example,
Malinvaud, 1972). An outcome is said to be Pareto optimal if no
one can be made better off without harming someone else. Two
important conditions required for this result are price-taking
behavior on the part of producers and consumers, and the existence of markets for every good in every time period. We consider whether these conditions are met in practice. In the discussion, however, it should be kept in mind that the failure of
a particular condition is not by itself sufficient to warrant
intervention. It must also be believed that public agencies,
with their different set of imperfections, do a better job than
the market in allocating resources.
     In the case of exhaustible resources, the lack of price-
taking behavior, which is obvious in many commodity markets, may
not be as important a problem as it initially seems. In general,
monopolization leads to increased conservation; that is, higher
price and lower consumption initially imply that a larger stock
of the resource remains for future generations.
     The requirement that futures markets exist for all time
periods is clearly not met; as a result, the competitive solution
may deviate from optimality. The direction of the bias, however,
is not clear. Neither is it clear that public agencies are
better forecasters of future scarcity and therefore do a better
job of intertemporal resource allocation.
     Another problem arises from the fact that future generations
are not here to have their preferences counted. Therefore, it
is only the current generation whose utility is maximized in
equation (6), and just as before, the market solution is likely
to be suboptimal. On the other hand, it is again not clear that
governments weigh future generations more heavily than private
individuals or firms do. As witness to this observation, consider the haste with which the current administration in the
United States is trying to withdraw lands from the public domain
and lease the right to explore for minerals on government-owned
property.
     For at least three reasons, therefore, the market solution
is likely to be suboptimal. However, whether these problems

call for some form of public control or central planning is a moot question. In contrast, there are other areas where the need for public intervention is more obvious. Information and knowledge possess elements of public goods (to be discussed shortly), and, to the extent that these commodities are public, the market undersupplies them. Public agencies should therefore collect and process information and should engage in research and development activities, especially in areas where the benefits are difficult to capture.


## Common-Property Resources

Common-property resources are those commodities for which the definition and enforcement of property rights present special problems. With the exhaustible resources discussed in the last section, the finite stock is the key feature, and the allocation of this stock over time is the key problem. With a common-property resource, the key feature is that there are many users, each of whom takes only himself into account and ignores the effect that his use has on others. Just as before, in the present section a simple model of common-property resource is set up, the optimality properties of a market solution are discussed, and the effects of population growth on the model predictions are analyzed. The discussion is by necessity brief; those wishing a more in-depth treatment are referred to Baumol and Oates (1975) and Dasgupta (1982).

Formally, suppose that there are N identical producers (countries or firms) who manufacture a homogeneous output q using the services of capital k, labor l, and a common-property resource P. This activity can be summarized by the following relationships:

$$q_i = h(k_i, l_i, P), \quad \Sigma q_i = Q, \quad \Sigma k_i = K, \quad \Sigma l_i = L ,$$

$$i = 1, \ldots, N , \tag{10}$$

where capital letters stand for aggregate quantities.

Suppose that the common-property commodity is a bad called pollution. Pollution is produced as a byproduct of the production of q, a relationship which for convenience is assumed to be linear,

$$P_i = \beta q_i, \quad \Sigma p_i = P . \tag{11}$$

Notice that it is aggregate pollution P that enters into the production relationship (10).

Under certain regularity conditions, there exists a cost function c dual to the production function h (see, for example, Diewert, 1974). The cost function has as arguments a vector of factor prices v (the rental price of capital $v_1$ and the wage rate $v_2$); the level of pollution P, which is unpriced; and the level of output $q_i$.

338                                                              Slade

Each producer wishes to maximize his own private profit $\pi_i$,

$$\max_{q_i} \pi_i = q_i - c(v,P,q_i) , \tag{12}$$

subject to the constraint (11). Without loss of generality, output price has been chosen to equal one. In what follows, the subscript i is suppressed; this suppression is justified because all producers are identical by assumption.

For a noncooperative solution (i.e., each producer chooses output independently and ignores the effect of his output decision on the behavior of others), a first-order condition for the maximization (12) is

$$d\pi_i/dq_i = 1 - \partial c/\partial P \;\; \partial P/\partial p \; dp/dq_i - \partial c/\partial q_i = 0 . \tag{13}$$

By (11), $\partial P/\partial p = 1$ and $\partial p/\partial q = \beta$. Therefore, (13) is equivalent to

$$c_q = 1 - \beta c_p , \tag{14}$$

where subscripted function denotes the partial derivative of the function with respect to the subscript variable.

Suppose that instead of each producer maximizing his own profit, a social planner maximizes joint profit $\Pi = \Sigma\pi_i$,

$$\max_{\{q_i\}} \Pi = \Sigma q_i - \Sigma c(v,P,q_i) , \tag{15}$$
$$\phantom{\max_{\{q_i\}}}\scriptstyle N \atop \scriptstyle i=1$$

subject to the N constraints (11). This is called the cooperative solution.

Because each producer is identical, (15) is equivalent to

$$\max_Q \Pi = Q - Nc(v,P,q) , \qquad q = Q/N . \tag{16}$$

A first-order condition for this maximization is

$$1 - N\beta c_p + Nc_q = 0 ,$$

or

$$c_q = 1 = N\beta c_p . \tag{17}$$

When equations (14) and (17) are compared, the difference between the two solutions is obvious. The planner takes into account the fall in every producer's output due to an increase in producer i's polluting activities. Therefore, i's output is increased only up to the point where his private marginal cost of polluting is equal to $1 - N\beta c_p$, not $1 - \beta c_p$ as in the noncooperative case.

With the market solution, too much pollution is produced. The market solution is therefore not Pareto optimal; that is, everyone could be made better off through cooperation. Moreover, when N is large, the difference can be substantial. Equations (14) and (17) are special cases of a result due to Samuelson (1954).

The lack of a market for pollution is what causes the market failure (i.e., it is why the market solution is not Pareto optimal). There are two aspects to this lack: pollution is not priced, and it is commonly owned. It is the second aspect, however, that is crucial.

To see this, consider the case where P is a private good, so that only $P_i$ enters the profit function $\pi_i$. In this case, even though pollution does not have a market price, it has a shadow price, $c_p$, which gives the correct signals. When P is a common-property resource, in contrast, the private shadow value is not equal to the social shadow value, and there is a market failure.

Here there is definite cause for public intervention. The marginal social damage of pollution is $Nc_p$. If the government charged the firm a tax T per unit of pollution generated equal to the difference between the social and private damage, $T = Nc_p - c_p = (N - 1)c_p$, optimality would be achieved. That is, the firm would set marginal benefit, $(1 - C_q)/\beta$, equal to marginal cost, $c_p + (N - 1)c_p$, which would result in (17).

To see how an increase in population affects pollution, consider the aggregate relationship

$$P = \beta Q = \beta H(K,L,P) . \tag{18}$$

Differentiating with respect to L, we have

$$dP/dL = \beta(H_K \ dK/dL + H_L + H_p \ dP/dL) . \tag{19}$$

Holding capital fixed, (19) simplifies to

$$dP/dL = \beta H_L/(1 - \beta H_p) . \tag{20}$$

Because $H_L$ is positive and $H_p$ is negative, $dP/dL$ is a positive number; that is, a larger population implies more pollution. If there are diminishing returns to labor, however, and if $|H_p|$ does not diminish with P (that is, if the marginal effect of pollution does not fall as pollution increases), then the marginal effect of population growth on pollution falls with increases in the population. Under these circumstances, for example, a doubling of the population results in a less than doubling of pollution. This is because pollution increases proportionately with output, but an increase in the labor force increases output less than proportionately. Also, as population and pollution increase, pollution is an ever more serious drag on output, reinforcing the first effect.

To derive these results, however, it was assumed that the relationship between pollution and output is linear. If the natural environment regenerates itself up to a point, but after that point can no longer cope with increases in pollution, the relationship between P and Q will be nonlinear with

$$P = \beta(Q), \qquad \beta'(Q) = 0 \qquad Q \leq \bar{Q} ,$$
$$\beta'(Q) > 0, \qquad Q > \bar{Q} . \qquad (21)$$

It may also be the case that, once pollution gets started, it increases more than proportionately with increases in Q ( $\beta''(Q) > 0$). In this case, there will be no environmental degradation up to a point, but after that point, increases in population may result in more than proportionate increases in pollution.

Special problems arise when the common-property commodity is a renewable resource, such as a stock of fish or other wildlife, a forest, or plains used for grazing. Here, in addition to the usual common-property problems, we must consider the rate of growth of the stock as a function of its size.

In the biological literature, it is often maintained that, in the absence of intervention, the size of the stock of a renewable resource follows an S-shaped path. For example, suppose that the resource is a forest that has just been cut down. Initially, because there are no mature trees to drop seeds, growth will be extremely slow. As trees begin to grow, however, more seeds will be produced and growth will become more rapid. In this initial phase, in fact, because trees produce trees, growth will be approximately exponential. Eventually, however, as the forest becomes crowded, growth will begin to taper off until finally it drops to zero when the carrying capacity is reached.

An S-shaped path, S = g(t), is depicted in Figure 1A. S represents the size of the stock, and t stands for time; C is the carrying capacity or ultimate limit to the size of the stock. The figure is drawn so that when the stock drops below some minimum, M, there is no growth. For example, it is obvious that if only one fish is left, it cannot reproduce, but even if several fish remain in a large ocean, the chances of a female fish finding a male at the time when eggs must be fertilized may be virtually zero.

The growth of the stock, S, is the slope of the function g(t),

$$\dot{S} = dS/dt = f(S) . \qquad (22)$$

We can analyze $\dot{S}$ as a function of S. When S is less than M, $\dot{S}$ is zero. As S increases beyond M, however, $\dot{S}$ begins to rise until it reaches a maximum at (C - M)/2 (assuming that the curve is symmetric); after this point, $\dot{S}$ begins to fall until it reaches zero again at C. $\dot{S}$ is graphed as a function of S in Figure 1B.

If the common-property resource is in steady-state equilibrium, the rate at which it is harvested each year, H, must equal the rate at which it replenishes itself, $\dot{S}$. Consider an arbitrary harvest rate H. Figure 1B shows that there are two points

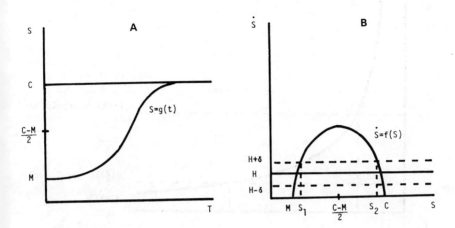

FIGURE 1   Growth Curves for a Renewable Resource

where $H = \dot{S}$, $S_1$, and $S_2$. At both $S_1$ and $S_2$, the rate at which the stock is harvested equals the rate at which it replenishes itself. From other points of view, however, the two points are very different.

Consider, for example, the ratio $H/S$. $H/S_1$ is close to one; that is, a very large fraction of the stock is harvested each year. In contrast, $H/S_2$ is large. In addition, there may be other differences.

Suppose, for example, that unit harvest cost, $C(H,S)/H$, is inversely proportional to the size of the stock, $S$,

$$C(H,S) = (\alpha/S)H .\qquad (23)$$

An inverse relationship could be due to many factors. For example, the time spent fishing for the same catch is much greater when the stock of fish is small. Similarly, for a forest, transport costs for the same number of trees cut are greater when the tree population is very sparse. Equation (23) implies that the cost per tree of harvesting $S_1$, $\alpha/S_1$ is much greater than the cost per tree of harvesting $S_2$, $\alpha/S_2$.

In writing down equation (22) and in drawing Figure 1, it was implicitly assumed that the relationship between $\dot{S}$ and $S$ is deterministic. For many renewable resources, however, the rate of growth may be stochastic and may depend on such exogenous factors as temperature and rainfall. For this reason, it may be more realistic to replace equation (22) with a stochastic version,

$$E(\dot{S}) = E(dS/dt) = f(S) ,\qquad (22')$$

where $E$ stands for the expected value. Now only the expected value of $\dot{S}$, $E(\dot{S})$, can be equated with $H$. What this means is

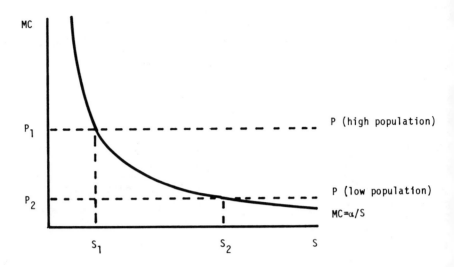

FIGURE 2   Marginal Cost as a Function of the Stock


that, although one can plan for a growth in the stock that equals
the harvest, the realized growth will differ from H by a random
factor.  Suppose, for example, that the expected value of $\dot{S}$ is
H, but that the realized value can fluctuate between H - $\delta$ and
H + $\delta$ .  These bounds are shown in Figure 1B as the dashed lines.
It should be noted that if S = $S_1$ and if the realized growth is
H - $\delta$ , the stock is very close to extinction (S $\simeq$ M).
     The two stocks $S_1$ and $S_2$ can be associated with different
populations.  Suppose, for example, that the commodity is sold
in a competitive market so that its price, P, equals the
marginal cost of harvesting, MC,

$$P = MC = \partial C / \partial H = \alpha / S .$$                                      (24)

When population is low, the ratio of consumption to the stock is
low, harvesting costs are low, and prices are low.  This corresponds to the point $S_2$ on the graph.  In contrast, when
population is large, H/S, harvesting costs, and prices are all
high.  One might ask why any society ends up at $S_1$ rather than
at $S_2$, paying more for the same consumption.  The answer is
that growth takes time.  Suppose, for example, that the resource
is a forest.  As the forest grows, harvesting costs fall.  If
people are willing to pay a price $P_1$ per tree, harvesting will
take place as soon as MC falls to $P_1$.  With less demand, people
are only willing to pay $P_2 < P_1$, and the trees remain in the
ground until MC reaches $P_2$.  This situation is depicted in
Figure 2.

Two things should be noted about the analysis. First, because the forest is commonly owned, all rents from it are dissipated. A private owner would perform an intertemporal profit calculation and would harvest when the present value of the profit stream from the forest was highest. In contrast, under common ownership, no individual could afford to wait for costs to fall because someone else would cut down the trees in the interim. There is thus a market failure.

Second, at point $S_1$, the chances of extinction or near extinction are much higher than at point $S_2$. At $S_1$, a random shock such as an extremely cold winter or a very prolonged drought could cause the stock to fall below M, where growth is zero. In contrast, at $S_2$ a similar shock would cause the stock to fall below $S_2$ where growth rates are higher than at $S_2$. With the first case, the species might never be seen again, whereas with the second, the stock would quickly renew itself and return to the steady-state level of $S_2$.

A final problem associated with the use of many environmental and renewable resources arises because they provide flows of unpriced services. For example, consider a forest. Forests are used for camping, hiking, and hunting. More important, however, they protect watersheds and keep agricultural soil from eroding. As a population grows, demands for all services from the forest increase, but, because commercial uses are priced whereas other uses are not, commercial activities dominate. Once again, because relative prices do not reflect relative values, there is a market failure.

To summarize the results of this section, we have seen that common-property environmental and renewable resources are sources of potentially serious market failures whose correction requires intervention or some form of cooperative behavior. When the common-property environmental resource is a bad (pollution) it is overproduced, and when it is a good (clean water, for example) it is underproduced. When the common-property resource is renewable (fish or grazing land, for example), it is generally overharvested and overgrazed to the point where the rents from the harvest are completely dissipated. In addition, problems associated with the combination of common ownership and population growth can lead to extinction of the species or to irreversible damage to the land.

It is the opinion of the author that the problems caused by common-property resources are much more serious than those posed by exhaustible resources (running out of oil, for example). One has only to glance at a newspaper to see that the foothills of the Himalayas are being deforested, that the sub-Sahara is becoming a desert, and that acid rain is destroying crops in most of the industrialized world. In addition, many of the effects of these problems are irreversible or at least onerous to counteract.

PROBLEMS WITH APPLYING THE THEORETICAL MODELS

In the previous section, formal models of production with
natural-resource inputs were derived. These models led to
seemingly simple testable relationships. For example, the size
of the elasticity of substitution between capital and natural
resources was seen to be an important parameter in determining
whether finite resources pose serious problems for sustained
consumption. In this section, empirical evidence bearing on
these matters is discussed. Particular attention is paid to the
difficulties encountered in trying to interpret this information.
The following areas are considered: problems with aggregation,
with measuring reserves and resources, with interpreting the
parameters of the aggregate production function, and with
measuring scarcity directly.


Aggregation

Theoretical models are attempts to condense real-world com-
plexities into a set of simple relationships that can be easily
analyzed. The process of condensation necessarily involves the
use of simplifying assumptions. One class of assumption enables
the modeler to treat broad groups of commodities as if they were
a single commodity and a large number of technologies as if they
were a single technology.

For example, in the last section "natural resources" were
modeled as a single homogeneous input, whereas in reality the
components, such as iron ore and crude petroleum, are very
dissimilar. In addition, the fiction of an aggregate production
function was maintained. This would make sense if an entire
economy were a giant factory that used natural resources for a
single purpose. In reality, however, an economy consists of
many dissimilar production processes that use resources for many
different purposes. It is therefore natural to ask whether, or
under what conditions, this sort of aggregation is valid.
Problems of aggregation across goods (inputs and outputs) and
across technologies are briefly touched on here. The subject is
very broad and cannot be covered in detail. The interested
reader is referred to Gorman (1953, 1968); Fisher (1965); and
Blackorby et al. (1978) for in-depth analysis.

In the modeling of production, the aggregate inputs capital,
labor, resources, and pollution were used. Each of these
consists of many heterogeneous commodities. To form an aggregate, it is necessary to condense many numbers (tons of iron ore
and barrels of petroleum, for example) into a single number R.
In addition, it was assumed that each aggregate commodity, with
the exception of pollution, has a price. Again, it is necessary
to condense many numbers (different wage rates, for example)
into a single number (the aggregate wage rate). In both cases,
an aggregator function or index number must be constructed.

A common practice is to construct a quantity (price) index
as a weighted average of individual quantities (prices) where

the weights are constant. If such a quantity index is constructed, the implication is that quantities are perfect substitutes so that prices move in a way that keeps their ratios constant. Further, if such a price index is constructed, the implication is that quantities are used in fixed proportions. The popularity of these indices lies in their ease of construction. Unfortunately, perfect price or quantity proportionality is rare, and therefore the implicit assumptions under which these indices are constructed are usually violated.

Another common practice is to choose a single characteristic (Btu value, for example, for energy) and form a quantity aggregate in terms of this characteristic. This practice is just a special case of the fixed weighted average. It suffers from an additional disadvantage: it is not clear that there exists a single important characteristic that all natural resources (capital equipment or workers) share. Lau (1982) discusses the construction of aggregates using several characteristics (strength, weight, and resistance to corrosion, for example, for materials); as the commodities aggregated become increasingly more diverse, however, the method becomes increasingly more complex.

There are more sophisticated methods of constructing indices that are less restrictive than the fixed weighted average. Diewert (1976), for example, discusses one class that he denotes "superlative." A larger question, however, is under what conditions a meaningful price or quantity aggregator exists, regardless of its functional form. The answer is well known: a price or quantity index for a subset of inputs used in production can be constructed from the prices and quantities of the constituent inputs alone if and only if the inputs in the subset are homothetically separable from other inputs used in production.

A technical discourse on the definition of homothetic separability can be found in the references cited earlier; the discussion here focuses on some of its implications. If a group of inputs (natural resources, for example) is homothetically separable from other inputs, then the way in which the inputs in the group can be substituted for one another in production is independent of the levels or characteristics of the inputs outside the group. This is a very strong assumption. To see its implications, consider the construction of an energy aggregate. Implicit in this construction is the assumption that the characteristics of the capital stock, for example, do not affect substitution possibilites among energy types. It is apt to be the case, however, that once a furnace or boiler is installed, it can burn only one type of fuel. Energy usage and substitution are therefore highly dependent on the capital stock. In addition, as the inputs that are aggregated are increasingly more dissimilar (fuel and nonfuel minerals, for example), the problems in forming a consistent aggregate are compounded. One might therefore ask why anyone attempts such an obviously inconsistent task. The answer is that it is necessary for tractability.

Often, in addition to aggregating inputs, one wishes to aggregate technologies, as, for example, when constructing an aggregate production function from the production functions of the individual plants or firms in the economy. It should be obvious that different firms and plants use inputs in different ways. Fortunately, from the modelers' point of view, if all commodities (inputs and outputs) are variable and if firms are price takers in input and output markets, there are no restrictions for consistent aggregation across technologies.

There are very strong assumptions, however. Most firms cannot freely vary their capital equipment, at least in the short run, and a regulated firm may be unable to choose certain levels of output production or input use. When some factors are fixed or when some agents have market power, the conditions for consistent technology aggregation are very restrictive (see, for example, Gorman, 1968).

The point of this discussion is not to master the conditions for consistent aggregation, but merely to realize the many underlying assumptions that are being tested when a seemingly simple hypothesis is subjected to scrutiny. For example, when one formulates and tests a statistical hypothesis about the elasticity of substitution between capital and resources in aggregate production, one is implicitly testing not only the magnitude of the elasticity, but also the conditions for consistent aggregation across inputs and technologies. This fact should be kept in mind when one examines empirical estimates of aggregate production parameters.

Measuring Reserves and Resources

In addition to the problems involved in constructing an aggregate measure of the flow of resources R, there are problems in measuring the stock S. In the following discussion, these aggregation problems are neglected, and the difficulties encountered in measuring the stock of a single commodity are discussed. It should be obvious that multicommodity stocks are still more difficult to deal with.

In modeling production with natural resources, it was assumed that the initial stock $S_0$ was known in advance with certainty. The way in which $S_0$ should be measured, however, was not considered. Three measures of resource stocks are commonly used by geologists: reserves, resources, and crustal abundance. The U.S. Geological Survey (1975:3) gives the following definitions:

A resource is a concentration of naturally occurring solid, liquid, or gaseous material in or on the earth's crust in such form that economic extraction of a commodity is currently or <u>potentially</u> feasible. A reserve is that portion of the identified resource from which a useable mineral or energy commodity can be economically and legally extracted <u>at the time of determination.</u>

The distinction between reserves and resources is based on economic factors, such as cost. In contrast, crustal abundance refers to the entire stock of a commodity in the earth's crust, regardless of extraction cost.

Suppose that we wish to construct a stock-supply curve--the total stock of a commodity that can be economically extracted at different prices. For this construction, we have only one point, "reserves," the quantity available at today's price and technology. In contrast, "resources" measures the quantity available at some conceivable price and state of knowledge. No one ever states what this price and knowledge might be--a doubling of price (halving of cost) or a change in these variables of several orders of magnitude--either of which could have been in the head of the geologist who made the estimate. In addition, "crustal abundance" may not be a quantity on the stock-supply curve at any price. A single atom of a commodity may be trapped in the earth's crust in such a way that no currently conceivable technology is capable of separating it from its surrounding material.

The distinction between reserves and resources on the one hand and crustal abundance on the other is very important. The ratio of crustal abundance to resources for many commodities is of the order of $10^6$; the ratio for reserves is still larger. Yet no one knows what fraction of this vast stock could be available under the most optimistic technology forecasts.

Reserves is the measure most often used by economic modelers. It is, however, unsatisfactory for many reasons. For one thing, it constantly shifts. A temporary decline in the price of copper on commodity markets, for example, may cause a substantial drop in estimated copper reserves. In addition, not only does extraction subtract from reserves, as in our simple model, but exploration adds to them. Because it is expensive to explore for ore bodies many decades in advance of potential use, reserves may be little more than working inventories. That is, companies may be happy with their reserve figures as long as they exceed yearly production by some factor. Perhaps companies explore only when reserves drop below this level.

In spite of the difficulties inherent in the use of any commodity-stock measure, reserves are analyzed here in some detail. Table 1 shows estimated world mineral reserves, in $10^6$ metric tons of contained metal, for seven major nonfuel mineral commodities in 1968 and 1979. It can be seen that, in spite of increased consumption of every commodity in almost every year, reserves grew faster than consumption.7

The second part of Table 1 shows consumption of the same commodities by developing and developed countries in 1980. It can be seen that, in spite of possessing only one-third of the world's population, the developed countries consume approximately 93 percent of the nonfuel minerals. The final row in Table 1 shows reserves divided by consumption, R/C. There are many ways to interpret this number: a pessimistic interpretation is that, at current consumption levels, we will run out of this commodity in R/C years; an optimistic interpretation is that mining companies are happy with reserves that will last R/C years and only

TABLE 1  World Nonfuel Mineral Reserves and Nonfuel Mineral Consumption
($10^6$ metric tons contained metal)

|  | Aluminum | Copper | Iron | Lead | Nickel | Tin | Zinc |
|---|---|---|---|---|---|---|---|
| Reserves |  |  |  |  |  |  |  |
| 1968[a] | 1,060 | 200 | 80,000 | 86 | 67 | 4.5 | 112 |
| 1979[b] | 4,717 | 494 | 103,000 | 127 | 60 | 10.0 | 162 |
| Percent change | 348 | 147 | 29 | 48 | -10 | 122 | 45 |
| Consumption (1980) |  |  |  |  |  |  |  |
| Developing[c] | 1.4 | 0.7 | 34.8 | 0.4 | 0.02 | 0.03 | 0.8 |
| Developed[c] | 18.4 | 8.8 | 435.7 | 4.7 | 0.72 | 0.22 | 5.5 |
| Total | 19.8 | 9.5 | 470.5 | 5.1 | 0.74 | 0.25 | 6.3 |
| R/C | 238 | 52 | 236 | 25 | 81 | 45 | 26 |

Note:  These figures are estimates.

[a]Data from Fishman and Landsberg (1972).
[b]Data from U.S. Bureau of Mines (1980).
[c]Data from U.N. Industrial Development Organization (1984).


explore when reserves drop substantially below this level. Undoubtedly, neither of these interpretations is completely correct.

An analysis of which nonfuel minerals are in short supply is beyond the scope of this chapter. It is interesting to note, however, that a recently published comprehensive study by Leontief et al. (1983) concluded that only four metals are likely to be exhausted on a global scale before 2030: lead, zinc, silver, and mercury. Two of these, lead and zinc, are included in Table 1, and they are the ones with the lowest reserve-consumption ratios. Leontief et al. foresee no problems in finding substitutes for the exhausted commodities.

The Leontief projections may be pessimistic for two reasons. First, they assume rates of growth for world GNP of over 3 percent per year, which is considerably above the rates experienced currently. Second, input-output models, even those as sophisticated as this, often underestimate substitution possibilities due to relative price changes.

The situation with respect to energy reserves is somewhat different. Table 2 shows estimated world crude petroleum reserves in $10^9$ metric tons for 4 years spanning three decades. The second column of this table shows estimated reserves divided by the corresponding year's consumption. This number increases for the first decade, but then begins to fall. Unlike the non-fuel minerals, each of which constitutes a small fraction of aggregate input cost, petroleum is a very important input to industrial production. In spite of OPEC, the world economy has

TABLE 2  World Crude Petroleum Reserves ($10^9$ metric tons)

| Year | Reserves | Reserves/ Consumption |
|------|----------|----------------------|
| 1950[a] | 11.8 | 22 |
| 1960[a] | 40.8 | 37 |
| 1972[a] | 91.4 | 35 |
| 1980[b] | 78.0 | 27 |

[a]Data from Institute of Petroleum Information, cited by Fisher (1981).
[b]Data from United Nations (1980).

become accustomed to cheap supplies of petroleum, and an adjustment to dwindling reserves could be extremely painful.

Table 3 shows world energy reserves and energy consumption by developing and developed economies in 1980, measured in $10^9$ tons of oil equivalent, for coal, crude petroleum, and natural gas. Just as with the nonfuel minerals, the developed economies consume a disproportionately large fraction of each type of fuel. The final row of Table 3 shows reserves divided by consumption. It can be seen that the other energy sources are not as problematic as petroleum.

Interpreting Parameters of the Aggregate Production Function

In the previous section, several important aggregate production parameters were identified. These include the capital-resource elasticity of substitution $\sigma$, capital and resource shares of total cost $\alpha_1$ and $\alpha_2$, the resource-augmenting rate of technical change $\lambda$, and the output-pollution proportionality parameter $\beta$. Empirical evidence about the signs and magnitudes of each of these parameters is discussed in turn.

The closest thing to the capital-resource elasticity of substitution $\sigma$ that is commonly measured is the capital-energy elasticity of substitution $\sigma_{KE}$.[8] Many researchers, including Berndt and Wood (1975), Griffen and Gregory (1976), Magnus (1979), and Pindyck (1979), have estimated this parameter at an economy-wide level. Table 4 contains their estimates.

A cursory glance at this table reveals that the experts do not agree even as to the sign of this parameter. Many explanations for this disagreement have been proposed. Griffen and Gregory (1976), Pindyck (1979), and Griffen (1981) note that their studies use cross-sectional data by country, whereas the other two studies use time-series data for a single country. They claim that because regional energy-price differences persist

TABLE 3  World Energy Reserves and Consumption in 1980 ($10^9$ tons of oil equivalent)

|            | Coal  | Percent | Petroleum | Percent | Natural Gas | Percent |
|------------|-------|---------|-----------|---------|-------------|---------|
| Reserves   | 539   |         | 78        |         | 66          |         |
| Consumption |      |         |           |         |             |         |
| Developing | 0.14  | .07     | 0.63      | .22     | 0.10        | .08     |
| Developed  | 2.01  | .93     | 2.25      | .78     | 1.09        | .92     |
| Total      | 2.15  |         | 2.88      |         | 1.19        |         |
| R/C        | 251   |         | 27        |         | 55          |         |

Sources:  U.N. (1980); U.N. Industrial Development Organization (1984).

over long periods of time, cross-sectional studies pick up long-run substitution possibilities that cannot be observed in time-series data.

Another explanation for the different findings is proposed by Berndt and Wood (1979), who note that their study uses four factors: capital K, labor L, energy E, and intermediate materials M, whereas Griffen and Gregory and Pindyck consider only K, L, and E. If K, L, and E are not separable from M, this exclusion biases the estimates of $\sigma_{KE}$ upward.

A third explanation is proposed by Field and Grebenstein (1980), who note that the treatment of the capital stock varies by study. Griffen and Gregory and Pindyck use a measure that includes working capital and land, whereas the measure used by Berndt and Wood and Magnus excludes these factors. Field and Grebenstein disaggregate the capital stock into working and physical capital, and find that physical capital and energy are predominantly complements, whereas working capital and energy are predominantly substitutes. What they do not emphasize is that their results cast doubt on the existence of a capital aggregate and thus on the meaningfulness of the entire question.[9]

A final $\sigma_{KE}$ issue, rarely discussed in the literature, is the choice of an elasticity of substitution measure. In the simple model, with labor fixed, there are only two inputs: capital and resources. Under these conditions, $\sigma$ is well defined by equation (7). With multiple inputs, however, the definition of  involves partial derivatives, and it makes a difference what is held constant when the derivatives are taken. Most research-ers use the Hicks-Allen elasticity of substitution (Allen and Hicks, 1934) because it possesses certain desirable theoretical properties (see, for example, Berndt and Christensen, 1973). There is, however, another partial elasticity of substitution--the Morishima elasticity (Morishima, 1967)--that is equally

TABLE 4  Estimates of the Capital-Energy Elasticity of Substitution

| $\sigma_{KE}$ | Country | Data | Source |
|---|---|---|---|
| -3.2 | U.S. | Time-series | Berndt and Wood (1975) |
| 1.02/1.07 | 9 industrial | Cross-section | Griffen and Gregory (1976) |
| -2.3 | Netherlands | Time-series | Mangus (1979) |
| .64/1.43 | 10 industrial | Cross-section | Pindyck (1979) |

desirable theoretically (see, for example, Blackorby and Russell, 1981), but rarely used in practice. When the Morishima elasticity is computed using the Berndt-Wood estimated parameters, the result is $\sigma_{KE} = .31$ and $\sigma_{EK} = .33$,[10] implying that the two inputs are substitutes. A change in the definition of $\sigma$ can thus reverse substitution-complementarity findings, even when the same data set and estimated parameters are used in the calculations.

Given the variability in the estimates of $\sigma$, it is difficult to conclude anything about its implications for sustained consumption. In addition, even if we knew the value of  for the factor shares observed today, what is important is the value when R is very small (when we are running out of resources).[11] Any information gleaned from current estimates of  is thus apt to be misleading when extrapolated to the issue of interest.

$\alpha_1$ and $\alpha_2$, capital and resource shares in total cost, are easier to measure than $\sigma$, but just as difficult to interpret. For example, Berndt and Wood (1975) find that in the United States, capital's share has historically been .054 and energy's share .045. Energy undoubtably accounts for the largest fraction of R, but it is not the total. $\alpha_1$ and $\alpha_2$ are therefore probably almost equal. Also, even if we could make definitive statements about the relative size of $\alpha_1$ and $\alpha_2$ today, we would not know what their sizes would be when R is very small. It is only with the simple Cobb-Douglas production function that these shares are constant.

The factor-using or factor-saving rate of technical change is another macroparameter of interest. Because of the difficulties involved in aggregating across technologies, technical change is most accurately measured at the firm or industry level. However, more aggregate estimates of technical change have been attempted. For example, Berndt and Kaled (1979) formulate and estimate a model of producer behavior for aggregate U.S. manufacturing; they find little evidence of technical change of any sort. This result is not surprising when studies at a more disaggregate level are considered (for example, Moroney and Trapani, 1981; Jorgenson and Fraumeni, 1981). These researchers find that technical change has been resource-using in some sectors and resource-saving in others. Meaningful conclusions about the size of  at the aggregate level are therefore not possible.

Statistical esimates of the output-pollution parameter $\beta$ are not common. One reason for this is the difficulty of measuring pollution. Most factors of production are bought and sold in markets where transactions are recorded. In contrast, firms have no incentive to measure polluting activity unless required to do so by law. It is widely believed, however, that threshold effects are common. That is, the earth's environment is capable of cleansing itself up to a point. After this point has been reached, degeneration may set in rapidly. This pattern implies that   is not a constant parameter, but is a nonlinear function of output.

The overall conclusion that can be drawn from the analysis of aggregate production-function parameters is that they do not tell us what we want to know. For this reason, it may be desirable to give up the attempt to measure potential scarcity effects indirectly through a production function. An alternative is to analyze direct indicators of scarcity.


Measuring Scarcity

As a resource becomes scarce, it is hoped that the market will signal impending shortages. Several indices that might measure scarcity have been proposed. The most common are relative price (the ratio of an extractive-industry price index to an overall price index), unit cost (labor or labor plus capital inputs per unit of extractive-industry output), and rental rate (the marginal value of the resource in the ground). Many authors have debated the merits of the different measures (see, for example, Brown and Field, 1978; Smith, 1978; and Fisher, 1979). It is not the purpose here to add to this debate; instead, empirical evidence concerning each index is examined in an attempt to see what sort of signals we are receiving.

The classic study is that by Barnett and Morse (1963), who looked at both relative-price and unit-cost trends. They concluded that, because both indices were falling over time, scarcity was not a problem. An update by Barnett (1979) reaches the same conclusion--that there is no sign of an upturn in either unit cost or relative price.

Other researchers who examine price trends, however, are not in complete agreement with Barnett. Smith (1979a) looks at the stability of the coefficients of the estimated price-trend relationships and concludes that the data are too volatile to support definitive conclusions. Slade (1982) finds that, after a substantial initial decline, in recent years there is evidence of an upturn in the price paths of many mineral commodities.

The finding of U-shaped price paths is not difficult to explain. Improvements in extractive technology and deterioration in ore quality are counter-balancing influences on production cost. The first may dominate initially, but may be superceded by the second in later years. Peterson and Maxwell (1979) document the history of ore grade-technology tradeoffs for many metals and claim that they have been the dominant determinants of metal prices in the long run.

Rent is more difficult to measure directly. Fisher (1979) and Devarajan and Fisher (1982) argue that rent can be measured indirectly. They advocate the use of unit-exploration cost as an approximation to scarcity rent and find evidence that, at least for petroleum, this cost has been rising. It is interesting to note that increases in exploration costs began prior to 1973, the first year of OPEC price increases; exploration costs were thus rising in a period of stable prices.

To summarize, if scarcity is measured by unit-extraction cost, there is little sign of an increase. If, on the other hand, relative price or unit-exploration cost is used as a scarcity index, and if these indices are examined on a commodity-by-commodity basis, there is weak evidence of increased scarcity for many commodities.

## SOME PARTICULAR PROBLEMS

### The Energy-GNP Relationship

Thus far, the analysis has been at a highly aggregate level. It is of considerable interest, however, to know how different countries, particularly those at different stages of development, use natural-resource commodities. For example, if it is found that as economies develop, they use natural resources at an ever-increasing rate, the implications of scarcity for development are grave. If in contrast it is found that, after an initial stage of rapid industrialization, natural-resource usage begins to taper off, the outlook is less dire.

In this section, the energy-per-capita/GNP-per capita relationship is examined in detail. The focus is on energy because it is by far the most important natural-resource input to production.

It seems clear a priori that increases in GNP per capita result in increases in energy use. What is not so clear is the shape of this relationship. It is possible that energy use grows at an ever-increasing rate. More likely, however, is that, as economies become mature, the importance of the service sector rises, while that of the industrial sector falls. Because services are less energy-intensive than manufacturing, energy use per capita may increase at a decreasing rate and even decline.

A statistical test of these conflicting hypotheses can be made as follows. Let $GPC_i$ and $EPC_i$ stand for GNP per capita and energy consumption per capita in economy i. An equation of the form

$$EPC_i = a_0 + a_1 GPC_i + a_2 GPC_i^2 \tag{25}$$

can be estimated. $a_1$, the linear-trend coefficient, is expected to be positive. It is $a_2$, the quadratic-trend coefficient, that is of interest: if energy use per capita grows at an ever-increasing rate, $a_2$ will be positive; if it increases at a decreasing rate and eventually falls, $a_2$ will be negative; and if the relationship is proportional, $a_2$ will be zero.

To conduct this test, cross-sectional data on GNP and energy consumption per capita are required for many countries at various stages of development. These data can be found in Geze, Valladao, and Lacoste (1983), who gathered data from many public sources, such as the U.N., the World Bank, and the Organization for Economic Cooperation and Development (O.E.C.D.), and recalibrated them so that the units would be as consistent as possible across countries. The data used here are for 1982.

Table 5 shows population (in $10^6$ people), GNP per capita (in $10^3$ U.S. dollars), and energy consumption per capita (in $10^9$ tons of coal equivalent) for 49 countries. These data were used to fit equation (25), with results as shown in Table 6 and Figure 3.

The first row of Table 6 shows estimated coefficients for equation (25). The numbers shown in parentheses under the estimated coefficients are the corresponding t statistics. It can be seen that $a_1$ is positive and statistically significant as expected. In addition, $a_2$ is negative and significant, implying that as economic development proceeds, energy use per capita increases at a decreasing rate and eventually falls.

Figure 3 locates the individual countries on the energy per capita/GNP per capita axes (the dots) and shows the estimated relationship (the center curve). The estimated relationship plus and minus two standard deviations is plotted above and below the center curve (the dashed lines); almost all countries fall within this band. It can be seen that the United States and Canada are obvious outliers. That is, energy consumption per capita in these countries is much higher than the equation predicts. For this reason, a dummy variable, DNA, equal to one for the U.S. and Canada and to zero for all other countries, was added to equation (22), with results as shown in the second row of Table 6. Adding the dummy variable does not change the conclusions. The signs of $a_0$, $a_1$, and $a_2$ are unchanged, and if anything the coefficients are more significant.

In addition to the data on GNP and energy consumption per capita, Geze, Valladao, and Lacoste give fractions of the working population that are associated with the agricultural, industrial, and service sectors for 33 of the 49 countries. The fractions in agriculture and in industry are shown in the fourth and fifth columns of Table 5; the residual is assumed to be in the service sector.

To test the hypothesis that per capita energy consumption goes up with industrial development and down as the service sector grows, two additional variables were added to equation (22): XIND is the fraction of the labor force associated with industry, while XSER is the fraction in the service sector. The final row of Table 6 shows the result of reestimating equation (22). Just as before, $a_1$ is positive and $a_2$ is negative; in addition, the coefficient of XIND is positive, whereas that of XSER is negative. All five coefficients are statistically significant.

TABLE 5   GNP and Energy Consumption per Capita

| Country | Population | GPC | PPC | XAGR | XIND |
|---|---|---|---|---|---|
| USSR | 270.00000 | 4.55000 | 5.68889 | 0.19000 | 0.38500 |
| USA | 232.00000 | 12.98700 | 10.10776 | 0.03100 | 0.21700 |
| China | 1008.00000 | 0.51600 | 0.56746 | 0.69000 | 0.19000 |
| India | 694.00000 | 0.20500 | 0.19597 | 0.64000 | 0.18000 |
| Japan | 118.00000 | 8.85400 | 3.56780 | 0.08700 | 0.33300 |
| Brazil | 125.00000 | 2.10900 | 0.73600 | 0.29900 | 0.24400 |
| Nigeria | 82.00000 | 0.09000 | 0.21341 | 0.52300 | 0.19000 |
| Indonesia | 153.00000 | 0.57300 | 0.23529 | 0.53800 | 0.12300 |
| Australia | 15.00000 | 10.45400 | 5.93333 | 0.05700 | 0.27200 |
| Pakistan | 87.00000 | 0.31700 | 0.21839 | 0.50800 | 0.19600 |
| Canada | 25.00000 | 11.75400 | 9.76000 | 0.04902 | 0.23500 |
| Argentina | 28.00000 | 2.88000 | 1.71429 | 0.11700 | 0.25500 |
| West Germany | 62.00000 | 10.65900 | 5.80645 | 0.05500 | 0.39900 |
| France | 54.00000 | 9.94100 | 4.72222 | 0.07900 | 0.31900 |
| United Kingdom | 56.00000 | 8.36800 | 5.55357 | 0.01800 | 0.33400 |
| Italy | 56.00000 | 6.17600 | 3.32143 | 0.12100 | 0.32400 |
| Spain | 38.00000 | 4.76300 | 2.36842 | 0.13600 | 0.34800 |
| Poland | 36.00000 | 3.90000 | 6.66667 | 0.38600 | 0.31900 |
| Yugoslavia | 23.00000 | 2.56800 | 2.26087 | 0.34500 | 0.20400 |
| Iran | 39.00000 | 0.79700 | 1.20513 | 0.36900 | 0.31000 |
| South Africa | 26.00000 | 3.01200 | 3.53846 | 0.17000 | 0.26700 |
| Mexico | 73.00000 | 3.07700 | 1.72603 | 0.35200 | 0.25300 |
| Turkey | 47.00000 | 1.12200 | 0.70213 | 0.55100 | 0.16100 |
| East Germany | 17.00000 | 7.18000 | 7.29412 | 0.10400 | 0.50900 |
| South Korea | 39.00000 | 1.63400 | 1.41026 | 0.28800 | 0.26600 |
| Egypt | 45.00000 | 0.69700 | 0.48889 | 0.38900 | 0.18700 |
| Philippines | 51.00000 | 0.78000 | 0.35294 | 0.48200 | 0.14000 |
| Thailand | 49.00000 | 0.75800 | 0.32653 | 0.71100 | 0.09600 |
| Zaire | 29.00000 | 0.17000 | 0.06897 | 0.73700 | 0.13000 |
| Algeria | 20.00000 | 2.11400 | 1.40000 | 0.24000 | 0.23500 |
| Ethiopia | 33.00000 | 0.13500 | 0.02424 | 0.78500 | 0.05000 |
| Cuba | 10.00000 | 2.68400 | 1.35000 | 0.22800 | 0.29900 |
| Israel | 4.00000 | 5.45000 | 2.25000 | 0.05800 | 0.29900 |
| Sweden | 8.30000 | 11.84000 | 5.16867 | | |
| Switzerland | 6.50000 | 14.79900 | 3.49231 | | |
| Denmark | 5.10000 | 10.92000 | 4.90190 | | |
| Norway | 4.10000 | 13.71300 | 5.95122 | | |
| Belgium | 10.00000 | 8.42000 | 6.10000 | | |
| Netherlands | 14.00000 | 9.65100 | 5.85714 | | |
| Austria | 7.50000 | 8.84500 | 4.00000 | | |
| New Zealand | 3.20000 | 8.22800 | 3.34375 | | |
| Romania | 22.50000 | 2.34000 | 4.40000 | | |
| Bulgaria | 8.90000 | 4.15000 | 5.39326 | | |
| Venezuela | 15.00000 | 2.81700 | 3.00000 | | |
| Ireland | 3.50000 | 5.04900 | 3.31429 | | |
| Chile | 11.50000 | 2.44900 | 0.91304 | | |
| Greece | 9.80000 | 4.00000 | 2.27551 | | |
| Panama | 2.00000 | 2.68800 | 0.90000 | | |
| Uruguay | 3.00000 | 3.04500 | 0.86667 | | |

TABLE 6  Estimated Energy-GNP Relationships

| Number | Constant | GPC | $GPC^2$ | DNA | XIND | XSER | $R^2$ | F | Number of Observations |
|---|---|---|---|---|---|---|---|---|---|
|   | $\alpha_0$ | $\alpha_1$ | $\alpha_2$ |   |   |   |   |   |   |
| 1 | -.091 | .942$^a$ | -.035$^a$ |   |   |   | .68 | 50 | 49 |
|   |   | (5.1) | (-2.6) |   |   |   |   |   |   |
| 2 | -.165 | 1.03$^a$ | -.049$^a$ | 4.84$^a$ |   |   | .80 | 60 | 49 |
|   |   | (6.9) | (-4.3) | (5.1) |   |   |   |   |   |
| 3 | -.006 | .996$^a$ | -.043$^a$ | 5.93$^a$ | 7.15$^b$ | -4.63$^a$ | .90 | 51 | 33 |
|   |   | (2.9) | (-1.7) | (5.0) | (2.2) | (-2.5) |   |   |   |

[a]Denotes significance at the 99 percent confidence level.
[b]Denotes significance at the 95 percent confidence level.

The statistical analysis thus shows that energy use per capita increases with industrialization and falls with the importance of the service sector. In addition, the relationship between per capita energy use and per capita GNP is not an ever-increasing one. As an economy becomes more mature, energy use per capita begins to taper off and eventually falls.

The implications of these results for the relationship between natural-resource constraints and increases in economic well-being are several. The slope of the graph in Figure 3 indicates the amount of energy required to move from one position to another. It can be seen that for poor countries, industrialization is very expensive in terms of increased energy use. When a poor country begins a program of rapid industrialization, resource constraints are apt to be very severe. On the one hand, per capita income is meager, and on the other, resource requirements are large. The income with which to purchase the natural-resource commodities (if the country is not a net supplier) may be difficult to come by. Moreover, if the scarcity of natural-resource commodities increases, as their prices rise, these constraints will become increasingly binding.

Problems are least severe for mature economies. Income per capita is highest, and resource requirements per capita are modest. The higher income should be sufficient to purchase the required resources, even for countries with low resource endownments.

## Destruction of Tropical Forests

An important event today is the destruction of moist tropical forests. The salient issues relating to this process are assessed here without any attempt at quantification. That is, the discussion is somewhat anecdotal, with no effort made to provide the sorts of numbers that could be used in a cost-benefit study.

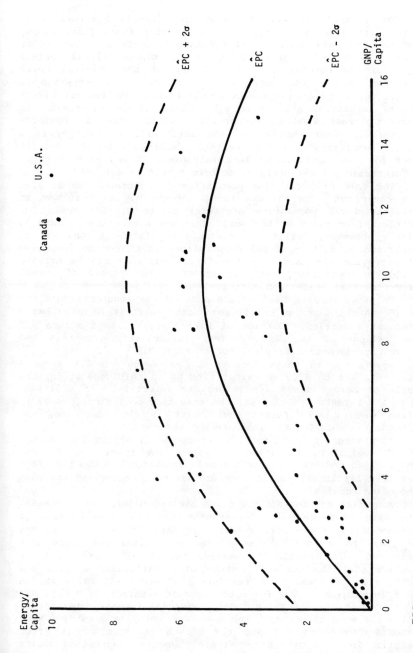

FIGURE 3  Per Capita Energy Use as a Function of Per Capita GNP

To original settlers of any region, forests are both great
assets and great problems.  Forests provide fuel, food, tools,
and building materials, but if the land is to be used for crops,
trees must be cut down and disposed of, commercially if markets
exist or by burning otherwise.  Many of the original North
American forests no longer exist; the land was converted to
agricultural use long ago.  It should be obvious that the clearing of forests is not per se a "problem;" it may be possible to
convert forest land to higher-value uses.  Just as obvious,
however, is that the destruction of forests is not per se a
social benefit; wood can be wantonly destroyed, and alternative
uses for the land may be less valuable.  In any assessment of
deforestation, these conflicting forces must be weighed.

The role of increasing population in deforestation is also
not clear cut.  On the one hand, forests may be cut down to
mitigate local population pressures or to provide homes for
settlers from parts of the world that are overcrowded.  Just as
likely, however, forests in sparsely populated regions may be
exploited by multi-national corporations that have no intention
of occupying the land.  In the latter case, it may be growing
worldwide population, with consequent higher prices of forest
products, that leads to clearing.

Tropical forests lie on each side of the equator around the
world.  A third are in Brazil and another quarter in other Latin
American countries.  Outside of Latin America, West Africa and
the islands of the East Indies, particularly Indonesia and
Zaire, are important tropical forest regions.

Vegetation in these forests is extremely dense.  Because
nutrients are to a large extent tied up in this vegetation, the
soils of forest lands are relatively infertile.  In addition,
when the forests are cleared, the resulting ecological change is
often severe.  The forest environment is thus delicate, and
alternative uses for the land are not abundant.

At present, forests house an enormous variety of life forms.
The biological interrelationships among these species can be very
complicated and are often only poorly understood.  Thus far there
has been little systematic research aimed at unraveling the many
ecological chains.

Many tropical forests are being cleared today.  In Indonesia,
the main force behind deforestation has been the logging of
hardwoods for the export market.  In many instances, there are
no plans for commercial use of the land after the trees have
been cut.  In Brazil, the extreme variety of types of trees
implies that the number of trees of a particular species per
hectare is low, and that therefore the commercial value of the
wood is marginal.  The force behind deforestation in Brazil has
been commercial ranching and not commercial forestry operations;
often the wood is burned.  Table 7 shows both the growth of wood
exports from Indonesia and the growth of meat exports from
Brazil.  These exports have certainly been an increasing source
of foreign exchange for the two countries.

There are several additional facts that are useful in
assessing the deforestation of tropical regions.  First, the

TABLE 7   Growth of Selected Exports from Countries That
Possess the Principal Tropical Forests

Growth of Roundwood and Sawnwood Exports from Indonesia,
1961-79 (1,000 m³)

| | |
|---|---|
| 1961 | 207 |
| 1970 | 8,031 |
| 1979 | 21,054 |
| | |
| Growth Rate<br>(% per year) | 27.5 |

Growth of Meat and Livestock Exports from Brazil,
1955-79 (1,000 mt.)

| | |
|---|---|
| 1955 | 2,590 |
| 1960 | 11,210 |
| 1970 | 125,210 |
| 1979 | 120,235 |
| | |
| Growth Rate<br>(% per year) | 16.6 |

Source:   Repetto and Homes (1983).

real prices of wood and wood products have consistenly risen
over the last century.  As an example, the real price of sawlogs
in the U.S. rose from $7 (per m. B. ft) in 1870 to $81 in 1979,
an increase of 1,150 percent over the period.  This corresponds
to a 2.2 percent growth rate per year.  The rise in real prices
of wood and forest products · is evidence of an increasing
scarcity of trees.

It may also be observed that the rate at which tropical
forests are being destroyed is not extremely fast.  For example,
a recent Food and Agriculture Organization (FAO) study (1982)
estimates the rate of deforestation of world tropical broadleaf
forests at 7.1 million hectares per year; this estimate implies
a rate of destruction of .60 percent per year.  The rate of
deforestation, of course, varies by country and by the source of
the estimate.  Some of these estimates are shown in Table 8.
The numbers in the table are uniformly lower than .60 percent,
the overall average.  This is because for some countries not
included in the table, the rate of deforestation is considerably
higher than .60 percent.

So far, the picture looks relatively rosy.  Developing countries are exploiting a vast natural resource of increasing value
to gain needed foreign exchange, and at the same time, the rate
of deforestation is not extremely high.  However, there are other
factors that indicate the many problems underlying this picture.

First, tropical-forest environments are very fragile, and
alternative uses for the land have low commercial value.  An

TABLE 8  Deforestation Rates for Selected Countries

| Country | Percent Annual Change[a] | Percent Annual Change[b] |
|---|---|---|
| Bolivia | -.44 | -.15 |
| Brazil | -.25 | -.41 |
| Indonesia | -.11 | -.47 |
| Zaire | -.23 | -.16 |

[a]Data from Food and Agriculture Organization Yearbook.
[b]Data from United Nations Environment Programme.

Source:  Sedjo and Clawson (1984).

important resource may therefore be destroyed for a one-time profit, resulting in a permanent loss to society.

Second, many of the services that the forests yield are unpriced. The most important of these is the protection of watersheds and downstream agricultural land. When the forests are destroyed, the result is apt to be a deterioration in water quality and the erosion of soil in more fertile areas.

In addition to local unpriced services, forests provide global unpriced services. A consequence of the destruction of the forests may be the extinction of many unique plant and animal life forms. It is estimated that 25 to 50 percent of the world's species reside in tropical forests, and it is clear that the habitats of many of these unique genetic resources are threatened. A final unpriced service of the forests is the absorption of $CO_2$. Concern is often expressed about the dire consequences for world climate that result from increased $CO_2$ in the atmosphere. In particular, the resultant warming effect can lead to radical changes in growing patterns. A combination of greater use of fossil fuels, particularly coal, and accelerated deforestation could speed up a process whose consequences are difficult to predict with any accuracy, but are surely undesirable.

The rising real price of wood signals increased prosperity for the owners of forest resources. It also signals increased scarcity of wood and wood products. If markets operate efficiently, owners of forests will use their resources in a way that maximizes the present value of the rent from the forests. There is much evidence, however, that markets do not operate efficiently. The common-property nature of tropical moist forests implies that trees will be cut too soon at high cost, and that therefore all rents will be dissipated. In addition, because owners are performing static profit calculations (because of the common-ownership problem), the price of wood may not reflect its true scarcity value. That is, when static calculations are performed, user costs are ignored. Finally, when there are rents to be earned, the beneficiaries may not be the owners of the forest. Instead, they may be multinational firms. Governments of developing countries have accelerated commercial logging operations in their countries through the use of generous incentives and concessions to foreign firms.

All of the above factors lead to the following conclusion: it is highly unlikely that tropical forests are being exploited at a rate and in a manner that maximizes social surplus. This conclusion is not surprising, given the difficulties involved in managing a resource that is commonly owned, yields valuable unpriced services, and involves markets for the priced services that function imperfectly.

The role played by growing population in the process of deforestation is not straightforward. In Indonesia, some forest clearing is due to programs of resettlement; in Brazil, however, the tropical population is sparse and is not in need of land for settlement. In both countries, a growth in worldwide population, coupled with higher prices for wood and falling transport costs, has been much more important than the growth of the local population in driving the destruction of the forests.


POLICY ISSUES

In addition to the physical problems of resource use and their relationship to economic well-being, there are many policy issues. These include the need for international cooperation about natural-resource objectives, the changes in income distribution that accompany policy decisions, and the choice among many instruments for achieving resource-policy goals. The purpose of this section is to discuss these policy issues.


International Cooperation

Most of the discussion of common-property problems was put in the context of competing firms. The model, however, applies equally well to different countries. The lesson to be learned is clear: noncooperative behavior is not optimal; everyone could be made better off through mutual cooperation. However, international enforcement of cooperative agreements presents special problems. In the case of firms in a single country, the government can play the role of monitor and enforcer. If firms are seen to cheat (by producing too much pollution, for example) they can be punished. Unfortunately, it is much more difficult to find an effective international monitoring and enforcement agency. Even when international organizations such as the United Nations exist, their powers are very weak.

To see why this is such a serious problem, consider the following example. Each of N countries can adopt a high-cost/low-pollution or a low-cost/high-pollution technology. All countries will be better off if they can cooperate and use the

low-pollution technology. However, given that N - 1 countries
have adopted the low-pollution technology, the N'th country will
prefer to adopt the high-pollution technology. Therefore, each
country unilaterally has an incentive to cheat, but when all
cheat, all are worse off.

The above example is a special case of a well-known problem
in economics called the "prisoner's dilemma." Other examples
abound in the literature (e.g., N countries extracting from the
same oil pool--all will extract too fast; N countries fishing in
the same waters--all will over-fish). Given the prevalence of
the problem and the difficulties inherent in its solutions, it
is not surprising that many of the most pressing natural-resource
issues faced by the world today (acid rain production, destruction of watersheds, pollution of international waterways, and so
forth) share this common pattern.

These problems are easy to describe; finding effective
solutions for them is a very different matter. It is all very
well to prescribe international cooperation. However, given the
difficulties of achieving such cooperation in other areas, such
as weapons control and tariff policy, the chances of success are
not high.


Income Distribution

Throughout this chapter, the concept of Pareto optimality is
used. An obvious problem with this concept, however, is that it
pays no attention to the distribution of income. To see this,
consider the example of two people who are to divide 100
dollars. Any distribution of the form X and 100 - X for $0 \leq X$
$\leq 100$ is Pareto optimal. On the other hand, giving all the
money to one person violates intuitive notions of fairness. The
implication of this example is that governments should not be
indifferent among various Pareto-optimal solutions. Often the
solutions have very different implications for income distribution. As an example, from the point of view of pollution
production, it may make no difference if a firm is taxed when it
pollutes or subsidized when it does not; from the point of view
of income distribution, however, the solutions are very
dissimilar.

Here again it is easy to describe problems, but difficult to
prescribe effective rules for their solution. In fact, without
being specific about society's goals and objectives, the task is
impossible.

One additional point is worth making. A Pareto-optimal
solution, once achieved, cannot be deviated from without making
someone worse off. Nevertheless, the move to the Pareto-optimal
point from a nonoptimal point can harm someone and can even harm
everyone.

To illustrate this point, another example may be used. Suppose that initially, all countries are using a polluting technology. We know that this noncooperative solution is not Pareto
optimal. It was shown above that a tax can achieve the Pareto-

optimal solution.  If, however, this tax is collected by a central agency and is not redistributed to the taxed countries,
every country is made worse off.  In contrast, the same outcome
from the point of view of pollution can be achieved by a tax
whose revenues are divided equally among the countries; in this
case, all are better off.  For a formal proof in a different context, see Weitzman (1976).

The moral is that not only are Pareto-optimal solutions not
necessarily "good" or "fair" in some intuitive sense, but also a
move from a suboptimal to an optimal solution may be preferred by
none.  The concept of Pareto optimality therefore must be used
with extreme care.


## Policy Instruments

At this point, the need for implementing resource policy should
be obvious.  Governing agencies have at their disposal many instruments for achieving policy goals.  These include taxes, subsidies, tariffs, quotas, licenses, and standards, to name only a
few.  The literature on the effects of tax policy instruments on
resource use is vast.  Summaries for environmental resources can
be found in Baumol and Oates (1975:Chapters 10-12), and for
exhaustible resources in Dasgupta and Heal (1979:Chapter 12).

A few words of caution are in order.  In the environmental
literature, the emphasis is on Pareto optimality, perhaps because
it is assumed that the no-tax solution is suboptimal.  Problems
with the Pareto-optimality concept have already been discussed.
In the exhaustible-resource literature, the emphasis is on
neutrality, perhaps because it is believed that competitive
markets in the absence of taxation achieve optimal solutions.
If the status quo is optimal, the government's objective may be
merely to extract resource rents from private firms.

Several points are worth making.  First, neutrality should
not be equated with productive efficiency.  It should be obvious
that if the initial situation is not optimal (because of tax
distortions in other sectors or market imperfections, for
example), then a neutral tax, which by definition does not
change outcomes, cannot be efficient.

Second, productive efficiency should not be equated with welfare.  In order to define welfare, one must be specific about
evaluation criteria.  In general, productive efficiency is only
one objective in society's welfare function.  Other objectives
may include equality of income distribution and smoothing of economic cycles.  If productive efficiency were the only goal, then
maximizing efficiency would be equivalent to maximizing welfare.
When there are multiple goals, however, there are almost always
tradeoffs between conflicting objectives.  For example, society
may be willing to sacrifice some output per capita to achieve a
more equitable distribution of income, both across individuals
and over time.

Finally, neutrality can usually be defined only with respect
to particular relationships.  For example, a tax may be called

neutral if it leaves the intertemporal pattern of extraction from known deposits unchanged. The same tax, however, may change a firm's profitability and therefore its willingness to explore for unknown deposits. Thus in a broader sense, the tax may not be neutral. It is therefore important to be clear about the context within which tax policy is said to be neutral or to achieve some other goal, such as conservation.

Again, the lesson is that the issues involved in the choice of policy instruments are complex. After objectives have been chosen, therefore, it is necessary to take considerable care in designing the way in which they will be implemented.


SUMMARY AND CONCLUSIONS

After a rather long survey, it is important to assess the salient issues discussed and the tentative conclusions reached.

It should be abundantly clear that all attempts here to draw conclusions about the effects of resource scarcity on the growth of population and economic well-being at the marco level failed. The examination of parameters of an aggregate production function proved futile. This was true regardless of whether the parameter examined was the capital-resource elasticity of substitution $\sigma$, capital and resource shares in aggregate cost $\alpha_1$ and $\alpha_2$, the resource-augmenting rate of technical change $\lambda$ , or the output-pollution proportionality factor $\beta$ . This failure should not be surprising. The problem is very complex, and a single number, if it could be calculated, is unlikely to contribute substantially to a solution. In addition, it is unrealistic to believe that we can measure these parameters accurately; the conditions required for accurate measurement are very restrictive and are unlikely to be met in practice.

On the other hand, the failure to predict the consequences of resource scarcity at the macro level does not imply that conclusions cannot be drawn. Tentative answers can be given at a somewhat less aggregate level.

In the Introduction, three questions were posed. It is now time to answer them. First, which problems are apt to be most important in the next few decades? It is the author's belief that the problems associated with common-property resources will be more constraining than those associated with nonrenewable resources. These problems include the destruction of watersheds, deforestation, desertification, and acid rain, to name only a few. One reason for this belief is that a policy of laissez-faire is apt to be much more disastrous when applied to common-property resources than when applied to exhaustible resources. In addition, many of these problems require international cooperation for their solution, and predictions made here about the viability of multicountry cooperative arrangements are not optimistic.

The second question is which exhaustible resources are apt to be most constraining? Petroleum was identified here as the resource that is both likely to be in short supply and apt to

pose serious adjustment problems. This conclusion is based on
several observations: petroleum reserve-to-consumption ratios
are small and falling, petroleum is a very important input to
industrial production, petroleum exploration has been extensive,
and petroleum exploration costs are rising.

The third question is which economies are most apt to be
constrained? The conclusion drawn here is that countries
attempting a rapid program of industrialization will be most
affected by exhaustible-resource constraints. This is true
because they lack the per capita income to spend heavily on
resource commodities, while at the same time requiring more
resource input per unit of output. As an economy moves from
service and agriculture to industry, constraints are apt to be
very severe. It is the highly developed economies that are in
the best position; they have high per capita incomes coupled
with a less intensive need for resource inputs per unit of
output.

It is also the rapidly developing economies that are most
apt to suffer from common-property problems. The industrialized
countries have become increasingly concerned about environmental
issues and have even in some cases been able to reverse detri-
mental trends. Many less developed countries, however, feel
that they cannot afford to be concerned with environmental
issues because remedies invariably raise production costs. The
very poorest nonindustrialized countries face common-property
constraints that are almost as severe as those faced by growing
economies. In these countries, the pressure of expanding
population on common-property resources, such as grazing land
and wood, can be very severe.

Any survey such as this raises many more questions than it
can possibly answer. This is as it should be. Without an
awareness of the complexity of the issues, viable solutions
cannot be found. It is hoped that through continued discussion
of the problems involved, progress will be made toward sensible
cooperative agreements that benefit all parties.


NOTES

1    This definition is used by Smith and Krutilla (1979),
     among others.

2    No distinction is made in this simple model between the popu-
     lation and the labor force.

3    The assumption of constant returns is not necessary, but it
     simplifies the analysis. Diminishing returns act as a drag
     on production, whereas increasing returns are a benefit to a
     growing economy.

4    It may seem unreasonable to discount the utility of future
     generations. Discounting, however, can be justified if un-
     certainty is present. For example, there may be a positive
     probability in each time period that a catastrophic event
     will put an end to the world.

5  The correct definition of $\sigma$ is the percent change in the factor-usage ratio due to a percent change in their marginal rate of technical substitution. In competitive markets, however, the marginal rate of substitution is equated to the price ratio.
6  If $\sigma$ is not constant, what is important is its value when R is very small (when we are running out of R).
7  Nickel is no exception to this statement. An estimate of nickel reserves made in 1980 puts them at 80.
8  Intermediate materials contain some elements of R. However, they consist primarily of processed materials.
9  If a group of inputs (capital) is homothetically separable from other inputs, then elasticities of substitution between two components of the group (physical and working capital) and an input outside the group (energy) must be equal.
10  The Morishima elasticity, unlike the Hicks-Allen, is not symmetric.
11  The studies discussed above use flexible functional forms. With a flexible functional form, the elasticities of substitution are not constant, but depend on the cost shares.

REFERENCES

Allen, R.D.G., and J.R. Hicks (1934) A reconsideration of the theory of value II. Economica 1:196-219.
Arrow, K.J., H.B. Chenery, B.S. Minhas, and R.H. Solow (1961) Capital-labor substitution and economic efficiency. Review of Economics and Statistics 43:225-250.
Barnett, H.J., and C. Morse (1963) Scarcity and Growth. Baltimore, Md.: The Johns Hopkins Press.
Barnett, H.J. (1979) Scarcity and growth revisited. Pp. 163-217 in V.K. Smith, ed., Scarcity and Growth Reconsidered. Baltimore, Md.: The Johns Hopkins Press.
Baumol, W.J., and W.E. Oates (1975) The Theory of Environmental Policy. Englewood Cliffs, N.J.: Prentice Hall.
Berndt, E.R., and L.R. Christensen (1973) The internal structure of functional relationships. Review of Economic Studies 40: 403-410.
Berndt, E.R., and M. Kaled (1979) Parametric productivity measurement and choice among flexible functional forms. Journal of Political Economy 87:1220-1245.
Berndt, E.R., and D.O. Wood (1975) Technology, prices, and the derived demand for energy. Review of Economics and Statistics 57:259-268.
Berndt, E.R., and D.O. Wood (1979) Engineering and economic interpretations of energy-capital complementarity. American Economic Review 69:342-354.
Blackorby, C., D. Primont, and R.R. Russell (1978) Duality, Separability, and Functional Structure. Amsterdam: North-Holland.
Blackorby, C., and R.R. Russell (1981) The Morishima elasticity of substitution. Review of Economic Studies 48:147-158.

Brown, G.M., and B. Field (1978)  Implications of alternative
    measures of natural-resource scarcity.  Journal of Political
    Economy 86:229-243.
Daly, H.E. (1977)  Steady-State Economics:  The Economics of
    Biophysical Equilibrium and Moral Growth.  San Francisco:
    Freeman.
Dasgupta, P. (1982)  The Control of Resources.  Oxford:  Basil
    Blackwell.
Dasgupta, P., and G.M. Heal (1974)  The optimal depletion of
    exhaustible resources.  Review of Economic Studies 41:3-28.
Dasgupta, P., and G.M. Heal (1979)  Economic Theory and Exhaus-
    tible Resources.  Cambridge, England:  Cambridge University
    Press.
Devarajan, S., and A.C. Fisher (1982)  Exploration and scarcity.
    Journal of Political Economy 90:1279-1290.
Diewert, W.E. (1974)  Applications of duality theory.  In M.
    Intrilligator and D. Kendricks, eds., Frontiers in Quanti-
    tative Economics.  Amsterdam:  North Holland.
Diewert, W.E. (1976)  Exact and superlative index numbers.
    Journal of Econometrics 4:115-145.
Field, B.C., and C. Grebenstein (1980)  Capital-energy substi-
    tution in U.S. manufacturing.  Review of Economics and
    Statistics 62:207-212.
Fisher, A.C. (1979)  Measures of natural-resource scarcity.  In
    V.K. Smith, ed., Scarcity and Growth Reconsidered.
    Baltimore, Md.:  The Johns Hopkins Press.
Fisher, A.C. (1981)  Resource and Environmental Economics.
    Cambridge, England:  Cambridge University Press.
Fisher, F.M. (1965)  Embodied technical change and the existence
    of an aggregate capital stock.  Review of Economic Studies
    32:263-288.
Fishman, L.L., and H.H. Landsberg (1972)  Adequacy of nonfuel
    minerals and forest resources.  In R.G. Ridker, ed.,
    Population, Resources, and the Environment.  Washington,
    D.C.:  Commission on Population Growth and the American
    Future.
Georgescue-Roegen, N. (1976)  Energy and Economic Myths.  New
    York:  Pergamon.
Geze, F., A. Valladao, and V. Lacoste (1983)  L'Etat du Monde.
    Paris:  La Descouverte/Maspero.
Gorman, W.M. (1953)  Community preference fields.  Econometrica
    21:63-80.
Gorman, W.M. (1968)  Measuring the quantities of fixed factors.
    In Value, Capital, and Growth:  Papers in Honor of Sir John
    Hicks.  Chicago:  Alden.
Griffen, J.M., and P.R. Gregory (1976)  An intercountry translog
    model of energy substitution responses.  American Economic
    Review 66:845-857.
Griffen, J.M. (1981)  Engineering and econometric interpretations
    of energy-capital complementarity:  comment.  American
    Economic Review 71:1100-1104.

Jorgenson, D.W., and B.M. Fraumeni (1981)  Substitution and
    technical change in production.  In E.R. Berndt and B.
    Field, eds., Measuring and Modeling Natural-Resource
    Substitution. Cambridge, Mass.:  M.I.T. Press.
Lau, L.J. (1982)  The measurement of natural-resource inputs.
    Pp. 167-200 in J.V. Krutilla and V.K. Smith, eds.,
    Explorations in Natural-Resource Economics. Baltimore,
    Md.:  The Johns Hopkins Press.
Leontief, W., J. Koo, S. Nasar, and I. Sohn (1983)  The Future
    of Nonfuel Minerals in the U.S. and World Economy.
    Lexington, Mass.:  D.C. Heath.
Magnus, J.R. (1979)  Substitution between energy and nonenergy
    inputs in the Netherlands.  International Economic Review
    20:465-484.
Malinvaud, M. (1972)  Lectures in Microeconomic Theory.
    Amsterdam:  North Holland.
Morishima, M. (1967)  A few suggestions on the theory of elasti-
    city. Keizai Hyoron (Economic Review) 16:149-150.
Moroney, J.R., and J.M. Trapani (1981)  Factor demand and sub-
    stitution in mineral-intensive industries.  Bell Journal of
    Economics 12:272-284.
Peterson, U., and R.S. Maxwell (1979)  Historic mineral produc-
    tion and price trends.  Mining Engineering 31(1):25-34.
Pindyck, R.S. (1979)  Interfuel substitution and the industrial
    demand for energy.  Review of Economics and Statistics
    61:169-179.
Repetto and Homes (1983)  The role of population in resource
    depletion.  Population and Development Review 9(4):609-632.
Samuelson, P.A. (1954)  The pure theory of public expenditure.
    Review of Economics and Statistics 36:387-389.
Sedjo, R.A., and M. Clawson (1984)  Global forests.  Pp. 128-170
    in J.L. Simon and H.Kahn, eds., The Resourceful Earth.  New
    York:  Basil Blackwell.
Slade, M.E. (1982)  Trends in natural-resource commodity prices:
    an analysis of the time domain.  Journal of Environmental
    Economics and Management 9:122-137.
Smith, V.K. (1978)  Measuring natural-resource scarcity:  theory
    and practice.  Journal of Environmental Economics and
    Management 5:150-171.
Smith, V.K. (1979)  Natural-resource scarcity:  a statistical
    analysis.  Review of Economics and Statistics 61:423-427.
Smith, V.K., and J.V. Krutilla (1979)  The economics of natural-
    resource scarcity:  an interpretative introduction.  In V.K.
    Smith, ed., Scarcity and Growth Reconsidered. Baltimore,
    Md.:  The Johns Hopkins Press.
Solow, R.M. (1974)  The economics of resources or the resources
    of economics.  American Economic Review, Papers and
    Proceedings, 64:1-14.
Stiglitz, J.E. (1974)  Growth with exhaustible resources:
    efficient and optimal growth paths.  Review of Economic
    Studies 41:123-138.

Stiglitz, J.E. (1979)  A neoclassical analysis of the economics
of natural resources.  In V.K. Smith, ed., Scarcity and
Growth Reconsidered.  Baltimore, Md.:  The Johns Hopkins
Press.
United Nations Industrial Development Organization (1984)
Second Study on Industrial Carrying Capacity.  Paper
prepared for the International Conference on Population,
Geneva.
United Nations (1980)  U.N. Yearbook of World Energy Statistics.
New York:  United Nations.
U.S. Bureau of the Mines (1980)  Mineral Facts and Problems.
Washington, D.C.:  U.S. Bureau of the Mines.
U.S. Geological Survey (1975)  Mineral Resource Perspective 1975.
Professional Paper No. 940.  U.S. Geological Survey,
Washington, D.C.
Weitzman, M. (1976)  Free access vs. private ownership as alter-
native systems for managing common property.  Journal of
Economic Theory 8:225-234.

# IV. Human Resources

# 10

## The Effect of Family Size on Family Welfare: What Do We Know?

Elizabeth M. King

### INTRODUCTION

Efforts to control fertility in developing countries have been based on the compelling proposition that a large population diverts scarce resources away from investment and productive activities that generate and sustain economic growth and development. Whereas this concern is based on the macroeconomic consequences of population growth, it is at the level of the family that fertility decisions take place. Moreover, through its roles as producer and consumer, the family contributes to economic development. As producer, it provides labor resources and allocates these to various productive activities; it distributes work effort among its members; it saves and accumulates human and nonhuman capital; it takes entrepreneurial risks, or seeks and implements new techniques of production. As consumer, it creates demand for various commodities and allocates consumption among its members. In these different ways, family behavior and the welfare of the larger economy are closely linked and mutually interactive. An important question to raise, then, is whether population pressure induces families to behave in such a way as to retard economic development. This might occur when costs and incentives are such that what is optimal for parents is not optimal from the social perspective.

Much of the demographic research on individual behavior has focused on how fertility choices respond to economic costs and incentives. How population pressure affects various consumption and production decisions made by a family is less understood. Because Third World countries have allocated increasing resources to the control of population, this issue deserves greater attention. This chapter reviews past research with the purpose of evaluating the consequences of population growth for the family's well-being. Past work in this area has explored the consequences of family size for the mental ability, health, and development of

This study was supported by the Rand Corporation and the National Research Council.

children. The present review starts with those studies. However, the discussion is not limited to the relationship between
family size and child welfare; it extends to the well-being of
parents and of other household members. Further, since fertility
decisions refer not only to family size but also to the spacing
of children, the relationship of birth spacing and birth order to
family welfare is also considered.

The review of past research presented here is grounded on an
economic paradigm of individual behavior. Although there are at
least two principal competing economic models of fertility behavior in the demographic literature (that have, in turn, in-
spired countless variations), the essence of these models is the
same: that the couple choose their family size, and that they
also choose the level of child-related expenditures, such as
schooling or health, as well as the level of their own consumption of leisure and other commodities (Easterlin, 1966; Becker,
1960; Becker and Lewis, 1973).[1] Using this theoretical framework, if high fertility reflects the decision of parents, it is
difficult to view it largely as a problem of population pressure
impinging on family welfare, _causing_ adverse effects. Rather,
the appropriate research question is what choices go hand-in-
hand with having large families. The cause for concern is that
the parents' decision may not be in the social interest. Here
the connection runs from individual choice to the creation of
population pressure that may interfere with the growth of the
larger economy.

Identifying the determinants of fertility is not the focus
of this chapter; rather, the focus is on the other areas of
decision making that constitute individual or family welfare--
expenditures for improving the nutrition and health, education,
shelter, leisure, and work of family members. The following
questions are addressed: What are the connections between the
fertility decisions of couples and other aspects of family life?
Are the findings of past studies consistent with the economic
paradigm--that is, are fertility and other aspects of family
life inherently intertwined because the couple or household are
the ultimate decision makers in these respects? If not, what
theoretical frameworks lie behind these findings? How have
other approaches been translated into empirical models? The
next section addresses the question of how family size affects
child welfare. This is followed by a discussion of the relationship between family size and intrafamily distribution. The
chapter then turns to the question of how family size affects
parental welfare. A final section presents concluding remarks.


HOW FAMILY SIZE AFFECTS CHILD WELFARE

Many studies have found a persistently negative relationship
between family size and various dimensions of child welfare.
However, there is less agreement about the factors that give rise
to this relationship. Three previous extensive surveys of the
literature have summarized the basis for the proposition that

family size adversely affects individual child welfare. Wray
(1971) focused on the effect of family size on the child's mental
and physical health. Terhune (1974) and Polit (1982) reviewed
studies that consider a broader set of effects, including the
child's health, intelligence, educational attainment, physical
development, and personality. The studies cited in these surveys
also address the consequences of family size for parents' marital
satisfaction and mental and physical health. While some of the
results cited are based on individual and family data from less
developed countries (LDCs), most are derived from data collected
in industrialized countries. To avoid repeating what these earlier surveys have achieved, the discussion here of the studies
included in these surveys is restricted to a summary of their
general findings, but with greater attention devoted to the implicit or explicit models of family behavior and empirical
formulations that they use; the focus is also on studies pertaining to developing countries.


## Adverse Effects on Child Development

Previous studies have concluded that large family size and short
birth intervals adversely affect various dimensions of the
child's welfare. The general results of these studies are
listed below:

- There is a persistently negative correlation between
  family size and intelligence (ranging from −.20 to −.30
  according to early psychological studies). When economic
  class is controlled for, the correlation is approximately
  halved, but remains significantly negative.

- Children from smaller families tend to perform better in
  school than those from larger families, partly because
  they tend to be more intelligent, as measured by IQ, and
  partly because they have more financial resources and receive greater parental encouragement. In larger families,
  each child receives less individual attention and other
  resources from parents.

- There is some evidence that personality traits of children
  are also correlated with family size. Psychological
  studies show that children from smaller families are
  generally more ambitious, more independent, and more
  dominant, and possess higher self-esteem than those from
  larger families.

- Moreover, children in large families tend to have poorer
  health and lower survival probabilities. A large family
  size also appears to inhibit or retard the physical development (e.g., height) of the child through lower quality
  of maternal care per child and higher incidence of malnutrition in larger families.

Past studies have attributed the adverse effects of a large family on the child's mental ability and health to two mechanisms--heredity, on the one hand, and environment, on the other. The heredity explanation relies on the hypothesis that duller people tend to have larger families. In 1962, Higgins et al. published the results of their study of the descendants of mentally retarded individuals in the United States observed 50 years earlier. They found the usual negative correlation between family size and intelligence; however, contrary to the heredity explanation, they also found that a relatively greater proportion of the low IQ group did not marry or did not reproduce. Furthermore, the IQs of the children so closely resembled those of the mothers that family size did not seem to matter much as an explanatory variable. Moreover, for families with one to five children, there was no observed relationship between family size and intelligence (Terhune, 1974). Olneck and Wolfe (1980), reexamining the effect of family size on intelligence among U.S. males, also did not find support for the heredity explanation of this relationship. In both the Kalamazoo and NBER-Thorndike-Regen samples that they examined, they did not find a negative relationship between ability and number of children. In fact, when the respondent's age, current marital status, education, and income were controlled for, the relationship became positive. Hence, they concluded that, contrary to the basis of the heredity explanation, individuals of low ability are not more likely to produce larger families.

More recently, the environmental hypothesis has received greater attention from researchers. This explanation is based on the argument that the larger the family, the more limited the amount of resources available to each child as more children compete for them. There is also less contact between the parents and each child, since the time of parents itself is a limited resource. This is called the dilution or strain-on-resources model. It implies that, at least with respect to the availability of goods resources per child, the negative relationship between family size and intelligence should be more pronounced in poorer families.

Belmont and Marolla (1973) found that, comparing correlations among social classes (defined by father's occupation) and controlling for birth order, the effect of family size on IQ is larger for males (Dutch 19-year-olds) whose fathers have manual rather than nonmanual occupations; among farmers, there is no effect. However, one must be careful in interpreting these results. First, income is not the only scarce resource of the family; parental time must be considered, too. Class division along father's occupation measures not only the probable effect of income constraints on the family environment (which is Belmont and Marolla's interpretation), but also the effect of the father's work hours and the mother's working status. Moreover, family size may itself be correlated with socioeconomic class.

To illustrate, suppose that parents in nonmanual occupations tend to have smaller completed families than parents in the other two groups. Parents in nonmanual occupations may have different

aspirations for their children and may prefer to spend more of
their resources for the development of each child's mental ability. We would then observe a negative effect between family size
and mental ability. However, since the observed variance in
family size among those in nonmanual occupations is smaller, the
negative correlation between family size and intelligence within
this class could also be smaller.

Blake (1981) found support for the dilution model in her
study of education and intellectual performance in the United
States and Europe. Controlling for socioeconomic background,
she found a negative relationship between total years of education and family size, and also between intelligence and family
size. She found that family size reduces ability and parental
encouragement among male youths in the U.S., thereby lowering or
dissipating college aspirations.

The amount of time that parents devote to each child may be
critical in that child's development. When parents have more
children to care for, this important resource is diluted. The
amount of care time per child is lower in larger families, as
Hill and Stafford (1980) have observed among U.S. families.[2]
But is the average time per child the appropriate measure of
child care? Undoubtedly, some parents will argue that it is not
the amount of time, but the quality of time spent with the child
that is more important; thus, lower care time per child does not
necessarily imply poorer care. Moreover, economies of scale may
be present in the care of young children. Vijverberg (1984)
found substantial economies of scale in child care time for U.S.
mothers. A later section discusses the effect of family size on
mothers' time allocation.


Birth Spacing and Birth Order

Past studies have explored the effects of birth order on the
intelligence, performance, and physical health of children, in
addition to, or outside the effect of, family size. Although
this is not our present focus, the arguments behind the family
size, birth order, and birth spacing effects are interrelated
and revolve around the dilution hypothesis. A child's birth
order may affect the amount of time that parents spend with that
child even more strongly than does family size. The following
questions arise: Does the effect of family size on the child's
welfare vary according to the child's birth order, or according
to the birth interval between that child and the preceding or
succeeding child? Or do birth order effects vary according to
family size?[3]

In the study by Belmont and Marolla (1973), intelligence
scores decline with family size within any particular birth order
and decline with birth order within each family size. However,
the birth order effect, which is regular and systematic in
smaller families, tends to be less consistent in middle-sized
families and inconsistent in large families. Moreover, intelligence scores seem to be discontinuously lower for last-born

children; further, only children, who are expected to be better off than all other children according to the dilution model, do not have the highest intelligence scores. To explain the birth order puzzle, Zajonc et al. (1979) explicitly considered in their "confluence model" the discontinuities observed for the only child and last-born children. The basic idea of the model is that the intellectual development of each family member is affected by the intellectual environment to which all members contribute. Hence, the birth order effect is not independent of the effect of family size and birth spacing. Short intervals force later-born children to spend a larger portion of their period of growth in a family environment where resources are diluted by the presence of young children. As spacing increases, the birth order effect on intelligence ceases to favor the earlier-born of any consecutive pair of siblings, but improves the growth of both the earlier-born and the later-born. Moreover, the nature and strength of the birth order effect depend on the age of the child and may be reversed as the child matures, depending on whether the child assumes a teaching function with respect to a younger sibling (also known as the sib-socialization hypothesis).

Zajonc and his associates found support for the confluence model from data on school children in Europe and the United States. These data indicate that intellectual level, as measured by IQ, generally declines with family size, even after controlling for socioeconomic status. Earlier-born children perform better on intelligence tests than do later-born children when intervals between successive births are relatively short. However, longer birth intervals appear to mitigate the negative effects of birth order, and short intervals seem to result in low IQs of children.

Lindert (1977) also found that greater family size appears to reduce schooling among children in a 1963 sample of New Jersey employees and their siblings. Birth order effects include first-borns' ending up with significantly better schooling than that of middle-born children in families with six or more children. Last-born children, however, have a slight edge over middle-born children in large families. Again, these findings provide support for the hypothesis of sibling crowding in large families. In Blake's (1981) study, for a given family size, the intelligence scores/birth-order relationship is not unambiguously negative. Her results suggest that children benefit from having other children around who facilitate their learning and socialization.

Short birth intervals may impinge on the development of the child through still another channel--the child's health.[4] According to various studies on childspacing practices in sub-Saharan Africa (Page and Lesthaeghe, 1981), the practice of prolonged postpartum taboo, which results in sexual abstinence by the mother after each birth, is primarily motivated by concern for child survival.[5] A longer lactation period for the mother, ensured by the prevention of another pregnancy following too soon, is believed to improve the survival chances of the

newborn child. Women whose infants die after birth may be
accused of witchcraft and punished accordingly. An earlier study
by Cantrelle and Leridon (1971) showed that in Senegal, the probability of child death is negatively related to age at weaning,
with 48 percent dying if the child is weaned at age 1 and only 23
percent if the child is weaned after age 2 (but not as a result
of infant death). Wolfers and Scrimshaw (1975) and de Sweemer
(1984) observed that the length of the (closed) birth interval is
significantly related to the survival of both the newborn child
and the older child in Guayaquil, Ecuador, and in Punjabi
villages, respectively. A major shortcoming of these studies,
however, is their failure to control for the interdependence between the effects of birth intervals and family size on the
child's health.

Most of the studies discussed above treat family size or
birth spacing as determinants of child welfare in much the same
way as parental characteristics and family background are determinants. The various aspects of child welfare are regarded as
consequences. This view implies that reductions in fertility
would necessarily increase the intelligence of children, as well
as their education and health. This view is justifiable only if
parents do not exercise adequate control over their family size;
it ignores the fact that parents also decide on their children's
nutrition, health, and education.

## Fertility, Child Mortality, and Child Quality

This section reviews studies on child mortality, focusing on the
relationship between child mortality and the choices that parents
make about child health and schooling, as well as other aspects
of a child's well-being. The relationship between child mortality and child quality is not independent of the relationship between fertility and child mortality. Past research has considerably enhanced our understanding of the relationship between fertility and child mortality.[6] However, the linkages between
mortality and fertility that can also affect parental decisions
about children's health or schooling have received much less
attention. These pertain to the impact on parents' decision
making of how they perceive the risk of investing family resources in any one child in the face of relatively high rates of
pre-adult mortality. High child mortality will undoubtedly
affect not only childbearing, but also childrearing patterns.
How parents choose to respond to expected or actual child
mortality will also be related to their intentions and choices
about child quality.

Previous studies have argued that parents respond to mortality in two ways.[7] Given the expected level of child
mortality, parents may have more births than their desired
family size to attain the desired number of surviving children;
this is also known as hoarding. Alternatively, parents may wait
to experience a death before having another birth as a replacement. In a single-period model, in which desired family size is

chosen once and for all and there is no uncertainty, parents who want a family of five but expect one child to die will decide to have six children in anticipation of experiencing a death. Parents' attitudes toward risk will determine how they respond to expectations about mortality. In a dynamic model, where risk is independent of expected mortality levels and uncertainty is involved, responses will be distributed according to the risk aversion of parents. Hence, parents who expect the same proba- bility of one child dying will not all respond similarly, but will differ according to their willingness to take risks. Furthermore, behavior will be different if uncertainty is posi- tively correlated with the level of expected mortality (as is probably the case in LDCs).

Whether the family hoards or replaces depends on the age at which the wife starts her family, how many children she and her husband want, and how fecund she thinks she is. The older the wife is, the less fecund she will be, and the greater the incen- tive for a hoarding strategy, particularly if she and her husband desire a large family. The choice of the response strategy also depends on the timing of costs and benefits associated with raising children (O'Hara, 1972).[8] Assuming a uniform stream of benefits over time, if most child-related costs are incurred earlier rather than later in the child's life, then a decrease in expected child mortality reduces the shadow price of children. In general, if the case of early costs and late benefits is more typical, then lower expected mortality will lead to a rise in desired family size (Ben-Porath, 1980). The cost stream of raising children itself will not be independent of the fertility response of parents. In some settings, the more reasonable strategy may be to hoard while minimizing the cost of resources allocated per child; in other settings, parents may decide to take their chances, but allocate more family resources per child to improve the survival probabilities of surviving children, and thus avoid another birth.

Under most circumstances, hoarding is a more costly strategy than replacement, since it requires incurring expenses early for more children than the desired number. An exogenous decline in expected mortality that raises the number of surviving children beyond the desired level increases the cost of hoarding. Like- wise, such an unanticipated decrease in mortality rates results in a wealth gain to those following the replacement strategy.

Figure 1 summarizes the above discussion. While this repre- sentation is simplistic, it shows how exogenous changes in infant or child mortality rates might affect the fertility and child quality decisions of parents.[9] When mortality rates are high, most of the fertility response to mortality is due to hoarding; the replacement effect tends to be quite weak. As aggregate in- fant mortality rates fall and the number of surviving children rises unexpectedly, parents adjust their expectations and behavior. The net result is a decline in total fertility rates (although completed [surviving] family size may remain the same). A large part of this adjustment in fertility comes from a decline in hoarding; most of the response to child mortality now takes

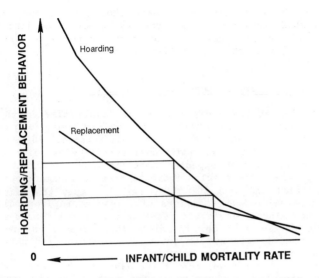

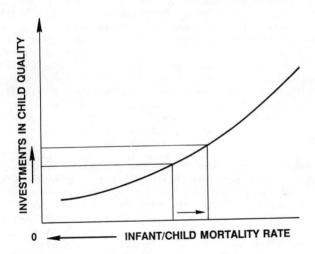

FIGURE 1   Effects of Exogenous Mortality Changes on Fertility and
Child Quality Choices of Parents

the form of replacement, and the replacement effect becomes
stronger. At the same time, because of the rise in the survival
chances of children, the rate of return to child quality investments increases considerably, inducing parents to allocate more
resources for child schooling or training.   Thus part of the

increase in child quality investments that parents make during the demographic transition is a mortality effect. The discussion below reviews the empirical evidence on the response of fertility and child quality to child mortality rates.

## How Fertility Behavior Responds to Child Mortality

Several studies at the individual level have estimated the response of fertility to child mortality, assuming sequential family behavior. They have examined differences in stopping probabilities or in desired additional fertility associated with levels of actual and/or expected mortality, at different parities. In general, the results indicate that replacement behavior is only partial and weak.[10] These results imply that improvements in general health conditions will lead to rapid population growth. They also indicate that fewer resources will be spent on the development of each child, unless these resources are made available more cheaply by the government through free nutrition and health centers or public schools.

Ben-Porath (1978) found that for a given parity among Israeli women, the stopping probability is lower where one of the preceding births ended in death, suggesting the extent of replacement to be about 23-80 percent at parities 2 and 3. Replacement decreases quite steeply for higher parities, but the decline is smaller for more-educated women. Prior mortality also reduces the length of the birth interval, though the effect is quite small (with elasticities at means of .03-.04 percent). In Colombia, Olsen (1980) observed that, if .5 of the correlation between mortality and fertility were due to a mixed strategy of hoarding and replacement, then the total response of fertility to mortality would be about .75. Mauskopf and Wallace (1984) found that the probability of replacing a lost child is about .6 in Brazil and that it increases with a mother's education. In contrast, Lehrer and Nerlove (forthcoming) found a weak and insignificant replacement effect in Malaysia. They obtained a significant negative coefficient for the husband's child survival expectations, which suggests hoarding, but not for the wife's equation. They explained this by the fact that the mother bears a disproportionate fraction of childbearing costs and of costs associated with infancy and early childhood, thus offsetting the hoarding effect. Lehrer (1984) examined the effect of child mortality on birth spacing, and found that mortality shortens the birth interval in the middle parities, but has no effect on earlier parities.

Newman and McCulloch (1984) estimated a proportional hazards model of the timing of births of Costa Rican women, with the regional probability of dying before age 5 as a regressor. Their coefficient estimates were positive and significant for younger women, suggesting that those in areas of higher mortality begin their childbearing earlier. The effect on the first birth is weaker for older cohorts, but this was attributed to the limitations of measuring the mortality variable at only one period,

1973. Also estimating a hazards model of time to next birth, Santow and Bracher (1984) found a strong positive coefficient among rural women in Central Java. Controlling for mother's age and education up to primary school, the probability of bearing another child increases greatly when the preceding child died, with the hazard increasing by a factor of four. The authors interpret this result as indicating the strength of biological factors rather than of replacement behavior. In the natural-fertility population of 14 nineteenth-century German villages, Knodel (1982) also found a persistent positive association between actual child mortality and subsequent fertility, with the size of the effect increasing across successive marriage cohorts, indicating the onset of deliberate family control in the population.

Wolpin (1984) has developed a dynamic model of fertility that derives the effect of the probability of death on the fertility decision.11 Parents decide whether to have a birth at each period, depending on the probability of child death, income levels, and family characteristics at each period. Child-bearing costs are allowed to vary across periods. In fact, mortality enters the model as an uncertain and exogenous quantity, its level depending on time and household characteristics. If a child survives up to age 1, it is assumed that it will out-live its parents. This assumption implies that it will be op-timal for parents to follow a replacement strategy. However, Wolpin's results using Malaysian data show that the replacement effect is quite small, inducing an increase in the number of children ever born by at most .015, and that the effect of survival probabilities is larger. A drop in percentage points of .05 reduces the number of births by about 25 percent.

## Child Mortality and Child Quality

Few studies have embedded child mortality in the quantity-quality model to measure the effect of mortality on both ferti-lity and child quality, and to make child mortality (at least partly) endogenous. Anderson (1983) estimated fertility, schooling, and survival functions for Guatemalan households. To test the endogeneity of child survival, which is measured as the ratio of actual to expected survival in each household, she com-pared the coefficient estimates obtained from fertility and schooling regressions with and without the survival rate as a regressor.12 The estimates are not significantly different. Thus, she concluded that the simultaneous equations bias when child survival is used simply as a regressor is small. The effect of child survival on fertility is strongly negative, but the effect on child schooling is not significant. Horton (1984) also estimated a quantity-quality model using data on rural Philippine households. Child mortality (measured as number of child deaths) enters as a regressor in the fertility and child quality equations. The index of child quality measures height for age of the child and weight for height. The results show a weak relationship between mortality and fertility, and also between mortality and child quality.

These two studies address a very important question--the effect of mortality rates on investments in children within an economic model of decision making in the household. However, their results may be biased because of methodological problems involved in estimating the replacement effect. As with other studies that have used children ever born to measure fertility, a shortcoming of these studies is that fertility and measures of child quality include uncompleted observations. Unless the data include only women who have completed their reproductive cycle, regressing children ever born on family mortality does not capture the true replacement effect. For the same reason, if child quality is not appropriately measured, the effect of mortality on child-related expenditures will also be biased. Children who are still enrolled have not completed their schooling. One further difficulty is that data are usually not available for children who have died. What is generally observed is the level of quality of surviving children.

A considerably different approach in relating health and fertility is taken by Rosenzweig and Wolpin (1984). Their dynamic model of parental investments in the health status of children incorporates into the decision-making process parents' learning about the family's health endowment and the child's initial health status. Parents' fertility and child quality choices together determine the health status of the child. At each period, parents decide whether to have a child and how many resources to allocate to that child and to existing children. The child's health at birth depends on its birth order, the timing of preceding births, the age of the mother at its birth, and the level of prenatal care, as well as on its health endowments. The child's health at any given age after birth depends on its initial health, the length of the interval to the next child, and the level of postnatal care.

To estimate how family health endowment in Colombian families is related to fertility and nutritional intake, the authors regressed the number of children less than 6 years of age, children ever born, and monthly per capita food consumption on an index of the family's health endowment. The results indicate that couples whose children have better health endowments tend to have larger families; however, they do not allocate significantly different levels of food per capita, implying that children born in healthier families will tend to receive less nutritional input.

Several important issues regarding the effect of mortality on parental investments in surviving children remain to be addressed in future research. First, consider the effect of a decrease in child mortality rates on child quality if decisions are made sequentially. When the family follows a hoarding strategy, an unexpected decline in mortality rates will yield a larger family size than desired. On the one hand, averted deaths represent a windfall gain in real income to parents; on the other hand, parents have more children to send to school than they had planned for. Parents may respond by increasing their labor supply if the net result of averted deaths is for the marginal utility of income to rise. Or, given income, parents may reduce their investments in quality per child because there are more children to spend on. This is similar to the effect of an unexpected increase in family size due to the occurrence of multiple births. Using twins data from India, Rosenzweig and Wolpin (1980b) found that the birth of twins both reduces the average educational attainment of all children, including the nontwins in the family, and decreases the family's expenditure on consumer durables.

A second issue is that the risk of mortality is also a risk of losing investments in child quality. Hence, among children in high-mortality areas, we would expect lower child quality. Although individual parents can protect their investments by improving their children's health and nutritional status, the cost of attaining good health may be too high. Moreover, parents can choose the timing of investments in child quality such that the risk of loss is small. Mortality rates are usually higher for young children and decline steeply for older children. Parents can revise their decisions about child quality as they experience child mortality and as they learn more about the health endowment of individual children. Nevertheless, although mortality affects the child quality decision, researchers may find no apparent effect of mortality on child quality because data are generally available only for surviving children. Clearly, this self-selection process must be considered in the estimation of these relationships.

Closely related to this issue is the idea that parents may also hedge their investments in child quality by allocating resources unevenly among offspring, according to efficiency and risk-of-mortality considerations. Past research has not addressed the distribution question in relation to child mortality. The next section below discusses the distribution of resources among offspring.


FAMILY SIZE AND INTRAFAMILY DISTRIBUTION

Economic models, including most applications of the quantity-quality model, are silent about the distribution of resources among offspring, considering only child quality averaged over all children in the family.[13] However, previous studies have found systematic differences in the quality of children within families, either by birth order or sex. In the model of Becker and Tomes (1976), inequality within the family may be the result of differences in the initial quality ("ability endowments") of children and the corresponding behavior response of parents to these differences. Do parents equalize the distribution of resources among children of different abilities, or do they compensate or reinforce the inequality in endowments? The Becker-Tomes model implies that, even when parents have "child-neutral preferences" (that is, when the marginal utility accruing to parents

from changes in child quality is the same for all children when
their qualities are equal), it costs less to add to the quality
of more able children than to add to that of less able children.
This result is quickly reversed if better-endowed, more able
children acquire quality at lower costs.14

In the model of Behrman et al. (1982), parents can secure the
future of children through education and/or bequests and inter
vivos gifts. Schooling, together with genetic endowments and
other parental inputs, determines the expected lifetime earnings
of the child. Family size is treated as a predetermined variable. Parents do not play favorites, such as sons over
daughters, or the eldest over the younger children. However,
this equal concern does not necessarily imply equal expected
earnings among children, which may result from differences in
their endowments.

The authors considered two alternative versions of parental
behavior--the separable earnings-bequest model and the wealth
model. In the former model, parents do not use bequests to
compensate for the expected low earnings of a particular child.
In the latter model, parents are indifferent between spending on
their children's schooling and transferring resources to them
through bequests or gifts. Since parents are concerned only
about the future wealth of children, they will allocate schooling
primarily on efficiency grounds, but will use bequests to equalize the distribution of wealth. Thus, parents will adopt a reinforcing strategy by giving more education to children who have
greater aptitude for schooling. In the separable earnings-
bequest model, parents are concerned with equalizing the earnings
of children, not just wealth. If they are absolutely averse to
inequality, they will adopt a compensating strategy by giving
more education to those who have lower rates of return to
schooling. If they are not averse to inequality, they will
follow a compensating or a reinforcing strategy, depending on
the properties of the earnings function. The estimates of the
separable earnings-bequest model using U.S. data on twins indicate that parents are averse to inequality among children and
thus tend to compensate less able children.

These models emphasize the role of genetic endowments in the
distribution of resources among offspring; they assume that
parents possess perfect knowledge about the endowments of
children. Rosenzweig and Wolpin (1984) have further improved
this class of models by allowing parents to learn about their
family-specific and child-specific characteristics over time.
Much of the empirical work on intrafamily distribution, however,
does not estimate the effect of the distribution of endowments
on the distribution of resources. Rather, the emphasis has been
on the allocation of resources by birth order and gender.

Birth Order Effects

Studies cited above have found that first-born children tend to
have higher IQs, attend school longer, and earn more than their
younger siblings. Last-born children appear to have an edge over

middle-born children, although there is more disagreement on
this.[15] First-born and last-born children appear to be better
off because they benefit from greater parental care, being reared
when there are fewer claims on family resources.[16]

Related to this is the effect of the earnings profile of
parents over the life cycle on the level of available family resources at any time period. Because of imperfect capital
markets, children who grow up during the peak in the earnings
profile may receive a greater share of lifetime family resources.
Expenditures may still be diluted if there are many children
growing up at about the same time. On the other hand, parents
may invest more heavily in older children (simply because they
are of the right age at the time) as regards formal schooling or
training, in hopes that these older offspring will later help
provide for younger children. Older offspring can then smooth
out the income stream of parents, serving as an alternative to
inaccessible capital markets.[17] If parents follow this strategy as a means of transferring resources across time, then they
might choose to invest in the offspring who is either more capable or more reliable in order to maximize returns from their
investment. For example, in certain settings, older sons are
chosen because they can earn higher returns on their education
or training; in other settings, older daughters are chosen because parents think they are more likely to remit earnings in
the future. (The next section discusses sex preference in the
family.)

Gomes (1984) found that Kenyan parents appear to favor first-
born children overwhelmingly.[18] Where completed family size is
4 or fewer children, the probability that a first-born child will
complete primary school is 48 percent, as compared with 31 percent for the second child, 11 percent for the third child, and 10
percent for the youngest child. In families with 5-7 children,
the differences in parental educational investments between
first-born and later-born children are even greater than those
in smaller families. In large families with 8 or more children,
first-borns are still much better off than younger siblings, but
the youngest children also have an advantage over middle-born
children. Gomes attributes this better position of the youngest
children to the fact that parents in Kenya are able to exert control over the income of older children; younger siblings as well
as parents gain from income remittances from older children.

Finally, there is a biological explanation for birth order
effects. Earlier-born children may be healthier because frequent
pregnancies erode the mother's health, thus adversely affecting
the health of younger children. Rosenzweig and Schultz (1983)
obtained a negative biological effect of birth order on infant
mortality in the United States. Heller and Drake (1979) and
Rozenzweig and Wolpin (1984), who analyzed the health status of
children in Candelaria, Colombia, also found a negative effect
of birth order on weight at birth. However, this effect dis-
appears by the time the child is 6 months old.[19]

Sex Preference

In several Asian countries, particularly India, Bangladesh, and Pakistan, there is evidence of preferential treatment of sons. This is indicated by the tendency of parents to adjust their childbearing according to the number of sons they have, and by the fact that boys and girls appear to have different survival probabilities and levels of education.

Ben-Porath and Welch (1976) found that, in Bangladesh, girls who are born into families with a high girl-boy ratio are less likely to survive than those born into families with a lower girl-boy ratio.[20] Chen et al. (1981) observed that parents in Bangladesh tend to allocate lower caloric and protein intake to daughters than to sons, and also discriminate against daughters in the use of health facilities in the community. The result is a substantially higher level of malnutrition among girls than boys.[21] In India, Rosenzweig and Schultz (1982) also found higher survival rates for boys than for girls, with a mean difference of 1.8 percent after standardizing for sex ratio in the family. These higher survival rates for boys appear to be to differences in the expected earnings opportunities for adult males and females in the district. When predicted women's employment rates are controlled for in the mortality difference equation, child survival rates do not appear to differ significantly for boys and girls, even in districts with a large proportion of Muslims. The Rosenzweig and Schultz estimates indicate that a rise in the adult female employment rate to 66 percent would erase the mean survival differential associated with gender.

Studies have found that son (or daughter) preference is partly a response of parents to differences in the perceived benefits from sons and daughters (Arnold et al., 1975; Williamson, 1976). In times of scarcity, families may distribute food according to allocation rules that favor men over women, adults over children, and boys over girls. If sons are more likely to earn higher incomes than daughters, then it is vital to the family that the health of their sons be ensured. In the rural Philippines, Fabella (1982) and others (Evenson et al., 1980) have noted that food is not equally shared among family members; but that a greater proportion is allocated to the family's breadwinners.

For the same reason that boys are favored in the distribution of food resources, they may be at a disadvantage relative to girls in other respects, such as schooling. For example, Rosenzweig and Evenson (1977) found that the school enrollment of boys is lower than that of girls in regions of India where the farm wages for child labor are higher. In the Philippines, the higher village-level wage rates of male children also partly explain why boys drop out of school earlier than do girls (King, 1982).

Family Size

Is intrafamily distribution affected by desired or actual family
size? Will couples who desire smaller (larger) families distribute resources among offspring more equally? If birth order
effects and other inequalities in the family are a consequence
of "crowding" within the family, then should they not be more
pronounced in larger than in smaller families? Above we noted
that Belmont and Marolla (1973) did not find strong birth order
effects in larger families. Blake (1981) also observed that
only children are not more intelligent (as measured by IQ) than
first-borns in two-child families, but are equally intelligent.
Moreover, last-born children appear to be relatively more
advantaged in larger than in smaller families.[22]
     Consider the effect of family size on child health through
its effect on the level and distribution of food nutrients within
the family. Although one can argue that there are economies of
scale to be realized in food preparation time in larger families,
evidence from LDCs does not show this to be important. Studies
on nutrition in Philippine rural households have found family
size to have a significant negative effect on the nutrient
adequacy of individual members.[23] Also, low-income families
do not distribute available nutrients equally: females receive
less, while family earners (males) and preschoolers receive relatively more. Mahmud and McIntosh (1980), in examining nutritional adequacy in Bangladesh, used per capita rice consumption
and per capita number of meals in the month prior to the survey
as measures of individual welfare in the family. They found that
larger families tend to have lower food consumption per head, and
that as family size increases, the distribution of food becomes
more unequal in favor of adult males. The negative effect of
family size is more pronounced in poorer villages.
     As part of a larger study on education in West Malaysia,
Lillard and King (forthcoming) explains how family size affects
the distribution of schooling among siblings in Malaysia. The
study presents only a partial test of the interaction between
family size and intrafamily distribution of child quality since
family size is treated as exogenous.[24] The authors found a
high correlation of about .5 for random-like sex pairs and cross-
sex pairs of siblings, suggesting that schooling inequality is
smaller within than between families.[25] The results imply that
the schooling levels of siblings will be more different in larger
than in smaller families, and that this inequality will be
greater among girls than boys. Controlling for family size, siblings who are farther apart in age tend to have more different
schooling levels, but this effect is less obvious for siblings
who are 5 years apart or more in age.


HOW FAMILY SIZE AFFECTS PARENTAL WELFARE

Issues of parental welfare that may be affected by family size
include wife's time allocation and labor supply, wife's health,
husband's labor supply, and child fosterage.

Wife's Time Allocation and Labor Supply

Because of the larger role that mothers play in childbearing and
in the early stages of childrearing, many studies have focused
on the wife's rather than the husband's labor supply decision in
relation to fertility choice.  In the static model of family
decision making, the wife's labor supply and fertility are determined simultaneously once and for all at the beginning of the
life cycle.  Attempts to estimate these two decisions within a
simultaneous equations model have yielded an unexpected, weakly
positive relationship.[26]  In contrast, single-equation studies
that treat the number of children as an exogenous factor have
found that the presence of young children inhibits female labor
supply.[27]  The basic idea of this model is that childbearing
is influenced by the direct costs associated with giving birth,
family income, and the value of alternative uses of the wife's
time, such as her marginal product in home production of her
market wage.  The wife's decision about market employment is
motivated by the same set of factors.  Rosenzweig and Wolpin
(1980a) use occurrence of twin births as a means of estimating
the effect of an exogenous or unanticipated increase in fertility
on female labor supply in the United States.[28]  For the youngest women, aged 15-24, with twins in the first birth, there is a
significant increase in home time early in the life cycle and a
substantial drop in the probability of working.  The negative
effect on labor force participation rates for women aged 25-34
is smaller.  For those aged 35-44, the effect is positive; labor
force participation rates increase and home time decreases.
These results indicate that, over the life cycle, there is some
substitutability of home time.
    Since twin birth is largely an unanticipated event, these
estimates reflect the impact on the wife's labor supply of an
exogenous increase in family size.  The authors compared these
results with coefficients obtained by simply regressing the labor
force participation rate (in a logit model) on commonly used
measures of fertility, such as children ever born or the number
of children under 6.  The impact on the wife's labor supply is
greatly underestimated when the simultaneity of fertility and
female labor supply is not considered.  The biased results indicate that women aged 15-24 will decrease their participation
rate by only .103 instead of .371; that women aged 25-34 will
increase their participation very slightly instead of decreasing
it; and that women aged 35-44 will increase participation by .041
as compared with .142.
    Several studies have argued that the effect of children on
women's labor supply depends also on whether some types of work
are more compatible with childrearing than others.  For example,
wage employment away from home may be less compatible with
raising children than are nonwage activities and unpaid family
work that have flexible hours and take place close to home.
    According to Ho (1979), mothers in the Philippines whose mar-
ket work takes place at home or close to home devote as much time
to the care of children as do mothers with no market activities,

while mothers employed outside the home tend to spend fewer hours on child care. DaVanzo and Lee (1983) found that about one-third of Malaysian women engaged in sales and cottage industry occupations, such as weaving and dressmaking, bring their young children to work, suggesting that these occupations are more compatible with child care. In agricultural occupations, even when children do not accompany their mothers, women with infants generally work fewer hours than other women. Hill (1983), examining work choices by Japanese women, found them also to be less likely (by 16 percent) to choose employment outside the home if they had preschool children.

Mason and Palan (1981) cast doubt on the importance of the role of the incompatibility hypothesis in explaining any relationship between employment and fertility in rural Malaysia. Among rural Malaysians, low income levels and the dependence of the family on the individual wage earnings of its members appear to explain a sometimes positive relationship between employment and fertility. Among urban families, there appears to be a more serious problem with arranging for child care, and thus a negative relationship is obtained. However, the presence of substitutes for the mother (e.g., a girl aged 10-15 or an older married woman) has the expected effect of reducing this negative relationship. Similarly, DaVanzo and Lee found that the number of hours that substitutes spend on child care depends on the wife's wage and the number of hours she works away from home. McCabe and Rosenzweig (1976) found an inverse relationship between wage rate of domestics and female labor supply in Puerto Rico.

The effect of number of children on female labor supply varies over the life cycle. When children are young, parents with more children to support may have to work longer hours to increase family income. At the same time, since childrearing requires the input of time by parents, having a large family may decrease parents' leisure or work hours, and induce specialization of work between husband and wife.[29] Using simple tabulations of time use, Ho (1979) found that, except during the first year of the child, the time spent by mothers on child care takes little time away from their market employment, but significantly more time away from their leisure.[30] During the child's infancy, the mother reduces both her leisure and her market time to increase child care time. Moreover, it is the age distribution of children rather than the number of children that appears to be the major determinant of the mother's time allocation.[31]

While this timing dimension cannot be treated properly in a static framework, it can be considered explicitly in dynamic models. In Hotz (1980), Moffitt (1984), and Vijverberg (1984), the fertility decision is modeled jointly with the wife's lifecycle time allocation decisions. These models view parents as making decisions about the timing and spacing of births in an environment in which the paths of their own future wages and incomes are uncertain. A prediction from these models is that, given wages, fertility tends to decrease hours worked during the early childrearing period, but that as children mature, hours worked rise (Moffitt, 1984). Rosenzweig and Wolpin (1980a) addressed this issue empirically, disentangling the simultaneity between these two outcomes using the case of multiple births. Rosenzweig and Schultz (1984) estimated an empirical model of sequential decision making in which predetermined fertility is allowed to affect subsequent fertility and labor supply. Their results indicate that women who have higher fertility will tend to have a substantially lower probability of participating in the labor market. Distinguishing between persistent and transitory effects, they found that a transitory increase in births has little or no lasting effect on female labor supply following a drop in the year after the birth.


## Wife's Health

Frequent pregnancies take their toll on the mother, resulting in what is termed "maternal depletion syndrome," particularly in poorer areas, where the higher dietary requirements of pregnant or lactating women are more likely to remain unfulfilled. Probably the clearest danger to mothers of high fertility are the obstetrical complications associated with very high parity (Terhune, 1974; Wray, 1971). Through this effect on the health of the mother, family size affects the level of the family's welfare.


## Husband's Labor Supply

Most of the studies on the relationship between family size and parents' economic activity have focused on the wife's labor supply. Few studies have explored the effect of family size on husband's employment and earnings.

Cramer (1980) analyzed data from the Michigan Panel Study of Income Dynamics for the period 1970-73 for a subsample of young married couples with at least one preschool child. He concluded that family size has a substantial effect on husband's labor supply and earnings. Having a second- or higher-parity birth is associated with an increase in husband's hours worked of about 200 hours per year and an increase in earnings of over $700, with most of this change coming from overtime work or increased moonlighting. The average increase in husband's earnings is about equal to the wife's average loss. The average effect on family income is small but positive.

A small sample of rural households in the Philippines indicates that employed husbands with six or more children work a substantially greater number of hours per day than those with smaller families (King and Evenson, 1983). This increased labor supply is obtained apparently at the expense of home production time and leisure hours. However, controlling for the age distribution of children (as well as the husband's wage and age), this large effect is greatly reduced. An additional child aged 1-15 will increase husband's labor supply by only about 20 minutes per day, on average. This discrepancy implies that the first result is due mostly to life-cycle effects.

Child Fosterage

One function of joint or extended family systems is the sharing of child care responsibilities. In other parts of the world, such as West Africa, this function is fulfilled by child fosterage. Child fosterage, or the transfer, giving out, or exchange of children among families, is a way by which parents can provide basic economic support or education for their children, by which adults may acquire domestic labor to perform various household tasks and small services, or by which mothers can join the labor force and secure care for their children at the same time. For whatever reason children are being fostered, this practice appears to be a means by which parents deal with the high costs of raising a large family and yet are able to benefit from having many children in later years when children become net contributors.

The benefit of fostering to working mothers is noted by Isiugo-Abanihe (1985), who reports that working women in West Africa, particularly in urban areas, are more likely to send their children away than are nonworking women. About one-third of working Ghanaian mothers aged 15-34 had sent children away, while only 25 percent of homemakers of the same age had. Among working mothers, those who are employees tend to send their children away more frequently than those who are self-employed. In Sierra Leone, women who work outside the home are more likely to foster out children and less likely to foster in children than are women who do not work (Bledsoe and Isiugo-Abanihe, 1985). In Nigeria, Ibadan working mothers in white-collar jobs are less likely to send their children away, perhaps because they are better able to afford alternative childrearing arrangements.

In areas where the practice is prevalent, child fosterage is an important issue in demographic research. Because it alters the cost of high fertility to parents, it can influence decisions concerning childbearing and child care, and thus affect child welfare. Estimates of the decision to foster out children must also consider the fertility goals or realized fertility of parents. Isiugo-Abanihe found a significant positive relationship between child fosterage and the number of surviving children in Ghana.[32] Bledsoe and Isiugo-Abanihe (1985) also obtained a strong positive relationship (using logistic regression) in their study of families in Sierra Leone. The jointness or interdependence of these two decisions, however, cannot be appraised correctly from a single-equation model. The number of children will be determined by the opportunities available to parents for fostering them out. In a dynamic framework, the number of children away affects the actual cost associated with childrearing, and hence influences future childbearing. Depending on why children are sent away, they can benefit or suffer from being fostered out. This is an issue that needs further research.

394                                                    King

ECONOMIC CONTRIBUTIONS OF CHILDREN

Children make economic contributions in primarily three ways--as
producers, as farm labor, and as old age security.


As Producers

So far, the discussion has focused on the adverse effects of high
fertility on the child's and the family's welfare. Yet children
are a source of satisfaction to parents. They often contribute
to the incomes of poor families and to household production, as
when older children care for their younger siblings. The benefits that parents derive from children have been discussed extensively in the works of Caldwell (1976, 1977), Cain (1980,
1984), De Tray (1974), Mueller (1976, 1981), and others. For
example, in Bangladesh, Cain (1980) found that children of both
sexes begin to work and put in long hours of work even at young
ages. Male children appear to become net producers by age 12.
In the Philippines, the contribution of children to family
income is also substantial. Calculating income from market work
and the value of home production, King and Evenson (1983) found
that children contribute about one-fifth of the family's market
income and one-third of the value of home production in rural
households.
     In Malaysia, girls perform traditional housekeeping activi-
ties for longer hours than boys, on average, but participation
rates and hours often differ little for other activities (De
Tray, 1983). Hence, under the broadest definition of productive
hours (that is, labor market employment plus household production), girls work longer hours. The importance of children as
income earners is indicated by the much greater labor force participation rates of children of mothers who are widowed, divor-
ced, or separated (9 points higher for those aged 5-14 and over
40 points for those aged 15-19). In Java and Nepal, children
spend an increasing amount of time in work activities as they
grow older, with the greatest increase occurring at ages 12-14
among girls and at 15-19 among boys in Java, and at ages 9-11
for both girls and boys in Nepal (Nag et al., 1978). By the time
Javanese boys and girls reach ages 15-19, they spend as much as 8
and 10 hours per day, respectively, in productive activities.
Nepalese boys and girls of the same age work 9.5 and 11 hours
per day, respectively. The fact of the longer work hours of
girls is due to the greater number of hours they spend in home
production, such as child care and food preparation.


As Farm Labor

In developing countries, agricultural production is usually the
dominant economic activity of workers in the family, employing
not only adult members, but also young children. The greater
the number of children (particularly sons), the greater the labor

resource of the family; however, the larger the family size, the greater also the pressure to consume own product and to market less. The interrelationships between the family's consumption and production are the essence of agricultural household models. Farmer parents must also allocate children's time among schooling, farm work, and leisure.

A relevant issue from production function studies is whether family labor is a perfect substitute for hired labor. If no specific human capital is embodied in own children and no consumption benefits are derived from having children work on the family farm, then children can substitute perfectly for hired labor.[33] If family and hired labor are imperfect substitutes, then the level of farm productivity and output depends on family size (or number of children present on the farm). To test the heterogeneity of family and hired labor, Bardhan (1973) estimated the production function coefficient of the proportion of hired to total labor. His results suggest heterogeneity of labor, but with hired labor being more efficient than family labor. Estimating a Cobb-Douglas production function for India (using district-level data), Deolalikar and Vijverberg (1982) suggested that family and hired labor should be treated as separate factors of production, although their results are not conclusive.

The issue of benefits to the farmer of a larger family size is not limited to whether or not family labor is more productive than hired labor. The small farmer may wish to employ his family because he would not have to borrow capital to hire workers during the plowing or sowing seasons,[34] and further may want a guaranteed supply of labor during crucial periods of a cropping cycle. Among the landless farmers in the Philippines, the farmer relies greatly on work by his wife, children, and relatives to fulfill his labor contract with landholders during the peak seasons (Ledesma, 1982). During harvests, children of landless farmers usually miss school for several days to help in the harvesting, threshing, and grain cleaning. The number of grown children who can work often determines the number and size of rice farm plots that the family can contract in one crop season. This dependence on the family will be most acute in areas where the wage labor market is undeveloped, and will be true for both landless workers and landowners.[35]


As Old Age Security

Cain (1984) attributes the strong son preference among Bangladeshi women to their relative economic dependence. In rural Bangladesh, women are excluded from all of the most important sources of wage employment and farm activities that would allow them to cultivate their own land. They may not seek employment in any of the field operations for paddy rice and jute that provide most wage employment. Sons are thus expected to provide security for them in their old age.

Respondents in the value of children surveys in East Asia frequently reported old age security as a reason for wanting children (Arnold et al., 1975). Among rural respondents in Korea and Taiwan, son preference can be linked mainly to economic reasons, such as old age support. On the other hand, economic support and old age security are rarely mentioned in connection with daughters, although help with household chores is often mentioned.

In contrast to these studies, Vlassoff and Vlassoff (1980) conclude that old age security is not important as a motive for fertility in Maharashtra State, India. They argue that in the Indian rural context, joint residence of adults with their parents (and/or with their children) represents only a stage in the life cycle of the family and can have both social and economic reasons. Hence, coresidence is not a sufficient test of the old age security motive. To ascertain dependence, the authors examined how active the elderly parents were and found that men over age 60 spent most of their time doing small jobs or caring for household animals and reported little leisure time. Moreover, they found that those who looked forward to a secure future and reported expecting economic support from their children were, on average, well-off landowners. Hence, the authors reject the hypothesis that old age security could be an important factor affecting fertility choices.

While the distinction between joint residence and dependence is a salient point to make, the argument that the presence of land assets should be taken as incompatible with the old age security motive is flawed. Land ownership provides elderly parents with the insurance they need against an economically insecure future. The expectation of receiving a bequest of land provides an economic incentive for children to support their parents in old age.[36]

CONCLUDING REMARKS

The aim of this chapter has been to assess the consequences of high fertility by examining its relationship to the welfare of the individual child, the mother, and the rest of the family. The evidence on this issue is scattered far and wide in the demographic, economic, sociological, and anthropological literatures. Although an attempt has been made to bring these literatures to bear on the discussion, some important strains of work have undoubtedly been missed. In this selective review, greater attention has been paid to economic-demographic research and to studies that pertain to developing countries.

The subject of the adverse consequences of rapid population growth has received a great deal of attention in past research. The thesis of past studies has been that a large family size undermines the welfare of the child and the parents. The mechanisms through which this is felt may be obviously biological in nature, as with frequent pregnancies' endangering the mother's or the child's health, or they may be behavioral. It has not always been clear in past studies that family welfare (as measured by child's health and education, and so on) is the result of decisions by parents and not simply a consequence of family size. A few studies have considered the jointness of family size and family welfare in parents' decision making, and see parents as altering both family size and investments in children in response to market and nonmarket forces.

Once the interrelationships among family size, child welfare, and parents' well-being are recognized, a different set of issues arises. Some of these issues have been addressed in the literature; others have not been given the attention they perhaps deserve. First, given that family size and child quality are simultaneously determined choices, it is erroneous to interpret the negative association between family size and the child's physical health or intellectual performance as evidence of causality. The same caveat applies to evaluating the relationship between fertility and the wife's (or the husband's) labor supply. Many related empirical studies have not been sufficiently grounded on a solid theoretical framework of decision making in the household. Analyses of family choices have mostly been partial--that is, limited to a single or a pair of decisions--and static, looking only at a single period. To be fair, we must note that data sets needed to support more rigorous analysis in developing countries are still relatively scarce.

The present review of existing work in this area indicates a near vacuum with respect to how survival probabilities influence the investments of parents in child quality. How much will parents spend on child quality when they are faced with high infant/child mortality rates? How much more will parents invest in their children's schooling, training, or health if these rates drop a certain number of points? How much does the distribution of resources among children depend on differences in survival probabilities? Further work is needed in the area of dynamic models of family behavior. Within a dynamic framework, the effects of changes in expected mortality levels and experienced mortality can both be considered. Dynamic models can also reflect the fact that parents make timing decisions, and that the chosen timing and spacing of births are associated with different levels of parents' labor supply and parental investments in child quality. In view of this, statistical methods must be adapted for handling both the dynamic aspect and the simultaneity of family behaviors. These developments will complement the increasing availability of life history data on vital events in the family, labor supply, and child outcomes. Finally, there is much empirical evidence of inequality among siblings. However, past research has not investigated the mechanisms that govern the relationship between intrafamily allocation of resources and family size, or how these mechanisms are affected by parents' characteristics, survival probabilities, and level of growth of the economy. Besides birth order and gender, there are other bases for the allocation of resources among offspring.

The view that population growth undermines individual welfare and inhibits economic development is not unanimously held. Some see rapid population growth as a driving force for development, arguing that population pressure motivates workers in poor countries to work harder and to invent and apply new techniques of production (Boserup, 1981; Caldwell, 1976; Easterlin, 1967; Simon, 1977). For example, increasing population density increases land rents. The response to the rising rental value of land relative to wages might be for producers to increase labor intensity by shortening fallow periods and applying methods that require more labor per unit area. Population growth and indivisibilities with respect to farm size induce specialization and may lead to organizational changes in rural labor markets, such as the creation of a class of landless laborers (Roumasset and Smith, 1981).

Moreover, as Boserup (1981) wrote, the "shrinking supplies of land and natural resources would provide motivation to invent better means of utilizing scarce resources or to discover substitutes for them," and "population increase would make it possible to use methods that are inapplicable when population is smaller." However, this view must be tempered by the consideration that only those who are willing and able to adopt the new technology may be said to benefit from population pressure; the others may be harmed. Success in disseminating new technology often depends on the level and distribution of resources available to the family and the willingness of the family to assume risks.

In work relating to developing countries, the relationship between family size and poverty is a primary concern for both research and policy. Past studies that have investigated the effects of high fertility do not show that it causes poverty; certainly, one cannot conclude from their findings that a drastic and immediate reduction in fertility levels would eradicate poverty in these areas. The question then that must be answered is whether, for families who do not possess much in the way of land or other productive assets, the addition of extra children exacerbates or alleviates poverty. Findings cited here indicate that siblings and parents suffer from a large family size. Particularly in poorer settings, the distribution of food resources may have to be greatly unequal in favor of males over females, or adults over children, to secure the family's survivorship. On the other hand, several studies have argued that the adverse consequences of a large family are mostly temporary, and that children grow up to be net contributors to the family's resources.

NOTES

1 For an historical review of the development of these two "schools," see, for example, Sanderson (1976). Followers of the two approaches tend to differ in their empirical implementations. Using the Becker-Lewis model, also known

as a quantity-quality model, the estimated relationship is considered a couple's demand function, hence, a demand function for the number of children, or a demand function for child schooling, and so on, where the most important determinants of the couple's decisions are income, wealth, and prices. On the other hand, those following the Easterlin approach distinguish between two sets of factors influencing actual fertility: biology and cultural patterns, which are considered to be outside the control of the couple; and individual preferences, which affect desired number of children, use of contraception, and breastfeeding practices. The volume edited by Bulatao and Lee (1983:Vol. 1, p. 3) is a collection of studies on the determinants of fertility that implement this approach. Biology and culture determine what is called the supply of children, "which is the number of surviving children a couple would have if they made no deliberate attempt at limitation," whereas preferences about family size, sex of children, and pace of birth, in conjunction with economic constraints on parents, determine what is called the demand for children.

2   However, education of the mother appears to mitigate this effect. The results they obtained indicate that a college-educated mother with two preschoolers present will spend as much time in care per child as will a high school-educated mother with only one preschooler, and substantially more than a grade school-educated mother with one preschooler.

3   In a later section, we return to birth order effects with respect to intrafamily distribution.

4   See Winikoff (1983) for a survey of studies on the effect of birth intervals on survival probabilities.

5   The practice does not seem to be motivated by fertility control since sexual abstinence does not apply to the husband who may have other wives.

6   Two important reviews of the literature and discussions of the issues involved in the mortality-fertility relationship are provided by Preston (1975) and Schultz (1976). Also see Mauskopf and Wallace (1984), Olsen (1980), and Williams (1977) for discussions of the empirical and statistical issues involved in estimating this relationship.

7   Past research has found a statistically significant positive association between the occurrence of child mortality and fertility. This relationship has been attributed to either biological mechanisms or behavioral responses, or both. According to the biological view, the death of an infant interrupts lactation, thus shortening the period of post-partum sterility and increasing the risk of another pregnancy within a short interval (Knodel and van de Walle, 1967; Cantrelle and Leridon, 1971). If parents can deliber-ately limit their family size, as is assumed in economic approaches, then a systematic relationship between mortality and fertility will also reflect a behavioral response. For example, parents might be viewed as deciding on the number of surviving children, with their expected level of child

mortality determining how many children they should have to
achieve the desired family size. Consequently, we would
observe high-mortality areas to be also high-fertility areas.
However, expected child mortality affects the shadow price
of children, and through this, desired family size. If the
utility that parents derive from children depends on whether
or not children survive to adulthood, then the expected return to fertility will be higher in low-mortality than in
high-mortality areas. Moreover, if the return to child
quality also depends on survival, then investments in child
quality will be more attractive in low-mortality areas as
well. The relative sizes of these effects will determine
parents' preferences for quantity or quality of children.

8  In the one-period model, expectations about mortality are
allowed to affect parents' decisions, but the effect of
actual child deaths is not considered. Hence, parents'
response to child mortality is limited to hoarding. In a
dynamic model, the actual loss of a child may induce parents
to revise their survival expectations and/or their fertility
goals. Similarly, averted deaths may result in parents'
stopping their childbearing sooner than previously planned,
not replacing actual losses or revising their fertility
goals. With respect to an unexpected child death, Ben-Porath
(1978) has argued that if the demand for surviving children
is income-inelastic, then parents will fully replace lost
children and will do so only partially if demand is somewhat
responsive to income.

9  I am grateful to Nancy Birdsall for suggesting these diagrams
to me; I have altered them somewhat, so I claim responsibility for any errors.

10 Cross-sectional studies have found the replacement effect to
be weak. In developing countries such as Bangladesh,
Senegal, and Morocco, about 25 percent of child deaths are
replaced. Since these countries are viewed as noncontra-
cepting populations, the effect is said to be purely bio-
logical--that is, caused by the interruption of breastfeeding
and the shortening of birth intervals when a nursing infant
dies. In developing countries such as Colombia, Peru,
Mexico, Taiwan, and Costa Rica, where contraception is
practiced, the replacement effect is even smaller (Preston,
1975). On the other hand, intercountry comparisons of individual survey data show that the effect can be large.
Schultz (1978) estimated that the derivative of births with
respect to child deaths varies greatly across countries,
ranging from 0.3-0.5 in rural India to 0.8-1.4 in Rio de
Janeiro. The replacement effect is larger for upper-income
classes, who have a lower probability of child mortality
than do lower-income classes. In an earlier study, Schultz
(1976) observed that child survival rates accounted for 4-19
percent of the relative variance in completed fertility among
low-income countries, suggesting that the response of fertility to mortality exceeds one-half of the amount needed for
total replacement. The magnitude of the effect was larger

for women who were older and were more likely to have completed their childbearing.

11  Newman's (1984) dynamic model of fertility and child mortality explicitly incorporates the stochastic nature of the birth and death processes. Parents affect the number and timing of births by choosing their probability of having a birth at any period. Their control lies in their choice of contraceptive efficiency. Children are subject to the risk of death at all ages, but this risk is constant over time and the same at all ages. Parents consider both the finite horizon for fertility decisions and the possibility of child mortality. The higher the probability of a death, the lower the control. This implies that in areas where the probability of mortality is higher, the occurrence of a death will mean a smaller decrease in control than in areas where the probability of mortality is lower. Hence, the replacement response will be smaller where the mortality rates are higher. This prediction coincides with the results obtained by Schultz (1978) for several countries. The model was not estimated.

12  The expected survival rate is measured as the sum of the probability of survival of each child up to the survey divided by the number of live births. The actual survival rate is the ratio of the number of children alive to the total number of live births.

13  In the United States, there has been a growing literature on the analysis of sibling data. The aim of this body of work has been to separate the effects of family environment and genetic endowments on similarities or differences between siblings. The collection of studies in Taubman (1977) addressed substantive and econometric issues related to education, income, and other measures of success between pairs of brothers. Griliches (1979) reviewed economic models of sibling behavior and an assessment of income returns to schooling. These studies, however, did not estimate the relationship between fertility and sibling resemblance.

14  Becker and Tomes also argue that investment in nonhuman capital will partially mitigate the effects of differential investment in children's human capital; that is, it is efficient for parents to invest more in their more able children and to compensate less able children through bequests of nonhuman capital. They further assert that parents may induce more able children to transfer resources directly to less able siblings.

15  According to psychological studies, the last child may be disadvantaged because the last-born, like the only child, has no younger sibling to teach (Zajonc, 1976; Zajonc et al., 1979).

16  For a discussion of the relevant issues pertaining to birth order effects, see Birdsall (1980).

17  Children can also provide future economic support for their parents. A later section discusses this benefit from children.

18  Her data come from two surveys conducted in 1979-80. One
    survey covers a cross-section of employees working in the
    formal wage sector, while the second covers rural school
    children and their families. Whereas data from the first
    survey would be free from the problem of observing indivi-
    duals who have not completed their schooling, data from the
    second survey would also include those who have not finished
    their schooling. This could yield a biased picture of educa-
    tional attainment.

19  Heller and Drake conclude that this effect is not only bio-
    logical or physiological, but also discriminatory, since
    later-parity children tend to receive one-half month less
    nursing than the preceding child, controlling for age of
    mother at nursing.

20  See also De Tray (1984), Khan and Sirageldin (1977) and
    Repetto (1972) for analyses of son preference in South Asia.

21  In the adolescent and childbearing years, the differences
    are less conclusive because of the difficulty involved in
    accurately quantifying the extra nutrient requirements
    associated with body weight, pregnancy and lactation, and
    activity. When body weight or level of physical activity
    adjustments are made, actual caloric intake between males
    and females remains highly unequal in the 0-4 age group;
    differences disappear for older age groups of 5-44 years,
    and are greatly reduced for the age group 45 and over.

22  As Blake noted, these birth-order results also reflect
    spacing patterns, since the data she used include only young
    children. For example, an 11-year-old child who is the
    youngest in a family of nine would not necessarily come from
    a tightly spaced sibset, whereas a child of the same age who
    is the eldest of nine children would.

23  These studies were reviewed by Evenson et al. (1980).

24  The family may be viewed as facing a two-stage decision
    process in which it decides first on the total number of
    children and a mean level of child quality and then on the
    actual distribution of child quality. Although the decisions
    are separated in time, fertility remains a family choice.

25  This correlation has been purged of the effect of observed
    family and individual characteristics.

26  A limitation of this approach is that since fertility and
    female labor supply are determined contemporaneously, the
    choice of identifying variables appears arbitrary (Rosenzweig
    and Schultz, 1984). For studies on the United States, see
    Cain and Dooley (1976), Carliner et al. (1984), and Fleisher
    and Rhodes (1979); for developing countries, see Maurer et
    al. (1973).

27  See DaVanzo and Lee (1983), Gronau (1974), Heckman and Willis
    (1977), Hill (1983), King and Evenson (1983), and Rosenzweig
    (1973).

28  Their data come from national random samples of women collec-
    ted in 1965 and 1973 by the Office of Population Research and
    the Department of Health, Education, and Welfare, respec-
    tively. The data contain information on life-cycle pregnancy

outcomes of 12,605 women. There were 87 twin births in the
first pregnancy. Their estimates show that the incidence of
twins in the first birth substantially alters the life-cycle
pattern of fertility, but has only a slight effect on completed family size.

29  Lindert (1977) found that lower-income wives in the United
    States, who have both more children and less leisure on
    average, will find time for an extra child mostly at the
    expense of other household work.

30  DaVanzo and Lee (1983) obtained similar results for West
    Malaysia--mothers who have more children of preschool age
    tend to reduce their nonchild-related household time.

31  For the United States, Cramer (1980) argues that the dominant
    effects are from fertility to employment in the short run and
    from employment to fertility in the long run. Employment
    before births tends to reduce the probability of having more
    children, and having a baby tends to discourage employment,
    with this latter relationship weakening as the child becomes
    older.

32  The dependent variable is measured as the ratio of the actual
    number of children living away to the number of children
    fostered out by the average mother of the same age. Perhaps
    because fostering is so prevalent, an alternative logit model
    did not yield significant coefficients.

33  Rosenzweig (1977) argues that this is a more accurate repre-
    sentation of conditions in developing countries where a
    market for child labor exists.

34  Contractual agreements of various forms that distribute the
    costs of capital (as well as risks) between farmers and
    workers are found in agricultural economies.

35  In one Indian village in Western India, Vlassoff (1979) found
    that adolescent boys showed little participation in produc-
    tive activities below age 16, much of it regarded as super-
    fluous. Sons living away did not contribute much to family
    income through remittances. Moreover, the author observed
    that parents who were employed as agricultural laborers
    secured much less help from their children than parents who
    were farmers, shepherds, or self-employed. This finding is
    not altogether surprising. Contrary to Vlassoff's argument,
    if the farm labor market is undeveloped, farmers with land
    or farm animals will have greater use for their children's
    labor since the marginal productivity of child time will be
    higher.

36  Nugent (1985) makes the same argument in reviewing the con-
    clusions of Vlassoff and Vlassoff.


REFERENCES

Anderson, K.H.  (1983)  The determinants of fertility, schooling,
    and child survival in Guatemala.  International Economic
    Review 24(3):567-589.

Arnold, F., R. Bulatao, C. Buripakdi, B.J. Chung, J.T. Fawcett,
T. Iritani, S.J. Lee, and T.-S. Wu (1975)  The Value of
Children.  A Cross-National Study.  Introduction and
Comparative Analysis.  Honolulu:  East-West Population
Institute.

Bardhan, P. (1973)  Size, productivity, and returns to scale:  an
analysis of farm-level data in Indian agriculture.  Journal
of Political Economy 81(6):1370-1386.

Becker, G.S. (1960)  An economic analysis of fertility.  In
Demographic and Economic Change in Developed Countries.  A
conference of the Universities-National Bureau Committee for
Economic Research.  Princeton, N.J.:  Princeton University
Press.

Becker, G.S. (1964)  Human Capital, a Theoretical and Empirical
Analysis with Special Reference to Education.  New York:
National Bureau of Economic Research.

Becker, G.S., and G.H. Lewis (1973)  On the interaction between
quantity and quality of children.  Journal of Political
Economy 81(2):S279-S288.

Becker, G.S., and N. Tomes (1976)  Child endowments and the
quantity and quality of children.  Journal of Political
Economy 84(4):S143-S162.

Behrman, J., R. Pollak, and P. Taubman (1982)  Parental preferences and provisions for progeny.  Journal of Political
Economy 90(1):52-73.

Belmont, L., and F.A. Marolla (1973)  Birth order, family size,
and intelligence.  Science 182:1096-1101.

Belmont, L., Z. Stein, and P. Zybert (1978)  Child spacing and
birth order:  effect on intellectual ability in two-child
families.  Science 202:995-996.

Ben-Porath, Y. (1978)  Fertility response to child mortality:
microdata from Israel.  Pp. 161-189 in S. Preston, ed., The
Effects of Infant and Child Mortality on Fertility.  New
York:  Academic Press.

Ben-Porath, Y. (1980)  Child mortality and fertility:  issues in
the demographic transition of a migrant population.  Pp. 151-
207 in R. Easterlin, ed., Population and Economic Change in
Developing Countries.  Chicago:  University of Chicago Press.

Ben-Porath, Y., and F. Welch (1976)  Do sex preferences really
matter?  Quarterly Journal of Economics 90(2):285-312.

Birdsall, N. (1980)  Birth Order Effects and Time Allocation.
Unpublished paper, World Bank, Washington, D.C.

Blake, J. (1981)  Family size and the quality of children.
Demography 18(4):421-442.

Bledsoe, C.H., and U.C. Isiugo-Abanihe (1985)  The Relationship
of Women's Status in Child Fosterage Transactions to Female
Fertility.  Unpublished manuscript, University of Pennsylvania.

Boserup, E. (1981)  Population and Technological Change.
Chicago:  University of Chicago Press.

Bulatao, R.A. (1981)  Values and disvalues of children in
successive childbearing decisions.  Demography 18(1):1-25.

Bulatao, R.A., and R.D. Lee, eds. (1983) Determinants of
    Fertility in Developing Countries, Vols. 1 & 2. New York:
    Academic Press.
Cain, G.G., and M.D. Dooley (1976) Estimation of a model of
    labor supply, fertility, and wages of married women.
    Journal of Political Economy 84(4, Pt.2)S179-S199.
Cain, M.T. (1980) The economic activities of children in a
    village in Bangladesh. Pp. 218-247 in H. Binswanger, R.
    Evenson, C. Florencio, and B. White, eds., Rural Household
    Studies in Asia. Singapore: Singapore University Press.
Cain, M.T. (1984) Women's Status and Fertility in Developing
    Countries: Son Preference and Economic Security. Center
    for Policy Studies Working Papers, No. 110. New York: The
    Population Council.
Caldwell, J.C. (1976) Toward a restatement of demographic transi-
    tion theory. Population and Development Review 2:321-366.
Caldwell, J.C. (1977) The economic rationality of high fertil-
    ity: an investigation illustrated with Nigerian survey data.
    Population Studies 31:5-27.
Cantrelle, P., and H. Leridon (1971) Breastfeeding, mortality in
    childhood, and fertility in a rural zone of Senegal. Popu-
    lation Studies 25(3):505-533.
Carliner, G., C. Robinson, and N. Tomes (1984) Lifetime models
    of female labor supply, wage rates, and fertility. Research
    in Population Economics 5:1-28.
Chen, L.C. (1983) Child survival: levels, trends, and deter-
    minants. Pp. 199-232 in R.A. Bulatao and R.D. Lee, eds.,
    Determinants of Fertility in Developing Countries, Vol. 1.
    New York: Academic Press.
Chen L.C., M.C. Gesche, S. Ahmed, A.I. Chowdhury, and W.M. Mosely
    (1974) Maternal mortality in rural Bangladesh. Studies in
    Family Planning 5:334-341.
Chen, L.C., E. Huq, and S. D'Souza (1981) Sex bias in the family
    allocation of food and health care in rural Bangladesh.
    Population and Development Review 7(1):55-70.
Cramer, J.C. (1980) Fertility and female employment: problems of
    causal direction. American Sociological Review 45(2):
    167-190.
Cramer, J.C. (1980) The effects of fertility on husband's
    economic activity: evidence from static, dynamic, and
    nonrecursive models. Pp. 151-182 in J.L. Simon and J.
    DaVanzo, eds., Research in Population Economics, Vol. 2.
    Greenwich, Conn.: JAI Press.
DaVanzo, J., and D.L.P. Lee (1983) The compatibility of child
    care with market and nonmarket activities: preliminary evi-
    dence from Malaysia. Pp. 62-91 in M. Buvinic, M. Lycette,
    and W.P. McGreevey, eds., Women and Poverty in the Third
    World. Baltimore Md.: The Johns Hopkins University Press.
Deolalikar, A., and W.P.M. Vijverberg (1982) The Heterogeneity
    of Family and Hired Labor in Agricultural Production: A
    Test Using District-Level Data from India. Center
    Discussion Paper No. 411, Economic Growth Center, Yale
    University.

De Sweemer, C. (1984)   The influence of child spacing on child
     survival. Population Studies 38(1):47-72.
De Tray, D. (1974)   Child quality and the demand for children.
     Pp. 91-116 in T.W. Schultz, ed., Economics of the Family
     (Marriage, Children, and Human Capital). Chicago:
     University of Chicago Press.
De Tray, D. (1983) Children's work activities in Malaysia.
     Population and Development Review 9(3):437-455.
De Tray, D. (1984)   Son preference in Pakistan:  an analysis of
     intentions vs. behavior. Research in Population Economics
     5:185-200.
Dooley, M.D. (1982)   Labor supply and fertility of married
     women:  an analysis with grouped and individual data from
     the 1970 U.S. census. Journal of Human Resources 17(4):
     499-532.
Easterlin, R.A. (1966)   On the relation of economic factors to
     recent and projected fertility changes. Demography 3(1):
     131-151.
Easterlin, R.A. (1967)   World population:  effects of population
     growth on the economic development of developing countries.
     Annals of the American Academy of Political and Social
     Sciences 369:98-108.
Evenson, R.E. (1983)   The Economic Consequences of Averting
     Births in North India. Unpublished manuscript, Economic
     Growth Center, Yale University.
Evenson, R.E., B. Popkin, and E.K. Quizon (1980)   Nutrition,
     work, and demographic behaviour in rural Philippine house-
     holds, a synopsis of several Laguna household studies.  PP.
     289-366 in H. Binswanger, R. Evenson, C. Florencio, and B.
     White, eds., Rural Household Studies in Asia.  Singapore:
     Singapore University Press.
Fabella, R. (1982)  Economies of Scale in the Household
     Production Model and Intra-Family Allocation of Resources.
     Unpublished Ph.D. dissertation, Yale University.
Fleisher, B.M., and G.F. Rhodes, Jr. (1979)   Fertility, women's
     wage rates, and labor supply. American Economic Review
     69(1):14-24.
Gomes, M. (1984)   Family size and educational attainment in
     Kenya. Population and Development Review 10(4):647-660.
Griliches, Z. (1979)   Sibling models and data in economics:
     beginnings of a survey. Journal of Political Economy 87(5,
     Part 2):S37-S64.
Gronau, R. (1974)   The effect of children on the housewife's
     value of time.  Pp. 457-488 in T.W. Schultz, ed., Economics
     of the Family (Marriage, Children, and Human Capital).
     Chicago:  University of Chicago Press.
Heller, P.S, and W.D. Drake (1979)   Malnutrition, child morbid-
     ity, and the family decision process. Journal of Development
     Economics 6(2):203-235.
Heckman, J., and R. Willis (1977)   A beta-logistic model for the
     analyses of sequential labor force participation by married
     women. Journal of Political Economy 85:27-58

Higgins, J.V., E.W. Reed, and S.C. Reed (1962)  Intelligence and
    family size:  a paradox resolved.  Eugenics Quarterly
    9:84-90.
Hill, C.R., and F.P. Stafford (1980)  Prenatal care of children:
    time diary estimates of quantity, predictability, and
    variety.  Journal of Human Resources 15(2):219-239.
Hill, M.A. (1983)  Female labor force participation in developing
    and developed countries--consideration of the informal
    sector.  Review of Economics and Statistics 65(3):459-468.
Ho, T.J. (1979)  Time costs of child rearing in the rural
    Philippines.  Population and Development Review 5:643-662.
Horton, S. (1984)  Birth Order and Child Nutritional Status:
    Evidence on the Intrahousehold Allocation of Resources in
    the Philippines.  Unpublished manuscript, University of
    Toronto.
Hotz, V.J. (1980)  A Life Cycle Model of Fertility and Married
    Women's Labor Supply.  Unpublished manuscript, Carnegie-
    Mellon University.
Hotz, V.J., and R. Miller (1984)  The Economics of Family Plan-
    ning.  Unpublished manuscript, Department of Economics,
    Carnegie-Mellon University.
Isiugo-Abanihe, U.C. (1985)  Child fostering in West Africa.
    Population and Development Review 11(1):53-73.
Khan, M.A., and I. Sirageldin (1977)  Son preference and the
    demand for additional children in Pakistan.  Demography
    14:481-496.
King, E.M. (1982)  Investments in Schooling:  An Analysis of
    Demand in Low Income Households.  Unpublished Ph.D.
    dissertation, Yale University.
King, E.M., and R.E. Evenson (1983)  Time allocation and home
    production in Philippine rural households.  Pp. 35-61 in M.
    Buvinic, M. Lycette, and W.P. McGreevey, eds., Women and
    Poverty in the Third World.  Baltimore, Md.:  The Johns
    Hopkins University Press.
King, E.M., and L.A. Lillard (1983)  A Censored Discrete Choice
    Model of School Attainment Level and Sibling Correlation in
    Schooling.  Paper presented at the Econometric Society
    Meeting, San Francisco.
Knodel, J. (1982)  Child mortality and reproductive behavior in
    German village population in the past:  a micro-level
    analysis of the replacement effect.  Population Studies
    36(2):177-199.
Knodel, J., and E. van de Walle (1967)  Breastfeeding, fertility,
    and infant mortality:  an analysis of some early German data.
    Population Studies 21:109-131.
Ledesma, A.J. (1982)  Landless Workers and Rice Farmers:  Peasant
    Subclasses under Agrarian Reform in Two Philippine Villages.
    Los Banos, Philippines:  International Rice Research
    Institute.
Lehrer, E. (1984)  The impact of child mortality on spacing by
    parity:  a Cox-regression analysis.  Demography 21(3):
    323-337.

Lehrer, E., and M. Nerlove (forthcoming) The impact of expected
    child survival on husbands' and wives' desired fertility in
    Malaysia: a log-linear probability model. Social Science
    Research.
Lillard, L.A., and E.M. King (forthcoming) Sibling Correlation
    in Schooling: Evidence from Malaysia and the Philippines.
    Santa Monica, Calif.: The Rand Corporation.
Lindert, P.H. (1977) Sibling position and achievement. Journal
    of Human Resources 12(2):198-219.
McCabe, J.L., and M.R. Rosenzweig (1976) Female labor force
    participation, occupational choice, and fertility in
    developing countries. Journal of Development Economics
    3:1-20.
Mahmud, S., and J.P. McIntosh (1980) Returns to scale to family
    size--who gains from high fertility? Population Studies
    34(3):500-506.
Mason, K.O., and V.T. Palan (1981) Female employment and fertil-
    ity in peninsular Malaysia: the maternal role incompatibil-
    ity hypothesis reconsidered. Demography 18(4):549-575.
Maurer, K.M., R. Ratajczak, and T.P. Schultz (1973) Marriage,
    Fertility, and Labor Force Participation of Thai Women: An
    Econometric Study. Santa Monica, Calif.: Rand Corporation.
Mauskopf, J. (1983) Reproductive response to child mortality: a
    maximum likelihood estimation model. Journal of the American
    Statistical Association 78(382):238-248.
Mauskopf, J., and T.D. Wallace (1984) Fertility and replacement:
    some alternative stochastic models and results for Brazil.
    Demography 21(4):519-536.
Michael, R.T. (1974) Education and the derived demand for
    children. Pp. 120-156 in T.W. Schultz, ed., Economics of
    the Family (Marriage, Children, and Human Capital).
    Chicago: University of Chicago Press.
Miyashita, H., P. Newbold, A.M. Pilarski, and J.L. Simon (1982)
    The effect of population growth upon the quantity of educa-
    tion children receive: a reply. Review of Economics and
    Statistics 64(2):352-355.
Moffitt, R. (1984) Optimal life-cycle profiles of fertility and
    labor supply. Research in Population Economics 5:29-50.
Mueller, E. (1976) The economic value of children in peasant
    society. Pp. 98-153 in R.G. Ridker, ed., Population and
    Development. Baltimore, Md.: The Johns Hopkins University
    Press.
Mueller, E. (1981) The Value and Allocation of Time in Rural
    Botswana. Discussion Paper No. 81-44. Washington, D.C.:
    World Bank.
Nag, M., B.N.F. White, and R.C. Peet (1978) An anthropological
    approach to the study of the economic value of children in
    Java and Nepal. Current Anthropology 19(2):293-306.
Newman, J.L. (1984) A Stochastic Dynamic Model of Fertility.
    Paper presented at the meeting of the Population Association
    of America, Minneapolis.
Newman, J.L., and C.E. McCulloch (1984) A hazard rate approach
    to the timing of births. Econometrics 52(4):939-961.

Nugent, J.B. (1985) The old-age security motive for fertility. Population and Development Review 11(1):75-97.

O'Hara, D.J. (1972) Mortality risks, sequential decisions on births and population growth. Demography 4(3):285-298.

O'Hara, D.J. (1975) Microeconomic aspects of the demographic transition. Journal of Political Economy 83(5):1203-1216.

Olneck, M.R., and B.L. Wolfe (1980) Intelligence and family size: another look. Review of Economics and Statistics 62(2):241-247.

Olsen, R.J. (1980) Estimating the effect of child mortality on the number of births. Demography 17(4):429-443.

Olsen, R.J. (1983) Mortality rates, mortality events, and the number of births. American Economic Review 73(2):29-32.

Olsen, R.J., and K.I. Wolpin (1983) The impact of exogenous child mortality on fertility: a waiting time regression with dynamic regressors. Econometrica 51(3):731-749.

Page, H.J., and R. Lesthaeghe (1981) Child-Spacing in Tropical Africa: Traditions and Change. New York: Academic Press.

Polit, D.F. (1982) Effects of Family Size: A Critical Review of Literature Since 1973. Final Report submitted to the Center for Population Research, National Institute of Child Health and Human Development. Washington, D.C.: American Institutes for Research.

Preston, S. (1975) Health programs and population growth. Population and Development Review 1:189-199.

Preston, S. (1980) Causes and consequences of mortality decline in less developed countries during the twentieth century. Pp. 289-360 in R. Easterlin, ed., Population and Economic Change in Developing Countries. Chicago: University of Chicago Press.

Razin, A. (1979) Number, birth spacing and quality of children: a microeconomic view. Pp. 279-293 in J. Simon and J. DaVanzo, eds., Research in Population Economics II. Greenwich, Conn.: JAI Press.

Repetto, R. (1972) Son preference and fertility behavior in developing countries. Studies in Family Planning 3(4):70-76.

Rodgers, G., and G. Standing (1981) Economic roles of children in low-income countries. International Labour Review 120(1):31-47.

Rosenzweig, M. (1977) The demand for children in farm households. Journal of Political Economy 85(1):123-146.

Rosenzweig, M. (1983) Estimating a household production func-function: heterogeneity, the demand for health inputs, and their effects on birth weight. Journal of Political Economy 91(5):723-746.

Rosenzweig, M., and R.E. Evenson (1977) Fertility, schooling, and the economic contribution of children in rural India: an econometric analysis. Econometrica 45(5):1065-1080.

Rosenzweig, M., and T.P. Schultz (1982) Market opportunities, genetic endowments, and intrafamily distribution: child survival in rural India. American Economic Review 72(4):803-815.

Rosenzweig, M., and T.P. Schultz (1983)   Consumer demand and
    household production:   the relationship between fertility
    and child mortality.   American Economic Review 73(2):38-42.
Rosenzweig, M., and T.P. Schultz (1984)   The Demand for and
    Supply of Births:   Fertility and Its Life-Cycle Consequences.
    Center Discussion Paper No. 464, Economic Growth Center,
    Yale University.
Rosenzweig, M., and K.I. Wolpin (1980a)   Life-cycle labor supply
    and fertility:   causal inferences from household models.
    Journal of Political Economy 88(2):328-348.
Rosenzweig, M., and K.I. Wolpin (1980b)   Testing the quantity-
    quality fertility model:   the use of twins as a natural
    experiment.   Econometrica 48(1):227-240.
Rosenzweig, M., and K.I. Wolpin (1984)   Heterogeneity, Intra-
    family Distribution and Child Health.   Economic Development
    Center, Bulletin Number 84-2, University of Minnesota.
Roumasset, J.R., and J. Smith (1981)   Population, technological
    change, and the evolution of labor markets.   Population and
    Development Review 7(3):401-419.
Sanderson, W.C.   (1976)   On two schools of the economics of
    fertility.   Population and Development Review 2(3-4):469-477.
Santow, G., and M.D. Bracher (1984)   Child death and time to the
    next birth in central Java.   Population Studies
    38(2):241-253.
Schultz, T.P. (1976)   Interrelationships between mortality and
    fertility.   Pp. 239-289 in R. Ridker, ed., Population and
    Development.   Baltimore, Md.:   The Johns Hopkins University
    Press.
Schultz, T.P. (1977)   The influence of fertility on labor supply
    of married women:   simultaneous equation estimates.   In R.G.
    Ehrenberg, ed., Research in Labor Economics, Vol. I.   Green-
    wich, Conn.:   JAI Press.
Schultz, T.P. (1978)   Fertility and child mortality over the life
    cycle.   American Economic Review 68(2):208-215.
Schultz, T.P. (1979)   An economic perspective on population
    growth.   Pp. 148-174 in National Academy of Sciences, ed.,
    Rapid Population Growth.   Baltimore, Md.:   The Johns Hopkins
    University Press.
Sewell, W.H., R.M. Hauser, and W.C. Wolf (1980)   Sex, schooling,
    and occupational status.   American Journal of Sociology
    86(3):551-583.
Simon, J.L. (1977) The Economics of Population Growth.
    Princeton, N.J.:   Princeton University Press.
Taubman, P., ed. (1977)   Kinometrics:   Determinants of Socio-
    economic Success Within and Between Families.   Amsterdam:
    North-Holland.
Terhune, K.W. (1974)   A Review of the Actual and Expected
    Consequences of Family Size.   Report to the Center for
    Population Research, National Institute of Child Health and
    Human Development.   Washington, D.C.:   National Institute of
    Health.

Vijverberg, W. (1984) Discrete choices in a continuous time model: life-cycle time allocation and fertility decisions. Pp. 51-87 in T.P. Schultz and K. Wolpin, eds., Research in Population Economics. Greenwich, Conn.: JAI Press, Inc.

Vlassoff, M. (1979) Labor demand and economic utility of children: a case study in rural India. Population Studies 33(3):415-428.

Vlassoff, M., and C. Vlassoff (1980) Old-age security and the utility of children in rural India. Population Studies 34(3):487-499.

Williams, A.D. (1977) Measuring the impact of child mortality on the number of births. Demography 14(4):581-590.

Williamson, N.E. (1976) Sons or Daughters (A Cross-Cultural Survey of Parental Preferences). Beverly Hills, Calif.: Sage Publications.

Winikoff, B. (1983) The effects of birth spacing on child and maternal health. Studies in Family Planning 14(10):231-245.

Wolfers, D., and S. Scrimshaw (1975) Child survival and intervals between pregnancies in Guayaquil, Ecuador. Population Studies 29(3):479-496.

Wolpin, K.I. (1984) An estimable dynamic stochastic model of fertility and child mortality. Journal of Political Economy 92(5):852-874.

Wray, J.D. (1971) Population pressure on families: family size and child spacing. Pp. 403-461 in National Academy of Sciences, ed., Rapid Population Growth, Consequences and Policy Implications. Baltimore, Md.: The Johns Hopkins University Press.

Zajonc, R.B. (1976) Family configuration and intelligence. Science 192:227-236.

Zajonc, R.B., H. Markus, and G.B. Markus. (1979) The birth order puzzle. Journal of Personality and Social Psychology 37(8): 1325-1341.

# 11

## School Expenditures and Enrollments, 1960-80: The Effects of Income, Prices, and Population Growth

T. Paul Schultz

INTRODUCTION

School systems have expanded rapidly during the last 25 years. Despite the unprecedented growth in the population reaching school age, enrollment rates at these ages have increased in virtually every country. However, school expenditures in some low- and middle-income countries have recently not increased as rapidly as enrollment; this growing gap in public educational expenditures per pupil between poorer and richer countries is a worrisome trend that suggests that a deterioration in the quality of schooling may be occurring in the low-income countries. To put these developments in perspective, this chapter proposes a production-demand framework for explaining the level and distribution of national expenditures on schooling and enrollment rates. Incomes, prices, production technology, and demographic factors are interrelated as constraints and conditions affecting the costs of, and demands for, educational services. Data for 89 countries from 1960 to 1980 are used to test empirically a variety of hypotheses within this framework, including whether rapid population growth, which has contributed to an increase in the relative size of a school-aged cohort, affects that cohort's educational opportunities and achievements. Differences in school enrollment between males and females are also examined. Finally, regional and religious deviations in educational expenditures and achievements are calculated, based on the fitted model. The uniformity and quality of the intercountry data and the simplicity of the statistical treatment of this mix of cross-sectional and time-series materials leave much room for future

The research assistance of Lynn Karoly, Andrew Levin, and Paul McGuire is greatly appreciated. The comments of Allen Kelley, Mark Rosenzweig, Raaj Sah, T.W. Schultz, and John Strauss and the Working Group were also valuable. This research was supported by a grant from the General Service Foundation and research assistance was provided by the National Research Council of the National Academy of Sciences.

analytical improvements; nevertheless, this initial examination
of educational systems confirms the usefulness of treating these
institutions as adapting to the constraints imposed by incomes,
relative factor prices, and population growth.

The hypothesis has been advanced that rapid population growth
makes it more difficult for a society to educate its youth
(Jones, 1971, 1975; Robinson, 1975; World Bank, 1974, 1984).
Obviously, a reduction in fertility leads to a reduction in the
number of children of school age in 6 to 8 years. In this sense,
this demographic development reduces the need for schools, and
these potential public savings due to fertility declines can be
used to achieve other social goals (Coale and Hoover, 1958:25).

To quantify the consequences of population growth for the
educational system and society, it is often assumed that the
allocation of resources to this public sector activity is fixed
and does not respond to the changing private demands of the
society for these services. Perhaps a more plausible institutional hypothesis is that public expenditures on the educational
system respond to private demands for schooling, and one determinant of these demands is the size of school-aged cohorts.
However, the public sector responds imperfectly and with lags
because of bottlenecks, for example, in the time required to increase the supply of trained teachers needed to educate a growing
student population. According to this view, educational expenditures and achievements per child may fall short of long-run
trends (equilibrium) in periods when the school-aged population
is a relatively large and growing fraction of the total population, while the opposite tendency may emerge when school staff
and structures exceed requirements temporarily because of a
decline in fertility. At issue is the importance of the relative
size of the school-aged population for the allocation of resources to the national educational system (e.g., Freeman, 1979;
Lee, 1979; Welch, 1979; Easterlin, 1980; Simon and Pilarski,
1979). Empirically measuring the elasticity of educational inputs and outputs with respect to the relative size of school-aged
cohorts is, therefore, a central objective of this study.[1]

The statistical problem is to hold constant for other exogenous factors that might explain the level and distribution of
public expenditures on schooling and school achievement across
countries and over time. It is particularly important to measure
and hold constant those factors that might help to account for
educational priorities in a society, or that represent supplementary private inputs to the educational process. When these
other factors are omitted from the empirical analysis and are
also associated with the relative size of the school-aged population, the observed partial association between schooling and
cohort size will be a biased measure of the hypothesized demographic effect of cohort size on schooling per child. The challenge is to minimize this potential source of bias.

One reason it is difficult to measure the relationship between relative cohort size and educational inputs and outputs is
because the size of the school-aged cohort is primarily a lagged
measure of period fertility rates. The fertility of parents is

closely related to what they privately invest in the schooling of each of their children, and this trade-off between quantity and quality has attracted the attention of many social scientists (e.g., Wray, 1971; Belmont and Marolla, 1973; Terhune, 1974; Becker and Lewis, 1974). The observation that fertility and schooling are inversely related does not imply that one causes the other. Indeed, both are jointly chosen to some degree by parents in response to their economic and biological endowments, constraints, and preferences. It is important, therefore, that the inverse correlation between fertility and child schooling not be mistaken for evidence confirming the effect of relative cohort size on public educational expenditures or enrollments (Schultz, 1971, 1981; Rosenzweig and Wolpin, 1980). The analytical problem is how to distinguish between two possible parallel associations: the first at the level of family choice between increases in parent investments in the schooling of their children and declines in their fertility, and the second at the aggregate level between the relative size of a school-aged cohort and the resultant squeeze on available school inputs and outputs per child. The strategy adopted here for separating these two relationships is to estimate the partial correlation between relative school-aged cohort size and indicators of school expenditures and outputs, holding constant for current total fertility rates; estimates are also reported in the Appendix without controlling for current period fertility. Information on a better indicator of the lifetime reproductive performance of the parents of the school-aged cohort is not available from the majority of countries. If the estimated effect of school-aged cohort size remains important after controlling for current total fertility, the aggregate "squeezing out" causal hypothesis is tentatively sustained.

This empirical strategy should be more successful when fertility and child mortality are in flux. At such times, it should be possible to discriminate statistically between (1) the covariance of current fertility and current parent investments in child schooling, and (2) the repercussions of lagged fertility (and child mortality) for cohort size and thus for the schooling system. The present framework may therefore be more discriminating in the study of the effects of cohort size on schooling at the secondary rather than the primary level because the lag separating fertility and the size of these school-aged cohorts is longer—about 12 compared to 8 years, on average.

To improve on this relatively crude method for evaluating the exogenous effect of changes in the relative size of school-aged cohorts on the allocation of public resources and the performance of school systems, more data and more explicit modeling would be required. Changes in fertility, child mortality, and age structure could be dynamically analyzed within countries over time, or determinants of cumulative fertility and parental investment in child schooling could be derived from an explicit model of household behavior. Both of these alternative approaches to estimating the effect of cohort size on the schooling system would require more data, and would therefore be based on

a smaller and probably less representative sample of countries
over time. Moreover, these alternative estimation strategies
would appear to call for a theory of fertility determination,
about which there is limited consensus today.

The next section of this chapter reviews world trends in
school enrollments and central government expenditures on education and identifies a number of issues for further study. The
next two sections model the determinants of demand for public
schooling to specify how to proceed with the empirical analysis.
This is followed by a report on the empirical findings of an
analysis of data from about 90 countries over the last three
decades. The concluding section uses these results to predict
the recent trends over time. A data Appendix describes the
sources, character, and limitations of these data and provides
supplementary tables.


WORLD TRENDS

Table 1 summarizes the levels and increases in enrollment ratios
at the primary, secondary, and higher education levels for countries grouped by income level, market/nonmarket economy, and oil
exporter status. For summary comparisons of overall levels of
schooling, a synthetic cohort measure is constructed, hereafter
called the "expected years of schooling." This measure is defined as the sum of six times the primary, six times the secondary, and five times the higher educational enrollment ratios,
where these weights (6, 6, and 5) correspond to the average
number of single-year age groups combined in the denominators of
these three standardized enrollment ratios.

Expected years of schooling increased 32 percent from 1960
to 1981 in the low-income class of countries, 46 percent gains
were achieved in the middle-income countries that imported oil,
and 50 percent gains occurred in the upper middle-income class.
The East European nonmarket countries increased their expected
years of schooling by 35 percent, while the industrial market
high-income countries advanced 16 percent. Oil exporters in the
middle-income class achieved a doubling of expected schooling
levels, while nearly a fourfold increase was reported among the
high-income oil exporters.

In general, the percentage gains in schooling were greater
for those countries that started from a lower level in 1960.
The gap in expected years of schooling between the low- and
high-income countries is therefore closing, on average, whether
expressed in relative terms or even as an absolute difference in
years. This closure in the education gap appears to be even more
rapid in relative terms than that achieved in health, analogously
summarized by life expectation at birth. The gap in expected
education and life at birth between the lowest-income countries
(excluding India and China in the World Bank categories) and the
high-income industrial market economies decreased markedly over
the last two decades. Life expectation stood at about 43 and 71
years in 1960 in these two groups of countries, respectively,

TABLE 1 Growth in Educational Enrollments by School Level and Countries by Income Classes, 1960-81

| World Bank Country Class[a] (number) | Primary (6-11) Education | | Secondary (12-17) Education | | Higher (20-24) Education | | Expected Years of Enrollment[b] | | Percent of Increase in Enrollment Ratios (1960-81) | | | |
|---|---|---|---|---|---|---|---|---|---|---|---|---|
| | 1960 | 1981 | 1960 | 1981 | 1960 | 1981 | 1960 | 1981 | Primary | Secondary | Higher | Expected |
| | (1) | (2) | (3) | (4) | (5) | (6) | (7) | (8) | (9) | (10) | (11) | (12) |
| Low Income (34) | .80 | .94 | .18 | .34 | .02 | .04 | 5.98 | 7.88 | 18 | 89 | 100 | 32 |
| Excluding China and India[c] | .38 | .72 | .07 | .19 | .01 | .02 | 2.75 | 5.56 | 89 | 171 | 100 | 102 |
| Middle Income (38) | | | | | | | | | | | | |
| Oil exporters | .64 | 1.06 | .09 | .37 | .02 | .08 | 4.48 | 8.98 | 66 | 311 | 300 | 100 |
| Oil importers | .84 | .99 | .18 | .44 | .04 | .13 | 6.32 | 9.23 | 18 | 144 | 225 | 46 |
| Upper-Middle Income (22) | .88 | 1.04 | .20 | .51 | .04 | .14 | 6.68 | 10.0 | 18 | 155 | 250 | 50 |
| High-Income Oil Exporters (5) | .29 | .83 | .05 | .43 | .01 | .08 | 2.09 | 7.96 | 186 | 760 | 700 | 281 |
| Industrial Market (18) | 1.14 | 1.01 | .64 | .90 | .16 | .37 | 11.5 | 13.3 | -11 | 41 | 131 | 16 |
| East European Nonmarket (8) | 1.01 | 1.05 | .45 | .88 | .11 | .20 | 9.31 | 12.6 | 4 | 96 | 82 | 35 |

[a] The low-income includes countries with an annual GNP per capita of less than $410 (U.S.) in 1982 prices; the middle-income class includes countries with GNP per capita between $410 and $1,650; the upper-middle-income class includes countries in the range from $1,650 to about $6,000.
[b] Synthetic cohort concept defined as six (years) times the sum of primary and secondary enrollment ratios plus five (years) times higher educational enrollment ratio.
[c] The lack of expenditure data for China and India in Table 2 justifies our consideration of the low-income class excluding these two large countries.

Source: World Bank (1984:Table 25).

and had increased to roughly 51 and 75 years by 1982. Expected years of schooling, on the other hand, increased for these two groups of countries from almost 3 and 11.5 years, respectively, in 1960, to almost 6 and 13.3 years in 1982, or from one-to-four to almost one-to-two. These achievements were recorded despite the fact that income (GNP) per capita in constant prices grew in the same period three times faster in the high-income countries than it did in this lowest-income group of countries.2

The salient fact is that all classes of countries, and indeed every country for which overall comparisons can be drawn, increased the expected schooling that it provided to the "average" child over these two decades, despite the extraordinarily rapid growth in the number of school-aged children in many of the poorest countries. The number of children between the ages of 6 and 17 more than doubled in the less developed regions from 1950 to 1980. The proportion of the population in these ages increased from 24.5 percent in 1950 to 29.1 percent in 1980, or by 19 percent.3 That the poorest countries and those that have suffered actual declines in their real income in this period were nonetheless able to expand their schooling systems rapidly enough to accommodate an increasing fraction of their children is a remarkable achievement.

However, a less sanguine picture of recent educational progress emerges from World Bank data assembled in Table 2. Central governmental expenditures on education (and health), when expressed in terms of constant GNP prices, have declined in many countries over the past decade. Among low- and middle-income countries that are not oil exporters, the share of central government expenditures allocated to education (and health) declined (columns 1-4). The share of total government expenditures in GNP also declined in the low-income countries and increased only slightly among the middle-income oil importers (columns 5 and 6). Resources allocated to education per capita by central governments appear to have declined in real terms by about two-thirds in the low-income countries (including or excluding India and China) and increased by only 22 percent in the middle-income oil-importing countries. In contrast, oil-exporting middle- and upper middle-income countries were able to more than double their per capita real public expenditures for education, while the high-income industrial countries increased their real outlays on education by 88 percent. A comparable decline occurred in the low-income countries in central government expenditures on health, which fell by about one-half, and grew less rapidly than educational expenditures in all other classes of countries (Table 2, column 9).

The puzzle is how the poorer countries sustained growth in enrollments in an era when central government real outlays for education per capita were tapering off. Several developments could be responsible for these seemingly divergent trends. The unit costs of producing educational services may have declined, which might occur, for example, if the price of educational inputs declined relative to the GNP deflator, or economies of scale in school systems were realized. Alternatively, the quality of schooling may have deteriorated.

TABLE 2  Central Government Expenditures, 1972 and 1981

| World Bank Country Class[a] (number) | Percent of Government Expenditures | | | | Total Government Expenditures as Percent of GNP | | Percent of Growth in Real per Capita GNP 1971-81[b] | Percent of Growth in per Capita Real Expenditures, 1972-81 | |
|---|---|---|---|---|---|---|---|---|---|
| | Education | | Health | | | | | Education | Health |
| | 1972 | 1981 | 1972 | 1981 | 1972 | 1981 | | | |
| | (1) | (2) | (3) | (4) | (5) | (6) | (7) | (8) | (9) |
| Low Income (34)[c] | 16.4 | 5.9 | 6.2 | 2.9 | 21.0 | 15.4 | 26 | -67 | -57 |
| Excluding China and India[c] | 16.4 | 11.5 | 6.2 | 4.4 | 21.0 | 17.6 | 7 | -63 | -37 |
| Middle Income (38) | | | | | | | | | |
| Oil exporters | 15.4 | 16.6 | 5.7 | 5.6 | 17.2 | 27.8 | 34 | +133 | +133 |
| Oil importers | 11.0 | 10.0 | 6.9 | 4.6 | 20.7 | 21.8 | 28 | +22 | -10 |
| Upper Middle Income (22) | 10.8 | 14.3 | 7.0 | 5.5 | 15.0 | 20.6 | 32 | +140 | +42 |
| High-Income Oil Exporters (5) | 13.5 | 9.2 | 5.5 | 5.5 | 36.6 | 26.3 | 0 | -51 | -28 |
| Industrial Market (18) | 4.3 | 5.1 | 9.9 | 11.4 | 21.7 | 28.3 | 21 | +88 | +87 |
| East European Nonmarket (8)[d] | | | | | | | | | |

[a]The low-income class has an annual GNP per capita of less than $410 (U.S.) in 1982 prices. The middle-income class includes countries with GNP per capita between $410 and $1,650, while the upper middle-income class ranges from $1,650 to about $6,000.
[b]Annual growth. Rate on per capita real GNP derived for 1970 to 1982 from World Bank tables and interpolated for the 9 years corresponding to expenditure data, 1972-81.
[c]The lack of data for China and India throughout this period makes the overall "low-income" country class comparisons of limited value.
[d]No data.

Source:  World Bank (1984:Appendix Tables 2, 19, and 26).

The dominant cost of primary and secondary school systems is teacher salaries. These salaries may have declined relative to the general wage level with development, as they have in the twentieth century in the United States (Williamson and Lindert, 1980:308). The supply of teachers may have outgrown the demand in many countries, while highly paid expatriates were replaced by less expensive indigenous personnel. Alternatively, the quality (and pay) of teachers may have deteriorated. Both phenomena may have occurred. In the first case, the real resources available to the school system may not have fallen as rapidly as (or grown more rapidly than) the figures suggest in column 8 of Table 2. Human and physical capital may also have been used more intensively over time, with teacher-to-student ratios increasing and capital expenditures as a share of total expenditures falling. These developments would be associated with larger classes, and perhaps less effective or lower-quality instruction.

Other developments may also explain the aggregate trends. Private school expenditures may have increased as a share of total educational outlays. However, this appears unlikely because private school enrollments are generally modest, and represent a declining share of total enrollments in most low-income countries.[4] Tuition and fees may also transfer some of the resource costs of public schools from public expenditures to parents.[5] The reliance on such user fees, though increasingly debated as an auxiliary means of supporting educational expansion, has nonetheless been eroded by recent inflation and policy changes, even in Africa (Jimenez, 1984). Subnational and local public expenditures on education are excluded from the worldwide figures reported in Table 2, and the central government's share of educational expenditures may have declined recently.

In sum, many factors could be behind the decline in central governmental expenditures on education in the lowest-income countries:

- The actual quality of schooling per student may have declined.

- The price of constant-quality educational services relative to the general price level (GNP deflator) may have declined.

- Central government revenues for education may have declined relative to other sources of support for public education.

- Private school expenditures may have increased their share of the market, though enrollment data do not support this conjecture.

- The underlying data may be in error.

The cross-country empirical analysis of public educational systems presented below is restricted to countries for which

there appear to be consistent data on enrollments, teachers, expenditures on current and capital account, estimates of GNP in
constant prices, urbanization, and the population's age composition. These restricted data are believed to be more reliable
than the comprehensive estimates reported in Table 2, but possibly less representative. Although UNESCO public expenditure
data also represent the sum of government outlays at all administrative levels, they probably in fact frequently omit local resources provided in kind for the construction and maintainence
of basic school structures. Estimates are later obtained of
changes in relative prices and changes in factor intensity or
quality in the use of teachers and physical capital. However,
there is no unambiguous way to distinguish between changes in
the quality of school inputs and changes in the prices of
quality-constant inputs, since the capacity of schools to raise
the market productivity and to augment the utility of students
remains unobserved.

The question raised in this review of world trends is how
enrollment rates were increased when central government expenditures slackened in real per capita terms or rose more slowly
than did the school-aged population. Before considering patterns
in these data from various countries, it is useful to have an
overall framework within which to account for variation in the
provision of educational services. This framework involves three
parts: an interpretation of the political economy translating
private demands into public expenditure decisions, a production
technology linking educational inputs to outputs, and the determinants of household demand for public educational services.

ADJUSTMENT OF THE EDUCATIONAL SYSTEM TO DEMAND AND SUPPLY

Analyses of the private demand for public goods have generally
assumed that citizens know about the costs of production and the
benefits of government spending (e.g., Borcherding and Deacon,
1972). The political process is assumed to be more or less demo-
cratic, in the sense that entrepreneur-politicians seek "elec-
tion" to deliver efficiently the public goods and services and
the associated tax burden that jointly command the support of a
majority of voters.[6] The essential idea is that public, as
well as private, institutions are constrained in their input
allocation and production decisions by consumer incomes, relative
input prices, and perceived benefits of outputs.

The private demand for public education, however, involves
several special features that warrant additional discussion.
First, education is demanded both as a consumer good that yields
direct utility and as a producer good that is expected to enhance
the future productivity of the educated individual (Schultz,
1961). Private demand for consumer goods depends on consumer income, relative prices, and tastes. The taste for education is
conventionally assumed uncorrelated with observed demand determinants, though this can be relaxed if an exogenous proxy for
taste can be distinguished; the examination below of male and fe-

male enrollment rates conditional on religion might be viewed as
assuming religion is such a proxy for exogenous cultural taste.

Education is also a produced means of production, and economists have reasoned that the private and social demand for education should be influenced by its private and social rates of return, relative to alternative investment opportunities (Becker,
1964). The cross-sectional relationship observed between the
rate of return to schooling and public (and private) expenditures
on schooling need not represent only the private supply function
of investment in this means of production. The rate of return is
also affected by the aggregate economy's derived demand for more
and less educated workers. Unless factors can be specified a
priori that shift one and not the other side of this market for
more educated labor, it is not generally possible to indentify
statistically the individual's investment supply response function from the aggregate derived demand function for educated
labor. It would be useful for our purposes to specify exogenous
endowments to the economy or technological dimensions to the
development process that affect the derived demands for relatively better-educated labor and hence displace the producer
returns to education. However, there is as yet no agreement on
what these factors might be. In the later empirical analysis,
income, relative prices, and technological constraints may influence the consumer's demand for education and also shift the
derived demand for educated labor, thereby varying the rate of
return to education as a producer good.[7]

The approach adopted here is to assume simply that the demand
for educated labor is primarily a function of the current level
of national income per worker, and other specified technological
and demographic constraints. Within these general long-run constraints, the political system seeks to allocate to the educational system the resources that are economically justified and
privately demanded. Hence, consumer demand for schooling is
itself a reduced-form relationship that embodies structural
parameters from an individual investment supply relationship and
an aggregate derived demand for relatively educated labor. The
identification of these underlying structural parameters is not
attempted here.

A second unusual feature of the educational system is that
it produces its own main input--teachers. It thereby affects,
by its past production, the current wage required to retain the
services of teachers and consequently the unit cost of producing
further education, other things being equal. This feedback
effect of output on unit costs suggests that choosing the best
expansion path for education involves issues of intertemporal
optimization and intergenerational equity, issues that implicitly
arise in the educational planning literature, but have not been
explicitly incorporated into empirical analyses (Bowles, 1969;
Freeman, 1971). For example, to expand a school system rapidly
from a very limited national educational base inevitably involves
temporarily bidding up the cost of teachers and may even require
the costly importation of trained personnel. These high initial
costs of expansion tend to decline as the pool of domestically

trained secondary school graduates increases and these new graduates compete for available teacher posts.  This decline in the
relative price of teachers then encourages, along with rising
incomes, more private demand for public education as both a consumption and investment activity.  Figure 1 illustrates this
downtrend in the relative price of teachers in a number of
African countries that have recently expanded their national educational systems.  The wages of teachers relative to those of
the average worker showed less obvious trends in the middle-
income countries, such as in Latin America.  In the high-income
market economies, this relative wage of public school teachers
followed a variety of paths, but there was often a tendency for
the relative wages of teachers to increase temporarily in the
1960s as the educational system expanded to accommodate the large
cohorts of babies born after World War II.
    Although there is no established framework for dealing with
these dynamic and recursive features of national educational
systems,  it is clear  that the current  wages of teachers depend

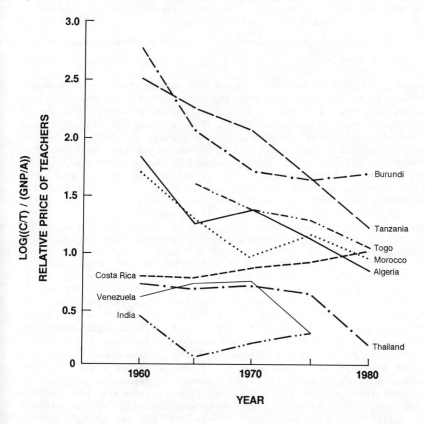

FIGURE 1   Relative Price of Primary Teachers to GNP per Adult
Over Time for Selected Countries

424                                                          Schultz

directly on the level of current demand for schooling. Consequently, the price of teachers is endogenous to a model determining the demand for educational services. To estimate without
simultaneous equation bias the effect of this price on current
demand, an instrumental variable method will be adopted. The
instruments will be selected such that they are correlated with
the current wages of teachers, but not with the errors in the
equation determining current educational demand.

A MODEL OF THE EDUCATIONAL SYSTEM

The technological possibilities for producing educational services are assumed to be identical across countries. This production function for educational services is also assumed in the
long run to exhibit constant returns; this does not seem to be
an unrealistic assumption if we exclude very small countries,
say, of less than 1 million persons, and concentrate separately
on the primary and secondary school systems (see the Appendix).
The production function may then be expressed in standard Cobb-
Douglas form:

$$X = Z \, L^{\alpha} \, K^{1-\alpha} ,$$                                        (1)

where X is the output of educational services, L is the labor
input, K is the physical capital input, and $\alpha$ is the share of
wages in output and $1-\alpha$ the capital share, while Z is a set of
exogenous technological shifters that affect the unit costs of
producing schooling in different environments, but are neutral
with respect to labor and capital productivity and use. One such
technological factor is the distribution of the population. Dispersed populations may incur greater private and public transportation costs, in terms of both time and money, in providing the
same effective schooling services.

Another technological factor that appears to influence the
effectiveness of the school's resources is children's home environment, and notably the education of parents (Leibowitz, 1974;
Rosenzweig, 1982). Consequently, it may be anticipated that,
other things being equal, the effective demand for schooling
services would be higher in a more urbanized population and in
one where parents are better educated. Finally, reductions in
mortality increase the expected returns from schooling to the
parent, the child, and society (Schultz, 1971; Ram and Schultz,
1979). This actuarial effect on average returns to education
may not be large since recent mortality declines occur disproportionately among preschool-aged children; nonetheless, returns
might increase in recent decades by one-tenth in a typical low-
income country because of this factor alone (Preston, 1980).

However, parent education and life expectation are factors
that also contribute to the market productivity of the parents
and hence to the current level of real GNP per person. Moreover,
with increased income, more resources in both the public and
private sectors may be allocated to health expenditures that

augment the expectation of life. If the education and expectation of life of parents were included as explanatory variables
in an educational expenditure or output equation, both of these
variables would be causally related to income in complex ways.
It would be unrealistic, therefore, to expect that country-level
data could separately distinguish the effects of parent income,
parent education, and expectation of life on the performance of
the schooling system. Merged family-level data and aggregate
community data might be able to sort out the effects of these
interrelated factors (Schultz, 1984); here only the technological
effects of urbanization on schooling costs will be estimated.

If the educational sector minimizes its unit costs, that is,
produces efficiently, the marginal cost or price of schooling
services, $P_x$, can be expressed as a multiplicative function of
the wage rate paid labor in the educational sector, W, and the
return, r, required on public capital (e.g., Borcherding and
Deacon, 1972):

$$P_x = (\frac{1}{z}) \, (\frac{W}{\alpha})^\alpha \, (\frac{r}{1-\alpha})^{1-\alpha} . \tag{2}$$

To some degree, world capital markets work to equalize the
rental rate on educational physical capital; then the only remaining constraints that would influence the marginal cost of education across countries and over time are the real wage paid to
teachers, W, and the exogenous technological conditions denoted
by Z. Teacher salaries are the bulk of recurrent expenses for
most school systems. In recent years, about 95 percent of current expenses in the primary school systems of low-income countries were teacher salaries, whereas in high-income countries
the proportion is about 75 percent (World Bank, 1983:99).
Therefore, current expenditures in a school system divided by
the number of teachers is a useful approximation of the wage
paid for labor by the educational system, and is the principal
factor determining the relative price of educational services in
a country. The price equation can be rewritten as the following,
if the rental rate on capital does not vary:

$$P_x = e^{\beta_0} \, z^{\beta_1} \, W^\alpha \, e^{ul} , \tag{3}$$

where $\beta_0$ is a constant, $\beta_1 = -1$, and $ul$ is a multiplicative error in the production technology affecting unit costs.
Because labor's share of educational expenditures, $\alpha$ , can be
observed, the effect of price variation can be estimated from
data on teacher wages (Gramlich and Rubinfeld, 1982).

Educational services are assumed to flow equally to all
citizens. The quantity demanded is defined as q,

$$q = X / P^\gamma , \tag{4}$$

where P is the population of children of school age, and $\gamma$ is
the "public good" parameter, equal to unity if it is a private
good and zero if it is a pure public good. Public externalities
of basic education are often cited as a reason for public subsidization of education, suggesting that $\gamma < 1$.

The median voter is assumed to pay a share to finance the output of educational services for each of his or her children:

$$t = (P_xX)/(FAq) = P_xP^{(\gamma - 1)} ,\qquad (5)$$

where t is the tax share per tax paying adult A, who has on average F children of school age, and hence FA = P.

Finally, the demand function for schooling of the median voter is conventionally assumed to be log-linear in the tax, t, paid (or price), in the taxpayer's income, Y, and possibly in technological factors, Z:[8]

$$q = Dt^{\eta} Y^{\delta} Z^{\epsilon} eu2 ,\qquad (6)$$

where $u_2$ is a multiplicative error in the demand relationship.

Combining equations (4) and (5) with (6), to eliminate the tax rate, an expenditure (E) function is obtained per school-aged child in terms of income, prices, children, and technological constraints:

$$E/P = tq = DY^{\delta} P_x (\eta +1) P(\eta +1)(\gamma -1) Z^{\epsilon} eu2.\qquad (7)$$

To simplify interpretation of the effect of the relative size of the cohort of school-aged children, X is assumed to be a purely private good, that is, $\gamma = 1$. In this case, after substituting (3) in for the price of educational services, logarithms are taken of (7); then the partial effects of income per adult, relative prices (teacher wage), and technological shifters on public educational expenditures per child can be expressed as a combination of household demand and production technology parameters:

$$\ln(E/P) = b_0 + b_1\ln Y + b_2\ln W + b_3\ln Z + v ,\qquad (8)$$

where   $b_0 = (\eta + 1)(\beta_0) + \ln D$ ,

$b_1 = \delta$ ,

$b_2 = \alpha(\eta + 1)$ ,

$b_3 = \beta_1(\eta + 1) +\epsilon$ ,

$v = u_1(\eta + 1) + u_2$ .

In sum, equation (8) is a reduced-form relationship derived from both the education production technology (1) and the form of household demand (6). The production and demand errors $u_1$ and $u_2$ are assumed to be independently distributed and serially uncorrelated and uncorrelated with Y, Z and lagged Y, and Z, and S/P, defined below. The income elasticity, $\delta$, that is directly estimated from a regression in the form of (8) would capture the effect of income on public expenditures for education that is due to both consumption demands and producer demands induced by

increasing rates of return to educated labor. Since   is known
from the input share of labor in total educational expenditures,
the Cobb-Douglas form of the technology permits one to identify
the price elasticity, $\eta$ . However, the wage of teachers is
likely to be endogenous and hence correlated with v, and it is
later transformed into a relative price of schooling that is
defined in terms of income and the component of current school
expenditures per teacher. Ordinary least squares (OLS) estimates
of  and  may thus be biased because of simultaneity and errors-
in-variables that are likely to generate spurious correlations
among measured relative price, income, and school expenditure
variables. An asymptotically unbiased instrumental variable
estimator is therefore later proposed.

The net effects of Z factors on educational inputs and outputs can also be inferred from estimates of (8). The estimated
impact of the relative size of the school-aged population on
schooling expenditure per child is an estimate of the cohort-
size effect squeezing out educational expenditures as hypothesized in the demographic-development literature. Alternative
interpretations could also be attached to a negative estimate of
the relative cohort-size effect.[9] The proportion of the population living in urban areas is a second technological variable.


EMPIRICAL FINDINGS

This section presents the empirical findings of an analysis of
data from about 90 countries over the last three decades. Included are an empirical decomposition of educational expenditures; estimates of school expenditure equations; and discussion
of sex differences in enrollment rates, the share of national
product expended on education, and patterns in residuals.


An Empirical Decomposition of Educational Expenditures

It is of practical interest to evaluate how the composition of
educational expenditures varies with price, income, and demographic factors, in addition to the behavior of overall educational expenditures. For this purpose, it is convenient to
divide school expenditures per school-aged child (E/P) into a
multiplicative function of four observable components:

$$\frac{E}{P} = (\frac{S}{P}) (\frac{T}{S}) (\frac{E}{C}) (\frac{C}{T}) . \tag{9}$$

The first term on the right-hand side is the ratio of students
enrolled to the number of children of school age, or the enrollment ratio, which can be computed in many countries for boys and
girls separately. The second term is the teacher/student ratio;
this will be treated as an indicator of the human capital "quality" of schooling (Pryor, 1968; Bowles, 1969), which may be contrasted with the "quantity" response in terms of enrollments.
The third term is the ratio of total to current expenditures, or

an index of the physical capital intensity of the educational
system. The fourth and final term is the current expenditures
per teacher. Logarithms of the four component ratios in equation
(9) are then regressed on the same income, price, technology, and
population composition variables used to explain expenditures per
child. The sum of the log-linear regression coefficients for
each conditioning variable in these four component regressions is
equal to that variable's coefficient in the overall expenditure
per child function. In this way, the effect of income, price,
and other factors on overall educational expenditures estimated
from equation (8) may be decomposed into the additive effects of
that conditioning variable operating on quantity, quality,
capital intensity, and teacher salaries.[10]

Educational expenditures are deflated to constant local
prices using the GNP deflator and converted to 1970 U.S. dollars
according to the prevailing average foreign exchange rate in
1969-71 (see the Appendix for details).[11] The wage of primary
and secondary school teachers is defined as the public current
expenditures on that level of schooling divided by the number of
teachers at that level. This "average" teacher salary should
then be deflated by the local price level to obtain a relative
price. The national productivity of the average adult has been
used here as a numeraire for the teacher's salary. Thus, this
relative price of teachers is defined as the ratio of teacher
salaries to GNP per person of working age (age 15 to 65).

This measure of the relative price or cost of educational
services is likely to be determined jointly and simultaneously
with production costs and consumer demands for schooling. The
endogeneity of the relative price of teachers is reflected in
the likelihood that unexplained variation in either production
costs ($u_1$) or consumer demands ($u_2$) will be correlated with
observed relative prices of teachers. OLS could overestimate
$b_2$ in equation (8) because of the resulting simultaneous
equation bias. Consequently, the model is estimated first by
OLS, under the assumption that the relative price of teachers is
exogenous, and then by instrumental variable (IV) techniques,
under the assumption that the price variable is endogenous, but
that the instrumental variables, specifically secondary school
enrollment rates, incomes, and urbanization, all lagged 10 years,
are uncorrelated with production and demand errors in the current
schooling system equations.[12] The IV estimates incorporate the
anticipation that the relative price of teachers today will be
reduced by increases in the supply of potential teachers trained
in the country in previous years. These estimates also eliminate
the errors-in-variable problem that arises because the logarithmic transformations of relative prices, incomes, and teacher
wages are linearly dependent on each other.[13] Although the
auxiliary instrumental variable equations for wages undoubtedly
simplify the structural process underlying time series of educational systems, these simultaneous equation techniques should
provide consistent estimates of the reduced-form equation (8)
based on demand/technology determinants of educational expenditures and enrollments.[14]

Income is measured as GNP in local constant prices, expressed in 1970 dollars by conversion at the average foreign exchange rate prevailing from 1969 to 1971.[15] To avoid definitional dependence on fertility, this measure of real GNP is divided by the population of working age, 15 to 65. Population density is measured as the proportion of the population living in an urban area, as defined by the World Bank and estimated from national censuses. The relative size of the school-aged cohort is the proportion of the population aged 6-11 for primary school and the proportion aged 12-17 for secondary school, following UNESCO conventions. For the consolidated expenditure and enrollment equations, the child cohort is defined as the proportion of the population aged 6 to 17. Period fertility is measured by the total fertility rate, which is equivalent to the sum of age-specific birth rates for women aged 15 to 49.

Data were first collected for 155 countries with populations greater than 1 million in 1983, for each five-year period from 1950-80. Data on all required series were obtained for at least 1 year in 89 countries, of which 30 were in Africa, 19 Latin America, 21 Asia, 2 Oceania, 1 North America, and 16 Europe (see Table A-1). The maximum number of country-year observations was 321 for primary schools and 258 for secondary schools. In the pooling of time series observations from a cross section, it is clear that all observations are not independent; neglect of covariation across observations on a particular country undoubtedly biases reported tests of statistical significance and may bias point estimates as well.

The variables are defined and sample characteristics summarized by region for primary and secondary school systems in Tables 3 and 4, respectively. Beneath the mean of the variable is its standard deviation in parentheses, and if the variable is expressed in logarithmic form, the antilog of the mean is reported as the third value in brackets to provide an absolute measure of level. For example, primary enrollment ratios are 59 percent in Africa and 95 percent in Latin America, while the teacher/student ratios and capital intensity are similar--.024 and .030, and 1.22 and 1.15, respectively. Primary school teachers are paid about the same in the two regions, but because GNP per adult is one-third as large in Africa, the relative price of teachers is twice as high in Africa as it is in Latin America. Expenditure per primary school-aged child is $20 in Africa, compared with $51 in Latin America. The potential explanatory role of income and relative prices in determining school expenditures and achievements is suggested from such gross regional comparisons. The large differences between enrollment ratios for boys and girls in Africa compared with Latin America may also stem from economic differences between regions. The next section proceeds to fit the multivariate production/demand relationships across country observations to estimate the magnitude of price and income effects, as well as the effects of urbanization and population growth.

TABLE 3  Characteristics of a Sample of Primary Schooling Systems, 1960-80, by Region[a]

| Variable | Region (sample size) | | | | | |
|---|---|---|---|---|---|---|
| | Africa (62) | Latin America (43) | East Asia (21) | South and West Asia (24) | Europe, Canada, and Oceania (36) | Total Sample (186) |
| **Dependent** | | | | | | |
| Enrollment Ratio - Total (S/P) | -.523 (.538) [.593] | -.0506 (.198) [.951] | -.0150 (.111) [1.02] | -.398 (.470) [.672] | .0315 (.0708) [1.03] | -.229 (.440) [.743] |
| Enrollment Ratio - Male (S/P) | -.339 (.479) [.713] | -.0235 (.181) [.977] | .0370 (.103) [1.04] | -.145 (.353) [.865] | .0332 (.0763) [1.03] | -.126 (.355) [.882] |
| Enrollment Ratio - Female (S/P) | -.737 (.619) [.479] | -.0717 (.231) [.930] | -.00466 (.121) [.995] | -.835 (.823) [.434] | .0277 (.0744) [1.03] | -.365 (.604) [.694] |
| Teacher-Student Ratio (T/S) | -3.73 (.266) [.0238] | -3.51 (.260) [.0299] | -3.48 (.238) [.0308] | -3.49 (.318) [.0305] | -3.06 (.345) [.0469] | -3.49 (.366) [.0305] |
| Capital Intensity Index (E/C) | .199 (.238) [1.22] | .141 (.162) [1.15] | .188 (.108) [1.21] | .270 (.184) [1.31] | .192 (.114) [1.21] | .192 (.184) [1.21] |
| Current Expenditures per Teacher (C/T) | 7.03 (.667) [1130.] | 7.35 (.613) [1156.] | 7.44 (1.02) [1703.] | 6.17 (.961) [478.] | 8.86 (.723) [7044.] | 7.39 (1.10) [1620.] |
| Real Expenditures per Child (E/P) | 2.97 (.885) [19.5] | 3.94 (.675) [51.4] | 4.16 (1.16) [64.1] | 2.55 (1.38) [12.8] | 6.02 (.847) [412.] | 3.87 (1.51) [47.9] |
| Expenditure Share of GNP | .0219 (.0087) -- | .0190 (.0067) -- | .0192 (.0063) -- | .0145 (.0095) -- | .0227 (.0098) -- | .0201 (.0087) -- |

Explanatory

| | | | | | | |
|---|---|---|---|---|---|---|
| GNP per Adult Real 1970 $ | 5.74 (.619) [311.] | 6.83 (.502) [925.] | 6.79 (.877) [889.] | 5.86 (.785) [351.] | 8.09 (.510) [3262.] | 6.58 (1.08) [721.] |
| Relative Price of Teacher | 1.29 (.565) [3.63] | .518 (.421) [1.68] | .644 (.387) [1.90] | .306 (.468) [1.36] | .771 (.482) [2.16] | .813 (.606) [2.25] |
| Proportion Urban Population | .227 (.137) -- | .479 (.155) -- | .533 (.320) -- | .284 (.183) -- | .626 (.169) -- | .404 (.240) -- |
| Proportion of Population Age 6-11 | .165 (.0119) | .170 (.0179) | .148 (.0271) | .167 (.0106) | .104 (.0127) | .153 (.0292) |
| Total Fertility Rate | 6.62 (.986) -- | 5.37 (1.18) -- | 3.88 (1.47) -- | 6.29 (.996) -- | 2.35 (.541) -- | 5.15 (1.91) -- |
| Proportion Adults Literate | .329 (.193) -- | .726 (.166) -- | .798 (.124) -- | .364 (.202) -- | .948 (.0733) -- | .598 (.299) -- |
| Life Expectation at Birth (years) | 47.9 (6.40) -- | 60.6 (6.81) -- | 65.0 (6.92) -- | 51.3 (8.88) -- | 72.0 (1.97) -- | 57.9 (11.2) -- |

aPrice is treated as exogenous and estimated with ordinary least squares. Absolute value of t ratio is reported in parentheses beneath regression coefficients. Antilog of the mean is reported in brackets if the variable is in logarithmic form.

TABLE 4  Characteristics of a Sample of Secondary Schooling System 1960-80, by Region[a]

| | Region (sample size) | | | | | |
|---|---|---|---|---|---|---|
| Variable | Africa (49) | Latin America (35) | East Asia (18) | South and West Asia (16) | Europe, Canada, and Oceania (21) | Total Sample (13) |
| **Dependent** | | | | | | |
| Enrollment Ratio - Total (S/P) | -2.45 (.836) [.0863] | -1.21 (.455) [.298] | -.779 (.455) [.459] | -1.59 (.612) [.204] | -.278 (.177) [.757] | -1.49 (1.00) [.225] |
| Enrollment Ratio - Male (S/P) | -2.13 (.807) [.119] | -1.20 (.424) [.301] | -.714 (.392) [.490] | -1.20 (.525) [.301] | -.271 (.141) [.763] | -1.33 (.882) [.264] |
| Enrollment Ratio - Female (S/P) | -2.95 (.956) [.0523] | -1.24 (.507) [.289] | -.852 (.523) [.427] | -2.35 (.960) [.0954] | -.295 (.233) [.745] | -1.78 (1.25) [.168] |
| Teacher-Student Ratio (T/S) | -3.05 (.284) [.0474] | -2.90 (.363) [.0550] | -3.22 (.276) [.0400] | -3.14 (.255) [.0433] | -2.67 (.275) [.0693] | -2.98 (.341) [.0508] |
| Capital Intensity Index (E/C) | .205 (.261) [1.23] | .127 (.113) [1.14] | .181 (.110) [1.20] | .304 (.171) [1.36] | .197 (.144) [1.22] | .192 (.193) [1.21] |
| Current Expenditures per Teacher (C/T) | 8.76 (.589) [6374.] | 8.09 (.725) [3262.] | 8.19 (1.01) [3605.] | 7.38 (.940) [1604.] | 9.18 (.628) [9701.] | 8.42 (.903) [4537.] |
| Real Expenditures per Child (E/P) | 3.47 (.867) [32.1] | 4.11 (.914) [60.9] | 4.37 (1.45) [79.0] | 2.96 (1.27) [19.3] | 6.42 (.931) [614.] | 4.14 (1.47) [62.8] |
| Expenditure Share of GNP | .0286 (.0113) -- | .0195 (.0098) -- | .0225 (.0017) -- | .0174 (.0105) -- | .0358 (.0108) -- | .0253 (.0123) -- |

Explanatory

| | | | | | | |
|---|---|---|---|---|---|---|
| GNP per Adult Real 1970 $ | 5.75 (.611) [314.] | 6.87 (.439) [963.] | 6.84 (.938) [934.] | 5.85 (.796) [347.] | 7.96 (.565) [2864.] | 6.52 (1.01) [679.] |
| Relative Price of Teacher | 3.01 (.615) [20.3] | 1.22 (.501) [3.39] | 1.35 (.570) [3.86] | 1.53 (.538) [4.62] | 1.21 (.315) [3.35] | 1.90 (.979) [6.69] |
| Proportion Urban Population | .220 (.137) -- | .489 (.153) -- | .567 (.326) -- | .290 (.196) -- | .560 (.166) -- | .392 (.237) -- |
| Proportion of Population Age 12-17 | .135 (.0102) -- | .143 (.0114) -- | .137 (.0199) -- | .139 (.0074) -- | .0996 (.0108) -- | .132 (.0185) -- |
| Total Fertility Rate | 6.68 (.973) -- | 5.34 (1.17) -- | 3.88 (1.57) -- | 6.70 (.600) -- | 2.41 (.602) -- | 5.34 (1.87) -- |
| Proportion Adults Literate | .328 (.183) -- | .744 (.146) -- | .798 (.119) -- | .285 (.123) -- | .936 (.0854) -- | .581 (.293) -- |
| Life Expectation at Birth (years) | 47.9 (6.39) -- | 61.3 (6.73) -- | 65.3 (7.44) -- | 49.0 (7.59) -- | 71.4 (2.28) -- | 57.2 (11.0) -- |

aThe price is treated as exogenous and estimated with ordinary least squares. Absolute value of t ratio is reported in parentheses beneath regression coefficients. Antilog of the mean is reported in brackets if the variable is in logarithmic form.

Estimates of School Expenditure Equations

The empirical findings are reported in two basic specifications—
one that assumes the relative price of teachers to be exogenous
and measured without error, and a second that treats this price
variable as endogenous and potentially measured with error.
Under the first set of assumptions, OLS estimates of the parameters to equation (8) may be satisfactory, and they are reported
in column 7 of Tables 5, 6, and 7 for the primary, secondary, and
overall public educational expenditures, respectively, per
school-aged child. Columns 3 through 6 provide the component
regressions designated in equation (9), although in the case of
the total school system, the transformation of enrollment rates
to expected years of schooling and the general gaps in data on
teachers in the public higher educational systems imply that the
analogous total components do not "add up." Because the relative
price of school teachers is defined as the wage of teachers
divided by GNP per adult, the logarithm of the teacher wage component in column 6 is precisely equal to the sum of the logs of
the income and price variables in the OLS estimates for the
primary and secondary school systems.

The second set of regressions in Tables 8, 9, and 10 report
IV estimates, which are preferred because they are consistent
under the more realistic assumptions specified above regarding
the endogeneity of relative prices. However, since these estimates depend on the availability of information on income and
secondary school enrollments a decade earlier, the working sample
for which these estimates can be obtained is reduced from 321 to
186 at the primary level, from 258 to 139 at the secondary level,
and from 250 to 132 at the level of the total school system.
Nonetheless, the countries in the samples do not change appreciably; only the time period shifts with the frequent omission of
the 1960s and the emphasis given to the 1970s (see Appendix
Table A-1). OLS estimates from the larger samples are similar
to those reported in Tables 5, 6, and 7, for which the samples
are restricted to those underlying the preferred IV estimates.

Alternatives to these preferred specifications of equation
(8) are reported in Appendix Tables A-2, A-3, and A-4 for OLS
estimates excluding total fertility rates, although in this form
the proportion of the population of school age may also proxy
for parental quality/quantity choices. Tables A-5, A-6, and A-7
report the analogous IV estimates without total fertility rates,
with the same caveat. Finally, Tables A-8, A-9, and A-10 report
the IV estimates of the preferred specification for the subsample
of less developed countries, which constitute about four-fifths
of the overall sample.

According to the OLS estimates, the income elasticities of
expenditures ($\delta$) on primary, secondary, and total school systems
exceed unity; they are specifically 1.37, 1.55, and 1.41, respectively. The IV estimates are similar—1.35, 1.47, and 1.35. The
share of income expended on each level of schooling tends to increase with real GNP per adult. The elasticity of educational
expenditures with respect to the relative price of teachers is

TABLE 5  Estimates of Primary School Expenditures and Components, with the Price of Teachers Exogenous[a]

| Explanatory Variable | Dependent Variable in Logarithms | | | | | | |
|---|---|---|---|---|---|---|---|
| | Enrollment Ratio | | | Teacher-Student Ratio (T/S) | Capital Intensity Index (E/C) | Teacher Salary (C/T) | Total Expenditure per Child Age 6-11 (E/P) |
| | Male (S/P) | Female (S/P) | Total (S/P) | | | | |
| | (1) | (2) | (3) | (4) | (5) | (6) | (7) |
| GNP per Adult in 1970 (log) | .158 (3.79) | .332 (5.07) | .224 (4.66) | .145 (3.75) | -.0002 (.01) | 1.0 | 1.37 (26.5) |
| Relative Price of Teachers (log)[a] | -.188 (5.13) | -.153 (2.67) | -.194 (4.61) | -.158 (4.65) | -.0428 (1.72) | 1.0 | .606 (13.4) |
| Proportion of Population Urban | .0898 (.54) | -.0173 (.07) | .0390 (.20) | -.308 (2.00) | -.0925 (.82) | 0.0 | -.362 (1.76) |
| Proportion of Population Age 6-11 | 2.44 (1.88) | 7.87 (3.88) | 4.25 (2.86) | -4.03 (3.36) | -1.22 (1.39) | 0.0 | -1.00 (.63) |
| Total Fertility Rate | -.0130 (.55) | -.110 (2.97) | -.0508 (1.87) | -.0270 (1.23) | .0155 (.97) | 0.0 | -.0623 (2.13) |
| Intercept | -1.36 (4.15) | -3.05 (5.97) | -1.95 (5.19) | -3.44 (11.3) | .372 (1.68) | 0.0 | -5.01 (12.4) |
| $R^2$ | .430 | .517 | .511 | .539 | .029 | 1.0 | .952 |
| Sample Size | 186 | 186 | 186 | 186 | 186 | 186 | 186 |
| Mean (standard deviation of dependent variable) | -.126 (.355) | -.365 (.604) | -.229 (.440) | -3.49 (.366) | .192 (.184) | 7.39 (1.10) | 3.87 (1.51) |

[a]Price is treated as exogenous and estimated with ordinary least squares.  Absolute value of t ratio reported in parentheses beneath regression coefficients.

435

TABLE 6 Estimates of Secondary School Expenditures and Components, with the Price of Teachers Exogenous[a]

| | Dependent Variable in Logarithms | | | | | | |
|---|---|---|---|---|---|---|---|
| | Enrollment Ratio | | | Teacher-Student Ratio (T/S) | Capital Intensity Index (E/C) | Teacher Salary (C/T) | Total Expenditure per Child Age 12-17 (E/P) |
| Explanatory Variable | Male (S/P) | Female (S/P) | Total (S/P) | | | | |
| | (1) | (2) | (3) | (4) | (5) | (6) | (7) |
| GNP per Adult in 1970 (log) | .399 (4.97) | .766 (9.13) | .526 (7.03) | .0377 (.69) | -.0132 (.37) | 1.0 | 1.55 (27.8) |
| Relative Price of Teachers (log)[a] | -.354 (6.84) | -.403 (7.45) | -.389 (8.05) | -.0927 (2.63) | -.0225 (.99) | 1.0 | .496 (13.8) |
| Proportion of Population Urban | -.219 (.71) | -.575 (1.78) | -.380 (1.32) | -.0181 (.09) | -.0766 (.56) | 0.0 | -.474 (2.21) |
| Proportion of Population Age 12-17 | 1.69 (.63) | 10.5 (3.74) | 4.53 (1.81) | -9.69 (5.29) | -2.14 (1.81) | 0.0 | -7.29 (3.91) |
| Total Fertility Rate | -.104 (2.91) | -.192 (5.13) | -.134 (4.03) | .0454 (1.87) | .0113 (.72) | 0.0 | -.0775 (3.12) |
| Intercept | -2.84 (4.05) | -6.15 (8.40) | -3.92 (6.00) | -2.01 (4.20) | .574 (1.86) | 0.0 | -5.35 (11.0) |
| $R^2$ | .763 | .872 | .839 | .261 | .039 | 1.0 | .959 |
| Sample Size | 139 | 139 | 139 | 139 | 139 | 139 | 139 |
| Mean (standard deviation of dependent variable) | -1.33 (.882) | -1.78 (1.25) | -1.49 (.999) | -2.99 (.341) | .192 (.193) | 8.42 (.903) | 4.14 (1.47) |

[a]Price is treated as exogenous and estimated with ordinary least squares. Absolute value of t ratio

436

TABLE 7  Estimates of Total School Expenditures and Components, with the Price of Teachers Exogenous[a]

| | Dependent Variable in Logarithms | | | | | | |
|---|---|---|---|---|---|---|---|
| | Enrollment Ratio | | | Teacher-Student Ratio (T/S) | Capital Intensity Index (X/C) | Teacher Salary (C/T) | Total Expenditure per Child Age 6-17 (X/P) |
| Explanatory Variable | Male (S/P) | Female (S/P) | Total (S/P) | | | | |
| | (1) | (2) | (3) | (4) | (5) | (6) | (7) |
| GNP per Adult in 1970 (log) | .237 (4.66) | .457 (5.98) | .314 (5.66) | .114 (3.22) | -.0085 (.23) | .919 (24.0) | 1.41 (24.4) |
| Relative Price of Teachers (log)[a] | -.250 (5.21) | -.239 (3.31) | -.276 (5.09) | -.103 (3.08) | -.0154 (1.50) | 1.17 (32.4) | .485 (8.87) |
| Proportion of Population Urban | -.0471 (.25) | -.314 (1.08) | -.161 (.76) | -.161 (1.20) | -.108 (.78) | -.0642 (.44) | -.334 (1.51) |
| Proportion of Population Age 6-17 | .432 (.52) | 3.31 (2.64) | 1.47 (1.61) | -2.92 (5.05) | -1.03 (1.73) | -.551 (.88) | -2.81 (2.96) |
| Total Fertility Rate | -.0381 (1.46) | -.127 (3.26) | -.0746 (2.62) | .0130 (.72) | .0166 (.89) | .0478 (2.43) | -.0365 (1.23) |
| Intercept | -.885 (2.05) | -1.11 (1.71) | -.221 (.469) | -3.09 (10.3) | .565 (1.83) | .527 (1.62) | -4.82 (9.82) |
| $R^2$ | .660 | .693 | .717 | .527 | .043 | .948 | .956 |
| Sample Size | 132 | 132 | 132 | 132 | 132 | 132 | 132 |
| Mean (standard deviation of dependent variable) | 2.03 (.461) | 1.72 (.728) | 1.90 (.551) | -3.31 (.271) | .195 (.196) | 8.80 (.886) | 3.89 (1.45) |

[a]Price is treated as exogenous and estimated by ordinary least squares.  Absolute value of t ratio reported in parentheses beneath regression coefficients.

TABLE 8  Estimates of Primary School Expenditures and Components, with the Price of Teachers Endogenous[a]

| Explanatory Variable | Dependent Variable in Logarithms | | | | | | |
|---|---|---|---|---|---|---|---|
| | Enrollment Ratio | | | Teacher-Student Ratio (T/S) | Capital Intensity Index (E/C) | Teacher Salary (C/T) | Total Expenditure per Child Age 6-11 (E/P) |
| | Male (S/P) | Female (S/P) | Total (S/P) | | | | |
| | (1) | (2) | (3) | (4) | (5) | (6) | (7) |
| GNP per Adult in 1970 (log) | .239 (3.96) | .430 (4.84) | .314 (4.53) | .168 (4.12) | .0008 (.03) | .870 (33.7) | 1.35 (20.2) |
| Relative Price of Teachers (log)[a] | -.627 (4.81) | -.760 (3.96) | -.698 (4.67) | -.181 (2.06) | -.0106 (.16) | 1.05 (18.8) | .161 (1.11) |
| Proportion of Population Urban | -.286 (1.44) | -.520 (1.41) | -.389 (1.35) | -.351 (2.08) | -.0736 (.60) | .193 (1.80) | .620 (2.23) |
| Proportion of Population Age 6-11 | 1.93 (1.08) | 6.39 (2.43) | 3.50 (1.71) | -2.98 (2.48) | -.773 (.88) | -7.07 (9.26) | -7.33 (3.71) |
| Total Fertility Rate | .0450 (1.23) | -.0277 (2.43) | .0163 (.39) | -.0268 (1.08) | .0102 (.57) | -.0120 (.76) | .0116 (.29) |
| Intercept | -1.60 (3.62) | -3.20 (4.92) | -2.18 (4.31) | -3.71 (12.5) | .291 (1.34) | 1.75 (9.27) | -3.86 (7.87) |
| F | 16.05 | 25.03 | 21.78 | 38.06 | .46 | 1383. | 441. |
| Sample Size | 186 | 186 | 186 | 186 | 186 | 186 | 186 |
| Mean (standard deviation of dependent variable) | -.126 (.355) | -.365 (.604) | -.229 (.440) | -3.49 (.366) | .192 (.184) | 7.39 (1.10) | 3.87 (1.51) |

aPrice is treated as endogenous and estimated with instruments of secondary enrollment ratio,
... GNP per adult, all lagged 10 years.  Absolute value of asymptotic t ratio reported in

TABLE 9  Estimates of Secondary School Expenditures and Components, with the Price of Teachers Endogenous[a]

| Explanatory Variable | Dependent Variable in Logarithms | | | | | | |
|---|---|---|---|---|---|---|---|
| | Enrollment Ratio | | | Teacher-Student Ratio (T/S) | Capital Intensity Index (E/C) | Teacher Salary (C/T) | Total Expenditure per Child Age 12-17 (E/P) |
| | Male (S/P) | Female (S/P) | Total (S/P) | | | | |
| | (1) | (2) | (3) | (4) | (5) | (6) | (7) |
| GNP per Adult in 1970 (log) | .304 (2.70) | .649 (5.13) | .428 (3.85) | .105 (1.53) | -.0087 (.24) | .942 (51.4) | 1.47 (21.9) |
| Relative Price of Teachers (log)[a] | -.905 (6.58) | -1.07 (6.92) | -.964 (7.11) | .194 (2.33) | -.0082 (.19) | 1.02 (45.5) | .242 (2.97) |
| Proportion of Population Urban | -.776 (1.76) | -1.25 (2.52) | -.963 (2.22) | .238 (.89) | -.0661 (.47) | .143 (1.99) | -.649 (2.49) |
| Proportion of Population Age 12-17 | -2.19 (.58) | 5.67 (1.33) | .593 (.16) | -6.16 (2.67) | -1.87 (1.53) | -5.22 (8.42) | -12.7 (5.61) |
| Total Fertility Rate | -.0049 (.09) | -.0597 (.98) | -.0203 (.38) | -.0093 (.28) | .0087 (.50) | -.0114 (1.28) | -.0322 (1.00) |
| Intercept | -1.02 (.97) | -3.92 (3.31) | -2.04 (1.97) | -3.27 (5.12) | .492 (1.46) | 1.03 (6.04) | -3.78 (6.08) |
| F | 48.99 | 86.87 | 69.58 | 6.42 | .88 | 1264. | 419. |
| Sample Size | 139 | 139 | 139 | 139 | 139 | 139 | 139 |
| Mean (standard deviation of dependent variable | -1.33 (.882) | -1.78 (1.25) | -1.49 (1.00) | -2.98 (.341) | .192 (.193) | 8.42 (.903) | 4.14 (1.47) |

[a]Price is treated as endogenous, and estimated with instruments of secondary enrollment ratio, urbanization, and GNP per adult, all lagged 10 years. Absolute value of asymptotic t ratio reported in parentheses beneath regression coefficients.

439

TABLE 10 Estimates of Total School Expenditures and Components, with the Price of Teachers Endogenous[a]

| Explanatory Variable | Dependent Variable in Logarithms | | | | | | |
|---|---|---|---|---|---|---|---|
| | Enrollment Ratio | | | Teacher-Student Ratio (T/S) | Capital Intensity Index (E/C) | Teacher Salary (C/T) | Total Expenditure per Child Age 6-17 (E/P) |
| | Male (S/P) | Female (S/P) | Total (S/P) | | | | |
| | (1) | (2) | (3) | (4) | (5) | (6) | (7) |
| GNP per Adult in 1970 (log) | .277 (3.80) | .496 (5.03) | .357 (4.54) | .126 (3.40) | -.0018 (.05) | .756 (12.9) | 1.35 (20.8) |
| Relative Price of Teachers (log) | -.767 (5.08) | -.863 (4.37) | -.816 (5.14) | .0267 (.36) | -.0223 (.30) | 1.43 (12.0) | .168 (1.28) |
| Proportion of Population Urban | -.473 (1.59) | -.821 (2.03) | -.614 (1.91) | -.0763 (.50) | -.0927 (.62) | .280 (1.17) | -.513 (1.93) |
| Proportion of Population Age 6-17 | -.479 (.39) | 2.02 (1.23) | .501 (.38) | -2.22 (3.57) | -.792 (1.31) | -3.13 (3.20) | -5.21 (4.80) |
| Total Fertility Rate | .0450 (1.06) | -.0292 (.51) | .0137 (.30) | .0022 (.10) | .0142 (.67) | -.0286 (.84) | -.0073 (.19) |
| Intercept | 1.27 (2.04) | -.529 (.63) | .623 (.93) | -3.49 (11.0) | .423 (1.37) | 2.28 (4.57) | -3.40 (6.15) |
| F | 27.85 | 36.23 | 34.25 | 23.38 | .69 | 134. | 414. |
| Sample Size | 132 | 132 | 132 | 132 | 132 | 132 | 132 |
| Mean (standard deviation of dependent variable) | 2.03 (.461) | 1.72 (.728) | 1.90 (.551) | -3.31 (.271) | .195 (.196) | 8.08 (.886) | 3.89 (1.45) |

[a]Price is treated as endogenous and estimated with instruments of secondary enrollment ratio, urbanization, and GNP per adult, all lagged 10 years. Absolute value of asymptotic t ratio reported in

.60, .50, and .49 at the three school levels, if we accept the assumptions underlying the OLS estimates. The preferred IV estimates of price elasticities are, as expected, substantially lower at .16, .24, and .17. According to these IV estimates, the elasticity of the quantity of schooling services demanded with respect to the price of labor, in the model $\eta$ , is equal to -.80, -.70, and -.80.16

The expenditure components underlying these income and price effects on public expenditures differ slightly by school level. In the primary schools, the income elasticity is about twice as large for enrollments as for teacher-student ratios; the IV estimates are .31 for quantity and .17 for quality (columns 3 and 4). The physical capital intensity index is not well explained by any of the economic or demographic variables, and may contain largely transitory variations in capital appropriations or unsystematic measurement error (column 5). There is no evidence of complementarity or substitutability of capital for labor. Teacher salaries increase 5 percent faster than do incomes per adult (column 6), contributing to the elasticity of the income-expenditure relationship (column 7).

At the secondary school level (Table 9), the income elasticity is four times larger for quantity (.43) than for quality (.11). The price elasticity of secondary enrollment is substantially larger in absolute value, -.97, than that at the primary level, -.70. The price elasticity of total expected years of schooling is also large, -.82 (Table 10, column 3), falling between the primary and secondary school estimates. A decline in the price of school teachers relative to national productivity is associated with a substantial increase in enrollment and a modest increase in the ratio of primary school teachers to students.

Urbanization exhibits a relatively weak, but consistent, relationship with public expenditures on schooling. According to the IV estimates, a country that has 10 percent more of its population in urban areas tends to expend 6 percent less on schooling per child at both the primary and secondary levels. This is accomplished at the primary level by a reduction in enrollments and in teacher-to-student ratios, whereas at the secondary school level, most of the reduction occurs through lower enrollments. These estimates, however, are based on the specification that permits urbanization a decade earlier to help determine the relative price of teachers today, and lagged urbanization is significantly associated with lower current relative prices for teachers. Thus, this indirect role of urbanization is to reduce the price of teachers and thereby induce an offsetting, but lagged, effect increasing enrollment rates. If urbanization is excluded from the list of instruments for estimating price effects, the net contemporary effect of urbanization on school expenditures is to reduce current outlays per teacher, with little net effect on enrollments or teacher/student ratios.17 Expenditures per child, in either case, are systematically lower in more urbanized countries when income levels and relative prices are held constant.

The data examined here are not very helpful in getting
behind these economies of urban schools to determine their
precise origin. The consolidation of schools into more
efficient-sized units to exploit specialized teaching functions
in more densely populated areas is often cited as an important
source of economies of scale in public schools.[18] Higher
population densities could also reduce the private opportunity
cost of travel time for students. However, the lack of large
effects of urbanization in reducing teacher/student ratios in
secondary schools, or increasing enrollments, suggests that
economies of scale or reductions in private student time costs
may not be important.

The relative size of the school-aged cohort, which is highly
correlated with recent levels of population growth, is associated
with lower expenditures on primary, secondary, and total school
systems; according to the preferred IV estimates, reported in
Tables 8, 9, and 10, the effect is statistically significant and
of a substantial magnitude. An increase in the proportion of
the population of primary school age by 10 percent, from .153 to
.168, is associated with an 11 percent decline in primary school
expenditures per child. In other words, the IV estimates suggest
that primary school expenditures do not increase in response to
an increase in the size of the school-aged cohort. There are
offsetting tendencies for primary school enrollment rates to increase for the larger cohorts, whereas teacher/student ratios
fall. Teacher salaries, in addition, are substantially lower (10
percent) for the larger school-aged cohort, and this appears to
be the main factor explaining the lower expenditures per child.

The IV estimates imply that a 10 percent larger cohort is
associated with an even larger decline in expenditures per secondary school-aged child, of about 17 percent. Secondary enrollments are unaffected, but teacher salaries and teacher/student
ratios are notably lower. In the OLS estimates, the cohort-size
effects are substantially smaller and less statistically significant, but similar offsetting movements in enrollment rates and
teacher/student ratios are still evident (see Tables 5, 6, and
7). Although larger birth cohorts do not seem to receive fewer
years of schooling, as is attested to by the pattern of enrollment ratios, they do appear to receive schooling of lower human
and perhaps physical capital intensity.

This adjustment in the factor intensity in schooling is a
plausible economic response to the relative scarcity of both
forms of capital in many poor countries recently experiencing
rapid population growth. Much thought has been given to how
health care delivery systems might be encouraged to use less
human and physical capital-intensive technologies in low-income
countries, rather than directly transferring the highly capital-
intensive procedures used in the industrially advanced high-
income countries. The current adoption of Western medical technologies in low-income countries is cited as contributing to
both great inefficiencies and inequities, since the services of
this modern medical system are so costly that they can be provided only to the elite living in a few metropolitan areas of

the low-income world. The tendency noted in this chapter of
low-income countries to substitute away from human and physical
capital-intensive educational production technologies therefore
appears on economic grounds to be a reasonable innovative response to different factor scarcities (e.g., Binswanger and
Ruttan, 1978; Hayami and Ruttan, 1984) until evidence is presented that the productive benefits for persons being schooled
by these less capital-intensive methods are greatly reduced.19
    To determine which country observations are giving rise to
this pattern, the model is reestimated within the small strata
of high-income industrially advanced countries and within the
rest of the sample (about 80 percent). The relative cohort-size
variable exhibits the same statistically significant effect on
primary, secondary, and total school expenditures in the sample
of lower-income countries, and increases in magnitude by 5 to 10
percent (see Appendix Tables A-8, A-9, and A-10). In the small
sample of industrially advanced countries, cohort size is also
generally significant (not reported). Among only the low-income
countries, for whom variation in cohort size relates clearly to
the pressures of rapid population growth, the relative number of
school-aged children is associated with lower teacher/student
ratios and lower wages per teacher. Income and price elasticities based only on the less developed countries are similar to
those reported above.
    Fertility, as anticipated, is inversely associated in the
OLS estimates with school expenditures per child, and this
correlation appears to stem from an inverse association between
enrollment and fertility, particularly at the secondary level.
Such a pattern could be expected if the private substitution by
parents of more schooling resources per child for having additional children led to an increase in the private demand for
schooling, and hence to greater enrollment rates. However, the
preferred IV estimates indicate no relationship between fertility
and school enrollments or expenditures, except perhaps for primary enrollments of girls. The deletion of fertility from
equation (8) leads to larger (more negative) estimates of the
effect of cohort size on schooling inputs, as anticipated (see
Appendix Tables A-2 through A-7), but the differences are not
substantial (less than 10 percent).


Sex Differences in School Enrollment Rates

Differences in the school enrollment rates of boys and girls may
have much to do with the levels of child mortality and fertility
as well as the rate at which women migrate from rural to urban
areas and leave domestic activities for employment in the market
labor force, in particular, for jobs in the nonagricultural
sector. The future economic status of women relative to men
depends heavily on their enrollment in school and their ability
thereby obtained to benefit directly from the increased productive opportunities created by modern economic growth.

First, all of the estimates imply that the income elasticity
is larger for female than for male enrollment rates. The preferred (IV) point estimates for female and male enrollment rates
are .43 and .24 at the primary level, .65 and .30 at the secondary level, and .50 and .28 for total expected years of schooling, respectively. Second, the price enrollment elasticities
are greater in absolute value for female than for male enrollments: -.76 and -.63 for the primary level, -1.07 and -.91 for
the secondary level, and -.86 and -.77 for total expected years
of schooling. A 50 percent increase in income per adult from
the sample mean of $721 (1970 U.S. dollars) would raise primary
enrollment rates for girls from 69 to 83 percent, while the rate
for boys would increase from 88 to 97 percent. The girls would
improve their relative achievement from .78 of the boys' to .85.
The "gender gap" in secondary schools would also close by a
fourth, with girls increasing their enrollment rates from 17 to
22 percent, while the rate for boys would increase from 26 to 30
percent. Reducing the relative price of schooling has an effect
of improving female enrollments relative to males that is similar
to that of raising incomes. According to these cross-sectional
estimates of income and price elasticities, economic development,
with its effects on adult income and relative wages of teachers,
is likely to be associated with an equalizing of schooling
opportunities between boys and girls; these tendencies are also
evident in the restricted sample of less developed countries.[20]
Here may be a potent dimension of the development process that
unleashes demand for the schooling of girls and young women,
which in turn plays a pivotal role in governing the timing and
pace of the demographic transition.

Religion is often cited as a traditional cultural force that
influences the status of women and their educational opportunities relative to men. Moslem culture, in particular, is often
singled out for its distinctive attitudes toward women's status,
education, employment, and, consequently, fertility (Kirk, 1966).
Adding to our framework the percent of the population that is
Moslem and the percent that is Catholic leads to the auxiliary
regressions reported in Table 11. At the primary school level
and for total expected years of schooling, the difference in the
Moslem coefficient for men and women is statistically significant
at the 10 percent level. Moving from a country with the sample
average percentage of Moslems at 37 percent to a country that is
entirely Moslem is associated with a decline in primary enrollments for males from 88 to 76 percent and for females from 69 to
50 percent. In relative terms, the ratio of female to male
enrollment rates would decline in this case from .78 to .66.
The regression coefficient on the Catholic variable is not
statistically significant, but works in the direction of increasing female relative to male enrollment rates. The general
direction of income and price effects is not altered by the
inclusion of the two religion variables, though the effect of
population growth via cohort size is eliminated because of
multicollinearity.[21]

TABLE 11 Enrollment Ratios for Males and Females, Including Proportion of Population Moslem and Catholic, with Price Endogenous[a]

| Explanatory Variable | Primary School | | Secondary School | | Expected Years of Schooling | |
|---|---|---|---|---|---|---|
| | Male | Female | Male | Female | Male | Female |
| GNP per Adult in 1970 $ | .234 (3.63) | .404 (4.18) | .337 (3.11) | .607 (4.42) | .274 (3.50) | .450 (4.09) |
| Relative Price of Teachers[a] | -.664 (4.79) | -.857 (4.14) | -.874 (6.68) | -1.07 (6.49) | -.796 (5.11) | -.966 (4.42) |
| Proportion of Population Urban | .228 (.85) | .422 (1.06) | .895 (2.13) | .1.24 (2.33) | -.417 (1.32) | -.632 (1.43) |
| Relative Cohort Size | 1.25 (.69) | 4.07 (1.40) | -1.13 (.31) | 4.52 (.98) | -.700 (.53) | .840 (.46) |
| Total Fertility Rate | .0763 (1.86) | .0477 (.78) | -.0283 (.52) | -.0573 (.83) | .0679 (1.43) | .0479 (.72) |
| Percent Moslem | -.0024 (2.22) | -.0053 (3.27) | .0031 (1.73) | -.0002 (.08) | -.0018 (1.35) | -.0059 (3.16) |
| Percent Catholic | -.0002 (.22) | .0010 (.70) | -.0001 (.10) | .0025 (1.30) | -.0004 (.35) | .0007 (.45) |
| Intercept | -1.56 (3.26) | -2.94 (4.11) | -1.27 (1.27) | -3.59 (2.82) | 1.29 (1.94) | -.144 (.15) |
| F | 11.08 | 18.01 | 39.90 | 55.54 | 17.49 | 24.15 |

[a]Price treated as endogenous variable and estimated with instruments of secondary enrollment ratio, urbanization, and GNP per adult, all lagged 10 years. Absolute value of asymptotic t ratio reported in parentheses beneath regression coefficients.

## The Shares of National Product Expended on Education

Another dimension of the educational system is the share of national resources (GNP) allocated to the various levels of the public educational system. In his sample of 20 countries, Pryor (1968) found few patterns accounting for differences in the share of GNP allocated to education, other than the tendency for non-market socialist countries to expend more than market economies on this activity. The proportion of children of school age (5-15) did appear in Pryor's study to be positively associated with the share of GNP spent on public education (1968:193).22 Table 12 extends his findings to include a larger sample with more low-income countries. Per adult real income is positively associated with the share of GNP allocated publicly to primary, secondary, and all educational levels combined, as implied by the earlier estimates of the income expenditure elasticities exceeding one in Tables 5 through 10. A doubling of real income per adult is associated with 0.6, 1.2, and 1.3 percent more of GNP

TABLE 12 Regressions on Share of GNP Expended on Public Schools, with Price of Teachers Endogenous[a]

| Explanatory Variable | Primary School | Secondary School | Total System |
|---|---|---|---|
| | (1) | (2) | (3) |
| GNP per Adult in 1970 $ (log) | .00636 (5.47) | .0117 (7.41) | .0131 (5.48) |
| Relative Price of Teachers (log)[a] | .00286 (1.14) | .00447 (2.31) | .00674 (1.39) |
| Proportion of Population Urban | -.0143 (2.96) | -.0205 (3.30) | -.0211 (2.16) |
| Proportion of School Age Population | -.00114 (.03) | -.0895 (1.67) | -.0490 (1.22) |
| Total Fertility Rate | .00089 (1.27) | .0006 (.73) | .00139 (1.00) |
| Intercept | -.0231 (2.71) | -.0428 (2.90) | -.0391 (1.91) |
| F | 8.18 | 18.97 | 10.79 |
| Sample Size | 186 | 139 | 132 |
| Mean (standard deviation of dependent variable) | .0201 (.0087) | .0253 (.0122) | .0404 (.0166) |

[a]Price is treated as endogenous and estimated with instruments of secondary enrollment ratio, urbanization, and GNP per adult, all lagged 10 years. Absolute value of asymptotic t ratio reported in parentheses beneath regression coefficients.

being allocated to primary, secondary, and all levels of public education combined, respectively, as compared with the sample mean levels of 2.0, 2.5, and 4.0 (recall that the composition of the samples differs by school level). Public expenditures on secondary schools are a slightly larger share of GNP in countries where the relative price of teachers is high, perhaps with the objective of increasing the pool of teachers and lowering their relative wage in the future. Urbanization reduces all three shares, presumably because of the reduction in teacher wages noted earlier. The relative size of the school-aged child population has no noticeable effect on the shares of GNP expended on education. Fertility is also uncorrelated with the share of GNP allocated to public education.[23]

Patterns in Residuals

In Table 3, the average characteristics of the primary school
sample were presented by region.  It is now possible to examine
the deviations of regions from the patterns explained by the
model.  In other words, holding constant for national incomes
per adult, prices, urbanization, and age composition, as estimated in Tables 8 and 9 for primary and secondary school systems,
respectively, how do the regions of the world differ in their
levels and patterns of school expenditures and enrollments?

Tables 13 and 14 report the regional averages of the residuals or deviations in country-level observations from those predicted by the fitted model.  Since all of the educational input
and enrollment variables are in logarithmic terms, with the exception of the final GNP shares, the average residuals can be
interpreted as approximately the proportion a region lies above
or below that predicted.  Expenditures per primary school-aged
child are 9 to 14 percent above average in East Asia and Africa,
but 24 percent below average in South and West Asia.  Enrollment
rates at the primary level are also notably above average in
Africa and East Asia, but 41 percent below average in South and
West Asia and 14 percent below in Latin America.  In the East
Asian region, which has invested heavily in basic education for
a number of years, the ratio of teachers to students is surprisingly below average, whereas the capital intensity is
slightly above average.  Teacher wages are higher than expected
in Latin American and South and West Asia, but lower in the
developed countries.  Finally, the share of GNP allocated to the
public support of primary education is above average for Africa
and less than expected in South and West Asia, controlling for
the economic and demographic constraints captured by the model.

At the secondary school level, the equations generally fit
enrollments more closely than at the primary level, but do less
well in explaining teacher/student ratios and teacher wages.
Secondary school expenditures per child are about 16 percent
above average in Africa, and some 18 percent below average in
Latin America.  Enrollment rates show more variation, with Latin
America and South and West Asia again reporting rates far below
those expected.  In contrast, Africa and East Asia again exhibit
enrollment rates far above expectations.  The teacher/student
ratio is above average in Latin America, but below in East Asia
and Africa.  Teacher wages are again higher in regions such as
South and West Asia and Latin America that have invested less
than the predicted amount in secondary schooling in the past.
Overall, the share of GNP spent on secondary schools is below
that expected for Latin America and above in Africa.

The primary and secondary school regressions are consistent.
They suggest a large and unexplained underinvestment in primary
and secondary schooling in the South and West Asian region and
in Latin America.  Enrollment rates, in particular, are below
the expected levels in these regions; teacher/student ratios
remain relatively high in Latin America at the secondary level,
while capital intensity is high in South and West Asia.  The

TABLE 13  Regional Average Deviations of Primary School Expenditures
and Outputs from Those Predicted, with Prices Endogenous

| Dependent Variable | Region (sample size) | | | | |
|---|---|---|---|---|---|
| | Africa (62) | Latin America (43) | East Asia (21) | South and West Asia (28) | Europe, Oceania, and Canada (36) |
| Total Enrollment Ratio (log) | .172 | -.142 | .147 | -.409 | .0605 |
| Male Enrollment Ratio (log) | .151 | -.164 | .110 | -.276 | .0558 |
| Female Enrollment Ratio (log) | .227 | -.106 | .202 | -.663 | .0601 |
| Teacher-Student Ratio (log) | -.0002 | -.0256 | -.0599 | .0633 | .0234 |
| Capital Intensity Index (log) | -.0062 | -.0370 | .0132 | .0632 | .0051 |
| Teacher Relative Wage (log) | -.0303 | .155 | -.0058 | .0385 | -.155 |
| Total Expenditures per Child (log) | .135 | -.0492 | .0941 | -.244 | -.0664 |
| Expenditures as Share of GNP | .0019 | -.0010 | .0011 | -.0023 | -.0012 |

Sources:  Estimates from Tables 8 and 12 and other data.

high level of teacher wages in Latin America and South and West
Asia may be traced in part to the failure to enroll more children
at the secondary level in earlier years.  The higher current wage
paid for teachers contributes to the higher price of educational
services today, which deters current public expenditures on the
school system in these regions.

Deviations from the pattern predicted by the model based on
income, price, demographic, and distributional characteristics
of the population may signal a disequilibrium that might encourage the private sector to provide schooling.  Although it was
not possible to obtain sufficient information to test this
conjecture, private schools in Latin America and portions of
Asia and Africa are not increasing their share of enrollments in
response to the sluggish public-sector provision of schooling
services (see Table A-11).  Another hypothesis might be that
stagnant economic conditions were not propitious for rewarding
education in the workforce, and that depressed social and private
rates of returns to education could explain the regional patterns

TABLE 14  Regional Average Deviations of Secondary School Expenditures and Outputs from Those Predicted, with Prices Endogenous

| Dependent Variable | Region (sample size) | | | | |
|---|---|---|---|---|---|
| | Africa (49) | Latin America (35) | East Asia (18) | South and West Asia (18) | Europe, Oceania, and Canada (21) |
| Total Enrollment Ratio (log) | .299 | -.437 | .184 | -.239 | .0555 |
| Male Enrollment Ratio (log) | .292 | -.502 | .170 | -.0742 | .0671 |
| Female Enrollment Ratio (log) | .356 | -.355 | .235 | -.615 | .0289 |
| Teacher-Student Ratio (log) | -.129 | .277 | -.188 | .0707 | .0295 |
| Capital Intensity Index (log) | -.0030 | -.0424 | .0199 | .0966 | -.0130 |
| Teacher Relative Wage (log) | -.0123 | .0753 | .0104 | .0338 | -.132 |
| Total Expenditure per Child (log) | .155 | -.177 | .0258 | -.0383 | -.0596 |
| Expenditures as Share of GNP | .0033 | -.0040 | .0007 | -.0007 | -.0012 |

Source: Estimates from Tables 9 and 12 and other data.

of low investment in schooling. Returns to education may not increase with modern economic growth because of limits to the regional and occupational mobility that rewards individuals on the basis of their skills and education. Public policies may also have failed to encourage technological change through adaptive research and development. Finally, the absence of competitive domestic factor and product markets, or distorting trade and foreign exchange regimes, may have eroded the incentives to invest in education or skewed the distribution of income so as to discourage broadly based educational programs. Exploring these possibilities would take us far beyond the scope of this chapter. However, at least in the case of Latin America, studies do not support the view that the underinvestment in secondary schooling is due to a low return to this activity; indeed, substantial private returns accrue to those in Latin America who manage to get a secondary education (Psacharopoulos, 1981). If the overall framework proposed in this chapter is tenable, then further study of regional- and country-level educational outlays and achievements is warranted, both to discover

why expenditures on schooling deviate from the economic pattern
estimated here, and to determine if these deviations could help
account for the rate and structure of modern economic growth
occurring in these countries.


CONCLUSIONS

The empirical association between public school expenditures and
enrollments, on the one hand, and real incomes per adult and the
relative price of teachers, on the other, confirms the view that
income and price variables contribute to determining the equilibrium level of expenditures on schooling within a country. The
working hypothesis that private demands for educational services
explain public expenditures is not rejected. Holding constant
for these dominant income and price constraints on the public
educational system, urbanization is found to be associated with
lower expenditures per school-aged child, and this reduction in
outlays on education in more urbanized countries is associated
with a lower price of teachers relative to other goods. A plausible interpretation of this pattern would presume that there are
economies in using teachers in the larger-scale urban schools and
perhaps compensating amenities in urban areas that teachers
value, such as attractive employment opportunities when schools
are not in session.
    The proportion of the population of school age is associated
with lower levels of public expenditures per child. Therefore,
rapid population growth, which tends to increase the youthfulness
of the population, plays an indirect role in diluting public resources allocated to the school system. This demographic squeeze
induced by a relatively large birth cohort depresses the teacher/
student ratio at both the primary and secondary school levels.
However, primary school enrollment ratios tend to be higher for
relatively large cohorts, leaving public outlays per primary
school-aged child less severely depressed. Estimates of the
demographic effects of cohort size on public-sector expenditures
on the educational system are smaller if one relies on OLS
estimates that ignore likely sources of bias arising from the
endogeneity of teacher prices within the current market for
teacher services.
    Disentangling the effect of fertility on school outlays is
not a simple task because fertility and decisions on the schooling of children are approached by parents jointly. Causation
cannot be inferred in this case from correlation. In this study,
however, the partial correlation between total fertility rates
and public educational outlays was not statistically significant.
    The separate examination of patterns of enrollment among
girls and boys confirms that female enrollments tend to increase
more rapidly with income per adult than do male enrollment rates.
Correspondingly, the decline in the relative wage of teachers, a
measure of the relative price of educational services, is associated with larger gains in schooling for girls than for boys.
Thus, the rise in income and the decline in relative price of

schooling that appear to occur at the onset of modern economic
growth contribute reinforcing gains to the educational attainment
of women that exceed those achieved by men. If the cross-
sectional patterns estimated here hold over time with development, the relative improvement in women's education is a major
and underemphasized concomitant of the development process, with
likely consequences for the rate of decline in child mortality
and fertility, and the long-term decline in population growth
rates.

Certain regions have been able to advance educational expenditures and enrollments beyond what might have been expected
based on incomes, cost of teachers, population distribution, etc.
East Asia and Africa stand out in this regard as "overachievers,"
while South and West Asia and Latin America are below the levels
expected on the basis of the fitted model. Africa's relative
performance, according to the criteria captured in the model, is
in striking contrast to the portrayal of a region suffering from
administrative inertia, an inability to achieve targets of universal primary schooling, and an overpaid cadre of teachers
(Jimenez, 1984; Lee, 1984; Sai, 1984). Since Africa has confronted relatively high prices for teachers, given the described
dynamics of expanding their school systems, it appears likely
that the decline in teacher relative prices will continue to
help this continent increase enrollments without necessarily
increasing outlays per student.

One method for evaluating the overall framework proposed in
this chapter is to calculate how well the educational changes in
the last decade are explained by the cross-sectional estimates
of the model and by the actual changes in the conditioning variables that occurred in this period. Cross-sectional patterns do
not always satisfactorily simulate changes over time. For this
purpose only, the small number of countries that report sufficient data for the decade of 1965 to 1975 are examined. Actual
proportionate changes in public expenditures per child and enrollment ratios are reported in the first column of Table 15.
The second column is the sum of columns 3 through 7, which
report the predicted changes due to the actual changes in each
of the five conditioning variables multiplied by the IV estimates in Tables 8, 9, and 10. The last column of Table 15
indicates how much of the change from 1965 to 1975 is accounted
for by the predicted or simulated change. There are several
possible reasons for divergence. First, the model is fit to a
pooled combination of cross-sectional data from several time
periods and not to just the 1965-75 time series changes within
countries. Second, the sample of countries for which the 1965-75
comparisons can be performed is much more restricted than the
sample used in estimating the model. A third reason is, of
course, the omission or misspecification of explanatory factors.

This parameterized model simulates the changes in expenditures and enrollments quite well for the primary school systems;
that is, 93 and 104 percent of the growth is explained from 1965
to 1975 in expenditures and enrollments, respectively. Public
expenditures per child at the primary level increased a third in

TABLE 15   Actual and Predicted Proportionate Changes in Expenditures per Child and Enrollment Ratios

| School Level (sample size) and Dependent Variable | Actual Change | Predicted Change | Predicted Change Due to Variable | | | | | Ratio of Predicted to Actual Change |
|---|---|---|---|---|---|---|---|---|
| | | | Adult Income | Relative Price | Urbani- zation | Relative Cohort Size | Total Fertility | |
| | (1) | (2) | (3) | (4) | (5) | (6) | (7) | (8)=(2)/(1) |
| **Primary Schools (63)** | | | | | | | | |
| Expenditures/child | .343 | .319 | .379 | -.027 | -.036 | .010 | -.007 | .93 |
| Enrollment ratio | | | | | | | | |
| Total | .160 | .166 | .088 | .115 | -.023 | -.005 | -.009 | 1.04 |
| Male | .128 | .125 | .067 | .108 | -.017 | -.003 | -.026 | .98 |
| Female | .228 | .224 | .121 | .125 | -.030 | -.008 | -.016 | .98 |
| **Secondary Schools (48)** | | | | | | | | |
| Expenditure/child | .385 | .234 | .413 | -.079 | -.038 | -.081 | .018 | .61 |
| Enrollment ratio | | | | | | | | |
| Total | .592 | .393 | .121 | .313 | -.056 | .004 | .011 | .66 |
| Male | .504 | .323 | .086 | .294 | -.045 | -.014 | .003 | .64 |
| Female | .663 | .582 | .183 | .347 | -.072 | .037 | .034 | .80 |
| **Total School System (45)** | | | | | | | | |
| Expenditures/child | .497 | .287 | .364 | -.030 | -.027 | -.023 | .004 | .58 |
| Expected years | | | | | | | | |
| Total | .303 | .186 | .096 | .131 | -.036 | .002 | -.008 | .61 |
| Male | .255 | .142 | .075 | .123 | -.028 | -.002 | -.025 | .56 |
| Female | .375 | .249 | .134 | .139 | -.049 | .009 | .016 | .66 |

Source:  Estimates from col. 1, 2, 3, and 7, Tables 8, 9, and 10.  Change data from separate tabulation of sample for all countries with complete 1965 and 1975 information.  See footnote 24 for list of countries included in secondary school sample.

452

this decade. The decadal increase in incomes per adult of about one-quarter would have contributed by itself to an even larger increase in expenditures, but this increase was moderated slightly by the relative decline in primary school teacher salaries and urbanization. The slight decrease in school cohort size increased expenditures marginally, whereas the decline in fertility was associated with a small decrease in school expenditures. Enrollment rates at the primary level responded predominantly to the decline in relative prices (of teachers), but also increased with incomes, particularly for females. Urbanization, relative cohort size, and fertility had relatively minor effects on primary enrollments.

At the secondary school level, the model underpredicts the substantial increases in expenditures and enrollments that actually occurred in this sample of 48 countries.[24] Again, income growth alone would have suggested a more rapid increase in expenditures than actually occurred, whereas the decline in prices, urbanization, and a small increase in cohort size restrained the growth in secondary school expenditures per child. Enrollments at the secondary level respond strongly to the decline in relative price of teacher salaries; these price effects are larger at the secondary level than they were at the primary level. Enrollments at the secondary level are not greatly affected by the changing demographic characteristics of the population.

When analysis focuses on the total school system, for which our data are less satisfactory, the underprediction of the fitted model remains substantial. Response patterns lie between those estimated for the primary and secondary school separately. Disaggregating enrollments (expressed as expected years of schooling) by sex indicates again how the increase in income per adult and decline in the relative price of teachers help to account in this decade for the more rapid proportionate increase in the enrollment of girls than of boys.

In conclusion, it is important to stress the need for much further work on these largely unexplored data and issues. There is no substitute for reliable data, be they across countries or across individuals or over time on either countries or individuals. The national observations examined here could undoubtedly be reconstructed from underlying government accounts and records for each country, and they might thereby be made more comparable and precise. However, it is doubtful that the salient patterns in the published compilations of data that are derived in this chapter would thereby be reversed.

The statistical significance of the relationships fit to the country observations may also be misstated somewhat because the repeated observations from some countries at five-year intervals are not independent; the "true" sample size might thus be viewed as less than that numerically reported. If the observations are restricted to an average for each country, that is, if the analysis is based on a simple cross-section of country averages, the estimated coefficients are not greatly affected, but their standard errors increase somewhat, and thus significant levels decline.[25]

The main finding of this analysis of international data from educational systems is that public expenditures on schools have conformed to regular patterns with respect to consumer incomes and prices and demographic constraints. Clearly at the secondary level, and probably also at the primary level, rapid population growth has depressed levels of expenditures per child of school age. This has occurred through an increase in class size and a lowering of teacher salaries, but notably not through the restriction of enrollments. The next step is to clarify the origins for many of the departures from this international standard, and to determine the extent to which the decline in public school expenditures per student that is associated with rapid population growth is an inefficient distortion in the allocation of social resources.

NOTES

1  For a relatively small number (20) of countries, market and centrally planned socialist, Pryor (1968) considered the level of public expenditures on education. In his effort to explain the share of GNP publicly expended on education, he observed a significant partial correlation with per capita income levels and share of population aged 5-15. Simon and Pilarski (1979) regressed primary and secondary enrollment ratios and educational expenditures against per capita income, the crude birth rate, life expectancy, and several other variables. They found enrollments and expenditures per child positively related to income and inversely related to birth rates. The partial correlation with crude birth rates was statistically significant only for secondary school enrollments. Because fertility and the schooling of children are partially determined by parents in response to similar constraints and related preferences, the covariation of these two choice variables does not confirm or reject the hypothesized causal effect that a relatively large cohort of school-aged children depresses the average educational resources and school achievements of that cohort. Lall (1969) and Kelley (1976) also explore patterns of government expenditures across low-income countries.

2  These illustrative figures are drawn from World Bank (1984:Tables 1, 23, and 25). See also Preston's (1980) comparisons of life expectation across more uniform and reliable data from a smaller number of countries.

3  The population of primary and secondary school age, according to UNESCO conventions ages 6 to 17, increased by an estimated 131 percent from 1950 to 1980 in the less developed regions of the world, while the total population increased 95 percent (United Nations, 1982). From 1960 to 1980, the corresponding figures were 68 and 58 percent.

4  See Appendix Table A-11 for a regional breakdown of existing data on private school enrollments and their limitations as an unweighted average over a relatively small set of reporting countries.

5  UNESCO Yearbook figures on public expenditures are generally designed to include all public-sector outlays, including subsidies from the public sector to private schools. Footnotes also indicate, particularly for some African countries, that school fees paid by parents to the public schools are included in public-sector expenditures. The data on public expenditures on education that are analyzed in the subsequent regressions are thus designed to include state and local government spending on schools.

6  The political process may not assign everyone's vote an equal weight, however. For example, urban populations in many low-income countries appear to exercise greater influence on public-sector decisions than do dispersed rural populations (Lipton, 1977). Without data on the distribution of income, public services, or taxes across subgroups within countries, it is not fruitful to speculate further here on the distributional implications of how this political process works.

7  Since relatively few studies have estimated the private or social returns to education, it is not possible here to even examine the correlation between unexplained deviation in public investments in schooling and the level of private and public returns to schooling. The most comprehensive comparison of rate of return studies is that by Psacharopoulos (1973; 1981). Differences in methodology across even these summarized country studies undermine the comparability of the return calculations.

8  For example, urbanization was hypothesized to reduce the unit costs of education for technological reasons. However, it might also be associated with higher relative demands for educated labor, and hence higher producer rates of return to schooling. Urbanization is one variable in Z which could thus influence education both by altering production technology and by increasing household demands.

9  Note that if the demand for educational services is relatively inelastic, $\eta > -1$, and education is a public good, $\gamma < 1$, the "cohort size effect" could be interpreted as a scale effect of schooling as a public good; that is, $(\eta + 1)(\gamma - 1)$.

10  Equation (9) may be rewritten in logarithms:

$$\ln(E/P) = \ln(S/P) + \ln(T/S) + \ln(E/C) + \ln(C/T).$$

Regressions would be calculated of the following form at each level of schooling:

$$\ln(E/P) = \beta_{11} + \beta_{12}\ln Y + \beta_{13}\ln P_x + \beta_{14}Z$$

$$\ln(S/P) = \beta_{21} + \beta_{22}\ln Y + \beta_{23}\ln P_x + \beta_{24}Z$$

$$\ln(T/S) = \beta_{31} + \beta_{32}\ln Y + \beta_{33}\ln P_x + \beta_{34}Z$$

$$\ln(E/C) = \beta_{41} + \beta_{42}\ln Y + \beta_{43}\ln P_x + \beta_{44}Z$$

$$\ln(C/T) = \beta_{51} + \beta_{52}\ln Y + \beta_{53}\ln P_x + \beta_{54}Z$$

The adding up of component effects implies that

$$\beta_{1i} = \sum_{j=2}^{5} \beta_{ji} \qquad \text{for } i = 1, \ldots 4 .$$

11  It may be argued that the use of foreign exchange (FX) rates
in 1969-71 to translate GNP from local currencies into the
common unit of dollars gives insufficient weight to nontraded
commodities. The tendency is to exaggerate differences
across countries in real consumer income per adult. Recent
work by Kravis et al. (1982), aimed at constructing a
purchasing power parity (PPP) basis for comparing incomes
across countries, is built on a sample of countries for which
price indexes were constructed; these results were generalized and revised to apply to other countries by Summers and
Heston (1984). As an example of these findings, FX-trans-
lated GNP per adult is 43 times larger in the U.S. than in
India in 1970, whereas the PPP real income per adult difference is only 13 to 1. Since consumer welfare may be
better approximated by the PPP income deflator, the PPP
deflated figures were used in reestimating the schooling
equations reported in this chapter. In general, PPP income
elasticities of school expenditures increased by as much as
one-quarter, as would have been expected since the sample
variance in log PPP incomes is markedly less than the
variance in log FX incomes. Price elasticities were reduced
somewhat, suggesting that some of the differences in the
relative price of teacher salaries are captured in the PPP
adjustment procedure. No systematic changes occurred in the
coefficients on relative size of school-aged cohorts, nor
were the estimated effects of urbanization noticeably changed
by this substitution of one measure of real GNP for the
other. Therefore, substantive conclusions of this chapter
are not particularly sensitive to this choice of procedure
for translating GNP across countries into common welfare
units.

12  The disturbances in the equation determining current demands
for schooling that would affect today's wages of teachers
might also be correlated with the unexplained disturbances in
the equation determining enrollment rates 10 years earlier,
such as might arise from a persistent country-specific unobserved effect. This form of error structure would imply
that the lagged enrollment variable was not actually exogenous to the wage equation. The two-stage estimates based
on the lagged enrollment instrument would then be subject to
the classical simultaneous equation bias and would also be
inconsistent. Although one cannot be confident of the
direction of the effect of this bias on the price elasticity,
it would seem likely to bias positively the estimate of the
enrollment effect on wages. In fact, the enrollment effect

is estimated to be negative and appears statistically significant for both the primary and secondary teacher wage rates, as reported in note 14.

13  An analogous errors-in-variable bias arises in the study of labor supply, where earnings are divided by hours worked to obtain a wage rate that is specified by theory as a determinant of hours.

14  The implicit primary and secondary school logarithmic wage equations for teachers were estimated as conditioned on the secondary school enrollment rate, income per adult, and proportion of the population urban, all of which explanatory variables were evaluated 10 years earlier:

$$\ln W_{pt} = -1.84 - .349 \ln E_{s_{t-10}} + .355 \ln GNP/A_{t-10} - .808U_{t-10}$$

    (3.38)   (6.22)            (4.30)            (2.67)

           n = 186              R2 = .264

$$\ln W_{st} = .931 - .646 \ln E_{s_{t-10}} + .305 \ln GNP/A_{t-10} - 1.25U_{t-10}$$

    (1.18)   (8.25)            (2.61)            (3.22)

           n = 139              R2 = .601

where $E_{st-10}$ refers to the secondary school enrollment proportion 10 years ago, $GNP/A_{t-10}$ indicates GNP per adult (age 15 to 65) measured 10 years earlier, $U_{t-10}$ is the urban proportion of the population 10 years ago, and $W_{pt}$ and $W_{st}$ are the current expenditures per primary or secondary school teacher divided by GNP per adult today.

15  See note 11.

16  From equation (8), the coefficient on the relative price or teacher wage variable in the expenditure function is $b_2 = \alpha (\eta + 1)$, and thus the estimated price elasticity, $\eta = (b_2/\alpha) - 1$. The sample mean of $\alpha$ is .82.

17  It appears to be generally cheaper to hire teachers in a more urbanized area, though GNP per adult augments teacher wages more than proportionately. Urban amenities, including summer employment opportunities, may be valued particularly strongly by teachers; thus it is costly to assign teachers to provincial rural schools where they must do without these amenities and relocate during vacations to obtain employment that rewards their educated skills maximally.

18  Economies of scale in producing school services might be distinguished at three levels:  (1) with the size of the national educational system, (2) with the size of the school measured in terms of its number of full-time teachers, and (3) with the size of the teacher's span of control or student-teacher ratio.  The importance of (1) in primary and

secondary school systems was assumed at the outset to be
negligible. The number of primary schools is reported for
some recent years in the UNESCO Yearbook. If the system's
average school size (i.e., log of teachers per school) is
added to equation (8), one might expect this added scale
variable to diminish the coefficient on urbanization if
larger urban schools realized economies that reduced unit
costs. In a sample of 60 countries for which these data are
recently available (UNESCO Statistical Yearbook, 1984),
school size is associated with greater expenditures per child
because of higher teacher-student ratios and higher current
outlays per teacher. The coefficients on urbanization are
not reduced in magnitude by the addition of the school-size
explanatory variable. Although consolidation economies
could remain important at the secondary level, no intercountry data were found to test this conjecture.

19  Standardized test comparisons do confirm that spending far
    less per student in low-income countries is associated with
    lower test scores (Heyneman and Loxley, 1983; Simons and
    Alexander, 1978). What is now needed is estimates of the
    marginal gains from additions to school quality and quantity
    that can be purchased with marginal increments in educational
    expenditures (Welch, 1966), and the effects of these alter-
    native expenditures on the future productivity of students
    (Heyneman, 1984).

20  The income elasticities are further apart for girls and boys
    in the low-income sample than for the entire sample, whereas
    price elasticities are closer together for boys and girls in
    the low-income sample at the primary level and further apart
    at the secondary level. The relatively large standard errors
    on the estimated income elasticities of male enrollment re-
    duce our confidence that male and female enrollments respond
    differently, whereas the price elasticity estimates are
    sufficiently precise to infer that they differ between sexes
    at a 10 percent confidence level in the low-income sample.

21  It should be noted that the religion variables are strongly
    intercorrelated with incomes, and thus income elasticity
    estimates are generally reduced by the inclusion of these
    variables. It should also be stressed that the distribution
    of religious preference within many countries is not known
    with great precision. The data analyzed here are drawn from
    Russet et al. (1964) and The Encyclopedia Britannica (1983).

22  Lall (1969) summarizes a study that found a cross-country
    relationship in the share of government expenditures on
    education and per capita real GNP in 1964. Within strata of
    low-income countries, the relationship was positive up to
    $250 per capita (1964 U.S. dollars) and then declined. The
    relationship of educational expenditures as a share of GNP
    was apparently not statistically significant and not
    reported, though it was positive and significant for public
    health expenditures.

23  This finding challenges the working assumption of Coale and
    Hoover (1958:267) that linked population growth to the share

of income allocated by poor countries to "less productive" expenditures on education and social welfare programs that are "diluted and delayed" in their effect on labor productivity or in their notation, $W_i$.

24  The countries included were Burundi, Kenya, Mauritius, Rwanda, Somalia, Uganda, Tanzania, Cameroon, Algeria, Morocco, Sudan, Tunisia, Ghana, Liberia, Togo, Sierra Leone, Jamaica, Costa Rica, El Salvador, Guatemala, Honduras, Mexico, Nicaragua, Panama, Argentina, Bolivia, Colombia, Ecuador, Paraguay, Peru, Venezuela, Hong Kong, South Korea, Singapore, Thailand, Afghanistan, Iran, Nepal, Pakistan, Iraq, Kuwait, Syria, Finland, Ireland, Italy, Portugal, Yugoslavia, and France.

25  Standard error-component models of time series of cross sections cannot be estimated here because the number of observations per country varies.


DATA APPENDIX

Data were initially compiled at five-year intervals from 1955 to 1980 for 155 countries with an estimated population of 1 million or more in 1983. Of these countries, 10 were eliminated for lack of numerous data series*; 11 nonmarket economies of Eastern Europe were also not examined, in part because they did not have convertible currencies and thus a free exchange rate with which to express their national income or educational expenditures (where available) in common currency units (1970 U.S. dollars). Yugoslavia is included. Since the bases for many demographic indicators, such as age composition and literacy, are population censuses that occur approximately every 10 years, data were linearly interpolated for up to 10 years and extrapolated for up to 5 years. Out of a possible 930 observations for all countries and years, complete data were obtained for only 321 observations for primary schooling systems (see Table A-1); 258 observations for secondary school systems; and 250 observations for combined systems including primary, secondary, and higher. Many countries have anomalous gaps in their published data that might be eliminated with further research, such as the omission of Taiwan because of the proscription of data from this country in recent U.N. data compilations.

More serious than these idiosyncratic gaps in the sample, which probably do not distort substantially the patterns des-

---

*Mozambique, Lesotho, Nambia, Guinea-Bissau, China, Mongolia, North Korea, Kampuchea, Laos, and Vietnam. The omission of particular series for the U.S. and Taiwan will be corrected in future work, and aggregations of early data for portions of Malaysia were compiled. Several countries, such as Chile and Argentina, were eliminated because of instability in their domestic GNP deflator over time, although it should be possible to include these countries in the future.

cribed here, are the poor quality and incomparability of some of
the reported data. Biases are obviously present in most school
systems that work to overstate enrollments, or at a minimum
contribute to a variable gap between initial enrollment and
average daily attendance rates. However, attendance rates are
not available from most countries, precluding reasonable adjustments. Enrollment is associated with changing numbers of days
of attendance over time and across countries. Expenditure data
are probably still less reliable, with changes in administrative
regimes leading to some unlikely year-to-year variations. Series
for only recurrent or current educational expenditures appear
more stable and reliable as compared with capital account expenditures that embody year-to-year variations not readily
explained by the economic and demographic constraints emphasized
here.

Total educational expenditures are often divided among primary, secondary (academic, vocational, and normal schools combined), and higher educational institutions. Those expenditures
not allocated among these three levels, such as central administrative expenses, are proportionately distributed to the three
levels according to their relative shares in the allocated total.
Current and capital expenditure shares of this total are also
assumed constant at the three levels, for lack of cross-tabula-
tions of capital expenditures. The consolidation of educational
expenditures at various levels of government may introduce
further error, for in federal governmental structures, state and
local expenditures on schools may not always be reported uniformly to the central government and hence not consistently included as intended in UNESCO figures across countries. The role
of the private sector in providing educational services may also
be an important factor in determining the amount and quality of
public-sector support for education and vice versa. Figures on
the numbers of teachers by level are also available for many
countries, but the treatment of part- and full-time teachers may
not be consistent across countries (Pryor, 1968) or how many
days per year they are required to teach. With all these mis-
givings, it is not possible in this chapter to more than summarize existing data as reported by governments on their educational systems and published in the UNESCO Statistical Yearbooks.
The wide range and variety of UNESCO data appear, nonetheless,
to warrant more comparative study than they have received.

The second major source of data is the World Bank Data Tape
(version dated April 1984). From this source, data are extracted
on GNP, both in current market and constant local prices; the implicit GNP deflator (price index); and the foreign exchange rate
into U.S. dollars (official International Monetary Fund figure).
Real GNP in constant U.S. dollars is then defined as the constant
local price GNP converted at the average exchange rate prevailing
in 1969, 1970, and 1971. The GNP deflator and exchange rate are
also used to derive estimates of the U.S. dollar equivalent of
government educational expenditures. To approximate the "price"
of public-sector educational services, the current educational
expenditures per teacher have been divided by the current value

of GNP per adult aged 15-64. This relative "price" of teachers is defined for the primary and secondary public school systems separately and averaged for the total system. UNESCO figures for educational expenditures are not always expressed in the same local currency units employed in the national income accounts reported by the World Bank. In some countries with substantial inflation and foreign exchange revaluations, such as Chile and Argentina, comparable expenditure and national income figures were not reconstructed, and these observations are omitted from this analysis.

Population figures are drawn from the United Nations (1982), and are linearly interpolated across decades as required or across ages to obtain the population of children aged 6-11 for primary school, 12-17 for secondary school, and 20-24 for higher education. These age groupings of potential students might differ from country to country given local schooling systems, but are standardized here to match the average definition of UNESCO enrollment ratios. Since children outside of a specific school age group may enroll in such schools, these ratios may exceed 100 percent. Enrollment ratios may also exceed 100 percent because of the upward reporting bias referred to earlier. To summarize school enrollments at all levels, a synthetic measure of cohort expected years of exposure to schooling is calculated. It is defined, as stated in the text, as the weighted sum of primary, secondary, and higher school enrollment rates, where the weights are 6, 6, and 5, respectively. The proportion of the population living in urban areas is drawn from the World Bank Data Tape. Educational attainment of parents of school-aged children is not readily available from standardized sources. Adult literacy rates are often published, but can be of doubtful reliability and are not uniformly available disaggregated by age or sex. The adult literacy rates considered here are interpolated from the 1983 World Development Report and augmented from early U.N. Demographic Yearbooks.

APPENDIX TABLE A-1   Countries Included in Sample, By Region, School Level, and Time Period

| Continent | Country Code | Country | Number of Observations | | | | | |
|---|---|---|---|---|---|---|---|---|
| | | | Primary | | Secondary | | Total | |
| | | | (a) | (b) | (a) | (b) | (a) | (b) |
| | | | (105) | (62) | (90) | (49) | (84) | (45) |
| Africa | 1 | Burundi | 5 | 3 | 5 | 3 | 5 | 3 |
| | 3 | Ethiopia | 3 | 2 | 2 | 1 | 2 | 0 |
| | 4 | Kenya | 4 | 2 | 4 | 2 | 4 | 2 |
| | 5 | Madagascar | 4 | 2 | 3 | 1 | 3 | 1 |
| | 6 | Malawi | 4 | 3 | 3 | 2 | 2 | 2 |
| | 7 | Mauritius | 5 | 3 | 4 | 2 | 4 | 2 |
| | 10 | Rwanda | 4 | 3 | 4 | 3 | 4 | 3 |
| | 11 | Somalia | 4 | 2 | 4 | 2 | 4 | 2 |
| | 12 | Uganda | 5 | 3 | 4 | 2 | 4 | 2 |
| | 13 | Tanzania | 5 | 3 | 4 | 2 | 3 | 2 |
| | 14 | Zambia | 3 | 2 | 2 | 1 | 2 | 1 |
| | 15 | Zimbabwe | 2 | 2 | 3 | 3 | 2 | 1 |
| | 17 | Ctrl. Af. Rep. | 2 | 0 | 2 | 0 | 1 | 0 |
| | 18 | Chad | 1 | 0 | 1 | 0 | 0 | 0 |
| | 19 | Congo Rep. | 4 | 2 | 4 | 2 | 4 | 2 |
| | 22 | Cameroon | 3 | 2 | 3 | 2 | 3 | 2 |
| | 24 | Algeria | 5 | 3 | 3 | 2 | 4 | 2 |
| | 27 | Morocco | 5 | 3 | 5 | 3 | 5 | 3 |
| | 28 | Sudan | 5 | 3 | 5 | 3 | 5 | 2 |
| | 29 | Tunisia | 4 | 2 | 4 | 2 | 4 | 2 |
| | 38 | Ghana | 4 | 2 | 4 | 2 | 4 | 2 |
| | 41 | Ivory Coast | 4 | 2 | 2 | 1 | 2 | 1 |
| | 42 | Liberia | 4 | 3 | 3 | 2 | 3 | 2 |
| | 43 | Mali | 2 | 2 | 1 | 1 | 1 | 1 |
| | 44 | Mauritania | 2 | 1 | 1 | 0 | 0 | 0 |
| | 45 | Niger | 1 | 0 | 1 | 0 | 0 | 0 |
| | 46 | Nigeria | 2 | 1 | 2 | 1 | 2 | 1 |
| | 47 | Senegal | 2 | 2 | 1 | 1 | 1 | 1 |
| | 48 | Togo | 4 | 3 | 3 | 2 | 3 | 2 |
| | 49 | Sierra Leone | 3 | 1 | 3 | 1 | 3 | 1 |
| Central and South America | | | (76) | (43) | (67) | (35) | (66) | (32) |
| | 53 | Dom. Rep. | 3 | 2 | 1 | 1 | 1 | 1 |
| | 55 | Haiti | 1 | 1 | 0 | 0 | 0 | 0 |
| | 56 | Jamaica | 4 | 2 | 4 | 2 | 4 | 2 |
| | 59 | Trin./Tobago | 3 | 2 | 2 | 1 | 2 | 1 |
| | 62 | Costa Rica | 5 | 3 | 5 | 3 | 5 | 2 |
| | 63 | El Salvador | 5 | 3 | 5 | 3 | 5 | 3 |
| | 64 | Guatemala | 5 | 3 | 4 | 2 | 4 | 2 |
| | 65 | Honduras | 4 | 2 | 3 | 1 | 3 | 1 |
| | 66 | Mexico | 5 | 3 | 4 | 2 | 4 | 2 |
| | 67 | Nicaragua | 5 | 3 | 4 | 2 | 4 | 2 |
| | 68 | Panama | 5 | 3 | 5 | 3 | 5 | 3 |
| | 69 | Argentina | 4 | 2 | 4 | 2 | 4 | 2 |
| | 72 | Bolivia | 4 | 3 | 3 | 2 | 3 | 2 |
| | 73 | Brazil | 4 | 2 | 3 | 1 | 3 | 1 |
| | 74 | Colombia | 5 | 3 | 5 | 3 | 5 | 2 |
| | 75 | Ecuador | 3 | 1 | 3 | 1 | 3 | 1 |
| | 77 | Paraguay | 3 | 1 | 4 | 2 | 3 | 1 |
| | 78 | Peru | 4 | 2 | 4 | 2 | 4 | 2 |
| | 80 | Venezuela | 4 | 2 | 4 | 2 | 4 | 2 |

Appendix Table A-1 (continued)

| Continent | Country Code | Country | Number of Observations | | | | | |
|---|---|---|---|---|---|---|---|---|
| | | | Primary | | Secondary | | Total | |
| | | | (a) | (b) | (a) | (b) | (a) | (b) |
| | | | (71) | (45) | (60) | (34) | (59) | (34) |
| Asia | 82 | Japan | 2 | 2 | 2 | 2 | 2 | 2 |
| | 83 | Hong Kong | 5 | 3 | 5 | 3 | 5 | 3 |
| | 86 | South Korea | 5 | 3 | 4 | 2 | 4 | 2 |
| | 88 | Burma | 3 | 1 | 3 | 1 | 3 | 1 |
| | 93 | Malaysia | 3 | 3 | 2 | 2 | 2 | 2 |
| | 94 | Philippines | 3 | 3 | 3 | 3 | 3 | 3 |
| | 95 | Singapore | 5 | 3 | 5 | 3 | 5 | 3 |
| | 96 | Thailand | 5 | 3 | 4 | 2 | 4 | 2 |
| | 98 | Afghanistan | 4 | 2 | 4 | 2 | 4 | 2 |
| | 99 | Bangladesh | 3 | 3 | 2 | 2 | 2 | 2 |
| | 101 | India | 4 | 2 | 3 | 1 | 3 | 1 |
| | 102 | Iran | 3 | 2 | 4 | 2 | 3 | 2 |
| | 103 | Nepal | 5 | 3 | 4 | 2 | 4 | 2 |
| | 104 | Pakistan | 4 | 2 | 4 | 2 | 4 | 2 |
| | 105 | Sri Lanka | 3 | 2 | 0 | 0 | 0 | 0 |
| | 108 | Iraq | 4 | 2 | 4 | 2 | 4 | 2 |
| | 110 | Kuwait | 0 | 0 | 0 | 0 | 0 | 0 |
| | 111 | Lebanon | 0 | 0 | 0 | 0 | 0 | 0 |
| | 115 | Syria | 5 | 3 | 4 | 2 | 4 | 2 |
| | 119 | Israel | 0 | 0 | 0 | 0 | 0 | 0 |
| | 120 | Turkey | 5 | 3 | 3 | 1 | 3 | 1 |
| | | | (8) | (4) | (2) | (0) | (2) | (0) |
| Oceania | 121 | Australia | 3 | 1 | 1 | 0 | 1 | 0 |
| | 122 | New Zealand | 5 | 3 | 1 | 0 | 1 | 0 |
| North America | 125 | Canada | 3 | 1 | 0 | 0 | 0 | 0 |
| | | | (58) | (31) | (39) | (21) | (39) | (21) |
| Europe | 134 | Denmark | 4 | 2 | 0 | 0 | 0 | 0 |
| | 135 | Finland | 5 | 3 | 5 | 3 | 5 | 3 |
| | 137 | Ireland | 5 | 3 | 5 | 3 | 5 | 3 |
| | 138 | Norway | 4 | 2 | 3 | 1 | 3 | 1 |
| | 139 | Sweden | 4 | 2 | 3 | 2 | 3 | 2 |
| | 142 | Greece | 3 | 2 | 0 | 0 | 0 | 0 |
| | 143 | Italy | 4 | 2 | 4 | 2 | 4 | 2 |
| | 145 | Portugal | 4 | 2 | 4 | 2 | 4 | 2 |
| | 146 | Spain | 4 | 2 | 3 | 1 | 3 | 1 |
| | 147 | Yugoslavia | 4 | 3 | 4 | 3 | 4 | 3 |
| | 148 | Austria | 3 | 2 | 2 | 1 | 2 | 1 |
| | 149 | Belgium | 4 | 2 | 2 | 1 | 2 | 1 |
| | 150 | France | 4 | 2 | 4 | 2 | 4 | 2 |
| | 151 | West Germany | 1 | 0 | 0 | 0 | 0 | 0 |
| | 153 | Netherlands | 4 | 2 | 0 | 0 | 0 | 0 |
| | 154 | Switzerland | 1 | 0 | 0 | 0 | 0 | 0 |
| Total Sample Size | | | 321 | 186 | 258 | 139 | 250 | 132 |

Note: (a) refers to entire sample that may not have included the ten-year lagged value of the instruments. This larger sample was the basis for only exploratory OLS estimations and tends to include a substantial number of observations from the 1960s for which the lagged instruments are not available. (b) refers to the restricted sample for which the lagged instruments (secondary school enrollment rates, GNP per adult, and urbanization) are available. These smaller samples are used for all of the OLS and IV estimates reported in this chapter.

TABLE A-2  Estimates of Primary School Expenditures and Components, with the Price of Teachers Exogenous, Excluding Fertility[a]

| | Dependent Variable in Logarithms | | | | | | |
| Explanatory Variable | Enrollment Ratio | | | Teacher-Student Ratio (T/S) | Capital Intensity Index (E/C) | Teacher Salary (C/T) | Total Expenditure per Child Age 6-11 (E/P) |
| | Male (S/P) | Female (S/P) | Total (S/P) | | | | |
| | (1) | (2) | (3) | (4) | (5) | (6) | (7) |
| GNP per Adult in 1970 (log) | .165 (4.10) | .384 (5.98) | .248 (5.33) | .158 (4.24) | -.0077 (.28) | 0.0 (32.7) | 1.40 (27.9) |
| Relative Price of Teachers (log)[a] | -.193 (5.45) | -.195 (3.44) | -.213 (5.19) | -.168 (5.10) | -.0369 (1.53) | 1.0 | .582 (13.2) |
| Proportion of Population Urban | .102 (.62) | .0854 (.32) | .0864 (.45) | -.283 (1.85) | -.107 (.96) | 0.0 | -.304 (1.48) |
| Proportion of Population Age 6-11 | 1.93 (2.12) | 3.60 (2.47) | 2.28 (2.16) | -5.08 (6.00) | -.620 (1.00) | 0.0 | -3.43 (3.01) |
| Intercept | -1.39 (4.33) | -3.32 (6.46) | -2.07 (5.57) | -3.51 (11.7) | .411 (1.88) | 0.0 | -5.17 (12.9) |
| $R^2$ | .429 | .493 | .501 | .535 | .024 | 1.0 | .951 |
| Sample Size | 186 | 186 | 186 | 186 | 186 | 186 | 186 |
| Mean (standard deviation of dependent variable) | -.216 (.355) | -.365 (.604) | -.229 (.440) | -3.49 (.366) | .192 (.184) | 7.39 (1.10) | 3.87 (1.51) |

[a]Price is treated as exogenous and estimated with ordinary least squares.  Absolute value of t ratio reported in parentheses beneath regression coefficients.

TABLE A-3 Estimates of Secondary School Expenditures and Components, with the Price of Teachers Exogenous, Excluding Fertility[a]

| Explanatory Variable | Dependent Variable in Logarithms | | | | | | |
|---|---|---|---|---|---|---|---|
| | Enrollment Ratio | | | Teacher-Student Ratio (T/S) | Capital Intensity Index (E/C) | Teacher Salary (C/T) | Total Expenditure per Child Age 12-17 (E/P) |
| | Male (S/P) | Female (S/P) | Total (S/P) | | | | |
| | (1) | (2) | (3) | (4) | (5) | (6) | (7) |
| GNP per Adult in 1970 (log) | .460 (5.77) | .877 (9.93) | .604 (7.91) | .0113 (.21) | -.0198 (.58) | 0.0 | 1.60 (28.7) |
| Relative Price of Teachers (log)[a] | -.394 (7.70) | -.478 (8.41) | -.441 (8.99) | -.0750 (2.19) | -.0181 (.83) | 1.0 | .466 (13.0) |
| Proportion of Population Urban | -.0426 (.14) | -.250 (.72) | -.152 (.51) | -.0953 (.46) | -.0959 (.72) | 0.0 | -.343 (1.58) |
| Proportion of Population Age 12-17 | -2.04 (.84) | 3.65 (1.36) | -2.68 (.12) | -8.06 (4.96) | -1.73 (1.67) | 0.0 | -10.1 (5.94) |
| Intercept | -3.29 (4.68) | -6.98 (8.96) | -4.50 (6.69) | -1.81 (3.85) | .623 (2.08) | 0.0 | -5.69 (11.6) |
| $R^2$ | .748 | .846 | .819 | .242 | .035 | 1.0 | .955 |
| Sample Size | 139 | 139 | 139 | 139 | 139 | 139 | 139 |
| Mean (standard deviation of dependent variable) | -1.33 (.882) | -1.78 (1.25) | -1.49 (.999) | -2.99 (.341) | .192 (.193) | 8.42 (.903) | 4.14 (1.47) |

[a]Price is treated as exogenous and estimated with ordinary least squares. Absolute value of t ratio reported in parentheses beneath regression coefficients.

TABLE A-4 Estimates of Total School Expenditures and Components, with the Price of Teachers Exogenous, Excluding Fertility[a]

| | Dependent Variable in Logarithms | | | | | | |
|---|---|---|---|---|---|---|---|
| | Enrollment Ratio | | | Teacher-Student Ratio (T/S) | Capital Intensity Index (E/C) | Teacher Salary (C/T) | Total Expenditure per Child Age 6-17 (E/P) |
| Explanatory Variable | Male (S/P) | Female (S/P) | Total (S/P) | | | | |
| | (1) | (2) | (3) | (4) | (5) | (6) | (7) |
| GNP per Adult in 1970 $ (log) | .283 (5.46) | .543 (6.96) | .355 (6.52) | .106 (3.15) | -.0177 (.51) | .892 23.8 | 1.43 (25.7) |
| Relative Price of Teachers (log)[a] | -.279 (5.58) | -.308 (4.10) | -.295 (5.62) | -.0979 (3.01) | -.0451 (1.34) | 1.19 (33.0) | .471 (8.79) |
| Proportion of Urban Population | -.0043 (.02) | -.165 (.54) | -.0564 (.27) | -.180 (1.36) | -.132 (.97) | -.131 (.90) | -.283 (1.30) |
| Proportion of Population Age 6-17 | .326 (.48) | 1.77 (1.13) | -.0430 (.06) | -2.66 (5.95) | -.696 (1.51) | .414 (.84) | -3.54 (4.81) |
| Intercept | .458 (1.02) | -1.69 (2.50) | -.0182 (.04) | -3.05 (10.4) | .619 (2.05) | .680 (2.09) | -4.93 (10.2) |
| $R^2$ | .648 | .664 | .701 | .525 | .037 | .946 | .955 |
| Sample Size | 132 | 132 | 132 | 132 | 132 | 132 | 132 |
| Mean (standard deviation of dependent variable) | 2.05 (.483) | 1.74 (.743) | 1.90 (.551) | -3.31 (.271) | .195 (.196) | 8.80 (.886) | 3.89 (1.45) |

[a]Price is treated as exogenous and estimated with ordinary least squares. Absolute value of t ratio reported in parentheses beneath regression coefficients.

TABLE A-5 Estimates of Primary School Expenditures and Components, with the Price of Teachers Exogenous, Excluding Fertility[a]

| | Dependent Variable in Logarithms | | | | | | |
|---|---|---|---|---|---|---|---|
| | Enrollment Ratio | | | Teacher-Student Ratio (T/S) | Capital Intensity Index (E/C) | Teacher Salary (C/T) | Total Expenditure per Child Age 6-11 (E/P) |
| Explanatory Variable | Male (S/P) | Female (S/P) | Total (S/P) | | | | |
| | (1) | (2) | (3) | (4) | (5) | (6) | (7) |
| GNP per Adult in 1970 $ (log) | .211 (4.09) | .447 (5.27) | .304 (4.86) | .184 (4.82) | -.0054 (.20) | .863 (35.0) | 1.35 (22.1) |
| Relative Price of Teachers (log)[a] | -.547 (5.24) | -.809 (4.73) | -.669 (5.31) | -.228 (2.96) | .0075 (.13) | 1.07 (21.6) | .181 (1.48) |
| Proportion of Urban Population | -.266 (1.51) | -.533 (1.41) | -.382 (1.37) | -.363 (2.13) | -.0689 (.56) | .199 (1.81) | -.615 (2.26) |
| Proportion of Population Age 6-11 | 3.51 (3.07) | 5.42 (2.89) | 4.07 (2.96) | -3.92 (4.65) | -.415 (.68) | -6.65 (12.2) | -6.92 (5.15) |
| Intercept | -1.50 (3.74) | -3.26 (4.95) | -2.15 (4.44) | -3.77 (12.7) | .313 (1.46) | 1.78 (9.31) | -3.83 (8.10) |
| F | 23.08 | 29.43 | 28.75 | 46.13 | .50 | 1638. | 571. |
| Sample Size | 186 | 186 | 186 | 186 | 186 | 186 | 186 |
| Mean (standard deviation of dependent variable) | -.126 (.355) | -.365 (.604) | -.229 (.440) | -3.49 (.366) | .192 (.184) | 7.39 (1.10) | 3.87 (1.51) |

[a]Price is treated as endogenous and estimated with instruments of secondary enrollment ratio, urbanization, and GNP per adult, all lagged 10 years. Absolute value of asymptotic t ratio reported in parentheses beneath regression coefficients.

TABLE A-6 Estimates of Secondary School Expenditures and Components, with the Price of Teachers Exogenous, Excluding Fertility[a]

| | Dependent Variable in Logarithms | | | | | | |
|---|---|---|---|---|---|---|---|
| | Enrollment Ratio | | | Teacher-Student Ratio (T/S) | Capital Intensity Index (E/C) | Teacher Salary (C/T) | Total Expenditure per Child Age 12-17 (E/P) |
| Explanatory Variable | Male (S/P) | Female (S/P) | Total (S/P) | | | | |
| | (1) | (2) | (3) | (4) | (5) | (6) | (7) |
| GNP per Adult in 1970 $ (log) | .303 (2.74) | .667 (5.02) | .434 (3.87) | .107 (1.61) | -.0114 (.32) | .946 (53.8) | 1.48 (21.4) |
| Relative Price of Teachers (log)[a] | -.899 (7.56) | -1.14 (8.00) | -.989 (8.20) | .183 (2.55) | .0026 (.07) | 1.01 (53.1) | .202 (2.73) |
| Proportion of Urban Population | -.778 (1.79) | -1.22 (2.32) | -.953 (2.16) | .242 (.92) | -.0704 (.50) | .148 (2.14) | -.633 (2.33) |
| Proportion of Population Age 12-17 | -2.00 (.63) | 3.44 (.90) | -.163 (.05) | -6.51 (3.39) | -1.54 (1.49) | -5.64 (11.1) | -13.9 (6.96) |
| Intercept | -1.02 (.98) | -3.93 (3.14) | -2.05 (1.94) | -3.27 (5.21) | .493 (1.47) | 1.03 (6.23) | -3.79 (5.84) |
| F | 62.33 | 96.37 | 83.59 | 8.28 | 1.04 | 1683. | 482. |
| Sample Size | 139 | 139 | 139 | 139 | 139 | 139 | 139 |
| Mean (standard deviation of dependent variable) | -1.33 (.882) | -1.78 (1.25) | -1.49 (1.00) | -2.98 (.341) | .192 (.193) | 8.42 (.903) | 4.14 (1.47) |

[a]Price is treated as endogenous and estimated with instruments of secondary enrollment ratio, urbanization, and GNP per adult, all lagged 10 years. Absolute value of asymptotic t ratio reported in parentheses beneath regression coefficients.

468

TABLE A-7 Estimates of Total School System Expenditures and Components, with the Price of Teachers Endogenous, Excluding Fertility[a]

| | Dependent Variable in Logarithms | | | | | | |
|---|---|---|---|---|---|---|---|
| | Enrollment Ratio | | | Teacher-Student Ratio (T/S) | Capital Intensity Index (E/C) | Teacher Salary (C/T) | Total Expenditure per Child Age 6-17 (E/P) |
| Explanatory Variable | Male (S/P) | Female (S/P) | Total (S/P) | | | | |
| | (1) | (2) | (3) | (4) | (5) | (6) | (7) |
| GNP per Adult in 1970 $ (log) | .283 (4.29) | .529 (5.31) | .350 (4.77) | .127 (3.60) | -.0086 (.25) | .769 (14.5) | 1.35 (21.6) |
| Relative Price of Teachers (log)[a] | -.689 (5.73) | -.942 (5.19) | -.792 (5.92) | .0228 (.35) | .0023 (.04) | 1.38 (14.2) | .155 (1.36) |
| Proportion of Urban Population | -.471 (1.67) | -.863 (2.03) | -.613 (1.964) | -.0763 (.51) | .0921 (.62) | .279 (1.23) | -.514 (1.93) |
| Proportion of Population Age 6-17 | 1.12 (1.33) | 1.96 (1.54) | .768 (.82) | -2.26 (5.00) | -.516 (1.16) | -3.69 (5.45) | -5.35 (6.70) |
| Intercept | .936 (1.60) | -.745 (.84) | .633 (.97) | -3.50 (11.1) | .432 (1.40) | 2.26 (4.81) | -3.41 (6.14) |
| F | 39.13 | 42.20 | 45.06 | 29.64 | .75 | 188. | 513. |
| Sample Size | 132 | 132 | 132 | 132 | 132 | 132 | 132 |
| Mean (standard deviation of dependent variable) | 2.05 (.483) | 1.74 (.743) | 1.90 (.547) | -3.31 (.271) | .195 (.196) | 8.08 (.886) | 3.89 (1.45) |

[a]Price is treated as endogenous and estimated with instruments of secondary enrollment ratio, urbanization, and GNP per adult, all lagged 10 years. Absolute value of asymptotic t ratio reported in parentheses beneath regression coefficients.

469

TABLE A-8 Estimates of Primary School Expenditures and Components Only in Low-Income Countries, with the Price of Teachers Endogenous[a]

| | Dependent Variable in Logarithms | | | | | | |
|---|---|---|---|---|---|---|---|
| | Enrollment Ratio | | | Teacher-Student Ratio (T/S) | Capital Intensity Index (E/C) | Teacher Salary (C/T) | Total Expenditure per Child Age 6-11 (E/P) |
| Explanatory Variable | Male (S/P) | Female (S/P) | Total (S/P) | | | | |
| | (1) | (2) | (3) | (4) | (5) | (6) | (7) |
| GNP per Adult in 1970 $ (log) | .195 (2.54) | .401 (3.44) | .270 (3.06) | .0936 (1.81) | -.026 (.62) | 1.067 (55.9) | 1.40 (15.5) |
| Relative Price of Teachers (log)[a] | -.559 (4.73) | -.667 (3.70) | -.621 (4.56) | -.236 (2.95) | .0012 (.02) | 1.02 (34.5) | .162 (1.16) |
| Proportion of Urban Population | -.147 (.52) | -.399 (.92) | -.249 (.76) | -.239 (1.23) | -.0575 (.37) | -.211 (2.95) | -.756 (2.23) |
| Proportion of Population Age 6-11 | -.918 (.37) | 2.50 (.65) | .266 (.09) | -2.74 (1.62) | .475 (.35) | -6.23 (9.97) | -8.23 (2.27) |
| Total Fertility Rate | .0524 (1.44) | -.0193 (.35) | .024 (.57) | -.0234 (.95) | .0007 (.03) | .0099 (1.10) | .0111 (.26) |
| Intercept | -1.02 (2.13) | -2.57 (3.53) | -1.56 (2.83) | -3.31 (10.3) | .286 (1.10) | .613 (5.14) | -3.97 (7.01) |
| F | 16.25 | 21.29 | 20.49 | 10.46 | .92 | 1527. | 146. |
| Sample Size | 148 | 148 | 148 | 148 | 148 | 148 | 148 |
| Mean (standard deviation of dependent variable) | -.167 (.387) | -.465 (.639) | -.296 (.470) | -3.599 (.289) | .190 (.198) | 7.009 (.823) | 3.305 (1.076) |

TABLE A-9  Estimates of Secondary School Expenditures and Components Only in Low-Income Countries, with the Price of Teachers Endogenous[a]

| Explanatory Variable | Dependent Variable in Logarithms | | | | | | |
|---|---|---|---|---|---|---|---|
| | Enrollment Ratio | | | Teacher-Student Ratio (T/S) | Capital Intensity Index (E/C) | Teacher Salary (C/T) | Total Expenditure per Child Age 12-17 (E/P) |
| | Male (S/P) | Female (S/P) | Total (S/P) | | | | |
| | (1) | (2) | (3) | (4) | (5) | (6) | (7) |
| GNP per Adult in 1970 $ (log) | .206 (1.40) | .622 (3.76) | .348 (2.41) | .0534 (.59) | -.0083 (.17) | 1.14 (53.3) | 1.53 (17.5) |
| Relative Price of Teachers (log)[a] | -.858 (6.25) | -1.04 (6.72) | -.923 (6.86) | .175 (2.09) | -.0103 (.23) | 1.02 (51.2) | .259 (3.17) |
| Proportion of Urban Population | -.405 (.73) | -1.14 (1.83) | -.674 (1.24) | .347 (1.03) | -.160 (.89) | -.343 (4.27) | -.830 (2.52) |
| Proportion of Population Age 12-17 | -2.90 (.47) | -.0433 (.01) | -1.62 (.27) | -4.50 (1.18) | -1.04 (.51) | -7.31 (8.11) | -14.5 (3.91) |
| Total Fertility Rate | .0153 (.26) | -.0678 (1.12) | -.0162 (.28) | -.0017 (.20) | .0011 (.06) | -.0232 (2.71) | -.0453 (1.29) |
| Intercept | -.620 (.51) | -3.03 (-2.21) | -1.47 (1.23) | -3.19 (4.29) | .456 (1.15) | .385 (2.19) | -3.82 (5.27) |
| F | 30.56 | 57.64 | 44.87 | 1.85 | .99 | 1030. | 150. |
| Sample Size | 116 | 116 | 116 | 116 | 116 | 116 | 116 |
| Mean (standard deviation of dependent variable) | -1.540 (.809) | -2.079 (1.156) | -1.738 (.911) | -3.046 (.323) | .188 (.201) | 8.265 (.867) | 3.670 (1.046) |

[a]Price is treated as endogenous and estimated with instruments of secondary enrollment ratio, urbanization, and GNP per adult, all lagged 10 years.  Absolute value of asymptotic t ratio reported in parentheses beneath regression coefficients.

TABLE A-10 Estimates of Total School System Expenditures and Components Only in Low-Income Countries, with Price of Teachers Endogenous[a]

| | Dependent Variable in Logarithms | | | | | | |
|---|---|---|---|---|---|---|---|
| | Enrollment Ratio | | | Teacher-Student Ratio (T/S) | Capital Intensity Index (E/C) | Teacher Salary (C/T) | Total Expenditure per Child Age 6-17 (E/P) |
| Explanatory Variable | Male (S/P) | Female (S/P) | Total (S/P) | | | | |
| | (1) | (2) | (3) | (4) | (5) | (6) | (7) |
| GNP per Adult in 1970 $ (log) | .194 (1.96) | .454 (3.21) | .251 (2.36) | .091 (1.70) | -.0067 (.13) | 1.08 (15.1) | 1.41 (15.0) |
| Relative Price of Teachers (log)[a] | -.686 (5.12) | -.824 (4.31) | -.746 (5.20) | .0059 (.08) | -.0160 (.22) | 1.39 (14.3) | .181 (1.43) |
| Proportion of Population Urban | -.152 (.42) | -.709 (1.39) | -.300 (.78) | .0120 (.06) | -.167 (.87) | .591 (2.29) | -.735 (2.18) |
| Proportion of Population Age 6-17 | -.198 (.11) | .493 (.19) | -.428 (.22) | -1.84 (1.88) | -.389 (.40) | -3.35 (2.56) | -5.39 (3.16) |
| Total Fertility Rate | .0396 (.93) | -.0321 (.53) | .0162 (.36) | -.0010 (.04) | .0030 (.13) | -.0382 (1.25) | -.0190 (.48) |
| Intercept | 1.51 (2.15) | .124 (.12) | 1.32 (1.76) | -3.40 (8.97) | .414 (1.11) | .780 (1.54) | -3.56 (5.38) |
| F | 22.31 | 26.42 | 25.86 | 3.55 | .88 | 88.28 | 149. |
| Sample Size | 109 | 109 | 109 | 109 | 109 | 109 | 109 |
| Mean (standard deviation of dependent variable) | 1.954 (.481) | 1.591 (.734) | 1.777 (.531) | -3.385 (.219) | .192 (.206) | 7.866 (.770) | 3.417 (1.067) |

aPrice is treated as endogenous and estimated with instruments of secondary enrollment ratio,

TABLE A-11  Unweighted Average of Percentages of Students Enrolled in Private Schools, by Level and Region, in 1965 and 1975

| Region | Primary Schools Number of Countries | 1965 | 1975 | Secondary Schools Number of Countries | 1965 | 1975 |
|---|---|---|---|---|---|---|
| East Africa | (8)[a] | 23 | 12 | (8)[b] | 33 | 23 |
| West Africa | (11) | 29 | 19 | (9) | 42 | 30 |
| Latin America | (18)[c] | 13 | 12 | (17)[c] | 39 | 30 |
| Asia (East) | (5) | 14 | 13 | (4) | 42 | 29 |
| N. Africa and Middle East | (9) | 7.4 | 6.2 | (10) | 18 | 8.2 |
| Total | (51) | 17 | 13 | (48) | 34 | 24 |

[a]Excluding high levels in Lesotho, Swaziland, and Burundi as small unrepresentative countries.
[b]Excluding high levels in Lesotho and Swaziland as unrepresentative.
[c]Excluding high levels in Haiti as a small unrepresentative country, where private shares have actually increased.

Source:  World Bank (1980).

REFERENCES

Becker, G.S. (1963)  Human Capital.  New York:  Columbia
    University Press.
Becker, G.S., and H.G. Lewis (1974)  Interactions between
    quantity and quality of children.  In T.W. Schultz, ed.,
    Economics of The Family.  Chicago:  University of Chicago
    Press.
Belmont, L., and F.A. Marolla (1973)  Birth order, family size,
    and intelligence.  Science 182:1096-1101.
Binswanger, H., and V.W. Ruttan (1978)  Induced Innovation:
    Technology, Institutions and Development.  Baltimore, Md.:
    The Johns Hopkins University Press.
Borcherding, T.E., and R.T. Deacon (1972)  The demand for the
    services of nonfederal governments.  American Economic
    Review 62(5):891-901.
Bowles, S. (1969)  Planning Educational Systems for Economic
    Growth.  Cambridge, Mass.:  Harvard University Press.
Coale, A.J., and E.M. Hoover (1958)  Population Growth and
    Economic Development in Low Income Countries.  Princeton,
    N.J.:  Princeton University Press.
Easterlin, R. (1980)  Birth and Fortune.  New York:  Basic Books.
Freeman, R. (1979)  The effect of demographic factors on age-
    earnings profiles.  Journal of Human Resources 14(3):289-318.
Freeman, R.B. (1971)  The Market for College-Trained Manpower.
    Cambridge, Mass.:  Harvard University Press.
Gramlich, E.M., and D.L. Rubinfeld (1982)  Microestimates of
    public spending demand functions and tests of the Tiebout
    and median voter hypothesis.  Journal of Political Economy
    90(3):536-560.
Heyneman, S. (1984)  Research on education in the developing
    countries.  International Journal of Educational Development
    4(4):293-304.
Heyneman, S., and W. Loxley (1983)  The effects of primary school
    quality on academic achievement across 29 high and low
    income countries.  American Journal of Scoiology 88(6):
    1162-1194.
Jimenez, E. (1984)  Pricing Policy in the Social Sectors:  Cost
    Recovery for Education and Health in Developing Countries.
    Unpublished manuscript, University of Western Ontario and
    the World Bank.
Jones, G. (1971)  Effects of population growth on the attainment
    of educational goals in developing countries.  In National
    Academy of Sciences Rapid Population Growth.  Baltimore,
    Md.:  The Johns Hopkins University Press.
Jones, G. (1975)  Population Growth and Educational Planning in
    Developing Nations.  New York:  Irvington Publications.
Kelley, A.C. (1976)  Demographic change and size of the govern-
    ment sector.  Southern Economic Journal 43:1056-1066.
Kirk, D. (1966)  Factors affecting Moslem natality.  In Family
    Planning and Population Programs.  Chicago:  University of
    Chicago Press.

Kravis, I.B., A. Heston, and R. Summers (1982) World Product and Income. Baltimore, Md.: The Johns Hopkins University Press.

Lall, S. (1969) A note on government expenditures in developing countries. Economic Journal 79(314):413-417.

Lee, R. (1979) Causes and consequences of age structure fluctuations: the Easterlin lypothesis. In Economic and Demographic Change: Issues for the 1980s. Liege: Ordina Publications.

Lee, K.H. (1984) Universal Primary Education: An African Dilemma. Unpublished manuscript, World Bank, Washington, D.C.

Leibowitz, A. (1974) Home investment in children. In T.W. Schultz, ed., Economics of the Family. Chicago: University of Chicago Press.

Lipton, M. (1977) Why Poor People Stay Poor: Urban Bias in World Development. Cambridge, Mass.: Harvard University Press.

Preston, S.H. (1980) Causes and consequences of mortality declines in LDCs during the twentieth century. In R.A. Easterlin, ed., Population and Economic Changes in Developing Countries. Chicago: University of Chicago Press.

Pryor, F.L. (1968) Public Expenditures in Communist and Capitalist Nations. Homewood, Ill.: Richard Irwin, Inc.

Psacharopoulos, G. (1973) Returns to Education. San Francisco: Jossey Bass-Elsevier Publications.

Psacharopoulos, G. (1981) Returns to education: an updated international comparison. Comparative Education Review 17(3):321-341.

Ram, R., and T.W. Schultz (1979) Life span, health, savings, and productivity. Economic Development and Cultural Change 27(3):399-421.

Robinson, W.C. (1975) Population and Development Planning. New York: The Population Council.

Rosenzweig, M.R. (1982) Educational subsidy, agricultural development and fertility change. Quarterly Journal of Economics 97(1):67-88.

Rosenzweig, M.R., and K.I. Wolpin (1980) Testing the quantity quality model of fertility. The use of twins as a natural experiment. Econometrica 48(1):227-240.

Russet, B.M., R.A. Hayward, K.W. Deutsch, and H.D. Lasswell (1964) World Handbook of Political and Social Indicators. New Haven, Conn.: Yale University Press.

Sai, F.T. (1984) The population factor in Africa's development dilemma. Science 226:801-805.

Schultz, T.P. (1971) An economic perspective on population growth. In National Academy of Sciences Rapid Population Growth. Baltimore, Md.: The Johns Hopkins University Press.

Schultz, T.P. (1981) Economics of Population. Reading, Mass.: Addison Wesley Publication Co.

Schultz, T.P. (1984) Studying the impact of household economic and community variables on child mortality. Population and Development Review 10(supplement):215-235.

Schultz, T.W. (1961)   Investment in human capital. American
    Economic Review 51(1):1-17.
Simon, J.L., and A.M. Pilarski (1979)  The effect of population
    growth upon the quantity of education children receive.
    Review of Economics and Statistics 61(4):572-584.
Simmons, J., and L. Alexander (1978)  The determinants of school
    achievement in developing countries.  Economic Development
    and Cultural Change 26(2):341-358.
Summers, R., and A. Heston (1984)  Improved international
    comparisons of real product and its composition, 1950-1980.
    Review of Income and Wealth, Series 30(2):207-262.
Terhune, K.W. (1974)  A Review of the Actual and Expected
    Consequences of Family Size.  Bethesda, Md.:  National
    Institute of Health.
United Nations, Department of International Economic and Social
    Affairs (1982)  Demographic Indicators of Countries:
    Estimates and Projections as Assessed in 1980.  New York:
    United Nations.
United Nations (various years)  Demographic Yearbook.  New York:
    United Nations.
United Nations, Education and Social Commission (various years)
    UNESCO Statistical Yearbook.  New York:  United Nations.
Welch, F. (1966)  Measurement of the quality of schooling.
    American Economic Review 56(2):379-392.
Welch, F. (1979)  The baby boom babies financial bust.  Journal
    of Political Economy 87(5):568-598.
Williamson, J.G., and P.H. Lindert (1980)  American Inequality.
    New York:  Academic Press.
World Bank (1974)  Population Policies and Economic Development.
    Baltimore, Md.:  The Johns Hopkins University Press.
World Bank (1980)  Education Sector Policy Paper, 3rd ed.
    Washington, D.C.:  World Bank.
World Bank (1981)  World Development Report 1981.  New York:
    Oxford University Press.
World Bank (1983)  World Development Report 1983.  New York:
    Oxford University Press.
World Bank (1984)  World Development Report 1984.  New York:
    Oxford University Press.
Wray, J.D. (1971)  Population pressure on families.  In National
    Academy of Sciences Rapid Population Growth.  Baltimore,
    Md.:  The Johns Hopkins University Press.

# V. Macroeconomic Issues and Models

# 12

## The Impact of Population Growth on Economic Growth in Developing Nations: The Evidence From Macroeconomic-Demographic Models

Dennis A. Ahlburg

ABSTRACT

This chapter reviews several economic-demographic models of developing countries, focusing on the predicted impact of population change on economic development. Early models found a very large negative impact of population growth on economic development. More recent models have found this negative impact to be smaller than previously thought, and a few have found the impact to be positive in the long run. Other models have shown the impact of population change to vary widely across countries and to have little impact on the degree of urbanization.

INTRODUCTION

It is widely believed that population growth has an adverse effect on economic growth in developing nations. In fact, Robert McNamara (1971:11) singled out population growth as the "greatest single obstacle to economic and social advancement of most of the societies of the developing world." However, a group of scholars have recently argued that the effects of population growth are neutral, or may even be positive. It is also commonly believed that the issue lacks its past urgency since fertility is declining in most areas. However, as McNicoll (1984:178) has remarked, this belief is "based on little more than heroic extrapolation and hope." Even if population growth rates are falling, they are still high and are expected to remain so. For example, India's population growth rate is not projected to fall below 1.5 percent per annum until after 1995, while Nigeria's rate of population growth is predicted to remain at 2.3 percent per annum through the year 2025 (McNicoll, 1984). Assuming that the demographic transition began in developing countries in 1930 and will extend

---

I would like to thank Geoffrey Greene, David Wheeler, Julian Simon, Richard Easterlin, and Nancy Birdsall for comments on and discussion of the material in this chapter.

for a century, the result would be a six- to ten-fold increase
in population in these countries during that period (McNicoll,
1984). Given population change of this magnitude, it is still of
critical importance to explore the impact of population growth
on economic development in developing nations.

This chapter reviews several economic-demographic models of
developing nations, focusing on the predicted impact of population change on economic development in each. Although the definition of economic development has been widened to include
social, political, economic, and demographic dimensions
(Horlacher, 1981), income per capita will be used here as the
principal index of economic development.

Formal economic-demographic models allow the investigator

> to evaluate the consequences of alternative demographic and
> nondemographic policies, to illuminate the interaction be-
> tween population and other variables in the development
> process, to provide projections of resources and require-
> ments, and to aid in achieving consistency in policy forma-
> tion, planning, and implementation. Many formal models also
> have the advantage that their underlying assumptions are
> made explicit, exposed to criticism, and thereby corrected
> and improved over time [unless disguised by overly complex
> structure] (Horlacher, 1981:6).

However, these models are not without shortcomings:

> They may provide decision makers with an incomplete or
> incorrect picture of the development process and the role of
> population factors in that transformation . . . by omitting
> essential qualitative aspects of the development process.
> The models may emphasize a single developmental factor as a
> sufficient condition [for development] when it may only be
> one of many conditions for development. Furthermore, these
> models may provide planners with an overly sanguine picture
> of the system's response to policy by assuming equilibrating
> adjustment mechanisms when in fact disequilibrating forces
> are pervasive . . . and may suggest incremented as opposed
> to structural policy changes (Horlacher, 1981:8).[1]

The next section briefly reviews the early growth models.
This is followed by a discussion of the various empirical models.
Next is a summary of areas for further research. The chapter
ends with a summary and conclusions.


THE EARLY GROWTH MODELS

Early neoclassical growth models in the Solow-Swan tradition
assumed population was exogenous and found that the equilibrium
growth rate of output (and capital) was the same as that of the
population. In these models, the highest feasible output per
capita was achieved with a stationary population, although even

higher levels of output per head could be achieved by making population growth negative. The absolute size of population played no essential part in determining the results of the models (Pitchford, 1974). Later models, with endogenous populations, came to similar conclusions. As Pitchford (1974:70) observed, "one of the striking features of [these] descriptive population growth models is that . . . they frequently take the economy into rather undesirable or even disastrous situations, such as, for instance, a subsistence stationary state."[2]

Simon and Steinmann (1981) argue that these models have failed to specify technical change correctly. When technical change is correctly specified, a higher population growth leads to a faster rate of economic growth and a higher level of consumption. The correct specification of technical change, it is asserted, is that of Phelps (1966):

$$\frac{A_t - A_{t-1}}{A_{t-1}} = \frac{A_{t-w-1}}{A_{t-1}} \ h \left(\frac{R_t}{A_{t-w-1}}\right), \tag{1}$$

where A = level of technology, R = number of researchers, and w = the retardation factor, which represents the delay in adoption of newly produced knowledge. R is considered to be proportional to the labor force; that is, a larger population implies more "ingenious men" (and women) who create economic progress (Simon and Steinmann, 1981:253).

Thus, depending on the assumptions made in the model, population growth can be shown to have a negative or positive effect on economic growth. This is a recurrent theme of this chapter.


EMPIRICAL MODELS

The empirical models discussed in this chapter vary as regards the source of data for the model, the method used for deriving parameter values, the treatment of key demographic and other variables (exogenous or endogenous), the policy issues explicitly addressed, and the direction and size of the impact of population change on economic development. These features are summarized in Table 1, which also provides a brief statement of the models' strengths and weaknesses. The remainder of this section looks at the key empirical models--the early simulation models (primarily Coale-Hoover); Barlow and Davies; the Bachue models; Wheeler; Simon; and models that include migration/urbanization (Kelly and Williamson; Mohan; and Schmidt).


Coale-Hoover

A development parallel to that of the neoclassical growth models was the specification of simulation models that attempted to capture the main structural features of growing economies. These models derived and compared alternative states of the economy at a point in time or over time under alternative demographic assumptions.

TABLE 1  Summary of Models

| Model Features | Coale-Hoover | Barlow-Davies | Bachue-Kenya | Wheeler |
|---|---|---|---|---|
| Data | Aggregate data for India | -- | Household and regional surveys | Aggregate .70 countries, 1960-80 changes |
| Parameters | Assigned on basis of data | Assigned | Estimated from data | Estimated from data |
| Labor Quality | -- | Endogenous | -- | Endogenous |
| Fertility | Exogenous | Endogenous | Endogenous | Endogenous |
| Mortality | Exogenous | Endogenous | Endogenous | Endogenous |
| Migration | -- | -- | Endogenous | -- |
| Effect of Population on Development | Negative, 50 percent fertility decline over 35 years increases income per capita 38-48 percent | Birth control, negative; a 37 percent decrease in births over 15 years increases income per capita 21 percent; a decrease in the death rate decreases income per capita 6 percent | Decrease in TFR of 30 percent, increase in GNP per capita of 14 percent; 46 percent TFR decrease, same increase in GNP per capita; impact of fertility reduction larger than life expectancy change; little impact of education or migration | Increase in education and family planning, decreased TFR; respective elasticities .25-1.05 and .39-.07 |
| Strengths | -- | Detailed endogenous demographic sector, endogenous government | Specification of the demographic sector | Interactive treatment of education and family planning |

482

| Weaknesses | Population exogenous, policy costless, no technology, no labor in production | No migration production function | Specification of several components of demand as exogenous (e.g., investment | One sector, no government or explicit technical change |
|---|---|---|---|---|
| Government | -- | Endogenous | Exogenous | -- |
| Health | -- | Endogenous | -- | -- |
| Education | -- | Endogenous | Exogenous | Exogenous |
| Technological Change | -- | Exogenous | Exogenous | -- |
| Policy Issues | Fertility reduction | Education and health policy | Demographic change on employment, economic policy on demography | Variations in education and family planning efficiency |

TABLE 1 continued on page 484

TABLE 1 (continued)

| Model Features | Simon | Kelley-Williamson | Schmidt | Mohan |
|---|---|---|---|---|
| Data | Aggregate | Aggregate, 40 countries | Same as Kelley-Williamson | Aggregate data for India |
| Parameters | Assigned from contemporary historical studies | Some assigned, some based on data | Some assigned, some based on data | Based on data |
| Labor Quality | Endogenous | Endogenous | -- | -- |
| Fertility | Exogenous | Exogenous | Endogenous | Exogenous |
| Mortality | Endogenous | Exogenous | Endogenous | Exogenous |
| Migration | -- | Endogenous | Endogenous | Endogenous |
| Effect of Population on Development | In long run (120-180 years), positive population growth gives higher economic growth than stationary population; in short run, reverse is true; declining population always reduces economic growth | Population increase has little impact on urbanization | -- | Population increase has little impact on urbanization; in short run, population growth decreases economic growth, but in long run, effect may not be negative |
| Strengths | Treatment of endogenous technical change and flexible hours worked | Strong theoretical basis (e.g., production, consumption sectors); treatment of service sector, nontradables | Specification of model schedules to complement general equilibrium models | Specification of consumption |

484

| Weaknesses | No feedback from economy to demography over simulation; no government sector | Demographically underdeveloped | Parameters of schedules largely exogenous |
|---|---|---|---|
| Government | -- | Endogenous | -- |
| Health | -- | -- | -- |
| Education | -- | Endogenous | -- |
| Technological Change | Endogenous | Exogenous | Exogenous |
| Policy Issues | Effect of changing fertility on economic development | Impact of population change, technical change, prices, and capital inflow on urbanization | Impact of population change, technological change, changing patterns of demand on urbanization |

Coale and Hoover's (1958) eight-equation model of the Indian economy is one of the earliest and is perhaps the most well known of the simulation models. Coale and Hoover assumed that the rate at which output can be expanded depends on (1) the resources devoted to investment in <u>productive</u> facilities and certain other developmental outlays, and (2) the incentives and energy of the labor force. For them, the prime determinant of the rate of development is the allocation of national output to public outlays plus private investment (F). The amount of funds available to finance these outlays is a function of national income (Y) and the average level of income per equivalent adult consumer (Y/C). After coefficients and base values are estimated from Indian data, the equation for public outlays and private investment is

$$F_t = .30Y_t - 49.27C_t .$$ (2)

However, F contains both "direct growth" expenditures and welfare expenditures that have a productive effect much less intensive and direct than that of the direct growth outlays. Welfare expenditures, such as the provision of schools, are taken to depend on population size and rate of increase and on levels of income per capita.[3] These expenditures include outlays designed to meet the current needs of the existing population and the needs of the future population. Equivalent growth outlays (G) are specified:

$$G_t = Y_t (.2275 - .725 \, p_t + .03625L_t)$$

$$+ .03625Y_{t-15} (1-L_{t-15}) - 49.27C_t ,$$ (3)

where L = the labor force participation rate and P = the ratio of annual population increment to current population.

The size and growth rate of population have an obvious ceteris paribus negative effect on "equivalent growth outlays" and consequently on economic growth. In simulations, a 50 percent linear reduction in fertility over 25 years is associated with a 38-48 percent higher income per consumer than would occur under constant fertility (Coale and Hoover, 1958:281). The absolute magnitudes of gain shown in Table 2 are sensitive to the parameter values, but the differential associated with reduced fertility is not. The differential occurs because more rapid population growth increases current consumption and welfare-type outlays at the expense of private savings and developmental expenditures.

Pitchford (1974) identified major weaknesses in the Coale-Hoover model. The transition to lower fertility is assumed to be costless, as is the assumed parallel decrease in mortality of 41 percent, and the use of an accelerator approach to production makes no explicit allowance for the effect of labor in production. Simon (1977:235) argued that, despite the enormous contribution of the work, "it has practically nothing to do with economic development" since output per worker and not income per

TABLE 2   Rates of Economic Growth in the Coale-Hoover Simulation

|                       | Percentage 1956-66 | Increases 1966-76 | Per Annum 1976-86 |
|-----------------------|--------------------|-------------------|-------------------|
| National Income       |                    |                   |                   |
| High fertility        | 3.3                | 3.4               | 3.5               |
| Medium fertility      | 3.3                | 3.5               | 3.9               |
| Low fertility         | 3.4                | 3.8               | 4.4               |
| Income Per Consumer   |                    |                   |                   |
| High fertility        | 1.3                | 1.0               | 0.9               |
| Medium fertility      | 1.3                | 1.4               | 2.5               |
| Low fertility         | 1.6                | 2.0               | 3.2               |

Notes:  High fertility equals unchanged fertility; medium
fertility equals 50 percent decline concentrated between 1966
and 1981; low fertility equals 50 percent decline between 1956
and 1981.  Decade averages are from a simple averaging of five-
year data given in Coale and Hoover (1958:273).

equivalent consumer is the relevant measure of economic development.   Omitting labor from the production function means that
population growth adds consumers but not producers.  This limits
the model to an analysis of "very short run effects of a short
run variation in population size," but not of economic development, which is a long-run phenomenon (pp. 236-237).

   In general, the specification of the production function in
economic-demographic models has a very significant impact on the
properties of the model.  If a model assumes that (1) the growth
of technology, the capital stock, and other factors in the production function are independent of the rate of growth of employment; (2) that the labor force/population ratio is constant;
and (3) that the production function exhibits constant returns
to scale, Sanderson (1980) has shown that decreasing the rate of
population growth will always increase the rate of growth of
income per capita, no matter what the parameter values.


Barlow and Davies

Barlow and Davies (1974) constructed a synthetic model of a
representative developing country that extended the Coale-Hoover
model and corrected many of its flaws.  They were primarily
interested in educational and health policy impacts on long-run
growth in per capita income.

The Model

Their model consists of six segments: population, income, labor
quantity, labor quality, capital quantity, and capital quality.
Fertility and mortality are endogenously determined (in Coale-
Hoover they were exogenous) as a function of income per equivalent consumer, a trend term capturing improvements in medical
technology, and an exogenous policy variable (public health
programs). Fertility is also specified to be a positive function
of child mortality. Population by single year of age, sex, and
educational attainment is endogenous as well. Endogenizing
population is necessary to obtain unbiased estimates of the
impact of population change on economic development (Kelley et
al., 1972).

Income per year is determined by a four-factor production
function that assumes a constant elasticity of substitution
between each pair of factors. The inputs are capital and labor,
specified by three educational classes.4 Labor is a quality-
weighted index of hours supplied. Quantity of hours is a
function of income per equivalent consumer and morbidity.
Morbidity is a function of income per equivalent consumer, a
trend, and of exogenous health projects. Labor quality (or
human capital) is a function of education, on-the-job-training
(proxied for by past hours of labor supplied), and debility
(determined by the same factors as mortality and morbidity).

Capital stock is a function of past capital stock plus new
investment. Investment is determined from the availability of
funds from private and public savings and depreciation. Private
savings are a function of personal disposable income, foreign
capital inflows, and the dependency ratio. Note here that
decreases in morbidity and debility can increase private savings
since they result in lower demand for medical care and thus
higher personal disposable income. A key assumption in the
savings function of this model and several others is the negative
relationship between savings and the percent of population below
15 and over 65 years of age. Fertility control reduces births,
increases private savings, increases investment, and increases
national income. Ram (1982:537-538) analyzed the relationship
between savings and the dependency ratio for 121 developing
countries for the 1970s and concluded that "contrary to the conclusions reached in Leff (1969), [and Coale and Hoover 1958; and
Barlow and Davies, 1974] there is little evidence of a significant adverse effect of a high dependency rate [particularly the
young dependency rate] on aggregate savings in the less developed
world where the issue has greatest relevance." Kelley (1980)
reached a similar conclusion, and in fact found that the relationship for Kenya was positive when education was considered to
be a form of saving.5

Barlow and Davies endogenized the government sector. Public
savings are determined by endogenous tax receipts plus foreign
aid minus endogenous government expenditures. These expenditures
are broken down into education, public health, defense, transfers, and other services, each of which is a function of revenue

available and the size of the client population.  Technology,
which was absent from the Coale-Hoover model, enters exogenously
to augment linearly the quality of domestic and imported capital
goods (embodied technical change), and to improve resource allocation arising from malaria eradication (disembodied technical
change).  In this last respect, it is, to some extent, affected
by population change.

## Policy Simulations

Two simulations run by Barlow and Davies are of particular
interest.  Both alter the growth rate of population--one by
instituting a birth control program to reduce the crude birth
rate by one point per year for 15 years from an initial level of
41 per 1,000, and the second by instituting a malaria eradication
program.  Both simulations involve increased costs in the public
health budget and run 30 years.  The birth control policy results
in an income per equivalent consumer 21 percent higher than that
of the baseline simulation with no birth control policy.  Reduced
fertility decreases labor input, but increases savings and investment though smaller family size.  Labor quality (human capital) increases as higher incomes mean less debility and better
education.  The payoff to birth control is invariant to cost per
births averted in the range of $10-$50.[6]  The malaria eradication program leads to decreased mortality (particularly child
mortality), morbidity, and debility, and increased fertility
(through reduced miscarriages).  Positive effects of the program
are felt for 8 years as the quantity and quality of labor,
savings, and efficiency of resource allocation increase.  These
effects are, however, outweighed by declines in investment as
growing population stimulates nonproductive current expenditures
in the public and private sectors.  Overall, income grows 15
percent and the population of equivalent consumers 22 percent,
leading to a 6 percent decline in income per equivalent consumer.
When the two simulations are run simultaneously, the result is
similar to the addition of the two separate simulations.

One problem with these simulations is the assumption of an
exogenous reduction in mortality and fertility.  While this
assumption may be reasonable for the former, it is less so for
the latter.  Recent work by Easterlin and Crimmins (1985) en-
dogenizes fertility control as a function of the difference
between the number of surviving children in the absence of
contraception (itself a function of a set of proximate determinants of natural fertility) and the number of children
desired, on the one hand, and the cost of contraception on the
other.  This approach represents a more fruitful avenue for
investigating the impact of policy on fertility.

The result for declining mortality depends critically on the
elasticity of factor substitution assumed in the production
function.  If the elasticity is low (0.3), then the effect of
declining mortality on income per consumer is positive, not negative.  It would be of interest as well to know the sensitivity

of the simulation results to the family size-savings relationship. The model also ignores migration and urbanization, which
Kelley et al. (1972) and Kelley and Williamson (1984a) have shown
alter the impact of population change on economic development (as
discussed below).

Despite these shortcomings, the Barlow-Davies model is a
good example of a detailed demographic model linked to a small
economic model and can be used to investigate a broad spectrum
of health and education policies. Although the model reaches
the same basic conclusion as do Coale and Hoover (1958)--that
population growth is associated with lower income per capita--
the pathways by which this result emerges may be more clearly
discerned.


The Bachue Models

A significant recent development in economic-demographic
modeling in developing countries is the advent of the Bachue
series of models. The five Bachue models (Kenya, Brazil,
Philippines, Yugoslavia, and International) all contain multi-
sectoral input-output models incorporating features of economic
dualism, such as modern and traditional sectors, and urban and
rural sectors. All treat population in a highly disaggregated
fashion (by age, sex, location, and education); endogenize the
components of population change; and determine both the level of
employment and the size distribution of incomes across households. The Bachue models are essentially long-run policy-
oriented simulation models rather than short-run forecasting
models. However, they are not identical; their structure,
assumptions, parameter values, and initial conditions reflect
country-specific conditions and concerns. Two of the models--
those for the Philippines and Kenya--are reviewed below.


Bachue-Philippines

Bachue-Philippines (Rodgers et al., 1978) focuses on issues
relating to the distribution of income and employment. In a
very detailed critique of this model, Sanderson (1980:7)
concludes that it may be of little use to planners except in
"analyzing the effects of changes in the economic and demographic environment on the distribution of income in those cases
where the changes themselves and the alterations in income
distribution have little or no effect on the rate of economic
growth." The major problem with the model is that, apart from
the agricultural sector, neither capital nor labor inputs affect
output. Output growth is determined exogenously, and investment, consumption, and government expenditure are thus independent of output. The model is essentially demand-driven and
is "not designed to answer questions concerning the effect of
policy discussions on the rate of economic growth" (p. 7). It
also contains several technical errors, particularly in the

treatment of prices and of the relationship between the total
fertility rate, proportions married, and age-specific ma ital
fertility. Sanderson feels that the model could be of us, to
planners if these technical problems were corrected and if
investment and output change were endogenized.


## Bachue-Kenya

Another of the Bachue models, Bachue-Kenya (Anker and Knowles,
1983), was designed to investigate the impact of demographic
change on employment and the potential impact of economic policy
on the demographic future of Kenya. This model differs fundamentally from Bachue-Philippines in that it is a supply-
constrained model estimated entirely on Kenyan household and
district-level survey data.


   The Model. Private consumer demand is derived from rural and
urban expenditure functions determined by income and household
size. The other components of aggregate demand--investment, exports, public consumption, and change in stocks--are assumed to
be exogenously determined by past rates of growth. These components are aggregated and adjusted for imports, taxes, and
subsidies to provide a sector of final demand for domestically
produced goods. The supply constraint is then introduced. Total
imports and exports are compared. If exports are greater (lower)
than imports, the sector of total demand (excluding exports) is
increased (decreased) in such a way as to maintain the given
relative rates of growth in the components of final demand. The
input-output model then produces new estimates of value-added
and imports, and the procedure is repeated until imports and
exports are within a given percentage range of each other. In
this way, "only the relative rates of growth of exogenous
components of final demand are determined exogenously" (Anker
and Knowles, 1983:290).
   The supply constraint "recognizes the Kenyan economy's heavy
reliance on imports and ensures that the projected overall rate
of economic growth is consistent with what is believed to be the
most important constraint on Kenya's economic growth--the
availability of foreign exchange" (Anker and Knowles, 1983:293-
294). The supply constraint is the key feature of the model and
drives the simulation results discussed below. This specification does not impose equality on savings investment, and makes
the availability of foreign exchange the sole constraint on
capacity. Anker and Knowles (1983) judge this to be appropriate
for Kenya since it uses expatriots and foreign capital and has a
pool of unemployed educated labor; this approach may, however,
limit the model to countries that share these features with
Kenya.

Baseline Simulation. The baseline simulation is designed to indicate the most likely future for Kenya, "a future which is dependent on the assumptions built into Bachue-Kenya" (Anker and Knowles, 1983:567). Some of the results are shown in Table 3. Gross domestic product (GDP) grows at 5 percent per year and population at 3.6 percent, resulting in a rise in GDP per capita of 54 percent, or an average of about 1.5 percent per year. However, by the 30th year of the simulation, this rate has fallen to 0.2 percent. The total fertility rate (TFR) falls from 7.6 to 7.0, life expectancy rises from 47.8 years to 59.2 years, and percent urbanized rises from 9.9 to 19.4 percent; however, urban unemployment rises from 8.6 to 18.9 percent. The assumptions built into Bachue-Kenya and/or the unspecified values of the exogenous variables allow for high economic growth despite a demographic pattern associated with the initial stages of the demographic transition. However, it is likely that an extension of the simulation beyond 30 years would show a negative correlation between population growth and economic growth because the rate of the latter slows considerably over the last 15 years of the simulation.

This relatively strong economic performance is driven largely by a 4.3 percent annual change in agricultural output, which is, in turn, driven by strong growth in largely exogenously determined factor inputs. Agriculture accounts for 30 percent of GDP, and in addition, the agricultural surplus drives exports and the foreign trade balance. The trade balance is the supply constraint in the model; if nonbinding, it turns the model into one driven by demand. Also contributing to the economic performance is explosive growth in education.

Why does agricultural output affect growth so strongly? It is determined in a Cobb-Douglas production function as a function of land, labor, capital, intermediate inputs, and technological change. Over the simulation, rural labor force grows 2-3 percent per annum; investment, of which agriculture gets a constant share, grows at an annual rate of 5.8 percent; rural literacy and the previous inputs determine intermediate input growth, and rural literacy grows 214 percent over the simulation; large-farm technical change progresses exogenously at a rate of 0.014 (determined so as to keep its share of gross marketed output constant); and small-farm technical change is determined endogenously, largely as a function of rising literacy. Thus, agricultural output and the supply constraint on the entire model are determined largely by exogenously determined investment, technological change, and literacy (or school enrollment rates). Since sensitivity analyses are not reported, it is not clear how sensitive the baseline simulation is to the exogenous variables.

TABLE 3   Economic and Demographic Outcomes of Bachue-Kenya Simulations

| Variable | Baseline | | | Percent Change from Baseline After 30 Years | | | | | |
| --- | --- | --- | --- | --- | --- | --- | --- | --- | --- |
| | Year 0 | Year 30 | Annual Percent Change | Slow Decline TFR | Rapid Decline TFR | Slow Increase in Life Expectancy | Rapid Increase in Life Expectancy | Declining Migration | Increasing Education |
| Population | 10,943.0 | 31,182.0 | 3.6 | -12.4 | -32.2 | 3.1 | 11.5 | 0.3 | -3.0 |
| GDP | 476.0 | 2,095.0 | 5.1 | -0.1 | -0.3 | 0.3 | 1.8 | 2.1 | -4.9 |
| GDP per capita | 43.6 | 67.2 | 1.5 | 14.0 | 47.1 | -2.7 | -8.7 | 1.8 | -1.9 |
| TFR | 7.6 | 6.5 | | -28.5 | -45.2 | -0.2 | -0.6 | 0.6 | -8.5 |
| Life Expectancy | 54.3 | 63.9 | | 0.4 | 1.1 | 7.4 | 13.2 | 1.9 | 0.5 |
| Rural-Urban Migration | 0.45 | 0.43 | | 1.1 | 1.1 | -0.3 | 0.3 | -38.5 | -2.5 |
| GINI Coefficient | 0.64 | 0.62 | | -0.1 | -0.2 | 0.1 | 0.4 | 3.7 | -0.1 |
| Urban Unemployment Rate | 8.6 | 18.9 | | -9.6 | -37.2 | 4.2 | 11.4 | -29.3 | 17.8 |
| Rural Informal Wages | 39.3 | 48.1 | | 26.3 | 157.7 | -6.4 | -21.9 | -12.1 | 11.4 |

Notes:  Slow decline in fertility equals decrease in TFR of 2.0 over simulation; rapid decline in fertility equals decrease in TFR of 3.5 in 10 years; slow increase in life expectancy equals increase of 4.5 years over simulation; rapid increase in life expectancy equals increase of 4.5 years in urban and 9.0 years in rural in first 5 years of simulation; declining migration equals decline of 50 percent over simulation; and increasing education equals education compulsory through second year of secondary school.  The simulations are assumed to be costless.

Demographic Simulations.    everal demographic simulations
were run; a selection of the results is reported in Table 3.
None of the demographic policy interventions (fertility decline,
mortality decline, reduced migration, increased education) affect
aggregate GDP growth.   The largest impact is a 5 percent reduction over 30 years that results from introducing compulsory education through the second year of secondary school.   Fertility
reduction does, however, have a significant positive impact on
GDP per capita:   a reduction in the TFR of 2.0 increases GDP per
capita by 14 percent over the base run, while a very large decline in the TFR of 46 percent results in a similar increase in
GDP per capita.   Demographic policies have relatively little
effect on urban employment or the distribution of income, but
declining population growth does have a large negative effect on
urban unemployment and a large positive effect on rural informal-
sector wages.   The impact of declining fertility is much greater
than that of adverse changes in life expectancy.   Education,
which has a powerful impact in some other models, for example
Wheeler (1984), has relatively little economic or demographic
effect in Bachue-Kenya because of the absence in the latter of
direct linkages between education and other variables.   The TFR
decreases only 9 percent over the base-run simulation despite
the extension of education.   The major impact of education is to
worsen urban labor market conditions as female labor force participation rates rise.
    One important feature of Bachue-Kenya that may limit the
generality of the simulation results from the fact that most of
the demographic linkages are indirect.   Fertility and mortality
changes have their impact through changes in the size and age
distribution of the population.   There is no link from fertility
to labor force participation7 or mortality, nor is the dependency rate linked to savings.   (Family size does, however,
influence food consumption, which affects agricultural exports
and foreign exchange earnings, and may serve the same purpose as
in models where it automatically reduces savings.)   Mortality
rates do not affect human capital investments or the rate of
labor productivity as might be expected.   In addition, there is
no feedback from economic or demographic variables to educational
attainment.
    The most powerful development strategy revealed by the simu-
lations is increased agricultural growth; however, as noted
above, this result is largely driven by increases in exogenously
determined investment, technology, and education.   Exogenous
growth in agricultural investment or output in turn has weak
demographic effects.   In a set agricultural policy simulation,
population growth is only 1.5 percent above the baseline, and
migration and life expectancy are similar.
    The strength of Bachue-Kenya lies in the specification of
its demographic sector and its careful investigation of micro-
and macro-level economic and demographic behavior in Kenya.
However, this specificity may limit its general application to
countries that are driven by the agricultural sector.

## Wheeler

Wheeler (1984) has constructed a small, closely specified, long-run economic-demographic simulation model that focuses on the growth outcomes associated with investments in education and family planning. The model is descriptive rather than "vigorously analytical," which Wheeler feels is appropriate for the broad sample of 70 countries in his data set.[8] The process of development entails a tremendously complex set of structural changes, some of which can be "captured qualitatively by econometric equations of the type employed [in his model]. The results can only be suggestive from the theoretical standpoint, but they do serve as a systematic basis for simulation modeling" (Wheeler, 1984:12).

### The Model

The five core equations are those determining decade percentage changes in output, investment, fertility, family planning, and infant mortality. Output change and investment are determined simultaneously. The demographic equations allow for joint determination of fertility, infant mortality, government family planning effort, and income per capita. Change in output is specified as follows:

$$g_t = \alpha_0 + \alpha_1 k_t + \alpha_2 l_t + \alpha_3 lf_t/PCI_t + \beta_i D_{it} , \qquad (4)$$

where $g$ = growth rate of GDP; $k$ = investment rate weighted by the World Bank management performance index; $l$ = percentage change in the labor force weighted by the lagged school enrollment rate (primary and secondary); $lf$ = percent change in the labor force divided by per capita income; and $D_i$ = dummy variables for internal violence, oil exporter, and mining state.

The rate of growth of unweighted capital has no effect on the growth of GDP, whereas the rate of growth of efficiency-weighted capital is an important determinant of output growth.[9] The rate of change of the labor force is combined in an interaction with the inverse of the change in income per capita to allow for the declining marginal contribution of raw (uneducated) labor as development occurs and with lagged school enrollment rates to allow for improved labor (human capital). The treatment of labor and capital in the model approximates factor-augmenting technical change in some other models of development.

Savings were found to be a positive function of income per capita and growth in GDP and a negative function of capital inflow.[10] This latter result is evidence in favor of the "revisionist" foreign aid perspective (Kelley and Williamson, 1984a: 56), which argues that the domestic savings effort is relaxed with the exogenous infusion of foreign aid. The dependency ratio was found to have a marginal positive effect on savings, while average life expectancy (longer expected time horizons may increase savings) was not significantly related to savings be-

havior.  Investment was found to be a positive function of income
per capita, foreign capital inflow, and past investment.

In Wheeler's model, demographics are handled in a fashion
similar to that in Wharton's POPMOD (Greene, 1983) and Bachue-
Kenya.  That is, fertility and infant mortality are specified as
functions of economic and demographic variables and then linked
to age-specific schedules.  The dynamic fertility equation is

$$f_t = \beta_i X_t + \beta_2 \, DPS_t \; ,$$  (5)

where f is the decadal percentage change in the TFR, and X is the
decadal percentage change in a set of independent variables (per
capita income, infant mortality rate).  DPS = [(dP/dt) $S_t$ +
(dS/dt) Pt] , where S is a measure of female schooling, and P is
an index of family planning activity.  Female education and planning effort are explicitly interrelated since it is assumed that
(1) increased planning effort affects fertility in proportion to
the level of female education, and (2) enhanced female education
affects fertility in proportion to the cost and availability of
contraception.[11]

A 1 percent increase in income per capita is associated with
a 0.16 percent decline in the TFR, and a 1 percent increase in
the infant mortality rate with a 0.32 percent increase in the
TFR.  (The TFR was not found to influence the infant mortality
rate.)  Education and program effectiveness are found to have
"impressive" negative effects on fertility with relatively long
lags.[12]  Wheeler (1984:25-26) stresses the importance of this
interactive effect.  Its policy implication is clear:  the rapid
expansion of family planning programs in societies where females
are being educated at low rates will not be very effective, and
the rapid expansion of educational opportunities for women will
have proportionally larger impacts on fertility where strong
family planning programs are in place.

Changes in infant mortality are found to be a function of
lagged infant mortality and a lagged interaction between education and family planning effectiveness.  Changes in family
planning effectiveness are, in turn, found to be a positive
function of lagged income per capita (a measure of ability to
finance); change in female secondary schooling; population
density (pressure on land availability sends a signal to
planners of impending increases in rural poverty and urbanization, creating a perception of political threat sufficient to
stimulate interest in population control); and the trend in fertility; and a negative function of the deviation of fertility
from trend.  These trend variables capture the effect of governments trying harder to reduce fertility in societies whose rate
of fertility decrease diminished from the 1960s to the 1970s,
and conversely for those whose rate of fertility decline increased.

Mortality in the model is solved in three steps.  Once the
values of the predetermined variables have been set, the infant
mortality rate for the simulation period is predicted.  This
prediction is plugged into a bivariate regression; this re-

regresssion generates a prediction of life expectancy at birth, which is, in turn, used to generate the position parameter in Brass' (1971) two-parameter model of mortality. The slope parameter is set at unity, and the Brass standard life table produces age-specific mortality rates.

The fertility rate is determined by adding the predicted change in the TFR to the initial rate. The Coale and Trussell (1974) fertility schedule for Peru is then used to allocate this fertility rate to 10-year age cohorts to produce age-specific cohort rates.[13] With all of these functions in place and given initial conditions, the model can produce population estimates by 10-year age groups.


## Simulations

Wheeler illustrated the properties of the model by assuming the initial conditions and schooling and family planning program costs of Togo and Malawi, two African nations with similar economic growth records but different social investment strategies. Some of the simulation results are reported in Table 4, which covers only the first 30 years of the seventy-year simulation period to allow comparison with simulation results from some of the other models discussed in this chapter.

The baseline simulation for Togo assumes no increase in family planning score or the female education ratio, but does assume a rise in the management efficiency score from 4 to 7. The policy simulation assumes an increase in family planning score and female education of 10 per decade, that is, an initial trebling of the former and a 30 percent rise in the latter. This policy has a marked negative impact on population and a positive impact on income per capita. These effects are also very strong in the remainder of the simulation, indicating a powerful "self-reinforcing process" (Wheeler, 1984:42) and the presence of lags in the model. The Togolese case "seems particularly fortuitous" since Togo is able to maintain a high investment rate, ensuring continued growth in per capita income, which in turn prevents downward pressure on the savings rate (Wheeler, 1984:43). Another feature of the model is the strong and almost immediate productivity impact of enhanced female secondary education, which gives a strong boost to economic activity, as can be seen from the long-run elasticities reported in the second half of Table 4.

The results from the Malawian simulation would seem to imply that there is little benefit to a policy involving an initial 60 percent increase in schooling and a 500 percent increase in family planning score. That is true for this policy and this time horizon, but not for a longer time horizon and stronger policy intervention. In fact, in the case of Malawi, a "big push" strategy is called for more strongly than in the case of Togo. Under the maximum policy intervention studied by Wheeler (30-point increases per decade in education and family planning), Malawi has a chance to stabilize population growth by the late twenty-first century, and its average income is three times the

TABLE 4  Economic and Demographic Outcomes from Thirty-Year Simulations from Wheeler (1984)

A. Results for Togo and Malawi

| Variable | Togo | | | | Malawi | | | |
|---|---|---|---|---|---|---|---|---|
| | Base Year | Baseline | Policy | Percent Difference | Base Year | Baseline | Policy | Percent Difference |
| Population | 2.6 | 25.3 | 16.5 | -34.8 | 6.0 | 20.5 | 19.9 | -2.9 |
| Per Capita Income | 363.0 | 947.0 | 1024.0 | 8.1 | 213.0 | 337.0 | 338.0 | 0.0 |
| TFR | 6.5 | 5.0 | 4.3 | -14.0 | 7.8 | 6.7 | 6.2 | -7.5 |
| Infant Mortality Rate | 107.0 | 43.2 | 38.8 | -10.2 | 169.0 | 76.9 | 74.4 | -3.3 |
| Life Expectancy | 48.0 | 66.0 | 66.8 | 1.2 | 44.0 | 59.8 | 60.3 | 0.3 |

B. Long-Run Response

Elasticities

| Country | Income Per Capita | | | Population | | |
|---|---|---|---|---|---|---|
| | Female Education | Family Planning | Both | Female Education | Family Planning | Both |
| Togo | .705 | .067 | .776 | -.152 | -.098 | -.252 |
| Malawi | .249 | .109 | .270 | -.057 | -.027 | -.084 |
| Kenya | 1.045 | .288 | 1.367 | -.353 | -.324 | -.673 |
| India | .471 | .357 | .841 | -.287 | -.448 | -.730 |
| Indonesia | .577 | .345 | .914 | -.442 | -.580 | -1.006 |
| Mexico | .601 | .305 | .866 | -.449 | -.808 | -1.214 |

Notes: Baseline assumes no change in 1980 levels of family planning and female education. Policy assumes a ten-point increase per decade in family planning score and in the female primary and secondary schooling ratio. The base year planning score and education ratio for Togo and Malawi were 11 and 105, and 6 and 51, respectively.

499

baseline level. What the simulations reveal is the continuing
burden of past policy decisions--little investment in education
and none in family planning. Simulations on nine additional
countries yielded a similar conclusion: social investments in
education and family planning reduce population growth and
increase per capita income.

The long-run elasticities shown in Table 4 reveal that for
long-run gains in income per capita, investment in female education is most effective, despite being more costly, while family
planning is generally a more effective means of reducing population growth as societies move higher in education and planning
simultaneously. Also note that the impacts of female education
on income per capita and population in Kenya were among the
highest found, while Anker and Knowles (1983) found small effects
for education in the Bachue-Kenya simulations. In Bachue-Kenya,
the main economic impact of increased education is to reduce the
rural labor force, agricultural output, agricultural exports, and
foreign exchange earnings needed to fuel growth. Only in the
second half of the simulation are the beneficial effects of a
more highly trained labor force felt. In contrast, in Wheeler's
model, increased education adds quickly to output growth.
Further work is needed to clarify the timing of education's
labor-augmenting role.

Wheeler's model is quite useful and provocative in illustra-
ting the impact of management efficiency, education, and family
planning on the economy and demography of developing nations.
However, while the management efficiency index and family planning scores are very important in the model, it is not clear how
they can be affected by policy. Management efficiency, the World
Bank's management performance index, is produced from fitted
values in a first-stage regression on predetermined variables.
It should be fully endogenized as a function of educational
enrollments and expenditures and the domestic share in output.
The 1982 family planning effort is an index of 30 items related
to policy and stage-setting activities, service and service-
related activities, record keeping and evaluation, and availability and accessibility of fertility-control methods (15 items
in 1972). Mauldin and Lapham (1985) discuss in detail the construction of the index and its usefulness. Some of the items
depend on judgments rather than observable facts, and all receive
equal weight, even though analysis showed that only 5 items and
the aggregate score for the availability and accessibility of
supplies and services were good predictors of fertility decline.
Further analysis may reveal more clearly the policy links to the
index components. Family planning expenditures and schooling
expenditures are assumed to occur at the expense of physical
capital accumulation. While this conservative strategy is
understandable given the purpose of the model, a useful extension
would be to introduce a government sector explicitly and treat
expenditure on education and health, including family planning,
as a form of public saving, as suggested by Kelley and Williamson
(1984a).

It is also debatable whether school enrollment rates should be treated as an exogenous policy variable or endogenized. Technological change is also absent, although the weighing of capital and labor in equation (4) serves as factor-augmenting technical change. Since this is a one-sector model, migration is absent. The model could be extended to two sectors and include migration, which is considered by some researchers to be "an essential feature of any developing country [model] perhaps more important even than endogenous fertility" (Moreland, 1982: 183).

Another aspect of the model that merits further attention is the treatment of labor. Output is increased by educated labor, created by education, and by raw labor, whose marginal contribution declines as development occurs. This latter term is important and "stacks the deck" against a positive contribution from population growth. When the term is dropped from the model, fertility control is not quite as effective, and the difference between the policy simulations and the baseline is decreased.[14]

Simon

Simon's model of the effects of population growth on the economic development of developing countries has attracted considerable attention because of its basic conclusion that "positive population growth produces considerably better economic performance in the long run (120 to 180 years) than does a stationary population, though in the short run (60 years), the stationary population performs slightly better. A declining population does very badly in the long run" (Simon, 1977:305). Simon is not alone in this belief. In a study of population and economic growth in 46 countries from 1961-63 to 1971-73, Clark (1978:147) concluded "that rates of population growth up to 3 percent per year seem to be increasingly beneficial from a point of view of improving rates of growth of real product per head, less favorable above the 3 percent per year," although McNicoll (1984:211) found that "a positive net productivity impact of rapid population growth is unsubstantiated as a general proposition." However, the problem of omitted variable bias hinders such gross cross-country comparisons.

The Model

Simon's model is a relatively small (18-equation), eclectic two-sector model. Output in the agricultural sector (QF) and the industrial sector (QI) is the outcome of a Cobb-Douglas production process:

$$Q_t = A \ K_t^{\alpha} M_t^{1-\alpha} J_t , \tag{6}$$

where A is the technology, K is the capital stock, M is labor in man-hours, and J is the quantity of social overhead capital; $\alpha$ =

.4 in agriculture and .5 in industry. Social overhead capital, J, also includes economies of scale because of the difficulty of separating the two. This variable captures better roads that accompany higher population, efficiencies in production that accompany larger markets, improved government organization, and health services and malaria eradication that accompany higher population density in agricultural areas (Simon, 1977:281). Simon's treatment of health services is quite different from that of Barlow and Davies (1974). In Simon's model, an increase in health expenditures directly increases output, whereas in the Barlow-Davies model, this effect is indirect, operating through the quantity and quality of labor.

Social overhead capital, J, is specified as a function of the labor force, L:

$$\frac{J_{t+1} - J_t}{J_t} = .20 \frac{L_t - L_{t-1}}{L_{t-1}} . \tag{7}$$

Social overhead capital enters the production function with an exponent of unity. Output may be doubled with a doubling of social overhead and no increases in other inputs, although Sanderson (1980) questioned the potency of this effect. Social overhead grows with the labor force (equation [7]) with an exponent of 0.2; thus, a doubling of the population would increase output by 20 percent. No government sector is modeled, and the financing of social overhead does not entail reductions in expenditure elsewhere; that is, policy is essentially costless, as it is in Coale-Hoover and Bachue-Kenya. Simon (1985) claims that "much of the social overhead in a poor economy, and almost all of it in agriculture, is likely not to be a diversion of consumption but rather the expenditure of labor in the off-season, and hence no conservation equation is appropriate. Such an equation would take us further from reality than having the social overhead appear costlessly in the system."[15]

Agricultural investment is specified as a function of the gap between the desired amount of capital stock and the actual amount minus depreciation. Industrial investment is a function of the change in industrial output, Q; the youth dependency ratio, YOU; and depreciation. This specification integrates an accelerator and the assumption that an increase in the youth dependency ratio decreases private savings and thus investment. The industrial investment equation is

$$I_t = 0.027 \left[ \log_{10} \frac{(Q_t - Q_{t-1})}{Q_t} \right] (1-.5YOU_t) K_t , \tag{8}$$

where I = net investment, K = capital stock, Q = industrial output, and YOU is an index of the youth dependency burden.

Sanderson (1980:63) pointed out what appears to be a critical flaw in this specification. Since output is usually growing, net investment seems always to be negative except for extremely high values of YOU. In addition, it appears that the greater the dependency burden, ceteris paribus, the greater (less negative) is net investment--the reverse of the usual assumption.  However, the specification as reported in Simon (1977:284) is missing a constant that was later added by Simon to avoid the problems noted by Sanderson; consequently, Simon claims that the simulations do not suffer from the shortcomings Sanderson has observed.[16]

Technological change in agriculture is a time trend, while technological change in industry is a function of time and the (log of the) change in output.  Simon (1981:197) stated that "it seems reasonable to assume that the amount of improvement [invention and adoption] depends on the number of people available to use their minds."[17]  He would probably now add population size or growth, or both, to the specification of technology.  In the simulations, the time trend and output change capture some of these effects, but a specification including population would clearly favor higher-fertility relative to lower-fertility regimes.

Simon's model is solved for a level of total output and total labor input in man-hours at the point of tangency between the aggregate production function $[Q_f(t) + Q_a(t)]$ and the highest attainable social indifference curve (see Sanderson, 1980:61-62 for more details).  This approach is unique to Simon's model, and it is claimed by Sanderson (1980:62), "immediately rules out the Simon approach [for policy use] because of the impossibility of estimating the parameters of families of shifting social welfare functions."  Simon disputes this and claims that his social welfare function is not subjective, but objectively determined by average income level and average number of children.[18]  As an alternative, Sanderson (1980) suggests the more conventional approach of specifying labor supply equations, wage equations, a dependency ratio equation, and an equation for nonlabor income.

Simon's model is relatively weak on the demographic side; fertility and labor force participation are assumed exogenous, mortality is a function only of per capita income, and education and migration play no part.  A number of fertility regimes are investigated in the model, including one in which fertility initially rises with income, then falls with an elasticity of one.  However, exogenizing fertility prevents the investigation of the effects of economic development on fertility and population growth, and thus biases the effect of population change on economic development.


The Simulations

Both very high and very low birth rate structures result in lower long-run per-worker outputs than do more moderate rates of fertility increase.  This result is produced by the combination of factors unique to Simon's model:  (1) the capacity of workers to vary hours worked in response to varying income aspirations and family size; (2) economies of scale and social overhead capital; (3) the specification of the industrial investment function; and (4) agricultural savings responsive to the agricultural capital/

output ratio. Higher fertility results in more hours worked, and
this "goes a long way to [offsetting the capital-dilution effect]
in the higher fertility variants" (p. 298). When there is no
increase in social capital as a function of labor force size,
there is "almost a monotonic (inverse) relationship between birth
rate and economic performance." This variable, however, is not
the dominant explanation of the findings, as other simulations
show (Simon, 1977:298). The determinants of physical investment,
in particular the large effect on investment of a small difference in industrial output, and the dependency effect of children,
"are critical in this model" and have "considerable impact on
the results." Small differences in output have a cumulative
effect on industrial investment because investors "project a
present period of decline (or increase) in output into a future
trend." Without the dependency of children, fertility and income
exhibit a monotonically positive relationship; otherwise, the
relationship is curvilinear (Simon, 1977:298-299).

    Two conclusions of the Simon model warrant particular
attention. First, the "advantage of moderate birth rates over
low birth rates generally appear[s] only after . . . 75-100
years" (p. 300). That is, the beneficial effects of population
are felt only in the long run. Depending on the rate at which
the future is discounted, moderate rates may be better or worse
than lower rates. The only generalization Simon states is that
"some population growth is beneficial in the long-run in all the
circumstances examined" (Simon 1977:302). Second, there "are
some reasonable sets of conditions under which fairly high fertility shows better economic performance at some times than does
low fertility, while there are also other reasonable sets of
conditions under which the opposite is true. That is, the
results depend upon the choice of parameters within the range
that seem quite acceptable [with the exception that fertility
below replacement always results in poorer economic performance
than any other rate]" (Simon, 1977:302, emphasis added).

    The model is constructed using parameter values from studies
of China for the seven centuries prior to World War II, eighteenth-century England, contemporary India, and contemporary
countries growing faster than India, all taken to be representative of contemporary developing countries. Two different simulations were run, one using economic parameters from eighteenth-
century England and one using parameters from twentieth-century
India (and other contemporary developing countries). Both used
1950s Indian demographic parameters. The main differences occur
in those aspects of the model that are unique. The simulations
indicate that high population growth is associated with the best
economic performance using parameters from eighteenth-century
England; very slow population growth is slightly better than
moderate growth when Indian parameter values are used. From
these results, Simon (1977:302) concludes that "any analytic
model of population which concludes that any one fertility
structure is unconditionally better than another must be wrong"
(with the exception noted above).

One problem with using parameter values from eighteenth-century England is that population growth and, accepting Simon's argument, economic growth, were mortality- not fertility-driven. As Preston (1982:174-175) has observed, "the mortality effects find no ready parallel in fertility effects, which are the focus [of Simon's model]," and thus may be inappropriate as a base for his parameter values. Mohan (1984:127) also criticizes the use of past European experience to approximate that of today's developing nations. In particular, high population growth and technological change have given rise to huge cities at low levels of income; these developments have no parallel in European economic history.

McNicoll (1984:213) has argued that Simon's alternative fertility assumptions result in populations of such widely different sizes that each simulation "reflects quite different socio-economic institutions and hence calls for quite different modeling assumptions." Thus, one strength of the Simon model—its long-run outlook—may be a liability if endogenous institutional change exists and is not captured by the model. One possible solution is to build models such as that of Kelley and Williamson that incorporate more institutional detail.

If we accept the basic assumptions of Simon's model—growth in social overhead capital with growth in the labor force, the existence of economies of scale, an accelerator effect in investment, technical change that is an increasing function of population, and a positive impact of children on labor supply—then the short-run dampening effects of population growth on economic growth have been overstated, and the long-run effect may be positive. Since the empirical support for many of these effects is at best inconclusive (McNicoll, 1984), the best strategy to take at present is one of agnosticism until Simon's model and its key assumptions have been more fully tested.

MODELS THAT INCLUDE MIGRATION/URBANIZATION

Up to this point, we have been reviewing models that investigate the impact of aggregate population growth on economic growth. Some, such as Bachue-Kenya, include the urban-rural distribution of population growth, while others, such as Simon and Wheeler, do not model migration. However, a fully developed economic/demographic model should include migration and its attendant degree of urbanization. Within a single country, a population growth rate of 2 to 3 percent per year typically coincides with growth rates for major cities of 4 to 5 percent per year (McNicoll, 1984). Such growth, it is feared, will cause Third World cities to "become unmanageable, environmental disasters, and centers of social revolution" (Williamson, 1985). Despite judgments on the potential magnitude of the urbanization problem, we do not clearly understand the demographic and economic "push" and "pull" factors that drive Third World city growth. What role does population growth play? Relative prices? Exogenous shocks?

## Kelley and Williamson

Kelley and Williamson (1980, 1982, 1984a, 1984b) have constructed
a computable general equilibrium model of urbanization designed
to answer the questions raised above.19

### The Model

The parameters of the model were derived from estimation performed on data from the 1960s and 1970s for a group of 40
developing nations and from the work of other researchers (for
instance, the production parameters). The model is able to
reproduce the qualitative dimension of Third World urbanization,
city growth, rural-to-urban migration, and unbalanced output
growth and industrialization for the period 1960-73, giving the
authors some faith in its parameter values. The model's key
features are first, that rural-urban migration is endogenously
determined by economic and demographic variables, and second,
that the model possesses "closure," that is, feedback and
interaction between sectors (notably price endogeneity), as well
as flexibility in production and consumption.

The model has eight sectors (five urban, three rural) and is
in the neoclassical, general equilibrium tradition. Firms are
driven by profit maximization and individuals by utility maximization. Each sector exhibits a different rate of technical
progress, factor intensity, and substitution elasticities.
Institutional and technological barriers are acknowledged and
lead to unequal sectoral rates of return to capital that may
persist. Prices of outputs and inputs are completely flexible,
and most are endogenous. Labor is heterogeneous (skilled and
unskilled), and skill bottlenecks may accompany rapid modern-
sector accumulation. The government sector is endogenous and is
assumed to allocate its budget to savings in response to increments in the resources available to it from taxes and foreign
services, and in response to demographic and urban pressures, by
assumption the main source of public investment demands.

The model is "savings-driven," with the aggregate pool of
savings being endogenously determined by retained corporate and
enterprise profits, government savings, and household savings.
The savings pool is allocated among investment in physical
(productive) capital, in human capital (training), and in ("unproductive") housing. The key exogenous variables in the model
are foreign capital inflow and aid; the total unskilled labor
force; total factor productivity advance, which favors the
modern sector and is labor-saving; prices of imported raw
materials and fuels; and the terms of trade.

A key element in the model is the distinction made between
tradable and nontradable sectoral outputs, which allows urban-
rural cost-of-living differences to arise. The inelastic supply
of urban land creates disamenities, raises rents and relative
urban-rural living costs, and inhibits in-migration to the city.
Thus, the model incorporates a "natural limit" to urban growth

that is missing from other models. This differentiates the Kelley-Williamson model from others that model migration, such as Bachue-Kenya.

Investment in housing and social overhead may lead to in-migration in the short run by decreasing disamenities. However, the implied decline in other forms of investment may limit the creation of future jobs and thus dampen migration. Therefore, in comparison to what one may expect from models that are con-fined to a strict trade-off between "productive" and "nonproduc-tive" investment, an increase in urban housing may well increase the long-run rate of city growth rather than retard it (Kelley and Williamson, 1984a:184).

Unlike some models in the Coale and Hoover tradition, the Kelley and Williamson approach does not treat demographically induced expenditures on education as unproductive consumption financed at the expense of productive investment. Education enters the model in a complex manner and is determined by the interplay of production possibilities, demographic forces, and government education policies. Educational expenditure is included in government savings since it yields consumption utility to its recipients and has an impact on future income as well. This approach is a "partial rectification of an antigrowth bias attributed to government in most development models" (Kelley and Williamson, 1984a:53).

Human capital accumulation in the form of skill formation plays a significant role in the model. Firms invest in skill accumulation through training programs, which compete with other forms of investment for funds. This accumulation is determined by its return to the using firms, as well as by demographic trends influencing the "stock of potential trainables." This stock is also influenced by government expenditures on education, which is a policy variable. Skilled labor is used in the manu-facturing sector and the modern service sector (electricity, gas, water, transport, communications, defense, education, urban housing, other government services), which is a leading growth sector in the model. Skilled labor is complementary to capital, and rapid capital accumulation raises the demand for skilled labor relative to that for unskilled labor and tends to generate earnings inequality.


Simulations

A baseline simulation was run incorporating expert assumptions about the most likely path for the key exogenous variables between 1980 and 2000. These assumptions are as follows: a 1.5 percent annual increase in fuel and raw material prices relative to those of primary product exports, a 0.6 percent annual decline in the relative price of manufactures, a steady decline in the foreign capital-to-GDP ratio from 3 percent in the 1970s to 2.4 percent by 2000, zero growth in arable land and 1 percent per annum growth in urban land, total factor productivity growing at 1.8 percent per annum, and labor force growth of 2.79 percent

per annum over 1981-90 and 2.84 percent over 1991-2000. This
simulation is contrasted with one in which pre-1973 conditions
prevail until 2000. Both simulations predict initially rising,
then falling urban population growth and immigration rates.
Urban growth rates of 5.15 percent per annum in 1970 are predicted to decline to less than 4 percent per annum in 2000,
"making it easier to cope with the accumulated problems associated with decades of rapid urban expansion" (Kelley and
Williamson, 1984b:429). The importance of immigration also
declines from 45.1 percent of urban population increase in the
1960s to 35 percent in the 1990s and zero in 2020.

Compared to projections based purely on demographics, the
baseline projection implies a higher degree of urbanization (4.7
percent per annum versus 4-4.5 percent per annum) and a later and
less pronounced slowdown in urban growth. These differences
arise from the positive impact on rural-urban migration, and thus
city growth, of the economic forces of development. Of particular importance are the terms of trade between primary products
and manufactures, as well as the relative price of imported raw
materials and fuels, and more rapid technological change in the
modern, urban-based manufacturing sector than in the traditional,
rural-based primary product sector.

One other finding of note is that while rapid population
growth does foster rural-to-urban migration and urban growth,
"it does not offer an explanation for Third World urbanization
experience since it has precisely the opposite effect" (Kelley
and Williamson, 1984:436, emphasis added). Higher population
growth increases the supply of labor, decreases its price, and
increases its relative use in the sector in which it is used
most intensively--agriculture. Accordingly, more rapid population growth leads to slower urbanization rates. A series of
four simulations, assuming different rates of population (labor
force) growth, show that future "Third World urban performance
is unlikely to be very sensitive to any relevant range of alternative demographic and labor force growth scenarios, at least
over the next two decades" (Kelley and Williamson, 1984a:169).
This finding is in direct contrast to that of a World Bank study
(Beier et al., 1976). It is important to recall that urbanization is defined as the percentage of the population classified
as urban; thus population growth does foster immigration and the
absolute size of cities, although not their relative size.

The Kelley-Williamson model has clearly made major contributions to the economic-demographic modeling of developing countries in its production functions, its treatment of savings and
consumption in the extended linear expenditure system, its endogenous allocation of investment funds, its treatment of migration
to include cost-of-living effects, and, finally, its introduction
of training to produce skilled workers. The model is, however,
not complete. It is demographically underdeveloped (Sanderson,
1980:18): fertility, mortality, family planning, and income
distribution are missing. Some of these deficiencies have been
remedied by Schmidt (1981, 1983), who has developed a demographic
framework for use with computable general equilibrium models,

such as that of Kelley and Williamson. Before discussing
Schmidt's demographic model, however, we will consider a recent
contribution by Mohan (1984) to the modeling of urbanization.


Mohan

Mohan (1984) has constructed a nonlinear, three-sector (agriculture, services, and manufacturing), two-region (urban, rural),
endogenous wage and price dynamic general equilibrium model,
which he uses to study the effects of population growth, pattern
of demand, and technological change on urbanization.[20] This
model has many features in common with that of Kelley and
Williamson (1984a), but is distinguished from it in approximating
a specific economy, that of postindependence India, and in being
a closed model, whereas Kelley and Williamson (1984a) explicitly
incorporate a foreign sector.[21] As in the Kelley-Williamson
model, the rate of population growth is exogenous.

In comparing a simulation of zero population growth with
simulations based on a higher rate of population growth, Mohan
(1984:138) concluded that with zero population growth, urbanization proceeds at a more rapid rate than with higher rates of
population growth. This occurs because lower population growth
means lower demand for food (lower demand for additional investment in agriculture); a faster shift to urban goods (real income
rises in the zero population growth simulation, and the income
elasticity of demand for food is less than unity); an increased
demand for urban labor; and, consequently, higher levels of
urbanization. This result depends on the assumed rates of technical change that release labor from agriculture (Mohan, 1984:
139). Both this model and that of Kelley and Williamson (1984a)
reject the notion of urbanization fostered primarily by population growth. They both also demonstrate that declining birth
rates (or population growth) will not "solve the urbanization
problem and that we can expect cities to grow along with the
development process" (Mohan, 1984:140).

Another simulation result of importance is that "over a long
enough period, a high population growth rate does not necessarily
mean a smaller growth in per capita income" (Mohan, 1984:142).
With zero population growth, there is a reversal in the terms of
trade, making urban goods more expensive. This dampens demand
for urban goods, including capital goods. The proportion of net
investment to gross national product (GNP) declines: the economy
endogenously adjusts for a slower growth in population. The converse occurs in the case of more rapid population growth. In
the short run, however, per capita income is increased by slower
population growth. In addition, the large short-run increase in
per capita income in the zero population growth simulation may
snowball and make further growth self-sustaining; such an effect
is likely if growth results in a large inflow of foreign investment and credit. If this is the case, the benefit of zero population growth relative to positive population growth is under-
stated.

If preferences change in favor of food, for example by a country-wide nutrition program that increases subsistence requirements for food, the demand for agricultural goods will also increase. Resources will move into that sector, and, with agriculture being the slowest-growing sector, per capita income growth will decline and urbanization slow. The reverse will occur when demand shifts or is shifted in favor of industrial goods or services. It should be pointed out that in this model, and in Kelley and Williamson (1984a), the service sector plays a prominent role. Models that omit this sector can lead to a conclusion that developing countries are currently "overurbanized" (Hozelitz, 1957). Mohan (1984:137) concludes that it is therefore essential to study structural change in at least a three-sector context.

In a simulation assuming a decline in neutral exogenous technical change in agriculture, Mohan (1984:148) found a very large decrease in the rate of urbanization. (A smaller rate of increase in income mitigates the Engel-type demand effects, and there is a smaller resultant demand for urban goods and urban labor.) In direct contrast, in the Kelley-Williamson (1984a) model, "rapid productivity advance in agriculture tends to forestall out-migration to the city." Immiserizing agricultural growth that "meets demand absorption problems, a declining farm terms of trade, and thus a 'labor surplus' which out-migrates to glut urban labor markets . . . is not an attribute of [their] open-economy model" (Kelley and Williamson, 1984a:102).22 Where technological progress is capital-augmenting, Mohan (1984: 148-149) finds that the urban demand for labor rises, and the level and rate of urbanization increase. However, "the effect is small in magnitude relative to the significant change in the nature of the technology that uses it."


Schmidt

The demographic framework uses model schedules to represent age patterns by sex and region for nuptiality, marital fertility, mortality, and rural-urban net migration; a constant age-sex-regional labor force participation rate schedule is also used. The individual model schedules are then integrated through standard demographic accounting into a complete demographic framework. The fertility model is that of Coale; it requires two model schedules (nuptiality and marital fertility) and four parameters, which are estimates from country cross-sectional data. The mortality model is that of Brass (1971), with the two parameters required also estimated from cross-sectional data. Schmidt (1983:324-325) derives a three-parameter (crude migration rate and two sex-specific shift parameters) net migration schedule. The Kelley-Williamson model determines the net number of individuals who migrate, and the schedule represents the age and sex patterns of these migrants. Schedules are useful where data are scarce and/or unreliable or where the level of the demographic event is determined in the economic rather than the demographic module.

Schmidt (1983) asks the following question:   Is the economic
effect of demographic change large enough to warrant a complex
demographic module?  He addresses this question by running three
simulations that assume a different level of population growth:
high (3.2 percent per annum); intermediate (2.7 percent per
annum); and low (declining from 2.7 percent in 1970 to 2.36
percent in 1990).  The overall regional distribution of population is relatively insensitive to different population growth
rates, but the age structure is not.  With declining fertility,
the youth dependency ratio falls, and its importance depends on
the way in which the economic model is specified.  If household
size and age structure influence demand, savings, and income,
then the demographic module is important; otherwise, it can be
assumed to be exogenous.  However, the different population
growth rates do affect labor force participation rates:  after
20 years, aggregate labor force participation is 7.3 percent
higher in the low-growth case.  Again, depending on the structure
of the economic model, these changes may affect income, saving,
investment, and average labor productivity.  What we learn from
this exercise is that it is worth constructing a demographic
module if the economic model contains demographic detail.

It should be noted that the parameters of Schmidt's demographic model are specified exogenously.  When linked to the
Kelley-Williamson model, the level of net urban-rural migration
will be endogenous, but the other demographic components (nuptiality, marital fertility, mortality, and labor force participation) will continue to be exogenous.  This is unfortunate
since these demographic components are important economic-
demographic linkages.  Two approaches could be pursued to endogenize these demographic components.  First, the parameters of
Schmidt's fertility and mortality schedules could be modeled as
functions of economic and demographic variables.  This approach
is used by Data Resources, Inc. (1981) to model income distributions.  A second approach, which could be used to model migration
in the Schmidt model, has been used to model fertility, mortality, and migration for Kenya by Anker and Knowles (1983), for the
United States by Greene (1983), and for Australia by the impact
group (Powell, 1983).  The aggregate rates are specified as
functions of economic and demographic variables, and age/sex
specific rates are then constructed from rate schedules that
reproduce the endogenous aggregate rates.  Both of these
approaches produce fully linked economic-demographic models and
are to be encouraged.[23]


FURTHER RESEARCH

From the review presented above, five main areas of difference
among the models emerge that require further research.

(1) Technological Change.  Most models assume that technical
change is exogenous, but is it?  Simon claims that technology is
endogenously determined as a function of population and growth;

Barlow and Davies assume it is embodied in imported capital;
Anker and Knowles assume it is exogenous in large-farm agriculture and industry, but endogenously determined by education in
small-farm agriculture. Mohan assumes that technical change in
agriculture is greater than that in industry, while Kelley and
Williamson assume the opposite. All models find that technical
change is a potent force in economic development, but its sources
are not well understood. More work needs to be done on the
sources of technical change, including induced innovation, and
on the effects of population on technological change.

(2) Fertility Control. In all the models, it is assumed
that population growth may be decreased through fertility
reduction. Very few of the models give us a hint as to how this
reduction can be attained and at what cost. Wheeler (1984)
endogenously determines family planning efficiency, which,
although something of a "black box," shows the path and cost (in
terms of reduced expenditure elsewhere) of the policy. Models
need to introduce a family planning variable in the fertility
equation, such as is done by Easterlin and Crimmins (1985), and
endogenize family planning expenditure, probably determined
simultaneously with fertility.

(3) The Government Sector. The government sector is often
ignored or enters exogenously, yet is a central actor in economic
and demographic policy. Simon's model attributes a significant
role to social overhead capital, yet ignores its financing; Coale
and Hoover assume it is less productive than other forms of expenditure; and some models assume no productive impact from
social overhead spending (Cassen, 1976). What impact does government expenditure on housing, health, education, and family
planning have? How is it financed? We need to know much more
about the role of the government in economic and demographic
development.

(4) Education. In some models, education is ignored, while
in others it plays an important role in improving labor quality
(Kelley and Williamson; Wheeler) and influencing fertility (Anker
and Knowles; Wheeler). Wheeler's simulation results are sensitive to variations in education, while those of Anker and Knowles
are not. Behrman and Wolfe (1984) have recently questioned traditional interpretations of the impact of education on fertility;
their argument has policy implications. Further analysis is
needed to establish the role of education and its financing in
economic and demographic change and to determine whether enrollment rates are exogenous or endogenous. The powerful interaction
between education and family planning modeled by Wheeler also
needs further investigation.

(5) Family Size. Several models assume that savings are
inversely related to family size (Coale and Hoover; Barlow and
Davies), while others explicitly reject this assumption (Wheeler;
Bachue-Kenya). The weight of recent evidence (Ram, 1982; Kelley,

1980) would lead us to be skeptical of such an effect in economic-demographic models. Two additional areas for further research on savings are the impact of foreign aid on savings
(Kelley and Williamson; Wheeler), and the treatment of education
(and health expenditures) as savings (Kelley and Williamson).

While Anker and Knowles do not include family size in the
savings function, they do include it in the consumption function
for food (which is an important equation in this model). Pollak
and Wales (1980) find that the number and age of children in a
family have a significant effect on consumption patterns, while
Denton and Spencer (1976) find no demographic effect on aggregate
consumption. Recent work by Rosenzweig and Pitt (1985) has
criticized and extended this work in a study of Indonesian farm
households. Work on consumption and saving should be carried
out within a consistent demand framework, such as that used by
Kelley and Williamson and Mohan.

One of the major strengths of formal economic-demographic
models--their ability to encompass direct and indirect effects
of population and economic policies--is also one of their major
weaknesses. Their attendant complexity often leads to a loss of
insight that limits their adoption and use in planning. A solution to this problem is discussed by James (1984). Sensitivity
analysis can be used to identify critical assumptions or parameters and give us a clear picture of the robustness of the
results to the specification of the model. Once the critical
equations of the model have been identified, "the essential
aspects of the general model can be pared away [yielding] a
submodel which should be much easier to understand" (James,
1984:235). Some of the model builders reviewed carry out sensitivity analysis; most do not. They do not identify either their
critical assumptions or their critical equations; this often
difficult task is left to the reader. Until James' suggestion
is adopted, the practical application of these models will be
impeded.[24]


SUMMARY AND CONCLUSIONS

The models discussed in this chapter exhibit the strengths and
weaknesses inherent in economic-demographic modeling. They
evaluate the consequences of alternative demographic and non-
demographic policies and illuminate the economic-demographic and
demographic-economic linkages in the development process. They
thus aid the achievement of consistency in policy formation,
planning, and implementation. As Sanderson (1980) has pointed
out, the Kelley-Williamson model is a "consistent and realistic
foundation" on which to build a complete economic-demographic
model. Fertility, nuptiality, and mortality could be added in
the ways suggested above. Material on income distribution could
be added from Adelman and Robinson (1978), material on family
planning and education from Tempo II or Wheeler (1984), and some
material on marriage rates from the Bachue models (Sanderson,
1980:18).

The models vary considerably in their complexity. Some, like
the Coale-Hoover and Wheeler models, have a relatively simple
structure and lay bare their key assumptions. Others have a
complex structure: the Barlow-Davies model is very detailed on
the demographic side, while relatively simple on the economic
side; the Kelley-Williamson and Mohan models are very detailed
on the economic side, while relatively underdeveloped on the
demographic side; the Bachue models are fairly detailed on both
the economic and demographic sides. The cost of the models'
increased complexity is that it is often very difficult to un-
cover the underlying assumptions and, particularly, since few
carry out sensitivity analysis, the key assumptions. Several of
the models are designed to focus on a particular problem, for
example urbanization, and thus may give an incomplete picture of
the development process.

As regards findings, the early models found a very large
negative impact of population growth on economic development.
Subsequent models have found that, while the short-run impact is
negative, it may not be as large as previously thought (Barlow
and Davies; Bachue-Kenya; Simon; and Kelley and Williamson) and
may even be positive in the very long run (Simon; Mohan). Other
models have shown that demographic effects can vary widely across
countries (Wheeler), and that population change has had little
impact on the degree of urbanization in developing countries
(Kelley and Williamson; Mohan).

On the basis of this review of economic-demographic models,
we concur with Preston (1982:175) that "population growth is not
so overwhelmingly negative a factor for economic advance as to
swamp the impact of all other influences. That is a worthwhile
lesson that bears repeating, but it is no argument for faster
demographic growth."


NOTES

1  In general, this chapter does not discuss models that have
   previously been discussed in the reviews of McNicoll (1976),
   Sanderson (1980), and Horlacher (1981). The one exception is
   Julian Simon's model. For a further discussion of the
   strengths and weaknesses of the formal modeling approach, see
   Arthur and McNicoll (1975), Rodgers et al. (1976), and
   Horlacher (1981).

2  Lee (1980:1151) deals with age structure and intergenerational transfers. He finds that "pending more careful empirical work, it appears likely that within the relevant range of
   population growth rates, the intergenerational transfer effect
   will never be large enough, even if positive, to offset the
   negative capital dilution effect [of population growth] and
   therefore if we (improperly) ignore utility from children, the
   'optimal' feasible growth rate would indeed be negative." For
   a discussion of growth models, see Pitchford (1974), McNicoll
   (1976), and Deardorff (1976).

3  Coale and Hoover (1958) concentrate on the effects of population growth rather than size because the size of the labor
   force is little affected by different fertility assumptions
   over a thirty-year simulation.
4  Barlow and Davies (1974) assume a constant elasticity of substitution (CES) production function with a single elasticity
   of substitution for the four factors of production. They
   view this as an acceptable oversimplification, but Kelley and
   Williamson (1984a) argue that the usual CES is inappropriate
   and a nested CES production function is needed. Given the
   nature of Barlow and Davies' model, it would seem important
   that they use a production function giving flexibility in
   substitution among labor of different types.
5  Ram (1982) explains the difference between his results and
   Leff's (1969) as being due to differences in the period
   studied, the sample covered, and the specification of the
   savings function. Kelley (1974) reports on an experiment
   replacing the standard "adult equivalency" consumption
   specification by one in which increased consumption from
   additional children is in part financed by the reduced consumption of other household members and the altered labor
   force behavior of parents. Simulations with the Tempo model
   show that this modification reduces the higher income per
   capita from lower population growth by 30 percent. Ram also
   cites work in which the impact of increased family size on
   saving is negative, positive, or zero depending on the source
   of the change in family size.
       McNicoll (1984) notes a further complication. It is
   highly plausible that high fertility is a consequence of low
   savings. In the absence of other forms of risk management,
   individuals may rely on children to provide future consumption. Moreland (1982) estimates separate savings functions
   for the agricultural and nonagricultural population, and finds
   that children compete with savings in rural areas, whereas in
   the nonagricultural urban areas, their impact is to increase
   savings. He explains this difference by the fact that rural
   children are seen as an income-generating asset.
6  Further experimentation could establish the unit cost per
   birth averted at which the policy's contribution to future
   income per equivalent consumer would be zero. Barlow and
   Davies have estimated this to be as high as $500.
7  The evidence on a link between fertility and labor force par-
   participation in developing countries is inconclusive. A
   positive relationship has been found in studies of India,
   Thailand, Egypt, and Sierra Leone; a negative relationship in
   Chile, Puerto Rico, Thailand, and Mexico; and no relationship
   in Taiwan and Peru. Smith (1981) suggested that the conflicting findings could reflect a failure to control for relevant variables, including whether work and childcare represent
   competing or noncompeting uses of maternal time. Using data
   for Mexico City, he found a negative relationship between work
   and fertility where work and childcare compete for maternal
   time and no relationship where they are noncompeting. Work
   is not a homogeneous activity in developing countries.

8    Wheeler's model assumes a much more stylized process of de-
     velopment than that assumed by more complex models, such as
     that of Kelley and Williamson. As a consequence, the assump-
     tions and linkages of the model are much clearer, but the
     risk of its being an incomplete picture of the development
     process is greater.

9    In a recent study of the United States, Bemmels (1984) intro-
     duced managerial efficiency into a translog production func-
     tion. Of the three types of managerial efficiency studied
     (participative management and goal setting, performance ap-
     praisal and feedback, and pay for performance), only pay for
     performance had a significant (and positive) effect on pro-
     ductivity.

10   Note that domestic savings decrease, not total savings. In
     the Kelley-Williamson model, the reduction of domestic
     savings occurs in the government sector, and domestic invest-
     ment increases by only one-third of the additional foreign
     aid (Kelley and Williamson 1984a:56). Wheeler's figure cor-
     responds roughly to this.

11   See Behrman and Wolfe (1984) for evidence of a positive asso-
     ciation between education and knowledge and use of modern
     contraceptives and a discussion of the policy implications of
     this association.

12   The effect of plan effectiveness is a drop of .4 percent per
     one-point increase in the index of program effectiveness (the
     data are from the Work Bank). For example, for a schooling
     index of 100 (out of a possible maximum of 200), and an in-
     crease in the plan effectiveness index from zero to 80
     (achieved by China in a decade), the associated decline in
     the TFR is 32 percent. The effect of a one-point increase
     in schooling is a decrease in the TFR of .2 percent; a 100-
     point increase in schooling would decrease fertility by about
     20 percent in the long run (Wheeler, 1984:25).

13   These proportions are assumed fixed over time even though it
     is recognized that they change with female education and life
     expectancy. Perhaps the Data Resources, Inc. (1981) method
     of forecasting parameters of the income distribution could
     be used to forecast these proportions.

14   Private communication with David Wheeler.

15   Private communication with Julian Simon.

16   Private communication with Julian Simon.

17   In a recent cross-sectional study using data from 1950-70,
     Simon and Gobin (1980) found that better economic performance
     comes from greater population density, with little indepen-
     dent effect from population size and growth. Density is
     associated with economies of scale in social overhead capital
     and communications.

18   Private communication with Julian Simon.

19   For a review of the model, see Sanderson (1980). The evalu-
     ation of general equilibrium models and their application to
     development planning is covered comprehensively by Dervis et
     al. (1982). Other useful discussions of general equilibrium
     models are found in Dixon et al. (1982) and Powell (1981).

20  The model, DYNURB, is relatively small (62 equations), is
    quite complex, and has a high degree of closure. Its para-
    meters are not systematically estimated, but are based on
    various empirical studies of the Indian economy. DYNURB
    tracks the Indian development record over 25 years and the
    trend of urbanization quite well.

21  Both models use consumer demand systems that are particularly
    useful in studying developing nations. Kelley and Williamson
    use the Extended Linear Expenditure System (LES), while Mohan
    uses the LES. Both capture Engel effects, incorporate dual-
    istic elements in demand behavior, provide an important role
    for demographic influences, and add explicit empirical con-
    tent to the concept of subsistence. The LES determines
    savings first, then committed expenditures for subsistence,
    and then discretionary expenditures. The Extended LES does
    not make this strong separability assumption between savings
    and expenditure, but determines expenditure allocation simul-
    taneously with total consumption (Kelley and Williamson,
    1984a:59; Mohan 1984:132).

22  Kelley and Williamson (1984a:102, 228-239) assume that the
    rate of productivity advance is higher in manufacturing than
    in agriculture, whereas Mohan (1984:137) makes the opposite
    assumption. Mohan also assumes a lower elasticity of factor
    substitution in manufacturing, a higher elasticity in agri-
    culture, and a similar elasticity in services. In simulation
    experiments, he found that, although the choice of technique
    or elasticity of substitution affects the results of the
    model, "the effects of changes within a reasonable range do
    not appear to be significant enough to warrant the large
    amount of literature devoted to the labor absorption issue"
    (Mohan, 1984:148).

23  See Ahlburg (forthcoming) for further discussion.

24  Forecasting models may have applications far beyond those
    usually recognized. For example, Ayres (1983:68-70) reports
    that the World Bank uses economic management and equity per-
    formance in the determination of country allocations of
    funds. Since there are few longitudinal data on income dis-
    tributions (although this is available from the Bachue family
    of models and Adelman and Robinson, 1978), "the Bank referred
    to such social indicators as life expectancy literacy, and
    infant mortality. Primary school enrollment ratios [also]
    received attention. By assigning scores to a number of per-
    formance indicators, and by combining such scores in an un-
    weighted manner with other factors such as a country's popu-
    lation size or absorptive capacity, a unit within the Bank's
    central economic staff attempted to arrive at very rough
    approximations of projected country allocations for the next
    five year lending period" (p. 69-70).

518                                                                                    Ahlburg

REFERENCES

Adelman, I., and S. Robinson (1978)  Income Distribution Policy
    in Developing Countries:  A Case Study of Korea.  Stanford,
    Calif.:  Stanford University Press.
Ahlburg, D.A. (forthcoming)  Modeling macroeconomic–demographic
    linkages:  a study of models of national and regional
    economies.  In K. Land and S. Schneider, eds., Forecasting
    in the Natural and Social Sciences.
Anker, R., and J.C. Knowles (1983)  Population Growth, Employment
    and Economic-Demographic Interactions in Kenya.  New York:
    St. Martin's Press.
Arthur, W.B., and G. McNicoll (1975)  Large scale simulation
    models in population and development:  what use to planners?
    Population and Development Review 4:251-265.
Ayres, R.L. (1983)  Banking on the Poor.  Cambridge, Mass.:  MIT
    Press.
Barlow, R., and G.W. Davies (1974)  Policy analysis with a
    disaggregated economic-demographic model.  Journal of Public
    Economics 3:43-70.
Behrman, J.R., and B.L. Wolfe (1984)  Knowledge and Use of Modern
    Contraceptives in a Developing Country:  Are the Effects of
    Women's Schooling Often Misunderstood?  Unpublished manu-
    script, University of Pennsylvania.
Beier, G.J., A. Churchill, M. Cohen, and B. Renaud (1976)  The
    task ahead for the cities of the developing countries.
    World Development 4:363-409.
Bemmels, B.G. (1984)  Managerial Efficiency, Unions, and Produc-
    tivity:  An Intergrative Analysis of Productivity at Manu-
    facturing Plants.  Unpublished Ph.D. dissertation, University
    of Minnesota.
Brass, W. (1971)  On the scale of mortality.  In W. Brass, ed.,
    Biological Aspects of Demography.  London:  Taylor and
    Francis.
Cassen, R.H. (1976)  Population and development:  a review.
    World Development 4:785-830.
Coale, A.J., and E.M. Hoover (1958)  Population Growth and
    Economic Development in Low Income Countries.  Princeton,
    N.J.:  Princeton University Press.
Coale, A.J., and T.J. Trussell (1974)  Model fertility schedules:
    variations in the age structure of child bearing in human
    populations.  Population Index 40:185-258.
Clark, C. (1978)  Population growth and productivity.  Pp. 143-
    154 in J. Simon, Research in Population Economics, Vol. 1.
    Greenwich, Conn.:  JAI Press.
Data Resources, Inc. (1981)  Demographic--Economic Models:  An
    Introduction.  Lexington, Mass.:  Consumer Research Division,
    Data Resources, Inc.
Deardorff, A.V. (1976)  The optimum rate for population:
    comment.  International Economic Review 17:510-515.
Denton, F.T., and B.G. Spencer (1976)  Household and population
    effects on aggregate consumption.  Review of Economics and
    Statistics 58:86-95.

Dervis, K., J. DeMelo, and S. Robinson (1982)  General Equilibrium Models for Development Policy.  Cambridge, England: Cambridge University Press.

Dixon, P.B., B.R. Parmenter, J. Sutton, and D.P. Vincent (1982) ORANI:  A Multisectional Model of the Australian Economy. New York:  North Holland.

Easterlin, R.A., and E. Crimmins (1985)  The Fertility Revolution:  A New Approach.  Chicago:  University of Chicago Press.

Greene, G. (1983)  Forecasting County and State Demographic Change:  A New Cohort-Component Algorithm for Estimating and Forecasting Population Using Econometric Models.  Paper presented at the Third International Symposium on Forecasting, Philadelphia, Pennsylvania.

Horlacher, D.E., ed. (1981)  Population and Development Modeling. New York:  United Nations.

Hozelitz, B.F. (1957)  Urbanization and economic growth in Asia. Economic Development and Cultural Change 5:42-54.

James, J.A. (1984)  The use of general equilibrium analysis in economic history.  Explorations in Economic History 21:231-253.

Kelley, A.C. (1974)  The role of population in models of economic growth.  American Economic Review 64:39-44.

Kelley, A.C. (1980)  Interactions of economic and demographic household behavior.  Pp. 403-448 in R.A. Easterlin, ed., Population and Economic Change in Developing Countries. Chicago:  University of Chicago Press.

Kelley, A.C., J.G. Williamson, and R.J. Cheetham (1972)  Dualistic Economic Development:  Theory and History.  Chicago: University of Chicago Press.

Kelley, A.C., and J.G. Williamson (1974)  Lessons from Japanese Development:  An Analytical Economic History.  Chicago: University of Chicago Press.

Kelley, A.C., and J.G. Williamson (1980)  Modeling Urbanization and Economic Growth.  Laxenburg, Austria:  International Institute for Applied Systems Analysis.

Kelley, A.C., and J.G. Williamson (1982)  The limits of urban growth:  suggestions for macro modeling third world economies.  Economic Development and Cultural Change 30:595-623.

Kelley, A.C., and J.G. Williamson (1984a)  What Drives Third World City Growth?  Princeton, N.J.:  Princeton University Press.

Kelley, A.C., and J.G. Williamson (1984b)  Modeling the urban transition.  Population and Development Review 10:419-442.

Lee, R.D. (1980)  Age structure, intergenerational transfers and economic growth:  an overview.  Demographic Economique 31: 1129-1156.

Leff, N.H. (1969)  Dependency rates and savings rates.  American Economic Review 59:886-896.

Mauldin, W.P., and R.J. Lapham (1985)  Measuring family planning
    program effort in developing countries:  1972 and 1982.  In
    N. Birdsall, ed., The Effects of Family Planning Programs on
    Fertility in the Developing World. Washington, D.C.:  World
    Bank.
McNamara, R. (1977)  Annual address to Board of Governors of the
    World Bank.
McNicoll, G. (1976)  Economic-demographic models.  Pp. 649-676 in
    L. Tabah, ed., Population Growth and Economic Development in
    the Third World. Liege:  Ordina Editions.
McNicoll, G. (1984)  Consequences of rapid population growth:
    overview and assessment.  Population and Development Review
    10:177-240.
Mohan, R. (1984)  The effect of population growth, the pattern of
    demand and of technology on the process of urbanization.
    Journal of Urban Economics 15:125-156.
Moreland, R.S. (1982)  Population, internal migration, and econ-
    omic growth: an empirical analysis.  Pp. 173-216 in J.L.
    Simon and P.H. Lindert, Research in Population Economics,
    Vol. 4.  Greenwich, Conn.:  JAI Press.
Phelps, E.S. (1966)  Models of technical progress and the golden
    rule of research.  Review of Economic Studies 33:133-146.
Pitchford, J.D. (1974)  Population in Economic Growth. New York:
    North Holland.
Pollak, R.A., and T.J. Wales (1980)  Comparison of the quadratic
    expenditure system and translog demand systems with alterna-
    tive specifications of demographic effects.  Econometrica
    48:595-612.
Powell, A.A. (1981)  The major streams of economy-wide modeling:
    is reapproachment possible?  Pp. 219-264 in J. Kmenta and
    J.B. Ramsey, Large-Scale Marco-Econometric Models.
    Amsterdam:  North-Holland.
Powell, A.A. (1983)  Aspects of the design of Bachuroo, an econ-
    omic-demographic model of labor supply.  Pp. 277-300 in A.C.
    Kelley, W.C. Sanderson, and J.G. Williamson, eds., Modeling
    Growing Economies in Equilibrium and Disequilibrium.  Durham,
    N.C.:  Duke University Press.
Preston, S.H. (1982)  Review of the ultimate resource.  Popula-
    tion and Development Review 8:176-177.
Ram, R. (1982)  Dependency rates and aggregate savings:  a new
    international cross-section study.  American Economic Review
    72:537-544.
Rodgers, G.B, R. Wery, and M.J.D. Hopkins (1976)  The myth of the
    cavern revisited:  are large-scale behavioral models useful?
    Population and Development Review 2:395-409.
Rodgers, G.B., M.J.D. Hopkins, and R. Wery (1978)  Population
    Employment and Inequality. New York:  Praeger.
Rosenzweig, M.R., and M. Pitt (1985)  Health and nutrient
    consumption across and within farm households.  Review of
    Economics and Statistics 67:212-223.
Sanderson, W.C. (1980)  Economic-Demographic Simulation Models:
    A Review of Their Usefulness for Policy Analysis. Laxenburg,
    Austria:  International Institute for Applied Systems
    Analysis.

Schmidt, R.M. (1981)   The Demographic Dimensions of Economic-
    Population Modeling.   Unpublished Ph.D. dissertation, Duke
    University.
Schmidt, R.M. (1983)   Incorporating demography into general
    equilibrium modeling.   Pp. 317-337 in A.C. Kelley, W.C.
    Sanderson, and J.G. Williamson, eds., Modeling Growing
    Economies in Equilibrium and Disequilibrium.   Durham, N.C.:
    Duke University Press.
Simon, J.L. (1977)   The Economics of Population Growth.
    Princeton, N.J.:   Princeton University Press.
Simon, J.L. (1981)   The Ultimate Resource.   Princeton, N.J.:
    Princeton University Press.
Simon, J.L. (1985)   Private communication.
Simon, J.L., and R. Gobin (1980)   The relationship between popu-
    lation and economic growth in LDCs.   Pp. 215-236 in J.L.
    Simon and J. DaVanzo, eds., Research in Population Economics,
    Vol. 2.   Greenwich, Conn.:   JAI Press.
Simon, J.L., and G. Steinmann (1981)   Population growth and
    Phelps technical progress:   interpretation and generali-
    zation.   Pp. 239-254 in J.L. Simon and P.H. Lindert, eds.,
    Research in Population Economics, Vol. 3.   Greenwich,
    Conn.:   JAI Press.
Smith, S.K. (1981)   Women's work, fertility, and competing time
    use in Mexico City.   Pp. 167-188 in J.L. Simon and P.H.
    Lindert, eds., Research in Population Economics, Vol. 3.
    Greenwich, Conn.:   JAI Press.
Wheeler, D. (1984)   Female education, family planning, income,
    and population:   a long-run econometric simulation model.
    In N. Birdsall, ed., The Effects of Family Planning Programs
    on Fertility in the Developing World.   Washington, D.C.:
    World Bank.
Williamson, J.G. (1985)   Regional economic-demographic modeling:
    progress and prospects.   In A. Isserman, ed., Population and
    the Economy.   Boston:   Kluwer-Nijhoff.

# 13

## National Saving Rates and Population Growth: A New Model and New Evidence

### Andrew Mason

### INTRODUCTION

In many assessments of the macroeconomic consequences of population growth, the link between demographic factors and saving or investment plays a key role. In their 1958 study of India, Coale and Hoover argue that lower population growth will encourage saving. Likewise, Mason and Suits' 1981 estimates of economic gains from fertility reduction derive from a model in which national saving is reduced by population growth. By contrast, the long-run economic benefits generated by Simon's 1976 model accrue, in part, because population growth is postulated to lead to higher rates of saving.

This chapter presents new analysis and evidence on the link between population growth and national saving. The analysis is based on the variable rate-of-growth effect model (Mason, 1981; Fry and Mason, 1982), which distinguishes two population growth effects: the rate of growth effect and the dependency effect. As in the traditional life-cycle model, an increase in the growth rate of aggregate income, given life-cycle patterns of household saving, leads to higher aggregate saving. To the extent, then, that population growth leads to higher growth of aggregate income, saving increases with population growth. An increase in child dependency operates in the opposite direction. By shifting consumption from nonchildrearing to childrearing stages of the

This chapter was prepared for the National Research Council and presented to a meeting on the consequences of population growth held August 2-4, 1984 at Woods Hole, Massachusetts. I benefited from useful discussions with Franco Modigliani, Arlie Sterling, Paul Schultz, Ernst Berndt, Arthur Lewbel, John Bauer, Ron Lee, and Dan Suits, as well as the research assistance of Leah Modigliani. During the preparation of this work, I was a visiting scholar at the Sloan School, Massachusetts Institute of Technology and gratefully acknowledge support provided for this research. Thanks to Norma Uejo and Gail Yamanaka for their help in the preparation of this manuscript.

household's life cycle, an increase in childrearing affects the timing of life-cycle saving. The impact on aggregate saving depends on the rate of growth of national income: a rise in the dependency ratio, given a higher rate of economic growth, leads to a greater decline in the saving ratio.

Crude support for this view is apparent in Table 1, which compares net national saving rates, averaged over the 1960 and 1980 period, for 79 countries. The highest saving ratios are observed among countries with both a low dependency ratio and a high rate of economic growth. Such countries average a saving ratio roughly twice that averaged by countries with high dependency ratios and low rates of economic growth.

The next section of this chapter reviews previous research on the saving-population growth link. Included are applications of the variable rate-of-growth effect model.

The third section presents an extension of the variable rate-of-growth effect model by linking factors that determine the number of children reared to the budget shares devoted to childrearing and, in turn, to the national saving rate. If a decline in childrearing results in a decline in the childrearing budget share, aggregate saving increases. Such a result will occur in two circumstances: (1) childrearing declines because of change in nonprice factors; and (2) childrearing declines elastically in response to increases in the relative price of children. If, however, the demand for children were inelastic, a price-induced decline in the number of children would result in an increase in the childrearing budget share and a decline in the national saving rate.

The fourth section presents estimates from international cross-section data covering the 1960 to 1980 period. The econometric evidence shows that countries, particularly those with moderate to high rates of economic growth, have achieved higher national saving via lower dependency ratios. In addition, estimates of childrearing budget shares varying from a high of 30 percent for high-fertility countries to a low of 15 percent for low-fertility countries are obtained. Budget share differences are primarily attributable to nonprice factors. By contrast,

TABLE 1  Average Net National Saving Ratio for 79 Countries, 1960-80

| Dependency Rate | Growth Rate of National Income | | |
| --- | --- | --- | --- |
| | Less than 0.5 | Greater than 0.05 | Combined |
| Greater than 0.6 | 0.089 | 0.146 | 0.124 |
| Less than 0.6 | 0.152 | 0.177 | 0.160 |

Note:  See Appendix for definitions of variables.

the relative price of children is shown to be roughly similar in high- and low-income countries.

In the fifth section, the neoclassical growth model is employed to show circumstances under which the rate-of-growth effect dominates the dependency effect, reversing the relationship between population growth and saving. In addition, the long-run relationship between population growth, saving, and capital and output per worker is analyzed.

The final section of the chapter reviews the evidence and presents conclusions. The Appendix defines the variables used in the model and details of the theoretical model.


PREVIOUS RESEARCH

That demographic factors have an important bearing on national saving rates is far from universally accepted. The evidence for such a relationship comes from two sources. First, simulation models, such as those of Tobin (1967) and Mueller (1976), have been used to analyze the complex relationship between saving and demographic factors. The conclusions reached, however, are quite sensitive to the relationship between household saving and age of head, and to the impact of the number of children on household consumption. Unfortunately, there is very little concrete evidence on these issues, particularly for developing countries. Thus, simulation models illustrate, but do not establish, the saving-population growth link. The second source of evidence comes from econometric studies of aggregate savings, based primarily on international cross-national data. A number of these studies, reviewed below, have concluded that high population growth depresses national saving rates, although the validity of this conclusion has been challenged on numerous grounds.


Simulation Studies

Tobin's 1967 article is the first of a number of studies to employ a simulation approach for assessing the impact of population on saving. Tobin describes a steady-state economy in which household consumption and earning, and hence saving, vary by age. With age profiles following the Modigliani-Brumberg path, that is, dominated by the pension motive, young households save and older households dissave. A high population growth rate generates an age distribution tilted toward young, saving households. Consequently, in contrast to empirical work cited below, aggregate saving is higher. By way of illustration, Table 2 presents from Tobin's study the ratio of wealth to labor income (W/L), wealth to total income (W/Y), and saving ratios (S/Y), given an interest rate of 0.05, a growth rate of worker productivity of 0.03, and several rates of population growth (n).

Tobin offers a refined model using more realistic consumption and earning profiles. The earning profiles are based on survey data for the United States. The consumption profiles are con-

TABLE 2  Tobin's Results Using a Simple
Life-Cycle Model

| n | W/L | W/Y | S/Y |
|---|-----|-----|-----|
| 0.0 | 9.1 | 6.2 | .19 |
| 0.01 | 8.4 | 5.9 | .24 |
| 0.02 | 7.6 | 5.6 | .28 |
| 0.03 | 7.0 | 5.2 | .31 |

structed using synthetic households with varying numbers of
equivalent adults: a husband, a wife, and children under 18
weighted by equivalent adult consumer units that vary from 0.1
to 1.0. This obviously complicates the role of population in an
interesting way. Changes in population growth affect both the
consumption profile and the age distribution of households. The
net effect on saving of a change in population growth is no
longer clear. Unfortunately, Tobin whets but fails to satisfy
our appetite; he provides refined estimates for only one rate of
population growth.

Several similar studies have been conducted (see, for
example, Kelley's 1968 analysis of economic growth in Australia
from 1861 to 1911, or Conroy's 1979 application of Tobin's model
to data from Peru). Of particular interest are studies by
Mueller (1976) and Lewis (1983).

Mueller uses an extensive amount of data to construct
earnings and consumption profiles appropriate to the developing
country context. In doing so, she establishes the importance of
child earning, not just consumption.[1] She concludes, in
general, that higher population growth results in a lower "potential" saving rate. For example, if one set of assumptions is
used, an increase in the gross rate of reproduction from 2 to 3
results in a decline in the "potential" saving rate from 11.9 to
4.8 percent.

Lewis examines the extent to which fertility decline explains
historical patterns in U.S. saving rates. Using the household as
the unit of analysis, he examines the effect of declining childbearing on the consumption profile of households, and hence on
the aggregate saving rate.[2] He concludes that fertility decline contributed about one-quarter of the increase in saving
rates observed from 1830 to 1900.

Household-Level Studies

All of the studies cited above suffer from a common problem:
the limited data on earning and, particularly, consumption age

profiles. Even where data are relatively ample, as in the
industrialized countries, differing conclusions are reached
about the importance of life-cycle saving. (For two recent
views, see Kotlikoff and Summers, 1981, and King and Dicks-
Mireaux, 1982). Little concrete evidence is available on the
effect of children on household consumption and earning patterns
among developing countries.

Both macrosimulation models and estimates from international
cross-section data reviewed below are based on the presumption
that the typical household's current consumption, income, and
hence saving are influenced by the number and demographic characteristics of its members. A number of studies of household consumption in industrialized countries provide support for this
view. Eizenga's 1961 analysis of the 1950 U.S. Survey of
Consumer Expenditures is one of the first efforts to estimate
the relationship of family size to saving. Controlling for
household income and age and occupation of head, Eizenga finds
that saving declines very substantially as family size increases
from one to three members, but declines much more gradually
thereafter. A number of other studies show that in industrialized countries, consumption is affected by the number of children
or household size (see, for example, Somermeyer and Bannink,
1973; Espenshade, 1975; and Mason, 1975).

Unfortunately, there is very little reliable evidence on the
relationship between the number of children and household saving
based on survey data for developing countries. Kwang Suk Kim's
1974 study of Korea is fairly typical. His analysis of 1964-72
Korean farm household saving data classified by farm size
provides no evidence that household saving is depressed by the
dependency ratio (ratio of employed members to total family
size). His analysis of per capita saving by urban households
during 1965 to 1972 shows that the average and marginal propensities to save are inversely related to household size. Kim's
study, like most of the others discussed below, is limited by a
lack of data (45 observations for the rural survey, for example);
it is also limited by the fact that many of the variables of
potential interest are not available, and that he had to rely on
published data tabulated in a way that restricts the analysis.

Peter Peek (1974) analyzes 1961, 1965, and 1971 data for the
Philippines classified by region (rural, Manila, and other urban)
and by income. He finds that, given household income, an increase in household size reduces household saving, but that the
number of children under age 18 has no significant effect on
saving.

Kelley and Williamson (1968) assess the saving behavior of
490 Indonesian households surveyed during 1958 and 1959.
Although the data will not support a direct analysis of the
relationship of saving to the number of children or family size,
Kelley and Williamson compare the average saving of households
classified into broad age categories to that predicted by simple
models in which saving varies with the number of "equivalent"
adults. The age variation "predicted" by the model is roughly
similar to that observed for rural households headed by persons

aged 30 or older. The observed variation among urban households, however, bears no relationship to variation in equivalent
household size.

Kelley (1980) analyzes the saving behavior of 400 Kenyan
nuclear households during 1968 and 1969. In this study, he
finds no evidence that the number of children affects household
saving.

Also of some relevance to understanding the saving-population
link in the developing context is an analysis of saving by households headed by employees of the U.S. iron, coal, or steel industry in 1889. Analysis by Kelley (1973) shows that saving rates
decline as family size increases above two members (see also
Espenshade, 1975). However, Kelley's 1976 reanalysis of the data
fails to find any significant relationship between family size
and saving.


Cross-National Studies

Two approaches have been taken to estimating the impact of population growth on aggregate saving. Leff (1969) and related
studies have analyzed international cross-section data using a
specification in which the demographic effects are captured by
including dependency ratios as regressors in the aggregate
saving function. The second approach employs the variable
rate-of-growth effect model discussed briefly above.


Leff and Related Studies

Leff (1969) analyzes gross national saving by 74 countries in
1964, and presents evidence that the saving rate is depressed by
an increase in either the youth dependency ratio, DR1 (population
younger than 15/population 15 to 64), or the old age dependency
ratio, DR2 (population older than 64/population 15 to 64). Leff
estimates the elasticity of saving with respect to the youth
dependency ratio to be -1.35, and with respect to the old age
dependency ratio to be -.40. Calculated and presented in Table
3 are saving ratios predicted, holding all other variables constant, using dependency ratios typical of low- and high-income
countries.

Leff's results have been subject to considerable scrutiny.
Adams (1971), Bilsborrow (1979, 1980), Goldberger (1973), and
Gupta (1971) have raised a number of issues. First, the theoretical basis of Leff's specifications has been questioned. The
use of the natural log of the saving ratio and of the rate of
growth of per capita income, variables that are not always defined, is one manifestation of the specification problem.
Second, it is argued that a more appropriate dependent variable
is household saving, while government and business saving should
not be included. Third, some critics suggest additional variables that should be included in the saving function; others
question the inclusion of per capita income. Fourth, simul-

TABLE 3  Calculated Saving Ratios Employing
Leff's Estimates

| Variable | Low Income | High Income |
|----------|------------|-------------|
| DR1      | .43        | .27         |
| DR2      | .04        | .10         |
| S/Y      | .17        | .22         |

Note:  Y/N set to $1,000 and g set to .03.

taneity issues have been raised.  Finally, a number of questions
have been raised about the use of international cross-section
data,   particularly   the   presence   of   sample   heterogeneity.
Perhaps the most damaging evidence presented to this point is
Ram (1982, 1984), who presents reestimates of Leff-like saving
functions based on 1970-77 cross-section data.  These results
provide very little support for the existence of a significant
dependency ratio effect in the form specified by Leff.    An
extensive review of the exchanges will not be undertaken here,
but the interested reader is referred also to Leff (1971, 1973,
1980, 1984).

Two other studies based on cross-national data also differ
in their conclusions about the importance of population growth.
Simon (1975) provides evidence that population growth has led to
additional investment in irrigation systems.  On the other hand,
Gupta (1975) employs World Bank data for the 1960s to estimate a
simultaneous equations model with a saving function that includes
the dependency ratio as an independent variable.  He concludes
that by using a single equation approach, Leff actually under-
estimates the impact of the dependency ratio.

## The Variable Rate-of-Growth Effect Model

Empirical results from four applications of the variable rate-of-
growth effect model are summarized in Table 4.  Mason (1981)
analyzes international cross-section data for 1960-70, while the
present study extends the analysis to the 1960-80 period.    Fry
and Mason (1982) analyze 1962-72 time series data for seven
Asian countries, and Fry (1984) extends the analysis to include
fourteen Asian countries over the 1961-81 period.  In each study,
the dependency ratio is found to have a significant adverse impact on saving:  a decline in the dependency ratio from 0.8 to
0.4 increases the saving ratio from 3.4 to 12.2 percentage
points, depending on the sample and type of data employed.

TABLE 4   A Comparison of Calculated Gross Saving Ratios
from Four Applications of the Variable Rate-of-Growth Model

| Source | Dependency Ratio [N(0-14)/N(15+)] | | |
|--------|------|-------|------|
|        | 0.4  | 0.611 | 0.8  |
| Mason (1981) | 0.239 | 0.203 | 0.170 |
| Fry and Mason (1982) | 0.245 | 0.203 | 0.165 |
| Fry (1984) | 0.265 | 0.203 | 0.143 |
| Mason (this chapter) | 0.224 | 0.203 | 0.190 |

Notes:   DR = 0.611 and S/Y = 0.203 are sample means from
Mason (this chapter); intercepts for Mason (1981), Fry and
Mason (1982), and Fry (1984) were adjusted to facilitate
comparison.  All calculated values assume a rate of growth
of national income equal to the sample mean from Mason
(this chapter) of 0.051.


Other Cross-National Research

The "consumer durable" role of children is the focus of most
research on the fertility-saving link.  With the exception of
Neher (1971), Lewis (1983), and Hammer (1984), the "provider of
old age security" role of children has been overlooked.  Children
and saving are substitutes or alternative ways that households
provide for their retirement.  Thus, a decline in "the rate of
return" to children vis-a-vis the rate of return to financial
assets should lead households to substitute financial assets for
children.
        Hammer develops such an approach and postulates that the
improvement of financial markets in developing countries has led
households to reduce their fertility while compensating with
increased saving.  In analyzing an international cross-section,
Hammer finds that the degree of monetization does lead to lower
fertility.  On the other hand, his model fails to explain
variation in personal saving rates.  Nonetheless, his approach
may be a promising way of incorporating the role of children
more fully into models of saving.


LIFE-CYCLE SAVING AND THE VARIABLE RATE-OF-GROWTH EFFECT

The basic idea behind the life-cycle saving model popularized by
Modigliani and his colleagues (see Modigliani, 1965, 1966;
Modigliani and Ando, 1957; and Modigliani and Brumberg, 1954) is
illustrated by Panel A in Figure 1, which represents the life-

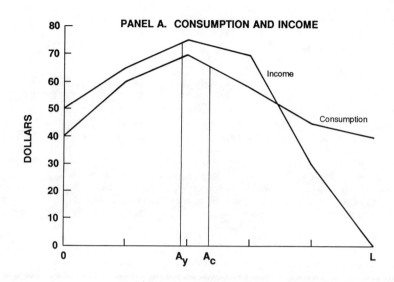

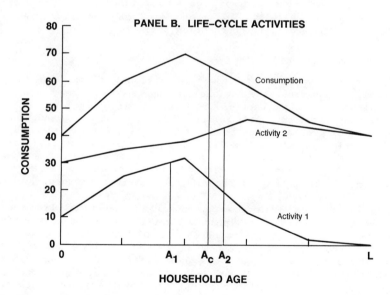

FIGURE 1   Life—Cycle Household

cycle patterns of consumption and earning of a "typical" household. Over the household's lifetime (OL measured on the horizontal axis), consumption is spread evenly, whereas earning is concentrated at preretirement years.   The household saves

during periods of relatively high earning in order to maintain
its consumption during periods of relatively low earning.

The household pictured accumulates no wealth over its lifetime, with dissaving during later years just matching saving
undertaken during earlier years. Even so, aggregate saving will
occur in an economy composed entirely of such households if that
economy is growing. The reason is simple: households at each
point of the life cycle are not equally represented. If the
population is a growing one, the young, saving households out-
number the old, dissaving households; if per capita income is
growing, young households have greater lifetime income than do
their elders. Hence, the absolute amount saved by the average
young household will exceed the absolute amount dissaved by the
average old household at any point in time. Effects of both
population and per capita income growth can be captured by the
growth rate of total income because, in equilibrium, the latter
measures the differences, across successive cohorts, of total
cohort lifetime earning.

The magnitude of the rate-of-growth effect, that is, the
effect on saving of a change in the rate of growth in national
income, depends on the extent to which household consumption lags
household earning. The consumption lag is measured by the difference between the average age of consumption, $A_c$, and the
average age of earning, $A_y$, both of which are identified in
Figure 1. The aggregate consumption ratio is given by

$$\ln c = a_0 + (A_y - A_c)g ,\qquad\qquad (1)$$

where g is the rate of growth of national income and c, of
course, is one minus the national saving ratio.[3]

Although the consumption lag has traditionally been treated
as constant,[4] recent research recognizes that the lag and hence
the rate-of-growth effect are variable--responding to changes in
childbearing (Mason, 1981; Fry and Mason, 1982), interest rates
(Fry and Mason, 1982), retirement programs (Modigliani and
Sterling, 1983), and other factors that affect the life-cycle
pattern of consumption or earning and their mean ages, $A_c$ and
$A_y$.

This chapter introduces a formal treatment of life-cycle
consumption and the determinants of variation in the consumption
lag. The essence of the model is captured by Panel B of Figure
1. The household participates in two activities--childrearing
and all other activities. The age patterns of the activities
(and their average ages, $A_1$ and $A_2$) are given, determined by
technological considerations rather than by prices or household
income. Expenditures on each activity and total expenditures
are plotted against household age. The average age of consumption, $A_c$, varies depending on the household's allocation of
its budget between the two activities: the greater the budget
share of activity 1 (childrearing), the younger the average age
of consumption; the greater the share of activity 2, the older
the average age of consumption. As is shown in the Appendix,
the average age of consumption can be calculated by

$$A_C = s1A1 + s2A2 . \tag{2}$$

$A_C$ is a weighted average of activity ages where the weights are the budget shares $s_1$ and $s_2$. Substituting $1-s_1$ for $s_2$,

$$A_C = s1(A1 - A2) + A2 . \tag{3}$$

The average age of consumption is determined by the share devoted to childbearing and the number of years, on average, by which expenditures on childrearing precede expenditures on other household activities.

In an algebraic sense, the budget share is determined by the price of children relative to adults $(P_1/P_2)$ and the quantity of children relative to the quantity of adults $(Q_1/Q_2)$. The childrearing share is calculated as

$$s_1 = \frac{P_1Q_1}{P_1Q_1 + P_2Q_2} = \frac{pq}{1 + pq} , \tag{4}$$

where p is the relative price of children and q is the relative quantity of children. In a behavioral sense, however, the relationship between share and quantity may be more complex because q and p need not be independent. The analysis carried out below distinguishes two cases.

Case I. Constant price (the equivalent adult consumer unit case). The simplest and most common approach to modeling the relationship of children to household consumption uses the equivalent adult consumer unit. Expenditures per child are held to be a constant fraction of expenditure per adult, with values used ranging from 0.1 upward. In terms of the model employed here, the relative price of children, p, is identical to the equivalent adult consumer unit. In this case, equation (4) describes the relationship of share to quantity. An increase in q unambiguously increases the share devoted to childrearing, with the magnitude depending on the value of the relative price.

Case II. Changing price and the demand for children. A more general representation of the relationship between share and quantity recognizes that the relative price of children may change and with it the number of children reared. The impact of price changes on the childrearing budget share will depend on the elasticity of demand. Figure 2 illustrates two possibilities. If demand is elastic, as is the case for the demand curve labeled DA, a relatively small price increase elicits a large decline in q and a decline in the share devoted to childrearing (judged by comparing the demand curve to the iso-share line). If, on the other hand, demand is inelastic, the case for DB, the price increase necessary to induce the observed decline in quantity is so large that the childrearing budget share actually increases.

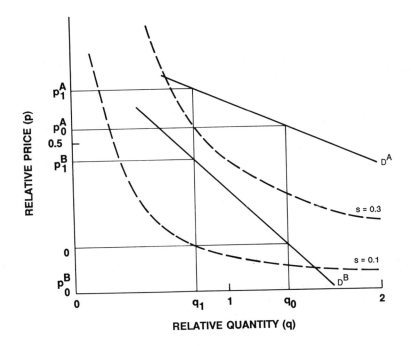

FIGURE 2   Relationship Between Budget Share, Elasticity of
Demand, and Demand Price

     In practice, the quantity of children will change in response
to both shifts in the demand for children and relative price
changes.   Shifts in the demand curve will unambigously affect
the budget share, while movements along the demand curve will
affect the budget share in keeping with the elasticity of demand.
Thus, the relationship of the budget share to the relative quantity of children rests on two issues:    (1) the extent to which
fertility has declined as a consequence of changes in relative
price as opposed to other factors, such as improved mortality
conditions, family planning programs, and higher female education; and (2) to the extent the price changes are important, the
elasticity of demand for children.   On these issues also rests
the extent to which a decline in the number of children reared
increases the aggregate saving rate.


AN APPLICATION TO INTERNATIONAL CROSS-SECTION DATA

Equations (1) and (3) are readily combined to yield a consumption
function amenable to estimation.    Substituting for the mean age
of consumption in equation (1) and rearranging terms, the consumption function is

$$\ln c = a_0 + s_1(A_2 - A_1)g + (A_y - A_2)g . \qquad (5)$$

The difference between the average age of childrearing and other activities, $A_2 - A_1$, is represented by $dA$; the difference between the average age of household earning and other activities, $A_y - A_2$, is estimated as a parameter of the model and is represented by $b_2$. The childrearing budget share is approximated[5] by

$$s_1 = a_1 + b_1 \ln q . \qquad (6)$$

Substituting into equation (5), the aggregate consumption function is

$$\ln c = a_0 + [a_1 + b_1 \ln q] \, dA \, g + b_2 \, g . \qquad (7)$$

The constant term $a_0$, as explained in the Appendix, contains two additive components: approximation error plus a behavioral component. If the error component is relatively small, $a_0$ will approximate the natural log of the average household's lifetime consumption ratio; in this case, $a_0$ will take a small negative value (the $\ln 0.9 = -0.105$, for example). The relationship between the childrearing budget share and the relative quantity of childrearing is discussed above. In either the equivalent adult consumer unit case or the elastic demand case, $b_1 > 0$. As measured here, $q$ essentially has an upper limit of 1 and $\ln q$ of 0, so that $a_1$ is an estimate of the maximum share devoted to childrearing if $b_1 > 0$. In the inelastic demand case, $b_1 < 0$, and $a_1$ is an estimate of the minimum share devoted to childrearing. In the unitary elasticity of demand case, $b_1 = 0$, and $a_1$ is an estimate of the constant share devoted to childrearing. In accordance with the life-cycle model, the average age of earning should be exceeded by the average age of adult consumption; thus the coefficient of $g$, $b_2$, is expected to be negative.

No direct statistical test is used to determine whether the equivalent adult consumer model is consistent with the data. However, calculated values for $p$ are easily obtained given values of $q$ and calculated shares. Rearranging equation (4),

$$p = s_1/(q - s_1 q) . \qquad (8)$$

The calculated price is an estimate of the equivalent adult consumer unit; the discussion below assesses the extent to which it varies with number of children reared.


Variables and Data

The quantity of childrearing activities, $Q_1$, is measured by the number of children (under age 15) per household. The quantity of other activities, $Q_2$, is measured by the number of adults (15 years and older) per household. Thus, the ratio of

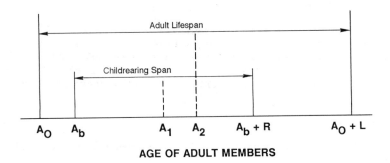

**AGE OF ADULT MEMBERS**

FIGURE 3   The Timing of Household Activities

the two quantities, $q$, is equal to the dependency ratio, the number of children per adult.

The approach taken to measuring dA is explained with the aid of Figure 3, which shows the timing of adult and childrearing activities. Households are formed by a group of adults, aged $A_0$ with a given lifespan of L. If adult consumption is distributed symmetrically with respect to age, then

$$A_2 = A_0 + L/2 . \tag{9}$$

$A_0$ is set to 20, and L is set to the average life-expectancy at 20 for the countries included in the sample.[6] Children are born to adults aged $A_b$. The childrearing span is equal to R, and if child consumption is distributed symmetrically with respect to age, then

$$A_1 = A_b + R/2 . \tag{10}$$

$A_b$ is measured by an estimate of the mean age at childbearing (see the Appendix for details), and R is determined by the level of enrollment observed in each country. Specifically,

$$R = 12 + 6*ENR2 + 4*ENR3 , \tag{11}$$

where ENR2 and ENR3 are the second- and third-level enrollment ratios; 12 years is the assumed minimum childrearing span; and 6 and 4 years are the durations of secondary school and college, respectively.

Analyses employing two measures of the consumption ratio are reported below. Because other cross-national studies use gross national saving as the dependent variable, the present study uses the "gross" consumption ratio equal to consumption (both private and government) divided by gross national income. The discussion focuses, however, on results obtained using consumption as a fraction of net national income, 1 minus the net national saving ratio, as the dependent variable.[7]

The growth rate of national income is obtained by calculating the growth rate of nominal national income, measured in each country's own currency, and subtracting the rate of inflation calculated using the consumer price index.

The model is estimated using quinquennial data from 1960-80 for countries with a labor force exceeding one million workers in 1960. Average values of the consumption ratio and the rate of growth of real national income are calculated for three ten-year intervals--1960-70, 1965-75, and 1970-80. The primary data sources are the 1976 and 1981 editions of the U.N. Yearbook of National Income Statistics. The consumer price index is taken from the International Monetary Fund's Yearbook of International Financial Statistics, 1981. Demographic data, calculated as of 1970, are taken from various issues of the U.N. Demographic Yearbook, and enrollment ratios are those reported by UNESCO's Statistical Yearbook, 1981. For more details on definitions, sources, and sample means, see Appendix Table A.1.

Multiplying dA g times the share terms in brackets, equation (7) can be estimated using ordinary least squares. The gross and net consumption ratios are denoted by c1 and c2; standard errors are reported below the estimated coefficients. The results are as follows:

$$\ln(c1) = -0.168 + [0.434 + 0.215 \ln DR]*dA*g - 4.32 g \ .$$
$$\quad\quad (0.020) \quad (0.159) \quad (0.032) \quad\quad\quad\quad (1.49)$$

$$N = 154 \quad\quad\quad R^2 = 0.283$$

$$\ln(c2) = -0.089 + [0.301 + 0.125 \ln DR]*dA*g - 3.46 g \ . \quad (12)$$
$$\quad\quad (0.010) \quad (0.136) \quad (0.026) \quad\quad\quad\quad (1.28)$$

$$N = 157 \quad\quad\quad R^2 = 0.253$$

All of the parameters are estimated with a fairly high degree of precision, and their signs and magnitudes are consistent with the present model. The coefficients of the gross consumption function are larger than the net coefficients, roughly in line with the ratio of gross to net saving for the sample of 1.5. In interpreting the results, the present analysis relies more heavily on the net estimates.

The estimate of the intercept is a reasonable value for the natural log of the lifetime consumption ratio. Approximation error aside, a lifetime consumption ratio of 0.91 is implied. The coefficient of g, estimated at minus three to four, is a plausible estimate of the number of years by which adult consumption lags earning. The point estimates of the share parameters are also reasonable. The "intercept" term, 0.301 for the net equation, is essentially an estimate of the upper limit of the share devoted to childbearing. As the dependency ratio declines, the budget share devoted to childrearing falls to a low of 15 percent for DR equal to 0.3. Table 5 reports estimated shares and the associated relative prices of children at selected dependency ratios.

TABLE 5  Calculated Shares and Prices of Children

|  | Gross Estimates | | Net Estimates | |
|---|---|---|---|---|
| Dependency Ratio | Share | Price | Share | Price |
| 0.3 | .18 | .71 | .15 | .59 |
| 0.5 | .29 | .80 | .21 | .55 |
| 0.7 | .36 | .80 | .26 | .49 |
| 0.9 | .41 | .78 | .29 | .45 |

Estimates based on gross national saving rates imply a very stable relative price of children quite in keeping with the equivalent adult consumer unit model. However, the estimated value of the equivalent adult consumer unit of close to 0.8 is somewhat higher than the values typically employed by other researchers. The estimated value of EACU (0.45 to 0.6) obtained from analyzing net national saving is more in keeping with other research. However, the variation in relative price suggests that changes in childrearing are, in part, a consequence of changes in relative price. There is nevertheless no way to judge on the basis of this analysis the extent to which fertility change is a consequence of relative price changes versus changes in exogenous factors. This is an issue to which we will return below.

The impact on saving of changes in the dependency ratio and the rate of growth of national income are assessed using Table 6, which reports calculated values of the saving ratio. The rate-of-growth effect, with the dependency ratio and dA set to their sample means, is close to one; an additional percentage point in growth yields roughly one additional percentage point of saving. Given a very high dependency ratio, say of 0.9, saving is much less influenced by growth: an additional percentage point in growth yields only one-half a percentage point in additional saving. By contrast, a very low dependency ratio of 0.3 yields a rate-of-growth effect in excess of one and one-half additional percentage points in saving for each percentage point in growth. These results are similar to those reviewed by Mikesell and Zinser (1973), but somewhat below estimates from previous applications of the variable rate-of-growth effect model (Mason, 1981; Fry and Mason, 1982).

The impact of a decline on childrearing depends on the rate of growth of income. Given no growth, rates of saving are independent of the dependency ratio. By contrast, given a 10 percent rate of growth per year, a decline in the dependency ratio from 0.9 to 0.3 generates an additional eleven percentage points of

TABLE 6   Calculated Saving Ratios

| Dependency Ratio | Rate of Growth of GNP | | | | | |
|---|---|---|---|---|---|---|
|  | 0.00 | 0.02 | 0.04 | 0.06 | 0.08 | 0.10 |
| Gross Saving Ratios | | | | | | |
| 0.3 | 0.155 | 0.198 | 0.239 | 0.278 | 0.314 | 0.349 |
| 0.5 | 0.155 | 0.180 | 0.206 | 0.230 | 0.253 | 0.276 |
| 0.7 | 0.155 | 0.169 | 0.183 | 0.197 | 0.210 | 0.223 |
| 0.9 | 0.155 | 0.160 | 0.166 | 0.171 | 0.176 | 0.182 |
| Net Saving Ratios | | | | | | |
| 0.3 | 0.086 | 0.122 | 0.156 | 0.189 | 0.221 | 0.252 |
| 0.5 | 0.086 | 0.111 | 0.135 | 0.159 | 0.182 | 0.204 |
| 0.7 | 0.086 | 0.103 | 0.121 | 0.138 | 0.155 | 0.171 |
| 0.9 | 0.086 | 0.098 | 0.110 | 0.122 | 0.134 | 0.145 |

saving. Given the average rate of growth for the sample of about 5 percent per year, a decline from a high-childrearing to a low-childrearing regime produces an increase in the net saving ratio of about five percentage points—roughly a 50 percent increase. Thus, the population dependency ratio has a substantial impact on saving given a moderate to high rate of economic growth.

## The Source of Fertility Change and the Saving Ratio

The estimates reported above are based on a model in which the share of the household budget devoted to childrearing is determined solely by the number of children reared relative to the number of adults. Such an approach is convenient in that it provides a straightforward summary of the statistical relationship between aggregate consumption and the dependency ratio—one that can be compared to estimates from previous studies. For several reasons, however, the approach is not entirely satisfactory.

First, the results have a clear theoretical basis only if tastes and other exogenous factors affecting the demand for children are constant. In this case only, the specification of the share equation employed above can be obtained from a utility function consistent with the basic tenets of consumer theory. International differences in childrearing may be attributed, in part, to differences in the price of children. However, a variety of nonprice factors undoubtedly play a key role.

Second, by failing to model explicitly the "instruments" by which fertility and, hence, the dependency ratio change, the model estimated above has limited policy applications. On theoretical grounds, the effect of reduced fertility on the aggregate saving ratio should vary depending on the means by which a fertility reduction is achieved: fertility decline accomplished via nonprice policies unambiguously reduces the share devoted to childrearing and increases aggregate saving; fertility decline induced via price changes has an ambiguous impact on saving that depends on the elasticity of demand.

A further difficulty with the simpler model is that the statistical relationship between the dependency ratio and aggregate saving will vary depending on the source of the observed variation in the dependency ratio. If the model employed fails to distinguish price and nonprice determinants of fertility, empirical results can vary substantially depending on the nature of the sample at hand.

A more complete analysis is possible if the demand for children is explicitly introduced. The demand schedule uniquely identifies combinations of p and q given exogenous determinants, while changes in the exogenous determinants shift the demand curve for children. The demand price for children is given by

$$p = f(q,x) , \tag{13}$$

where x is a vector of exogenous determinants. Substituting for price in equation (4), the budget share is a function of q and x, that is,

$$s = \frac{f(q,x)q}{1 + f(q,x)q} . \tag{14}$$

Complete specification of the share equation can proceed only if the form of the demand function is known. Analysis here is based on the share equation associated with the direct homogeneous translog utility function (Christensen et al., 1975). The budget share is given by

$$s = b_0 + b_1 \ln q + b_2 x_1 + \ldots .$$

The impact on share of a change in quantity, given exogenous factors, is determined by the elasticity of demand. If demand is inelastic, $b_1 < 0$; if demand is elastic, $b_1 > 0$; and if demand has unitary elasticity, the null case, $b_1 = 0$. The partial effect of any exogenous factor, x, on share depends on the change in the demand price for specified quantities that results from shifts in the demand schedule. If demand shifts to the right in response to a change in x, a higher demand price and a higher budget share will prevail at each quantity. Thus, the coefficient of factors that increase the demand for children will be greater than zero; for factors that reduce the demand for children, the coefficient will be less than zero.

Four factors that affect fertility are included: the proportion of the adult population that is literate (LIT); the proportion of the labor force employed in agriculture (LFAG); a dummy variable equal to one for countries in which the dominant culture

and/or religion (Islamic or Catholic) is pronatalist (REL); and
a time variable (YEAR, equal to 0 for 1960–70 observations).
(For more information on these variables, see the Appendix.)  The
equation estimated is

$$\ln c = a_0 + [b_0 = b_1 \ln DR + b_2 LIT + b_3 LFAG$$
$$+ b_4 REL \quad b_5 YEAR]*dA*g + a_1 g \ . \tag{15}$$

The interpretation of $a_0$ and $a_1$ is unaffected by the inclusion of additional determinants of the budget share.  The term
$b_0$, however, no longer has a useful interpretation.  An increase in education or a decline in the labor force in agriculture should lead to a downward shift in the demand for children.
Pronatalist countries should have a higher demand for children.
The secular trend in the demand for children should be downward,
capturing Caldwell's "westernization" process and/or the impact
of family planning programs.  Thus, the coefficients of LIT and
YEAR should be negative, while the coefficients of LFAG and REL
should be positive.  For a detailed discussion of the relationship of these factors to fertility and, hence, the dependency
ratio, the interested reader is referred to the vast literature.
Estimated coefficients and standard errors are as follows:

$$\ln c1 = -0.171 + [0.024 + 0.089 \ln DR + 0.133 LIT + 0.391 LFAG$$
$$(0.010) \quad (0.165) \quad (0.046) \quad\quad (0.053) \quad\quad\quad (0.077)$$

$$+ 0.051 REL - 0.0076 YEAR]*dA*g - 3.294 g \ . \tag{16}$$
$$(0.021) \quad\quad (0.0022) \quad\quad\quad\quad (1.389)$$

$$R^2 = .431 \quad\quad\quad\quad N = 154$$

$$\ln c2 = -0.093 + [0.021 + 0.053 \ln DR + 0.120 LIT + 0.263 LFAG$$
$$(0.009) \quad (0.153) \quad (0.042) \quad\quad (0.050) \quad\quad\quad (0.073)$$

$$+ 0.040 REL - 0.0058 YEAR]*dA*g - 2.849 g \ . \tag{17}$$
$$(0.020) \quad\quad (0.0022) \quad\quad\quad\quad (1.300)$$

$$R^2 = .337 \quad\quad\quad\quad N = 157$$

Empirical results are generally consistent with the model
proposed.  Of the exogenous determinants of the dependency ratio,
the effects of LFAG, REL, and YEAR are in the expected direction
and significantly different than zero.  The coefficient of g is
significantly less than zero, as expected.  The coefficient of
the dependency ratio is small, positive, and not significantly
different from zero, consistent with an elasticity of demand near
unity.

LIT, contrary to our expectations, is significantly greater
than zero.  There are a number of plausible explanations for this
positive effect.  First, the measure does not distinguish female
from male education, which may have a positive effect on fertility.  Second, the relationship may be spurious, picking up the
effect of excluded variables.  Child mortality is an obvious

example of such a variable.8  Of course, even direct estimates
of the determinants of fertility, based on international cross-
sections, generally fail to untangle the various effects of education, urbanization, religion, etc. (see Hazeldine and Moreland,
1977, for example).  It is hardly surprising, then, that an indirect approach is not entirely successful.  In any case, the
results will not support an analysis of the effect on saving of
any particular antinatalist policy.

A somewhat less demanding issue can be addressed:  the effect
of price- versus nonprice-induced changes in the dependency
ratio.  Figure 4 presents calculated demand curves obtained by
varying dependency ratios, holding other determinates of the
budget share constant.  The budget share devoted to childrearing
is obtained and the relative price of children calculated using
equation (4).  Two demand curves are shown:  the demand curve
labeled "nonindustrialized" is calculated using sample means for
countries with a GNP per capita in 1973 under $1,000; the other
demand curve, "industrialized," is calculated using sample means
for countries with an income exceeding $1,000.  Also shown in
the figure are the average dependency ratios of the two subsamples and the implied prices.  This figure illustrates several
key points.  It is quite clear that the difference in fertility
observed between the industrialized and nonindustrialized countries is not the consequence of a difference in the price of
children.  The price of children evaluated at the means for both
samples is about one-third.  Differences in the quantity of

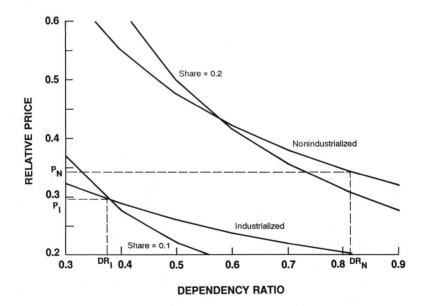

FIGURE 4   Demand for Children

TABLE 7  Calculated Net National Saving Ratios
for Industrialized and Nonindustrialized Countries

| Rate of Growth | Industrialized (low fertility) | Nonindustrialized (high fertility) |
|---|---|---|
| .02 | .124 | .106 |
| .04 | .158 | .122 |
| .06 | .190 | .139 |
| .08 | .221 | .155 |
| .10 | .251 | .170 |

childrearing are dominated by shifts in the demand for children. This "finding" will come as no surprise to students of fertility change. Nonetheless, it is critical to our finding that a decline in fertility is accompanied by a decline in the budget share devoted to childrearing.

Aside from their implication for aggregate saving, the estimate of the equivalent adult consumer unit and the finding that it does not vary substantially with economic development are interesting results in their own right. Although simulation studies cited earlier have used the equivalent adult consumer unit, no estimate based on aggregate consumption data has yet been available. Furthermore, no evidence has been presented that so simple an approach has any empirical validity in comparing countries at different stages of development. The evidence presented here indicates that the idea that adults and children share resources in fixed proportions has more than intuitive appeal. The equivalent adult consumer unit approach provides a fairly accurate description of differences between the industrialized and nonindustrialized countries.

The effect on saving of the shift in the demand for children shown in Figure 4 is substantial. The share of the budget devoted to children declines from over 20 percent to just at 10 percent for the industrialized countries. At the mean rate of growth of national income, the calculated net national ratio rises from 13.5 percent to 18.2 percent. The impact of the shift in the demand for children at other rates of growth is shown in Table 7. Again for moderate- and high-growth economies, a decline in the dependency ratio has a substantial effect on saving.

Robustness of Findings

Critics of cross-national studies of saving and population growth have focused, in particular, on two issues: (1) the inclusion of government saving or consumption in the dependent variable, and (2) the sensitivity of results to sample selection. These issues are addressed in this section.

## Are Government and Private Saving Perfect Substitutes?[9]

Studies of aggregate saving or consumption are frequently criticized for their choice of dependent variable. Bilsborrow (1979,
1980), in his critiques of Leff's analysis, argues for a narrow
concept--household saving. That such an approach is unattractive
is evident when it is examined from the perspective employed
here. Current consumption is "constrained" by lifetime resources, and whether those resources are paid in the current
period as wages, distributed as profits, or retained by corporate
(or unincorporated) enterprises is irrelevant. On a priori
grounds, then, private consumption is preferable to household
saving. On the other hand, it is arguable that government and
private saving are perfect substitutes. The analysis that
follows shows that, other things being equal, private saving (or
its consumption counterpart) should be employed. However, there
are costs to doing so, because data on private saving are not
available for many low-income countries. Analysis shows that
using national saving as a dependent variable may not result in
substantially biased estimates.

The traditional application of the life-cycle model focuses
on private consumption, $C_p$, as a fraction of disposable income,
that is,

$$C_p = MPC [Y - T] , \qquad (18)$$

where Y is national income, T is taxes net of transfers, and the
marginal propensity to consume is MPC. This approach has
recently been challenged by Barro, who argues that government
deficits, D, are indistinguishable from taxes in their impact on
private consumption, so that

$$C_p = MPC [Y - T - D] . \qquad (19)$$

If Barro's model is employed, government saving (-D) and private
saving are close substitutes depending on the MPC.

The model used above implies that government and private
saving are perfect substitutes. The government acts as an agent
of households, so that government and private consumption
together are "constrained" by total national income, that is,

$$C_p + C_g = MPC[Y] . \qquad (20)$$

Noting that $C_g$ is equal to T + D, dividing both sides by Y,
and using lower case letters to represent the resulting ratios,
a general model of consumption is given by

$$c_p = MPC[1 + a_1 t + a_2 d] , \qquad (21)$$

where the three models differ with respect to the values of $a_1$
and $a_2$:

| Model | $a_1$ | $a_2$ |
|---|---|---|
| Life-cycle | -1 | 0 |
| Barro | -1 | -1 |
| Mason | -1/MPC | -1/MPC |

It is not possible to test directly the validity of all three specifications from the general model. A second model will be estimated, however, to analyze the approach employed here:

$$c_p = MPC + a_1 t + a_2 d , \tag{22}$$

where the Mason specification is consistent with $a_1 = a_2 = -1$. A somewhat simpler specification of the marginal propensity to consume than that employed above is used:

$$\ln MPC = b_0 + b_1 g \ln DR + b_2 g . \tag{23}$$

This differs from the specification employed above in that the difference in the ages of consumption, dA, is subsumed in the coefficient $b_1 \simeq s_1 dA$ and the intercept term, $b_0$.

The alternative models are estimated applying nonlinear least squares to the 96 observations, out of the full sample, for which the required additional data are available. Equation (24) presents the LCH-Barro model:

$$c_p = \exp[-0.081 - 0.532g + 0.953 \ g \ln DR][1 - 1.019t - 0.290d]$$
$$\quad\quad (0.031) \ (0.299) \ \ (0.306) \quad\quad\quad (0.101) \ \ (0.181) \ . \tag{24}$$

$$N = 96 \quad\quad\quad\quad -2 \ \lambda = 167.59$$

The results are consistent with the "pure" LCH ($a_2 = 0$) or with substantial substitution between government and private saving. We can reject the "pure" Barro specification, however.

Equation (25) presents the Mason specification:

$$c_p = \exp[-0.086 - 0.503g + 0.714g \ln DR] - 0.909t - 0.273d$$
$$\quad\quad (0.028) \ (0.226) \ \ (0.240) \quad\quad\quad (0.106) \ \ (0.160) \ . \tag{25}$$

$$N = 96 \quad\quad\quad\quad -2 \ \lambda = 167.90$$

Again the traditional LCH approach is clearly more consistent with the data than is the approach using national saving as the dependent variable. A deficit ratio coefficient of -1 is soundly rejected by the data. Thus, using national saving as a dependent variable gains efficiency, by enlarging the sample, at the expense of introducing specification error. How serious is the error? Equation (26), in which equation (25) is reestimated with $a_2$ and $a_3$ constrained to -1, provides some evidence on the issue:

$$c = c_g + c_p = \exp[-0.100 - 0.790g + 0.757g \ln DR]$$
$$\phantom{c = c_g + c_p = \exp[}(0.015) \quad (0.251) \quad (0.287) \; . \tag{26}$$

$$N = 96 \qquad\qquad -2 \; \lambda = 152.134$$

As compared with equation (24), employing the total consumption
ratio as the dependent variable leads to an estimate of the impact of the dependency ratio and an estimate of the partial
effect of g, evaluated for possible values of DR, that are closer
to zero. Thus, available evidence suggests that the standard
approach, using national saving, may <u>underestimate</u> the importance of demographic factors.

## Sensitivity to Sample Selection

Previous studies of the dependency ratio–saving link have noted
the sensitivity of the results to both sample selection and the
inclusion of additional variables. The analysis carried out
above provides one explanation of the sensitivity of previous
results. Nonetheless, estimates of the model employed here are
sensitive to sample selection. Table 8 reports estimates of the
consumption function obtained by fitting equation (15) to the two
subsamples--industrialized and nonindustrialized countries--
referred to above. The effect of the dependency ratio in industrialized countries is quite similar to that found for the all-
country sample; for nonindustrialized countries, however, the
effect of the dependency ratio is significantly less than zero,
consistent with an inelastic demand for children. Where significantly different than zero, the effects of other determinants
of the budget share are in the expected direction. For the
industrialized sample, literacy and the trend variable lead to a
lower budget share; in the nonindustrialized countries, the labor
force in agriculture, religion, and the trend variable are significant and have the expected impact on the share.

If the equations are evaluated at their respective sample
means, the calculated childrearing share for nonindustrialized
countries substantially exceeds that for industrialized countries. In general, this supports the conclusion reached above--
that shifts in the demand curve reduce both fertility and budget
share devoted to childrearing, and hence increase the aggregate
saving ratio. However, the differences in the shares are implausibly large. The estimates based on the subsamples will not
support the demand analysis carried out for the full sample.
Calculated shares frequently exceed one for the nonindustrialized
countries and are negative for the industrialized countries.

## NEOCLASSICAL GROWTH AND SAVING

The analysis of the dependency ratio carried out above is a
partial one. The effect of the dependency ratio is estimated
given the rate of growth of national income. Changes in the

TABLE 8  Results from Extended Analysis; Coefficients and Standard Errors (in parentheses)

| Dependent Variable | Industrialized | | Nonindustrialized | |
|---|---|---|---|---|
| | Gross Consumption | Net Consumption | Gross Consumption | Net Consumption |
| $a_0$ | -0.168 (0.020) | -0.086 (0.017) | -0.167 (0.012) | -0.093 (0.011) |
| $b_0$ | 0.384 (0.293) | 0.160 (0.246) | 0.368 (0.384) | 0.669 (0.304) |
| ln DR | -0.062 (0.086) | -0.048 (0.072) | -0.239 (0.144) | -0.225 (0.097) |
| LIT | -0.719 (0.324) | -0.446 (0.272) | 0.078 (0.066) | 0.088 (0.060) |
| LFAG | 0.101 (0.188) | -0.013 (0.158) | 0.341 (0.110) | 0.274 (0.100) |
| REL | -0.028 (0.047) | -0.041 (0.039) | 0.079 (0.033) | 0.088 (0.031) |
| YEAR | -0.0116 (0.0039) | -0.0078 (0.0032) | -0.0050 (0.0028) | -0.0050 (0.0024) |
| g | 0.247 (1.426) | 0.485 (1.194) | -7.048 (3.702) | -9.765 (2.974) |
| N | 67 | 67 | 87 | 90 |
| R2 | 0.387 | 0.404 | 0.315 | 0.417 |

rate of growth of population may affect both the dependency ratio and the rate of growth of aggregate income. The discussion below employs the neoclassical growth model to broaden the analysis of saving and, at the same time, to examine the impact of population growth on capital output ratios and output per worker. Although the chief attraction of the analysis is its simplicity, the comparative static results presented below are primarily of academic interest because steady state results obtain over such extended periods that they are of little value in framing economic policy. Unfortunately, there are no widely accepted models that capture the short-run effects of population growth on growth of per capita income. Research conducted on this subject finds that growth in aggregate income does not generally decline point-for-point with population growth. Thus, the neoclassical model is a very conservative approach to the impact of population growth.

The analysis follows Solow (1956), with exogenous labor augmenting technological growth. Output is a linearly homogeneous function of capital and effective labor, E, so that output per effective worker, y, depends only on capital per effective worker, k; that is,

$$y_t = f(k_t) ,\qquad (27)$$

where $f' > 0$ and $f'' \leq 0$. The effective labor force grows at rate $\lambda + n$, where $\lambda$ is the growth in effective labor per worker and n is the growth of the labor force (and the population). Letting . stand for the growth rate,

$$\dot{E}_t = \lambda + \dot{L}_t = \lambda + n . \qquad (28)$$

The growth of the capital stock is determined by the saving ratio and the ratio of output to capital; that is,

$$\dot{K}_t = s_t Y_t / K_t = s_t\, y_t / k_t . \qquad (29)$$

Equilibrium is attained with $\dot{k}_t = \dot{y}_t = 0$. Because $\dot{k}_t$ is equal to

$$\dot{k}_t = \dot{K}_t - \dot{E}_t = s_t y_t / k_t , \qquad (30)$$

the equilibrium capital-output ratio $(k/y)*$ is equal to

$$(k/y)* = s*/( \lambda + N) . \qquad (31)$$

The equilibrium saving ratio, $s*$, is determined by $g = \lambda + n$ and the dependency ratio associated with n employing the consumption function estimated above.

TABLE 9  Equilibrium Saving and Capital-Output Ratios for Selected Values of $\lambda$ and n

| n | $A_y - A_c$ | $\lambda = 0$ | | $\lambda = .02$ | | $\lambda = .04$ | |
|---|---|---|---|---|---|---|---|
| | | s* | (k/y)* | s* | (k/y)* | s* | (k/y)* |
| 0.00 | -2.0 | 0.085 | -- | 0.121 | 6.0 | 0.155 | 3.9 |
| 0.01 | -1.4 | 0.098 | 9.8 | 0.123 | 4.1 | 0.147 | 2.9 |
| 0.02 | -1.0 | 0.103 | 5.2 | 0.121 | 3.0 | 0.138 | 2.3 |
| 0.03 | -0.7 | 0.104 | 3.5 | 0.117 | 2.3 | 0.129 | 1.8 |

Note:  Saving ratios are calculated using $\ln c = -0.089 + (A_c - A_y)$, where the relationship of the consumption lag to the dependency ratio is based on the net consumption variant of equation (27) with dA set at its sample mean.  The values of DR used at the selected population growth rates are based on Mason (1981).

TABLE 10  Equilibrium Output Per Worker

| n | $\lambda = .00$ | $\lambda = .02$ | $\lambda = .04$ |
|------|------|------|------|
| 0.00 | -- | $167e.02t$ | $149e.04t$ |
| 0.01 | 174 | $137e.02t$ | $129e.04t$ |
| 0.02 | 124 | $115e.02t$ | $113e.04t$ |
| 0.03 | 100 | $100e.02t$ | $100e.04t$ |

Note: Cobb-Douglas production function with
capital elasticity of 0.35 is used to calculate
output per worker ratios.

Table 9 shows calculated saving ratios and capital-output
ratios for selected values of n and $\lambda$ . Table 10 provides an
index of output per worker where the Y/L is set to 100 for n =
0.03.

Table 9 demonstrates that, given slow productivity growth,
the rate-of-growth effect dominates the dependency effect; higher
population growth leads to higher saving. In the extreme case,
g = 0, a change in the dependency ratio has no impact on saving
at all, and the rate-of-growth effect necessarily dominates. At
higher values of g, the dependency effect is of greater importance and eventually dominates the rate-of-growth effect; thus,
increased population growth leads to reduced saving.[10]

For all values of productivity growth, an increase in the
population growth rate leads to a decline in equilibrium capital/
output and output/worker ratios. On a percentage basis, the
high-productivity-growth economies have the smallest differentials in output per worker. For $\lambda$ = 0.04, output per worker for
the ZPG case is 50 percent above that obtained when n = .03. In
absolute terms, of course, differences in output per worker will
be greater the higher the growth in productivity.

The association between the capital/output and output/worker
ratios and the rate of population growth is a consequence of the
capital-dilution effect. If higher population growth leads to
higher saving, as is the case for low values of g, the capital-
dilution effect is offset. If, on the other hand, higher population growth leads to higher saving, the capital-dilution effect
is compounded. Were the saving ratio constant at 0.129 for $\lambda$ =
0.04, for example, the capital/output ratio and index of output
per worker, given ZPG, would be 3.2 and 137 versus the table
values of 3.9 and 149.[11]


CONCLUSIONS

Available evidence from the international cross-section supports
the proposition that a higher dependency ratio leads to lower
saving, particularly among countries with moderate to high rates

of income growth. At the mean rate of growth observed over the
last two decades for the seventy countries analyzed here, a decline from a high- to a low-childbearing regime generates an
increase in the net national saving rate of about five percentage
points--nearly a 50 percent increase. In addition to this central finding, the results reported above also address the magnitude and validity of the equivalent adult consumer unit. Aggregate consumption data imply an equivalent adult consumer unit of
about one-third, a value surprisingly constant across the stage
of development. This analysis implies that simulation models
based on the equivalent adult consumer unit can provide useful
insights about the relationship between population growth and
aggregate consumption and saving rates.

There are a number of important issues, however, that are
not adequately addressed by the preceding analysis. For one,
the analysis presented here does not fully resolve the issue of
the relative importance of the rate-of-growth and dependency
effects. The importance of the population rate-of-growth effect
is determined in part by the impact of the rate of population
growth on the rate of growth of national income. The analysis
above is based on the neoclassical growth model, for which the
equilibrium rate of growth of national income increases point-
for-point with an increase in the rate-of-growth of population.
If, however, the growth rate of per capita income is inversely
related to the population growth rate, the population rate of
growth effect is overstated by the above analysis. Given the
long periods required to adjust from one equilibrium to another,
the steady-state results of the neoclassical model may have
limited relevance to the design and evaluation of development
and population policy. Furthermore, there is no consensus that
the neoclassical model accurately describes the relationship of
population growth to national income, even in the long run.

Further, although the model proposed here clearly delineates
the link between children, household saving, and national saving,
the role ascribed to children is limited. The model acknowledges
only that children require household resources for their support.
A more complete analysis would focus, as well, on the varied
institutions by which households provide for their old age
security. The mechanism emphasized here is the accumulation of
financial assets. No attention has been paid to old age support
provided by children, or to investment in the human resources of
children by parents as a substitute for the accumulation of
financial assets. Furthermore, in many developed countries,
governments play an increasingly pervasive role in the provision
of old age security, further clouding the relationship between
children and saving. A more comprehensive model of saving should
acknowledge the joint determination of investment in human resources and the accumulation of financial resources and their
dependence on publicly funded social insurance schemes.

Although this study relies entirely on aggregate-level data,
the findings are verifiable, in principle, at the micro level as
well. The critical relationship is that of the number of children to the average age of consumption. Unfortunately, few

studies of the impact of household composition on household consumption or saving have been conducted in developing countries. Furthermore, most studies tend to emphasize the impact of current composition on current consumption. Analysis of the timing of consumption requires estimates of the impact of children on the entire age–consumption profile, or alternatively, analysis of the impact of children on current assets. Until richer survey data are available and analyzed, the importance of demographic factors to national saving rates is likely to be the subject of continued debate.

## NOTES

1   This is a point made by Kelley (1968, 1973, 1976, 1980), as well, in his analysis of micro data.

2   Lewis does not consider the impact of fertility on the subsequent age distribution of the adult population. Thus, his analysis does not admit the rate-of-growth effect.

3   See the Appendix for the derivation.

4   Empirical studies show that a one percentage point increase in growth generates between one and four percentage points worth of saving, consistent with a lag between earning and consumption averaging 1 to 4 years (Mikesell and Zinser, 1973).

5   The choice of this particular functional form is clarified below. It is based on the direct homogeneous translog utility function (Christensen et al., 1975).

6   L is not allowed to vary from observation to observation, because an adequate modeling of the role of mortality would recognize that all timing variables are affected by mortality change.

7   The use of gross national saving as a dependent variable has been criticized by Bilsborrow and others, who argue that either private saving or household saving would be more appropriate to the household model on which the empirical studies are based. Using household saving as the dependent variable would be appropriate if for some inexplicable reason, lifetime wealth, as perceived by households, were not affected by undistributed corporate profits. In the absence of evidence to support this view, most studies of life-cycle saving have not analyzed household saving. The choice between private and total net saving is a more ticklish affair, given the considerable interest in the impact of government deficits on private consumption. Barro (1974) provides the theoretical grounds for the argument that government and private saving may be close to perfect substitutes. Supporting empirical evidence is provided for the U.S. by Kormendi (1983) and for Turkey by Fry (1979). Recent analysis of cross-section data by Modigliani et al. (1984) also shows government and private saving to be partial substitutes. Of course, even were government and private saving totally independent, including government saving in

the dependent variable would not necessarily lead to biased
estimates. On the other hand, private saving as distinct
from total saving is available for a substantially reduced
sample. Analysis presented below provides evidence that the
dependency ratio depresses private as well as national
saving.

8  The model was also estimated using life expectancy at birth
as a proxy for child mortality. The life expectancy variable
was not significant, nor does it reverse the sign of the
literacy variable.

9  This section draws heavily from a recently completed study
by Modigliani, Mason, and Sterling (1984).

10  The first-order condition for a maximum saving ratio is that
the percentage changes in the consumption lag and the percentage change in g with respect to n are of equal magnitude
and of opposite sign. This result is easily obtained by
equating to zero the partial derivative of $\ln c = a_0 + (A_y - A_c)g$. This result does not depend on use of a
neoclassical growth model.

11  These conclusions bear on recent theoretical work by Arthur
and McNicoll (1978), Lee (1982), and Willis (1983) on the
relationship of population growth to the equilibrium capital
labor ratio. Arthur and McNicoll elaborate on the neoclassical growth model to show that, in the presence of age-
dependent consumption and earning, Solow's capital-dilution
effect may be offset or complemented by what they term the
"intergenerational transfer effect." The latter is just
another manifestation of the rate-of-growth effect. Based
on illustrative calculations, Arthur and McNicoll conclude
that the rate-of-growth effect reinforces the capital-
dilution effect. The analysis presented here supports a
more complex view.

APPENDIX

This Appendix describes in detail the life-cycle model presented
in this chapter.

The Life-Cycle Household

The household is assumed to have a known lifetime, commencing at
age 0 and ending at age L. The household engages in two
utility-yielding activities and chooses activity levels that
maximize its utility function:

$$U = U(Q_1, Q_2) ,$$   (A-1)

subject to

$$V > P_1Q_1 + P_2Q_2 ,$$   (A-2)

where V is the household's lifetime resources. Given a well-behaved utility function, the demand prices for each activity level are given by

$$P_1 = F1(Q_1, Q_2, V)$$
$$P_2 = F2(Q_1, Q_2, V) .$$  (A-3)

The budget share of each activity, $s_i$, is equal to

$$s_i = P_iQ_i/V = Q_iF_i(Q_1,Q_2,V)/V .$$  (A-4)

If the utility function is homothetic, as assumed below, $s_1$ is independent of lifetime resources and is uniquely determined by the quantity of childrearing relative to the quantity of other activities; that is,

$$s_1 = f(q) ,$$  (A-5)

where $p = P_1/P_2$ and $q = Q_1/Q_2$. The share devoted to activity 2 is equal to $1-s_1$.

The Age Consumption Profile

Households engage in activities at one or more ages, and the proportion of $Q_i$ "consumed" at each age is designated by $k_i(a)$, where $k_i(a) \geq 0$ and $\int k_i(a) da = 1$. The proportion is assumed to be independent of prices, income, and the total level of each activity. The amount "consumed" at age a is equal to $k_i(a)Q_i$, and the value of expenditures on activity i at age a is given by

$$C_i(a) = P_iQ_ik_i(a) .$$  (A-6)

The age distribution of activity i is summarized by its average age, $A_i$, where

$$A_i = \int_0^L aC_i(a) da/ \int_0^L C_i(a) da = \int_0^L ak_i(a) da .$$  (A-7)

Expenditure on all activities at age a is equal to

$$C(a) = P_1Q_1k_1(a) + P_2Q_2k_2(a) .$$  (A-8)

The fraction of lifetime earnings expended at age a, c(a), is equal to

$$c(a) = C(a)/V = s_1k_1(a) + s_2k_2(a) .$$  (A-9)

The timing of consumption is summarized by its average age, $A_c$, where

$$A_c = \int_0^L ac(a)\ da\ . \tag{A-10}$$

The average age of consumption is a weighted average of the average ages of each activity, where the weights are the activity budget shares. Substituting equation (A-9) into (A-10) and rearranging terms,

$$A_c = \sum_{i=1}^{2} s_i \int_0^L ak_i(a)\ da = \sum_{i=1}^{2} s_i A_i\ . \tag{A-11}$$

The Age Earning Profile

The household's age earning profile is described in similar fashion to the household's consumption profile. The fraction of lifetime earnings accruing at age a is given by

$$y(a) = Y(a)/V\ , \tag{A-12}$$

where $Y(a)$ is the age a earnings by the household.

The timing of earning is summarized by its average age, $A_y$, where

$$A_y = \int_0^L ay(a)\ da\ . \tag{A-13}$$

The Aggregate Consumption Rate

The aggregation of life-cycle households requires that consumption and earning profiles, $c(a)$ and $y(a)$, be independent of lifetime resources, V. This condition is fulfilled if life-cycle activities are homothetic. It is assumed, as well, that steady-state growth in both per capita income and population prevails, so that the lifetime resources of all members of the cohort currently aged are given by

$$H(a)V(a) = e^{-ga}\ H(0)V(0)\ , \tag{A-14}$$

where $H(a)$ is the number of households aged a, $V(a)$ is the lifetime resources per age a household, g is the rate of growth of national income, and $H(0)V(0)$ is the lifetime resources of all members of the cohort of newly formed households.

Current consumption by the age a cohort is equal to $c(a)H(a)V(a)$, and aggregate consumption, C, is obtained by summing across all household ages:

$$C = \int_0^L c(a)H(a)V(a)\ da = H(0)V(0) \int_0^L e^{-ga}\ c(a)\ da\ . \tag{A-15}$$

Likewise, current income of the age a cohort is equal to $y(a)H(a)V(a)$, and aggregate income, $Y$, is

$$Y = \int_0^L y(a)H(a)V(a) \ da = H(0)V(0) \int_0^L e^{-ga} y(a) \ da \ . \quad (A\text{-}16)$$

Taking the ratio of C to Y yields the aggregate rate of consumption, c:

$$c = \int_0^L e^{-ga} c(a) \ da / \int_0^L e^{-ga} y(a) \ da \ . \quad A\text{-}(17)$$

Finally, taking the logarithm of both sides and approximating the integral terms using a Taylor series expansion (see Mason, 1981),

$$\ln c = a_0 + (A_y - A_c)g \ , \quad (A\text{-}18)$$

where $a_0 = \ln \int c(a) \ da + e$, and e is an error term associated with the Taylor series approximation. $A_y - A_c$ is the average consumption lag.

This representation of the life-cycle model is quite similar to its extensively analyzed cousins. In the absence of growth, and the error term aside, the consumption rate for the economy as a whole is equal to the lifetime consumption rate of the average household, $\int c(a) \ da$. The rate-of-growth effect, the partial effect of change in the rate of growth of national income, is $A_y - A_c$. This term has a straightforward interpretation: it is the average lag between the point at which the household earns and the point at which it spends its income. If households, on average, earn before they spend, that is, they are net creditors over their lifetimes, an increase in the rate of growth of total income leads to a lower aggregate consumption rate, and, consequently, a higher saving ratio.

TABLE A.1   Description of Variables and Sources (mean values in brackets)

---

Gross Consumption Ratio (c1) [.797]
　　　Ratio of total consumption to gross national income. Gross
　　　national income defined as net national income plus capital
　　　consumption.  Sources:  United Nations (1976b, 1981) and World
　　　Bank (1976; 1981).

Net Consumption Ratio (c2) [.862]
　　　Ratio of total consumption to net national income.  Net national
　　　income corresponds to U.N. classification "national disposible
　　　income"; excludes capital consumption and taxes paid to
　　　supranational organizations; includes net current transfers from
　　　abroad.  Sources:  United Nations (1976b, 1981).

Rate of Growth of Income (g) [.051]
　　　Rate of growth of net national income.  Calculated as the
　　　difference between the rate of growth of nominal income and the
　　　inflation rate as measured by the rate of growth of the consumer
　　　price index (CPI).  Source for CPI:  IMF (1981).

Dependency Ratio (DR) [.611]
　　　Ratio of population under 15 years of age to population 15 years
　　　and older in 1970.  Source:  United Nations (various years).

Mean Age of Childbearing (MACB) [28.5]
　　　The mean age of childbearing was not used directly in the measure
　　　of dA because a major source of variation in MACB is the age at
　　　marriage, which should not affect dA.  However, variation in MACB
　　　due to fertility variation should affect dA.  The MACB was
　　　regressed on the total fertility rate using a logistic functional
　　　form.  Predicted values of MACB were used to construct dA.
　　　Source:  United Nations (various years).

Labor Force in Agriculture (LFAG) [.412]
　　　Ratio of labor force employed in agriculture to the total labor
　　　force.  Source:  United Nations (1976a).

Literacy Rate (LIT) [.674]
　　　Ratio of literate population to population over age 14.  Source:
　　　United Nations (1976a).

Religion (REL) [.357]
　　　Dummy variable equal to one for countries that are predominantly
　　　Islamic or Catholic.

Time Variable (YEAR)
　　　Year of observation of the dependent variable:  for 1960-70
　　　observation YEAR is 0; for 1965-75 observation YEAR is 5; for
　　　1970-80 observation YEAR is 10.

---

Notes:  All monetary variables were calculated using nominal values of a
country's currency.  Consumption ratios were calculated for three
ten-year intervals:  1960-70, 1965-75, and 1970-80.  For each interval,
ratios were calculated using three values:  the endpoints and the
midpoint.  Where all three values were not available, decadal estimates
are the average of available data.  Growth rates were calculated over the
ten-year interval or the longest available subinterval using the
inflation rate over the corresponding interval.

REFERENCES

Adams, N. (1971)  Dependency rates and savings rates:  comment.
    American Economic Review 61:472-475.
Arthur, W.B., and G. McNicoll (1978)  Samuelson, population and
    intergenerational transfers.  International Economic Review
    19(1):241-246.
Barro, R.J. (1974)  Are government bonds net wealth?  Journal of
    Political Economy 6:1095-1117.
Bilsborrow, R.E. (1979)  Age distribution and savings rates in
    less developed countries.  Economic Development and Cultural
    Change 28:23-45.
Bilsborrow, R.E. (1980)  Dependency rates and aggregate savings
    rates revisited:  corrections, further analysis, and
    recommendations for the future.  Pp. 183-204 in J.L. Simon
    and J. DaVanzo, eds., Research in Population Economics, Vol.
    2.  Greenwich, Conn.:  JAI Press.
Christensen, L.R., D.W. Jorgenson, and L.J. Lau (1975)  Trans-
    cendental logarithmic utility functions.  American Economic
    Review 65:367-383.
Coale, A.J., and E.M. Hoover (1958)  Population Growth and
    Economic Development.  Princeton, N.J.:  Princeton
    University Press.
Conroy, M. (1979)  Population growth, life-cycle saving, and
    international differences in steady-state optimal saving
    rates.  Demography 16:425-438.
Eizenga, W. (1961)  Demographic Factors and Savings.  Amsterdam:
    North-Holland Publishing Co.
Espenshade, T.J. (1975)  The impact of children on household
    saving:  age effects versus family size.  Population Studies
    29:123-125.
Fry, M.J. (1979)  The cost of financial repression in Turkey.
    Savings and Development 3:127-135.
Fry, M.J. (1984)  Terms of Trade and National Saving Rates in
    Asia.  Unpublished manuscript, University of California,
    Irvine.
Fry, M., and A. Mason (1982)  The variable rate of growth effect
    in the life-cycle saving model.  Economic Inquiry 20:426-442.
Goldberger, A. (1973)  Dependency rates and savings rates:
    comment.  American Economic Review 63:232-233.
Gupta, K.L. (1971)  Dependency rates and savings rates:  comment.
    American Economic Review 61:496-471.
Gupta, K.L. (1975)  Foreign capital inflows, dependency burden,
    and saving rates in developing countries:  a simultaneous
    equation model.  KYKLOS 28:358-374.
Hammer, J.S. (1984)  Children and Savings in Less Developed
    Countries.  Unpublished manuscript, World Bank, Washington,
    D.C.
Hazeldine, T., and R.S. Moreland (1977)  Population and economic
    growth:  a world cross-section study.  The Review of
    Economics and Statistics LIX:253-263.
International Monetary Fund (IMF) (1981)  Yearbook of Inter-
    national Financial Statistics, 1981.  Washington, D.C.:  IMF.

Kelley, A.C. (1968) Demographic change and economic growth:
  Australia, 1861-1911. Explorations in Entrepeneurial
  History, 2nd Series, 5:207-277.
Kelley, A.C. (1973) Population growth, the dependency rate, and
  the pace of economic development. Population Studies
  27:405-414.
Kelley, A.C. (1976) Savings, demographic change, and economic
  development. Economic Change and Cultural Development
  24:683-693.
Kelley, A.C. (1980) Interactions of economic and demographic
  household behavior. Pp. 403-470 in R.A. Easterlin, ed.,
  Population and Economic Change in Developing Countries.
  Chicago: National Bureau of Economic Research.
Kelley, A.C., and J.G. Williamson (1968) Household saving
  behavior in the developing economics: the Indonesian case.
  Economic Development and Cultural Change 16:385-403.
Kim, K.S. (1974) The Household Saving Behavior in Korea.
  Interim Report 7402, Korea Development Institute, Seoul.
King, M.A., and L.-D. L. Dicks-Mireaux (1982) Asset holdings
  and the life-cycle. The Economic Journal 92:247-267.
Kormendi, R.C. (1983) Government debt, government spending and
  private sector behaviour. American Economic Review
  73:994-1010.
Kotlikoff, L.J., and L.H. Summers (1981) The role of inter-
  generational transfers in aggregate capital accumulation.
  Journal of Political Economy 89:706-732.
Lee, R.D. (1982) Age structure, intergenerational transfers and
  economic growth: an overview. Revue Economique 33:
  1129-1155.
Leff, N.H. (1969) Dependency rates and savings rates. American
  Economic Review LIX:886-895.
Leff, N.H. (1971) Dependency rates and savings rates: reply.
  American Economic Review 61:476-480.
Leff, N.H. (1973) Dependency rates and savings rates: reply.
  American Economic Review 63:234.
Leff, N.H. (1980) Dependency rates and savings rates: a new
  look. Pp. 205-214 in J. Simon, ed., Population Economics,
  Vol. 2. Greenwich, Conn.: JAI Press.
Leff, N.H. (1984) Dependency rates and savings: another look.
  American Economic Review 74:231-233.
Lewis, F.D. (1983) Fertility and savings in the United States:
  1830-1900. Journal of Political Economy 91:825-839.
Mason, A. (1975) An Empirical Analysis of Life-Cycle Saving,
  Income and Household Size. Unpublished Ph.D. dissertation,
  University of Michigan.
Mason, A. (1981) An Extension of the Life-Cycle Model and its
  Application to Population Growth and Aggregate Saving.
  East-West Population Institute Working Papers 4. Honolulu:
  East-West Population Institute.
Mason, A., and D.B. Suits (1981) Computing the level and
  distribution of gains from fertility reduction. Pp. 255-272
  in J. Simon and P. Lindert, eds., Research in Population
  Economics, Vol. 3. Greenwich, Conn.: JAI Press.

Mikesell, R.H., and J.E. Zinser (1973)   The nature of the savings
    function in developing countries:   a survey of the
    theoretical and empirical literature.   Journal of Economic
    Literature 11:1-26.
Modigliani, F. (1957)   Tests of the life cycle hypothesis of
    saving. Bulletin of the Oxford University Institute of
    Statistics 19:99-124.
Modigliani, F. (1965)   The Life Cycle Hypothesis of Savings, the
    Demand for Wealth and the Supply of Capital.   Paper
    presented to the Rome Congress of the Econometric Society,
    Rome.
Modigliani, F. (1966)   The life cycle hypothesis of savings, the
    demand for wealth and the supply of capital. Social Research
    33(2):160-217.
Modigliani, F., and R. Brumberg (1954)   Utility analysis and the
    consumption function:   an interpretation of cross-section
    data.   In K. Kurihara Post-Keynesian Economics.   New
    Brunswick, N.J.:   Princeton University Press.
Modigliani, F., and A. Sterling (1983)   Determinants of private
    saving with special reference to the role of social
    security--cross-country tests.   Pp. 24-55 in F. Modigliani
    and R. Hemming, eds., The Determinants of National Saving
    and Wealth.   New York:   St. Martin's Press.
Modigliani, F., A. Mason, and A. Sterling (1984)   The Effect of
    Fiscal Policy on Saving.   Unpublished manuscript,
    Massachusetts Institute of Technology.
Mueller, E. (1976)   The economic value of children in peasant
    agriculture.   Pp. 99-153 in R. Ridker, ed., Population and
    Development:   The Search for Selective Interventions.
    Baltimore, Md.:   The Johns Hopkins University Press.
Neher, P.A. (1971)   Peasants, procreation, and pensions.
    American Economic Review 61:380-389.
Peek, P. (1974)   Household savings and demographic change in the
    Philippines.   Malayan Economic Review 19:86-104.
Ram, R. (1982)   Dependency rates and aggregate savings:   a new
    international cross-section study.   American Economic Review
    72:537-544.
Ram, R. (1984)   Dependency rates and savings:   reply.   American
    Economic Review 74:234-237.
Simon, J.L. (1975)   The positive effect of population growth on
    agricultural savings in irrigation systems.   The Review of
    Economics and Statistics LVII(1):75-79.
Simon, J.L. (1975-76)   Population growth may be good for LDCs in
    the long run:   a richer simulation model.   Economic
    Development and Cultural Change 24:309-337.
Solow, R.M. (1956)   A contribution to the theory of economic
    growth.   Quarterly Journal of Economics 70:65-94.
Somermeyer, W.H., and R. Bannink (1973)   A Consumption-Savings
    Model and Its Application.   New York:   North Holland/
    American Elsevier.
Tobin, J. (1967)   Life cycle saving and balance economic growth.
    Pp. 231-256 in W. Fellner, ed., Ten Economic Studies in the
    Tradition of Irving Fisher.   New York:   Wiley Press.

United Nations (various years)  Demographic Yearbook.  New York:
    United Nations.
United Nations (1976a)  World Tables, 1976.  New York:  United
    Nations.
United Nations (1976b)  Yearbook of National Income Statistics.
    New York:  United Nations.
United Nations (1981)  Yearbook of National Income Statistics.
    New York:  United Nations.
Willis, R.J. (1983)  Life Cycles, Institutions, and Population
    Growth:  A Theory of the Equilibrium Interest Rate in an
    Overlapping Generations Model.  Liege:  IUSSP.
World Bank (1976)  World Tables, 1976.  Baltimore, Md.:  The
    Johns Hopkins University Press.

# 14

## Trade and Capital Mobility in a World of Diverging Populations

Alan V. Deardorff

INTRODUCTION

Background and Purpose

According to the modern theory of international trade, the basis for much of that trade lies in international differences in relative factor endowments. Such differences certainly exist, most notably between the developed and less developed parts of the world. Moreover, if recent projections of population growth in the two areas are to be believed, it appears that their labor forces, at least, will become even more divergent over the next few decades. Whether this implies greater divergence in relative factor endowments, of course, depends on whether the accumulation of other factors, such as capital, can keep pace with population growth. If not, then we can expect international differences in factor endowments to become progressively more pronounced over the coming years, with consequent implications for the extent of trade and perhaps also for the disruptions that such trade may cause.

The purpose of this chapter is to examine these issues. The approach will be largely theoretical, using simple economic models of growth and trade, though there will also be an effort made to select among alternative theoretical possibilities by quantifying one of the models and using it to simulate some alternative paths that the world economy may follow. It is hoped that this approach will provide at least a framework for thinking about these issues.

The author has benefited from discussions of an outline of this chapter at a meeting of the Working Group on Population Growth and Economic Development of the Committee on Population held at Woods Hole, Massachusetts, August 2-4, 1984. Versions of this chapter have also been presented to seminars at the University of Western Ontario and the University of Michigan. I would like to particularly thank F. Gerard Adams, Geoff Greene, David Lam, Ron Lee, Jim Markusen, T.N. Srinivasan, and Bob Stern for their helpful comments.

Organization of This Chapter

Before examining issues of international trade, it is necessary
first to clarify what is likely to happen to relative factor endowments. For this purpose, the next section draws on a model
of growth with international investment presented elsewhere
(Deardorff, 1985). In this two-country model, population growth
rates differ in the two countries. The possibility of international direct investment provides an opportunity for the more
slowly growing country to escape from the constraint of the law
of diminishing returns by investing abroad. Several possible
outcomes in terms of steady-state growth are described.

     In the next section, an attempt is made to sort out the
several possibilities presented earlier by quantifying the
parameters of a modified version of the growth model. The main
modifications allow for nonidentical technologies and imperfect
capital mobility, both permitting escape from the implausible
condition of international factor price equalization that underlies the simpler model. This section also presents several
simulation results with the modified model, indicating aspects
of possible growth paths for the world economy.

     Both of these growth models are made tractable through the
assumption of one-sector economies. Trade takes place in these
models only in the sense of an exchange of final output for
factor services. However, while not rigorously correct, it is
helpful to interpret the production of the one-sector models as
actually representing an aggregate of the production of a great
many goods of different factor intensities. At each point in
time along the growth path, then, one can examine in static terms
the implications for trade of the factor endowments that have
been derived dynamically from the growth model; this is discussed
in the final section.


Notes on the Literature

Before proceeding, a few notes on the literature are in order.
The topic of this chapter does not seem to have received very
much attention, but there have been a few contributions that
should be mentioned.

     First, Leontief et al. (1977), in a study for the United
Nations, did very detailed projections of world economic performance for the years 1980, 1990, and 2000. For this purpose,
they used an elaborate input-output model, and focused attention
on the feasibility of suggested growth paths in terms of the need
for such things as food, mineral resources, pollution abatement,
and balance-of-payments financing. They took as given not only
the trajectories of population growth, but also several scenarios
for the growth of developed and developing country gross national
product (GNP). The latter, however, were not based on what might
be expected to occur on the basis of likely savings and investment behavior in the two regions considered in the study; instead, these growth rates were based either on target rates of

growth set by the International Development Strategy, or on even
more optimistic criteria of reducing world income inequality.
Thus, the Leontief et al. projections had to do with the feasibility of desired growth, and not with the likelihood of actual
growth, which the present discussion attempts to consider. Nor
can one really say that Leontief et al. focused on the implications of different population growth rates, even though they did
use such different rates to forecast population for their model,
since they were primarily concerned with the difficulties of
accommodating the world's total population rather than its increasingly uneven geographical distribution.

Sapir (1983) has directed attention more specifically to
unequal population growth, and the ways that countries can deal
with large and growing differences in labor abundance. In a
thoughtful, nontechnical discussion, he examines the roles that
trade and international factor movements can play in reconciling
these differences. His most striking point is the difference
between Europe and Japan in the way they have responded to perceived labor shortages:  Europe has made considerable use of
imported labor, brought in under guest worker programs, while
Japan has dealt with similar problems almost exclusively by
exporting capital.

Swamy (1984) also looks at this problem, but focuses on the
relative merits of trade and migration in accommodating uneven
population growth. She observes that current levels of migration are only a small fraction of developing country population
growth, and, noting the cultural factors likely to inhibit the
increase in levels, concludes that migration will not deal
adequately with the problem. Instead, since world trade has
proven itself capable of considerable expansion in recent years,
she favors reliance on trade and therefore reduced protectionism, although it is not clear why she expects even a substantial
amount of trade to be enough to serve the purpose, or why she
neglects international capital movements as an alternative.

A final contribution to be mentioned is a statement by Demeny
(1984). Examining the implications of the United Nations (1982)
population projections, he expresses concern that migration will
not be permitted, while trade and capital flows will not be
adequate, to alleviate the strains that will follow from projected uneven population growth. In the end, the only hope he
offers is that developing country population growth rates may
somehow be reduced.

In the discussion below, these sentiments that migration will
not resolve the problem are implicitly accepted, while the possibility that trade in goods alone will offer anything more than
partial factor price equalization is discounted. Current differences in relative factor endowments between the North and South--
and the differences that will appear in the future unless capital
is very mobile--are simply too large for free trade alone to lead
to nonspecialization. Instead, like Krueger (1977), this discussion takes a model with complete specialization and unequal
factor prices as being most descriptive of relations between the
North and the South unless factors themselves are very mobile.[1]

For this reason, in all but the final section of the chapter, the
focus is on a one-sector model in which the role of trade is
severely limited. What is important instead is first, the ability of different parts of the world to accumulate capital apace
with their population growth, and second, the international
mobility of that capital. Thus the chapter examines various
scenarios in terms of population growth, savings, and--in the
third section--frictions on international investment to determine how the world's economies may evolve over time.

## ALTERNATIVE STEADY STATES WITH DIVERGING POPULATIONS

Two salient features of the world economy today are first, that
population growth has slowed markedly in developed countries
(DCs) as compared to less developed countries (LDCs), and second,
that to a great extent, capital is no longer tied, if it ever
was, to the countries in which the saving that finances it takes
place. That is, partly within the institution of the multi-
national corporation, capital has become more mobile internationally in the last few decades than it was in the earlier
part of this century. To a considerable extent, capital is
being installed in locations where it can take advantage of the
inexpensive LDC labor force that is still expanding rapidly
through population growth.

In combination, these two phenomena of unequal population
growth rates and international direct investment give rise to
some interesting possibilities of steady-state growth that could
not otherwise occur. International two-country growth models,
such as that of Oniki and Uzawa (1965), have typically been built
on the assumption of equal population growth rates. This was
done to prevent one of the countries from becoming infinitely
large relative to the other and thus dominating the model completely. However, Deardorff (1985) shows that, when international investment is permitted in the model, interesting outcomes are possible even with unequal population growth rates, or
what the author calls diverging populations. The reason is that
the country with the more slowly growing population can save and
invest abroad in such quantity that it becomes a nation of
capitalists, with labor income present but of negligible proportion. As a result, this country can achieve growth rates in
excess of its own population growth rate, and may even come to
own, in steady state, a significant share of world capital
although its share of world labor is insignificant.

## Model Description

The model from which these results derive is as follows. Let
there be two countries, indexed i = 1,2, each with a labor force,
$L_i$, and a capital stock owned by its residents, $K_i$. These
factors of production are used to produce a single good, Y, by
means of a neoclassical production function, $Y/L = f(K/L)$, that

is available in both countries. With capital freely mobile between countries, this production function, applied to world
endowments of K and L, determines world output of the good, as
well as competitive factor payments to labor, w, and to capital,
r, that are the same in both countries. Adding the requirement
that world factor endowments be fully employed, these assumptions
lead to the equations given below that describe the static behavior of the model at each point in time.

## Static Equations

$$L = L_1 + L_2 \tag{1}$$

$$K = K_1 + K_2 \tag{2}$$

$$Y/L = f(K/L) \tag{3}$$

$$r = f'(K/L) \tag{4}$$

$$w = f(K/L) - rK/L . \tag{5}$$

With only one good produced anywhere, demand conditions need
not be specified as part of the static model. However, demand
conditions do play a role as residents of the two countries
choose to set aside a portion of what they earn of that good for
future use as capital. This savings behavior can be characterized by a single average propensity to save in each country,
$s_i$, which applies to its residents' gross income from both
labor and capital, the latter including that which may happen to
be installed abroad.[2] Adding proportional rates of population
growth, $n_i$, and depreciation of capital, $\lambda$ , these considerations lead to the following dynamic equations, which complete the
model.

## Dyanmic Equations

$$dL_i/dt = n_i L_i \qquad i = 1,2 \tag{6}$$

$$dK_i/dt = s_i[wL_i + rK_i] - \lambda K_i \qquad i = 1,2 \tag{7}$$

Note that both savings rates and population growth rates are
assumed in general to be different in the two countries. In
particular, it is assumed that

$$n_2 \geq n_1 \quad ,$$

so that Country 1 can be thought of as representing the developed countries--which will be called North--and Country 2
represents the less developed countries--or South.

## Three Cases

The behavior of this model has been analyzed in some detail by
Deardorff (1985).  There it is shown that the long-run behavior
of the model resolves into three cases, depending primarily on
the relative sizes of $s_1$, $s_2$, $n_1$, and $n_2$.  To describe
the dividing lines between the three cases, it is convenient
first to define $k^*$ as the steady-state capital-labor ratio that
would obtain in South if it were closed and were thus to conform
to the standard Solow (1956) one-sector growth model.  Thus $k^*$
is defined implicitly by the following equation:

$$s_2 f(k^*) = (\lambda + n_2)k^* .$$

It is also useful to introduce $r^*$ as the return to capital that
would correspond to this capital-labor ratio,

$$r^* = f'(k^*) .$$

It is clear that $r^*$ incorporates information about both $s_2$
and $n_2$, as well as the technology.  In particular, $r^*$ will be
higher the lower is $s_2$ and the higher is $n_2$.  Also, following the
literature on golden rules of growth, it is reasonable to assume
that savings in South is no greater than the Golden Rule, which
would maximize steady-state per capita consumption, and thus[3]

$$r^* > \lambda + n_2 .$$

The three cases may now be described.  Each constitutes a
steady-state solution in the sense that all variables are either
constant or change at a constant, exponential rate.  These rates
need not be the same, however, which is what makes them
interesting.

Case I:   $s_1 < (\lambda + n_1)/r^*$

In this case, it turns out that North's growth approaches a
steady state of the usual sort.  That is, North's capital grows
in the long run only at the rate $n_1$, approaching a constant
ratio to its own population, $L_1$.  Since both capital and labor
in South are growing at the higher rate, $n_2$, North's share of
world capital, like its share of world labor, goes asymptotically
to zero.  In effect, South behaves as if it were a closed
economy, its transactions with North becoming insignificant.
North, on the other hand, behaves somewhat differently from a
closed economy because of its opportunity to invest abroad.
North's technology is augmented by the ability to borrow and
lend at the rate $r^*$, and this leads in general to a higher level
of per capita income in North than the country would have sustained if it were closed.  Nonetheless, the case is conventional
in the sense that both per capita income and per capita consumption in North are constant in the steady state.

Case II:   $(\lambda + n_1)/r^* \leq s_1 \ (\lambda + n_2)/r^*$

Here it turns out that North's savings are large enough to remain permanently above what would be needed for it to keep up with both depreciation and its own population growth, so that its ownership of capital per person grows at an exponential rate forever. This is possible since, by investing this capital abroad, North avoids the diminishing returns that would otherwise set in if it tried to operate this capital using only its own limited labor force. North's rate of growth of capital becomes, it turns out, $s_1r^* - (\lambda + n_1)$. This rate of growth is above $n_1$, but it is below $n_2$ if $s_1$ is within the bounds stated above. The latter is important, since it means that North's ownership of capital in South remains insignificant from South's point of view, even though that ownership grows exponentially in importance to North. Thus, again South behaves essentially as a closed economy, while North displays the very unconventional result of permanent positive per capita growth. Furthermore, since North's ownership of capital grows exponentially relative to its labor, and since both the wage and the rental are pegged by South, it follows that North's share of income from capital as opposed to labor asymptotically approaches one.[4]

Case III:   $s_1 > (\lambda + n_2)/r^*$

Now North is saving so much that its share of world capital becomes positive and diminishing returns set in after all, South's labor force being the constraining factor. In this case, North and South behave as if they together constitute one of Pasinetti's (1962) two-class economies, North being the capitalist class that, because of its neglible income from labor, appears to derive income only from capital. As Pasinetti showed, the steady-state return to capital is no longer $r^*$, but becomes

$$r^{**} = (\lambda + n_2)/s_1 \ ,$$

which depends on $s_1$ and $n_2$, but not at all on $s_2$. In this steady state, all variables grow at the rate $n_2$, which means again that per capita income and consumption in North are increasing exponentially.


Results

Deardorff (1985) establishes several propositions that indicate how the results in the three cases described above depend on the parameters. These propositions include the following:

- Not only can North, by varying $s_1$, determine which of the above cases it falls into, but within Case II, North can also increase its steady-state rate of growth by increasing $s_1$.

• Steady-state per capita consumption in South is unaffected by $s_1$ in Cases I and II and increases with that savings propensity in Case III.

These results indicate the potentially extreme importance of savings in the North, which may determine not only its own rate of growth, but also the steady-state level of welfare in the South. If Northern savings are high, the model predicts an extreme amount of direct investment from North to South, and this might appear to constitute exploitation; however, according to the second of the above results, this investment is actually to the benefit of South.

Consider now what this model and these results tell us about the issue considered in this chapter: What is likely to be the outcome of differences in population growth rates between the DCs and the LDCs, and what can be done about it? Useful implications are limited, given the extreme assumptions of this simple model and the exclusive focus thus far on very long-run, steady-state outcomes. Still, the model suggests that high rates of population growth in LDCs are hardly harmful to the DCs, at least in their aggregate effects.[5] On the contrary, rapid population growth abroad provides an extraordinary opportunity for capital investment there, and this can make it possible for DCs to sustain positive per capita growth forever. Nor, in economic terms, is this growth gained at the expense of the LDCs, who actually may benefit in terms of their own per capita consumption even when their economies come to be dominated by capitalists from the DCs.

It remains to be seen, of course, which of these three cases is most plausible in terms of empirically relevant savings and other parameters. However, all three cases say something interesting about the ability of international direct investment to deal with unequal population growth rates.


NONSTEADY-STATE GROWTH PATHS

The minimum information needed to identify the three cases described above would be the savings and population growth rates of North and South, plus rates of return and depreciation on capital. However, this information alone would determine only the steady state that would eventually be approached by the model, and would say nothing at all about where the world is now and the path that would be followed to get there. For this, it is necessary to model the nonsteady-state dynamics of growth in the two regions, and this requires somewhat more information.

It will also be easier to use this information if the model itself is modified somewhat. First, it will be easier to use the model computationally if it is specified in discrete rather than continuous time. Second, the assumption that technologies are necessarily the same in North and South will be relaxed, and the assumption of an explicit Cobb-Douglas technology with an efficiency parameter that may differ between the two regions

will be made instead. Finally, the extreme assumption that
capital is perfectly mobile is relaxed as well. Instead, it is
assumed that owners of capital require a premium to invest
abroad, so that they do so only if the return to capital abroad
is, say, $\psi$ percent higher than what they can earn at home.[6]
This assumption means in turn that the model must distinguish
between capital owned by a country, which will now be denoted
$KO_i$, and capital installed in that country, $K_i$. It also
means that the solution to the model can fall into different
regimes, depending on which country is investing in the other
and whether any such international investment is taking place at
all, and the system can switch from one regime to another over
time. This complicates things considerably as compared to the
theoretical model described in the previous section; however,
these complications are easily handled with the computer
simulations that will be used here.


Model Description

The model again includes both static and dynamic equations. The
first four static equations below are essentially analogous to
those of the previous section, but with separate capital-labor
ratios, $k_i$, rentals, $r_i$, and wages, $w_i$, in the two countries as a result of imperfect capital mobility. The net capital position, $N$, is defined in equation (12) as North's ownership of capital in South, if positive, or South's ownership of
capital in North, if negative. This net capital position is
related to capital rentals in the three regimes represented in
equation (13) and is used to determine each country's ownership
of foreign capital in equation (14). The latter is needed in
equation (15) to determine each country's national income, $I_i$,
which includes all income from domestic labor, the income from
that portion of domestically installed capital that is not owned
by foreigners, and the incomes from domestic residents'
ownership of capital abroad.

### Static Equations

$$K_1 + K_2 = KO_1 + KO_2 \tag{8}$$

$$k_i = K_i/L_i \qquad\qquad i = 1,2 \tag{9}$$

$$r_i = \theta A_i k_i^{(\theta - 1)} \qquad\qquad i = 1,2 \tag{10}$$

$$w_i = (1 - \theta)A_i k_i^{(\theta)} \qquad\qquad i = 1,2 \tag{11}$$

$$N = KO_1 - K_1 \tag{12}$$

$$N > 0, \quad r_2 = (1 + \psi)r_1 \tag{13a}$$

or

$$N = 0 \ , \quad r_2/(1 + \psi) < r_1 < (1 + \psi)r_2 \qquad\qquad (13b)$$

or

$$N < 0 \ , \quad r_1 = (1 + \psi)r_2 \qquad\qquad\qquad\qquad (13c)$$

$$N_1 = \max(N,0) \ , \quad N_2 = \max(-N,0) \qquad\qquad (14)$$

$$I_i = w_iL_i + r_i(K_i - N_j) + r_jN_i \quad j \neq i = 1,2 \ . \qquad (15)$$

The dynamic equations of this model are completely analogous to equations (6) and (7), though their appearance is modified somewhat by the use of discrete time.

## Dynamic Equations

$$L_i(t + 1) = (1 + n_i)L_i(t) \qquad\qquad i = 1,2 \qquad (16)$$
$$KO_i(t + 1) = (1 - \lambda)KO_i(t) + s_iI_i(t) \quad i = 1,2 \qquad (17)$$

Parameters and Initial Values

To simulate this model, one must first assign values to its parameters and to the initial stocks of capital and labor. The values indicated in Table 1 have been selected; these values are intended roughly to characterize North as the DCs of the world and South as the LDCs. Sources for these values are also indicated, but a few remarks are in order for some of them.

The efficiency parameter of the North, $A_1$, was calculated so as to make the Cobb–Douglas production function consistent with 1980 U.S. GNP and population, given a capital-output ratio of 1.91 as estimated by Laitner (1984). The parameter $A_1$ was then held constant in all simulations. However, the parameter of South, $A_2$, was varied across simulations in an effort to explore its importance for the results; thus $A_2$ is set equal to various fractions of $A_1$.

For initial values, it was possible to use population data directly, as indicated in the table. For capital stocks, however, direct information was not used. Instead, values were calculated values that, together with the assumed production functions, would be compatible with certain observed characteristics of the world economy. That is, $K_1$ and $K_2$ were calculated to yield a world GNP of \$11,124 billion and a developing country share in that GNP of 21.5 percent.[7] Since this calculation depends on both of the Cobb–Douglas efficiency parameters, and one of these, $A_2$, was set differently in different runs, it follows that the initial capital stock values are also variable across simulations.

Finally, the premium that is required for foreign investment, $\psi$, is also allowed to take on various assumed values in different simulations. Here again, the effect that various degrees of capital mobility would have on the results was of interest, and there was no convincing prior information as to what this parame-

TABLE 1   Values of Parameters and Initial Values Used in Simulations and Their Sources

| Paramenters and Initial Values | Value | Scorce |
|---|---|---|
| **Parameters** | | |
| Constant population growth rates | $n_1 = 0.28\%$<br>$n_2 = 2.57\%$ | Demeny (1984) |
| Savings propensities | $s_1 = 21.1\%$<br>$s_2 = 22.0\%$ | World Bank (1983) |
| Capital depreciation<br>Capital share | $\lambda = 6\%$<br>$\theta = 35\%$ | Laitner (1984), based in turn on national accounts data |
| Cobb-Douglas scale parameters | $A_1 = 5.12$<br>$A_2$ = various assumed values relative to $A_1$ | See text |
| Capital friction parameter | $\psi$ = various assumed values | |
| **Initial Values** | | |
| Labor | $L_1 = 742.4$ million<br>$L_2 = 1877.4$ million | United Nations (1982)<br>Population age 15-64 |
| Capital | $K_1$ = various values<br>$K_2$ = various values | See text |

ter should be.  In the reported simulations, $\psi$ is taken to be either 50 or 5 percent.


Simulations

A number of simulations were run with this model, each using somewhat different values for the parameters A2--the efficiency parameter in South--and $\psi$ --the parameter describing the friction that impedes international capital movement.  Four of these simulations are reported in Tables 2 through 5 and are labeled Simulations 1-4.  In the first three of these simulations, the tables report year-by-year results for the first 10 years, followed by results for less frequent intervals up to year 300. In the fourth simulation, annual results are reported for 45 years, based on variable population growth rates projected by the United Nations (1982).  In all cases, those parameters and initial values that are variable across simulations are reported below each table.

The columns of each table report, first, North's share of the world labor force as it evolves over time because of the different population growth rates, $n_1$ and $n_2$.  This share starts at 28 percent and declines, in the runs with constant population growth rates, to near zero after 200 years.

The world capital labor ratio, reported next, grows substantially over time in all of the runs, indicating that the
world begins well below its steady state. This is also reflected in the behavior of the regional capital labor ratios for
North and South that follow. Interestingly, in Simulations 1-3,
which extend to 300 years, the world capital labor ratio rises
above its long-run value and then falls back down; this is the
result of early growth in North that later becomes insignificant
as the size of South comes to dominate.

After these various capital labor ratios, the tables next
report the net capital position, in two columns. In both cases,
this is the amount of capital owned by North but installed in
South, as a fraction first of world capital and second of capital
owned by North alone. These columns, then, indicate the extent
of international direct investment.

The last three columns in the tables all suggest the relative
economic sizes of the two regions by reporting North's share of
world capital, production, and income. The latter differs from
production since it includes income on capital invested abroad.

## Simulation 1

The first simulation has LDC efficiency only 25 percent of DC
efficiency, while capital requires a 50 percent premium to be
invested abroad. In combination, these two parameters turn out
to prevent any international investment from taking place at
all, as the two "Net Capital" columns indicate. Thus in this
run, the countries follow autarkic growth paths.

As seen in Table 2, in this situation and with the other
assumed parameters, North's share of world capital, and therefore of income, goes ultimately to zero. This is as it should
be, since the two economies are effectively closed and are
therefore constrained in their growth by their respective population growth rates. Furthermore, the steady-state capital-labor
ratio in South is much smaller than that in North, because of
both South's higher population growth rate and its technological
disadvantage.

## Simulation 2

In the second simulation, the capital friction parameter is reduced to 5 percent, while the LDC efficiency parameter remains at
25 percent. As a result of the reduced friction, international
capital movement now does take place. The movement is from North
to South, but only 3 percent of world capital moves, even initially, as a result of the inferior technology that is assumed
for South.

Over the first 15 years of the simulation, capital accumulation in South replaces some of this capital from North, and the
share of world capital that North invests in South declines.
This movement is then reversed for a time, apparently because

TABLE 2  Simulation 1:  Growth with Constant Population Growth Rates, Low LDC Technical Efficiency, and Low Capital Mobility

| Year Simulation | North's Share of Labor | World Capital Labor Ratio | North's Capital Labor Ratio | South's Capital Labor Ratio | Net Capital Position, Share of World Capital | Net Capital Position, Share of North's Capital | North's Share of Capital Owned | North's Share of Production | North's Share of Income |
|---|---|---|---|---|---|---|---|---|---|
| 1 | 0.28 | 3.76 | 10.77 | 0.99 | 0.0 | 0.0 | 0.81 | 0.78 | 0.78 |
| 2 | 0.28 | 4.35 | 12.57 | 1.18 | 0.0 | 0.0 | 0.80 | 0.78 | 0.78 |
| 3 | 0.27 | 4.94 | 14.39 | 1.37 | 0.0 | 0.0 | 0.80 | 0.77 | 0.77 |
| 4 | 0.27 | 5.52 | 16.23 | 1.56 | 0.0 | 0.0 | 0.79 | 0.77 | 0.77 |
| 5 | 0.27 | 6.08 | 18.07 | 1.75 | 0.0 | 0.0 | 0.79 | 0.77 | 0.77 |
| 6 | 0.26 | 6.63 | 19.91 | 1.94 | 0.0 | 0.0 | 0.78 | 0.76 | 0.76 |
| 7 | 0.26 | 7.16 | 21.73 | 2.12 | 0.0 | 0.0 | 0.78 | 0.76 | 0.76 |
| 8 | 0.25 | 7.66 | 23.53 | 2.30 | 0.0 | 0.0 | 0.78 | 0.75 | 0.75 |
| 9 | 0.25 | 8.15 | 25.31 | 2.48 | 0.0 | 0.0 | 0.77 | 0.75 | 0.75 |
| 10 | 0.24 | 8.61 | 27.07 | 2.65 | 0.0 | 0.0 | 0.77 | 0.74 | 0.74 |
| 15 | 0.22 | 10.56 | 35.33 | 3.42 | 0.0 | 0.0 | 0.75 | 0.72 | 0.72 |
| 20 | 0.20 | 11.94 | 42.62 | 4.04 | 0.0 | 0.0 | 0.73 | 0.70 | 0.70 |
| 25 | 0.19 | 12.84 | 48.90 | 4.55 | 0.0 | 0.0 | 0.71 | 0.68 | 0.68 |
| 30 | 0.17 | 13.34 | 54.24 | 4.94 | 0.0 | 0.0 | 0.69 | 0.66 | 0.66 |
| 40 | 0.14 | 13.51 | 62.47 | 5.48 | 0.0 | 0.0 | 0.65 | 0.61 | 0.61 |
| 60 | 0.09 | 12.22 | 71.95 | 5.98 | 0.0 | 0.0 | 0.56 | 0.50 | 0.50 |
| 80 | 0.06 | 10.52 | 76.23 | 6.15 | 0.0 | 0.0 | 0.45 | 0.39 | 0.39 |
| 100 | 0.04 | 9.13 | 78.13 | 6.21 | 0.0 | 0.0 | 0.35 | 0.29 | 0.29 |
| 120 | 0.03 | 8.13 | 78.96 | 6.23 | 0.0 | 0.0 | 0.25 | 0.21 | 0.21 |
| 140 | 0.02 | 7.46 | 79.32 | 6.23 | 0.0 | 0.0 | 0.18 | 0.14 | 0.14 |
| 160 | 0.01 | 7.02 | 79.48 | 6.23 | 0.0 | 0.0 | 0.12 | 0.10 | 0.10 |
| 180 | 0.01 | 6.74 | 79.55 | 6.23 | 0.0 | 0.0 | 0.08 | 0.06 | 0.06 |
| 200 | 0.0 | 6.56 | 79.58 | 6.24 | 0.0 | 0.0 | 0.05 | 0.04 | 0.04 |
| 220 | 0.0 | 6.44 | 79.59 | 6.24 | 0.0 | 0.0 | 0.03 | 0.03 | 0.03 |
| 240 | 0.0 | 6.37 | 79.60 | 6.24 | 0.0 | 0.0 | 0.02 | 0.02 | 0.02 |
| 260 | 0.0 | 6.32 | 79.60 | 6.24 | 0.0 | 0.0 | 0.01 | 0.01 | 0.01 |
| 280 | 0.0 | 6.29 | 79.60 | 6.24 | 0.0 | 0.0 | 0.01 | 0.01 | 0.01 |
| 300 | 0.0 | 6.27 | 79.60 | 6.24 | 0.0 | 0.0 | 0.01 | 0.0 | 0.0 |

Parameters:  $A_2/A_1$ = 0.25; psi = 0.50; $n_1$ = 0.28%; $n_2$ = 2.57%.

573

TABLE 3  Simulation 2:  Growth with Constant Population Growth Rates, Low LDC Technical Efficiency, and High Capital Mobility

| Year Simulation | North's Share of Labor | World Capital Labor Ratio | North's Capital Labor Ratio | South's Capital Labor Ratio | Net Capital Position, Share of World Capital | Net Capital Position, Share of North's Capital | North's Share of Capital Owned | North's Share of Production | North's Share of Income |
|---|---|---|---|---|---|---|---|---|---|
| 1 | 0.28 | 3.76 | 10.38 | 1.14 | 0.03 | 0.04 | 0.81 | 0.77 | 0.78 |
| 2 | 0.28 | 4.35 | 12.16 | 1.34 | 0.03 | 0.03 | 0.80 | 0.77 | 0.78 |
| 3 | 0.27 | 4.94 | 13.96 | 1.53 | 0.02 | 0.03 | 0.80 | 0.77 | 0.77 |
| 4 | 0.27 | 5.52 | 15.77 | 1.73 | 0.02 | 0.03 | 0.79 | 0.76 | 0.77 |
| 5 | 0.26 | 6.09 | 17.58 | 1.93 | 0.02 | 0.03 | 0.78 | 0.76 | 0.77 |
| 6 | 0.26 | 6.63 | 19.38 | 2.13 | 0.02 | 0.03 | 0.78 | 0.75 | 0.76 |
| 7 | 0.25 | 7.16 | 21.16 | 2.33 | 0.02 | 0.03 | 0.78 | 0.75 | 0.76 |
| 8 | 0.25 | 7.67 | 22.92 | 2.52 | 0.02 | 0.03 | 0.78 | 0.75 | 0.75 |
| 9 | 0.25 | 8.15 | 24.64 | 2.71 | 0.02 | 0.03 | 0.77 | 0.74 | 0.75 |
| 10 | 0.24 | 8.61 | 26.33 | 2.89 | 0.02 | 0.03 | 0.77 | 0.74 | 0.74 |
| 15 | 0.22 | 10.57 | 34.18 | 3.76 | 0.02 | 0.03 | 0.75 | 0.71 | 0.72 |
| 20 | 0.20 | 11.96 | 40.92 | 4.50 | 0.03 | 0.04 | 0.73 | 0.69 | 0.70 |
| 25 | 0.19 | 12.86 | 46.52 | 5.11 | 0.04 | 0.05 | 0.71 | 0.67 | 0.68 |
| 30 | 0.17 | 13.36 | 51.07 | 5.61 | 0.04 | 0.06 | 0.69 | 0.64 | 0.66 |
| 40 | 0.14 | 13.53 | 57.52 | 6.32 | 0.05 | 0.08 | 0.65 | 0.59 | 0.61 |
| 60 | 0.09 | 12.26 | 63.19 | 6.95 | 0.07 | 0.13 | 0.56 | 0.47 | 0.50 |
| 80 | 0.06 | 10.57 | 63.91 | 7.03 | 0.08 | 0.17 | 0.45 | 0.37 | 0.39 |
| 100 | 0.04 | 9.18 | 62.83 | 6.91 | 0.07 | 0.20 | 0.35 | 0.27 | 0.29 |
| 120 | 0.03 | 8.18 | 61.34 | 6.74 | 0.06 | 0.23 | 0.26 | 0.19 | 0.21 |
| 140 | 0.02 | 7.50 | 60.00 | 6.60 | 0.05 | 0.26 | 0.18 | 0.13 | 0.15 |
| 160 | 0.01 | 7.05 | 58.96 | 6.48 | 0.03 | 0.28 | 0.12 | 0.09 | 0.10 |
| 180 | 0.01 | 6.76 | 58.21 | 6.40 | 0.02 | 0.29 | 0.08 | 0.06 | 0.07 |
| 200 | 0.0 | 6.57 | 57.70 | 6.34 | 0.02 | 0.30 | 0.05 | 0.04 | 0.04 |
| 220 | 0.0 | 6.45 | 57.35 | 6.31 | 0.01 | 0.30 | 0.04 | 0.02 | 0.03 |
| 240 | 0.0 | 6.37 | 57.13 | 6.28 | 0.01 | 0.31 | 0.02 | 0.02 | 0.02 |
| 260 | 0.0 | 6.32 | 56.98 | 6.26 | 0.0 | 0.31 | 0.01 | 0.01 | 0.01 |
| 280 | 0.0 | 6.29 | 56.88 | 6.25 | 0.0 | 0.31 | 0.01 | 0.01 | 0.01 |
| 300 | 0.0 | 6.27 | 56.82 | 6.25 | 0.0 | 0.31 | 0.01 | 0.0 | 0.0 |

Parameters:  A2/A1 = 0.25; psi = 0.05; n₁ = 0.28%; n₂ = 2.57%.

| Year Simulation | North's Share of Labor | World Capital Labor Ratio | North's Capital Labor Ratio | South's Capital Labor Ratio | Net Capital Position, Share of World Capital | Net Capital Position, Share of North's Capital | North's Share of Capital Owned | North's Share of Production | North's Share of Income |
|---|---|---|---|---|---|---|---|---|---|
| 1 | 0.28 | 3.15 | 6.15 | 1.96 | 0.42 | 0.43 | 0.97 | 0.54 | 0.69 |
| 2 | 0.28 | 3.97 | 7.79 | 2.49 | 0.34 | 0.39 | 0.89 | 0.54 | 0.66 |
| 3 | 0.27 | 4.81 | 9.50 | 3.03 | 0.29 | 0.35 | 0.83 | 0.53 | 0.63 |
| 4 | 0.27 | 5.66 | 11.24 | 3.59 | 0.25 | 0.32 | 0.79 | 0.52 | 0.61 |
| 5 | 0.27 | 6.51 | 13.02 | 4.16 | 0.22 | 0.29 | 0.75 | 0.52 | 0.60 |
| 6 | 0.26 | 7.35 | 14.80 | 4.72 | 0.20 | 0.27 | 0.72 | 0.51 | 0.58 |
| 7 | 0.26 | 8.19 | 16.57 | 5.29 | 0.18 | 0.25 | 0.70 | 0.51 | 0.57 |
| 8 | 0.25 | 9.00 | 18.33 | 5.85 | 0.16 | 0.24 | 0.67 | 0.50 | 0.56 |
| 9 | 0.25 | 9.80 | 20.07 | 6.41 | 0.15 | 0.22 | 0.66 | 0.50 | 0.55 |
| 10 | 0.24 | 10.58 | 21.79 | 6.96 | 0.14 | 0.21 | 0.64 | 0.49 | 0.54 |
| 15 | 0.22 | 14.04 | 29.78 | 9.51 | 0.10 | 0.17 | 0.57 | 0.46 | 0.50 |
| 20 | 0.20 | 16.80 | 36.61 | 11.69 | 0.08 | 0.16 | 0.53 | 0.43 | 0.46 |
| 25 | 0.19 | 18.87 | 42.25 | 13.49 | 0.07 | 0.15 | 0.49 | 0.41 | 0.43 |
| 30 | 0.17 | 20.36 | 46.77 | 14.94 | 0.07 | 0.15 | 0.46 | 0.38 | 0.40 |
| 40 | 0.14 | 22.03 | 53.05 | 16.94 | 0.07 | 0.16 | 0.40 | 0.33 | 0.35 |
| 60 | 0.09 | 22.44 | 58.49 | 18.68 | 0.06 | 0.20 | 0.31 | 0.24 | 0.26 |
| 80 | 0.06 | 21.53 | 59.51 | 19.01 | 0.05 | 0.23 | 0.22 | 0.17 | 0.18 |
| 100 | 0.04 | 20.52 | 59.15 | 18.89 | 0.04 | 0.26 | 0.16 | 0.11 | 0.13 |
| 120 | 0.03 | 19.73 | 58.51 | 18.69 | 0.03 | 0.28 | 0.11 | 0.07 | 0.08 |
| 140 | 0.02 | 19.17 | 57.95 | 18.51 | 0.02 | 0.29 | 0.07 | 0.05 | 0.06 |
| 160 | 0.01 | 18.80 | 57.54 | 18.38 | 0.01 | 0.30 | 0.05 | 0.03 | 0.04 |
| 180 | 0.01 | 18.55 | 57.25 | 18.28 | 0.01 | 0.30 | 0.03 | 0.02 | 0.02 |
| 200 | 0.0 | 18.39 | 57.06 | 18.22 | 0.01 | 0.31 | 0.02 | 0.01 | 0.02 |
| 220 | 0.0 | 18.29 | 56.94 | 18.18 | 0.0 | 0.31 | 0.01 | 0.01 | 0.01 |
| 240 | 0.0 | 18.23 | 56.86 | 18.16 | 0.0 | 0.31 | 0.01 | 0.01 | 0.01 |
| 260 | 0.0 | 18.19 | 56.81 | 18.14 | 0.0 | 0.31 | 0.01 | 0.0 | 0.0 |
| 280 | 0.0 | 18.16 | 56.77 | 18.13 | 0.0 | 0.31 | 0.0 | 0.0 | 0.0 |
| 300 | 0.0 | 18.14 | 56.75 | 18.12 | 0.0 | 0.31 | 0.0 | 0.0 | 0.0 |

Parameters: A2/A1 = 0.50; psi = 0.05; $n_1$ = 0.28%; $n_2$ = 2.57%.

TABLE 5  Simulation 4:  Growth with Variable Population Growth Rates, Low LDC Technical Efficiency, and High Capital Mobility

| Year of Simulation | n1 (%) | n2 (%) | North's Share of Labor | World Capital Labor Ratio | North's Capital Labor Ratio | South's Capital Labor Ratio | Net Capital Position, Share of World Capital | Net Capital Position, Share of North's Capital | North's Share of Capital Owned | North's Share of Production | North's Share of Income |
|---|---|---|---|---|---|---|---|---|---|---|---|
| 1980 | 0.96 | 2.68 | 0.28 | 3.76 | 10.38 | 1.14 | 0.03 | 0.04 | 0.81 | 0.77 | 0.78 |
| 1981 | 0.96 | 2.68 | 0.28 | 4.34 | 12.09 | 1.33 | 0.03 | 0.03 | 0.80 | 0.77 | 0.78 |
| 1982 | 0.96 | 2.68 | 0.28 | 4.92 | 13.82 | 1.52 | 0.02 | 0.03 | 0.80 | 0.77 | 0.78 |
| 1983 | 0.96 | 2.68 | 0.27 | 5.49 | 15.55 | 1.71 | 0.02 | 0.03 | 0.79 | 0.77 | 0.77 |
| 1984 | 0.96 | 2.68 | 0.27 | 6.04 | 17.26 | 1.90 | 0.02 | 0.02 | 0.79 | 0.76 | 0.77 |
| 1985 | 0.57 | 2.53 | 0.27 | 6.58 | 18.96 | 2.08 | 0.02 | 0.02 | 0.78 | 0.76 | 0.77 |
| 1986 | 0.57 | 2.53 | 0.26 | 7.12 | 20.70 | 2.28 | 0.02 | 0.02 | 0.78 | 0.76 | 0.76 |
| 1987 | 0.57 | 2.53 | 0.26 | 7.63 | 22.42 | 2.46 | 0.02 | 0.02 | 0.78 | 0.75 | 0.76 |
| 1988 | 0.57 | 2.53 | 0.26 | 8.13 | 24.10 | 2.65 | 0.02 | 0.02 | 0.77 | 0.75 | 0.75 |
| 1989 | 0.57 | 2.53 | 0.25 | 8.60 | 25.75 | 2.83 | 0.02 | 0.02 | 0.77 | 0.74 | 0.75 |
| 1990 | 0.38 | 2.18 | 0.25 | 9.05 | 27.36 | 3.01 | 0.02 | 0.02 | 0.77 | 0.74 | 0.75 |
| 1991 | 0.38 | 2.18 | 0.24 | 9.51 | 29.00 | 3.19 | 0.02 | 0.02 | 0.76 | 0.74 | 0.74 |
| 1992 | 0.38 | 2.18 | 0.24 | 9.94 | 30.60 | 3.36 | 0.02 | 0.02 | 0.76 | 0.73 | 0.74 |
| 1993 | 0.38 | 2.18 | 0.24 | 10.36 | 32.16 | 3.54 | 0.02 | 0.02 | 0.76 | 0.73 | 0.74 |
| 1994 | 0.38 | 2.18 | 0.24 | 10.75 | 33.67 | 3.70 | 0.02 | 0.02 | 0.75 | 0.73 | 0.73 |
| 1995 | 0.49 | 2.09 | 0.23 | 11.12 | 35.14 | 3.86 | 0.02 | 0.02 | 0.75 | 0.72 | 0.73 |
| 1996 | 0.49 | 2.09 | 0.23 | 11.47 | 36.55 | 4.02 | 0.02 | 0.02 | 0.75 | 0.72 | 0.73 |
| 1997 | 0.49 | 2.09 | 0.23 | 11.80 | 37.91 | 4.17 | 0.02 | 0.02 | 0.74 | 0.72 | 0.72 |
| 1998 | 0.49 | 2.09 | 0.22 | 12.12 | 39.22 | 4.31 | 0.02 | 0.02 | 0.74 | 0.71 | 0.72 |
| 1999 | 0.49 | 2.09 | 0.22 | 12.41 | 40.50 | 4.45 | 0.02 | 0.02 | 0.74 | 0.71 | 0.72 |
| 2000 | 0.38 | 1.96 | 0.22 | 12.69 | 41.72 | 4.59 | 0.02 | 0.02 | 0.74 | 0.71 | 0.71 |
| 2001 | 0.38 | 1.96 | 0.22 | 12.96 | 42.96 | 4.72 | 0.02 | 0.03 | 0.73 | 0.70 | 0.71 |
| 2002 | 0.38 | 1.96 | 0.21 | 13.22 | 44.15 | 4.85 | 0.02 | 0.03 | 0.73 | 0.70 | 0.71 |
| 2003 | 0.38 | 1.96 | 0.21 | 13.46 | 45.30 | 4.98 | 0.02 | 0.03 | 0.73 | 0.70 | 0.70 |
| 2004 | 0.38 | 1.96 | 0.21 | 13.68 | 46.41 | 5.10 | 0.02 | 0.03 | 0.72 | 0.69 | 0.70 |
| 2005 | 0.38 | 1.96 | 0.21 | 13.89 | 47.47 | 5.22 | 0.02 | 0.03 | 0.72 | 0.69 | 0.70 |

| Year | | | | | | | | | | | |
|------|------|------|------|-------|-------|------|------|------|------|------|------|
| 2006 | 0.38 | 1.96 | 0.20 | 14.08 | 48.50 | 5.33 | 0.02 | 0.03 | 0.72 | 0.69 | 0.70 |
| 2007 | 0.38 | 1.96 | 0.20 | 14.25 | 49.49 | 5.44 | 0.02 | 0.03 | 0.72 | 0.68 | 0.69 |
| 2008 | 0.38 | 1.96 | 0.20 | 14.41 | 50.44 | 5.55 | 0.02 | 0.03 | 0.71 | 0.68 | 0.69 |
| 2009 | 0.05 | 1.96 | 0.20 | 14.56 | 51.35 | 5.65 | 0.02 | 0.03 | 0.71 | 0.68 | 0.69 |
| 2010 | 0.05 | 1.56 | 0.19 | 14.70 | 52.23 | 5.74 | 0.02 | 0.03 | 0.70 | 0.67 | 0.68 |
| 2011 | 0.05 | 1.56 | 0.19 | 14.88 | 53.25 | 5.85 | 0.02 | 0.03 | 0.70 | 0.67 | 0.68 |
| 2012 | 0.05 | 1.56 | 0.19 | 15.04 | 54.24 | 5.96 | 0.02 | 0.03 | 0.70 | 0.66 | 0.68 |
| 2013 | 0.05 | 1.56 | 0.19 | 15.19 | 55.19 | 6.07 | 0.02 | 0.04 | 0.70 | 0.66 | 0.67 |
| 2014 | 0.05 | 1.56 | 0.18 | 15.33 | 56.11 | 6.17 | 0.02 | 0.04 | 0.69 | 0.66 | 0.67 |
| 2015 | 0.05 | 1.56 | 0.18 | 15.46 | 56.99 | 6.27 | 0.03 | 0.04 | 0.69 | 0.65 | 0.66 |
| 2016 | 0.05 | 1.56 | 0.18 | 15.58 | 57.84 | 6.36 | 0.03 | 0.04 | 0.69 | 0.65 | 0.66 |
| 2017 | 0.05 | 1.56 | 0.18 | 15.68 | 58.65 | 6.45 | 0.03 | 0.04 | 0.68 | 0.65 | 0.66 |
| 2018 | 0.05 | 1.56 | 0.17 | 15.78 | 59.44 | 6.53 | 0.03 | 0.04 | 0.68 | 0.64 | 0.65 |
| 2019 | 0.05 | 1.56 | 0.17 | 15.86 | 60.19 | 6.62 | 0.03 | 0.04 | 0.68 | 0.64 | 0.65 |
| 2020 | -0.09 | 1.19 | 0.17 | 15.94 | 60.91 | 6.70 | 0.03 | 0.04 | 0.68 | 0.64 | 0.65 |
| 2021 | -0.09 | 1.19 | 0.17 | 16.05 | 61.73 | 6.79 | 0.03 | 0.04 | 0.68 | 0.64 | 0.65 |
| 2022 | -0.09 | 1.19 | 0.17 | 16.16 | 62.53 | 6.87 | 0.03 | 0.04 | 0.67 | 0.63 | 0.64 |
| 2023 | -0.09 | 1.19 | 0.17 | 16.26 | 63.29 | 6.96 | 0.03 | 0.04 | 0.67 | 0.63 | 0.64 |
| 2024 | -0.09 | 1.19 | 0.16 | 16.35 | 64.03 | 7.04 | 0.03 | 0.04 | 0.67 | 0.63 | 0.64 |

Parameters:  A2/A1 = 0.25; psi = 0.05.

577

population growth in South catches up and creates new opportunities for capital. Eventually, however, North's savings are inadequate to sustain an increased share, and that share falls again toward zero. Ultimately, in the very long run, North's ownership of world capital, both domestically and world wide, again declines toward zero just as it did without capital flows in the first simulation. In fact, since even the share of North's own capital that it invests in South stabilizes at about 31 percent, it is clear that North fails to achieve sustained per capita growth. Instead, in spite of the capital flows, North's steady state is like Case I of the previous section.

Comparing Simulations 1 and 2, the opportunity for capital to flow has not had much effect on South, except to increase somewhat its installed capital-labor ratio in the early years while the capital flows themselves remain marginally significant. In North, however, the opportunity to invest in South permits a reduction in its installed capital-labor ratio that lasts forever and becomes considerable after half a century or so. This in turn means that the return to capital is increased permanently, and the wage reduced, as a result of North's opportunity to invest abroad.


Simulation 3

In the third simulation, the efficiency of the LDC technology is raised to 50 percent of that in the DCs, while the capital friction parameter is held at 5 percent as it was in Simulation 2. To account for the LDC's very small share of world income requires a substantial reduction in the amount of capital that is ascribed to them. Thus, virtually all of the capital is initially owned by the North. On the other hand, over 40 percent of it is initially invested in the South, and international investment is now initially very important.

Over time, however, this share again declines to zero as North's share of world capital again becomes insignificant. Once again, North's savings propensity is insufficient to pull it out of Case I of the previous section. Even though sustained per capita growth would have been possible for North had it been able to save at a greater rate, it fails to do so.

Of the three simulations reported so far, Simulation 2 appears to have most merit. This is partly because both the extent of initial international investment and the rates of growth of capital in Simulation 3 seem excessive. In addition, as alluded to earlier, there was some difficulty involved in selecting initial values for capital stocks in this case. It is difficult to explain South's small share of world income, given its large share of the world labor force, unless its technology for using that labor is decidedly inferior to that in North.[8] Simulation 3 should, therefore, be regarded as being primarily for illustrative purposes.

Simulation 4

In the fourth and final simulation, all of the parameter settings
of Simulation 2 are retained, but the assumption that population
growth in the North and South proceeds at constant rates has been
dropped.    Instead, these rates have been allowed to vary from
year to year as projected by the United Nations (1982).    The
assumed values for the two population growth rates over time are
reported in the second and third columns of Table 5.    They were
inferred from the U.N. projections of population at five- and
ten-year intervals, and thus vary discretely at these intervals.
The years of the simulation are now listed as 1980 through 2024,
since these are the years for which these projections were made.

The first thing to note here is the substantial drop in
North's share of world labor, which falls from 28 percent in 1980
to 16 percent in 2024.    This projection is of course the main
reason for the present chapter, and while in 45 years North's
share does not fall anywhere near to the zero that it ultimately
approaches in the other simulations, this is still a sizable
decline.

It is clear in this simulation that North dominates the
situation in the early years.    It owns most of the world's
capital and therefore, with its superior technology, derives
over three-quarters of world income even though it has less than
one-third of world population.    In this simulation, only a small
portion of North's capital is invested abroad, largely because
of the inferior technology that is assumed to be available in
South.

North's dominance changes over time, however.    Even though
South's savings rate is only a shade larger than North's, applied
to its substantial and growing income from both labor and
capital, this is enough for it to gain on North as an owner of
capital.    North's share of world capital drops from 81 percent
initially to only 67 percent by the end of the simulation in
2024.    At the same time, capital labor ratios rise in both North
and South, but because of the assumed capital mobility, they
remain fixed relative to one another.

As this growth in capital occurs, the portion of it that
moves internationally remains remarkably stable, fluctuating
around 2 or 3 percent.    It appears that, over this limited time
horizon, the displacement of North's capital by new saving in
South is just about offset by population growth there.


Results

In all of the simulations described above, the picture that
emerges is one in which North becomes of diminishing importance
relative to South over the years, as South accumulates its own
capital to serve its rapidly growing labor force.    The possibility noted in the previous section that North might save
enough to continue to dominate the ownership of world capital
does not, in fact, seem to occur, which is not surprising given

the nearly equal savings propensities that were found in the
data.

It is not even the case, apparently, that North takes much
advantage of the vast availability of labor in South. North's
saving, it seems, is sufficient to maintain in steady state a
capital stock that is somewhat larger than it needs to service
its own labor force. However, that saving is not large enough
to provide the ever-growing stock of capital per man that could
have been the basis for sustained per capita growth.


IMPLICATIONS FOR INTERNATIONAL TRADE IN GOODS

As already noted, the theoretical model and the simulation model
of the previous two sections both assume the production of only
a single good. This facilitates the analysis, but makes it
impossible to say anything interesting directly about the pattern
of trade. Still, these models will be used here as the basis for
such a discussion, assuming now, in a very nonrigorous way, that
the single good has actually been some sort of composite of the
many goods that may be produced and traded in the real world.[9]
The analysis here, then, will use what was learned from the
growth models to indicate what may happen over time to factor
endowments, and use these results in turn in the context of a
static Heckscher-Ohlin (H-O) framework to examine what would
happen to trade.

The H-O model to be used for this purpose is the two-factor,
many-good model with internationally unequal factor prices that
has been examined before by Krueger (1977) and Deardorff (1979).
In this model, while technology is such as to lead to factor
price equalization if there is free trade and if factor endowments are sufficiently similar, it is assumed instead that
factor endowments are too far apart for this to happen, even
with limited capital mobility. Given the divergent growth paths
that have been found in earlier sections, this seems an appropriate assumption here.

The H-O model does not normally assume international factor
mobility, of course; however, the model is consistent with some
movement of capital so long as this can be taken as given and
the resulting stocks of capital, once relocated, treated as
factor endowments. Thus, the capital stocks installed in North
and South, derived from the above growth models, will be used as
the capital endowments that provide the basis for an H-O discussion of trade.

In the Krueger-Deardorff version of the H-O model, goods may
be arranged in order of their capital intensities. Then, depending on the relative sizes of the two trading countries, this
chain of goods is broken at some point, with the more capital-
abundant country producing only those goods that lie above this
point in terms of capital intensity, and the more labor-abundant
country producing only those goods below. With this pattern of
complete specialization, each country must import those goods it
does not itself produce; thus each exports some of each good

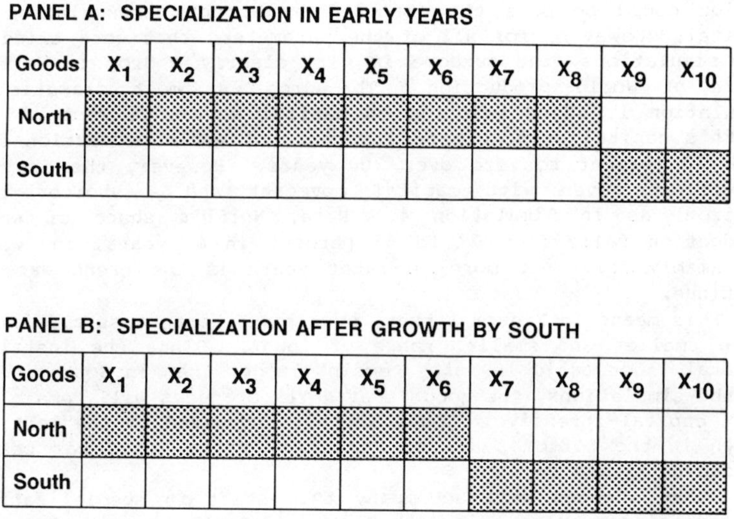

## PANEL A:  SPECIALIZATION IN EARLY YEARS

| Goods | $X_1$ | $X_2$ | $X_3$ | $X_4$ | $X_5$ | $X_6$ | $X_7$ | $X_8$ | $X_9$ | $X_{10}$ |
|-------|-------|-------|-------|-------|-------|-------|-------|-------|-------|----------|
| North | ▓ | ▓ | ▓ | ▓ | ▓ | ▓ | ▓ | ▓ | | |
| South | | | | | | | | | ▓ | ▓ |

## PANEL B:  SPECIALIZATION AFTER GROWTH BY SOUTH

| Goods | $X_1$ | $X_2$ | $X_3$ | $X_4$ | $X_5$ | $X_6$ | $X_7$ | $X_8$ | $X_9$ | $X_{10}$ |
|-------|-------|-------|-------|-------|-------|-------|-------|-------|-------|----------|
| North | ▓ | ▓ | ▓ | ▓ | ▓ | ▓ | | | | |
| South | | | | | | | ▓ | ▓ | ▓ | ▓ |

FIGURE 1  Alternative Patterns of Specialization for Goods $X_1$-$X_{10}$

that it does produce to the other, except perhaps for at most one good that the two may produce in common.

Such a pattern is shown in the top panel of Figure 1. Goods are arranged from $X_1$ to $X_{10}$ so that $X_1$ is the most capital-intensive and $X_{10}$ the least. The break point in the specialization pattern here is between goods 8 and 9, so that North, with more capital, produces and exports goods 1-8, while South produces and exports goods 9-10. This break point was determined primarily by total capacity to produce. With complete specialization, each country must make enough of each of the goods it produces to satisfy all of world demand. Thus, the range of goods that it produces is limited by its factor endowments, including any imported factors, and the level of world demand for the goods to which its factor endowments are appropriate. In the top panel of Figure 1, for example, if the demand for the less capital-intensive goods were greater and the demand for the more capital-intensive goods less, North would be able to satisfy world demand for even more goods, $X_1$-$X_9$, say, and the break point would move to the right. On the other hand, if South were to grow in its factor endowments relative to North, thus becoming able to satisfy world demand for more goods itself, then the break point would move to the left.

This is precisely what the simulations of the previous section suggest as the likely outcome of population growth in South. In all of the simulations, North's share of world production falls over the years. This did not logically have to be the case, since it is conceivable that South's growth of popu-

lation could be more than matched by North's accumulation of
capital. However, for all of the parameters that were tried in
the simulations, the outcome is very clearly a drop in North's
share of world production. The drop was most dramatic in
Simulation 1, where friction on capital movements kept all of
North's capital at home, and its share of world production fell
from 78 percent to zero over 300 years. However, the drop is
significant even with capital movement and a shorter time
horizon, as in Simulation 4. Here, North's share of world
production falls from 77 to 63 percent in 45 years, and would
presumably fall much more in later years if the trend were to
continue.

This means in Figure 1 that, over time, North must specialize
in a smaller and smaller range of goods. Since the installed
capital labor ratio in North remains larger than in South in all
of the simulations, the goods that North produces will remain the
most capital-intensive. Thus, North is squeezed to the left, as
shown in the bottom panel of Figure 1, where North has ceased
producing $X_7$ and $X_8$.

Other changes will accompany this shift in specialization.
As capital accumulates in both North and South, wages everywhere
will rise and the return to capital will fall. This in turn will
lower the relative prices of capital-intensive goods and thus
worsen the terms of trade of North, which exports such goods.
Counteracting this, however, will be South's accumulation of
factors generally, which, if there were no rise in capital labor
ratios, would require a fall in the prices of South's products
relative to North's. Thus the net effect on the terms of trade
is unclear.

What is clear is that North's structure of production will
change. As the range of goods in which North can remain competitive is reduced, whole industries will have to shut down,
such as $X_7$ and $X_8$ in Figure 1, and the factors of production
that were employed there will have to be relocated. There will
be no shortage of demand for the services of these factors, since
it is growth in the South and the consequent rise in demand for
all goods, including the most capital-intensive, that are giving
rise to this adjustment. However, the familiar difficulties of
accomplishing such an adjustment in the real world are bound to
arise. Adjustment is needed in South, too, of course, but since
the range of industries expands there and since factor endowments
are growing, South's adjustment problems seem likely to be less
severe.[10]

What is the extent of the adjustment that will be needed?
Using Simulation 4 as a very rough guide, North's share of world
production falls from 77 percent in 1980 to 71 percent in 2000.
This means industries that currently provide for 6 percent of
world production and that are located in the developed countries
of North will, if forces of competition are allowed to govern,
go out of existence by the year 2000 and be replaced by production in the LDCs. This would appear to be a substantial burden
of adjustment. It is true, of course, that this adjustment takes
place in the context of a growing economy, even in North, and

this must ease the burden somewhat. However, the need for a
number of industries to disappear from North entirely is bound
to pose severe problems in some Northern regions.


## Nontraded Goods

So far, it has been assumed that all goods are traded, and this
could have been important for some of the results. It is worth
considering for a moment what would happen in this scheme of
things if there were also a substantial sector of both North and
South producing nontraded goods. These would have to be produced, regardless of their capital intensities, within each
country, and prices of factors and goods would have to accommodate this fact.

The main effect of this modification is easily derived.
Suppose that nontraded goods comprise, say, 50 percent of world
demand. Then each country must devote a portion of its resources
to producing nontraded goods in a value equal to 50 percent of
its income. Suppose that as a result of investment abroad, a
country's income from domestic factors were ever to fall below 50
percent of its total income. Then all of its domestic factors
would be needed to produce the required nontraded goods, and
nothing would be left for producing traded goods. The country
would then cease exporting any goods at all and would import all
traded goods from abroad, paying for these with its income from
foreign investment. This is an extreme result, but one that
would have to happen eventually in both Cases II and III in the
second section above, since there we found that income from
foreign investment grows asymptotically to constitute eventually
100 percent of North's income. Incidentally, once exports of
traded goods cease and growth of income continues in these cases,
the prices of domestic factors and of nontraded goods will begin
to increase as needed to induce enough capital to remain at home
and provide the needed quantities of the nontraded goods.

In the simulations, nothing this extreme occurs. Judging
from a comparison of the production and income shares that are
reported, North's production never falls enough short of its
income so that a substantial reduction in exports is required to
free resources for the production of nontraded goods. Indeed,
North's production as a share of income (compare the last two
columns of the tables) is at its smallest in the first year of
Simulation 3, and even then is over 78 percent. The ratio then
rises quickly and approaches 100 percent in the long run. Thus,
while it is true that some resources in North will have to be
employed in nontraded sectors, thus reducing somewhat the range
of traded goods that can be produced, it does not appear that
this consideration substantially alters the conclusions above.

Other Extensions of the Model

There are quite a number of other ways that one might wish to
modify or extend the models considered in this chapter. While
there is not space enough to pursue any of these in detail, some
deserve to be mentioned since they may serve as the basis for
further research.

## Endogenous Population Growth

The extension most often mentioned in discussions of this topic
is to endogenize the rates of population growth. Aside from what
was done in Simulation 4, where population growth rates were
variable though still exogenous, it has not been possible to
follow up on this suggestion for the present analysis. Much
would certainly depend on the particular function used to determine population growth, and there does not seem to be a consensus
as to what variables should be included in such a function, nor
even on what the direction of the relationship with particular
variables should be. However, it is possible to speculate on the
implications of two different lines of analysis that might be
followed.

On the one hand, if population growth were determined by
similar functional relationships in both North and South, but the
function for South were simply shifted upward as compared to that
of North, then the results described in this chapter should be
essentially unchanged. In particular, it would remain true that
South would tend to accumulate the bulk of world labor, and
eventually the bulk of world capital and production as well,
even though the time paths followed by the two parts of the
world would be different.

On the other hand, suppose that population growth is determined by the same relationship in both North and South, and that
the higher observed rates of growth in South are merely the result of different values for the variables that determine population growth. If the latter include economic variables, such
as income, that will change in the course of growth, then differences in population growth rates might disappear over time.
This could invalidate the analysis, though in view of the
already substantial lead that South has over North in terms of
population, it would be surprising if North were nevertheless
not to decline considerably in relative economic size over time
as South proceeded to accumulate capital as well as labor.

## Endogenous Savings Rates

The simple constant proportional savings propensities assumed in
this chapter could perhaps be improved on. Deardorff (1985)
describes ways in which the theoretical model presented above is
altered by allowing savings to depend on the interest rate, and
also by allowing savings to be the result of dynamic optimization

subject to a rate of time preference that may differ across
countries. In both cases, it appears that much of the behavior
of the model remains qualitatively the same, though in the optimizing model, it turns out to be difficult to get the two
countries to share ownership of the world capital stock in steady
state. It is not clear that these alternative assumptions lead
to improved descriptions of the world.

## Resource Constraints

A study of long-run growth that does not recognize constraints
on the availability of certain natural resources may seem of
little use. Indeed, if it is true that resources will pose
effective constraints on growth in the long run, then the problems discussed here that arise from differences in population
growth rates will fade into irrelevance. However, if the main
effects of limits on some resources will involve changes in
relative prices and substitution toward alterative resources
that are not so limited, then the analysis of this chapter still
has something useful to say. Naturally, one could learn more
from a model that included more, and an enhanced model that
could capture this process of substitution and its interactions
with growth would be of interest. However, the main conclusions
of this chapter should not be undermined.

## Technical Change

It appears that a good deal of economic progress is accounted
for more by technical change than by capital accumulation.
Furthermore, international capital movements seem to provide the
means for the diffusion of technical change around the world.
The models here have not explicitly captured either technical
progress or its transmission abroad. On the other hand, much of
technical progress is the deliberate result of investment in
research and development, and thus bears a closer relationship
to the processes included in the models here than might first
appear to be the case. Again, while it would certainly be
preferable to model these processes explicitly, the results of
doing so would not necessarily be significantly different.

## More Goods, More Countries

Finally, some have suggested that the models used here,
especially the simulation model, should include more goods to
allow explicitly for trade. To that might be added the even
greater need to allow for more countries, to account for the
considerable differences that exist among countries within the
developed and developing parts of the world as regards population
growth and savings rates. These would be important extensions,
but they would turn the model from a theoretical one with a

numerical application into a massive empirical simulation
exercise. This would be a worthwhile undertaking, but far beyond
what can be attempted here.


CONCLUSION

The question addressed in this chapter has concerned the implications of projected differences in population growth rates between
the developed North and the less developed South. These differences must inevitably cause problems for the relations between
the two parts of the world. Either their economies will be
forced to adjust to these differences in one way or another, or
their governments will be forced to erect higher and higher
barriers to prevent that adjustment. Adjustment could come
about through international migration, but sufficient adjustment
through that means seems unlikely given existing attitudes and
policies. Failing that, adjustment must come about through
international capital movement and through trade. It is these
latter two mechanisms that have been examined in this chapter.

Based on the models treated here, international investment
can be seen as a potentially important source of capital for the
less developed world over the next several decades. However,
saving in the developed world is not enough to enable it to provide significant capital forever; rather, North could be expected
to dwindle in importance over the longer run if Southern population growth continued to exceed that in North indefinitely. Even
in the nearer term, in fact, the most plausible simulations do
not show direct investment from North to be terribly great.

With or without much international direct investment, the
less developed world will never catch up to North in terms of
its available capital per man. As a result, international trade,
if it continues to be permitted, will continue to favor North's
exporting capital-intensive goods to South in exchange for labor-
intensive goods. Furthermore, as both labor and capital endowments grow in South relative to North, the range of goods that
South will provide will expand, requiring that the least capital-
intensive of those industries still in North be displaced. Thus
it should be anticipated that the list of industries that are
located in developed countries will become gradually shorter over
the years as more and more production moves to ever-growing
South.

These adjustments may be resisted in North, where workers
and owners of capital in the threatened industries will naturally
find it preferable to lobby for protection, rather than move into
those industries that still remain viable. The point is, however, that the forces that create the need for this adjustment
arise not from a once-and-for-all change, but from the ever-
growing share of population in South. Therefore, efforts to
resist adjustment, if they are to succeed, will also have to become stronger and stronger over the years.

NOTES

1  Although the models of this chapter use the terms North and
   South as convenient names for the developed and developing
   parts of the world, respectively, they should not be con-
   fused with what has come to be called the North-South Model
   of development associated with Findlay (1980).
2  This particular savings assumption can be modified in
   various ways without changing the qualitative nature of the
   results.  For example, the savings propensity could be
   applied to income net of depreciation of capital, or savings
   could be made dependent on source of income and the interest
   rate.
3  This is not necessary for the model to work, but without it,
   Case III below could not arise.
4  Note that labor supply is pegged exogenously to population
   here.  If it were not, and if workers in North shared evenly
   in the ownership of capital, then wealth effects could
   presumably drive the labor supply, and thus labor income, to
   zero.
5  The final section of this chapter will look at the dislocations among sectors in North that these growth paths may
   entail.
6  The need for this premium could reflect risk aversion, together with a perceived uncertainty associated with operating in a foreign country, though, of course, such
   uncertainty is not a part of the model.
7  These calculations were done assuming no international movement of capital between North and South.  Thus, South's
   initial share in world income will differ from this percentage in the simulations to the extent that capital is found
   to move significantly between the regions.  An alternative
   calculation taking capital movement into account was
   attempted, but turned out to be inconsistent with this
   percentage for some values of the assumed parameters.
8  See Footnote 7.  The attempt to allow for capital movements
   in calculating initial capital stocks led to a negative
   capital stock in South using the parameters of Simulation 3.
9  Since relative prices are unlikely to remain constant over
   any nonsteady-state growth path, this aggregation cannot be
   justified as a Hicksian composite.  Thus, the model of this
   section is really a different one from those in the earlier
   sections, and it is not explored fully.
10 Note, however, that within the countries that comprise South,
   a similar process of changing specialization is going on,
   with the most capital-abundant of the southern countries
   specializing in the more capital-intensive goods.  As growth
   proceeds, the identities of these most capital-intensive
   goods for South will change, and thus the most capital-
   abundant of the southern countries may have to adjust
   completely out of some industries and into others.

REFERENCES

Deardorff, A.V. (1979)  Weak links in the chain of comparative
    advantage. Journal of International Economics 9:197-209.
Deardorff, A.V. (1985)  Growth and International Investment with
    Diverging Populations. Unpublished manuscript.
Demeny, P. (1984)  A note on global population growth and its
    influence  on  the  world  economy.  In  Population  Notes.
    Center  for  Policy  Studies.  New  York:  The  Population
    Council.
Findlay, R. (1980)  The terms of trade and equilibrium growth in
    the world economy. American Economic Review 70:291-299.
Krueger, A.O. (1977)  Growth, Distortions, and Patterns of Trade
    Among Countries. Princeton Studies in International Finance,
    No. 40. Princeton, New Jersey.
Laitner, J. (1984)  Transition time paths for overlapping-
    generations models. Journal of Economic Dynamics and Control
    7:111-129.
Leontief, W. et al. (1977)  The Future of the World Economy. New
    York: Oxford University Press.
Oniki, H., and H. Uzawa (1965)  Patterns of trade and investment
    in  a  dynamic  model  of  international  trade.  Review  of
    Economic Studies 32:15-38.
Pasinetti, L. (1962)  The rate of profit and income and income
    distribution  in  relation  to  the  rate  of  economic  growth.
    Review of Economic Studies
Sapir, A. (1983)  Some Aspects of Populations Growth, Trade and
    Factor Mobility. Unpublished manuscript.
Solow, R.M. (1956)  A contribution to the theory of economic
    growth. Quarterly Journal of Economics 70:65-94.
Swamy, G. (1984)  Population, International Migration, and Trade.
    Unpublished manuscript.
United Nations (1982)  Demographic Indicators of Countries:
    Estimates and Projections as Assessed in 1980. New York:
    United Nations.
World Bank (1983)  World Tables, 3rd ed. Washington, D.C.:
    World Bank.

# 15
## Distribution Issues in the Relationship Between Population Growth and Economic Development
## David Lam

INTRODUCTION

Among the possibly deleterious effects of rapid population growth, distributional issues have frequently been mentioned. The World Bank's (1984) recent analysis of population issues in developing countries in the World Development Report 1984, for example, focuses considerable attention on the undesirable con-sequences of population growth for both the interhousehold distribution of income and the intrahousehold distribution of economic well-being by age and sex. Some have found the evidence persuasive enough to conclude that negative distributional con-sequences of population growth can be expected even when the consequences for per capita variables are difficult to predict. An earlier World Bank report (1974:35) argued that "whereas some people regard the effect of reduced fertility on per capita in-come growth as ambiguous, there appears to be no explicit dissent from the view that lower fertility contributes to greater income equality."

While the 1974 World Bank report may have overstated the degree of unanimity on the topic, there does appear to be a fairly broad consensus among economists that rapid population growth is likely to have negative distributional consequences.[1] This chapter analyzes the theoretical arguments and empirical evidence that have contributed to this consensus. The focus is on causation from population growth to inequality, with possible effects in the other direction ignored except when direct effects of inequality on fertility and mortality might affect the inter-pretation of empirical results. As will be seen below, a criti-cal survey of the evidence on the distributional effects of pop-ulation growth leads to mixed conclusions: some widely held arguments for negative distributional consequences appear theo-retically sound and receive support from empirical evidence;

This chapter has benefited from the comments of Theodore Bergstrom, Severin Borenstein, Chin-Yi Chu, Lowell Taylor, and T. Paul Schultz.

other arguments either appear less convincing theoretically, arecontradicted by data, or in many cases simply cannot be tested carefully given the data currently available.

Though the point will be obvious to most readers, it is important to note at the outset that the question "Would a lower rate of population growth reduce inequality?" is too broad and ill-defined to have a simple answer. First, it is necessary to define inequality and identify operational definitions that correspond to particular distributional criteria. We will see below, for example, that the effect of population growth on the ratio of wages to rents may provide a much different answer to the question than does the effect of population growth on a standard inequality measure such as the Gini coefficient. Second, as will become clear in the discussion below, it is necessary to identify the proximate cause of a change in the population growth rate. A reduction in the fertility of the highest-income groups will have a very different effect on inequality from an across-the-board fertility decline for all income classes that produces the same change in the overall population growth rate. Finally, it is important to consider the underlying causes of changes in fertility or mortality that are responsible for changing population growth rates. The rate of population growth is not a variable policy makers can autonomously control, but rather is the outcome of the behavior of individual couples responding to a complex set of social and economic variables. The question of how population growth affects inequality cannot be answered in the same way as a question about the distributional effect of some true policy instrument such as a tariff or an inheritance tax. From a policy perspective, it is meaningful only to consider the distributional effects of specific policies that indirectly affect population growth rates. Such policies may have direct distributional consequences of their own that are more important than any indirect effects working through the relationship between population growth and inequality.

In considering the distributional effects of population growth, this chapter attempts to identify explicitly the distributional criteria that underlie each part of the analysis. It should be emphasized, however, that there is a difficult, ultimately philosophical, problem involved in choosing an appropriate criterion for evaluating the effect of population growth on economic development. Even when distributional issues are ignored, it is not clear on economic grounds whether per capita income, total income, or some other measure should be the criterion used to evaluate the costs and benefits of population growth.2 Criteria for incorporating distributional concerns raise similar philosophical issues, issues that are often substantively related to the complex methodological problems inherent in the use of summary inequality indexes. The following discussion will not resolve these larger issues. However, in the process of evaluating the state of current knowledge on the distributional effects of population growth, the chapter identifies areas in which important conceptual issues have been neglected and attempts to give these more careful consideration.

The discussion below first briefly summarizes the existing cross-national evidence on the effects of population growth on inequality. The next two sections represent an attempt to disentangle the compositional and welfare effects of population growth: first is a discussion of compositional effects associated with changing age structure, household composition, and differential fertility; this is followed by a discussion of welfare effects, including effects on wages, and on intrahousehold distribution and intergenerational mobility. Finally, a summary and conclusions are presented.

## CROSS-NATIONAL EMPIRICAL EVIDENCE

The possibility that population growth could affect the distribution of income was recognized in a number of the cross-national empirical investigations that grew out of the concern with inequality among development economists in the 1960s and 1970s. A large number of studies have used cross-national regressions in attempting to identify the effects of population growth on inequality, and it is instructive to examine their results as a backdrop for the analysis that follows.

In their well-known work on social equity in developing countries, Adelman and Morris (1973) include both crude fertility rates and population growth rates among their explanatory variables, concluding that high values of both lead to greater inequality. They attribute this result to a tendency for high fertility rates in rural areas to generate a larger "reserve army" of urban unemployed (1973:35), and to the fact that the poor have higher fertility than the rich. "To the extent that poor households have more children than rich households," the authors argue, "and to the extent that they contribute less to family income than they consume, higher rates of population growth would . . . increase the skewness of the distribution of income" (1973:105).

Population growth is also included as an explanatory variable in Ahluwalia's (1976) analysis of income distribution using data from 60 countries. Ahluwalia's single-equation cross-national regressions indicate a significantly positive effect of population growth on the income share of the top 20 percent and a significantly negative effect on the income shares of the middle 40 percent, the bottom 60 percent, and the bottom 40 percent. According to Ahluwalia's results, a 1 percentage point increase in the population growth rate would lead to a 1.2 percentage point decrease in the income share of the bottom 40 percent of the population. On the other hand, the causal interpretation of these single-equation results has been questioned by authors suggesting a causal link in the opposite direction. The contention that income distribution might directly affect fertility and mortality was suggested in the early 1970s by authors such as Kocher (1973) and Rich (1973) and has become most closely associated with Repetto (1978, 1979).[3]

Recognizing the possibility of effects in both directions, simultaneous-equations models of fertility, mortality, and income distribution have been estimated by Repetto (1979), Winegarden (1978, 1980), Ogawa (1978), and Rodgers (1983). These studies report mixed results on the causal effects in both directions. Most authors have estimated a positive effect of inequality on fertility, results consistent with Repetto's hypothesis that, because of a nonlinear relationship between income and fertility, a transfer of income from the rich to the poor decreases fertility at low incomes by a greater proportion than it increases fertility at high incomes. The major dissenter from this view is Winegarden (1980), who finds insignificant or negative direct effects of inequality on fertility. There is greater unanimity in the estimated effects in the other direction, with all studies prior to Rodgers (1983) supporting the single-equation studies' conclusion that higher population growth causes greater inequality. Rodgers, using a somewhat different specification than previous authors, finds effects of population growth on inequality that are statistically insignificant.

The number of empirical studies investigating the relationship between population growth and inequality might lead us to hope for a consensus on empirical regularities. Unfortunately, as with many other debates that have been fought in the arena of cross-national regressions, the results are disturbingly sensitive to the choice of country groupings, the specification of lags in independent variables, and decisions about whether to treat specific variables as endogenous or exogenous. Because there is no convincing theoretical justification provided for the identifying restrictions in the simultaneous-equations models, it is difficult to have confidence in any of the estimated results.

Even if there were a consensus regarding the empirical evidence on the effects of population growth on inequality, we would still face a difficult problem in interpreting those effects. The commonly cited reasons for the effects of population growth on inequality include both significant welfare issues, such as declines in wage incomes relative to returns to capital and land, and other issues of minimal welfare significance, such as the pure compositional effects of a younger age structure. In an attempt to move closer to disentangling compositional effects from more directly welfare-related effects, attention is given below to the compositional effects associated with age structure, household composition, and differential fertility. This discussion demonstrates the serious problems of measurement and interpretation that plague research on distributional issues. It also raises conceptual issues regarding the exact nature of our concerns about inequality and the distributional objectives that should guide policy choices.

COMPOSITIONAL EFFECTS OF POPULATION GROWTH

The Effects of Changing Age Structure on Inequality

One of the factors often cited in discussion of the effects of population growth on inequality is the shift to a younger age structure caused by higher rates of population growth. The potential importance of age structure for cross-sectional measures of inequality has been noted by a number of authors, an important example being Paglin's (1975) proposal of an age-standardized Gini coefficient. Morley (1981) has applied a variant of Paglin's approach in identifying the contribution of changes in age structure to increased inequality in Brazil between 1960 and 1970. Morley concludes, as most authors have, that the compositional effect of a younger age structure was to increase inequality in Brazil, although the magnitude of the pure age structure effects is quite small. Winegarden (1978, 1980) also cites the effects of a younger age structure as one reason why more rapid population growth would lead to high inequality.

On the other hand, not all authors have agreed that a younger age structure should lead to greater inequality. Repetto (1979) and Lindert (1978) suggest an effect in the opposite direction. Repetto (1979:21) argues that "lower fertility and mortality rates, by elongating the age pyramid and increasing the variation in age among earners, would tend to increase the current inequality in the distribution of earned income." An almost identical argument is made by Lindert (1978:182), although, like Repetto, he expects other, more powerful effects of slower population growth to lead to net decreases in inequality.

The answer to the confusion over the effects of a younger age structure on inequality is that in some sense both sets of authors are correct. Those arguing that a younger age structure will increase inequality are referring to the effects of increased proportions of young workers on intercohort variance. Because the young have relatively low mean incomes, an increase in their share in the population tends to increase the "between group" component of total inequality. On the other hand, Lindert is correct that if the age-specific variance of earnings tends to increase with age, a decline in population growth will have a disequalizing effect by shifting the population into the higher-variance older age groups. The complete picture is that total inequality is the combination of the intercohort and intracohort components, with conflicting statements about the effect of a younger age structure reflecting the fact that these two components may be affected in opposite directions by an increase in the population growth rate.

## Decomposition of Age Structure Effects

Schultz (1981) has provided the most detailed analysis of age structure effects using age profiles of income and the variance of the logarithm of income from the United States, the

Netherlands, and Colombia. Schultz's decomposition of each age
group's contributions to intra- and intercohort inequality indicates that increases in the proportion of the population in
younger age groups should increase inequality in the United
States and the Netherlands. The decompositions for Colombia,
however, indicate only slight differences in the contributions
of different age groups to total variance, suggesting that the
age structure effects of more rapid population growth on inequality would be quite small.

As demonstrated in Lam (1984), the potentially offsetting
effects of changes in intra- and intercohort inequality brought
on by a younger age structure can be summarized analytically with
a stable population model of income distribution. The basic
result is that for stable populations, the total variance of income (or the variance of the logarithm of income, a more defensible measure of inequality) will increase when the population
growth rate increases if the mean age of the population is
greater than a weighted average of the "mean ages" of intra- and
intercohort variance. The intuition is straightforward: if both
intracohort variance (because of high age-specific variance) and
intercohort variance (because of age-specific mean incomes far
from the population mean) are relatively concentrated in young
ages, higher population growth will tend to increase inequality.

The weighted mean ages that determine the sign of the derivative of the variance of the logarithm of income with respect to
the population growth rate can in principle be estimated given
an actual or hypothetical age structure and age profiles of
income and income variance. Lam (1984) presents results based
on profiles for the United States and Brazil, with the estimated
mean ages giving conflicting evidence regarding the age structure effects of population growth on inequality. When the 15-19
age group is included in the U.S. age profiles, the results
indicate the kind of disequalizing effect of population growth
suggested by authors such as Winegarden and Morley; the Brazilian
profiles, however, indicate an effect that is much smaller in
magnitude and opposite in sign. A similar small but equalizing
age structure effect of population growth is estimated for the
United States when the 15-19 age group is omitted. These results
do not take account of the potential effects of population
growth on the age profiles of income and income inequality themselves, but assume constant age profiles and hence abstract to
what might be thought of as the pure first-order compositional
effects. The direct effects of age structure on age-specific
income and income variance are discussed in more detail below.

The reason for the difference in the estimated direction of
the effect of age structure on inequality for the United States
and Brazil can be seen in Figures 1 and 2, which plot recent
age-income profiles for the two countries.[4] The U.S. data show
mean incomes with the characteristic life-cycle profile--low at
young and old ages and highest from ages 35 to 55. The U.S. age
profile for the variance of the logarithm of income is inverted,
taking lower values in the high-income middle ages than it does
at the youngest and oldest ages. Such a pattern is consistent

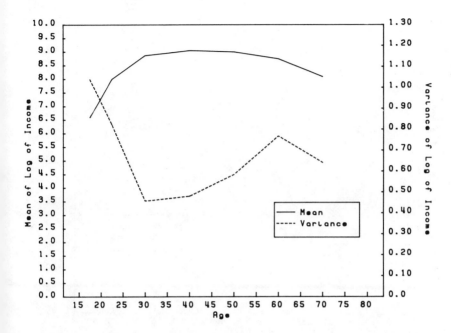

FIGURE 1  Age Profiles of Income and Inequality for U.S. Males,
1970

Source:  Schultz (1975).

with Mincer's human capital explanation of differences in life-
cycle income profiles (Mincer, 1974).  At young ages, some
individuals will be trading off current earnings for schooling
and training, creating relatively high intracohort inequality.
As these better-trained individuals reach the "overtaking" age
at which their faster-rising age income profiles cross the profiles of individuals with less schooling, there will be relatively low inequality.  Beyond the overtaking age, the income
profiles for those with larger investments in human capital will
rise above the profiles for less well-trained individuals,
causing a return to the high inequality of the younger ages.
    Age profiles such as that shown for the United States in
Figure 1, in which the youngest groups have low means and high
variances, will tend to give the result that a younger age
structure increases cross-sectional inequality, since both intra-
and intercohort inequality will tend to increase when the proportion of young persons increases.5  The data for Brazil
exhibit a different pattern.  In the Brazilian case, the profiles
for the mean and variance have similar shapes, both having lower
values at extreme ages than they have in the intermediate ages.
Given the Brazilian profile, intercohort variance will tend to

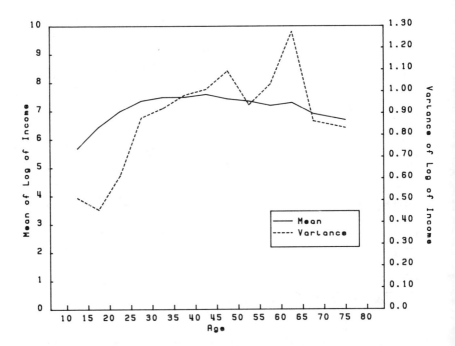

FIGURE 2   Age Profiles of Income and Inequality for Brazilian
Males, 1976

Source:   Calculated from 1976 PNAD Survey.


increase with a younger age structure, since the young have
relative low mean incomes; intracohort variance, on the other
hand, will tend to decrease with a younger age structure because
of the low variance in the young ages.   Profiles like Brazil's,
then, produce offsetting effects, as indicated in the small net
effect estimated using the weighted mean ages derived from the
stable population model (Lam, 1984).   The inconsistency of the
Brazilian profiles with the Mincer human capital explanation of
age-inequality profiles is noteworthy and suggests a need for
further research on possible differences in returns to human
capital in the United States and Brazil.
        There are difficult conceptual and methodological problems
involved in the treatment of the youngest age groups in age profiles such as those shown in Figures 1 and 2.   Previous research
has demonstrated the sensitivity of inequality measures to the
inclusion or exclusion of unpaid family workers, most of whom
are in the younger age groups.[6]   As a simple test of one
extreme potential effect of omitting unpaid family workers,
Figure 3 shows a comparison of the age-specific coefficients of
variation when these workers are excluded and when they are

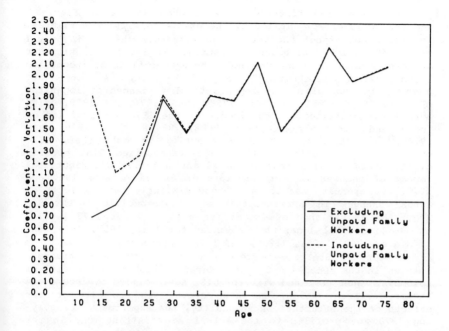

FIGURE 3   Coefficient of Variation of Earnings by Age for Brazilian Males, 1976

Note:   Excluding unpaid family workers and including unpaid family workers with income set to zero.

included with an assigned income of zero. If the exclusion of unpaid family workers has the effect of artificially lowering measured inequality at young ages by omitting a large group of poor workers, then including them with zero income should significantly raise inequality at young ages, and possibly change the direction of the age-inequality profile to something closer to the U.S. pattern shown in Figure 1. Figure 3 shows that, while the inclusion of the unpaid family workers does increase inequality in the youngest age groups, the effect is sufficient to alter the sign of the slope of the age-inequality profile only for the 10-15 age group.[7]

## Trends in Age-Standardized Inequality

As an alternative to the hypothetical stable population estimates derived in Lam (1984), this discussion here is based on estimation of the variance of the logarithm of income for the United States, Brazil, and Colombia using the actual age distributions over the last 30 or 40 years, and the age profiles of mean income and age-specific logarithm variance that existed around

1970.8  Given the offsetting effects demonstrated in Figure 2
and the small effect implied by the stable population estimates,
we should not expect the actual age structure changes in Brazil
from 1940 to 1980, although substantial, to lead to significant
changes in inequality when we hold the age profiles of income and
income variance at their 1970 levels.   In fact, the changes are
almost imperceptible.  The implied total variances of logarithm
of income for Brazil for 1940, 1950, 1960, 1970, and 1980, using
actual age distributions combined with the 1970 age profiles of
income and income variance, are .9688, .9683, .9749, .9780, and
.9746, respectively.   It is interesting to note that, like
Morley's results using Paglin's age-standardized Gini coefficient, these results indicate a slight negative distributional
impact of changes in age structure in Brazil between 1960 and
1970.   The results for Colombia show similarly small effects of
actual changes in age structure when age-specific income and
logarithm of variance of income are held at their 1973 levels.
The implied total logarithm variances for 1938, 1957, 1964, and
1973 are 1.790, 1.792, 1.806, and 1.799, respectively.

     The United States experienced more dramatic age structure
changes in the decades under consideration than either Brazil or
Colombia.  When combined with the U.S. age profiles of income and
income variance, which, as shown above, tend to give greater
effects of age structure on inequality, the experiment of applying 1970 age profiles to the actual age distributions in the
United States leads to more noticeable effects than those for
Brazil and Colombia.  The implied total variances of logarithm
of income in the United States for 1950, 1960, and 1970 are
1.117, 1.154, and 1.212, respectively, when each year's actual
age distribution is combined with the 1970 profiles of income
and income variance.   The increasing inequality results from
increasing proportions in the youngest working ages, as the
profiles shown in Figure 1 would suggest.

## Direct Welfare Effects of Population Growth on Age Profiles of Income and Inequality

It is important to go beyond pure compositional effects in considering the role of age structure in the relationship between
population growth and inequality.  The analysis above assumes
that the age profiles of income and income inequality do not
themselves change as a result of changing age structure.  This
is clearly an unsatisfactory assumption given the extensive
recent research, both theoretical and empirical, on the effects
of age structure fluctuations on wages and employment in industrialized countries.9  In addition to the potentially depressing effect of cohort size on mean earnings, Dooley and Gottschalk
(1984) have recently argued that age-specific inequality may
increase when cohort size increases.  They find supporting evidence in recent trends in age-specific inequality in the United
States.  If, as the U.S. evidence suggests, a younger age structure causes lower mean incomes and higher inequality of income

for young workers, then there will be a greater tendency for
population growth to increase inequality in the cross-section.
The effects on the distribution of lifetime income are more
difficult to predict since mean incomes should increase at older
ages, while the effect on inequality at older ages is unclear.

There is a need for additional research using developing
country data to extend our knowledge of the direct (welfare)
effects of age structure on age profiles of income and income
inequality. In analyzing such effects, it is important to distinguish between short-term age structure fluctuations, such as
the U.S. baby boom, and the long-term age structure changes that
are caused by patterns of fertility and mortality in developing
countries. The mechanisms described by Easterlin, Welch,
Freeman, and Dooley and Gottschalk have a large component of
what might be considered short-run disequilibrium effects.
Theoretical attention should be given to the difference between
a population that has one large cohort passing through the labor
force and one that has a permanently higher proportion of young
workers because of a permanently higher population growth rate.
If long-run elasticities of substitution between young and old
workers are higher than short-run elasticities of substitution,
then it will not be appropriate to transfer the estimates of
Welch and Freedman for the effects of cohort size to the case of
long-term age structure differences resulting from long-term
differences in population growth rates. This is an important
area for research, which, it may be hoped, will move beyond the
cohort-size issue for the United States and begin to explore the
interactions of age structure with income and inequality profiles
under the demographic and economic conditions typical of developing countries.

## The Role of Changing Household Composition

In addition to a changing age structure, changes in population
growth rates are associated with changes in household composition, which can affect measured income inequality. As with the
age structure effects discussed above, however, it is difficult
to separate the pure compositional effects of changing household
composition from more substantive structural effects representing
changes in the relative welfare of particular groups.

Among the numerous issues surrounding the choice of appropriate inequality indexes is the treatment of household composition in the choice of the income-recipient unit. Many economists have argued that the family or household is a more
appropriate unit than the individual for income distribution
analysis because of the household's primary role in consumption
and resource allocation. However, treating the household as the
focus of income distribution analysis raises complex questions
about the interaction between changes in household composition
and changes in the distribution of income. The work of Kuznets
(1976, 1978, 1981) has been particularly important in illuminating the interactions among household income, household size,

and inequality. One of the consistent cross-national empirical regularities demonstrated by Kuznets is an almost universal tendency for household size to vary directly with total household income, but inversely with per capita household income (i.e., total household income divided by the number of persons in the household). This pattern can cause the income rankings of particular households to change dramatically when the unit of analysis is changed from total household income to per capita household income, and causes inequality comparisons across populations and over time to be highly sensitive to the choice of recipient unit.

Kuznets has argued that a household per capita income measure is a better indicator of family members' welfare than is total family income, a position shared by a number of other researchers, including Danziger and Taussig (1979), Visaria (1979), and Datta and Meerman (1980). Danziger and Taussig show that the changes over time in U.S. income distributions depend critically on the choice of income unit. Gini coefficients indicate that U.S. incomes became less equal between 1967 and 1976 based on a total household income criterion, but became more equal based on a per capita household income criterion. Danziger and Taussig also show that the relative position of particular groups can be highly sensitive to the unit of analysis; this is demonstrated by the aged, of whom 25 percent fell within the lowest-income decile in 1976 based on total household income, but only 6 percent based on per capita household income.

The effects of changing from total household income to per capita household income have been analyzed for developing countries by Visaria (1979) and Datta and Meerman (1980). Visaria (1979:293), using data from Nepal, Sri Lanka, Taiwan, and two states in India, finds that indexes based on per capita income indicate significantly lower inequality than those based on total household income. He interprets this as meaning that total household income measures "overstate the degree of inequality because they overlook the fact that low total income is associated with a lower average household size." As an indicator of the sensitivity of household rankings to the unit of analysis, Visaria finds that fewer than 20 percent of the households in Nepal, Sri Lanka, and the two Indian states fall in the same decile when the unit of analysis is changed from total household to per capita household income. Similar results are obtained for Malaysia by Datta and Meerman (1980), who point out that the choice of target groups for reducing poverty can be influenced by the unit of analysis. Female-headed families in Malaysia, for example, appear to have significantly lower than average incomes on a total income basis, but have a mean income identical to that of male-headed households on a per capita basis.

The choice between total and per capita household income as the appropriate unit of analysis depends in part on the presumed source of variations in household size.[10] If fertility is viewed entirely as a choice variable, then from the parents' perspective there may be no welfare distinctions between a couple

with \$10,000 income and no children and a couple with \$10,000 and
four children.  If, on the other hand, fertility is viewed as
exogenous and outside the scope of choice, a per capita income
measure may provide a more appropriate welfare comparison.  A per
capita measure may also be justified on the grounds that children
should be given equal weight independent of their parents in
welfare comparisons across households, or may be thought of as
an indirect index of second-generation inequality since per
capita household income or wealth may be a rough proxy for per
capita endowments to children.

These issues are important in understanding the relationship
between population growth and inequality since they suggest that
changes in household composition over time are likely to lead to
changes in the distribution of income.  Such an effect has been
cited in the case of Taiwan, for example.  The extensive study
by Fei et al. (1979:256) points to a decline in both the mean
and variance of family size between 1966 and 1972, and concludes
that "changes in the size and composition of families must have
contributed to the reduction of inequality."  The precise mechanism for such an effect is not described, however, and the
authors point out that interpretation of causality is difficult
since the changes in household size were probably themselves
stimulated by changing economic conditions, including improvements in income distribution caused by other factors.

Some insights into the relationship between household size
and inequality are provided by a simple decomposition similar to
that used by Schultz (1982).  The logarithm of per capita household income can be written as $\ln y = \ln Y - \ln N$, where $Y$ is
total household income, $N$ is household size, and $y = Y/N$.  The
variance of the logarithm of $y$, then, can be decomposed as

$$V(\ln y) = V(\ln Y) + V(\ln N) - 2\text{Cov}(\ln Y, \ln N) , \qquad (1)$$

where $V$ denotes variance and Cov denotes covariance.  Comparing
inequality in per capita household income, $V(\ln y)$, with inequality in total household income, $V(\ln Y)$, we see from equation
(1) that $V(\ln y) > V(\ln Y)$ if $V(\ln N) > 2\text{Cov}(\ln Y, \ln N)$.  A regression of $\ln Y$ on $\ln N$, assuming it is behaviorally meaningful,
will imply an elasticity of household income with respect to
household size equal to

$$\frac{\text{Cov}(\ln Y, \ln N)}{V(\ln N)} .$$

The magnitude of this elasticity then exactly describes whether
per capita or total household income is more equally distributed.
If the elasticity of total household income with respect to
household size is less than .5, implying that $V(\ln N) > 2\text{Cov}(\ln Y, \ln N)$, then per capita household income will be more unequal
than total household income, at least according to the logarith-
mic variance measure.

The two terms determining the direction of the difference
between per capita and total household income inequality are

worth noting. Inequality in household size, V(ln N), has the
direct effect of increasing per capita household income inequality according to equation (1). The covariance of household
size and household income, which as shown by Kuznets is typically
positive, appears to have the direct effect of reducing per
capita household income inequality. It is important to remember,
however, that these two terms will not in general be independent.
A reduction in the variance in household size will not necessarily imply a reduction in per capita household income inequality
since it may imply a simultaneous reduction in the equalizing
positive covariance of household income and household size.
Identifying the relationship between reductions in the mean and
variance of household size and changes in the distribution of
household income requires a more complete understanding of the
behavioral relationship between household income and household
composition than existing research can provide.

The most detailed empirical evidence on the interactions
among household composition, household income, and inequality is
provided in the decompositions of household income inequality by
Schultz (1982). He separates total household size into the
numbers of adults and children, producing an expanded analog of
equation (1) with three variance and three covariance terms.
These variances and covariances are then estimated using data
from Colombia and rural India. In Colombia, Schultz finds total
household income more equally distributed than per capita household income, while the opposite pattern (and the pattern observed
in the developing-country studies cited above) is found in rural
India. The overall levels of inequality by both measures are
also significantly higher in Colombia than in rural India.
Looking at the role of adult household composition in inequality,
Schultz estimates an elasticity of family income with respect to
the number of adults that is close to one for all age groups in
Colombia. This is the result that would be expected, he argues,
if the propensity of adults to live together were not correlated
with the potential income contributions of family members. For
a sample from rural India, he finds a lower elasticity, ranging
from .44 to .59, implying that household income increases less
than proportionately with increases in the number of adults. He
suggests this may be due to the absorption of poor widows and
other disadvantaged adult members, and concludes that "the distribution of families by number of adults contributes substantially to Indian family per capita income inequality, with the
families having many adults being notably poorer in terms of per
adult income" (1982:146). Turning to the contribution of fertility to inequality, Schultz concludes that the negative covariance of fertility and total household income tends to increase
inequality in per capita household income in both India and
Colombia, with the effect in Colombia significantly larger. He
tentatively suggests that the greater income differentials in
fertility in Colombia may result from Colombia's being further
advanced in its demographic transition, with the initial fertility reductions in the country occurring primarily among
higher-income families.

Whether larger income differentials in fertility are an important explanation of the higher level of inequality in Colombia than in India cannot be determined from Schultz's evidence alone. The results do suggest an important and relatively unexplored mechanism for effects of changing fertility levels on inequality. Potter (1979) has also pointed to income differentials in fertility as an important factor in the effect of fertility decline on inequality. He provides evidence from Colombia and Costa Rica that fertility tends to be lower for families with higher income, although the behavioral interpretation of these results is difficult since he uses income per equivalent adult consumer as the measure of family income, and thus introduces a possible spurious negative correlation between fertility and family income. Potter also provides limited evidence from Colombia suggesting that the difference between the fertility of high- and low-income groups has increased with the decline in the overall level of fertility in recent years. He argues that this increase in income differentials in fertility means that initial declines in overall fertility may increase inequality in subsequent generations.

Research on the relationship between household composition and inequality has documented the sensitivity of inequality comparisons to the treatment of household composition, and has demonstrated that changes in the mean and variance of household composition over time can have substantial effects on the distribution of household income. The magnitude and even the direction of these effects are poorly understood, however, since they depend on the complex relationship between changes in the mean and variance of household size, and changes in the covariances of household size and household income. Although income differentials in fertility and their changes over time clearly play a critical role in the interactions among population growth, household composition, and inequality, the dynamics of differential fertility and inequality have received only limited attention in the existing literature. The next section analyzes some of the implications of differential fertility, emphasizing the complex compositional effects it implies; a later section considers the relationship of differential fertility to the intergenerational transmission of inequality.

## The Dynamics of Differential Fertility and Inequality

There are two kinds of questions we might ask about the distributional effects of a factor such as population growth. The first is of the form "Does this factor have a more negative (or less positive) effect on the incomes of the poor than on the incomes of the wealthy?" The second, which is the question most empirical studies have attempted to answer, is of the form "Does this factor increase some measure of dispersion of incomes in the population?" It has begun to be recognized in the development economics literature that these are not necessarily the same question. In some of the earliest discussions of inequality and development, Kuznets (1955) pointed out that transferring indi-

viduals from a poor traditional sector to a higher-income modern
sector might increase measures of inequality without any real
deterioration in the relative welfare of the poor. Robinson
(1976) and Fields (1979) formalized this important point, demonstrating the increase in inequality measures, such as the Gini
coefficient, that can occur when some of the poor experience
increases in their incomes by transferring to the modern sector
while the incomes of the rich and all remaining poor remain
unchanged. The confusing signals given by the inequality
measures in such a case occur because the composition of income
classes changes between two periods. In the absence of such
changes, a "good" inequality measure will translate real gains
in the relative incomes of the poor into declines in measured
inequality.

When we examine the distributional effects of population
growth, compositional effects similar to those explored by
Robinson and Fields can be pervasive. It is therefore essential
to define distributional issues carefully, taking care to examine
whether given operational measures correspond to those issues.

It is possible that one distributional issue of concern is
in fact the value of some measure of dispersion. Following the
arguments of such authors as Hirschman and Rothschild (1973), it
is possible that a measure of dispersion directly enters individual utility functions, with individuals affected by the level
and distribution of the incomes of those around them, as well as
by their own direct consumption possibilities. In the case of
rural-urban migration, for example, we might want to argue that
there really is a negative welfare effect when we transfer some
of the poor to the modern sector, even though some of the poor
end up better off and none end up worse off than they were before. Generally, however, the use of dispersion seems to have
been motivated not by such concerns, but by the implicit assumption that these measures are appropriate indexes of actual
increases or decreases in the relative incomes of particular
groups of individuals in the distribution. The comparison of
the share of income received by the bottom 40 percent of the
population in one period with that received by the bottom 40
percent in another period is presumably made not because of an
assumption that individuals directly care about the value of
that share, but because it is an index of whether the incomes
received by the poorest groups in the population rose or fell
relative to the incomes of richer groups.

A serious weakness of the extensive empirical literature
surveyed earlier has been inadequate attention to the simple
mathematics of inequality in growing populations. Whenever new
individuals are added to a population, we will in general
observe changes in measures of the distribution of income.
Given differential fertility across income groups, potentially
serious compositional effects will be included in the observed
relationships between population growth and measured inequality.
As demonstrated below, compositional effects on measures of
dispersion are considerably more complex than compositional
effects on mean values, and can lead to misleading inferences

from cross-national or time series comparisons of inequality measures.

Although the literature analyzing the properties of inequality measures is extensive, relatively little attention has been given to the effects of adding new members to the population or altering the population's composition. Exceptions include Robinson (1976) and Fields (1979), who have demonstrated that changing the sectoral composition of the population can generate the empirically observed inverted-U pattern of inequality over time, and Morley (1981), who has pointed out that the effect on percentile income shares of adding new poor members to the population can be either positive or negative.

An important contribution to recent literature on inequality has been the systematic analysis of the consistency between inequality measures and social welfare functions with explicitly desirable properties.11 This research has provided insights into the implicit value judgments inherent in particular inequality measures, and has provided at least partial guidance in going beyond ad hoc comparisons of summary measures. We are thus now able to choose between, say, the Theil Index and the Gini coefficient on the basis of their sensitivity to particular patterns of inequality.

Unfortunately, this literature is of less help when we must compare populations of different sizes. This is to be expected, since social welfare functions that are capable of ranking allocations across different numbers of people raise significantly more complex philosophical issues than social welfare functions defined for allocations across a fixed population.12 While we know that a transfer of income from a richer to a poorer person will decrease inequality for a number of "good" summary measures, we have little guidance regarding the effect of adding an additional person with some given income. In a recent paper (Lam, 1985), the compositional effects of population growth on measured inequality are explored in detail. The paper concludes that in the presence of differential fertility, standard measures of inequality give confusing, often misleading signals regarding changes in the relative welfare of income groups. This conclusion has important implications for our understanding of the dynamics of population growth and inequality and is discussed below.

## The Mathematics of Population Growth and Income Variance

The nature of compositional effects involved in the relationship between population growth and inequality can be demonstrated by considering the effect on the mean and variance of income of adding a group of immigrants to a population. Suppose that we begin with a population of n natives with mean income $\mu_n$ and variance of income $\sigma_n^2$ and add a new group of m immigrants with mean income $\mu_m$ and variance $\sigma_m^2$. The new mean income for the augmented population, which we will denote $\mu_{m+n}$ is

$$\mu_{n+m} = \frac{1}{n+m} \left[ n\mu_n + m\mu_m \right].$$

Naturally, the mean income will rise or fall as the immigrants' mean income is above or below that for the native population. This simplest of compositional effects depends only on the difference in the two groups' mean incomes, and is affected in magnitude but not in direction by the size of the entering group.

If we think of the new population as consisting of two groups, the natives and the immigrants, the new variance, $\sigma^2_{n+m}$, can be expressed in a standard decomposition of between-group and within-group variance as

$$\sigma^2_{n+m} = \frac{nm}{(n+m)^2} (\mu_m - \mu_n)^2 + \frac{n}{n+m} \sigma^2_n + \frac{m}{n+m} \sigma^2_m . \quad (2)$$

Equation (2) indicates that the new variance is a simple function of the two population sizes, the two group variances, and the difference between the two group mean incomes.[13] It is easy to see from equation (2) that the new variance can in general be greater than, less than, or equal to the variance of the original native population.

Would a group of immigrants with incomes below those of the original population mean tend to increase or decrease inequality as measured by the variance? Equation (2) tells us that any effect is possible. If the immigrants have a variance no larger than that of the natives and a mean within one standard deviation of the natives' mean, then the population variance will decline. More interestingly, however, the variance can decline even if the new group's mean is much lower (or much higher) than the original mean. Consider the case in which the immigrants' variance is smaller than that of the natives, but their mean is more than one standard deviation from that of the natives. Equation (2) gives us the result that the new combined variance will be greater than, less than, or equal to the original variance according to the following relationship:

$$\sigma^2_{n+m} \begin{Bmatrix} < \\ = \\ > \end{Bmatrix} \sigma^2_n \quad \text{as} \quad m \begin{Bmatrix} > \\ = \\ < \end{Bmatrix} \frac{n(\mu_m - \mu_n)^2}{\sigma^2_n - \sigma^2_m} - n . \quad (3)$$

Equation (3) implies that whatever the mean and variance of income in the immigrant population, as long as their variance is less than that of the natives' and their mean is more than one standard deviation from that of the natives, we can find some size for the immigrant group that will cause the variance in the new, augmented population to be identical to the original variance of the native population. That is, we can always find an m to satisfy the equality condition in equation (3) given any values for the means and variances that fall into the case being considered. Not only can we always satisfy the equality in

equation (3) by an appropriate choice of m, but we can also
satisfy either of the inequalities, increasing or decreasing the
variance depending on the size of the group added. We thus see
the fundamentally more complex nature of compositional effects
on measures of dispersion as compared to compositional effects
on means. While we know that the addition of our hypothetical
group of immigrants will unambiguously decrease mean income when
they enter a higher-income population, the effect of the group
on the variance can be in any direction and cannot be predicted
without knowing all of the parameters in equation (3).

These simple results have implications for the effects of any
changes in population composition, such as migration or natural
increase. In particular, they have important implications for
the patterns of inequality to be observed whenever income classes
grow at different rates. Suppose that a segment of the population with some mean and variance of income begins to grow at a
faster rate than the rest of the population. From equation (1),
we can track the change in the variance of incomes at different
points in time as m, the number of additional members of the
fast-growing class, increases. If the class has a mean income
more than one standard deviation from the original mean and a
variance smaller than that of the original population, a small
increase in its relative size will tend to increase the variance
of incomes. However, we know from equation (3) that if the group
grows large enough, the variance will eventually return to that
of the original population. As m increases beyond that level,
the variance will begin to decline, converging in the limit to
the intragroup variance of the rapidly growing group as that
group approaches 100 percent of the population.

The variance is a poor measure of inequality, in part because
it is not invariant with respect to mean income. We need only
define income as the natural logarithm of income, however, and
the results apply to the variance of logarithm of income, a
standard scale-independent inequality measure. Similarly, it is
easy to see that the coefficient of variation, another standard
measure, will also fall eventually if any income class that
itself has a smaller within-group coefficient of variation
increases its share of the population. As with the variance, an
initial increase in the size of a group with an extreme mean
income can increase the coefficient of variation. However,
appealing to the limiting case once again, as the more rapidly
growing class approaches 100 percent of the population, the
coefficient of variation will converge to the group's coefficient of variation.

Analogous arguments can be made for all measures of dispersion, including standard inequality measures such as the Gini
coefficient and percentile income shares. Considering, for
example, the income share of the bottom 40 percent of the population, it is easy to see that if a low-income group with identical incomes grows more quickly than the rest of the population
long enough to approach 100 percent of the population, the income
share of the bottom 40 percent will approach 40 percent, the
share in a perfectly egalitarian economy. Results analogous to

those given above for the variance can be derived to show that
the effect of an increase in the size of a low-income group on
the income share to the bottom K percent of the population can
be positive, negative, or zero, depending on the number of
persons added.  As with the variance and the coefficient of
variation, if we start a low-income group growing faster than
the rest of the population, its growth may initially reduce the
share to the bottom K percent.  However, at some point this
share must reach a minimum after which continued growth will
cause the share to rise, eventually exceeding its original level.

## Implications for Empirical Research

The potentially misleading signals that standard inequality
measures provide in the presence of income differentials in
fertility are easily demonstrated by simulations of income-
differentiated population growth.  Lam (1985) presents a series
of simulations based on differing assumptions about the causal
relationship between income and fertility and the extent of
intergenerational mobility.  A simple projection of the 1970
quintile income shares for the Brazilian population, for example,
shows a confusing pattern of intertemporal changes in standard
inequality indexes when the original quintiles are assigned
different population growth rates.  Even if the incomes of every
group are held constant, differential fertility will cause inequality to increase in some periods and decline in others, with
the changes unrelated to the actual relative economic positions
of income groups.  Given higher fertility rates for the poorest
groups, it can be demonstrated that the incomes of the poorest
groups can be rising unambiguously relative to those of higher-
income groups at the same time that all standard inequality
indexes show increasing inequality.

   Stated in their strongest form, these results suggest that
in the presence of income differentials in fertility, hypotheses
about the effect of population growth on the relative economic
position of the poor cannot be tested using cross-national or
time-series observations of standard inequality measures.  The
compositional effects of income-differentiated population growth
can cause standard inequality measures to move in the opposite
direction from changes in the earnings of the poor relative to
earnings of the rich, a result that raises serious concerns about
what information is actually contained in comparisons of inequality measures when populations are changing in composition.
The interpretation of empirical results regarding the effects of
population growth on inequality is called into serious question;
we have no way, for example, of rejecting the hypothesis that
population growth tends to raise wages relative to rents, even
though we observe declining shares of income to the bottom 40
percent of the population whenever population growth rates
increase.

While disconcerting, the results surveyed in this section increase our understanding of the dynamics of population growth and inequality and improve the prospects for meaningful tests of the hypotheses in which we are directly interested. If researchers are ever to establish firmly any positive or negative distributional consequences of rapid population growth, the complex compositional dynamics of population growth and inequality must be fully understood and carefully accounted for. The results suggest that many of the hypotheses about the distributional consequences of population growth would be better framed as hypotheses about relative incomes of particular income groups, rather than as hypotheses about standard inequality measures. Much of the literature suggests that analysis of functional distributions or relative factor payments would be appropriate. Since many of the theoretical arguments regarding the distributional effects of population growth are based on the effects on relative wages, and since direct observation of relative wages may avoid the compositional biases confounding inequality indexes, we turn now to an analysis of the relationship between population growth and wages.

## WELFARE EFFECTS OF POPULATION GROWTH

### The Effects of Population Growth on Wages

The most standard argument for negative distributional consequences of higher population growth rates is the depressing effect of increased labor supply on wages. The tendency of population growth to reduce wages relative to the returns to other factors of production is perhaps the most fundamental of the distributional consequences of population growth, and is given unambiguous theoretical support by standard neoclassical models of economic growth such as Solow (1956). The depressing effect of population growth on relative wages is also well established empirically, and indeed is one of the only empirical issues raised in this chapter for which existing research appears to provide a consistent answer.

It was argued above that hypotheses about the distributional effects of population growth should in many cases be tested directly with data on wages and rents rather than with summary inequality measures. Unfortunately, data on factor payments are difficult to obtain, particularly for developing countries, and are subject to many of their own problems of definition, measurement, and interpretation.

The most useful research on the relationship between population growth and wages has been based on historical time-series data from currently industrialized countries. The pioneering research by Lee (1973, 1978, 1980) on preindustrial England provides convincing evidence that exogenous increases in population size (due, for example, to mortality declines unrelated to economic conditions) had a strong depressing effect on relative wages. Analyzing population and wage data for England

from 1540 to 1800, for example, Lee (1980) estimates an elasticity of the real wage with respect to population size of -1.5,
implying that a 10 percent increase in population size would
have caused a 15 percent decline in the real wage.

Although both theory and empirical evidence confirm the
tendency of population growth to lower relative wages, it does
not necessarily follow that the direction of the resulting
effects on standard inequality measures will be predictable.
The theoretical prediction regarding functional shares, for
example, is well known, indicating that labor's share of total
output will decrease (increase) when the population growth rate
increases if the elasticity of substitution between labor and
capital is less than (greater than) one. Given evidence that
elasticities of substitution are not likely to be greater than
one (see, for example, Morawetz, 1976), and given that wages are
typically a larger share of the income of low-income groups than
of high-income groups, the argument is often made that a decline
in labor's share will also imply a decline in the share of income
received by the lowest-income groups. The same argument is
applied to the relative shares of wages and land rents or the
relative shares of unskilled and skilled wages, each case
assuming that the poorest groups in the population begin with
relatively smaller endowments of productive assets (physical
capital, land, and human capital) whose returns increase when
the population growth rate increases.

However, the argument that a declining factor share to labor
will imply a declining income share to the poor whenever the poor
receive a higher proportion of their earnings as wages is not
necessarily correct. Consider a case in which the poor receive
only wage income, but the rich receive both wage income and income from capital, all labor being homogenous. Suppose that the
elasticity of substitution between labor and capital is one, so
that the share of total output paid out as wages does not change
with the size of the labor force. If the number of poor workers
increases, wages will fall, total income will increase, and the
share of total income paid as wages will remain constant. If the
number of rich workers does not change, the share of total income
paid as wages to the rich must decline, since wages have fallen
and total income has increased. The share of total income paid
to poor workers must increase, then, in order for labor's total
share to remain constant. In other words, when the number of
poor workers increases, the share of income paid to capital
remains constant, the share paid as wages to the rich declines,
and the share paid as wages to the poor increases. Even if the
elasticity of substitution were less than one, it is easy to see
that it would be possible for the share of income paid to the
poor to increase even if labor's total share were to decline, as
long as the rich received some labor income.

One must use caution, then, in moving from factor payments
to factor shares to individual shares in predicting the effects
of population growth on the distribution of income. As suggested
by the results set forth earlier, however, we may in fact be more
interested in relative wages directly than in potentially con-

fusing income shares. It is little consolation to the poor that their collective share of total income is remaining constant if they are becoming an increasingly large percentage of the population and individually face declining wages. Ideally, we would like to examine both relative wages and standard inequality indexes over time in an attempt to identify the possible distributional effects of population growth.

One of the few sources of historical data on both factor payments and inequality measures is the work by Williamson and Lindert on the history of inequality in the United States (Lindert, 1978; Williamson and Lindert, 1980), in which a number of results relevant to the present discussion are presented. Williamson and Lindert investigate the extent to which wage differentials between skilled and unskilled workers move in the same direction as summary inequality measures in their time series. For periods in which data on both wage differentials and summary inequality measures are available, they find high correlations between the movements of the two series over time. In the period 1913-34, for example, regressions of the annual share of income earned by the top one percent of the population on annual unemployment rates and the ratio of skilled to unskilled wages show that the "wage gap" has a statistically significant positive effect on the income share of the top one percent (Williamson and Lindert, 1980:80-82). The authors conclude that the series move enough in parallel to justify using wage ratios alone to infer movements in inequality measures during periods when the latter are unavailable.

Williamson and Lindert, then, do not find evidence of the kind of confounding compositional effects analyzed above, with relative incomes and inequality measures moving in opposite directions. Of course, we cannot conclude from their limited evidence for the United States that relative wages and inequality measures can always be assumed to move in parallel when we are analyzing cross-national or time-series data from developing countries. However, the Williamson and Lindert results are among the only good comparisons of such series, and suggest a useful area of investigation as more complete cross-sectional and time-series data on wages and inequality measures become available from developing countries.

Williamson and Lindert's analysis of historical patterns of inequality in the United States leads them to conclude that population growth, whether from immigration or natural increase, has had unequalizing effects on the income distribution in the United States, with the wage-depressing effect of increased labor supply playing a major role. Lindert writes in his earlier book (1978:257), "No other potential influence on the distribution of income fits the long-run movements in inequality as well as the behavior of the labor supply." Having documented the role of fertility as a major determinant of historical movements in U.S. labor supply, Lindert concludes (p. 259) by arguing, "If this reading of the macroeconomic evidence is correct, the case for collective policies to encourage birth restriction in countries with rapid population growth is strengthened."

U.S. historical experience, then, appears to support the argument that more rapid population growth causes significant deterioration in the wages of unskilled relative to skilled workers and is returned to capital and land. This deterioration in turn appears to have negative effects on the personal distribution of income. Unfortunately, there is little evidence from developing countries to compare to the Lindert and Williamson work for the United States. Data on wage differentials from developing countries are more difficult to obtain, and the data that do exist have not been analyzed systematically from the standpoint of the possible influence of population growth.

The limited time-series data that do exist for individual developing countries give a mixed picture of changes in relative wages or other measures of inequality over time. Fields (1980b) surveys a number of existing studies and finds no consistent pattern in the relationship between the rate of economic growth and changes in inequality in the thirteen countries that have reliable measures for more than one point in time. He does not compare these countries according to population growth rates, but it seems clear from a survey of his brief description of the countries that no simple relationship between population growth rates and trends in measured inequality will be strongly supported by the data. Argentina, for example, with relatively low population growth, appears to have had an increase in its Gini coefficient during the 1950s, while Costa Rica, with a much higher growth rate, experienced a decline in its Gini coefficient during the 1960s.[14] Other cross-country comparisons would suggest an opposite relationship. In general, the data are much too limited, both within and across developing countries, for the kind of careful multivariate analysis that would be necessary to identify a relationship between population growth and inequality measures based on time-series observations.

In addition to data on changes in summary inequality measures, limited data also exist on changes in relative incomes in a small number of developing countries. Ahluwalia and Chenery (1974) present data on the rate of growth of mean incomes for specific income groups, comparing the rate of growth of income for the lowest 40 percent to that for the middle 40 percent and top 20 percent. Like the data on inequality measure trends surveyed by Fields, these comparisons of income growth rates across income groups provide no consistent pattern for the thirteen developing countries considered. Four countries (Panama, Brazil, Mexico, and Venezuela) indicate faster income growth for the highest-income groups; four countries (Colombia, El Salvador, Sri Lanka, and Taiwan) indicate faster income growth for the poorest groups; while the five remaining countries (Korea, the Philippines, Yugoslavia, Peru, and India) show no significant differences in the growth rates of different income groups. It seems unlikely that any systematic relationship between population growth and income growth rates of specific income groups can be supported by data such as those provided by Ahluwalia and Chenery.

Thus there are simply insufficient data to test whether the wage-reducing impact of population growth found by Williamson and Lindert in the United States is having a substantial effect in the same direction in developing countries. As new data become available, it may be hoped that we will begin to get a clearer picture of recent trends in relative wages and inequality measures in a number of developing countries. We may then be able to identify the role of population growth in these trends, although, as the results reported above demonstrate, even with a wealth of data it will be essential to use caution when inferring changes in relative welfare among the population from time-series observations of standard income distribution measures.

## Intrahousehold Distribution and Intergenerational Mobility

The discussion thus far has concentrated on the interhousehold distribution of income and wealth. Possible effects of population growth on the intrahousehold distribution of economic well-being have often been raised as well, particularly as regards distribution by sex and age. The microeconomics of economic allocations inside the family are too complex to be treated with justice here and have only recently begun to receive the serious attention they deserve. The discussion below presents a brief overview of the issues that have been raised and of the limited theoretical and empirical evidence that bears on them.

## Intrahousehold Inequality by Sex

The distribution of economic welfare between men and women in households may be affected by the number of children if the costs and benefits of children are unequally distributed. Although numerous studies have attempted to measure the costs and benefits of children in both developed and developing countries,[15] few have explicitly attempted to identify the distribution of these costs and benefits within the household. The latter is conceptually difficult since these costs and benefits include both goods and time, occur over the entire life cycle, and are realized through a variety of reallocations within the household that are not directly observable to the researcher. It may be quite misleading, in fact, to attempt to isolate the distribution of costs and benefits of any particular component of a household's expenditures. All household expenditures are interrelated, and there is no particular reason why what appear to be the direct costs and benefits of any single item should be equally distributed among household members.[16] With this warning in mind, there is some limited evidence on the costs and benefits of children that is relevant to the distributional issues being considered here.

The component of the costs of children that can be most easily separated among household members is the time inputs required for childcare. Evidence provided by recent time-use

surveys in developing countries suggests, not surprisingly, that
women bear most of the burden of the time costs of children.
Ho's (1979) analysis of time-use data from the Philippines, for
example, indicates that the time demands of additional children
are met primarily by a reduction in the leisure time of women.

It is also possible that the benefits of children, whatever
their magnitude relative to the costs, are not distributed
equally between husbands and wives. It is difficult to say much
about the distribution of the benefits of children when they are
young, given the complex set of factors, both directly economic
and psychic, involved. The East-West Center's value of children
studies (Arnold et al., 1975) did not find striking differences
in male and female assessments of the costs and benefits of
children, although there were some differences. Women generally
reported higher values than men for the emotional rewards of
children and for the value of children as economic support in
old age, while men placed higher value than women on the continuity of the family name. Men also reported being more concerned than women about the direct economic costs of children
(Arnold et al., 1975:97-98). Old age support is the principle
area in which the literature suggests there may be a greater
benefit of children to women than to men, especially in certain
cultural settings. DeTray (1983), for example, finds the time
contributions of children significantly higher for female-headed
households than for male-headed households in Malaysia. Cain
(1978) has argued that the importance of children in supporting
widows in Bangladesh is a major factor encouraging high fertility
in that country. Similarly, Goodstadt (1982:52) discusses concerns about potential declines in intrafamily old age support due
to the one-child policy in China and quotes local Chinese fears
that "the old, the weak, and the women often get the worst of the
deal."

It seems difficult to argue that large family size itself has
any direct effect on intrahousehold distribution by sex that can
be unambiguously identified in either direction. Whether a particular family planning policy will be advantageous to women
clearly depends on the nature of the policy. Public health measures that increase the availability of contraceptives and family
planning information to women, or policies that increase women's
educational or labor force opportunities, appear defensible on
equity grounds regardless of any direct connection between family
size and intrahousehold inequality. On the other hand, policies
that restrict family size without providing substitutes for such
benefits from children as old age support might easily have distributional effects that are deleterious to women.

## Intrahousehold Allocations Affecting Children

From the standpoint of children in the household, there are
distributional issues regarding the allocations between adults
and children and the allocations among children. Since investments in children will affect the level of inequality the

children experience as adults, these issues are also linked to issues of the intergenerational transmission of inequality.

As discussed above in the case of adult intrahousehold distribution, one of the major distribution issues at the level of children in the household is inequality by sex. While there is considerable evidence for unequal distribution of resources between boys and girls in households in a number of developing countries (e.g., Chen et al., 1981), there is little evidence on the relationship of this inequality to family size itself. Studies that have explored sex differentials in child mortality, for example, have typically not investigated the effect of the number of children on these differentials.[17] Evidence on time use by children also suggests a possible sex bias against female children. Data from Bangladesh (Cain, 1977) and Malaysia (DeTray, 1983), for example, indicate that girls contribute more total productive time than boys when both market work and household production are considered. However, neither study analyzes the effect of family size directly on sex differentials in hours worked. Whatever the causes of unequal treatment of male and female children within households, there does not seem to be any compelling reason why reductions in family size would have a direct equalizing effect. The possibility that the effect could even be toward greater inequality in some circumstances is suggested by reports of the effects of China's one-child policy. It appears that at least that version of policy-induced fertility reduction may exacerbate sex differentials in mortality, possibly even leading to female infanticide.[18]

A more direct concern about the effects of family size on intrahousehold distribution as regards children relates to the effect on the allocation of resources per child. A number of authors have argued that a higher mean level of fertility leads to greater inequality because the higher mean is associated with higher variance in fertility. According to this argument, increased family size leads to a decline in per child bequests and investments in human capital, so that greater variance in fertility leads to greater inequality in the second generation. Lindert (1978), for example, argues that declining fertility in the United States in the twentieth century led to increasing income equality in part because lower fertility was associated with lower variance in family size, and therefore caused greater equality in per child endowments across generations.

It is generally true that larger numbers of children are associated with lower child "quality," where quality is measured by such indicators of parental investment as levels of schooling or health status;[19] however, we cannot necessarily conclude that if fertility were reduced through some policy intervention (perhaps directly by quantity restrictions or indirectly by reductions in the price of contraceptives), then per child investments would increase. The desired quantity and quality of children of a particular couple are not chosen independently, representing at least in part a simultaneous decision based on the couple's preferences and economic constraints. The observed cross-sectional relationship between child quantity and quality,

then, represents the outcome of decisions by parents who face
different sets of constraints and may have different preferences,
and therefore should not be interpreted as demonstrating the
causal effect of family size on per child endowments.

Fortunately, there has been some success in solving the identification problem involved in the child quantity-quality relationship. Rosenzweig and Wolpin (1980) use the occurrence of
twins as an exogenous unplanned increase in fertility, which
makes it possible to identify the direct effect of fertility on
variables such as investments in child schooling. Household-
level data from India suggest that the additional unplanned birth
associated with twins leads to a reduction in the average educational attainment of all children in a household. According to
Rosenzweig and Wolpin (1980:239), the results "suggest that a
decrease in family size brought about, say, by exogenous improvements in birth control technology, would increase schooling
levels of Indian children."

There is some evidence from the United States on the relationship between family size and direct financial bequests, based
on estate records. Menchik (1980) and Tomes (1981) both find a
negative effect of the number of siblings on the size of an
individual's inheritance, evidence that supports the argument
given above regarding the potentially unequalizing tendency of
high variance in fertility. However, evidence that larger family
size leads to lower per child endowments does not necessarily
imply that incomes would be more equal if there were no variance
in fertility. If it were higher-income parents who had higher
fertility and lower per child endowments, then the observed
pattern of fertility and endowments would imply a "leveling" of
incomes across generations and potentially greater equality than
would exist if fertility were identical across income groups.
While high fertility is often associated with lower-income groups
(see, for example, Birdsall, 1980), the income-fertility relationship in developing countries is complex, with considerable
evidence suggesting that pure income effects are positive[20]
and much stronger evidence suggesting that the effects of some
forms of wealth, most importantly land, are positive (Mueller
and Short, 1983; Rosenzweig and Evenson, 1977). If fertility
decline initially implies reduced fertility among the wealthy,
then inequality may increase in subsequent generations because
of a reduction in the previously offsetting effect of wealthy
parents' larger family sizes diluting per child bequests and
human capital endowments.

The relationships between income and wealth, fertility, and
the intergenerational transmission of inequality are complex and
require more research at both the theoretical and empirical
levels before much can be said precisely about the intergenerational component of the effect of population growth on inequality. There can be no general answer to the question of whether
reduced population growth rates would have an equalizing effect
through greater intergenerational mobility. A decline in the
fertility of the highest-income groups while the fertility of
the poor remains constant could have unequalizing effects, while

an equal proportional decline in all households' fertility might
have no effect at all. Furthermore, it is worth repeating the
warning given above that the observed effects of any particular
pattern of fertility decline will be different, often even of
opposite sign, for different measures of inequality. A change
to replacement fertility for all income groups, for example, may
lead to a smaller percentage of the population being poor, but
may lead to increased inequality as measured by Gini coefficients
or the income share of the bottom 20 percent of the population.
If we can decide on welfare grounds which measures correspond to
our social objectives, then we must ensure that we get correct
signals from the inequality indicators used in any analysis of
alternative population policies.


SUMMARY AND CONCLUSIONS

Existing evidence on the distributional effects of population
growth leads to mixed conclusions. The certainty of negative
distributional effects of population growth expressed in the 1974
World Bank report quoted at the beginning of this chapter seems
a much stronger conclusion than empirical and theoretical analysis of the issue can currently support.
    As surveyed above, empirical work on this issue has primarily
taken the form of cross-national regressions that include population growth as an independent variable explaining some summary
inequality index. Most of these cross-national studies have
concluded that population growth increases inequality, although
recent results of Rodgers (1983) suggest no significant direct
effect of population growth. These empirical studies are subject
to standard criticisms of attempts at inference from cross-
national comparisons and suffer from the absence of theoretical
justifications for their identifying restrictions. In addition,
there are a number of reasons to believe that the issue of the
distributional effects of population growth is particularly ill-
suited to cross-national investigations of the type common in the
literature. In particular, complex compositional effects make it
difficult to infer the real welfare effects of population growth
from data on summary inequality measures alone. It seems unwarranted, then, to attach a great deal of weight to empirical
evidence on the overall relationship between population growth
and inequality. Understanding the relationship in a way that
meaningfully distinguishes between compositional effects and
substantive welfare issues requires probing deeper into the
specific mechanisms at work.
    One such mechanism through which population growth affects
inequality is through changes in age structure, as outlined
above. The easiest aspects of age structure effects to analyze
are those that can be thought of as pure compositional effects.
These effects can in principle be in offsetting directions, since
young workers may receive low incomes but at the same time have
low intracohort inequality. Age profiles from the United States
and Brazil give conflicting evidence on the net direction of

these effects, with the Brazilian profiles suggesting that a
shift toward a younger age structure could have a small equalizing effect on cross-sectional income distribution.  It may be
hoped that future research will provide additional evidence
based on income and inequality profiles from a variety of developing countries.  More important, future research in this area
should investigate the direct effects of age structure on the
age profiles of income and inequality themselves, since these
effects may be more important quantitatively and have more
substantive welfare implications.

Changes in household composition associated with changing
fertility are also likely to have significant effects on measured
inequality, but as with changes in age structure, the effects can
in principle be in any direction.  Even in a simply statistical
sense, reductions in the variance of household size will not
necessarily imply reductions in interhousehold income inequality
since the variance of household size and the covariance of household size and household income are not independent.  The role of
household composition in the relationship between population
growth and inequality depends on poorly understood behavioral
links between income, fertility, and adult household composition.
As discussed above, if overall fertility decline initially leads
to increases in income differentials in fertility, then measured
inequality may increase.

The existence of income differentials in fertility implies
that measured inequality will change over time in part simply
because of changing proportions of the population in different
income groups.  Welfare interpretations of such changes are
difficult, since children of the poor may be no worse off relative to higher-income groups than their parents were, but measured inequality may increase or decrease as the proportion of
the population that is poor increases.  The analysis above demonstrates that the effect of higher fertility among the poor on
standard inequality measures can be either positive or negative
and may reverse direction if the differentials persist for long
periods.  Simple simulations show that in the presence of income
differentials in fertility, it is possible for the incomes of
the poor to fall relative to higher-income groups at the same
time that standard indexes show decreasing inequality.
Similarly, incomes of the poor may rise relative to those of
higher-income groups at the same time that standard indexes show
rising inequality.  These results demonstrate the importance of
defining distributional criteria carefully and the need for
caution in drawing inferences from cross-national or intemporal
differences in measured inequality.

Given the complex compositional effects that may confound
measures of dispersion, it is necessary to examine direct evidence on relative income differentials in addition to standard
inequality indexes.  Unfortunately, such data are limited and
have received little attention in developing countries.  The
argument that more rapid population growth reduces wages is well
supported by both economic theory and empirical evidence.  As
discussed above, Williamson and Lindert conclude from their

analysis of the historical U.S. experience that this effect is important in explaining intertemporal trends in inequality in the United States. However, comparable studies from developing countries do not exist. Furthermore, it is important that caution be used in deriving policy implications from the wage-reducing effect of population growth. A decline in relative wages of the poor may increase measured inequality, but need not imply that the poor are worse off in absolute terms. While it is important to combine distributional criteria with criteria such as maximizing per capita income, distributional criteria alone may not be consistent with maximizing the welfare of the poor.

The area in which the most important welfare issues arise appears to be the intergenerational transmission of inequality. As long as we are concerned with inequality among current adults, it is inherently confusing to consider the effects on inequality of a variable that is essentially the outcome of those individuals' behavior. However, if we choose as our criterion inequality within future generations, there may in principle be a defensible case for arguing that the fertility behavior of the current generation is inconsistent with the welfare of subsequent generations. This would appear to be the point of view implicit in the many studies in which it is argued that large income differentials in fertility lead to greater inequality in the second generation because of a decline in per child endowments (including human capital investments) associated with high fertility. The possibility that policy-induced fertility reductions would increase child "quality" is supported by the empirical evidence, even after controlling for possible simultaneity bias. This is an important area for additional research, with hopes that empirical evidence will be supplemented by theoretical analysis of the complex "intergenerational externality" issues that are implicit in most discussions of the distributional effects of high fertility, but have not been carefully thought through.

In conclusion, it is worth reemphasizing the obvious but often neglected point that population growth cannot be independently controlled as a policy instrument, but rather results from the behavior of individual couples. It is misleading to attempt to analyze the distributional effects of population growth in the same way that we might examine the distributional effects of a direct policy instrument such as an income tax. For policy purposes, we can meaningfully consider only the distributional effects of policies that indirectly affect population growth, and are likely to have direct distributional consequences of their own that are far more important than any indirect effects working through the relationship between population growth and inequality. A family planning policy that provides information and health services to the poor is more easily justified on the grounds that it involves a direct redistribution of resources than on the grounds that lower fertility will lead indirectly to greater equality. Similarly, the distributional effects of policies such as direct restrictions on fertility should be evaluated from the standpoint of their direct

welfare effects on different income groups in the population.
If the current burden of the policy falls hardest on the poor,
it would seem unsound to justify such a policy on the grounds
that lower population growth will lead indirectly to a more
equal distribution of income.

As a final caveat regarding policy implications, it is worth
mentioning the standard economic argument that if we seek to
maximize distributional goals, it is best to use the most direct
instruments available. The evidence surveyed here suggests that
it is too complex and difficult to divide the distributional
implications of population growth between compositional and welfare effects for those implications to serve as an important
foundation for population policy. If the goal is to redistribute
resources to the poor, there are surely more direct means, even
under severe political constraints, than influencing individual
fertility decisions. Even from the perspective of intergenerational inequality, the area in which probably the best case for
policy intervention can be made, we are likely to be much more
effective in decreasing differentials in child endowments by
increasing expenditures on schooling directly (or by instituting
compulsory education laws) than by attempting to alter individual
fertility decisions. As mentioned above, this does not mean that
family planning programs cannot serve important distributional
objectives. If the poor benefit directly from increased availability of family planning services, then such programs may have
a positive distributional effect directly, as would the increased
provision of any health or education service to the poor.

From the perspective of understanding the dynamics of economic development, the demographic transition, and inequality,
there is clearly a great deal more to be learned about the
relationship between population growth and inequality. In this
broader sense, there are important policy issues surrounding the
research surveyed here. To evaluate recent trends in inequality
in developing countries and formulate policies that may offset
any disequalizing tendencies associated with economic growth, it
is essential to understand the demographic component of changing
inequality. The results surveyed here suggest that this component can be substantial, but also suggest that the effects are
not well understood. It may be hoped that future research will
move us further toward a separation of these demographic effects
into those that are purely compositional and those that have
substantive welfare implications requiring legitimate policy
attention.


NOTES

1  For a history of thought on the subject and for more detailed
   discussion of certain issues not treated extensively here,
   see the previous surveys of the distributional effects of
   population growth by Sirageldin (1975), Boulier (1977),
   Potter (1979), Visaria (1979), Kuznets (1980), and Rodgers
   (1978, 1983).

2  See, for example, Meade (1965), Dasgupta (1969), and the
   survey by Pitchford (1974).

3  For a detailed critique of Repetto's work, see Boulier
   (1982).

4  U.S. data are taken from Schultz (1975). Brazilian data were
   compiled from the 1976 Pesquisa Nacional de Amostra Domicilar
   (IBGE, 1976); very similar profiles for Brazil are implied by
   the estimates of Langoni (1973) from 1970 Brazilian census
   data.

5  Since there is also higher inequality at older ages, the
   effect of shifting workers into the high-variance young ages
   will be partially offset by the reduction in the proportion
   of workers in the oldest age groups.

6  See the debate between Fishlow (1972, 1980) and Fields (1977,
   1980a), for example. Some indicators of poverty and inequality in Brazil showed improvements between 1960 and 1970 when
   unpaid family workers were included, but showed deterioration
   when those workers were excluded.

7  The coefficient of variation was used for this exercise since
   the preferred measure of the variance of the logarithm of
   income cannot include zero incomes. Since the coefficient
   of variation is less sensitive to changes at low income
   levels, it is not well suited to this particular test.
   Experiments of assigning low but nonzero values to unpaid
   family workers for calculating the variance of the logarithm
   of income showed sharp increases in inequality at young ages.
   Such comparisons are hard to evaluate, however, given the
   arbitrariness of the incomes assigned.

8  The age profiles for the United States are taken from Schultz
   (1975); the profiles for Colombia are from Schultz (1981);
   the profiles for Brazil are from Langoni (1973).

9  The effects of cohort size on earnings have been an integral
   part of Easterlin's theories of economic-demographic cycles
   (e.g., Easterlin et al., 1978). Two major pieces of empirical work on the labor market impact of the U.S. baby boom
   are Welch (1979) and Freeman (1979).

10 See, for example, the discussion by Kusnic and DaVanzo (1980:
   9-12).

11 See the seminal article by Atkinson (1970). A useful survey
   of subsequent developments in this literature is provided by
   Kakwani (1980).

12 See Lam (1985) for further discussion of this literature and
   its applicability to welfare comparisons of changes in inequality caused by population expansion.

13 See Robinson (1976) for similar analysis of the pattern of
   inequality generated when one sector increases its share of
   the population over time.

14 See Fields (1980b:87-98) and the sources he cites.

15 See, for example, Mueller (1976), Cain (1980), Lindert
   (1980), and DeTray (1983).

16 Suppose a wife's clothing is purchased entirely out of her
   husband's market earnings, while the husband's meals are
   prepared entirely with the wife's time. It would be

artificial to look at either clothing or meals in isolation and attempt to identify the distributional impact of that item in the household. The fact that one member is specializing in production of a certain good does not mean that this member would be better off if less of the good were produced.

17  Evidence from Bangladesh is analyzed by D'Souza and Chen (1980) and Chen et al. (1981). Evidence from India is analyzed by Rosenzweig and Schultz (1982). One possible indirect effect of family size might work through the effect of per capita resources in the family. The results reported by Rosenzweig and Schultz suggest that there may be a pure income effect in the direction of decreasing sex differentials in mortality. Chen et al. do not identify any direct relationship between wealth and intrafamily equity in Bangladesh.

18  For a discussion of some indirect data regarding recent trends in sex differentials in mortality in China, see Coale (1984).

19  See, for example, the evidence surveyed by Wray (1971) and Birdsall (1977).

20  For instance, the effect of income on fertility, controlling for the endogeneity of household income, due to factors such as the simultaneous choice of fertility and female labor supply.

## REFERENCES

Adelman, I., and C.T. Morris (1973)  Economic Growth and Social Equity in Developing Countries.  Stanford, Calif.: Stanford University Press.

Ahluwalia, M.S. (1976)  Inequality, poverty and development. Journal of Development Economics 3(4):307-342.

Ahluwalia, M.S., and H. Chenery (1974)  The economic framework. Chapter 2 in H. Chenery et al., eds., Redistribution with Growth.  London: Oxford University Press.

Arnold, F., R.A. Bulatao, C. Buripakdi, B.J. Chung, J.T. Fawcett, T. Iritani, S.J. Lee, and T.-S. Wu (1975)  The Value of Children, A Cross-National Study:  Introduction and Comparative Analysis.  Honolulu:  East-West Population Institute.

Atkinson, A.B. (1970)  On the measurement of inequality. Journal of Economic Theory II:244-263.

Birdsall, N. (1977)  Analytical approaches to the relationship of population growth and development.  Population and Development Review 3(1):63-102.

Birdsall, N. (1980)  Population and Poverty in the Developing World.  World Bank Staff Working Paper No. 404.  World Bank, Washington, D.C.

Boulier, B.L. (1977)  Population policy and income distribution. In C.R. Frank and R.C. Webb, eds., Income Distribution and Growth in the Less-Developed Countries.  Washington, D.C.: Brookings.

Boulier, B.L. (1982) Income redistribution and fertility decline: a skeptical view. In Y. Ben-Porath, ed., Income Distribution and the Family. Supplement to Vol. 8 of Population and Development Review 159-173, New York.

Cain, M. (1977) The economic activities of children in a village in Bangladesh. Population and Development Review 3(3):201-227.

Cain, M. (1978) The household life cycle and economic mobility in rural Bangladesh. Population and Development Review 4(3):421-438.

Chen, L.C., E. Huq, and S. D'Souza (1981) Sex bias in the family allocation of food and health care in rural Bangladesh. Population and Development Review 7(1):55-70.

Coale, A. (1984) Rapid Population Change in China, 1952-1982. Washington, D.C.: National Academy Press.

D'Souza, S., and L. Chen (1980) Sex differentials in mortality in rural Bangladesh. Population and Development Review 6(2):257-270.

Danziger, S., and M. Taussig (1979) The income unit and the anatomy of income distribution. Review of Income and Wealth 25(4):365-375.

Dasgupta, P. (1969) On the concept of optimum population. Review of Economic Studies 36:295-318.

Datta, G., and J. Meerman (1980) Household income or household income per capita in welfare comparisons. Review of Income and Wealth 26(4):401-417.

DeTray, D. (1983) Children's work activities in Malaysia. Population and Development Review 9(3):437-455.

Dooley, M., and P. Gottschalk (1984) Earnings inequality among males in the United States: trends and the effect of labor force growth. Journal of Political Economy 92(1):59-89.

Easterlin, R.A., M.L. Wachter, and S.M. Wachter (1978) Demographic influences on economic stability: the United States experience. Population and Development Review 4(1):1-23.

Fei, C.H., G. Ranis, and S.W.Y. Kuo (1979) Growth with Equity: The Taiwan Case. New York: Oxford University Press.

Fields, G. (1977) Who benefits from economic development? A reexamination of Brazilian growth in the 1970s. American Economic Review 67(4):570-582.

Fields, G.S. (1979) A welfare economic approach to growth and distribution in the dual economy. Quarterly Journal of Economics 93(3):327-353.

Fields, G. (1980a) Who benefits from economic development? Reply. American Economic Review 70(1):257-262.

Fields, G. (1980b) Poverty, Inequality, and Development. Cambridge, England: Cambridge University Press.

Fishlow, A. (1972) Brazilian size distribution of income. American Economic Review 62(2):391-410.

Fishlow, A. (1980) Who benefits from economic development? Comment. American Economic Review 70(1):250-256.

Freeman, R. (1979) The effect of demographic factors on age-earnings profiles. Journal of Human Resources 14(3):289-318.

Goodstadt, L. (1982)   China's one-child family:   policy and
    public response.   Population and Development Review
    8(1):37-58.
Hirschman, A.O., and M. Rothschild (1973)   The changing toler-
    ance for income inequality in the course of economic develop-
    ment.   The Quarterly Journal of Economics 87:544-566.
Ho, T.J. (1979)   Time costs of child rearing in the rural
    Philippines.   Population and Development Review 5(4):643-662.
IBGE (Instituto Brasileiro de Geografia e Estatistica) (1976)
    Pesquisa Nacional por Amostra de Domicilios.   Rio de
    Janeiro:   IBGE
Kakwani, N.C. (1980)   Income Inequality and Poverty:   Methods of
    Estimation and Policy Applications.   Oxford:   Oxford
    University Press.
Kocher, J. (1973)   Rural Development, Income Distribution, and
    Fertility Decline.   New York:   The Population Council.
Kusnic, M., and J. DaVanzo (1980)   Income Inequality and the
    Definition of Income:   The Case of Malaysia.   Santa Monica,
    Calif.:   The Rand Corporation.
Kuznets, S. (1955)   Economic growth and income inequality.
    American Economic Review 45(1):1-28.
Kuznets, S. (1976)   Demographic aspects of the size distribution
    of income.   Economic Development and Cultural Change 25(1):
    1-94.
Kuznets, S. (1978)   Size and age structure of family households:
    exploratory comparisons.   Population and Development Review
    4(2):187-224.
Kuznets, S. (1980)   Recent population trends in less developed
    countries and implications for internal income inequality.
    In R. Easterlin, ed., Population and Economic Change in
    Developing Countries.   National Bureau of Economic Research
    Conference Report Number 30.   Chicago:   University of Chicago
    Press.
Kuznets, S. (1981)   Size of household and income disparities.   In
    J. Simon and P. Lindert, eds., Research in Population
    Economics.   Greenwich, Conn.:   JAI Press.
Lam, D. (1984)   The variance of population characteristics in
    stable populations, with applications to the distribution of
    income.   Population Studies 38:117-127.
Lam, D. (1985)   The Dynamics of Population Growth, Differential
    Fertility, and Inequality.   Research Report No. 85-69.
    Population Studies Center, University of Michigan.
Langoni, C.G. (1973)   Distribuicao da Renda e Desenvolvimento
    Economico do Brasil.   Rio de Janeiro:   Editora Expressao e
    Cultura.
Lee, R.D. (1973)   Population in preindustrial England:   an
    econometric analysis.   Quarterly Journal of Economics
    87(4):581-607.
Lee, R.D. (1978)   Models of preindustrial population dynamics
    with applications to England.   In C. Tilly, ed., Historical
    Studies of Changing Fertility.   Princeton, N.J.:   Princeton
    University Press.

Lee, R.D. (1980)  An historical perspective on economic aspects
of the population explosion:  the case of preindustrial
England.  In R.A. Easterlin, ed., Population and Economic
Change in Developing Countries.  National Bureau of Economic
Research Conference Report Number 30.  Chicago:  University
of Chicago Press.

Lindert, P. (1978)  Fertility and Scarcity in America.
Princeton, N.J.:  Princeton University Press.

Lindert, P. (1980)  Child costs and economic development.  In R.
Easterlin, ed., Population and Economic Change in Developing
Countries.  National Bureau of Economic Research Conference
Report Number 30.  Chicago:  University of Chicago Press.

Meade, J.E. (1965)  Efficiency, Equality and the Ownership of
Property.  Cambridge, Mass.:  Harvard University Press.

Menchik, P.L. (1980)  Primogeniture, equal sharing, and the U.S.
distribution of wealth.  Quarterly Journal of Economics
94(2):299-316.

Mincer, J.A. (1974)  Schooling, Experience, and Earnings.  New
York:  Columbia University Press.

Morawetz, D. (1976)  Elasticities of substitution in industry:
what do we learn from econometric estimates?  World
Development 4(1):11-15.

Morley, S. (1981)  The effect of changes in the population on
several measures of income distribution.  American Economic
Review 71(3):285-294.

Mueller, E. (1976)  The economic value of children in peasant
agriculture.  In R. Ridker, ed., Population and Development:
The Search for Selective Interventions.  Baltimore, Md.:
The Johns Hopkins University Press.

Mueller, E., and K. Short (1983)  Effects of income and wealth
on the demand for children.  Pp. 590-642 in R. Bulatao and
R. Lee, eds., Determinants of Fertility in Developing
Countries.  New York:  Academic Press.

Ogawa, N. (1978)  Fertility control and income distribution in
developing countries with national family planning pro-
grammes.  Pakistan Development Review 17(4):431-450.

Paglin, M. (1975)  The measurement and trend of inequality:  a
basic revision.  American Economic Review 65(3):520-531.

Pitchford, J.D. (1974)  Population in Economic Growth.
Amsterdam:  North Holland.

Potter, J. (1979)  Demographic factors and income distribution
in Latin America.  In International Union for the Scientific
Study of Population, Economic and Demographic Change:  Issues
for the 1980s 1:321-336.

Repetto, R. (1978)  The interaction of fertility and the size
distribution of income.  Journal of Development Studies
(London) 14(3):22-39.

Repetto, R. (1979)  Economic Equality and Fertility in Developing
Countries.  Baltimore, Md.:  The Johns Hopkins University
Press.

Rich, W. (1973)  Smaller Families Through Social and Economic
Progress.  Washington, D.C.:  Overseas Development Council.

Robinson, S. (1976)  A note on the U hypothesis relating income inequality and economic development. American Economic Review 66(3):437-440.

Rodgers, G. (1978)  Demographic determinants of the distribution of income. World Development 6(3):305-318.

Rodgers, G. (1983)  Population growth, inequality and poverty. International Labour Review 122(4):443-460.

Rosenzweig, M.R., and R. Evenson (1977)  Fertility, schooling, and the economic contribution of children in rural India: an econometric analysis. Econometrica 45(5):1065-1079.

Rosenzweig, M.R., and T.P. Schultz (1982)  Market opportunities, genetic endowments, and intrafamily resource distribution: child survival in rural India. American Economic Review 72(4):803-815.

Rosenzweig, M.R., and K.I. Wolpin (1980)  Testing the quantity-quality fertility model: the use of twins as a natural experiment. Econometrica 48(1):227-240.

Schultz, T.P. (1975)  Long-term change in personal income distribution theoretical approaches, evidence, and explanations. Pp. 147-169 in D.M. Levine and M.J. Bane, eds., The Inequality Controversy. New York: Basic Books.

Schultz, T.P. (1981)  Age of Individuals and Family Composition as Factors Underlying the Distribution of Personal Income. Economic Growth Center Discussion Paper No. 383, Yale University.

Schultz, T.P. (1982)  Family composition and income inequality. Population and Development Review, Supplement to Volume 8, 137-150.

Sirageldin, I.A. (1975)  The demographic aspects of income distribution. In W.C. Robinson, ed., Population and Development Planning. New York: The Population Council.

Solow, R.M. (1956)  A contribution to the theory of economic growth. Quarterly Journal of Economics 70(1):65-94.

Tomes, N. (1981)  The family, inheritance, and the intergenerational transmission of inequality. Journal of Political Economy 89(5):928-958.

Visaria, P. (1979)  Demographic factors and the distribution of income: some issues. In IUSSP Economic and Demographic Change: Issues for the 1980s 1:298-320.

Welch, F. (1979)  Effects of cohort size on earnings: the baby boom babies' financial bust. Journal of Political Economy 87(5), part 2:S65-S97.

Williamson, J.G., and P.H. Lindert (1980)  American Inequality: A Macroeconomic History. New York: Academic Press.

Winegarden, C.R. (1978)  A simultaneous-equations model of population growth and income distribution. Applied Economics 10:319-330.

Winegarden, C.R. (1980)  Socioeconomic equity and fertility in developing countries: a block-recursive model. De Economist 128, NR 4.

World Bank (1974)  Population Policies and Economic Development. Baltimore, Md.: The Johns Hopkins University Press.

World Bank (1984)  <u>World Development Report 1984</u>.  New York:
  Oxford University Press.
Wray, J.D. (1971)  Population pressure on families:  family size
  and child spacing.  Pp. 403-457 in National Academy of
  Sciences <u>Rapid Population Growth:  Consequences and Policy
  Implications</u>.  Baltimore, Md.:  The Johns Hopkins University
  Press.

# VI. Welfare and Ethics

# 16
## The Ethical Foundations of Population Policies
Partha Dasgupta

INTRODUCTION

In his recent book, Parfit (1984) distinguishes three types of policy options: same people choices, same number choices, and different number choices. The first affects neither the number of persons nor their personal identities, as in the classic problem of dividing a cake fairly among a given group of people; much of social choice theory is concerned with such choices. The second type of choice affects the identities of future persons, but not their numbers. The last affects both.

National economic plans are most often cast within the context of same number choices. This is a good approximation when the available set of economic policies is restricted, for either technical or political reasons, to those that do not impinge on the size of future populations. The idea, then, is to forecast future numbers (which, by assumption, are unaffected by choice of policy) and then to rank alternative policies. In same people choices, "social states"--or "end states," to use Nozick's (1974) terminology--need not include in their characterization the personal identities involved, since the same persons are affected by all the policies. In contrast, in same number choices, a social state includes in its characterization the identities of the people involved, although, of course, the number of lives associated with all end states is, by assumption, the same. To be sure, one may argue that personal identities ought not to matter in same number choices, but only the quality of lives. The point is that the kind of moral reasoning associated with the idea of "impersonal preference" (Harsanyi, 1955, 1977), or "extended sympathy" (Arrow, 1963), which has often been restricted to analyses of same people choices, can also be invoked for same number choices.1 If policy option $A_1$ is pursued, then ego 1 will be born and will enjoy a given level of well-being. If policy option $A_2$ is pursued, then ego 2 will be born instead and will enjoy a (possibly) different level of well-being. (Thus $A_1$ and $A_2$ may differ by way of the timing of conception.) In either event, there will be an ego (in addition to all the other egos that will exist under either of the policies); there will

631

be an additional life.  Confronted with $A_1$ and $A_2$, I can be
asked which one I would choose if I did not know which person's
circumstances I would inherit under either policy.  This is the
classic way of posing the problem of social choice using the extended sympathy route.  An end state in a same people choice is
an allocation of the good (e.g., welfare).  The desire for imper-
sonality implies that names do not matter; that is, we should be
socially indifferent between a distribution of well-being and any
of its permutations across persons.[2]  In exactly the same way,
the extended sympathy argument implies that the allocation of the
good (e.g., welfare) is morally the only relevant feature of an
end state, even in a same number choice.

Of course, extended sympathy is not the only moral route
available for exploring problems of social choice.  One may invoke "anonymity" or "symmetry" as a primary moral--that is, invoke it as a moral axiom--and assert that in same number choices,
personal identities must not matter, but only the qualities of
lives lived under each policy option.  This is precisely the way
in which the issue has been handled by Koopmans (1960, 1972) and
Diamond (1965).[3]  Frank Ramsey's classic formulation of the
optimum savings problem concerned same number choices and also
invoked the anonymity, or symmetry, axiom (see Ramsey, 1928).
In the Ramsey formulation, an end state is an intertemporal distribution of the good (i.e., welfare):  the names or identities
of persons under each option are of no moral consequence; only
lives matter.

For the most part, welfare economics has addressed same
people choices and same number choices, and has not distinguished
the two.  It has not done so because for the most part, the ob-
ject of study has been the quality of lives under various policy
options.  The quality index is often referred to as "welfare,"
and on occasion as "utility."  In this chapter, these terms are
used synonymously, and it is assumed that they correlate perfectly with agreeable consciousness, the level of well-being, the
standard of living, and so forth.  Nothing will be lost by this
assumption.

Far and away the most difficult kind of question option is
that involving different number choices.  There is a small literature in welfare economics under the heading "Optimum Population" that addresses the moral issues involved in such types of
social choice.  This chapter argues that different number choices
pose conceptual problems far more intricate than those involved
in same number choices, partly because the anonymity or symmetry
axiom is not readily defensible in different number choices.
Before presenting such arguments, however, it is worthwhile to
review the conceptual problems that arise in analyzing same
number choices and to discuss related issues, such as the choice
of social discount rates.  This is done in the next section
below.  The following section presents the classical utilitarian
answer to the optimum population problem, a central aspect of
different number choices.  It is argued then that classical
utilitarianism invokes the anonymity or symmetry axiom for different number choices because it views the problem of optimum

population as a genesis problem.  In an actual problem, the symmetry axiom is otiose.  However, if one drops the symmetry axiom,
there are new difficulties.  This is illustrated in the next section by means of a set of examples.  The final section presents a
brief summary and conclusions.


SAME NUMBER CHOICES

Social Welfare Functions

Begin by considering a simple but fairly general formulation of
the problem of normative economics involving same number choices.
We suppose that there are N social states (or end states), labeled $S_j$ (with $j=1, \ldots, N$).  The number of persons in each
social state is M, and we label persons by $i=1, \ldots, M$.  The
problem of social choice involving same number choices is to
rank the N social states.  There is of course no reason why we
should expect of a moral theory the ability to coax a complete
ranking; that is, the morally defensible social ordering may be
only a partial ordering.  However, at this level of generality,
it makes no sense not to impose a complete ordering on the N
objects of choice.  We do this, and we write by $W(S_j)$ a numerical representation of this complete ordering.  This is a social
welfare function in its most general form.
    No restriction has been imposed on the concept of a social
state.  Thus, a social state embodies in its characterization
everything that is morally relevant for social choice.  A social
state embodies not only the consequences of actions, but also
possibly the actions themselves.
    The social welfare function is, of course, an aggregator.
As a numerical function, it aggregates a variety of possible
social objectives or goals.  Take, for example, a sample of the
many social objectives that are often proclaimed:  national income per head must be increased; the degree of inequality and
wealth (in the light of some summary measure, say) needs to be
reduced; poverty must be made to disappear; the level of unemployment ought to be lessened; the rate of inflation has to be
pruned; the nation's resources must be conserved; the citizens'
fundamental rights (suitably defined) must not be encroached
upon; life expectancy must be raised; the "basic needs" of the
citizens must be met within T years; and so on.  Some of these
goals are, at least approximately, quantifiable, but not all.
They are most often nonbasic, in the sense that they are implied
by a combination of some other goals (often only implicitly held)
and contingent facts--e.g., in any discussion that attempts to
establish the evils of high inflation rates.  Moreover, they are
usually noncompulsive, in that when in conflict, each of them is
usually given some weight; no objective overrides all others.[4]
    In fact, of course, much of welfare economics imposes a good
deal further structure on W.  For the most part, it sees W as
being defined directly on the welfare, or utility, consequences
of the social states.  For purposes of this chapter, nothing will

be lost in imposing this restriction. The discussion here therefore takes it that social welfare depends solely on the M-tuple
of numerical indexes of the good, which for the sake of concreteness is called here the "standard of living" or alternatively,
the "living standard." It is naturally assumed that this corre-
lates with utility, welfare, the quality of life, agreeable consciousness, preference satisfaction, and so forth. Let $U_i(S_j)$
be the standard of living in social state $S_j$ of the person labeled i. Then social welfare at $S_j$ is

$$W(U_1(S_j), \ldots, U_i(S_j), \ldots, U_M(S_j)) .^5 \qquad (1)$$

A person's living standard is determined, among other things,
by the sorts of activities he can engage in, his consumption
level, the size of his family, and so forth. Later in the chapter, the ingredients that enter into the standard of living index
are discussed. Until then, we consider social orderings of end
states $(S_1, \ldots, S_N)$ without asking what characterizes
these end states. The numerical index of the good is termed
"living standard" because it is assumed in what follows that the
good is fully comparable interpersonally. Any other term, such
as utility or welfare, might jar against this assumption, whereas
the standard of living probably will not. A living standard is
positive if it is good that a person lives at that state. This
involves comparison with a life just worth living, that is, the
worst state such that we do not count it a positively bad thing
that people live at that state. The standard of living is nil at
such a state. A formal definition is provided later in the chapter. However, we may note here that this is not to be thought
of as a state at which a person is indifferent between remaining
alive and committing suicide, or as the state between which and
the "state" of not having been born a person is indifferent.


## Multiple Goals and Rights

In the previous subsection, it was seen that the social welfare
function (1) incorporates basic social goals expressed in terms
of the distribution of the good, what we call here the living
standard. This formulation does not deny that there may be
multiple social objectives. When these objectives conflict,
they are weighted, and the social welfare function expressed in
(1) implicitly incorporates these weights.
        Where do rights come in? Certain types of rights--those that
are not inviolable--are eschewed when we define the social welfare function directly on the M-tuples of living standards. However, if certain rights are deemed inviolable, they can be incorporated as additional moral constraints. Thus, we would wish to
maximize (1) subject to the technological, informational, and
institutional constraints facing the economy. However, if there
are certain rights that must not be violated, these rights can
be described by additional constraints in the planning exercise.
For example, Sen (1982), using torture as an analogy, has re-

cently argued that future generations may have a right to a clean
environment, a right that is not based on welfare or utility
claims in the manner of (1). For present purposes, the point is
not so much whether this is a compelling argument, but rather
that if rights to a clean environment (suitably defined) are inviolable, then the imposition of constraints on pollution emission and concentration levels (e.g., ambient air quality standards) is the way to articulate such rights.[6]

## Accounting Prices

Suppose that a planner wishes to maximize the social welfare
function (e.g., (1)) subject to the technological, informational,
and institutional constraints facing him. Institutional constraints consist, among other things, of the responses of the
private sector to the planner's decisions. The extent to which
the planner can exercise control over the economy can be great
or small, depending on the economy in question. For expositional
ease, we assume away uncertainty.[7] It is then a well-known
theorem in welfare economics that under certain circumstances
(for example, W is concave and the constraint sets convex), the
optimum plan can be decentralized, in the sense that there exists
a system of "accounting prices" or "shadow prices" for goods and
services which, if used in production plans, can sustain the desired program, and thus the desired social state.

To link this to the general formulation presented at the beginning of this section, we may consider N to be the set of all
conceivable social states, where a social state is characterized
by an allocation of goods and services and so forth among the M
people in society. The social welfare function (1) ranks these
N states completely. However, technological and institutional
constraints (and possible constraints capturing the inviolability
of certain types of rights) ensure that not all N social states
are feasible; these constraints together determine which ones are
feasible. The planner's problem is to locate the (socially) best
social state from the feasible set. A system of accounting
prices can be of help in implementing the best (or optimal) feasible plan, that is, the plan that sustains the best (or optimal)
feasible social state.

## The Symmetry Axiom

So far, there has been no mention of time. To avoid for the
moment the special considerations introduced by time, the discussion continues to assume a timeless world.

In (1), the social welfare function has been defined on the
M-dimensional space of living standards. Let $u_i$ denote the
living standard of label i. Then we have $W(u_1, \ldots, u_i, \ldots, u_M)$ as the social welfare level. Let us now impose some
(moral) conditions on W so as to simplify the exposition.

The first assumption we will impose on W is that it is a continuous function; that is, standard of living M-tuples that are not too different are not far apart in the social ordering as reflected by W. A distinguished social welfare function that violates this condition is lexicographic maxi-min.[8] Therefore, it may be felt that in continuity too much is assumed. In fact, lexicographic maxi-min is an extreme moral ordering, and in any case, it can be approximated, as closely as one likes for all practical purposes, by a continuous function. Continuity is in fact a very mild restriction.

The second, and most important, assumption we will make is symmetry, that is, that all permutations of an M-tuple of living standards are awarded the same numerical value by W. Figure 1 depicts the case where M = 2. Symmetry amounts to the claim that the iso-welfare contours--$(u_1, u_2)$ pairs for which W has the same value--are symmetric about the 45° line.

Symmetry is not an innocuous assumption. It can be defended, as was done by Harsanyi (1955), by an appeal to a particular form of the extended sympathy framework. While not innocuous, however, it is at the same time difficult to reject since to do so is to claim that a person's label matters in the social treatment of that person's standard of living.[9]

These two assumptions imply, as Figure 1 demonstrates, that associated with every M-tuple of living standards, $(u_1, \ldots, u_i, \ldots, u_M)$, there is a corresponding living standard, $\mu$, which, if awarded to each of the M lives, leads to a situation that is exactly as good as $(u_1, \ldots, u_i, \ldots, u_M)$. $\mu$ is therefore an "average" living standard associated with $(u_1, \ldots, u_i, \ldots, u_M)$ (though unless W is Utilitarian, it is not the arithmetic average; see below). This feature of W will greatly facilitate our subsequent discussion. Since corresponding to any end state there is an equally desirable one in which all lives enjoy the same living standard, we may as well restrict the discussion to such end states. Thus, by $W_M(\mu)$ we will now mean the numerical social welfare value associated with an end state in which each of the M lives enjoys $\mu$.[10]

Finally, it is assumed that $W_M(\mu)$ is increasing in $\mu$. (In Figure 1, this means that northeasterly points on the 45° line are more desirable.) This last assumption is very innocuous.

A distinguished example of a social welfare function forsSame number choice satisfying these requirements is provided by utilitarianism. Here $W(u_1, \ldots, u_M) = u_1 + u_2 + \ldots + u_M$. It should be noted that the equally distributed equivalent living standard under utilitarianism is the arithmetic mean; that is, $\mu = (u_1 + u_2 + \ldots + u_M)/M$. Advocating as it does the sum, utilitarianism is indifferent between all distributions of a given aggregate living standard. There is a precise sense in which all moral theories that are equality-seeking entail that the equally distributed living standard, $\mu$, is less than the arithmetic average (see Dasgupta et al., 1973).

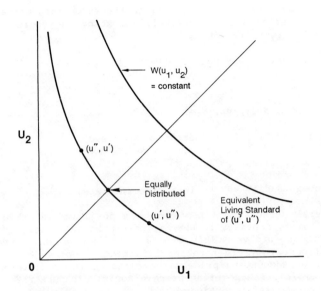

FIGURE 1   Loci of Living Standards Yielding Equal Welfare in
Same Number Choice


## Time and Social Discount Rates

So far, the framework used here for discussing same number
choices has been timeless. In fact, time can be readily incorporated by suitable reinterpretation. First, not all of the M
lives under consideration are lived by present persons; some are
future people. Second, goods, services, and resource flows may
be labeled not only by their physical characteristics and location, but also by the date at which they make their appearance.
Thus a social state is a complete specification of the goods,
services, and so forth flowing to and from each person at each
date.

Consider then an intertemporal planning problem in which a
social welfare function, such as (1), is to be maximized subject
to the variety of constraints the planner faces. Let t denote
time, and without loss of generality, label "today" as $t = 0$,
the date at which the planning problem is posed. Suppose that
it is possible to implement the optimal plan--that is, the solution of the planning problem--by the use of accounting prices.
Let the planner select a given commodity as a numeraire, which
we label by all its characteristics except its date. Let $P_t$
be its accounting price for date t. It is a present value
price, the accounting price to be used today for the numeraire
of date t. Suppose that $P_t > 0$ for all $t \geq 0$; that is, the
numeraire is never a free good. Consider two adjacent moments,
t and t+1. We define the social rate of discount between t and

t+1 as the percentage rate of fall in the accounting price of the numeraire over this unit interval. Denoting the social rate of discount by $r_t$, we thus have

$$r_t = - (P_{t+1} - P_t)/P_{t+1} ,$$

or

$$r_t = (P_t - P_{t+1})/P_{t+1} . \qquad (2)$$

Now, equation (2) can be rearranged to yield

$$P_{t+1} = P_t/(1+r_t) , \qquad (3)$$

which shows readily why $r_t$ is a discount rate.

Several observations need to be made about social discount rates. First, contrary to what is often thought, social discount rates do not involve solely ethical considerations, in particular, notions of intergenerational justice. Representing as they do a set of accounting prices, their status is no different from that of any other accounting price. Social discount rates depend not only on social objectives, as, say, captured in (1), but also on the constraints with which the economy is faced, which include a description of where the economy is; that is, social discount rates in particular, and accounting prices in general, reflect both welfare judgments and feasibility constraints.

Second, social discount rates depend on the numeraire good. Thus, suppose the optimum solution of a planning exercise yields as accounting prices \$15 and \$10 for bananas at dates t and t+1, respectively, and \$30 and \$15 for apples at dates t and t+1, respectively. Using (2), we conclude that if bananas are the numeraire good, the social rate of discount between t and t+1 is 1/3, whereas it is 1/2 if apples are the numeraire good. It is only when the optimum policy sustains a steady (or stationary) economic state that social discount rates do not depend on the numeraire good, for, along a steady state, relative accounting prices at all dates are the same.[11] We need hardly add that, irrespective of whether the economy is at a stationary state, the choice of policies is not affected by the numeraire.

Third, it is sometimes held that social discount rates ought to be nil, since otherwise one would be discriminating against future generations. This is essentially the argument used by Georgescu-Roegen (1979) in his criticism of Hotelling's (1931) analysis of the optimal depletion of exhaustible resources. Much depends on what the numeraire is, for as we may note from (2), the claim that the social discount rate ought to be nil amounts to the assertion that $P_t$ ought to equal $P_{t+1}$ for all t. However, as we have already observed, social discount rates (2) are exclusively a function of accounting prices, and they in turn depend on welfare judgments and feasibility constraints. Social discount rates are derived from optimization exercises; they are not a primitive concept, and they depend crucially on the numer-

aire chosen. Thus, suppose the numeraire good is some index of
per capita aggregate consumption. Now suppose along an optimal
program (i.e., optimal social state), this is expected to grow.
Then we should, under conventional hypotheses, expect the social
rates of discount to be positive, because future generations
will have a higher living standard (and thus diminished marginal
utility of consumption).

On the other hand, what is meant occasionally by the assertion that the social discount rate ought to be nil is the belief
that the social welfare function in (1) ought to be symmetric in
living standards. Thus suppose the index i in (1) represents the
ith generation, and, for simplicity of exposition, let us suppose that all generations are of equal size. Now suppose that
$u_i$ represents the living standard of generation i. For the
social welfare function (1) to be symmetric in living standards,
it must be the case that all permutations of any given allocation of living standards, $(u_1, \ldots, u_M)$, must be equally
valued by W. In his classic formulation of the optimum savings
problem, Ramsey (1928) assumed a utilitarian formulation and
took it that

$$W = u_1 + u_2 + \ldots + u_i + \ldots + u_M . \qquad (4)$$

Here, future living standards are not being discounted when evaluated by the generation i = 1. However, even if one chooses to
work with (4), the social discount rate may well be positive if
the numeraire is not the standard of living, but rather an ingre-
dient of the standard of living, such as aggregate consumption.

Now, it may be argued that if M is large, there is a case for
abandoning the symmetry in general and formulation (4) in particular, for the reason that future generations (at least those in
the distant future) may not exist. The possibility of future
extinction looms large if for no other reason than the redoubt-
able Second Law of Thermodynamics, a law that Georgescu-Roegen
himself has skillfully invoked to decry the manner in which economists are prone to modeling production possibilities. No doubt
there is a chance that future generations will exist no matter
how far into the future we peer, the chance being smaller the
farther we peer. However, this is an argument for including all
future generations in a planning exercise, not for awarding the
same social weight, by generation i = 1, to the living standard
of all future generations. Thus, suppose $q_i$ is the (subjective) probability that the ith generation will exist. (Presumably $q_i \geq q_{i+1} \geq 0$ for all i.) Then a defendable
generalization of (4) is

$$W = u_1 + q_2u_2 + \ldots + q_iu_i \ldots + q_mu_m + \ldots , \qquad (5)$$

the indefinite sum reflecting the possibility that i = 1 is not
certain which the terminal generation is. Here, $q_i$ is rather
like a discount factor. In fact, the form of the social welfare
function, as given in (5), can be deduced from an extended sympathy argument along the lines pursued by Harsanyi (1955) in his

pioneering essay. In a sense, even (5) preserves the symmetry
axiom, which in Harsanyi's formulation becomes the equi-probabil-
ity hypothesis of being in anyone's state. However, if future
generations are less likely to exist, then "equiprobable" must
translate directly into "less probable" to be in the shoes of future generations. If, for analytical tractability, it is assumed
that the extinction process is Poisson-like, then of course

$$q_i = (1+\delta)q_{i+1} ,$$

where $\delta > 0$ is the rate of decay. In this case, (5) reduces to
the form

$$W = u_1 + u_2 + \ldots + \frac{u_i}{(1+\delta)^{i-1}} + \ldots \tag{6}$$

The formulation in (6) has dominated the literature on optimum
savings.

   A great deal has been written on the subject of social discount rates and the arguments involved in estimating them. (See
for example, Baumol, 1968; Arrow and Kurz, 1970; and Lind, 1982.)
Much has been made of the possibility that social discount rates
ought to differ from private ones. In fact, the subject is open-
ended because social discount rates depend, among other things,
on social objectives, and of course one would expect accounting
prices to differ from market prices.

   We have supposed so far that for each value of M, there is a
complete ordering of end states, represented by $W_M(\mu)$. Population theory concerns different number choices. One must,
therefore, provide a link between each of the same number choice
orderings. The remainder of the chapter addresses this issue.
In what follows, social welfare is written as $W(\mu,M)$, to express
the feature that M is subject to choice.


## DIFFERENT NUMBER CHOICES

### The Genesis Problem and the Repugnant Conclusion

In the genesis oroblem, there are no actual persons: all persons
are potential. In its purest form, the genesis problem asks how
many lives there should be and at what (living) standards they
should be lived. Most theoretical exercises in the genesis problem have been conducted within the framework of classical utilitarianism (see, e.g., Meade, 1955 and Dasgupta, 1969).

   However, the application of classical utilitarianism in a
world with finite resources often implies a large population
size; that is to say, the average standard of living is embar-
rassingly low. (See Dasgupta, 1969:307; a simplified version is
presented in the Appendix to this chapter.) Rawls (1972:162-163)
notes in passing one implication of classical utilitarianism:
" . . . so long as the average utility per person falls slowly
enough when the number of individuals increases, the population

should be encouraged to grow indefinitely no matter how low the
average has fallen." Since there are possible worlds in which
the average utility per person falls "slowly enough" as the population size increases, this feature of classical utilitarianism
must not be ignored.

Parfit (1984) finds this idea repugnant, hence his term the
repugnant conclusion. One may, of course, ask why it is repugnant. The answer presumably is that the standard of living is a
good and therefore matters, that from the universal point of
view, mere numbers cannot compensate for a barely tolerable
living standard. However, what of two worlds with different M's
but the same $\mu$ ? How should we rank them? It may be supposed
that if the living standard is positive, the larger world is the
better one, and the worse one if the living standard is negative.
That will be the supposition here, not because it is needed for
the main thesis, but because it is a necessary condition for the
repugnant conclusion, which is discussed in this section.

The repugnant conclusion is implied not only by the classical
utilitarian form, $\mu M$, but also wherever all iso-welfare curves
of $W(\mu, M)$ tend to $\mu = 0$ for large M (see Figure 2).

If we find the repugnant conclusion repugnant, such functions
should be rejected or accepted repugnantly! The obvious move is
to consider those possessing the property that different iso-
welfare curves tend to different values of $\mu$ as M is made to
increase; the higher the iso-curve, the larger the value of $\mu$ to
which it converges (see Figure 3). Such welfare functions reflect "average utilitarianism" in an approximate manner for large
population sizes, and thereby avoid the repugnant conclusion.


The Pareto-Plus Principle

Personal identities ought not to matter in the genesis problem.
Indeed, it can be argued that they cannot matter: in the genesis
problem, all persons are potential. In a comparison of possible
worlds, there is no privileged person or group; the fact that
different worlds may have different persons is of no consequence.
For comparison purposes, all that is morally relevant is the
vector (or distribution) of living standards.

Consider a possible world that would consist of M persons,
where each would enjoy a standard of living $\mu$ . Social welfare
associated with this world is $W(\mu, M)$. Now consider another possible world that would consist of M + 1 persons, where again
each would enjoy $\mu$ as his living standard. Social welfare associated with this second world is $W(\mu, M+1)$. In what follows, it
is assumed that there is a unique value of $\mu$ such that for all
$M \geq 0$, $W(\mu, M) = W(\mu, M+1)$. This $\mu$ is calibrated as zero. This
defines the zero standard of living.

Consider two possible worlds, $(u_1, \ldots, u_i, \ldots, u_M)$ and
$(u_1, \ldots, u_i, \ldots, u_M, u_{M+1})$. Call them X and Y, respectively. They differ solely by the fact that Y has an additional
(labeled M+1) with a living standard $u_{M+1}$. The identities of
persons in the two worlds may well be different, but as we have
argued, this is of no consequence. We now wish to rank X and Y.

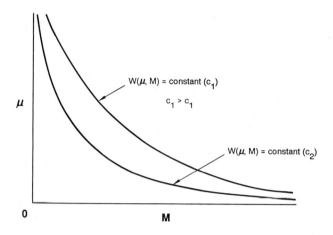

FIGURE 2   Social Indifference Curves Between Population and
Equally Distributed Equivalent Living Standards in the Genesis
Problem


It may be agreed that X is the better world if $u_{M+1}$ is
negative. However, what if $u_{M+1}$ is positive?
    In a thoughtful essay, Sikora (1978:42) has reasserted the
classical thesis that " . . . it is prima facie wrong to prevent
the existence of anyone with reasonable prospects of happiness,"
implying thereby that in the event $U_{M+1}$ is positive, Y ought
to be ranked over X. Sikora calls theories based on this thesis
"obligation theories." His idea of preventing the existence of
someone is curious; it suggests an image of potential immigrants
to a land of reasonable plenty condemned instead to languish in
an eternal limbo. The error to avoid, of course, is regarding
potential persons as a special type of persons. The claim that
$u_{M+1}$ is positive amounts to no more than a comparison of the
standard of living for person M + 1 in Y with the worst state
such that we do not count it a positively bad thing that people
live at that state. It would be wrong to claim that in choosing
Y we would be benefiting this person.
    The only morally relevant difference between X and Y is that
Y has an additional person, and his living standard is positive.
Call the conception which says that in such circumstances Y is
the better world the Pareto-plus principle. There are many who
find the principle appealing, and some find it so compelling that
they feel no requirement to justify it (see, e.g., Sikora, 1978).
The problem is that under fairly weak conditions, it implies the
repugnant conclusion.[12] There is no paradox in this; rather,
if we find the repugnant conclusion repugnant, something will
have to give. Parfit (1982:164) offers a way out of suggesting
that perhaps the welfare ranking is merely a partial ordering,
that if $u_{M+1}$ is not too large (but above zero), we simply
acknowledge that we cannot compare X and Y.

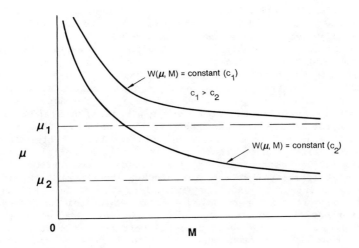

FIGURE 3   Avoiding the Repugnant Conclusion in the Genesis
Problem

It would be astonishing if a pluralist theory did not yield
a partial ordering of alternative worlds.  One would suppose that
where different principles are in conflict, we would typically
not be able to impute precise weights to them.  However, at this
general level of discourse, Parfit's suggestion is not really a
way out:  it does not address the problem, but merely evades it.
If we find the repugnant conclusion repugnant, we must ask why.
If we do not find the Pareto-plus principle compelling, we must
say why.

Is the Pareto-plus principle appealing?  Is Y a better world
than X?  In the genesis problem, the relevant difference between
X and Y is that Y has an additional person and his living standard is positive.  Suppose the living standard of all persons in
X is very high (that is, $u_i$ is large, $i = 1, \ldots, M$), and
suppose $u_{M+1}$, though positive, is very small.  Might one not
have grounds for thinking the worse of Y for that?  Notice that
one could consistently think the worse of Y for just that while
acknowledging the Pareto principle when applied to same people
choices.  Indeed, this would be consistent with acknowledging
the Pareto principle when applied to same number choices.  X and
Y contain different numbers of persons.  Person M+1 in Y is not
better off in Y than in X, nor is he denied a life of positive
welfare if X is chosen.  The Pareto-plus principle requires
further justification than is normally provided.

Parfit provides one.  He finds it difficult to rank Y below
X if the inequality in Y involves no social injustice.  This is
because he cannot bring himself to think that " . . . on the
ground that the extra group are worse off than some other group
 . . . it would have been better if the extra group had never

existed" (Parfit, 1982:159). Perhaps so. However, the problem with this sentiment is that it presupposes Y to be the world that has actually been chosen, and the world we live in. In this event, X is not attainable; it is not a possible world. We cannot move from Y to X, because in X the additional person does not exist, in the sense of never having existed. To be sure, we can still ask whether X would have been the better world, but there are good reasons why our answer if Y is the actual world is likely to be different from our answer if both X and Y are available for choice (as discussed further below). "Better if you hadn't existed" is a different sentiment from "better if an additional life isn't created." In an influential essay, Williams (1973) has reminded us of a consideration overlooked in theories of morality that are scrupulously impersonal: the idea of personal integrity and, in particular, its value. Williams did not suggest that personal integrity is overriding, merely that it needs to find room in moral discourse. Granted that he was in the main writing about personal morality; it must then be granted that if a person ought to find such a consideration pertinent, so should others when judging his situation. We are here discussing the genesis problem. This is different from the moral problem confronting actual people when they choose from among possible future worlds. Considerations relevant for the genesis problem are pertinent for actual persons when they contemplate alternative savings and population policies. However, an actual problem involves additional issues that make it quite different, as is argued below.

Suppose, however, that the identities of the first M persons in X and Y are the same, and suppose now that in Y, each of them enjoys a slightly higher living standard. Would this not provide a compelling reason for ranking Y over X? In Y, these M persons are certainly better off than in X, but the additional person in Y is neither better nor worse off. We conclude that the Pareto-plus principle is not the same as the Pareto principle: it is stronger. Even if we can justify the latter on the basis of prior moral reasoning, it does not follow without further deliberation that we can justify the Pareto-plus principle. This is discussed next.

The Pareto principle involves same number choices. What moral theories are there that may justify it? There would appear to be three distinguished ones: (1) social contract theories based on an "original position" argument; (2) teleological theories that identify happiness, or agreeable consciousness, or the level of well-being, or preference fulfillment as the sole good; and (3) pluralistic intuitionist theories.

It is obvious that the second theory yields the Pareto principle. The first does not, at least not without qualification. In his celebrated work, Rawls (1972) argued that parties behind the veil of ignorance will give priority to equal basic liberties over the lexical maxi-min principle concerning the distribution of income and wealth. It follows that the parties would have no allegiance to subsuming the Pareto principle, at least, that is, if the principle were defined on income and wealth. Neverthe-

less, it would be cheating to invoke this as a way of arguing
against the Pareto principle here.  Let us take it, therefore,
that allocations satisfying the Pareto principle do not require
for their attainment either unequal basic liberties or a reduction in equal basic liberties.  In such situations, a party behind the veil of ignorance will not choose a Pareto-dominated
outcome.  In such circumstances, contract theories do recommend
the Pareto principle.

Intuitionist theories are not wedded to the Pareto principle
at all.  Suppose, for example, that an increase in the aggregate
standard of living and a better distribution of living standards
are both valued, and suppose we are in agreement about how to
weight these social objectives relative to each other.  So long
as the aggregate does not have priority over the distribution,
and so long as the index (or measure) of distribution does not
itself subsume the Pareto principle (and there is no reason why
it should), the overall theory will violate the principle.

We conclude that, roughly speaking, only the first two categories of moral theories subsume the Pareto principle, and therefore might seem to have some chance of implying the Pareto-plus
principle as well.  In fact, however, teleological theories
generally do not.  For example, classical utilitarianism subsumes
the Pareto-plus principle, but average utilitarianism does not.
What of contract theories?

In his account of a consideration leading to average utilitarianism, Rawls (1972:161-166), extending an argument of
Harsanyi (1955) and Vickrey (1960), suggests that if an individual in the original position were to maximize expected utility,
and if he were to assume an equal chance of being in any person's
circumstance, he would choose the society with the highest average utility.  Hare (1973:245-256), in his review of Rawls, cari-
catures the conception by admitting an interpretation of the
original position which, if pursued, would imply that justice
demands the world to be thickly populated with people, all
existing at just about subsistence level.  Thus (POPs being
parties in the original position):

> We may note here an embarrassing consequence of the inclusion
> of possible people among the POPs, if Rawls' own normative
> principles are adopted, and if it is assumed that to have
> any life at all is better than not to be born.  The unborn
> will then be his least advantaged class; and so his differ-
> ence or maxi-min principle will require him to say that
> before anything is done for the rest of us we ought to
> secure the birth of all these possible people.  This would
> lead us to a duty of procreation on a vast scale; we would
> stop only when the earth would support no more people above
> the starvation level.

There are two separate points to be noted.  One concerns the
interpretation of the various authors, the other the pertinence
of the original position as a conception for population theory.
To take the first point, neither Harsanyi nor Vickrey was addres-

sing population theory when developing choice theoretic Utilitarianism. It is not plain whether Rawls' account of the reasoning leading to average utilitarianism for the population
problem would be accepted by Harsanyi and Vickrey. At the same
time, nowhere in the elaboration of his own theory of justice
does Rawls discuss the question of population policies; he
assumes that a same number problem is faced by actual people.
It would appear, then, that Hare's observation about the size of
population and the level of well-being in a Rawlsian world is
beside the point, because Rawls can argue that Hare is utilizing
the Rawlsian apparatus to analyze a problem for which the apparatus was not designed.

The more important point is whether contract theories make a
sensible basis for population policies. Rawls' "original position" is not a congress of souls. It is a conceptual apparatus
designed to capture the consideration "suppose I were in his
circumstances" when contemplating a social order in which "he"
receives the worse end of the bargain. However, there must be a
well-defined "he" for this consideration to make sense. Nonexistence is not a state in which one can imagine oneself. It
is not to be viewed on a par with a zero living standard (for
just such a view, see Kavka, 1975). Nonexistence is like nothing
for us--not even like a very long night--because there is no
longer any us to imagine. One cannot be asked what it would be
like to experience one's own nonexistence because there is no
subject of experience in nonexistence. This difficulty in
imagining our own nonexistence renders spurious the view that
nonexistence must be a long dismal night from which we must try
to rescue people. We can, of course, feel grateful to the persons who created us for doing just that, not because they thereby
rescued us from anything, but because they are responsible for
all our experience. Contract theories have credence when applied
to actual lives, and in Rawls' theory, such is the application.
The original position was designed to illuminate one's conception
of justice; it cannot be expected to sharpen our understanding of
every moral concept.

We may conclude, therefore, that the only avenue open for exploring whether or not the Pareto-plus principle is defensible is
to appeal to intuition. Intuitively, however, there is not
enough to commend it: the principle is totally insensitive to
distributional issues. Unless one adds living standards, as
classical utilitarianism would have us do, there is no reason to
rank X and Y on a par with each other if all the persons in X
have high standards of living and the additional person in Y has
nil. The mistake would lie in equating a person experiencing a
zero living standard with nonexistence. If one refrains from
equating the two, the intuitive appeal of the Pareto-plus principle weakens.

Consider an evaluation that is sensitive to distribution.
Let X be a world consisting of M persons, each of whom enjoys the
same (positive) living standard $\mu$, and let Y be a world consisting of X and an additional person, whose living standard is $\mu^*$.
For X and Y to be judged equally good, $\mu^*$ must be positive,

less than $\mu$ , and increasing as a function of $\mu$ . Such an axiom
would be consistent with the welfare contours depicted in Figure
3.


DIFFERENT NUMBER CHOICES:  ACTUAL PROBLEMS

A Fundamental Asymmetry

In the previous section, we considered certain difficulties involved in making different number choices (and we noted that certain problems arise even if all people are potential), the central hypothesis of the genesis problem.  The question we may now
ask is whether the genesis problem is the right one to pose.  We
ask this with some trepidation because most of the formal literature on optimum population theory has addressed the Genesis
Problem.

    In an actual problem, there are actual people--existing per-
sons called here the current generation--who deliberate over future population sizes, and current and future living standards.
The size of the current generation is given; it is a datum.

    Consider the following problem.  There is a child whose life-
time standard of living is firmly expected to be nil unless additional resources are diverted to his needs.  Option A is to give
him some resources so as to raise his living standard to $\bar{u}$.
Option B is to create an additional person and award him resources, thereby enabling him to enjoy the standard of living $\bar{u}$,
while the existing child remains at a zero living standard.
Assume that all other effects are the same under the two options.
Which option should we choose?  If, as Sidgwick (1907) would have
it, pleasure, or agreeable consciousness, is the sole good, and
if the fact that something good would be the result of one's
action is the basic reason for doing anything--the ground of
binding reasons--then we should be indifferent between A and B.
Indeed, this is precisely what unbridled classical utilitarianism
would dictate.  However, classical utilitarianism presupposes a
conception of a person--as solely a location of agreeable con-
sciousness--that can be questioned.

    Modern statements of utilitarianism, such as Hare's prefer-
ence fulfillment theory, cannot be applied to different number
choices.  Hare (1981, 1982) argues that his conception of the
principle of universalizability leads unerringly to utilitarianism.  He says (1982:26):

    . . . what the principle of utility requires of me is to do
    for each man affected by my actions what I wish were done for
    me in the hypothetical circumstances that I were in precisely
    his situation; and, if my actions affect more than one man
    . . . to do what I wish, all in all, to be done for me in the
    hypothetical circumstances that I occupied all their situa-
    tions . . . .  This . . . emphasizes that I have to give the
    same weight to everybody's equal interest; and . . . in so
    far I am one of the people affected . . . my own interests
    have to be given the same . . . weight . . . .

The reason that this conception cannot be used to discuss different number choices is similar to the one offered earlier in the discussion of attempts to use an "original position" argument for such choices. Potential persons are not a special type of persons. If, in the foregoing example, we were to regard A as the more desirable of the two alternatives, we would not be violating Hare's principle of utility. What is more to the point, we would not know how to use the principle: it is not, even hypothetically, possible to occupy the "situation" of a nonexistent, and never-to-be-existent, person.

In his statement of classical utilitarianism, Mirrlees (1982: 81) argues that moral ignorance in different number choices may well be the correct position, because it may in practice be impossible to remove personal bias in conducting utilitarian calculations:

> To get preference information relevant to comparing states of the society with different numbers, the individual has to perform a thought experiment in which the number of alternative selves varies, and to decide which of the two positions he prefers. I suppose this is the purified question of choice about length of life. Can one consider this question without the corruption of thinking about it as one's own life, rather than variation of the number of experiences?

It is doubtful that one can, but in any case, it may be asked why it would be wrong if one did not. We have already noted that the principle of universalizability, as formulated by Hare (1981, 1982), does not tell us why we should be committed to classical utilitarianism in different number choices, and indeed why, in the choice of the numbers of future lives, an actual person must on linguistic and moral grounds award the same weight to his living standard (his "interest") as to a potential living standard. Mirrlees' formulation of the population problem, on the other hand, would appear to be based on an ideal observer theory. However, then one may ask why in a different number choice, the feelings of an ideal observer should be the sole guide. Mirrlees merely asserts they should; he does not provide an argument.

We may conclude that modern statements of utilitarianism do not provide any guidance for a choice between A and B. There would be a great many people whose moral sense would urge them to rank A over B on the ground that in A, an actual child's living standard will improve, the moral sentiment being that one ought not to add new people without looking after existing ones. What has been argued here is that such a basic intuition is consonant with the language of morals. To be sure, average utilitarianism would also rank A over B, but not for the reason that in a choice over future numbers, actual persons' living standards ought to be awarded greater attention, that is, ought to count for more, than potential living standards.

What is the source of this moral sense that the living standards of actual and future persons ought to count for more than potential living standards? It may well stem from a distinction between different sorts of goods.[13] Begin by distinguishing between "categorical goods," those that give you a reason to stay alive in order to get them (e.g., projects you may have), and "conditional goods," those worth having if you are alive. Both sorts of goods are components of what makes life good, and good lives are worth having, but only categorical goods make life worth living. Thus, of course, nothing can be a categorical good for a potential person (i.e., an unconceived person). The concept of living standard that has been used in this chapter incorporates both sorts of goods in principle, and so for actual (or future) persons, it includes more of them, namely categorical ones.

However, if we accept this, we are abandoning the symmetry axiom for different number choices: actual and future persons are thus to count for more than potential persons. It is important to emphasize that this is consistent with imposing the symmetry axiom for same number choices. What it means is that given future numbers, savings decisions ought to be arrived at on the basis of a symmetric social welfare function (as discussed earlier), but that the symmetry axiom ought to be abandoned when we are choosing from among world histories that contain different numbers. We shall see how this can be achieved. First, however, let us enlarge on what is implied by the abandonment of the symmetry axiom in different number choices. The first thing to notice is that along any world history, certain potential persons "become" actual persons. When these future persons in their turn come to consider different number choices, they, like current actual persons, will count their (and future persons') living standards for more than potential living standards, and so on with the passage of time as certain potential persons become actual persons, and thus become moral agents. However, if this is the characteristic of moral reasoning in different number choices, then moral goodness is conditional on what exists: it is "state-dependent," or rather agent-relative, and it is agent-relative because the question of who will appear as actual agents is itself subject to choice.

## State-Dependent Morality as an Implication of the Asymmetry: An Example

To see this in the simplest of contexts, consider five possible worlds, $X_1$, $X_2$, $X_3$, $X_4$, and $X_5$. There are two persons (1 and 2) in $X_1$, each firmly expecting to enjoy a living standard of 40. In $X_2$ and $X_3$, there is an additional person (labeled 3). In $X_2$, their living standards are 30, 45, and 15, respectively; in $X_3$, they are 30, 14, and 45, respectively. In $X_4$ and $X_5$, there is a further person (labeled 4). In $X_4$, the persons' living standards are 25, 25, 40, and 10, respectively; in $X_5$, they are 25, 25, 9, and 40, respectively (see Table 1).

TABLE 1  Illustration of State-Dependent
Morality

| Person | World | | | | |
|--------|-------|-------|-------|-------|-------|
|        | $X_1$ | $X_2$ | $X_3$ | $X_4$ | $X_5$ |
| 1      | 40    | 30    | 30    | 25    | 25    |
| 2      | 40    | 45    | 14    | 25    | 25    |
| 3      |       | 15    | 45    | 40    | 9     |
| 4      |       |       |       | 10    | 40    |

We are now discussing an actual problem and not the genesis problem. Suppose $X_1$ is the actual world. Then persons 1 and 2 are actual people. When choosing numbers, they count their own living standards for more, although in a same number choice they of course award equal treatment to all living standards. For concreteness, suppose, without loss of generality, that the living standards of actual lives count for twice potential living standards, and that the social ranking is based on weighted classical utilitarianism.

Consider first the ranking of $X_2$ and $X_3$. It is a same number choice. Since (30+45+15) exceeds (30+14+45), $X_2$ is better than $X_3$. Likewise, $X_4$ and $X_5$ present a same number choice, and, since (25+25+40+10) exceeds (25+25+9+40), $X_4$ is better than $X_5$. Thus, what remains for persons 1 and 2 is to rank $X_1$, $X_2$, and $X_4$. Now, awarding the living standard of an actual life a weight of 2, social welfare in $X_1$ is (2x40) + (2x40) = 160; in $X_2$ and $X_4$, as viewed from the moral perspective of the persons in $X_1$, it is (2x30) + (2x45) + 15 = 165 and (2x25) + (2x25) + 40+10 = 150, respectively. We conclude, therefore, that $X_2$ is superior to $X_1$, which in turn is superior to $X_4$. In particular, $X_2$ is superior to $X_4$.

However, suppose $X_2$ is the actual world. $X_1$ is, of course, not a feasible alternative world now, but $X_3$, $X_4$, and $X_5$ are. The ranking of $X_2$ and $X_3$ remains the same, since they offer a same number choice; likewise for $X_4$ and $X_5$. Therefore it remains to rank $X_2$ and $X_4$. Social welfare in $X_2$, from the perspective of the persons in it, is (2x30) + (2x45) + (2x15) = 180, whereas social welfare in $X_4$, from the same vantage point of $X_2$, is (2x25) + (2x25) + (2x40) + 10 = 190. Thus $X_4$ is superior to $X_2$. We may conclude that $X_2$ is superior to $X_4$ if $X_1$ is the actual world, but is inferior to $X_4$ if $X_2$ is the actual world. This is the incoherence in ranking mentioned earlier. There is no overall moral ordering of alternative worlds. (This does not mean there can be no rational choice. If $X_2$ is the actual world, then plainly $X_4$ should and indeed will be chosen. However, if $X_1$ is the actual world, it may be rational for persons 1 and 2 collectively to persist with $X_1$, since they know that if they choose what they see as the best world, namely $X_2$, then $X_4$ will subsequently be seen as the best. Nevertheless, from their existing vantage point, $X_4$ is morally the least desirable among $X_1$, $X_2$, and $X_4$.)

## Social Choice Rules and Backward Induction

There are two attitudes one can adopt to the incoherence discussed above. One is that it is otiose because it flagrantly violates moral reasoning. In this case, the way out is immediate: the symmetry axiom must be reinvoked for different number choices. If we go this route, we will, as argued earlier, identify actual problems with the genesis problem. Indeed, this may well be the reason why the genesis problem has so long dominated discussion. The other attitude is to accept the implication of asymmetry: that morality is person-relative (or generation-relative), and that all moral reasoning can provide in different number choices is a rule for selecting social states, a rule that is not based on an overall ordering of these states. (In the language of social choice theory, this amounts to being satisfied by a social choice rule that is generated by a noncyclic binary relation.)

If we adopt this second attitude, the manner in which a representative generation chooses would be as follows. It would first partition all social states into sets, each consisting of social states offering same number choice. (Thus, in the example given earlier, the partition would obviously be $\{X_1\}$, $\{X_2, X_3\}$, and $\{X_4, X_5\}$.)[14] That is, all social states in a given set would consist of the same number of lives, and the numbers of lives in social states belonging to different sets in the partition would be different. Choice would then be made from each such set on the basis of a symmetric social welfare function, $W_M(\mu)$ (see the discussion earlier). Thus, $W_M(\mu)$, with $M = 1, 2, \ldots$, would yield a best element from the set in the partition consisting of social states involving precisely $M$ lives. One would then be left with an undiluted different number choice. This would then be made on the basis of a criterion that awards a higher weight to the living standards of actual (and future) persons. This two-step procedure offers a rule for selection. The rule, however, is not based on an overall ordering; rather, it adheres strictly to the underlying reasoning discussed in same number choice problems and different number choice problems.[15]

We have one more step to take. The two-step procedure for selecting a social state was described for a representative, actual generation, and as we noted earlier, the asymmetry implies that choice (via the two-step procedure) among alternative future worlds depends on which world is the actual one. The problem of savings and population is seen from the moral perspective of actual people, because with the passage of time, some potential lives become actual lives as the world unfolds along a path de-

termined by the choices made by Mother Nature and actual people
of the past. No doubt the present generation plays God in
choosing the next generation's size and its resource and capital
base. However, there is no unique present generation. Each future generation will in time become the present and will have to
choose. So long as there are future generations, no generation
is privileged in this sense. Each will view the future in much
the same way as the present generation does; in particular, each
will, given the asymmetry, on moral grounds award a greater
weight to its own living standard when proposing the sizes of
future generations and choosing the size of the next generation.
Thus in fact, each actual generation will use a different social
choice rule. To be sure, each actual generation will use the
two-step procedure, and may even use the same weight on actual
living standards. However, the choice rule will change as potential generations become actual. There is, therefore, a recursion
here, and the way to resolve it is the familiar backward induc-
tion argument (see the earlier discussion). An actual generation
applies its choice rule (via the two-step procedure), taking into
account that the generation that comes into being because of its
choice will in turn apply its choice rule (via the two-step procedure) when deciding on its savings and procreation policy, and
in turn will take into account . . . and so on.

This backward-induction argument works if there is a terminal
date from which to work back. Under our present knowledge, however, it is difficult to justify postulating in advance a terminal date for the world. The appropriate thing to do, then, is
to conduct this backward-induction argument for every finite
possible terminal date (that is, the set of positive integers).
Associated with each chosen terminal date, there is an optimal
temporal population and savings policy, from the present to the
terminal date. Now let the terminal date tend to infinity.
Presumably, the sequence of associated optimal intertemporal
population and savings policies has limit points, and in simple
economic models it will have a unique limit point. Such limiting
policies are then the optimal policies for the infinite-horizon
case.

These are the immediate implications of the asymmetry. If
they jar against one's intuitive moral sense, this is because we
usually think of moral reasoning as being able to generate a
universal ordering over social states. Certainly, that is what
the overwhelming majority of modern welfare economics has
assumed. If agent-relative morality is found wanting, symmetry
of treatment of actual and potential living standards must be
invoked. However, the gnawing question would then be whether
they should be awarded equal weight.


SUMMARY AND CONCLUSIONS

This chapter has suggested that for the most part, welfare economics has addressed same number choice problems. It has argued
that in such contexts, the requirement that the social welfare

function be symmetric in living standards is entirely justified. Moral frameworks based on extended sympathy (Arrow, 1963) or impersonal preferences (Harsanyi, 1955) readily yield symmetry as a necessary requirement of social welfare functions. Classical utilitarianism provides a distinguished example of such social welfare functions. The chapter argued that discounting of future living standards (i.e., giving a lower weight to the standard of living of future people) can nevertheless be justified on the ground that there is a positive (exogenous) probability of extinction. Thus, for example, an often-used social welfare function, the sum of discounted living standards, can be interpreted as the expected value of aggregate living standards, and this can be obtained directly from Harsanyi's framework; such an approach does not violate the symmetry axiom.

The chapter then turned to defining social discount rates, noting that they depend on the choice of the numeriare good, though of course the choice of numeriare does not affect policy. Being accounting prices, social discount rates depend not only on objectives (i.e., the social welfare function), but also on feasibility constraints. They are a derived concept.

Next, the discussion turned to different number choices. Optimum population theory is an aspect of such choice theory. First, the genesis problem, in which all persons are assumed to be potential was, surveyed. It was argued that much of the discussion on optimum population theory has concentrated on the genesis problem (e.g., Blackorby and Donaldson, 1979), in which the symmetry axiom is compelling. Next, the discussion focused on the repugnant conclusion, which is implied by classical utilitarianism when applied to different number choices. It was then shown that for all intents and purposes, the repugnant conclusion is implied by the Pareto-plus principle, and it was argued that a rejection of the Pareto-plus principle is entirely congruent with the language of morals. The discussion further addressed various types of social welfare functions that violate the Pareto-plus principle when applied to different number choices and thus avoid the repugnant conclusion.

The chapter then turned to actual problems concerning different number choices. In an actual problem, there are actual people who deliberate over future numbers and future living standards. It was argued that the symmetry axiom is otiose in the formulation of an actual problem, and that there are good moral reasons for awarding a higher weight to the living standards of actual (and future) people as compared to the living standards of potential people. However, it was then noted that this necessarily introduces a new class of problems since some of the potential persons become actual people, and they, presumably, are equally justified in awarding themselves a higher weight when comparing their living standards with those of potential people. Not only is there an intertemporal inconsistency, but there is a more glaring problem: moral principles pertaining to an actual problem are not, in a sense, universalizable. They are agent-relative; they depend on the actual person who is thinking of the problem. In particular, this means

that even if there is a social welfare function for a same number
choice, there can be none for a different number choice in an
actual problem. Finally, a brief sketch was offered of how a
different number choice may nevertheless be made in an actual
problem.


NOTES

1    Hare (1981) and Mirrlees (1982) contain recent discussions of
     extended sympathy from a utilitarian standpoint, Sen (1973)
     from a non-utilitarian one.
2    This is called "anonymity" or "symmetry" in the social choice
     literature. See Hammond (1976), d'Aspremont and Gevers
     (1977), and Maskin (1978).
3    Koopmans (1960, 1972) and Diamond (1965) were, among other
     things, concerned with showing that in intertemporal social
     choice, if there is an infinity of future generations,
     "anonymity" conflicts with other seemingly plausible moral
     axioms, leading to the impossibility of social choice. For
     a nontechnical account of the matter, see Dasgupta and Heal
     (1979:Chapter 9).
4    From this definition, it follows that a compulsive social
     goal is one that has an overriding weight over others. A
     lexicographic ranking of social objectives would have this
     characteristic. No trade-offs are allowed in such a case.
5    The point that you do need certain additional moral axioms to
     move from the domain of social states to the domain of living
     standards in defining the social welfare function was noted
     and demonstrated in the important article of d'Aspremont and
     Gevers (1977).
6    Nozick (1974) contains an excellent discussion of rights as
     constraints.
7    For present purposes, nothing is lost in my making this as-
     sumption.
8    It should be noted that the lexicographic maxi-min principle
     was invoked by Rawls (1972) to rank alternative distributions
     of an income and wealth index.
9    A true monarchist would deny the moral force of the symmetry
     axiom.
10   The device of restricting attention to end states in which
     all persons are equally treated has been used earlier by
     Kolm (1969), Atkinson (1970), and Mirrlees and Stern (1972).
     Blackorby and Donaldson (1979) have used it fruitfully to ex-
     plore the axiomatic foundations of what is called the genesis
     problem below. In Figure 1, this means that we may as well
     restrict our attention to the 45° line.
11   In our example, the economy is not at a steady state during t
     and t+1, since the relative prices of bananas in terms of
     apples at t and t+1 are 1/2 and 2/3, respectively.
12   Blackorby and Donaldson (1979) provide a proof of this for a
     restricted class of social welfare functions. Parfit (1982:
     158-169) presents a diagrammatic argument; the precise con-

ditions required to generate the result are therefore not entirely transparent. The algebraic reasoning is as follows.
Suppose $X_0$ is a world consisting of M persons, each enjoying $\mu_0$, where $\mu_0$ is positive. Continuity of $W(\mu, M)$
and the Pareto-plus principle imply that $X_0$ is ranked on a
par with $X_1$, where $X_1$ is a world consisting of M persons,
each enjoying $\mu_0$, and an additional person, whose living
standard is nil. However, there then exists a positive
living standard $\mu_1$ such that $X_1$ is in turn ranked on a
par with a world in which each of the M + 1 persons is
awarded $\mu_1$. (This follows from the third condition imposed on $W_M(\mu)$ for same number choices.) Now, any conception of social welfare for same number choices that is "more
egalitarian" than the royalist lexical maxi-max would have
it that $\mu_1 < \mu_0$. Let us assume this. Next, construct
$X_2$ from $X_1$ in the same way as $X_1$ was constructed from
$X_0$, and define $\mu_2$ analogously. Then $\mu_2 < \mu_1$, and
so $\mu_2 < \mu_1 < \mu_0$. Proceeding in this way, we can create
more and more populous worlds. In particular, for the k-th
extension, $\mu_k < \mu_{k-1} < \ldots < \mu_2 < \mu_1 < \mu_0$, and $\mu_k >$
0. It follows that $\mu_k$ must tend to a limit as k tends to
infinity. If the limit is zero, we have the repugnant conclusion; if not, we do not. (We should note that if $W_m(\mu)$
in same number choices is utilitarian or any function more
equality conscious, then $\mu_0 \geq (M+k) \mu_k/M$. This means
that $\mu_k$ tends to zero as k tends to infinity, which is the
repugnant conclusion.)

13  This distinction is owed to John Broome of the University of
Bristol, who in turn bases it on Bernard Williams' distinction between two sorts of desires. See Williams (1982).

14  An initial pruning of social states might at this stage be
required to eliminate those that are dominated by the Pareto-
plus principle, if this principle is invoked and is regarded
as compulsive.

15  This two-step procedure was illustrated in the previous section.


APPENDIX

The Genesis Problem

Suppose K is the quantity of a consumption good available in the
world. If x is the consumption level of a person, his utility
index is U(x), where U is a numerical function, increasing in x
(i.e., $U'(x) > 0$), with diminishing returns (i.e., $U''(x) < 0$). Let
$x_0$ denote the level of consumption at which utility is nil;
that is, $U(x_0) = 0$. The utility subsistence level of consumption is $x_0$; we suppose that $x_0$ is positive (see figure
below).
Let N denote the number of persons and we shall, with little
loss in accuracy, suppose that N is a continuous variable (i.e.,
it can assume fractional or even irrational values). Since all
persons have, by hypothesis, identical utility functions, and

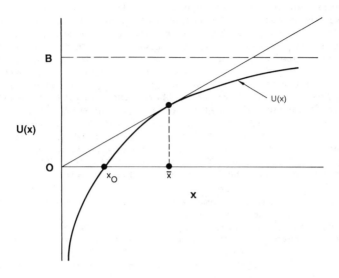

FIGURE A-1

since marginal utility, by hypothesis, is a decreasing function
of consumption, an equal distribution of K among all actual persons is the optimum distribution under classical utilitarianism.
This means that if there are N persons, each should receive K/N
units of the resource. Total utility is then NU(K/N), and in
the genesis problem, we search for that value of N which maximizes this.

Thus we differentiate NU(K/N) with respect to N, which yields
the derivative U(K/N) - (K/N)U'(K/N). This we equate to zero.
The optimum population size is the solution of this equation.
Write x = K/N. Since we know K, locating the optimum N is the
same as locating the optimum x. The condition that yields
optimum x is therefore

$$U(x) = xU'(x) ,  \tag{A-1}$$

that is, the value of x at which marginal utility of consumption
equals average utility per unit of consumption.

Equation (A-1) is fundamental to classical utilitarianism
(see Meade, [1955] and Dasgupta [1969] for successive generalizations of this). Let us here call it the Sidgwick-Meade Rule.
Its intuitive basis is simple. Suppose we have located the
optimum population. Then a marginal increase in the size should
not change total utility, nor should a marginal decrease. Thus
suppose we were to contemplate a marginal increase (the argument
associated with a marginal decrease is analogous). Then this
"additional" person would share K equally with the "original"
population. The gain in introducing this additional person is

his utility, which is $U(x)$. However, there is also a loss, which is that each of the remaining persons has slightly less consumption. This utility loss is $xU'(x)$. At the optimum population size, this gain and loss must be equal; the Sidgwick-Meade Rule asserts this equality. Figure A-1 shows diagrammatically how we may locate the optimum per capita consumption level with the help of the Sidgwick-Meade Rule. The solution is denoted by x.

Let us now specialize the utility function to obtain some quantitative results. Consider the following class of utility functions:

$$U(x) = \beta - x^{-\alpha} , \tag{A-2}$$

where $\beta$ and $\alpha$ are positive constants.

(A-2) is a useful class of utility functions to analyze because it is defined by two parameters, $\beta$ and $\alpha$. Ramsey romantically called $\beta$ the "bliss level," for obvious reasons: $\beta$ can be approached, but not attained (see Figure A-1).

With (A-2) as the utility function, it is simple to check that the utility subsistence level of consumption, $x_0$, is given by the expression

$$x_0 = (1/B)^{1/\alpha} . \tag{A-3}$$

Now use (A-2) in the Sidgwick-Meade Rule (A-1) to obtain the optimum per capita consumption level as

$$\bar{x} = \left[ (1+\alpha)/\beta \right]^{1/\alpha} . \tag{A-4}$$

Finally, use (A-3) in (A-4) to reexpress (A-4) as

$$\bar{x}/x_0 = (1+\alpha)^{1/\alpha} . \tag{A-5}$$

However, $\alpha$ is a positive number, and it is a well-known mathematical fact that when $\alpha$ is positive, $(1+\alpha)^{1/\alpha}$ is less than e (the base of natural logarithms), which in turn is approximately 2.74. We may conclude, therefore, that

$$\bar{x}/x_0 = (1+\alpha)^{1/\alpha} < e \simeq 2.74 . \tag{A-6}$$

Taking exact figures, suppose $\alpha = 1$. Then $\bar{x}/x_0 = 2$, which is to say that optimum per capita consumption is only twice as large as the utility subsistence consumption level. Quite obviously, the larger is $\alpha$, the closer is $\bar{x}/x_0$ to unity. This is the precise sense in which classical utilitarianism advocates "overly large" population sizes for the genesis problem in plausible worlds, and where the repugnant conclusion to which Rawls and Parfit have drawn our attention is not to be ignored.

REFERENCES

Arrow, K.J. (1963)  Social Choice and Individual Values, 2nd ed.
    New York:  John Wiley.
Arrow, K.J., and M. Kurz (1970)  Public Investment, the Rate of
    Return and Optimal Fiscal Policy.  Baltimore, Md.:  The
    Johns Hopkins University Press.
Atkinson, A.B. (1970)  On the measurement of inequality.  Journal
    of Economic Theory 2(3):244-263.
Baumol, W.J. (1968)  On the social rate of discount.  American
    Economic Review 57.
Blackorby, C., and D. Donaldson (1979)  Moral Criteria for
    Evaluating Population Change.  Unpublished manuscript,
    University of British Columbia.
Dasgupta, P. (1969)  On the concept of optimum population.
    Review of Economic Studies 36(7):295-318.
Dasgupta, P., and G. Heal (1979)  Economic Theory and Exhaustible
    Resources.  Cambridge, England:  James Nisbet and Cambridge
    University Press.
Dasgupta, P., A.K. Sen, and D. Starrett (1973)  Notes on the
    measurement of inequality.  Journal of Economic Theory
    6(2):180-187.
d'Aspremont, C., and L. Gevers (1977)  Equity and informational
    basis of collective choice.  Review of Economic Studies
    44(2):199-209.
Diamond, P.A. (1965)  The evaluation of infinite utility streams.
    Econometrica 33.
Georgescu-Roegen, N. (1979)  Comment.  In V. K. Smith, ed.,
    Scarcity and Growth Reconsidered.  Baltimore, Md.:  The Johns
    Hopkins University Press.
Hammond, P.J. (1976)  Equity, Arrow's conditions and Rawls'
    difference principle.  Econometrica 44(4):793-804.
Hare, R. (1973)  Rawls' theory of justice, part II.  Philosophi-
    cal Quarterly 23.
Hare, R. (1981)  Moral Thinking:  Its Levels, Method and Point.
    Oxford:  Clarendon Press.
Hare, R. (1982)  Ethical theory and utilitarianism.  In. A.K. Sen
    and B. Williams, eds., Utilitarianism and Beyond.  Cambridge,
    England:  Cambridge University Press.  Originally published
    in H.D. Lewis, ed., Comtemporary British Philosophy.  London:
    Allen and Unwin.
Harsanyi, J. (1955)  Cardinal welfare, individualistic ethics,
    and interpersonal comparisons of utility.  Journal of
    Political Economy 63.
Harsanyi, J. (1977)  Essays on Ethics, Social Behaviour, and
    Scientific Explanation.  Dordrecht, The Netherlands:  D.
    Reidel Publishing Company.
Hotelling, H. (1931)  The economics of exhaustible resources.
    Journal of Political Economy 39.
Kavka, G. (1975)  Rawls on average and total utility.  Philoso-
    phical Studies.
Kolm, S. Ch. (1969)  The optimal production of social justice.
    In J. Margolis and H. Guitton, eds., Public Economics.
    London:  Macmillan.

Koopmans, T.C. (1960) Stationary ordinal utility and impatience. *Econometrica* 28.

Koopmans, T.C. (1972) Representation of preference orderings over time. In C.B. McGuire and R. Radner, eds., *Decision and Organization*. Amsterdam: North Holland.

Lind, R., ed. (1982) *Discounting for Time and Risk in Energy Policy*. Baltimore, Md.: The Johns Hopkins University Press.

Maskin, E. (1978) A theorem on utilitarianism. *Review of Economic Studies* 45(1):93-96.

Meade, J.E. (1955) *Trade and Welfare*. Oxford: Oxford University Press.

Mirrlees, J.A. (1982) The economic uses of utilitarianism. In A.K. Sen and B. Williams, eds., *Utilitarianism and Beyond*. Cambridge, England: Cambridge University Press.

Mirrlees, J.A., and N.H. Stern (1972) Fairly good plans. *Journal of Economic Theory* 4(2):268-288.

Nozick, R. (1974) *Anarchy, State and Utopia*. Oxford: Basil Blackwell.

Parfit, D. (1982) Future generations: further problems. *Philosophy and Public Affairs* 11.

Parfit, D. (1984) *Reasons and Persons*. Oxford: Oxford University Press.

Ramsey, F.P. (1928) A mathematical theory of saving. *Economic Journal* 38.

Rawls, J. (1972) *A Theory of Justice*. Oxford: Oxford University Press.

Sen, A.K. (1973) *On Economic Inequality*. Oxford: Oxford University Press.

Sen, A.K. (1982) Approaches to the choice of discount rate for social benefit-cost analysis. In. R. Lind, ed., *Discounting for Time and Risk in Energy Policy*. Baltimore, Md.: The Johns Hopkins University Press.

Sidgwick, H. (1907) *The Methods of Ethics*, 7th ed. London: Macmillan.

Sikora, R. (1978) It is wrong to prevent the existence of future generations? In R. Sikora and B. Barry, eds., *Obligations to Future Generations*. Philadelphia: Temple University Press.

Sikora, R., and B. Barry, eds. (1978) *Obligations to Future Generations*. Philadelphia: Temple University Press.

Vickrey, W. (1960) Utility, strategy, and social decision rules. *Quarterly Journal of Economics* 74.

Williams, B. (1973) A critique of utilitarianism. In. J.J.C. Smart and B. Williams, *Utilitarianism For and Against*. Cambridge, England: Cambridge University Press.

Williams, B. (1982) *Moral Luck*. Cambridge, England: Cambridge University Press.

# 17
# Externalities and Population
## Robert J. Willis

INTRODUCTION

A demographic transition from high to low levels of mortality and fertility has accompanied the economic growth and development of all of the currently developed countries, and the beginnings of such a transition are suggested by the recent demographic and economic performance of a number of developing countries, such as Taiwan and South Korea. At the same time, many other countries in the Third World are experiencing rapid population growth because dramatic reductions in mortality following World War II have not yet been matched by decreasing fertility. In most of these countries, levels of income are extremely low, and the rate of economic development is not rapid. We do not yet know whether these countries will eventually follow the path of other countries that have completed the transition to low fertility and high income, or whether rapid population growth will continue until it is checked by Malthusian factors.

To many observers, it seems self-evident that the rate of population growth in this latter group of countries is too high from a social point of view. Advocates of reduced population growth have often argued that fertility is also too high from a private point of view, and that the central requirement for fertility reduction is the dissemination of family planning knowledge and methods. However, the mixed success of family planning programs in reducing fertility suggests that high fertility may be privately optimal in many low-income countries. Moreover, if it is true that population growth is too rapid from a social point of view, it follows that there must be some divergence be-

I would like to thank participants at the committee workshop held at Woods Hole in August 1984 for their help in getting me started on this chapter and for their patience in waiting for its completion. I am grateful to Gary Becker, Geoffrey Greene, Ronald Lee, Alain Nairay, Marc Nerlove, and Samuel Preston for their comments on the first draft of this chapter and absolve them from blame for any errors of commission or omission that it contains. The opinions expressed are my own.

tween the private and social costs of childbearing that leads to
excessively high fertility.

One of the triumphs of modern economic theory is the rigorous
confirmation of Adam Smith's famous theorem that self-interested
economic agents are led "as if by an invisible hand" to behave in
a fashion that leads, via their interactions in the market, to a
socially desirable outcome. In its modern incarnation, the validity of Smith's theorem is confirmed under a set of specific
assumptions about the structure of the economy and a carefully
delimited concept of the term "socially desirable." In particular, it is shown that the economy will achieve a Pareto-efficient
allocation of resources if markets are complete and perfectly
competitive and if there are no technological externalities
(i.e., direct, nonmarket interactions among economic agents such
as households and firms). Although first proven in the context
of static general equilibrium theory, the theorem has been extended to cover situations of intertemporal equilibrium under
uncertainty in the work of Arrow, Debreu, and many others. (See
Debreu's [1984] Nobel Lecture for a brief history of modern
general equilibrium theory.)

It is natural for a modern economist to ask whether Smith's
invisible hand might be expected to operate in the context of
population growth. Specifically, should we expect a socially
desirable outcome to flow from the decentralized decisions of
individuals to marry, bear children, and invest in the human and
physical capital with which their children and their children's
children will work? Has a demographic invisible hand operated
successfully in the United States, France, and Japan, and has it
failed to operate in Ecuador, Ethiopia, and Bangladesh? If so,
why?

Until quite recently, these questions have not been addressed
explicitly, either in the purely theoretical sense of establish-
ing conditions under which such a theorem would hold, or in the
empirical sense of determining whether private demographic behavior either does or does not tend to lead to socially desirable
outcomes. Very recently, several economists (e.g., Pazner and
Razin, 1980; Willis, 1981; Becker, 1983; Eckstein and Wolpin,
1982) have more or less independently proposed general equilibrium models of population growth in which decentralized family
fertility decisions have the same sort of optimality properties
as those of standard competitive general equilibrium models in
which population is exogenous.[1] Specifically, under certain
conditions, it can be shown that "altruistic" parents (i.e.,
parents who care about the number and welfare of their children)
are capable of internalizing the effects of their childbearing
and childrearing decisions on the welfare of future unborn generations within the family. If these conditions are satisfied by
all families in a society, private fertility decisions are socially optimal in the sense of Pareto. That is, in equilibrium,
no possible reallocation of resources or change in fertility can
improve the welfare of any individual in the current generation
without reducing the welfare of some other individual in current
or future generations.

The major focus of this chapter is on possible externalities and other failures of market and nonmarket institutions that are associated with the size, distribution, and growth of population, and that may lead to socially undesirable outcomes. However, a large portion of the discussion is devoted to presenting and examining a simple version of a theoretical model that produces socially optimal outcomes.

There are several reasons for this strategy. First, the theory provides a benchmark against which to assess the effects of externalities or other market imperfections that may cause a population to grow "too quickly" or "too slowly." Specifically, it is important to know with precision the conditions under which socially optimal outcomes will occur if we are to identify possible sources of nonoptimal outcomes implied by the failure of these conditions. In addition, the concept of social optimality itself involves some subtle and controversial issues in the context of endogenous population that can be clarified according to an explicit model. For example, within the theory presented here, maximization of per capita income or consumption is not socially optimal; therefore, a finding that reduced fertility would increase per capita income does not, in itself, constitute evidence that policies designed to reduce fertility are necessarily desirable.

A second reason for presenting the theory is that, as the author has argued elsewhere (Willis, 1982), its implications are broadly consistent with some of the major features of changes in economic and demographic behavior and institutions that occur at both the micro and aggregate levels during the process of demographic transition. Given that conditions for the social optimality of private decisions are met, the theory suggests that, in response to technological improvements in the returns to investment in physical and human capital, a society will tend to experience a "successful" economic and demographic transition; this transition will be characterized by growth in income and education, fertility reduction, a shift from an extended to a nuclear family system, and changes in the direction and magnitude of intergenerational transfers within families similar to those stressed by Caldwell (1976) in his well-known theory of demographic transition.

In addition to parents' having altruistic preferences, two other conditions appear to be important in ensuring a successful transition: one is the existence of well-functioning financial markets in which parents can borrow and lend at the market rate of interest; the other is the ability of parents to make implicit loans to their children without "default risk" or, equivalently, to be confident of receiving old age support from their children. The failure of market and family institutions to support these conditions may lead to an "unsuccessful" response to technological improvements, in which improved technology causes a population explosion and underinvestment in the human capital of children caused by such institutional failure. The discussion below also shows how the growth of public transfer programs, such as social security in modern "welfare states," can cause a diver-

gence between the social and private costs of children that results in excessively slow population growth and high capital
intensity relative to the social optimum.

The chapter is organized as follows. It begins with a brief
look at the concept of externalities and market failures and
applies these to some demographic phenomena in which conventional
tools of analysis are adequate. The discussion turns first to
technological externalities, and then to pecuniary externalities
and the distribution of welfare. The chapter then examines a set
of questions concerning the conditions under which the private
and social costs and benefits of parental fertility decisions
coincide or diverge; this set of questions requires the explicit
treatment of intergenerational issues as described above.

## TECHNOLOGICAL EXTERNALITIES

Formally, a direct or technological externality can be represented by a situation in which the consumption of a given person
or the output of a given firm is a function of the consumption
or output of another person or firm. For example, suppose that
the utility function of the ith person is

$$U^i = U^i(X^1, X^2, \ldots, X^i, \ldots, X^N) ,  \tag{1}$$

where $X^j$ is the n-dimensional vector of goods consumed by person j in a population of N persons. A direct consumption externality exists if variations in $X^j$ $(j \neq i)$ cause variation in the
ith person's utility. Obviously, we could introduce external
effects caused by the activities of firms by assuming that some
of the X vectors measure the inputs or outputs of firms, and
could represent external effects involving firms by interpreting
(1) as a production rather than a utility function; however, for
simplicity, firms are ignored in the discussion. Externalities
can be classified according to whether the direct interaction is
beneficial or harmful to a given agent. Thus, an external economy exists if an increase in an element of $X^j$ has a positive
effect on i's utility, while an external diseconomy exists if
that increase has a negative effect.

### Externalities and the Coase Theorem

Meade (1952) used the bucolic case of a beekeeper and an apple
orchardist in what became a classic textbook example of (reciprocal) technological external economies. Bees pollinate fruit
trees and use the pollen to make honey. The supply of blossoms
is an input into the production of honey, and, symmetrically, the
supply of bees is an input into the production of apples. If the
beekeeper increases his stock of bees, he benefits by the additional honey they produce. He also confers an "external" benefit
on the orchardist who finds that his apple crop has increased because of additional pollination. The benefit is "external" be-

cause the farmer does not pay the cost of bees. Symmetrically, if the orchardist plants more apple trees, he receives a private benefit of additional apple production and confers an external benefit on the beekeeper by increasing the honey production of his bees.

According to the conventional analysis, the externalities in this example are assumed to lead to inefficiency. The private optimum for the beekeeper is to purchase bees up to the point at which the marginal revenue product of the bees from honey production is equal to their marginal cost. If he took into account their productivity in pollination, he would increase the supply of bees until their full marginal revenue product in both honey and apple production was equal to their marginal cost. Similarly, the orchardist tends to undersupply apple trees because he has no incentive to take into account their productivity in the production of honey.

In a classic paper, Coase (1960) criticized this line of argument for its narrow focus on the technological nature of externalities and its failure to consider the incentives of economic agents to overcome inefficiencies. That is, since both the beekeeper and the orchardist could be made better off if they were to achieve a Pareto-efficient allocation of resources, Coase's argument predicts that they would bargain to an agreement yielding that allocation.

One mechanism for such a bargain would be for one of the agents to buy out the other and form a single firm producing both bees and honey. Clearly, the owner of this firm would have an incentive to "internalize" the direct interactions in the production process because it would be privately profitable to do so. Indeed, as Coase argued in an earlier paper (1937), allocational activities within firms tend to be based on nonmarket (e.g., command) mechanisms, and it is the efficiency of such mechanisms relative to the price system that determines which activities take place within firms and which involve market transactions. Situations in which there are direct interactions among factors of production tend to be ones in which nonmarket methods have a comparative advantage and therefore tend to become internalized within firms. Samuelson (1956) makes much the same point about the family as an institution that can internalize consumption externalities among its members. More recently, this argument has been greatly elaborated by Becker (1981) and other writers in the "new home economics" tradition.

It may be inefficient for the beekeeper and the orchardist to merge into one firm because the external effects involved may extend beyond the two agents in the example. Another possible solution is for the beekeeper and orchardist to enter into a contractual arrangement in which one would pay the other for the services of the factors of production that he owns. In fact, when Cheung (1973) investigated the organization of the beekeeping industry in the State of Washington, he obtained strong evidence verifying the predictions of Coase's argument. For instance, beekeepers pay "apiary rents" to orchardists for the right to keep bees on the latter's property for crops that provide large honey yields, while orchardists pay "pollination fees" to beekeepers for crops with low honey yields.

Apart from its title, the tale of the bees and the flowers does not bear directly on demographic issues. However, several points can be drawn from it that are of relevance to the topic of this chapter. First, it illustrates the so-called Coase Theorem, which states, in part, that if costless negotiation is possible and property rights are well-specified, then the allocation of resources will be efficient so that there is no problem of externality. Conversely, the theorem suggests that externality problems will be most severe when property rights are not well-specified or transaction costs are high. Examples of both of these problems are discussed below in connection with "collective externalities" and "common property resources," where negotiation is costly because of the large number of individuals affected by the externality and the characteristics of certain resources, such as an airshed, preclude private ownership. Second, the Coase Theorem directs attention toward an important set of questions concerning the efficient division of activities between market and nonmarket institutions and the nature of the interdependencies among these institutions. In the case of demographic externalities, the theorem suggests that special attention should be given to the institutional role of the family and to the interrelationships among families, firms, and the government. Finally, the tale itself emphasizes the importance of empirical verification of alleged externalities. Of course, the converse point should also be made--that it is important to seek empirical verification of allegedly efficient institutional arrangements.

## Public Goods and Collective Externalities

Public goods (or bads) and what will be called here "collective externalities" are important special cases of external effects that are of potential demographic significance because their benefits and costs depend on the size and distribution of population. Pure public goods, such as national defense, clean air, or the stock of basic knowledge, are defined as goods consumed in equal quantity (although not necessarily equally valued) by all inhabitants of a given area, with the boundaries of that area determined by features of the geographical, physical, cultural, and political environment that vary with the type of collective good under consideration (Samuelson, 1954). The term "collective externality" is used here to refer to situations in which the utility of a given person depends on the aggregate consumption of "externality-producing" goods. In practice, as illustrated below with the example of pollution caused by automobile emissions, such situations combine elements of pure public goods and externalities.

In the case of a collective externality, we may write person i's utility function as

$$U^i = U(c^i, e^i, Z) \ , \tag{2}$$

where $c_i$ is a purely private consumption good, $e_i$ is an externality-producing private good, and $Z$ is a pure public good that is consumed in the same amount by all persons within the relevant region. Assume that $Z$ is produced according to the production function

$$Z = F(E, R) \ , \tag{3}$$

where $E = \sum_{i=j}^{N} e^j$ is the aggregate "input" to the production of the public good caused by the spillover effects of private consumption of the externality-producing good, and $R$ represents the relevant environmental characteristics. If $E$ has a positive (negative) marginal product, the consumption of $e$ involves an external economy (diseconomy). The conventional case of pure public goods occurs if the inputs to the production of $Z$ (i.e., $e_j$) do not themselves provide direct utility to consumers.

Classic examples of externalities such as air pollution caused by automobile emissions are represented by (2) and (3) as follows. Suppose that $e_i$ represents the amount of automobile travel by person $i$ and that $Z$ represents the quality of the air shared by the $N$ persons within a given airshed, and assume that emissions are proportional to the amount of travel. Thus, $e_i$ provides direct utility to $i$ and, because of an incidental "spillover" effect, also constitutes a negative (i.e., harmful) input into the production of the public good, air quality.

The private marginal benefit (measured in dollars) to person $i$ of a unit of auto travel is given by

$$PMB^i = MRS_e^i + MRS_Z^i \cdot F_E \ , \tag{4}$$

where $MRS_e{}_i$ is the marginal rate of substitution between auto travel and the purely private good, $MRS_Z{}_i$ is the marginal rate of substitution between air quality and the private good, $F_E$ (which is negative) is the marginal damage to air quality caused by emission from $i$'s auto, and the private good $c_i$ is assumed to be a composite good measured in dollars. The environmental cost person $i$ imposes on himself, $MRS_Z^i F_e$, is probably negligible relative to the private value of auto travel, $MRS_e{}_i$. Thus, the privately optimal choice of the amount of travel will occur when $MRS_e{}_i$ is (approximately) equal to the private marginal cost of travel, $MC_e$.

The social marginal benefit of person $i$'s auto travel is

$$SMB^i = MRS_e^i + F_E \cdot SMB_Z \ , \tag{5}$$

where $SMB_Z = \sum_{j=1}^{N} MB_Z^j$ is the marginal benefit of increasing

the public good, which is given by the sum of the marginal values
of air quality to each individual. Note that the second term in
(5), which measures the marginal aggregate damage done by person
i's auto emissions to all other individuals in the airshed (including himself), may be large even though the marginal damage to
each individual is small. The latter term provides an (approximate) measure of the difference between the social and private
cost of automotive travel.

The socially optimal amount of automobile travel occurs when
the social marginal benefit of travel is equal to its marginal
cost, or alternatively, when the private marginal benefit of
travel is equated to its social marginal cost. Using (4) and
(5), the latter form of this statement can be expressed as the
condition that optimal travel occurs when

$$PMB^i = MC_e - F_E \cdot SMB_Z ,  \tag{6}$$

where $MC_e$ is the private marginal cost of travel, and $-F_E \cdot SMB_Z$
is the marginal cost of environmental damage caused by emissions.
Since a given person has no incentive to take into account the
damage he inflicts on others, privately optimal behavior will
lead to overconsumption of automobile travel from a social point
of view.

An analogous argument can be used to show that there will
tend to be underconsumption of goods that have beneficial spill-
over effects (i.e., when $F_E$ is positive). For example, a
chemistry professor may obtain private benefits from his research
activities because he enjoys the act of discovery or because his
salary is based, in part, on his research productivity. If the
economic value of his discoveries cannot be captured either by
the chemist or by his employer (i.e., the new knowledge is not
patentable), it will not pay either party to devote the socially
optimal level of effort to research. For the same reason, it
has long been argued that there would be underproduction of pure
public goods in a private market system. As a result, inputs to
the production of the public good would not appear directly in
individual utility functions, and hence the privately optimal
supply of these inputs would tend to zero in a large economy.


Demographic Implications of Technological Externalities and
Public Goods

In the pollution example given above, population size interacts
with the damage caused by emissions in two distinct ways. First
(and most obviously), the aggregate quantity of emissions may
tend to increase with the aggregate amount of auto travel, which
in turn is positively related to population size, other things
being equal. It should be stressed, however, that the volume of
auto emissions is not mechanically linked to the size of the
population, and that policies attempting to reduce air pollution
by reducing population generally would be exceedingly inefficient
relative to alternative policies attacking emissions directly.

The latter policies might involve direct controls, such as the mandated installation of antipollution equipment or emission surcharges attempting to bring the marginal private cost of automobile travel into equality with its marginal social benefit. Similar remarks can be made about most other examples of collective external economies or diseconomies.

An examination of equation (5) suggests a second way in which population size may interact with a collective externality. Specifically, the final term in (5) involving $MB_Z$ implies that the marginal social damage caused by person i's auto emissions is an increasing function of the number of people living in i's airshed, other things being equal, and consequently that the marginal social value of reducing emissions is greater the larger the population. Suppose that government policy always manages to produce a socially optimal level of emissions. As population size increases, holding per capita income and other variables constant, the rising marginal value of clean air implies that the socially optimal level of automobile usage per capita will become ever more restricted, and that the composition of private consumption will shift away from the harmful externality-producing good. Similarly, the rising marginal value of public goods will induce an increase in the production of public goods and beneficial externality-producing goods as the population increases. If public goods are normal, it may be noted that increases in per capita income have a similar effect since $MRS_Z^j$ (for j = 1, ..., N) will tend to be larger the higher the level of income.

The discussion in the preceding paragraph is closely related to the issue of external economies and diseconomies of scale with respect to population distribution and density, as well as population size.

## Population Distribution and Density

If the total population of a given society is taken as given, social policy should be designed to distribute the population in a way that will equate social marginal costs and benefits across regions. For example, suppose that different geographic areas of the country are differentially productive because of the location of waterways, the quality of climate, and the like. Also assume that each region has its own airshed and that automobile emissions are the only source of externalities. In the absence of government intervention, population will be nonoptimally concentrated in the relatively more productive regions. In effect, the airshed of a region is a common property resource that is not priced and therefore is subject to overuse. An optimal policy would impose a price on this scarce resource by charging region-specific emission surcharges (or their equivalent) that would reflect the marginal social benefit of air quality within each region. Mobility of workers and firms would then take place until net advantages (including the appropriate charge for air quality) were equalized across regions. Of course, this is easier said than done. For example, governmental jurisdictions

may not coincide with airsheds; the empirical measurement of the
value of air quality and the effect of emissions on it is extremely difficult; and the imposition of "optimal" surcharges
would tend to redistribute income away from owners of fixed factors in high-density regions, creating conflicts between equity
and efficiency in theory and political obstacles in practice.
Such problems are compounded by the existence of many potential
externalities that differ in direction (external economies versus
diseconomies) and in geographic scope (local versus national
versus global).

## Population Size

Diseconomies of Scale. The earliest examples of diseconomies
of scale to population size follow from Malthusian diminishing
returns to a fixed resource base. If the resources in question
are ordinary private ones, such as land, increases in population
cause (eventually) a diminishing average and marginal product of
labor, and an increase in the average and marginal products of
land. Assuming that competitive markets for labor and land
exist, the equilibrium allocation of resources will tend to be
Pareto-optimal with reference to any given population size. In
particular, the equilibrium rental value of land (which is equal
to its marginal product) will properly reflect its social opportunity cost.

It may be noted that a positive rental value for land indicates that per capita income could be increased by a reduction
in population size. That is, per capita income is maximized at
a point at which the average product of labor reaches a maximum
and the marginal product of land is zero. If per capita income
is adopted as a welfare criterion, as is sometimes advocated,
population size is surely too large in virtually all important
societies. However, as is argued below, per capita income (or
per capita utility) is probably an inappropriate criterion, and
therefore the phenomenon of diminishing returns to land and other
private resources does not in itself involve a divergence between
private and social interests. Moreover, the classical economists' emphasis on diminishing returns to a fixed resource base
as the primary limiting factor in economic growth finds little
empirical support in modern studies of resource scarcity, which
show that technological change has steadily increased the effective supplies of supposedly fixed stocks of nonrenewable resources (Dasgupta and Heal, 1979).

This sanguine conclusion does not extend, however, to situations in which a natural resource is not privately owned. As is
clear from the pollution example above, collective external diseconomies are often associated with a "common property resource"
such as an airshed. Overfishing of whales and salmon, highway
and urban congestion, and radio and television interference on
the radio spectrum are symptoms of the common property aspects
of other resources, such as the ocean fisheries, physical space,
and the radio spectrum. Such common property resources are

typically subject to diminishing returns and, therefore, become more valuable as population size increases. If these resources are managed optimally through appropriate governmental intervention, no issues arise other than those discussed above with respect to diminishing returns to land. On the other hand, if appropriate policy is not followed, growth of both population and income may lead to a "tragedy of the commons," to use the title of Garrett Hardin's (1968) well-known paper. While our analysis suggests that these issues become more important as population and/or income increases, it is worth reiterating that it is unlikely that the most efficient policy response involves direct attempts to manipulate population size.

Increasing Returns to Scale. In surely the best known statement about increasing returns to scale, Adam Smith argued that the specialization and division of labor are limited by the extent of the market. While the empirical validity of this insight has been compelling to all economists since Smith, it has so far eluded precise theoretical statement and proof. In one modern attempt, Stigler (1951) argued that unspecialized production tends to be vertically integrated. For example, peasant production of bread may involve growing wheat, milling it into flour, baking the bread, and, finally, consuming it at the family table. Each component of this process may be subject to differential ranges of decreasing and increasing cost due to differences in the divisibility of capital equipment and labor skills required for a given stage of production. As the size of the market grows beyond a self-sufficient family, it becomes efficient for individual parts of the process to be divided into separate enterprises (e.g., wheat farm, flour mill, bread baker, household consumer), each of which can operate at the most efficient scale (i.e., minimum average cost) for that part of the process. As a consequence, the average cost of the final product tends to decrease as specialization increases.

While Stigler's theory explains certain important aspects of the specialization and division of labor, it is not clear that increased specialization associated with growth in the size of the market always involves vertical disintegration. More important from the point of view of this chapter, it is not clear whether the gains to specialization involve external economies, and, if they do, precisely how such externalities are related to demographic issues. Concretely, the list of issues that could be examined under this heading is extremely large. For example, it might include "agglomeration economies" associated with the urban development; the provision of "social overhead capital" or an "infrastructure," such as transportation and communication networks, power generation, and other industries characterized by decreasing average costs; increasing returns to specialization in human capital (Becker, 1981; Rosen, 1983); and many other issues. Although each of these topics is of potential interest and relevance, space constraints preclude more extended discussion here.

## PECUNIARY EXTERNALITIES AND THE DISTRIBUTION OF WELFARE

The tern "externality" is often used in the demographic and economic development literature to refer to "pecuniary" externalities, which operate through the price system, in contrast to "technological" externalities, discussed above, which involve interaction among economic agents outside the price system. For example, an immigrant into a country causes a small increase in the aggregate supply of labor. Because of diminishing returns, this will cause a small reduction in the real wage received by members of the existing population. It might be argued that the immigrant fails to take into account the "harmful" effect of his entry into the society on the wage received by others, and, consequently, that the level of immigration will tend to be larger than is socially optimal. This argument might then be used as a rationale for restricting immigration.

This argument is incorrect. To illustrate, consider a hypothetical society in which a homogenous private good (e.g., food) is produced with labor and land according to a constant returns production function, and assume that the supply of land is fixed. The demand for labor, given by its marginal product, corresponds to the negatively sloped curve MP in Figure 1. Suppose that the initial labor supply is $L_0$ and the corresponding equilibrium wage rate is $w_0$. Total national income is given by the sum of the areas A, B, and C, where total labor income is A+B and the total rental income of landowners is C. Per capita income, $y_0$, is given by the height of the average product curve, AP. Now consider an immigration that increases the aggregate labor supply to $L_1$. From a welfare point of view, it is tempting to conclude that the initial population would benefit from a restriction of immigration because both the equilibrium wage and per capita income fall to $w_1$ and $y_1$, respectively, as a consequence of the inflow of labor.

A more careful examination of the diagram reveals that this conclusion is not necessarily valid. In the new equilibrium, the incomes of the original population of laborers are reduced: of the total labor income given by area A+D, the new immigrants receive an amount equal to area D, while the initial population of laborers now receive area A instead of the area A+B they received before the immigration. However, landowners gain as a consequence of the immigration. Total rental income rises from area C to area C+B+E. Of this increase, area B represents an income transfer from the initial group of laborers to landowners, while area E is the new "surplus" generated by the additional labor of the immigrants. Note that it would be possible for the landowners, as a group, to benefit from the immigration and to secure the agreement of the initial group of laborers to allow it by "bribing" them with an income transfer whose aggregate value would be any amount between areas B and B+E.

This example illustrates several relevant points. Unlike technological externalities, pecuniary externalities do not lead to economic inefficiency. Specifically, note that the post-migration equilibrium is Pareto-efficient; that is, no individual

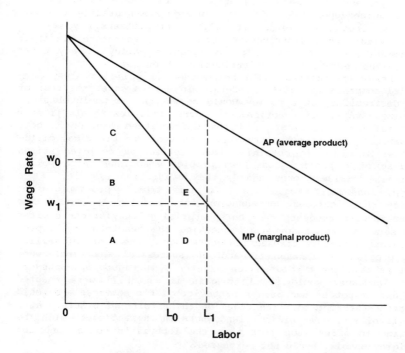

FIGURE 1   Welfare Effects of Immigration

in the society (excluding consideration of the immigrants themselves) can be made better off without harming someone else by
restricting immigration.   This is true whether or not the initial
group of laborers are compensated for the losses they have incurred as a consequence of the migration.

From an ex ante (i.e., premigration) perspective, however, a
policy allowing migration will be a Pareto improvement (i.e.,
will make at least one individual better off without harming any
other) only if compensation is actually paid to those who otherwise would suffer as a consequence of the policy.   If compensation is not paid, a strict Paretian cannot evaluate the merits
of the policy because it intermingles changes in efficiency with
changes in the distribution of income.   To judge the merits of
such a change, conventional welfare economics requires the introduction of a "social welfare function" that weighs each individual's contribution to social welfare and can thus be used to
determine whether the benefits of a policy to the "gainers" out-

weigh its costs to the "losers." The primary difficulty with
this approach to policy evaluation is that there is no universally agreed--upon basis for the interpersonal utility comparisons required to implement it.  Different citizens may vary in
their views about distributive justice and, therefore, in their
judgments about the merits of immigration policy or any other
policy that entails the redistribution of income.

These difficulties would be avoided if policies always included compensation of the losers.  In such a case, the test of
the desirability of a policy would be whether it could obtain a
unanimous vote.  In practice, of course, policies rarely if ever
contain such provisions, and the difficulties mentioned above
remain.  It may be noted that one aspect of the practical difficulties involved in obtaining Pareto-efficient policies arises
because of a public goods-like problem associated with policy
making.  Consider, once again, the immigration example.  As a
group, landowners would stand to gain from a pro-immigration
policy that included compensation for existing laborers.  The
Coase Theorem suggests that an enterprising lobbyist could offer
his services to landowners in seeking the enactment of a pro-
immigration bill if transaction costs (e.g., the costs of selling
his program to landowners and of successful lobbying) were
smaller than the surplus given by area E in Figure 1.  However,
each landowner would stand to gain if the bill were enacted
whether or not he had paid for the lobbyist's services and would
therefore attempt to "free ride" on the efforts of others.  As a
result of such free-riding, landowners in the aggregate might be
willing to offer much less than the lobbyist's costs, and the
immigration bill would not be passed.

Pecuniary externalities arise in many demographic contexts.
For example, a parent inflicts a pecuniary external diseconomy on
society by having an additional child, who will add to the future
labor supply and lower the wages of other people's children.
Within a static framework, the issues raised by private fertility
decisions are analytically identical to those discussed in the
immigration example.  (See Blandy, 1974, for a more extensive
discussion).  As is discussed below in detail, however, fertility
behavior and population growth do involve potential intergenerational externalities that require going beyond a static framework.

## INTERGENERATIONAL EXTERNALITIES, THE FAMILY, AND POPULATION GROWTH

Beginning with Malthus, economists have consistently pointed to
a conflict between increased population and individual economic
well-being.  In classical economics, the "Iron Law of Wages"
expressed the conclusion that the acquisition of new resources
through discovery, conquest, or the redistribution of income to
the poor could only temporarily improve the lot of the common
man.  Malthus assumed that the standard of living of workers,
measured by wage, has a positive effect on the rate of popula-

tion growth through its effects on mortality and/or fertility;
he assumed further that there exists a particular wage level--
the "subsistence wage"--at which the birth rate equals the death
rate so that population growth is zero. Beginning from an
initial equilibrium, the discovery of new land (or income redistribution), which increases the standard of living, will induce
positive population growth. Assuming that the resource base
remains fixed at its new level, population growth causes
diminishing returns, which reduce both the wage and the rate of
population growth until long-run equilibrium is reestablished at
the initial subsistence wage and the population ceases growing.
The only hope for long-run improvement in welfare lies in preventive checks, which in effect reduce the level of fertility at any
iven wage, and therefore increase the required level of living at
which the population is willing to reproduce itself.

As a positive model, Malthusian theory has long since been
discredited. The proximate reasons are well known. The growth
and spread of new knowledge and technology caused a vast cumulative increase in the effective supply of resources that permitted
unprecedented growth in both population and income. In addition,
the fertility transition indicates that the standard of living
at which the population is willing to reproduce itself has steadily increased. Modern theories of economic growth embody the
idea of cumulative progress, which was foreign to the classical
economists, and allow for the possibility of steady growth for
an unlimited period into the future; moreover, modern economic
theories of fertility behavior emphasize the possibility that the
"subsistence wage" will tend to rise as an economy develops.

Despite the elimination of a fixed resource base (in theory,
and possibly in fact), modern neoclassical economic growth
theories (e.g., Solow, 1956) predict a trade-off between the
rate of population growth and the level of per capita consumption. This is because increased population growth requires that
a larger fraction of economic output be invested in physical (or
human) capital if a given capital-labor ratio is to be maintained, even though, given an assumption of constant returns to
scale, the size of the population has no effect.

More recently, it has been shown that, in principle, this so-
called "capital-dilution effect" may be offset by an "intergenerational transfer effect." With the latter, the benefits of
(net) transfers from the younger to the older generation are
enhanced by the shift to a younger age distribution, which is
associated with a more rapid population growth rate (Samuelson,
1975; Arthur and McNicoll, 1978; Lee, 1980). Empirically, however, it appears unlikely that the intergenerational transfer
effect is sufficient to outweigh the capital dilution effect in
either developing or developed countries; moreover, at least in
the developed countries, it is likely that the direction of net
transfers is from the older to the younger generation.[2] Thus,
apart from the possibility that there are increasing returns to
scale with respect to population, modern economic theory suggests
that population growth is costly.

The basic question to be addressed now is not whether population growth is costly, but whether population growth involves externalities that cause the rate of growth to be too fast or too slow from a social point of view. The rest of this chapter is devoted to an examination of this question. As mentioned in the Introduction, as a first step, a simple overlapping generation model is presented. In this model, fertility decisions lead to a Pareto-optimal outcome in the sense that the level of utility of any individual in a given generation cannot be increased without reducing the utility received by some other individual in the same or a later generation.

## The Model

Assume that individuals live for three periods called childhood, middle age, and old age. The individual's life-cycle consumption path is $c_j = (c_j^0, c_j^1, c_j^2)$, where $c_j^a$ is the consumption of an individual of age a (a=0,1,2) born in period j. Individuals marry and have $n_j$ children at the beginning of middle age. For simplicity, no distinction is made between males and females, and the assumption is made of no mortality before the end of the old age period. Thus, $n_j$ may be regarded as the net reproduction rate (i.e., the number of girls per mother surviving through the reproductive period) in time period t=j+1, and the life-cycle consumption and income profiles may be regarded as averages of the sex-specific profiles. The rate of population growth in period t is $g_t$, where $n_j=1+g_j$. In addition, for simplicity, it is assumed that all individuals in all cohorts have identical preferences and capacities, that technology remains constant over time, that there is no uncertainty, and that all decision makers have perfect foresight concerning the behavior of all of their descendants.

## Altruistic Preferences

In standard economic models such as those discussed in the first part of this chapter, individuals are assumed to be selfish in the sense that they care only about their own consumption. While the hypothesis of self-interested behavior is both appropriate and fruitful for explaining the interaction of economic agents within markets, it does not appear to be adequate for addressing a number of other forms of social interaction that take place outside the market. In particular, it is clear that social relationships among members of a family often involve sacrifices of one member's self-interest for the benefit of another. In an important paper, Becker (1974) suggested that self-interest in the market and self-sacrifice within the family can be reconciled by the hypothesis that at least one family member has "altruistic preferences." In this terminology, individual A is altruistic toward individual B if A's utility increases when B is made better off.

Recently, Becker (1983) has suggested an interesting version of an altruistic utility function embodying "dynastic altruism," which is employed in this chapter.[3] Let the total lifetime utility of an individual who is born in period $t-1=j$, reaches middle age in period $t$, and enters old age in period $t+1$ be

$$U_j = V(c_j) + \delta\alpha(n_j)\sum_{i=1}^{n_j} U_{j+1}^i . \qquad (7)$$

This utility function states that the individual's total lifetime utility is the sum of the utility he receives from his own lifetime consumption,

$$V(c_j) = V(c_j^0, c_j^1, c_j^2)$$
$$= v(c_j^0) + \delta v(c_j^1) + \delta^2 v(c_j^2) , \qquad (8)$$

plus the sum of the levels of lifetime utility, $U_{j+1}^i$, achieved by each of his $n_j$ children, multiplied by the product of the individual's "time preference," $\delta$ ,* and his "generational preference," $a(n_j)$.

The introduction of generational preference and the conceptual distinction between it and time preference is an innovative feature of the utility function in equation (7). In this utility function, time preference refers to the rate at which an individual discounts his own future consumption. Thus, the higher is $\delta$ (i.e., the lower is $\partial$ ), the more weight the individual places on the utility received from future relative to present consumption. Generational preference measures the degree of a parent's altruism toward his children. Although the individual has a finite life, his generational preference determines the degree to which he cares about his offspring and, through them, about the welfare of his grandchildren, great grandchildren, and so on.

Specifically, by repeated substitution into (7) of $U_{j+1}$, $U_{j+2},...,$ the utility function of an individual in cohort $j$ becomes

$$U_j = V(c_j) + \delta\alpha(n_j)n_j V(c_{j+1})$$
$$+ \delta\alpha^2(n_j)\ \alpha(n_{j+1})\ n_j n_{j+1} V(c_{j+2}) +... , \qquad (9)$$

where, for simplicity, it is assumed that each child in a given generation in the family dynasty enjoys the same life-cycle consumption pattern and has the same number of children as other members of his generation. Note that (9) implies that, where the discount factor is the product of time preference and genera-

---

*$\delta = 1/(1+\gamma)$, where $\gamma$ is the rate of time preference.

tional preference, the full lifetime utility of an individual in cohort $j$ is equal to the discounted sum of the levels of utility from own consumption of all descendants in all generations in the dynasty. If (9) is to be a meaningful preference function, this sum must be finite (i.e., $U_j$ must be bounded). Assuming that there are an infinite number of future generations, a sufficient condition for $U_j$ to be finite is that $\delta\alpha$ $(n_{j+\tau})$ $n_{j+\tau}$ is less than one for all $\tau = 0,1,\ldots$ .[4] In turn, this implies that generational preference, $a(n_{j+\tau})$, must (eventually) decrease as $n_{j+\tau}$ increases (i.e., $a'(n_{j+\tau}) < 0$). In addition, we would expect that the marginal utility of an additional birth to an individual in generation $j$ should be positive, but diminishing (i.e., $\partial U_j/\partial n_j > 0$, $\partial^2 U_j/\partial n_j < 0$). It is easy to verify that these conditions would be satisfied if, for example,

$$a(n) = (1 - e^{-\alpha} n)/\beta n , \qquad (10)$$

where $\alpha > 0$ and $\beta > \delta > 0$ are constants.

Let $p(n_{j+\tau}) = \delta a(n_{j+\tau})n_{j+\tau}$ for $\tau = 0,1,\ldots$ . Then, the total utility of an individual in cohort $j$ may be written as the discounted sum of the levels of per capita utility from own life-cycle consumption of each generation in the family dynasty, i.e.,

$$U_j = V(c_j) + p(n_j)V(c_{j+1})$$

$$+ p(n_j)p(n_{j+1})V(c_{j+2}) + \ldots . \qquad (11)$$

Given (10), this sum converges because

$$p(n_{j+\tau}) = \frac{\delta}{\beta} (1-\exp(-\alpha n_{j+\tau})) < 1 \text{ for all } \tau .$$

In addition, the marginal utility of children, $MU(n_j)$, is positive, i.e.,

$$MU(n_j) = \frac{\alpha U_j}{\alpha n_j} = \frac{\alpha p(n_j)}{\alpha n_j} [V(c_{j+1}) + p(n_{j+1})V(c_{j+2}) + \ldots]$$

$$= \frac{\delta}{\beta} \exp(-\alpha n_j)U_{j+1} > 0 , \qquad (12)$$

but diminishing (i.e., $\partial^2 U_j/\partial n_j^2 = -(\alpha\delta/\beta)\exp(-\alpha n_j)U_{j+1} < 0$).

## Resources and Technology

For simplicity, assume that there is a single nonstorable consumption good that is produced with inputs of labor services (i.e., no physical capital is used in production). Labor productivity varies with age and depends on the amount of human capital investment in a child's education. Specifically, let $y_{ja}$ denote the labor productivity (in terms of the con-

sumption good) of an individual of age a (a = 0,1,2) in cohort
j. In the absence of any investment in human capital, that
individual's age-specific earning capacity is $y^0$.

Human capital investment in education is assumed to take
place during childhood, so that the individual's net childhood
income is

$$y_j^0 = \bar{y}^0 - e_j \ , \tag{13}$$

where $e_j$ is the sum of the direct (e.g., tuition) and indirect
(e.g., foregone earnings) costs of his education. Note that net
childhood income is negative if the direct and indirect costs of
the child's income exceed his earnings capacity, as is typically
the case in societies in which child labor is insignificant.

Educational investment influences the child's future earnings
according to the human capital earnings functions

$$y_j^1 = h_1(e_j)$$

and

$$y_j^2 = h_2(e_j) \ , \tag{14}$$

where the marginal product of education is assumed to be positive, but diminishing (i.e., $h_a' \ 0$ and $h_a' \ 0$ for a=1,2).

In period t=j+1, aggregate output $(Y_t)$ is equal to aggregate consumption $(C_t)$. Aggregate output and aggregate consumption, respectively, are equal to the sum of age-specific
labor income $(Y_{t+a}^a)$ or age-specific consumption $(c_{t-a}^a)$ multiplied by the number of individuals $(N_{t-a}^a)$ of each age a = 0,1,2.
That is, the social budget constraint in period t is

$$Y_t = N_{j+1}^0 y_{j+1}^0 + N_j^1 y_j^1 + N_{j-1}^2 y_{j-1}^2$$

$$= C_t \quad = N_{j+1}^0 c_{j+1}^0 + N_j^1 c_j^1 + N_{j-1}^2 c_{j-1}^2 \ . \tag{15}$$

It is convenient to normalize this aggregate constraint by
dividing through by $N_j^I$, the number of individuals of reproductive age, to obtain

$$n_j y_{j+1}^0 + y_j^1 + \frac{1}{n_{j-1}} y_{j-1}^2 = n_j c_{j+1}^0 + c_j^1 + \frac{1}{n_{j-1}} c_{j-1}^2 \ . \tag{16}$$

Intuitively, (16) may be interpreted as expressing the total resource constraint of a "representative" three-generation extended
family in period t from the point of view of one of its middle-
aged members. This individual is one of $n_{j-1}$ siblings who are
assumed to receive equal shares of their elderly parents' labor
income and to provide equal shares of their parents' consumption.
In addition, the individual pools his own income with the net in-

come (after educational investment) of his $n_j$ children, and from this he provides for his own and the children's consumption. It should be stressed, however, that from a formal point of view, (16) is simply a feasibility constraint that is consistent with any possible distribution of decision-making power among family members, with any institutional structure of the family, and with any familial or nonfamilial (e.g., market or government) institutional mechanisms through which consumption goods are distributed.

In period t+1, the $n_{j+1}$ children of the representative parent in period t will have reached maturity, and their aggregate income and consumption are given by

$$\left[ n_{j+1} y^0_{j+2} + y^1_{j+1} + \frac{1}{n_j} y^2_j \right] n_j = \left[ n_{j+1} c^0_{j+2} + c^1_{j+1} + \frac{1}{n_j} c^2_j \right] n_j , \quad (17)$$

where the bracketed sum on the left side is the total income "controlled" by a typical family head in the next generation of the family "dynasty," and the bracketed sum on the right side is the total consumption of the family.

More generally, let

$$N^1_{j+\tau} = \prod_{k=j}^{j+} n^{-1}_k \quad (18)$$

be the number of middle-aged parents in the $ $ th generation of descendants of the representative parent in period t+ $ $ = j+ $ $ +1, where $N_j1 = 1$. Also, let

$$s^a_{j+\tau} = y^a_{j+\tau} - c^a_{j+\tau} \quad (19)$$

denote the age-specific difference between productivity and consumption of individuals in cohort j+ $\tau$. Then the aggregate resource constraint of the $\tau$ th generation of the family may be written as

$$N^1_{j+\tau} \left[ n_{j+\tau} s^0_{j+\tau+1} + s^1_{j+\tau} + \frac{1}{n_{k-1}} s^2_{j+\tau-1} \right] = 0 . \quad (20)$$

## Socially Optimal Population Growth

As we have seen, parental altruism as expressed by generational preference implies that parents care about the number and welfare of their children, and through them, about the number and welfare of all of their descendants. An omniscient and omnipotent parent in generation j who could control not only his own fertility and allocation of resources, but also those of his descendants, would choose values for these variables in each generation that would maximize his total utility, $U_j$ (which, of course, includes the utility of all of his descendants), subject to the sequence of resource constraints faced by each generation in the family.

The solution to this maximum problem implicitly provides one possible definition of socially optimal population growth. Formally, this problem can be stated as finding an "optimal program" that specifies the levels of age-specific consumption, $c_k a$ (a = 0,1.2), education investment, $e_k$, and fertility, $n_k$, for all generations k = j,j+1,... such that

$$U_j^* = \max V(c_j) \; \delta + a(n_j)n_j U_{j+1}$$

$$+ \sum_{k=j}^{\infty} \lambda_k N_k^1 \left[ n_k s_{k+1}^0 + s_k^1 + \frac{1}{n_{k-1}} s_{k-1}^2 \right], \tag{21}$$

where $U_j^*$ is the maximum level of utility of the representative parent in cohort j as defined by the utility function in (7) or, in alternative forms, in (9) or (10); $\lambda_j$, $\lambda_{j+1}$,... are Lagrangian multipliers associated with the aggregate resource constraints faced by the $k^{th}$ generation in the family dynasty defined in (20); and $N_k^1$ and $s_k^a$ are defined, respectively, in (18) and (19). Also note that $n^{j-1}$ and $c_{j+1}^2$ are treated as exogenous. The program that solves (21) may be termed the "*" program.

It is important to note that the recursive form of the utility function (7) implies that the "*" program is dynamically consistent (Razin and Ben-Zion, 1975). That is, the analogous maximum problem generation j+1 will yield the same optimal values of $(c_k^a, e_{k+1}, n_k)$ for k = j+1,j+2,... as the "*" program does if the values of $c_j^a, e_{j+1}, n_j)$ from the "*" program are given as initial conditions for the new problem. Thus, let the elements of the vector $(U_j^*, U_{j+1}^*, U_{j+2}^* ...)$ denote the levels of total utility received by members of each successive cohort in the family in the "*" program, where the elements of the vector $(1, N_{j+1}^*, N_{j+2}^*, ...)$ give the number of individuals in each of the cohorts. This dynamic consistency property implies that the "*" program is Pareto-efficient because members of each successive generation achieve the maximum feasible level of utility, given the utility levels achieved by preceding generations, as well as the resource constraints they and their descendants face.

It is also important to note, however, that the "*" program is optimal only from the viewpoint of one generation of parents (i.e., generation j) in an arbitrarily chosen family line (i.e., the "representative" family). Since all families are assumed to be identical, the choice of one family for the analysis is innocuous. However, the choice of generation j is not innocuous. For example, it would be possible to find a program, say the "**" program, that would give members of generation j+1 a level of utility higher than the utility level $U_{j+1}^*$, they receive in the

"*" program.  Clearly, this could be accomplished by increasing
the initial resources of the j+1 cohort through additional investment in their human capital or through a reduced commitment
to the consumption of their elderly parents.  As a result of
their altruism toward their offspring, the improvement in the
initial wealth of the j+1 cohort would tend also to lead to
higher levels of utility for future generations.  Thus, relative
to the "*" program, the "**" program would be characterized by a
lower level of utility for generation j and by higher levels of
utility for members of all subsequent generations.

From a social point of view, the "**" program might be judged
superior to the "*" program if one felt that parents place too
little weight on the welfare of their children, that is, that
they are not sufficiently altruistic.  (Apparently, no one seems
to feel that parents are excessively altruistic.)  For now, let
us assume that parental preferences with regard to discounting
the utilities of future generations are regarded as "appropriate"
from a social point of view.  This assumption is probably not
controversial in a world in which everyone is assumed to have
identical preferences, capacities, and initial resources.  However, the presumption of "parental sovereignty" may become more
controversial with the introduction of heterogeneity in preferences and inequalities in individual capacities and resource
endowments, together with a social concern for the degree of inequality in the distribution of welfare.  We shall return to this
issue later.


## Characterization of Optimal Population Growth

The implications of the "*" program for the allocation of resources to age-specific consumption and investment in education
and for fertility behavior can be characterized by examining the
first-order conditions associated with the maximum problem in
(21).  To derive these conditions, it is convenient to rewrite
(21) as

$$\max \sum_{k=j} \left\{ N_k^1 \left[ R_k \left[ v(c_k^0) + \delta v(c_k^1) + \delta^2 v(c_k^2) \right] \right. \right.$$
$$\left. \left. + \lambda_k \left[ n_k s_{k+1}^0 + s_k^1 + \frac{1}{n_{k-1}} s_{k-1}^2 \right] \right] \right\} ,$$  (22)

where

$$R_k = \overset{k-j}{\phantom{x}} \prod_{i=j}^{k-1} a(n_i) \qquad \text{for } k = j+1, j+2, \ldots$$  (23)

and

$$R_j = N_j^1 = 1 .$$

The first-order conditions for the kth generation (k = j, j+1,...) are given by the following equations. The optimal current and future consumption, respectively, of a parent in generation k (i.e., $c_k 1$ and $c_k 2$) satisfy

$$N_k^1 \left[ R_k \, \delta \, v'(c_k^1) - \lambda_k \right] = 0 \tag{24}$$

and

$$N_k^1 \left[ R_k \, \delta^2 v'(c_k^2) - \lambda_{k+1} \right] = 0 . \tag{25}$$

The optimal levels of childhood consumption and educational investment allocated to each of their children (i.e., $c_{k+1}^0$ and $e_{k+1}$), respectively, satisfy

$$N_k^1 \left[ R_{k+1} v'(c_{k+1}^0) - \lambda_k n_k \right] = 0 \tag{26}$$

and

$$-N_k^1 \frac{\lambda_k}{k} n_k + N_{k+1}^1 \lambda_k h_1'(e_{k+1}) + \frac{N_{k+2}^1 \lambda_{k+2} h_2'(e_{k+2})}{n_k} = 0 . \tag{27}$$

Finally, their optimal number of births satisfies

$$N_k^1 \left[ R_k MU(n_k) - \lambda_k s_{k+1}^0 + \frac{\lambda_{k+1} s_k^2}{n_k} \right] = 0 , \tag{28}$$

where the marginal utility of a birth, $MU(n_k)$, is defined in (12).

A standard result of conventional life-cycle theory is that optimal life-cycle consumption occurs when the marginal rate of substitution between current and future consumption is equal to one plus the interest rate. Thus, dividing (23) by (24) and rearranging the result, we have

$$MRS(c_k^1, c_k^2) = \frac{\lambda_k}{\lambda_{k+1}} = \frac{v'(c_k^1)}{\delta v'(c_{k+1}^2)} = 1 + \hat{r}_k , \tag{29}$$

where $\hat{r}_k$ is the "shadow" interest rate between period k and k+1. Note that the slope of the individual's life-cycle consumption profile is positively related to the difference between the interest rate and his rate of time preference. That is, $c_k 2 \gtreqless c_k 1$ as $\hat{r}_k \gtreqless \partial$, where $\delta = 1/(1 + \partial)$ and $\partial$ is the rate of preference.

The relationship between the parent's current consumption and his child's current consumption is obtained by dividing (26) by (23) and rearranging to obtain

$$\frac{v'(c^0_{k+1})}{v'(c^1_k)} = \frac{n_k}{a(n_k)} \quad . \tag{30}$$

Given diminishing marginal utility (i.e., $v''<0$), it is clear that childhood consumption will be higher relative to the parent's consumption the more altruistic the parent (i.e., the higher is $a(n_k)$) and the smaller the number of children, $n_k$.

Optimal educational investment in the "*" program is chosen so as to maximize the present value of the lifetime earnings of each child net of the cost of his education. To see this, divide (27) by $\lambda_k$, and use (24) to obtain

$$\frac{h'_1(e_{k+1})}{(1+\hat{r}_k)} + \frac{h'_2(e_{k+1})}{(1+\hat{r}_k)(1+\hat{r}_{k+1})} = 1 \quad . \tag{31}$$

This equation states that the present value of the marginal returns to investment, given by the left side of (31), is equal to the marginal cost of investment of the right side.

It is important to note that (31) implies it is optimal for parents to invest in each child's human capital so as to maximize the present value of the child's lifetime earnings. Consequently, optimal human capital investment in children depends not on the degree of parental altruism or on other aspects of parental preferences, but on only two things: the child's capacity to benefit from investment, as determined by the human capital production functions (i.e., $ha(\cdot)$ for $a = 1,2$), and the shadow interest rates, which determine the degree to which the returns to investment are discounted.

This implication of the altruism model was first emphasized by Becker and Tomes (1976). They stress the importance of distinguishing between optimal intergenerational wealth transfers from parents to a child and optimal parental investment in the child's human capital. For example, a relatively altruistic parent might desire to make a net wealth transfer of $10,000 to each of his children, while a less altruistic parent might wish to transfer only $5,000 to each child. If the optimal human capital investment for children of either parent costs $8,000 per child, (31) implies that both parents will invest this amount. However, the more altruistic parent will transfer an additional $2,000 to each of his children in the form of a gift or bequest of money, while the less altruistic parent will wish each of his children to transfer $3,000 to him as compensation for the portion of the investment cost he incurred that exceeds the net wealth transfer he wishes to make.

The optimal net wealth transfer per child measures the marginal social cost per child and influences optimal births per parent. This can be seen if we divide (28) by $\lambda_k$ to obtain the following condition for optimal births per parent:

$$MB(n_k) = \frac{MU(n_k)}{\lambda_k} = MC_s(n_k) = [c^0_{k+1} - e_{k+1} + \bar{y}^0]$$

$$+ \frac{y^2_k - c^2_k}{n_k} \cdot \frac{1}{1+\hat{r}_k} , \tag{32}$$

where the marginal benefit of a birth, $MB(n_k)$, measures the dollar value of the marginal utility of the birth to a parent, and $MC_s(n_k)$ is the social marginal cost of the birth. Note that if the marginal utility of a birth is bounded away from zero, then the social marginal cost of a birth must be positive.

The social marginal cost of a birth consists of two components. One of these, represented by the first set of bracketed terms, is the cost of childrearing (i.e., the cost of the child's consumption and education net of his earnings during childhood). The other component, given by the second bracketed term, is the present value of an implicit or explicit intergenerational transfer made by an elderly parent to his middle-aged child (if $y_k^2 - c_k^2 < 0$) or a transfer made by the middle-aged child to his elderly parent (if $y_k^2 - c_k^2 > 0$). The institutions through which the social marginal cost of a birth is paid include the family, the government, and even financial markets. Later we shall examine the extent to which the private and social marginal costs of a birth tend to coincide or to diverge.

The growth rate of age-specific consumption in the "*" program can be determined by considering the ratio of the marginal utilities of age-specific consumption for two successive generations, k and k+1. Thus, using (24)-(26), and $1+\hat{r}_k = \lambda_k/\lambda_{k+1}$ from (29), we obtain the relationship

$$\frac{v'(c^a_k)}{v'(c^a_{k+1})} = \delta\, a(n_k)(1+\hat{r}_k) . \tag{33}$$

Given diminishing marginal utility (i.e., $v'' 0$), (33) implies that

$$\Delta c^a_{k+1} \gtrless 0 \quad as \quad \frac{1}{\delta a(n_k)} \gtrless 1+\hat{r}_k , \tag{34}$$

where $\Delta c^a_{k+1} = c^a_{k+1} - c^a_k$ ($a = 0,1,2$) is the change in age-specific consumption in successive generations. In other words, (34) states that age-specific consumption will grow, remain stationary, or decrease across generations as the reciprocal of the product of time preference and generational preference (i.e., $\delta a(n_k)$) is greater than, equal to, or less than the shadow interest factor (i.e., $1+\hat{r}_k$).

Beginning from any arbitrarily chosen initial conditions, assume that the optimal program asymptotically approaches a steady state in which the levels of age-specific consumption, educational investment, and births per parent are stationary (i.e., constant from one generation to the next). As is clear from (33) and (34), this implies that the steady-state shadow interest rate, r, is given by

$$1+r = \frac{1}{\delta a(n)} \ .$$

(35)

Recall that $\delta a(n)n$ must be less than one if $U_j$ is to be bounded (e.g., see (10)). Using this fact and (35), it follows that

$$\hat{r} > g \ ,$$

(36)

where g=n-1 is the rate of population growth in steady state. This conforms with a well-known result, due to Starrett (1972), which shows that the interest rate is equal to or greater than the growth rate in any efficient program.

Starrett's result is closely related to Samuelson's (1958) famous "biological interest rate" result, which shows that it is always possible for an age-structured population to make inter-generational transfers that provide an implicit rate of return equal to the rate of population growth. Beginning from an ini-tial steady-state program in which the (market or shadow) rate of interest is smaller than the biological interest rate, it is possible, for instance, to devise a "pay-as-you-go" social secur-ity scheme that increases the welfare of all those alive when it goes into effect and also increases the welfare of members of all future generations. Since the reallocation accomplished by the social security scheme is a Pareto improvement, it follows that the initial program is inefficient. Conversely, if the rate of interest in the initial program is equal to or greater than the population growth rate, it is not possible to find any inter-generational transfer scheme that increases the welfare of some-one in a given generation without reducing the welfare of someone else in the same or a different generation relative to the util-ity they would have received in the initial program. Hence, in this case, the initial program is Pareto-optimal.[5]

One popular definition of optimal population growth is that rate of growth that maximizes per capita utility from own con-sumption. (In the terms of this chapter, this concept of the optimal rate of population growth involves choosing the rate of growth so as to maximize V(c) as defined in (8).) For example, Nerlove et al. (1982) trace this idea back to John Stuart Mill; more recently, Samuelson (1975) has employed this definition.

An important implication of (36) is that the rate of popula-tion growth in the "*" program does not satisfy this criterion. Specifically, a standard result in neoclassical economic growth theory is that the maximum steady-state level of per capita util-ity from own consumption corresponding to any given rate of popu-lation growth occurs in the "golden rule program," in which the rate of interest is equal to the rate of population growth. Since $\hat{r}$ is strictly greater than g in (36), it follows that the steady-state level of per capita utility in the "*" program is lower than the maximum feasible steady-state level of V(c).

Intuitively, there are two reasons for this result. First, the fact that parents are assumed to derive utility from the number of children implies that they would be willing to sacrifice some utility from consumption in order to have children. Second, taking fertility as given, parents in each generation could achieve the golden rule if they made a sufficiently large net wealth transfer to each child. In effect, a larger net transfer to each child increases both the child's lifetime utility and his optimal savings; the latter effect tends to reduce the rate of interest (Willis, 1985). The assumption that parents in each generation discount the utility of their offspring (i.e., $\delta\, a(n) < 1$) implies that parents are unwilling to make net wealth transfers sufficiently large to drive the interest rate down to equality with the growth rate. It may be noted that the greater the degree of parental altruism, the larger are net wealth transfers from the older to the younger generation, the higher is the steady-state level of V(c), and the smaller is the difference between the rate of interest and the rate of growth.

Finally, it is worth reemphasizing a point made earlier: the "*" program is optimal from the perspective of the current generation of parents, and not necessarily from the perspective of someone who wishes to weight the welfare of current and future generations differently than the current parental generation does. In optimal growth theory, it is customary to distinguish between the private and social rate of time discount (see, e.g., Arrow and Kurz, 1970). In the model presented here, the private rate of time discount is given by the shadow interest rate, which, in steady state, is related to the product of parental time preference and generational preference parameters as expressed in (35). While parents' preferences incorporate concern for both the number and per capita welfare of future generations in their own family line, those preferences do not incorporate any broader ethical concern with the distribution of economic welfare, either within or between generations of members of other family lines within the society, or, a fortiori, among members of current and future generations in other societies.

In welfare economies, these broader ethical concerns are often expressed in the form of a social welfare function and used as a justification for policies aimed at redistributing income. Note that issues of equity within generations are irrelevant in the model presented here because all family lines are assumed to have identical preferences and resources; however, the intergenerational distribution of welfare is relevant. Ethical views concerning the intergenerational distribution of welfare can be summarized by a social rate of time discount. For example, Arrow and Kurz (1970: xvii-xviii) assume that the social welfare function may be expressed as the discounted sum of the utilities from own consumption of all individuals in current and future generations. If, for instance, the social rate of time preference is smaller than $1/\delta\, a(n)$, then the privately optimal "*" program will give too little weight to the utility of future

generations.  In this case, policy measures designed to increase
the savings rate might be justified on the basis of the ethical
views embodied in the social welfare function, even though such
measures would not be justified in Paretian terms because they
would reduce the utility of members of the current generation.


## The Optimality of Private Fertility Decisions

As we have seen, the "*" program is optimal from the point of
view of an omniscient and omnipotent dynastic family head in a
given generation who has the power to control the allocations
and fertility behavior of all his descendants for an infinite
number of generations.  In actuality, of course, a family head
controls only the allocation of resources over which he has property rights; most likely, moreover, he directly controls the
behavior of his own children only during their childhood, although it is conceivable under some forms of family organization
that the head would directly control the behavior of his offspring as long as he lived.  However, even under the most favorable circumstances, a family head from a given generation cannot
directly control the allocational decisions and fertility behavior of his more distant descendants.

   Superficially, therefore, it appears that private fertility
decisions should be plagued by externalities because the parent's
utility function (7) is implicitly a function of the allocations
and fertility behavior of all of his descendants (i.e., see (9)).
Happily, the potential for externalities need not be realized in
this model.  Specifically, as is shown in this section, private
fertility decisions and other allocative decisions by family
heads in a competitive economy with perfect markets lead to allocations identical to those chosen by an omnipotent social planner
in the "*" program.  Thus, the model of dynastic parental altruism extends the scope of the "invisible hand" so that the optimality of decentralized private decisions by families concerning
reproduction and investment in their children's human capital is
included among the standard efficiency results in competitive
general equilibrium theory.  The model therefore provides a
natural benchmark for the analysis of failures of market or
nonmmarket institutions that may result in nonoptimal outcomes.

   In addition to the usual assumptions concerning perfect
markets, this happy result is a consequence of the additively
separable recursive form of the altruistic utility functions of
individuals in each generation and the associated dynamic consistency properties of this function noted earlier.  As Becker
(1974) has shown in his "rotten kid theorem," an altruistic
parent need not directly control the behavior of his children to
induce them to make allocations that are optimal from the
parent's point of view.  Rather, it is sufficient for the parent
to exert indirect control over his children's behavior through
his control of transfers to them.  As is shown below, this result
carries over to the case of endogenous fertility in the sense
that if parents in each generation are free to choose the magni-

tude of the net wealth transfer to each child (and if certain
other conditions hold), each grown child will voluntarily choose
the level of fertility, investment per child, and consumption
levels for himself and his children that his parent would have
chosen for him given the power to do so. The same is true for
his children, his children's children, and so on for all future
generations in the family.

Although the discussion here drops the assumption of parental
omnipotence in showing the optimality of private fertility decisions, for simplicity the assumption of parental omniscience is
retained. That is, parents in each generation are assumed to
have perfect foresight concerning the resources and technology
available to each subsequent generation in the family dynasty,
as well as perfect foresight about the decisions to be made by
members of each subsequent generation. Similar optimality results could be supposed to carry over for a "rational expectations" equilibrium in a model with uncertainty, but it is beyond
the scope of this chapter to investigate this case.

Assume that, upon reaching maturity at the beginning of
middle age (i.e., $a=1$) in period $t=j+1$, an individual can choose
how many children to have $(n_j)$, how much to spend on his own
consumption $(c_j^1)$, how much to spend on his children's current
consumption $(n_j c_{j+1}^0)$, and how much to save $(z_j)$. Note that $z_j$
may be either positive if he is a net saver (or a net lender) or
negative if he is a net dissaver (or a net borrower). His net
income is equal to his own income $(y_j^1)$ plus his children's income $(n_j y_{j+1}^0)$ plus a bequest from his parent or minus an old age
transfer he makes to his parent, which is denoted by $b_{j-1}$. Thus,
we may write his current budget constraint as

$$y_j^1 + n_j y_{j+1}^0 + b_{j-1} = c_j^1 + n_j c_{j+1}^0 + z_j . \tag{37}$$

when the individual enters old age at the beginning of period
$t+1$, his budget is

$$y_j^2 + (1+r_j)z_j = c_j^2 + n_j b_j , \tag{38}$$

where $r_j$ is the market rate of interest, and $n_j b_j$ is the
amount of his estate that he leaves to his children (if $b_j$ is
positive) or the amount of old age support he receives from his
children (if $b_j$ is negative).

There are two key assumptions in this section: first, that
the individual faces a "perfect" credit market, so that he can
borrow or lend at the same market rate of interest, $r_j$; and
second, that the sign and magnitude of $b_j$ are subject to the
parent's choice. The latter assumption requires little justification if the parent wishes to leave a positive estate; however, if he wishes to receive old age support from his children,
a question arises concerning whether his grown children will
comply with this desire. At this point, let us assume that the

children consider a negative value of $b_j$ chosen by the parent as a binding commitment. Using the terminology of Becker and Tomes (1984), we may call this assumption the absence of "default risk." Later, possible determinants and consequences of default risk will be considered.

The two budget constraints in (37) and (38) can be combined into a "net wealth" constraint

$$w_j = y_j^1 + \frac{y_j^2}{1+r_j} + b_{j-1} = c_j^1 + \frac{c_j^2}{1+r_j} + \pi_j n_j \ , \tag{39}$$

where the individual's net wealth, $w_j$, is equal to the present discounted value of his lifetime income, plus his share of his parent's estate (if $b_{j-1} > 0$) or minus his old age support obligation to his parent (if $b_{j-1} < 0$), and where

$$\pi_j = c_{j+1}^0 + e_{j+1}^{-0} - y_{j+1}^{-0} + \frac{b_j}{1+r_j} \tag{40}$$

measures the net cost per child over the lifetime of the parent. It is important to point out that $\pi_j$ is an endogenous variable subject to parental choice; thus, the parent chooses whether the child is a net "investment good" (i.e., $\pi_j < 0$) or a net "consumption good" (i.e., $\pi_j > 0$).

Let $x_k = (c_k^1, c_k^2, n_k, c_{k+1}^0, e_{k+1}, b_k)$ be the set of "control" variables that a prospective parent in cohort k can choose directly. Thus, an individual who reaches maturity in period $t=j+1$ directly controls the values of $x_j$, treats $b_{j-1}$ as a predetermined exogenous variable, and also treats the sequence of current and future market interest rates (i.e., $r_j, r_{j+1}, \ldots$) as exogenous. In addition, his utility is affected by variables that are controlled by his children, grandchildren, and more remote descendants (i.e, $x_{j+1}, x_{j+2}, \ldots$). He is assumed to know their preferences (i.e., $U_k$ as defined in (7)) and the constraints they face. The net wealth constraints of successive generations in the family are obtained in the same way as in (39) and can be expressed by replacing the index j in (39) with the index k for the kth generation for $k = j+1, j+2, \ldots$ .

The maximization problem for a parent in cohort j is written in the form of a dynamic programming problem in equation (A-1) in the Appendix and the first-order conditions associated with this problem are stated in equations (A-2)-(A-7). Using these first-order conditions, it is easy to establish that the parent in cohort j will make the identical choices when he can control only $x_j$ that he would make if he were omnipotent and could also control $x_k$ for all $k = j, j+1, \ldots$, as is assumed in (21); this is given the assumption that he faces a market interest rate, $r_j$, that is equal to the shadow interest rate, $\hat{r}_j$, determined in the *·* program (see (29)).

To demonstrate, note that the family head adjusts the value
of $b_j$ so as to make the ratio of his own marginal utility of
income to that of each of his children equal to one plus the market rate of interest; that is, by rearranging (A-7) we obtain

$$\frac{\mu_j}{\mu_{j+1}} = \frac{1}{1+r_j} , \tag{41}$$

where the Lagrangian multipliers $\mu_j$ and $\mu_{j+1}$, respectively,
measure the marginal utility of income of the parent and each of
his children. Since it is assumed that the market interest rate
faced by the parent is equal to the shadow rate of interest, it
follows that $\mu_j/\mu_{j+1} = \lambda_j/\lambda_{j+i}$, where the $\lambda$ 's are the values
of the Lagrangian multipliers associated with the "*" program.
(A similar argument will establish that $\mu_k/\mu_{k+1} = \lambda_k/\lambda_{k+1}$ for all $k = j, j+1,\dots$ .) Using this fact, the substitution of $\lambda_k/\lambda_{k+1}$ for $\mu_k/\mu_{k+1}$ and $1+r_k$ in (A-2)-(A-7), to-
gether with some simple algebra, permits one to show that (A-1)-
(A-7) are identical to each of the first-order conditions in the
"*" program (i.e, (24)-(28)). Hence, privately optimal parental
choices in each generation coincide with those in the socially
optimal "*" program.

It is important to stress that this result depends crucially
on the assumption that parents view their children's consumption
and fertility choices in the same way that the children themselves do. This assumption is embodied in the additively separable parental utility function

$$U_j = V(c_j) + \delta a(n_j) n_j U_{j+1}$$

in (1), and it implies that, for any given budget, children will
voluntarily make the same decisions their parent would have made
for them. Because of this property, a parent can indirectly control the behavior of his offspring simply by controlling the
amount of wealth transferred to them.

If parental preferences do not have this property, private
fertility behavior <u>will</u> be plagued by externalities. This is
because the variables under control of a given generation of
parents will be insufficient to induce their descendants to behave as those parents wish them to behave. Thus, as was stressed
earlier, the question of the importance of intergenerational externalities involving population is uncomfortably model-dependent
because it depends so critically on the specific form of parental
utility functions.

This raises the question of whether dynastic altruism provides a reasonable approximation of actual parental preferences.
On a priori grounds, arguments can be made on both sides of this
issue. It has been noted, for example, that altruistic preferences are "nonpaternalistic" because an altruistic parent simply
honors his children's preferences, and therefore does not seek
to interfere with their decisions. Alternatively, it can be
argued that a major part of childrearing involves parents' trying
to shape their children's preferences so that those children

will display "good behavior" (as viewed by the parents) when not
subject to parental control. In this sense, altruistic preferences would tend to hold if parents were, in fact, successful in
this enterprise. At root, however, assessment of the reasonable-
ness of the hypothesis of dynastic altruism, as well as of conclusions based on this hypothesis concerning the optimality of
private fertility decisions, is an empirical question that depends on the degree to which such preferences are or are not
consistent with observed behavior.

## DIVERGENCE BETWEEN SOCIALLY AND PRIVATELY OPTIMAL POPULATION GROWTH

Elsewhere, the author has argued (Willis, 1982) that a theoretical model of the type outlined here does appear to be broadly
consistent with changes in demographic behavior and institutional family structure that are observed to accompany economic
development during the process of demographic transition. Among
other things, the model provides an explanation for changes in
the direction of intergenerational transfers during the transition process that are emphasized in Caldwell's (1976) well-known
theory of demographic transition, although the causal interpretation of these changes differs from his.

In particular, it is assumed that the basic causal force
underlying economic development is technological change. Given
this assumption, it can be shown that technological change will
lead to a "successful" demographic transition from high to low
fertility and a "successful" economic transition from low to high
levels of income if the conditions hold under which parental fertility decisions are socially optimal. Conversely, the underlying causes of "unsuccessful" transitions marked by continuing
high rates of population growth and poverty may be found in the
failure of certain of these conditions to hold. In addition, it
is possible that the development of the welfare state in post-
transitional societies may lead to a divergence between social
and privately optimal fertility that results in nonoptimally low
rates of population growth and overinvestment in human capital.

Although it remains for future theoretical and empirical
research to verify these conjectures rigorously, this chapter
concludes with a brief and intuitive discussion of their underlying reasoning. The discussion begins with the case of a
successful demographic transition, in which it is assumed that
private fertility decisions are socially optimal.

## The Direction of Intergenerational Transfers and Demographic Transition

Given the assumption that the marginal utility of children is
always positive, it has been shown that altruistic parents
equate the marginal utility and marginal cost of children by
choosing to make a positive net intergenerational transfer to

each child. However, the direction of transfers need not be from
the older to the younger generation at each point in the life
cycle. For example, a parent might obtain a net surplus from
his children's labor during the childrearing period, but leave
them bequests of higher present value when they are grown. Alternatively, a parent might wish to receive old age transfers
from his grown children to defray part of the costs incurred in
rearing them.

The optimal life-cycle pattern of intergenerational transfers
depends on both the state of technology, and the degree of generational and time preference. For instance, in a primitive technological environment in which child labor is useful and the
productivity of investment in human capital is low, a life-cycle
pattern of parental "exploitation" of child labor followed by
positive bequests may be optimal. This pattern is more likely
the lower is the rate of time preference, which implies a willingness to postpone consumption to later stages of the life
cycle, and the higher is the degree of generational preference,
which reflects parents' desires to make relatively large
transfers to their children.

Assuming stable preferences, and holding the level of wealth
and rate of interest constant, a life-cycle pattern involving
positive expenditures on childrearing followed by old age transfers from children to parents is more likely the more productive
is investment in human capital. As the return increases, it is
optimal for parents to invest more in their children during the
childrearing period; however, if per capita wealth and the rate
of interest remain constant, there is no change in the net transfer parents wish to make to each child. Consequently, the parent
finances the higher level of investment in the child with an
implicit loan, which is later repaid by the child with an old
age transfer to the parent. Holding the productivity of investment constant, as the level of wealth increases, the size of the
desired net wealth transfer per chid tends to increase, and the
size of the desired old age transfer decreases. At a sufficiently high level of wealth, parents will wish to leave positive net bequests to their children; in this case, parents make
positive net transfers to children throughout the life cycle.

The discussion suggests that, beginning from a "pretransitional" situation characterized by primitive technology, improvements in technology that increase the general level of productivity and raise the return to investment in human capital will
tend to cause an accompanying change in the life-cycle pattern
of intergenerational transfers within the family. At the earliest stage, there is an emphasis on the role of children in
family production. As the return to investment increases, this
is followed by a stage of increased investment in children and a
growing importance of old age transfers. Finally, growth in the
level of wealth and an associated increase in net transfers to
the young may lead to a modern nuclear family structure in which
children provide no pecuniary benefits to their parents at any
stage in the life cycle. During this process, increases in the
optimal net parental transfer per child, and hence increases in

the marginal cost of children, cause a downward trend in the
optimal level of fertility, while increased investment per child,
together with general productivity increases, causes rising
levels of per capita income.


## Institutional Failure and Unsuccessful Transition

In the scenario outlined above, it is assumed that all social
institutions perform efficiently, so that privately optimal
parental decisions are also socially optimal at each stage of
the transition.   There are two key institutional assumptions
underlying the proposition that private fertility behavior is
socially optimal:   first, that parents face a "perfect" credit
market in which they can borrow and lend as much as they wish at
the market rate of interest, and second, that the parent may, if
he so chooses, obligate each of his grown children to support
him in old age and have confidence that his children will not
default on this obligation.  To the extent that these conditions
fail to hold, privately optimal parental decisions concerning
fertility investment in children will tend to diverge from
social optimality.
    The consequences of the failure of these two conditions de-
pend on the life-cycle pattern of intergenerational transfers
that would be socially optimal given the state of technology and
preferences.   Thus, default risk is unimportant if parents wish
to make bequests to children, borrowing constraints are unimportant if parents do not need to borrow to finance investment in
their children's human capital, and lending constraints are
unimportant if parents do not need to save for their old age.
For example, neither capital market imperfections nor default
risk is likely to be a significant cause of socially nonoptimal
fertility behavior in the pretransitional situation described
above in which parents first appropriate a surplus from their
children's labor and later leave bequests to them.  When children
are young, parents can exercise direct control over their children's level of consumption and over their allocation of time
between investment and labor.   Of course, the children will
welcome a positive bequest when they are grown.
    If a successful demographic and economic transition is to
take place, the changing life-cycle pattern of intergenerational
transfers within the family that is caused by improvements in
technology will necessitate changes in both family and market
structure.   Conversely, the failure of these institutions to
adapt appropriately to a changed environment may lead to economic
stagnation and high rates of population growth.  The latter possibility is illustrated in the following scenario.
    Consider, initially, a pretransitional agrarian society
characterized by high mortality and a primitive technology;
parents invest little in their children's human capital, and the
family land is bequeathed in equal shares to each surviving
child upon the parent's death.  Now assume that the introduction
of new medical technology causes a decrease in mortality rates,

and that improvements in production technology create increases
in the demand for skilled labor in urban industrial areas. The
decline in mortality and increase in demand for skilled labor
will tend to increase the productivity of investment in human
capital of the young, which will be realized, in part, through
the migration of labor to urban areas. In addition, the reduction of mortality at older ages may increase the period of
economic dependence during old age, especially if morbidity does
not fall.

For the sake of argument, assume that the socially optimal
response to these changes involves reducing the level of fertility; increasing the level of investment per child by enough to
make the net cost of childrearing positive; and generating a
demand by parents for old age transfers from their children to
defray part of the cost of financing their investment in human
capital and to provide additional consumption during old age.
As noted earlier, this life-cycle pattern of intergenerational
transfers means that parents make implicit loans to their children to pay part of the cost of financing the higher level of
investment in their human capital, which is repaid by old age
transfers from the children. To finance this investment,
parents may need to borrow in a credit market, and to be repaid,
they must somehow induce their children to make old age transfers.

Even in societies with sophisticated legal and financial
institutions, it is difficult for households to obtain unsecured
loans at market interest rates. In a newly developing economy,
the assumption of efficient credit markets for either borrowing
or lending is still less likely to conform to reality. In addition, the institutional task of the family is made more difficult because of the parent's need to find a way of reducing the
risk that his children will default on implicit parental loans
by failing to provide old age support. These difficulties may
be exacerbated by changes in the institutional and geographical
structure of the economy that lead to a shift in productive
activities from the family to the firm and from rural to urban
areas.

If parents are credit-constrained and are unable to guard
against the risk of default, the net private cost of a child
with the socially optimal level of investment is greater than
his social cost. If parents were constrained to make the
socially optimal investment, fertility would tend to fall by
more than is socially optimal. However, parents are not so
constrained. Thus, it may be privately optimal for parents to
maintain the initial low level of investment per child and high
level of fertility. Moreover, parents may alter both the composition and level of their investment in their children to
reduce the default risk. For example, if physical proximity
influences a child's sense of obligation to his parents, rural
parents might discourage their children from acquiring skills
whose utilization requires migration to urban areas. Such
failures of market and family institutions to adapt to new conditions may present serious obstacles to a successful demographic
and economic transition.

## Fiscal Distortions

It is reasonable to hypothesize that the development of the modern welfare state may be traced, in part, to the inability of private capital markets and the traditional family to adapt efficiently to rising demands for investment in human capital and old age security caused by technological change and decreased mortality. In particular, the emergence of public schools and social security both represent means by which intergenerational transfers through the public sector substitute for private intrafamily transfers, thereby reducing the reliance of the family on capital markets and decreasing its need to enforce obligations of the young toward their parents.

The altruism hypothesis has powerful implications for the effect of government transfer programs on family fertility, savings, and investment programs. Perhaps the best-known example of this involves analysis of the effect of social security on savings in models that treat population growth as exogenous. Using a nonaltruistic life-cycle model, Feldstein (1974) argues that a "pay-as-you-go" social security program would reduce aggregate savings because it would reduce the need for individuals to save for their retirement. In contrast, in an altruistic model, Barro (1974) shows that the introduction of social security would induce exactly offsetting changes in intergenerational transfers within families, so that there would be no effect on aggregate savings. More generally, given perfect capital markets and the absence of default risk, changes in intrafamily transfers will tend to offset any attempt by the government to redistribute income among generations. For instance, Pelzman (1973) argues that tax-financed public schooling induces families to reduce private expenditures on schooling and provides some evidence of such effects. Of course, even in the altruism model, it is possible for the government to alter the distribution of income among families through lump sum taxes and transfers and to affect their behavior by altering the prices they face through marginal taxes and subsidies. Moreover, in practice, all fiscal policies combine redistributive and marginal effects.

Neutrality results such as Barro's are overturned when population is endogenous. For instance, given altruism, perfect markets, and no default risk, the offsetting of public social security transfers by the family causes a divergence between the private and social costs of children that leads to lower fertility than is socially optimal. The argument is simple.

Consider a social security program that imposes a lump sum tax on middle-aged workers and transfers the proceeds to elderly retirees. Before the introduction of the program, each family distributes its income so as to equate the ratio of the marginal utilities of wealth of the two generations with one plus the interest rate (see (29)); fertility is chosen so as to equate the private marginal benefit and marginal cost of a birth (see (32)), where, recall, the marginal cost of a birth is equal to the present value of the sum of the net costs of rearing the child, plus the net bequest to each child or minus the net old age transfer received from each child.

Taking fertility and the interest rate as given initially, the transfer increases the wealth of the older generation, and the tax reduces the wealth of the middle-aged generation; this is turn causes the ratio of marginal utilities of wealth to fall. To reestablish the optimal distribution of income between generations, the elderly increase their bequests or reduce the amount of old age support they desire from their children until the ratio of marginal utilities is once again equal to one plus the interest rate. This occurs, as Barro has shown, when the intrafamily transfer exactly offsets the public transfer, and the optimal levels of age-specific consumption and investment remain unchanged. Note, however, that the increase in bequests (or the reduction in old age support) implies that the private marginal cost of a birth to a parent has risen, and consequently, that the privately optimal level of fertility will decrease. To the extent that the reduction in the aggregate rate of population growth causes a reduction in the equilibrium interest rate, the social security program will cause the capital intensity of the economy (including human capital) and the level of per capita output to exceed what is socially optimal.[6]

It is important to point out that the distortionary effect of government fiscal programs on fertility incentives depends on their overall impact on the intergenerational income distribution, rather than on the impact of a single program such as social security. For instance, ignoring its effects on the marginal cost of education, public schooling represents a public transfer from the older to the younger generation, and the offsetting behavior of altruistic families tends to reduce the private marginal cost of children. Since the growth of public-sector programs tends to generate benefits to both tails of the age distribution, this may help to explain the mixed results, reported in a recent survey by Wildsasin (1984), of empirical tests of the hypothesis that social security tends to reduce fertility. That is, if social security and public schooling are both introduced, it is possible that their net effect on the cost of children is neutral, and that private fertility decisions are not distorted by fiscal policy. However, Preston (1984) suggests that the distribution of public benefits in the U.S. has been tilting notably toward the elderly in the past two decades. If so, the growth of the welfare state may result in excessive private costs of children and lower than optimal population growth.

NOTES

1    Also see Nerlove et al. (1983) for discussion of a variety of other aspects of the welfare economics of population growth within this framework.

2    This was the conclusion reached by Willis (1985) on the
     basis of crude estimates of the capital dilution and
     intergenerational transfer effects by Arthur and McNicoll
     (1978) and Lee (1980).

3    The concept of dynastic altruism was first introduced by
     Barro (1974) and was first employed in a model of endogenous
     population growth by Ben Zion and Razin (1975).

4    For completeness, it must also be assumed that utility from
     age-specific consumption must be finite as the level of
     age-specific consumption approaches infinity (i.e., $\lim$
     $v(c_{j+}^{a} \tau) = $ constant as $c_{j+}^{a} \tau \to \infty$).

5    The logic of these results can be explained most easily by
     assuming that the society consists of two age groups, the
     young and the old, and that the rate of population growth is
     g percent per generation. Note that this implies an age
     structure such that there are 1+g young people for every old
     person in each period. Assume initially that the society is
     in a steady-state equilibrium in which the young and the old
     each consume 100 units of a nonstorable consumption good each
     period. Now consider an alternative allocation such that,
     beginning in some period t=0, each young person is required
     to pay a tax equal to 1 unit of the consumption good into a
     fund that is redistributed equally to each old person.
     Assume that this transfer scheme remains in force forever.

         Clearly, the old in period zero are made better off
     because each receives an additional 1+g units of the con-
     sumption good. The effect of this scheme on the welfare of
     the young in period zero is ambiguous: their consumption in
     period zero is reduced from 100 to 99, but their consumption
     in period 1 when they are old is increased from 100 to 101+g.
     Since the scheme remains in force in all future periods,
     note that each individual in every future generation will
     also have a consumption profile (99, 101+g). If the shadow
     rate of interest was initially $\hat{r}$, we know from revealed
     preference that $U(100,100) \geq U(99, 100+r)$ where $U(c^0,$
     $c^1)$ denotes the individual's lifetime utility from the
     life-cycle consumption page $(c^0, c^1)$. It follows that
     the welfare of the young must fall if $\hat{r}_g \geq g$ because $U(99,$
     $100+\hat{r}) \geq U(99, 100+g)$. Conversely, if $\hat{r} < g$, it will always
     be possible to find some social security scheme that permits
     both the old and young in period 0 and members of all future
     generations to enjoy a higher level of welfare.

6    After completing the first draft of this chapter, I dis-
     covered that a nearly identical argument has been made
     independently by Wildasin (1985).

APPENDIX

A parent in cohort j is assumed to maximize the following expression with respect to his control variables,

$$x_j = (c_j^1, c_j^2, n_j, c_{j+1}^0, e_j, b_j),$$

treating the control variables of subsequent generations,

$$x_k = (c_k^1, c_k^2, n_k, c_{k+1}^0, e_k, b_k) \text{ for } k = j+1, j+2,\ldots$$

as exogenous:

$$\max_{x_j} \left[ \delta v(c_j^1) + \delta^2 v(c_j^2) + \delta a(n_j) n_j v(c_{j+1}^0) \right] \tag{A-1}$$

$$+ a(n_j) n_j \left[ \max_{x_{j+1}} \left[ \delta v(c_{j+1}^1) + \delta^2 v(c_{j+1}^2) + \delta a(n_{j+1}) n_{j+1} v(c_{j+1}^0) \right] \right] \ldots$$

$$+ a(n_{j+\tau-1}) n_{j+\tau-1} \right] \ldots \max_{x_{j+}} \left[ \delta v(c_{j+\tau}^1) + \delta^2 v(c_{j+\tau}^2) \right.$$

$$\left. + \delta a(n_{j+\tau}) n_{j+\tau} v(c_{j+\tau+1}^0) \right] + \ldots$$

$$+ \mu_j \left[ s_j^1 + \frac{s_j^2}{1+r_j} + b_{j-1} - r_j n_j \right]$$

$$+ n_j \mu_{j+1} \left[ s_{j+1}^1 + \frac{s_{j+1}^2}{1+r_{j+1}} + b_j - \pi_{j+1} n_{j+1} \right] \ldots$$

$$n_j \ldots n_{j+\tau-1} \mu_{j+\tau} \left[ s_{j+\tau}^1 + \frac{s_{j+\tau}}{1+r_{j+\tau}} + b_{j+\tau-1} - \pi_{j+\tau} n_{j+\tau} \right]$$

$$+ \ldots ,$$

where $\mu_j$, $\mu_{j+1},\ldots$ are Lagrangian multipliers associated with the wealth constraints of generations $j$, $j+1,\ldots,$ where $b_{j-1}$ is exogenous, and where

$$s_k^a = y_k^a - c_k^a , \text{ and}$$

$$\pi_k = c_{k+1}^0 - e_{k+1} + \bar{y}^0 + \frac{b_k}{1+r_k}$$

for $k = j, j+1,\ldots$ and $a = 0,1,2.$

Assuming that there exists an internal solution to this maximum problem, the parent's choice of $c_j^1$, $c_j^2$, $n_j$, $c_{j+1}^0$, $e_j$, $b_j$, respectively, satisfies the following first-order conditions:

$$\delta \, v'(c_j^1) - \mu_j = 0 \ , \tag{A-2}$$

$$\delta^2 v'(c_{j+1}^2) - \left[\frac{1}{1+r_j}\right] \mu_j = 0 \ , \tag{A-3}$$

$$MU(n_j) - \mu_j \, \pi_j = 0 \ , \tag{A-4}$$

$$\delta \, a(n_j) n_j v'(c_{t+1}^0) - \mu_j = 0 \ , \tag{A-5}$$

$$-n_j \, \mu_j + n_j \, \mu_{j+1} \left[ h_1'(e_{j+1}) + \frac{h_2'(e_{j+1})}{1+r_{j+1}} \right] = 0 \ , \tag{A-6}$$

$$\frac{-n_j \, \mu_j}{1+r_j} + n_j \, \mu_{j+1} = 0 \ , \text{ and} \tag{A-7}$$

where $MU(n_j)$ is given by (6) in the text. The first-order conditions corresponding to the optimal choices of their controls, $x_k$, by each member of the $k = j+1, j+2, \ldots$ successive generations in the family will be identical to (A-2)-(A-7), with the index $j$ replaced by the index $k$ and with $b_{k-1}$, which is chosen by their parent, being treated as exogenous by each member of the $k$th generation.

REFERENCES

Arrow, K.J., and M. Kurz (1970)  Public Investment, the Rate of
    Return and Optimal Fiscal Policy. Baltimore, Md.:   The
    Johns Hopkins University Press for Resources for the Future.
Arthur, W.B., and G.McNicoll (1978)  Samuelson, population and
    integenerational transfers. International Economic Review
    19:241-246.
Barro, R.J. (1974)  Are government bonds net wealth?  Journal of
    Political Economy 82:1095-1118.
Becker, G.S. (1974)  A theory of social interaction.  Journal of
    Political Economy 82:1063-1093.
Becker, G.S. (1981)  A Treatise on the Family.  Cambridge, Mass.:
    Harvard University Press.
Becker, G.S. (1983)  Some Notes on Population Growth and Economic
    Growth. Unpublished manuscript, University of Chicago.
Becker, G.S., and N. Tomes (1976)  Child endowments and the
    quantity and quality of children. Journal of Political
    Economy 84:S142-S163.
Becker, G.S., and N. Tomes (1984)  Human Capital and the Rise
    and Fall of Families. Working Paper No. 84-10, Economic
    Research Center, National Opinion Research Center.
Blandy, R. (1974)  The welfare analysis of fertility reduction.
    Economic Journal 84:109-129.
Caldwell, J.C. (1976)  Toward a restatement of demographic
    transition theory. Population and Development Review
    2:321-366.
Cheung, S.N.S. (1973)  The fable of the bees:  an economic
    investigation. Journal of Law and Economics 16:11-34.
Coase, R. (1937)  The nature of the firm.  Economica 386.
Coase, R. (1960)  The problem of social cost.  Journal of Law and
    Economics (3):1-44.
Dasgupta, P.S., and G.M. Heal (1979)  Economic Theory and
    Exhaustible Resources. Cambridge, England:  Cambridge
    University Press.
Eckstein, Z., and K.I. Wolpin (1982)  Endogenous Fertility in an
    Overlapping Generations Growth Model.  Economic Growth
    Center, Discussion Paper No. 416, Yale University.
Feldstein, M. (1974)  Social security, induced retirement, and
    aggregate capital accumulation. Journal of Political
    Economy 82:905-926.
Hardin, G. (1968)  The tragedy of the commons.  Science 162:
    1243-1248.
Lee, R.D. (1980)  Age structure, intergenerational transfers,
    consumption and economic growth. Revue Economique 1129-1156.
Meade, J.E. (1952)  External economies and diseconomies in a
    competitive situation. Economic Journal 62:54-67.
Nerlove, M., A. Razin, and E. Sadka (1982)  Population size and
    the social welfare functions of Bentham and Mill.  Economic
    Letters 10:61-64.
Nerlove, M., A. Razin, and E. Sadka (1983)  Some Welfare
    Theoretic Implications of Endogenous Fertility.  Paper
    prepared for the Conference on the Economics of the Family,
    University of Pennsylvania.

Pazner, E.A., and A. Razin (1980) Competitive efficiency in an overlapping generation model with endogenous population. Journal of Public Economics 13:249-258.

Pelzman, S. (1973) The effect of government subsidies in kind on private expenditures: the case of higher education. Journal of Political Economy 81:1-27.

Preston, S.H. (1984) Children and the elderly: divergent paths for America's dependents. Demography 21:435-458.

Razin, A., and U. Ben-Zion (1975) An intergenerational model of population growth. American Economic Review 65:923-924.

Rosen, S. (1983) Specialization and human capital. Journal of Labor Economics 1:43-49.

Samuelson, P.A. (1954) The pure theory of public expenditure. Review of Economics and Statistics 36:387-389.

Samuelson, P.A. (1956) Social indifference curves. Quarterly Journal of Economics 70:1-22.

Samuelson, P.A. (1958) An exact consumption loan model of interest with or without the social contrivance of money. Journal of Political Economy 66:467-482.

Samuelson, P.A. (1975) The optimum growth rate for population. International Economic Review 16:531-538.

Solow, R.M. (1956) A contribution to the theory of economic growth. Quarterly Journal of Economics 70:65-94.

Starrett, D. (1972) On golden rule, the "biological rate of interest" and competitive inefficiency. Journal of Political Economy 80:276-291.

Stigler, G.J. (1951) The division of labor is limited by the extent of the market. Journal of Political Economy 59:185-193.

Wildasin, D.E. (1984) Old Age Security and Fertility. Project paper prepared for the Fertility Determinants Group, Indiana University.

Wildasin, D.E. (1985) Non-Neutrality of Debt with Endogenous Fertility. Unpublished paper, Department of Economics, Indiana University.

Willis, R.J. (1981) On the Social and Private Benefits of Population Growth. Unpublished manuscript, SUNY at Stony Brook.

Willis, R.J. (1982) The direction of intergenerational transfers and demographic transition: the Caldwell hypothesis reexamined. Population and Development Review Supplement to Vol. 8:207-234.

Willis, R.J. (1985) A theory of the equilibrium rate of interest: life cycles, institutions, and population growth. In B. Arthur, G. Rogers, and R. Lee, eds., Economic Consequences of Alternative Population Patterns. Oxford, England: Oxford University Press.